- Assist the classroom teacher in selecting books, technology-based information, and nonprint materials representing multiple levels, broad interests, and cultural and linguistic backgrounds.

- Demonstrate and model reading and writing for real purposes in daily interactions with students and education professionals. Assist teachers and paraprofessionals to model reading and writing as valued life-long activities.

Standard 5: Professional Development

- Use methods to effectively revise instructional plans to motivate all students. They assist classroom teachers in designing programs that will intrinsically and extrinsically motivate students. They demonstrate these techniques and they can articulate the research base that grounds their practice.

- Articulate the theories related to the connections between teacher dispositions and student achievement.

- Conduct professional study groups for para-professionals and teachers. Assist classroom teachers and paraprofessionals in identifying, planning, and implementing personal professional development plans. Advocate to advance the professional research base to expand knowledge-based practices.

- Positively and constructively provide an evaluation of their own or others' teaching practices. Assist classroom teachers and paraprofessionals as they strive to improve their practice.

- Exhibit leadership skills in professional development. They plan, implement, and evaluate professional development efforts at the grade, school, district, and/or state level. They are cognizant of and can identify and describe characteristics of sound professional development programs. They can articulate the evidence base that grounds their practice.

Simeck

FIFTH EDITION

INSTRUCTING STUDENTS WHO HAVE LITERACY PROBLEMS

Sandra McCormick

Professor Emerita
The Ohio State University

PEARSON

Merrill
Prentice Hall

Upper Saddle River, New Jersey
Columbus, Ohio

Library of Congress Cataloging-in-Publication Data

McCormick, Sandra.

Instructing students who have literacy problems/Sandra McCormick.—5th ed.

p. cm.

Includes bibliographical references and index.

ISBN 0-13-171879-7

1. Reading—Remedial teaching—United States. I. Title.

LB1050.5.M373 2007

372.43—dc22   2006044400

Vice President and Executive Publisher: Jeffery W. Johnston
Senior Editor: Linda Ashe Bishop
Senior Production Editor: Mary M. Irvin
Design Coordinator: Diane C. Lorenzo
Senior Editorial Assistant: Laura Weaver
Production Coordination and Text Design: Carlisle Publishing Services
Cover Designer: Kristina Holmes
Cover Images: Anthony Magnacca/Merrill
Photo Coordinator: Monica Merkel
Production Manager: Pamela D. Bennett
Director of Marketing: David Gesell
Marketing Manager: Darcy Betts Prybella
Marketing Coordinator: Brian Mounts

This book was set in Melior by Carlisle Publishing Services. It was printed and bound by Hamilton Printing Company. The cover was printed by The Lehigh Press, Inc.

Photo Credits: Barbara Schwartz/Merrill, pp. 2, 126, 228, 470; Anne Vega/Merrill, pp. 22, 271, 312, 354, 380, 418, 431, 456, 476; Richard Haynes/Prentice Hall School Division, p. 23; Scott Cunningham/Merrill, pp. 30, 52, 65, 115, 224, 264, 326, 353, 445; Anthony Magnacca/Merrill, pp. 46, 70, 72, 96, 154, 159, 278, 406; KS Studios/Merrill, p. 76; Linda Kauffman/Merrill, p. 98, 342; Lynn Saville/Prentice Hall School Division, p. 120; Karen Mancinelli/Pearson Learning Photo Studio, pp. 133, 217; David Mager/Pearson Learning Photo Studio, p. 172; Silver Burdett Ginn, pp. 186, 414; Modern Curriculum Press/Pearson Learning, p. 191; Laura Bolesta/Merrill, p. 246; Jean Greenwald/Merrill, p. 308.

Pearson Prentice Hall™ is a trademark of Pearson Education, Inc.
Pearson® is a registered trademark of Pearson plc
Prentice Hall® is a registered trademark of Pearson Education, Inc.
Merrill® is a registered trademark of Pearson Education, Inc.

Pearson Education Ltd.   Pearson Education Australia Pty. Limited
Pearson Education Singapore Pte. Ltd.   Pearson Education North Asia Ltd.
Pearson Education Canada, Ltd.   Pearson Educación de Mexico, S.A. de C.V.
Pearson Education—Japan   Pearson Education Malaysia Pte. Ltd.

10 9 8 7 6 5 4 3 2 1
ISBN: 0-13-171879-7

This book is dedicated to Robert and Karen
for their help and kindness with Mamma
and
to Bob for his help and kindness to me.

Author Biography

Before assuming a teaching position at a university, Sandra McCormick taught as a fourth- and fifth-grade classroom teacher in schools comprised primarily of at-risk youngsters, served as a Title I reading teacher for elementary and middle school students, worked as a Reading Resource Teacher assisting teachers in inner-city schools with their classroom reading and language arts programs, and supervised a citywide reading program that served 129 elementary schools in a large Midwestern city. She also was a television reading teacher, teaching children in eight cities in Ohio via a PBS program aimed at students with reading delays.

After receiving her Ph.D. at The Ohio State University, Dr. McCormick joined the faculty in the College of Education at that university, where she taught courses on remedial and clinical reading assessment and instruction, and on methods for instructing students with learning disabilities. She also supervised a university-based reading clinic for a number of years.

Dr. McCormick is the author or editor of several books in addition to this one, including *Remedial and Clinical Reading Instruction* and *Cognitive and Social Perspectives for Literacy Research and Instruction* (the latter with Jerry Zutell). She publishes articles frequently in journals such as *Reading Research Quarterly, The Reading Teacher, Journal of Reading, Journal of Reading Behavior, Journal of Educational Research, Exceptional Children, Journal of Learning Disabilities*, and *Language Arts*. Dr. McCormick was coeditor of the National Reading Conference Yearbook for 3 years and on the editorial advisory review board for several journals. Her research interest, as might be expected, is with students having literacy problems. Although her research focus was on comprehension instruction and reading/learning disabled students for several years, she also has investigated ways to facilitate word learning with severely delayed readers, including nonreaders.

Dr. McCormick has served as a member of the Board of Directors of the International Reading Association, was a distinguished finalist in 1990 for the Albert J. Harris Award presented annually for significant research on reading disabilities, and has been elected to Fellow in the National Conference on Research in English. Dr. McCormick is a frequent presenter at national and international conferences, and she has regularly reviewed research and development proposals for the United States Department of Education.

Preface

Beginning with the first edition of *Instructing Students Who Have Literacy Problems*, this text has been research based and has long been popular with instructors who want their students to gain knowledge that is supported by quantitative and qualitative data. Likewise, preservice and inservice teachers value this book because it presents scores of practical applications that have been translated from the research. The newly revised fifth edition follows the same traditions.

The fifth edition, like prior editions, also reflects the balanced view of literacy instruction held by most educators today. While acknowledging that the fundamental purpose of reading is to comprehend text, the current perspective also recognizes that accurate, automatic word recognition and knowledge of word identification strategies are necessary precursors for understanding printed material. The fifth edition thoroughly treats both issues—word learning and comprehension—for students who have difficulties in learning to read. The balanced conception of reading programs is further exhibited in suggestions for integrating reading, writing, and spelling.

This book is intended for upper-level undergraduates and graduate students in courses focusing on corrective, remedial, and/or clinical reading instruction and assessment. It is also suitable for coursework with teachers who work with students who have learning disabilities because the educational problems of those students most frequently are rooted in difficulties in learning to read.

NEW TO THE FIFTH EDITION

There are a number of additions to the existing content in this latest edition.

- **The first chapter of the book has been comprehensively revised**. Now, in this foundational chapter, the reader will find the following:
  - **A section on educational initiatives has been added that features the No Child Left Behind Act (NCLB) of 2001 and one of its key programs, Reading First.** Although controversial, teachers need to know the law's purposes and have information and strategies to meet its program requirements. In addition to **a concise summary** of the legislation in Chapter 1, **an icon**, like the one to the left, is placed in margins throughout the book to alert readers to information that can assist in fulfilling the intent and obligations of this act.

NCLB
READING FIRST

- In addition, printed on the inside front cover are standards the International Reading Association advocates for reading specialists and literacy coaches.
- Updated, detailed discussions are included on new definitions and new issues related to the concepts of (a) disabled readers/delayed readers, (b) learning disability, and (c) dyslexia.
- New entries for 2000–2005 have been added to the extensive history table that outlines milestone events in remedial and clinical reading instruction.

- In all chapters, a new WEBSITE margin note highlights Internet resources related to chapter topics, focusing on websites genuinely useful to teachers. Look for the icon like the one to the left.
- New illustrations in Chapter 1 include (a) a table delineating the differences in terminology used by professionals across various literacy-related fields, with the intent of facilitating understanding and communication; and (b) a table specifying teaching activities that scaffold reading experiences for students.

- Like Chapter 1, **the final chapter in this new edition (Chapter 14) has been significantly revised.** This chapter, which describes reading instruction for students with special needs, includes these new features:
  - **An extensively expanded section on literacy instruction for new English Language learners (ELLs) begins the chapter.** In the 1990s the number of individuals immigrating to the United States and Canada was the largest of any decade on record. Now, reading teachers in all parts of these countries are working with ELLs. Special considerations for the oral language and literacy instruction and assessment of ELLs are discussed. Specific teaching suggestions are offered and illustrated.
  - Other helpful Chapter 14 information includes a Research Box, summarizing selected research pertinent to reading instruction for ELLs; a vignette of an exemplary sheltered English lesson; a table listing the many similarities between learning to read in a second language and in a first language (and some differences); a website for obtaining a list of Spanish-English cognates; and an illustrative example of high-quality books that are helpful for budding English speakers.
  - The remainder of Chapter 14, with its attention to at-risk students and to adult literacy, has been shortened and reorganized to accommodate the expanded ELL section.

- **The section on fluency has been moved to Chapter 8 and lengthened to include a comprehensive research review on techniques for improving fluency, along with a myriad of practical ideas based on the research.**
- **The well-received causation chapters, Chapters 2 and 3, have been combined into one, slightly longer chapter** (now Chapter 2). To keep the chapter from becoming too long, issues presently of less interest have been removed or the amount of coverage reduced. At the same time, in-depth, research-based information reflecting still-existing concerns has been retained. Further, a new section has been added, based on Barone's (1999) ground-breaking study regarding the literacy development of students who have been exposed to crack/cocaine prenatally.

- **The icons that signal the popular student case studies have been renamed and used more widely to make the case studies easier to locate:**

Brian's Case Study

David's Case Study

Bridget's Case Study

Dan's Case Study

Neal's Case Study

Frederick's Case Study

- In addition to the case study narratives focusing on children, the fifth edition presents **five instructional narratives about teachers**, each labeled as **Vignette: Real Teachers in Action**, and illustrating a variety of assessment and instructional activities, all conducted in an exemplary manner.
- **The Instructor's Manual is now available electronically on the Instructor's Resource Center (IRC).** This manual presents chapter-by-chapter materials including: (a) multiple transparency masters for each chapter which are especially supportive for conveying important chapter information through a number of interactive means; (b) a comprehensive listing of suggested course activities, designed to give students opportunities to learn course content in a variety of ways, and which also provide useful instructional models for their own teaching; and (c) test questions of a variety of types that assess literal, interpretive, and applied understandings, along with the answers to these questions. Instructors adopting this text may contact their Prentice Hall sales representative for access to the IRC.
- **A new PowerPoint program**, for those who prefer this presentation mode to that of overhead projector and transparencies.

POPULAR FEATURES THAT HAVE BEEN RETAINED

Certain features have been retained from the previous editions. These features offer a cohesive blend of theory, research, and practice. Features you will continue to see in the fifth edition are the following:

- A focus on both *elementary and secondary students*
- *Four comprehensive chapters on literacy assessment*, conveying in-depth, timely information on formal and informal procedures
- A chapter-long presentation of *research-based principles for working with delayed readers*
- Two separate, thorough *chapters on word recognition and word identification*
- A chapter presenting rich and innovative methods for helping students to increase their *meaning vocabulary knowledge*

- *Two chapters on comprehension instruction,* one discussing comprehension of narrative material and the other exploring expository text
- *A full, detailed chapter devoted to severely delayed readers and nonreaders*
- *Student study aids, titled "Learning From Text,"* interspersed throughout chapters to help students understand and apply information presented in this book (also designed to provide models for teachers on how to teach their own students to read expository text and to study)
- In every chapter, *visuals to clarify, inform, extend, generate interest, and provide actual materials teachers can use*
- Throughout, an emphasis on use of high-quality literature with delayed readers
- A *Reflections section* at the end of each chapter focusing on questions and activities to prompt thinking about chapter content, some providing the basis for exercises that can be carried out during class sessions in college courses
- *Q & A (Questions and Answers)* boxes that pose questions and report answers found in the literature search conducted by the National Reading Panel
- *Margin notes* sprinkled liberally through all chapters to highlight critical points of information
- *Key terms* defined in text printed in **bold**

A review of the text will disclose many other topics beneficial for teachers.

ACKNOWLEDGMENTS

My thanks go to my professional colleagues across the country who have used and informally reviewed this book, and to Maria Elena Arguelles, University of Miami; Francine R. Johnston, University of North Carolina at Greensboro; Michael Kibby, University of Buffalo; and Priscilla M. Leggett, Fayetteville State University for their comprehensive, formal reviews. Warm thoughts and many thanks go to Linda Bishop, the editor everyone would like to have, for her good ideas and great spirit—and to Laura Weaver, editorial assistant, whose care and feeding of authors makes the job much, much easier. Finally, I recognize Bob Ruddell, who as my husband brings love and joy into my life and as my colleague inspires me through professional discussion. Input from conscientious educators such as these has provided helpful guidance in preparation of this fifth edition.

My wish is that everyone reading this book will work hard to bring the best instruction to those who need it the most, delayed readers.

Sandra McCormick

Teacher Preparation Classroom

Your Class. Their Careers. Our Future. Will your students be prepared?

We invite you to explore our new, innovative and engaging website and all that it has to offer you, your course, and tomorrow's educators! Organized around the major courses preservice teachers take, the Teacher Preparation site provides media, student/teacher artifacts, strategies, research articles, and other resources to equip your students with the quality tools needed to excel in their courses and prepare them for their first classroom.

This ultimate online education resource is available at no cost, when packaged with a Merrill text, and will provide you and your students access to:

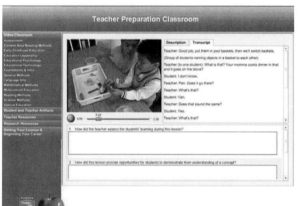

Online-Video Library. More than 150 video clips—each tied to a course topic and framed by learning goals and Praxis-type questions—capture real teachers and students working in real classrooms, as well as in-depth interviews with both students and educators.

Student and Teacher Artifacts. More than 200 student and teacher classroom artifacts—each tied to a course topic and framed by learning goals and application questions—provide a wealth of materials and experiences to help make your study to become a professional teacher more concrete and hands-on.

Research Articles. Over 500 articles from ASCD's renowned journal *Educational Leadership*. The site also includes Research Navigator, a searchable database of additional educational journals.

Teaching Strategies. Over 500 strategies and lesson plans for you to use when you become a practicing professional.

Licensure and Career Tools. Resources devoted to helping you pass your licensure exam; learn standards, law, and public policies; plan a teaching portfolio; and succeed in your first year of teaching.

How to ORDER *Teacher Prep* for you and your students:
For students to receive a *Teacher Prep* Access Code with this text, instructors **must** provide a special value pack ISBN number on their textbook order form. To receive this special ISBN, please email: **Merrill.marketing@pearsoned.com** and provide the following information:
- **Name and Affiliation**
- **Author/Title/Edition of Merrill text**

Upon ordering *Teacher Prep* for their students, instructors will be given a lifetime *Teacher Prep* Access Code.

Brief Contents

Contents

LOOK FOR Myths Versus Possible Hypotheses for Explaining Reading Difficulties

LOOK FOR David's Case Study, a Continuing Case Report Across Four Chapters Describing Assessment Procedures With a Delayed Reader

LOOK FOR A Vignette Illustrating Ways a Reading Teacher Used Observation Instead of Formal Tests for Assessment

LOOK FOR Easy, Sound Ways to Assess Phonemic Awareness

LOOK FOR Ways to Combine Teaching and Assessment to Evaluate Comprehension

PART **III**   INSTRUCTIONAL INTERVENTIONS   185

CHAPTER **7**   *Important Principles of Instruction for
Delayed Readers*   186

LOOK FOR Materials That
Motivate Delayed
Readers and Assist
Learning

LOOK FOR Teacher- and Research-Tested Strategies for Developing Fluency

CHAPTER **9** *Word Identification* **264**

LOOK FOR Sound
Instructional Strategies
for Teaching Phonics
and Structural Analysis

LOOK FOR Teacher-Guided Strategies That Promote Rich Development of Students' Meaning Vocabularies

LOOK FOR Comprehension Instructional Strategies to Use Before, During, and After Student Reading

LOOK FOR Teacher-Designed Strategies to Help Students Access Expository Text

LOOK FOR The Multiple-Exposure/Multiple-Context Strategy for Nonreaders

LOOK FOR Reading and Oral Language Instructional Suggestions for New English Language Learners

Special Features

CASE STUDIES

TEACHING RESOURCES

TEST BANKS

TEACHERS' STORE

STEPS: ADMINISTERING ASSESSMENTS IN YOUR OWN CLASSROOM

FOUNDATIONS OF REMEDIAL AND CLINICAL READING INSTRUCTION

1

Basic Concepts and Definitions in Reading

A developmental reading program should include many opportunities to read narrative and informational materials, to learn strategies, and to practice study skills.

LEARNING FROM TEXT

Teachers of reading are responsible not only for helping students *learn how to read*, but also *how to learn from reading*. Throughout this book I include aids called "Learning From Text" to help *you* study effectively. These aids also suggest ideas you can use with *your students* to help them comprehend text. The best study guides (a) assist in learning a lesson's content and (b) teach general strategies for understanding and remembering. The study aids in this text are in *shaded boxes* and signaled by the icon shown here, labeled "Learning From Text."

—*The Author*

*I*f you were asked to name the most important invention in history, what would you say? The Almanac of World History (Daniels & Hyslop, 2003) suggests this answer: the printing press. In the mid-1400s, after Johannes Gutenberg modified wine presses to accommodate moveable type and develop a practical printing process, book printing multiplied amazingly from the single Bible that was Gutenberg's first product to several million copies of several thousand works a mere 50 years later (Daniels & Hyslop, 2003). With the proliferation of books came the proliferation of literacy. The proliferation of literacy, in turn, led to a diffusion of ideas and hastened many of humankind's other achievements.

Literacy became an increasingly respected accomplishment and eventually was seen as a necessary one. For example, in 17th-century Sweden, being literate to read religious books was considered so important that parents were fined if they failed to teach their children to read, and marriage was denied adults until they could demonstrate literacy (Venezky, 1991). In the 1800s, literacy was promoted in Western countries so citizens could participate effectively in politics and the military, and as a means of improving the nation's economic condition as a result of a better educated workforce.

Being able to read is even more critical in contemporary life (see Table 1–1). For individuals, reading provides access to employment, educational opportunities, social adjustment, and entertainment. In addition, a literate population is crucial for generating ideas that lead to social change; thus, many governments, including our own, mandate universal education, with literacy as a prime objective.

Fortunately, as a result of typical educational experiences, most students attain reading skill. In fact, data from many sources show that students in U.S. schools exhibit reading achievement surpassing that from any other period in American education (e.g., Klenk & Kibby, 2000; "SAT, ACT," 2004; Snow, Burns, & Griffin, 1998).

Unfortunately, this is not true for all. Since you are reading this text, likely you are a teacher who is concerned about those elementary and secondary students who show serious delays in literacy achievement. The consequences of low literacy, for the individual and for society, are serious. Thus, although such students are a relatively small segment of the population, your concern for them is shared by the public and by educational agencies.

TABLE 1–1 *Reading Levels of a Sampling of Items and Materials Encountered in Adult Life*

Items and Materials	Approximate Grade Level of Reading Ability Needed
Help-wanted ads in newspapers	6–7
Front-page stories in newspapers	9–12$^+$
Dosage and symptom information on aspirin bottle labels	10
Preparation directions on boxes of frozen dinners	8
Directions for filling out the 1040 income tax forms	9–10
Training materials for military cooks	7–8
Articles in *Reader's Digest, Saturday Evening Post, Ladies' Home Journal, Popular Mechanics,* and *Harper's*	12$^+$
Articles in romance, TV, and movie magazines	8
Recent presidential inaugural addresses	9
Information on financial statements	11–16$^+$
Life insurance policies	12
Apartment leases	College

Sources: Compiled from: Bargantz and Dulin (1970); Bittner and Shamo (1976); Bormuth (1973–74); Felton and Felton (1973); Hirshoren, Hunt, and Davis (1974); Hoskins (1973); Kilty (1976); Kwolek (1973); Pyrczak (1976); Razik (1969); Sticht (1975); Worthington (1977).

EDUCATIONAL INITIATIVES

Local school districts, states, provinces, and national governments often propose reform measures to improve reading achievement.

The No Child Left Behind Act of 2001

NCLB

READING FIRST

In the United States, an educational initiative referred to as the No Child Left Behind (NCLB) Act of 2001 (U.S. Public Law 107-110, 2002) has caused change and controversy. This act champions an important cause: It proposes that no students in American elementary or secondary schools—regardless of race, ethnicity, disability, first language, or socioeconomic status—will fail to meet important educational standards. That is, *no* child will be "left behind."

This law affects the responsibilities of professionals who teach reading. Thus, you should know something of NCLB's mandates and impact.

NCLB is intended for students from low-income families. While its requirements apply only to educational bodies receiving federal funds, this represents large numbers of U.S. schools and districts.

One central purpose of the act is for all students to obtain a rating of "proficient" in core academic areas by the year 2014. To this end, the act requires all states to have *content standards* for (a) reading or language arts, (b) mathematics, and (c) science. These must be linked to *student-achievement standards* that indicate what represents "mastery" of the content standards at each of three levels: (a) an *advanced* level of performance (the highest level), (b) a *proficient* level, and (c) a *basic* level of performance (the lowest level).

School districts serving economically disadvantaged students receive funds to implement plans for helping their students meet these standards. The plans must conform to NCLB requirements, including curriculum that takes into account scientifically based research, as well as diagnosis and teaching of the lowest-achieving students.

After a district's plan has been put into effect, another part of the law comes into play. This part requires states to annually verify—and make public—whether each school receiving NCLB funds has or has not made **adequate yearly progress (AYP)** toward the year 2014 goal. Based on achievement the year NCLB was enacted (2001–2002), schools determined the amount of yearly growth necessary for all students to reach the proficient level in that 12-year period. This figure must be attained annually for progress to be deemed adequate.

NCLB calls for frequent assessment using valid, reliable instruments to judge whether students have made AYP toward meeting the standards. For reading/language arts, students are tested yearly in grades 3 through 8, and once during grades 10 through 12. Ninety-five percent of a school's students must participate in these assessments. AYP must be demonstrated for the student body as a whole and for: (a) economically disadvantaged students, (b) English-language learners, (c) major racial and ethnic groups, and (d) students with disabilities.

When AYP is not achieved after 2 years, the school is given academic assistance and additional funding to support further efforts. However, if failure to make AYP continues, schools are subjected to sanctions.

A second, different but related, directive specifies that schools receiving NCLB funds employ highly qualified teachers. Each state must ensure that low-income students are not taught at higher rates than others by unqualified or out-of-field instructional staff. Parents may request information about a teacher's license or certification and must be notified if their child is taught for 4 consecutive weeks by someone not highly qualified. Furthermore, school districts are expected to collaborate with colleges and other agencies to refine and update knowledge and instructional skills of fully certified teachers in the focal subjects of reading, language arts, math, and science.

NCLB's scope is much larger than the highly publicized requirements discussed in the preceding paragraphs. Its wide-ranging focus—to close the achievement gaps with accountability, flexibility, and choice-details various initiatives including Title I, *Improving the Academic Achievement of Disadvantaged*, Title III, *Language Instruction for Limited English Proficient and Immigrant Students*, and Title V, *Promoting Informed Parental Choice and Innovative Programs*.

NCLB
READING
FIRST

Reading First. A subcomponent of the larger NCLB law, Reading First provides grants to strengthen reading instruction in regular classrooms for low-income students in grades kindergarten through 3. To obtain a grant, school districts must follow specific guidelines. Foremost is use of **research-based instruction.** That is, programs may not base instructional decisions on someone's opinion—not even the opinion of an "authority"—but rather must ground instruction on findings from carefully and appropriately conducted research.

After their review of many studies meeting this standard, the National Reading Panel reported certain factors that were associated with success in reading (National Institute of Child Health and Human Development [NICHD], 2000).

Five of these were deemed essential components for primary-grade instruction. No school may receive Reading First funds unless its program demonstrates instruction in five *essential components*:

1. *Phonemic awareness*—hearing individual sounds that make up *spoken* words
2. *Phonics*—the relationship between the sounds of spoken language and letters in written language
3. *Fluency*—reading both accurately and reasonably quickly
4. *Vocabulary*—knowledge of word meanings
5. *Comprehension*—understanding what is read

Classroom teachers in Reading First schools must be knowledgeable about instructional methods, materials selection, and assessment related to these five components. So, too, must reading specialists, who are often called upon to assist classroom teachers in these areas and to organize professional development programs around those components.

Pros and Cons.   Everyone applauds NCLB's intent to eliminate achievement gaps between mainstream and low-income students, and most educators support a number of the implementation measures—for example, emphasis on highly qualified teachers and research-based instruction. Furthermore, investigation by the Education Trust, a nonpartisan, nonprofit organization, shows that many school districts are narrowing academic gaps under this plan, even if not as quickly as had been hoped (Wiener & Hall, 2004).

On the other hand, there are major concerns. Perhaps the most heated disagreement is with sanctions that can be applied if students do not make AYP; these include placing students' education in the hands of commercial tutoring ventures, change of school status to a charter school, and other options unlikely to solve the problem. There also is apprehension about the many testing demands and uneasiness that instruction may center on "teaching to the tests." Another issue relates to money: Many states complain that insufficient funds are granted to fulfill the law's obligations. In some cases, NCLB's requirements seem in conflict with other federal and state laws.

Teacher Assistance.   Regardless of one's views about this law, literacy educators must deal with its challenges unless or until the U.S. federal government decides on modifications. Throughout this book the icon combining the **NCLB** acronym and the **Reading First** program title is placed in margins to signal sections that are informative about the legislation or particularly helpful for meeting its instructional and assessment obligations. You have seen two such icons on previous pages in this section. Follow the icons for useful ideas.

📖 TYPES OF READING PROGRAMS

Teachers wishing to participate in efforts to improve the reading skills of children, older youth, or adults may work in one of several programs. A *developmental* reading program is a regular classroom program designed for most school-age students. These programs should provide students with many opportunities to read narrative and informational texts as well as specific activities to develop reading strategies. In addition to the five essential components of reading instruction

Five essential components of reading instruction recommended by the National Reading Panel are phonemic awareness, phonics, fluency, vocabulary, and comprehension.

specified by the National Reading Panel (NICHD, 2000)—phonemic awareness, phonics, fluency, vocabulary, and comprehension—teachers in developmental programs help students develop

1. automatic recognition of words on sight as an aid to fluency,
2. use of structural analysis as a word identification strategy to supplement phonics,
3. knowledge of study skills in conjunction with informational text comprehension, and
4. other literacy-related understandings.

Classroom teachers also engage in *corrective* reading programs when they assist students who have mild reading delays within the regular classroom.

Remedial programs are characterized by ongoing assessment and flexibility in adapting instruction to individual differences.

In *remedial* reading programs, students with moderate to severe reading delays receive instruction from a specially trained reading teacher. Often instruction is conducted in groups of about five to eight students. More comprehensive assessment of students' reading problems is undertaken in remedial programs than in most developmental or corrective programs to determine weaknesses, reasons for these, and strengths that may help alleviate problems. Since students are grouped according to common needs, some instruction may be carried out with all of the small group participating. Other times, students work one-to-one with the teacher. The teacher's special training and the small class sizes make possible frequent ongoing assessment and flexibility in adapting instructional techniques to individual differences.

A *clinical* program is designed for students with severe reading delays; therefore, the clinician, with only rare exception, works with one student at a time. Assessment is more extensive, including formal testing and informal observation. Remediation is intensive and highly individualized. A case study report is often developed for the student; it includes assessment results and the student's responses to instructional techniques (see the Appendix for an example). School systems, hospitals, and social agencies may sponsor reading clinics, but they are especially prevalent at universities because clinics furnish opportunities for reading teachers-in-training to have supervised practice in specialized literacy instruction. A recommended source of information on reading clinics is *Reconsidering the Role of the Reading Clinic in a New Age of Literacy* (Evensen & Mosenthal, 1999).

Although developmental, corrective, remedial, and clinical reading programs differ in individualization and pace, they all deal with the same major components of reading.

Although developmental, corrective, remedial, and clinical reading programs differ in individualization and pace, they are based on the same principles of learning, and all deal with the same major components of reading. Most techniques suggested in this text are equally useful in all programs.

📖 ROLES OF READING SPECIALISTS

The term **reading teacher** can be defined as anyone whose work includes reading instruction, but more often it refers to a teacher with special training to address the needs of students who have reading problems. The designation **reading specialist** is increasingly employed as a substitute for *reading teacher*. An often-cited report on preventing reading difficulties recommends that every school have a reading specialist (Snow et al., 1998). Another influential document, Standards for Reading Professionals (Professional Standards and Ethics Committee, 2004), advises that reading specialists have graduate-level education, including a clinical practicum, in order to perform their tasks related to (a) assessment, (b) instruction, and (c) leadership, as discussed in the following sections.

Assessment and Instructional Tasks

Reading specialists go about assessment and instructional tasks in a number of ways. Many work directly with students who leave the regular classroom for this special instruction in the reading specialist's class. Such an arrangement is sometimes referred to as a "pull-out program."

LEARNING FROM TEXT

Make a Prediction. The following section discusses inclusion programs. Make a guess about the answer to this question about inclusion program: do they or don't they work as well as pull-out programs for students with literacy problems? (Making predictions before reading engenders interest, supports comprehension, and helps readers remember what they have read.)

Push-in versus pull-out: The critical variable is quality of teaching in either arrangement.

In other cases, reading specialists work within regular classroom settings. That system often is referred to as an *inclusion*, or "push-in," *program*, because students who might have left the regular classroom for special instruction under this plan remain, or are "included," in the regular class for that instruction.

Reading specialists and learning disability teachers have used both arrangements in recent years, and there has been debate about whether students fare better academically under pull-out or push-in programs. For many years, research tackling this issue has shown that the critical variable is quality of teaching—that is, excellent teaching in either program results in better achievement than mediocre teaching in the other (Dunn, 1973; Gottlieb, 1974; Payne, Polloway, Smith, & Payne, 1981). This is not too great a surprise and is echoed in more recent studies. For example, push-in programs have been beneficial when the in-class instruction is preplanned, systematic, intensive, and research-based, and when additional time is provided for struggling learners (e.g., Cunningham, Hall, & Defee, 1998).

On the other hand, push-in programs have poorly served students with learning difficulties at other times. Researchers have documented inclusion programs where instruction is not matched to the levels and needs of delayed readers, who as a result make no advances in literacy development (e.g., Klingner, Vaughn, Schumm, Hughes, & Elbaum, 1997; Zigamond et al., 1995). O'Sullivan, Ysseldyke, Christenson, and Thurlow (1990) found that students with learning difficulties even get short-changed in regular classrooms in terms of time allotted for reading instruction in comparison to that for average readers. This study showed pupils to be more actively engaged and responsive in pull-out programs rather than inclusion programs.

In addition to academic concerns, another argument made for instructing students with learning difficulties within regular classrooms is that students' affective needs are better served. A research review by Gresham and MacMillan (1997) indicates this hoped-for circumstance has not necessarily proved to be the case. This review pointed out that higher-achieving students often are contemptuous of students with learning difficulties and that this, along with challenges in learning, has unfortunate effects on peer relations and on self-concept for low-achieving students.

Drame (2002) reported a study of teacher preferences in which those using whole-class reading instruction preferred pull-out programs more than teachers who grouped students within their classrooms to teach reading; Spear-Swerling (2004) speculated that this probably was due to the complexity of assisting individuals with diverse needs in large groups.

A compromise to the pull-out/push-in issue is integration of content covered in regular classrooms with that covered in pull-out programs. At the least, teachers should communicate about programs of mutual students, with the classroom teacher sharing knowledge about a student's learning behaviors that comes from spending many in-school hours with a learner and the reading specialist sharing expertise about literacy instruction.

Leadership Tasks

Reading specialists who assume leadership responsibilities across many schools may be called *reading consultants*, *reading coordinators*, or *reading supervisors*. Presently, however, the predominant leadership activity occurs within single buildings and is that of literacy coach.

NCLB
READING FIRST

Literacy Coaches. Customarily, reading specialists based in a single school have worked not only with students, but also for improvement of literacy education throughout their buildings. With the advent of NCLB, the second part of this role has been encouraged as a way to foster ongoing professional development required by the law. This role has even been given a name, **literacy coach** (or **reading coach**). Not all reading specialists work as literacy coaches, but growing numbers do.

A literacy coach has multifaceted duties and may engage in any of the following:

1. *Working with teachers,* including making suggestions, answering questions, modeling techniques, linking teachers with resources, helping with assessments and their interpretation, working on collaborative lessons, and observing students to plan corrective instruction.

2. *Coordinating schoolwide literacy activities,* including planning inservice programs, developing curriculum, selecting materials, informing administrators of current research, and guiding paraprofessionals.

3. *Working with parents,* including initiating outreach, getting families involved in family literacy programs, complying with NCLB mandates regarding parents, and planning meetings on home-based activities that can help children (e.g., monitoring homework).

Two essentials for being a literacy coach are (a) to be highly informed about literacy instruction and assessment, and (b) to have skill in working with adults.

If a teacher is going to coach another educator, that teacher must have excellent breadth and depth of knowledge about the subject coached. Regrettable stories exist about teachers with no experience in teaching reading who are sent to one-day workshops and then deemed literacy coaches ("Coaches, Controversy, Consensus," 2004). Dole (2004) reports on literacy coaches she studied in

TABLE 1–2   *Minimum Qualifications for Literacy Coaches*

Literacy coaches . . .
- are excellent teachers of reading, preferably at the levels at which they are coaching.
- have in-depth knowledge of reading processes, acquisition, assessment, and instruction.
- have expertise in working with teachers to improve their practices.
- are excellent presenters and group leaders.
- have the experience or preparation that enables them to model, observe, and provide feedback about instruction for classroom teachers.

From: International Reading Association. (2004). *The role and qualifications of the reading coach in the United States.* [Brochure]. Newark, DE: Author.

12 schools over 7 years. While many demonstrated expertise, she describes some who did not:

- The reading coach in this school did not know enough about the content and curriculum of phonemic awareness to know what to do once students have mastered one stage. As a result, the students and teachers stagnated. (p. 468)
- The reading coach in the school did not know enough about comprehension instruction to assist teachers in the intermediate stage of professional knowledge. (p. 469)

A successful literacy coach must have much classroom teaching experience, experience as a reading teacher, and graduate-level coursework in literacy education.

Sensitivity in working with adults also is vital. Teachers are more receptive to collaboration than to directives. A willingness to roll up one's sleeves to work side by side with colleagues for problem solving leads to growth in professional skill. Offering compliments about strengths eases the discomfort of change in areas of weakness. Addressing first what *teachers* see as their *own* needs opens the way for extending learning to other objectives. In short, social perceptiveness must work in tandem with academic knowledge.

Table 1–2 lists the *minimum* qualifications the International Reading Association considers acceptable for a literacy coach (International Reading Association [IRA], 2004a). However, they advocate that within 3 years the literacy coach should meet the more rigorous Standards for Reading Specialists and Literacy Coaches (IRA, 2004b) reprinted in this textbook's inside front cover. Examine those now.

To learn how to obtain a helpful book, *The Literacy Coach's Survival Guide,* go to www.reading.org/publications/

📖 IMPORTANT DEFINITIONS

As a professional, you should know meanings of important terms associated with literacy.

LEARNING FROM TEXT

Preview.   Terminology is used differently among different groups, sometimes leading to misunderstanding. Table 1–3 provides a preview of the upcoming section. Previewing helps you mentally organize potentially confusing material. Take a side trip to Table 1–3 to consider the information there.

TABLE 1–3 *Terminology: Differences Sometimes Found Among Professionals Interested in Literacy*

Reading Educators Might Say:	LD Educators Might Say:	Educational Psychologists Might Say:	Medical Personnel Might Say:
Disabled reader/ reading disability Basic terms used for literacy problems	**Learning disabled/ learning disability** Basic terms used for learning problems, including reading difficulties	**Disabled reader/ reading disability** Currently, for many, replacing the terms *dyslexic/ dyslexia*	**Learning disabled/ learning disability** Terms often used
Delayed reader Increasingly replacing the term *disabled reader*	**Disabled reader/ reading disability** Sometimes equated with *learning disabled/ learning disability*; sometimes used instead of *dyslexic/ dyslexia*	**Learning disabled/ learning disability** Some believe same as *reading disabled/ reading disability*	**Dyslexic/ dyslexia** Terms often used
Struggling reader Current synonym for *delayed/ disabled reader*	**Dyslexic/ dyslexia** Sometimes, terms still used	**Dyslexic/ dyslexia** Sometimes, terms still used	**Disabled reader/ reading disability** Terms sometimes used
Learning disabled/ learning disability Many now believe same as *reading disabled/ reading disability*		**Garden-variety poor readers** Believed to have experientially based literacy problems and to respond more readily to instruction than "disabled readers"	
Dyslexic/ dyslexia Use of these terms often avoided because of conflicting definitions			

Disabled Readers/Delayed Readers

The classification **disabled readers** traditionally has been used by reading educators to refer to individuals who have difficulty learning to read despite adequate intelligence and adequate instruction. Recently, some favor an alternate description, **delayed readers,** to depict the same students and to indicate that, while these students are progressing more slowly than the norm, the capacity to achieve is present (e.g., Gaskins, 1998; McCormick, 2006). This is your present author's preference. Currently, the expression *struggling reader* is used synonymously with these terms.

There are two approaches for designating a student as a delayed (or disabled) reader. The most frequently used is based on a *discrepancy model*; the other proposes a *treatment-resistance model* (Speece & Shekitka, 2002).

One approach for designating a student as a delayed reader is based on a *discrepancy model*, another on a *treatment-resistance model*.

The Discrepancy Model. Those who subscribe to the discrepancy model define a disabled or delayed reader as anyone reading significantly below his or her own potential. A comparison is made between (a) *present* reading ability and (b) reading *potential*—that is, where an individual *should* be reading. (Note that the criterion is potential, not grade level.) The difference between the two is referred to as a **discrepancy.** If the discrepancy is large, the student is said to warrant special reading instruction.

Obviously, to use this approach, one must know a person's probable reading potential. Procedures for determining this are explained in Chapter 3.

A Treatment-Resistance Model. Some literacy professionals have proposed a different way of defining reading disability. They advocate a treatment-resistance model in which the guiding point is whether a student is resistant to high-quality interventions that are fruitful for others. "Resistant" in this case means the student has not shown noteworthy improvement over an extended time.

Differentiating severe, moderate, and mild reading delays can be useful in planning instruction, especially when a student's learning phase is taken into account.

This approach is frequently suggested by those who distinguish between *reading disability* and what they call *garden-variety poor readers* (e.g., Spear-Swerling, 2004). In this view, reading disability is characterized as innate, severe, and existing in individuals of average or above intelligence. In contrast, "garden-variety poor readers" are thought to have experientially based problems (e.g., detrimental influences of poverty), to have more moderate delays, and thus to be more easily remediable. Making a distinction between these groups has loss some popularity as differences between the two are found to be less apparent than once believed. However, differentiating severe, moderate, and mild delays can be useful in planning instruction, especially when a student's learning phase is taken into account (see Chapter 8). The treatment-resistance concept may take hold for that reason. (Note that "resistance" does *not* mean that the learning difficulty is without a solution. Informed literacy professionals believe that all literacy difficulties are remediable. See Chapter 13.)

LEARNING FROM TEXT

Summarize. Based on the previous section, orally and briefly answer the question, "Who is a disabled/delayed reader?" (Research indicates that summarizing information aids recall of major ideas.)

Learning Disability

The term **learning disability (LD)** was adopted in 1963 as a generic description replacing many different labels applied to difficulties in listening, mathematics, reading, speaking, spelling, thinking, or writing. Although this description covers several academic areas, in reality, 80% to 90% of students in LD programs are enrolled because of reading difficulties (McCormick & Cooper, 1991; Moats & Lyon, 1993; Snow et al., 1998; Spear-Swerling, 2004). In fact, recent research and thinking indicate strong conceptual and practical similarities between the designations *reading disability* and *learning disability*. Accordingly, for this 80% to 90% at least, many professionals today believe no distinction should be made between the two concepts (see Klenk & Kibby, 2000; Snow et al., 1998; Spear-Swerling, 2004).

These similarities exist in a number of ways. First, data show that whether students are labeled *reading delayed*, *reading disabled*, or *learning disabled*, there may be several different causes for their reading difficulties, and across these groups, the causes tend to be the same (see Chapter 2). Second, in most states, criteria for judging students' need for LD program placement is determined exactly as for most remedial reading programs—simply by examining discrepancies between achievement and potential—and no longer through tests designed to identify alleged processing disorders or other outmoded means. Third, although the intent of the law mandating LD services was to provide interventions only for those with severe learning delays (approximately 3% of the population), in practice, LD teachers, like reading teachers, work with students having moderate as well as more serious reading problems. For all these reasons, the student communities found in reading programs and LD programs are quite comparable.

As a final point, another similarity is the instructional focus in contemporary LD programs and reading programs: There are few major differences. This was not true in the early days of the LD movement when old theories for working with brain-injured and retarded individuals often found their way into LD classrooms. At that time, in place of reading activities, LD students might walk balance beams and perform other motor exercises, complete visual perception tasks, or carry out auditory perception drills, all believed to improve defective brain processing functions. After a period, LD professionals became disillusioned with these perceptual-motor techniques when, repeatedly, their research demonstrated that direct teaching of reading was effective for students with learning disabilities, whereas treatment of "underlying processes" was not (e.g., Black, 1974; Bryan, 1974; Hammill & Larsen, 1974; Saphier, 1973). Today, LD teachers directly teach what students need to learn, rather than hoping to remediate difficulties in a roundabout fashion. Reading teachers and LD teachers teaching in programs based on current research use no significantly different methods for teaching reading.

LEARNING FROM TEXT

Note Taking. Write a brief, paraphrased list of similarities between students, and their programs, who have been designated *learning disabled* and those labeled *reading disabled*. (One factor on which success in studying depends is *depth of processing*. Some techniques, such as paraphrasing, induce you to expend more cognitive effort, which is associated with greater recall of information.)

LEARNING FROM TEXT

Make a Prediction. Dyslexia! What in the world is it?

Dyslexia

When asking someone to define **dyslexia,** the answer you get depends on who you ask.

Proposed in the late 1800s as an alternate name for the now-discounted notion of "congenital word-blindness," the theory of dyslexia was characterized in numerous, contradictory ways over the next century. For example, some used the term to indicate only profound reading disabilities; others applied it to any reading delay of any kind. Some specified an unknown origin for dyslexia; others spelled out a catalog of causes, including faulty teaching and other environmental factors. Many other inconsistencies regarding symptoms and causes of dyslexia were found, especially in the lay press. Furthermore, professionals in different fields often defined dyslexia differently.

A Categorical Definition. In the last few years, however, several educational and medical researchers have examined the concept of dyslexia using new brain scan technologies and other research methods (for discussions, see Gillet, Temple, & Crawford, 2004; Goswami, 2000; Johnson, 1995; Olson & Gayan, 2002; Rumsey et al., 1997; Shaywitz et al., 2000; Vaughn, Bos, & Schumm, 1997; Verrengia, 2004). The quality of this research has varied, but certain conclusions have been fairly consistent. As a result, some educators, medical personnel, and psychologists have now converged on definitions that are at least similar. If asked to define *dyslexia*, they likely would include the following manifestations and causes: (a) *serious delay in acquiring reading skill*, despite adequate *intelligence, hearing, vision, and oral language*; (b) a *congenital* (i.e., existing at birth), *neurological cause* (not environmental causes, like poverty, cultural customs, or poor teaching); (c) sometimes an *hereditary* factor, but sometimes not; (d) *difficulty mastering other written language skills* (i.e., spelling and writing); (e) *problems with phonological processing* (and, less frequently, with visual processing); and (f) *treatment resistance*, as demonstrated by the necessity for intensified instruction and extended time frames to achieve learning goals. This view of dyslexia is called a *categorical model* because it categorizes individuals evidencing these characteristics differently from other poor readers. Many educators consider a definition of dyslexia based on these criteria to be acceptable.

One should use caution in depending on the media or commercial vendors for a description of dyslexia; misinformation abounds in those sources.

Nonprofessional Definitions. On the other hand, the media, and especially vendors of commercial products claiming to treat dyslexia, sometimes fall back on outdated beliefs clearly rejected by research long ago. While there certainly are exceptions, one should use caution in depending on the media or commercial vendors for a definition and description of dyslexia. Misinformation abounds in these sources, ranging from commonly held myths (e.g., letter reversals are signs of dyslexia) to preposterous assertions (e.g., drinking whole milk causes word recognition difficulties). Too often, erroneous statements are accompanied by claims for controversial treatments unsupported by valid evidence.

Some experts question the concept of *dyslexia* and prefer to dispense with the term entirely.

A Dimensional Approach.   There is a final, important perspective to consider when attempting to define *dyslexia*. For several reasons, a small, but growing group of experts prefers to dispense with the concept entirely. For example, the influential report *Preventing Reading Difficulties in Young Children* (Snow et al., 1998) describes data indicating more similarities than differences between those deemed dyslexic and other poor readers. To confirm this, reexamine factors (a) through (f) presented previously in this section. Clearly, most factors apply to any struggling reader. More importantly, designating an individual as dyslexic, or not, does nothing to inform instruction. The same skills must be learned by all readers—and odd, unusual methods are neither needed nor successful with any reader. What *is* useful to know is (a) the gravity of the problem (mild, moderate, or severe) in order to pace instruction and (b) the individual's specific learning phase in order to precisely target lessons.

Thus, instead of a categorical model, many researchers favor a *dimensional model* focusing on differences, not defects. Such a model conceptualizes reading achievement across the dimensions of a bell-shaped curve indicating the normal distribution of human behaviors. In this view, individuals may have a strong, average, or low aptitude for reading, as they might for any ability (for example, aptitudes for musical, mathematical, writing, or athletic achievement). Perceived this way, poor readers simply fall in the curve's left-hand portion indicating low functioning when it comes to reading-skill aptitude.

Echoing this standpoint, Spear-Swerling and Sternberg (1998) say that all reading disability cases are likely a part of a normal continuum of individual differences. Roller (1996) titles her book on struggling readers *Variability, not Disability*, reflecting this trend. Today the term *dyslexia* is used in definitions for disabilities in some states, but rejected in others.

To end our section on definitions and terminology, consider the following outlook offered by Spear-Swerling and Sternberg (1998):

> Because there is little evidence that most school-labeled children with reading disabilities suffer from an intrinsic abnormality, the terms *reading disability* and *learning disability* are at best misleading. . . . In our opinion, children who are currently called "learning disabled" or "reading disabled" should receive labels using purely descriptive terminology, as in "poor readers," "children with reading difficulties," "children with word-recognition problems," and the like. (p. 317)

📖 THE INCIDENCE OF READING DELAY

Accurate figures on individuals with serious reading delays are difficult to obtain, largely because criteria for determining if students should receive special reading services differ. Some programs include students with a 1-year discrepancy, while others specify a larger or smaller delay. To be eligible for U.S. Title I reading programs, students often, but not always, must score in the lower 33rd percentile on reading achievement tests. LD program eligibility can vary somewhat from state to state. Prevalence studies—that is, studies estimating numbers of individuals with reading delays found in a geographic area—may use strict, or less stringent, criteria for defining a reading delay (e.g., 2 vs. 1.5 standard deviations below the mean). Because of such differences, accounts of numbers of delayed/disabled readers may disagree.

Snow et al. (1998) report that U.S. Department of Education figures show approximately 3.5% of American youngsters in the United States are enrolled in learning disability classes because of reading difficulties. Similar figures have been given for serious reading delays in Great Britain (Yule, Rutter, Berger, & Thompson, 1974). In considering students with mild delays as well as those with moderate and severe problems, it has been suggested that as many as 15% of students probably warrant special instruction in reading—and indeed prevalence studies in the United States (Shaywitz & Shaywitz, 1996) and Canada (Commission on Emotional and Learning Disorders in Children, 1970) have produced comparable statistics. In U.S. poverty areas, one in five first graders participates in Title I remedial reading programs (Institute for Education Sciences, 2001).

Relating Information to Your Own Experiences. How do these estimates compare to your own experience? (Relating information to your background experiences assists understanding and recall.)

📖 MILESTONES IN THE HISTORY OF REMEDIAL AND CLINICAL READING INSTRUCTION

Reading instruction has been subject to cyclical movements. While many old ideas still have validity, others do not. Sometimes old ideas resurface that prove to be as unsuccessful the second time around as they were the first. Furthermore, reading theories tend to swing from one extreme to another. Being familiar with the field's history helps teachers examine questionable notions that arise in the present and avoid either/or positions that deny students adequate instruction.

Setting a Purpose for Reading. The history of reading instruction is summarized in a long table (Table 1–4). For this kind of information, ask instructors what they think you should learn. Teachers should help students set purposes for reading. If the instructor wants you to note general trends, you would study differently than if you were expected to know specific details. To note trends, read the columns vertically. First, read down through the entire column titled "Instructional Approaches," and then try to orally summarize significant trends. Do this for the other three columns.

Using Illustrative Aids. Many students consider information on reading models to be complex. Rumelhart, along with Ruddell and Unrau, provide diagrams to accompany their explanations. USE the diagrams. Alternately read the text and examine the diagram. Read the text and examine the diagram as you study the sections on these models. Encourage your own students to use illustrative aids to bolster their understanding.

TABLE 1–4 *Some Trends and Issues in Remedial and Clinical Reading Instruction*

Time Period	Instructional Approaches	Suggested Causes of Reading Disability	Prevalent Assessment Techniques and Tools	Milestones
Prior to the 1800s	• The alphabetic method of reading instruction is used almost exclusively until the 1700s; students spell out words letter by letter and reading is mainly oral. • The whole-word method is introduced in the 1700s.			
1800s	• Phonics methods become popular.	• Kussmaul suggests "word blindness" as a cause of reading disability.		• Research in reading has its beginnings in Europe with Valentius's work on perceptual processes.
1900–1909		• Perinatal difficulties, such as injuries during birth, are postulated by Bronner as causal factors.		
1910–1919	• The "non-oral" method, consisting of an exaggerated emphasis on silent reading, is introduced. • Russell and Schmitt suggest a method for teaching nonreaders consisting of elaborate phonics stories and the acting out of action words.	• "Congenital word-blindness" is popularized as *the* cause of reading disability.	• The first edition of the *Gray Standardized Oral Reading Paragraphs* is published; it provides teachers with the opportunity to observe and analyze students' reading errors. • The first standardized reading achievement tests are used.	• The first journal article on reading disabilities is published (Uhl, W. L. [1916]. "The use of the results of reading tests as bases for planning remedial work." *Elementary School Journal, 17,* 266–275).
1920–1929	• The kinesthetic method is introduced. • A swing away from phonics and an emphasis on the whole-word approach reemerges. • An emphasis on silent reading is prevalent.	• Lack of cerebral dominance is believed by some to be the major etiological factor in reading disability. • Inappropriate eye movements are postulated as a cause.	• The first informal reading inventory is developed. • Diagnosis usually involves compiling a case history.	• The first reading clinic is begun at UCLA. • The first remedial reading textbook is published in the United States (Gray, C. T. [1922]. *Deficiencies in Reading Ability: Their Diagnosis and Remedies.* Boston: D. C. Health).

(continued)

TABLE 1–4 *Some Trends and Issues in Remedial and Clinical Reading Instruction* *(continued)*

Time Period	Instructional Approaches	Suggested Causes of Reading Disability	Prevalent Assessment Techniques and Tools	Milestones
1930–1939	• The language experience approach (LEA) is developed.	• Emotional disturbance is suggested as a cause. • The concept of multiple causation is introduced.	• Machines begin to be used in diagnosis (e.g., eye-movement cameras).	• Monroe writes *Children Who Cannot Read*, a classic book advocating a phonic-kinesthetic approach to remediation.
1940–1949	• Both oral and silent reading are advocated. • Interest in LEA subsides.	• Much emphasis is given to emotional disturbance as a cause. • Interest in eye defects (myopia, astigmatism, etc.) as causes of reading disabilities is seen. • The concept of multiple causation gains popularity after Robinson publishes *Why Pupils Fail in Reading*, a classic interdisciplinary study that examines etiology of reading disability.	• Use of informal reading inventories is popularized by Betts. • The notion of independent, instructional, and frustration levels of reading is introduced.	• The work of Strauss and Lehtinen forms the roots of the LD movement.
1950–1959	• Interest in LEA revives. • There is a trend away from the whole-word method and back toward phonics again.	• Emotional disturbance as a cause continues to receive attention in the beginning of the decade; reading problems begin to be attributed to neurological impairments and brain-processing deficiencies in the late 1950s. • The concept of multiple causation is considered to be most viable by many.		• Many universities begin programs to train reading specialists.

1960–1969	• Body management activities (e.g., walking balance beams) are suggested as remedial activities. • The linguistic approach gains some popularity. • The training of students' visual perception skills is advocated. • Interest in teaching to the "strongest modality" emerges.	• Brain damage is thought by many to be a major causal factor. • Belief in multiple causation continues.	• The Illinois Test of Psycholinguistic Abilities (ITPA) is introduced and influences the focus of instructional interventions in many reading and LD programs for the next decade. • Prediction of reading failure before it occurs (called "early identification") is advocated.	• Title I programs begin. • Goodman's model of the reading process is introduced. • Certification of reading teachers begins in many states. • The term *learning disability* is suggested to replace many diverse labels for the same general condition. • Research begins on differences in mental processes in the left and right brain hemispheres.
1970–1979	• There is strong interest in reading instruction based on psycholinguistic research, with an accompanying emphasis on LEA. • Another major interest is diagnostic/prescriptive teaching. • There is a movement away from training visual, auditory, and motor processes.	• Inappropriate diet is purported to be a causal factor in lay press articles. • An interest in the role of defective memory processes as etiology in reading disabilities is seen. • There is a de-emphasis on brain damage as a cause. • The concept of multiple causation continues to be supported by most authorities.	• Criterion-referenced tests are widely used. • The Reading Miscue Inventory (RMI), devised to promote qualitative as well as quantitative judgments about reading errors, receives much attention and use. • The cloze procedure is considered an important diagnostic technique.	• The National Right-to-Read Effort is begun. • The Education for All Handicapped Children Act is passed; this increases the number of LD classes in public schools. • An interactive model of the reading process is proposed by Rumelhart.
1980–1989	• There is a heavy emphasis on techniques for improving comprehension. • Computer-based instruction is being used and its value debated. • There is interest in how reading and writing are linked.	• The concept of multiple causation continues to be the causal theory most widely accepted.	• Investigations into improved ways to assess comprehension are undertaken. • The RMI and cloze technique continue to be used.	• There is a growing closeness of the reading disability and learning disabilities fields.

(continued)

TABLE 1–4 *Some Trends and Issues in Remedial and Clinical Reading Instruction* *(continued)*

Time Period	Instructional Approaches	Suggested Causes of Reading Disability	Prevalent Assessment Techniques and Tools	Milestones
1990–1999	• There is an interest in whole-language and literature-based instruction. • Interest in word recognition processes revives. • The Reading Recovery Program shows success with at-risk first graders. • "Balanced reading instruction" becomes a watchword, advocating attention both to connected text reading and to direct instruction of strategies.	• Research demonstrates that a strong characteristic distinguishing good from poor readers is the latter's lack of phonemic awareness. • The cyclical effects of a student's reading history (or, Matthew Effects) is considered to have serious impact on achievement.	• Portfolio assessment is popular. • For both reading and writing, authentic assessment is advocated.	• Marilyn Adams publishes *Beginning to Read: Thinking and Learning About Print*, providing a research base supporting phonics instruction. • Research specifying natural phases of word learning receives attention.
2000–present	• Emphasis on early intervention expands. • There is interest in effects of tutoring, partly the result of the U.S. Department of Education program, America Reads. • Research-based reading instruction is urged, even required, in many programs.	• Research support continues to build specifying lack of phonemic awareness as a major source of reading delays. • Interest in neurobiological factors revives with availability of technologies such as MRIs for examining brain behaviors. • A dimensional model is proposed suggesting reading disability as simply a part of a normal distribution of individual differences.	• Statewide literacy tests are mandated in most U.S. states. • Assessment practices are linked to literacy standards. • Issues of testing for improvement of learning vs. testing for accountability are prevalent. • Pressures to meet state and federally imposed goals for adequate yearly progress (AYP) influence curriculum.	• The Report of the National Reading Panel is issued providing a review of scientific research findings in reading. • The No Child Left Behind Act of 2001 and its subcomponent, Reading First, shape literacy programs in schools with high percentages of low-achieving students.

Sources: Table 1–4 draws upon numerous sources. Some of the most useful historical sources are listed here: Cook (1977); Critchley (1970); Evans (1982); Hall (1970); Hildreth (1965); Harris (1968, 1976, 1981); Matthews (1966); Ribovich (1978); H. A. Robinson (1966); Schreiner and Tanner (1976); N. B. Smith (1965); Thompson (1966).

📖 MODELS OF THE READING PROCESS

Reading researchers have attempted to learn what our brains do to recognize words, combine them into sentences, and understand messages from written language. These researchers have developed "models" to explain their conclusions. The term **reading model** can mean a verbal explanation of the reading process or a diagram to clarify that verbal explanation.

Many believe understanding these processes is crucial to solving the problems of low literacy. Several models are presently considered important.

Cognitive-processing models attempt to explain how we know that little lines, squiggles, and shapes on paper represent specific words, thus enabling us to read.

Cognitive-Processing Models

The term **cognitive** derives from the word *cognition*, which refers to thinking. Cognitive-processing models attempt to explain how thinking processes allow us to know that little lines, squiggles, and shapes on paper represent specific words, thus enabling us to read.

The Rumelhart Model. In 1976, David Rumelhart proposed an **interactive model** now widely accepted in the literacy profession.

Several older "serial" models previously had described text processing as occurring in serial steps, one after the other, with no immediate interaction among the steps. The serial models were divided into two types, and these have significance for understanding the Rumelhart model. One type, **bottom-up models,** suggested that a reader starts with smaller elements of language (such as letters and words) and goes up to larger portions and meaning. The second type, **top-down models,** described readers moving in the other direction, starting first by predicting meaning and then identifying words.

In contrast, Rumelhart's model proposes that readers begin word identification and predict meaning *at the same time* and that lower-level processes (word identification) and higher-level processes (meaning) *help* each other. Thus, the model is designated "interactive."

Rumelhart diagrammed the interactive process he proposed (Figure 1–1). In this model, the lines, squiggles, and shapes making up print (the "graphemic input") are registered in the brain's "visual information store," a temporary storage place for lines and squiggles, labeled VIS in the diagram. While there, graphemic input is acted on by a "feature extraction device." It determines the features (i.e., lines, circles, and positions or combinations of these) that identify what particular ink marks on the page represent. Next, a "pattern synthesizer" acts on these features, using four knowledge sources, simultaneously. These are the reader's **syntactical knowledge** (intuitive knowledge of sentence patterns based on the reader's knowledge of oral and written language), **semantic knowledge** (knowledge of meaning), **orthographic knowledge** (knowledge of letters, spelling patterns, and sounds), and **lexical knowledge** (knowledge of words)—all used to get at meaning (i.e., the most probable interpretation).

Many reading professionals agree that bottom-up and top-down models do not explain things we know to be true about the reading process, and experimental findings seem to confirm that the process is interactive.

An important way to improve reading ability is to do a great deal of reading.

FIGURE 1–1   *A Stage Representation of an Interactive Model of Reading*

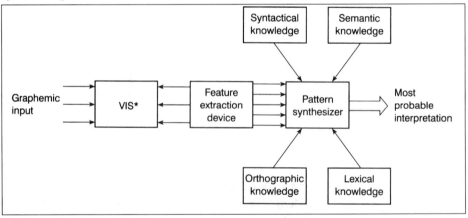

Source: From Rumelhart, David E. (2004). Toward an Interactive Model of Reading. *Theoretical Models and Processes of Reading*, 5th edition, Robert B. Ruddell & Norman J. Unrau, editors, International Reading Association, 1149–1179. Reprinted with permission of the International Reading Association. All rights reserved.

*VIS = Visual Information Store

Practical implications.   Programs should emphasize both word identification and meaning since lower-level and higher-level processes aid each other. Because some decisions are based on knowledge of print structures, students need abundant opportunities to read; the more students read, the more efficient their print and meaning predictions can be.

Orthographic and lexical knowledge are important, but students also have syntactical knowledge, based on their use of oral language, which can assist in

When students discuss their interpretations of text meanings, comprehension is enhanced.

encounters with printed text. One must remember, however, that although there are more similarities than differences, written syntactic structures do vary somewhat from oral language patterns. Therefore, teachers should attempt to increase students' knowledge of written language patterns. One way to do this is by reading *to* them.

For semantic knowledge to be accessible, meanings must be stored in the student's background knowledge. Students can add to their store of meanings through direct experiences, discussions before reading, vicarious experiences (such as viewing pictures and other audiovisuals), and reading. Instructional strategies should lead students to apply their prior knowledge when they are reading.

LEARNING FROM TEXT

Applying What You've Learned. What practical applications might the Rumelhart model suggest for use in your own classroom? Consider this question for the other models you read about below.

The Stanovich Model. Keith Stanovich (1980) proposed an **interactive-compensatory model** that has significance for delayed readers. Agreeing with Rumelhart that reading involves interactions of several knowledge sources, the added term *compensatory* extends that view. Stanovich advanced the notion that when there is a deficit in any of these knowledge sources, the reader compensates by using one or more of the others. As an illustration, Stanovich uses this frequently seen example: a poor reader, deficient in automatic word recognition (lexical knowledge), turns to context clues (based on syntactic and semantic knowledge). This reader guesses unknown words based on what would seem correct—in terms of sentence patterns and in terms of meaning—as suggested by words that are known. In this case, context clues compensate for limited word knowledge. At some stages of learning, using one knowledge source to compensate for another at least allows readers to work their way through text.

However, in relation to this example, Stanovich believes his model explains individual differences in reading fluency and comprehension. He cites studies showing that poor readers use context more than good readers, and as a result have slower word recognition times as they guess their way through printed material. Conversely, good readers are more proficient in context-free word recognition (i.e., they recognize words immediately on sight) and have more effective phonological decoding skills (i.e., they easily use letter sounds to identify words). Both factors produce fluent reading. Proficient word recognition also may account for good readers' superior comprehension: since less attention is needed for word identification, more is available to focus on meaning.

Practical implications.   The interactive-compensatory model suggests that readers need a variety of knowledge sources to call on and also implies that readers must be flexible in strategy use. If one strategy does not work, students should ask themselves, "What could I try next?" "What other information could help me?"

> Readers need a variety of knowledge sources to call on and must be flexible in strategy use.

If poor readers are to become good readers, they must eventually learn to recognize words automatically. Moreover, during reading stages in which many words are still unknown, adept use of phonic and structural analysis strategies is an aid to fluent reading. Students should master these strategies so undue attention to word recognition does not detract from gaining meaning.

A Sociocognitive-Processing Model

> Sociocognitive-processing models consider both thinking processes and environmental/contextual factors related to learning.

Sociocognitive-processing models not only consider thinking processes, as the Rumelhart and Stanovich models do, but also take into account "social" factors related to learning. In this case, the designation *social* refers to environmental influences (sometimes called "contextual influences") that affect understanding.

The Ruddell and Unrau Model.   While the two previously discussed models center largely on word recognition/identification, the Ruddell and Unrau (1994) reading model focuses on processes for obtaining meaning. This model looks at several interacting elements in the learning environment: (a) the reader, (b) the teacher, and (c) the text and classroom context. The model suggests the following.

The reader.   The reader's own knowledge-construction processes are important for obtaining meaning from text (see Figure 1–2). The term *construction* in this description is used to indicate that readers mentally engage in activities to build, develop, and "get at" meaning. Knowledge construction involves cognitive functions such as purpose-setting, planning, and organizing (e.g., the reader might, instinctively or deliberately, adopt different reading strategies depending on whether the text is a story or informational material). The reader's knowledge-construction activities lead to tentative interpretations of what the text means.

However, consciously or unconsciously, preliminary interpretations may be affected by the reader's prior beliefs and prior knowledge. As seen in Figure 1–2, these preexisting factors include affective conditions (such as sociocultural

FIGURE 1–2   *Reading as a Meaning-Construction Process: The Ruddell and Unrau Model*

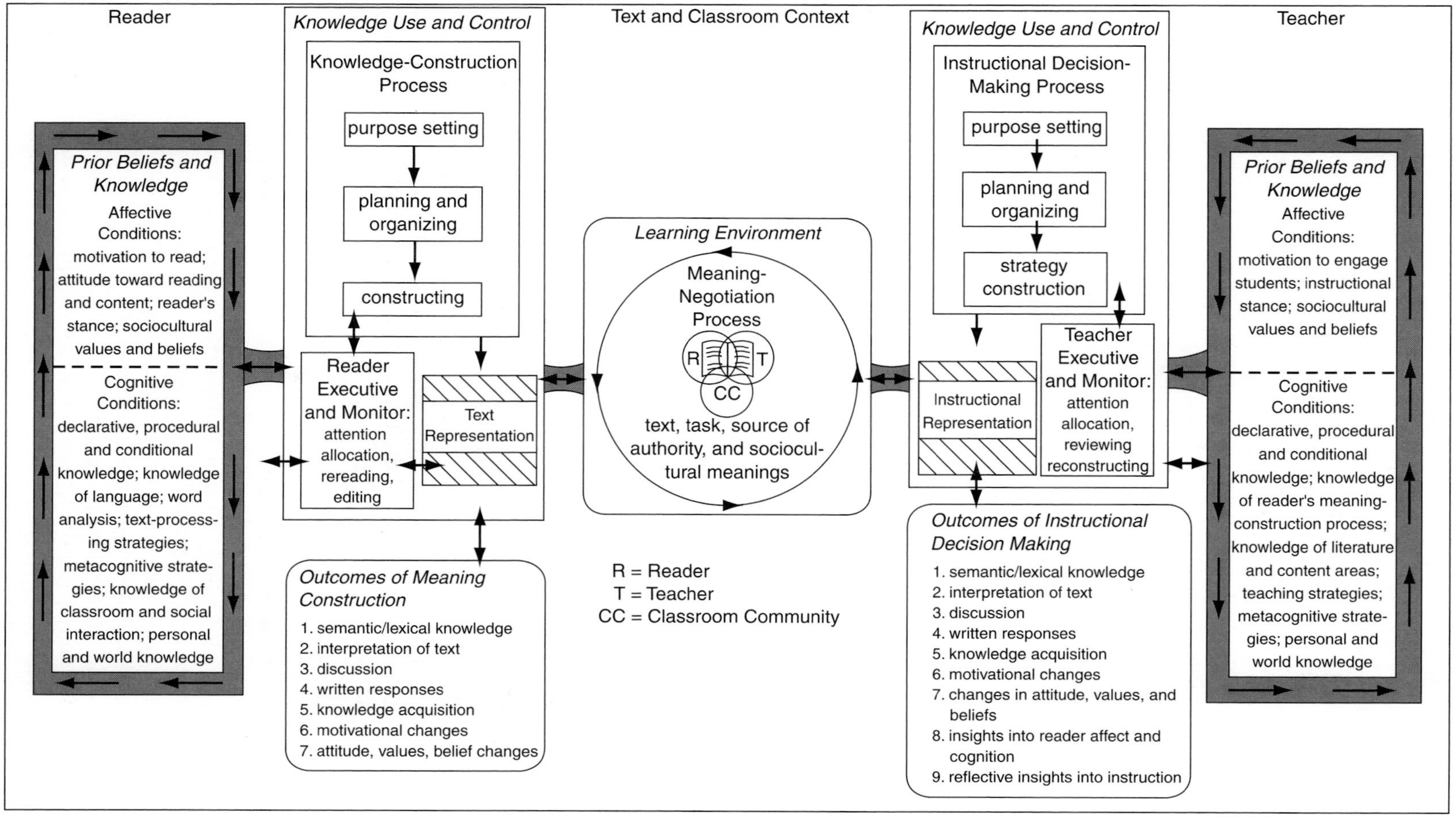

Source: Figure p. 1465, from Ruddell, Robert B., & Unrau, Norman J. (2004). Reading as a meaning-construction process: The reader, the text, and the teacher. *Theoretical Models and Processes of Reading,* 5th edition, Robert B. Ruddell & Norman J. Unrau, editors, International Reading Association, article 51, pp. 1462-1521. Reprinted with permission of Robert B. Ruddell and the International Reading Association.

values) and cognitive conditions (such as language knowledge). Based on these factors, readers may confirm or reject their initial interpretations.

The teacher. The teacher's beliefs and knowledge, which have critical impact on learning conditions, come into play through a variety of factors, such as instructional philosophy and familiarity with content areas. These influence the teacher's purpose setting, planning, and organizing, which, in turn, influence strategy construction—that is, the selection or development of teaching strategies the teacher perceives to be relevant to a lesson's goal and learners' needs. The teacher may monitor and, if necessary, reconstruct activities if, based on that teacher's standards, sufficient understanding is not occurring.

The text and classroom context. There are additional interacting factors through which comprehension is mediated, beginning with the presence of the text that provides ideas and information, but also incorporating discussions and exchanges of interpretations with others in the classroom learning community (teacher and classmates).

Practical implications. Ruddell and Unrau specify a number of classroom suggestions based on their model. For one, readers should review their existing knowledge about a topic to build understanding of new content. Developing a purpose for reading aids comprehension as readers vary their approach to the material based on that purpose. Exchanges of meaning interpretations among all in the classroom community extends comprehension because considering divergent points adds to richness of understanding, dispels misconceptions, and provides new meanings from which to draw in the future.

A General Learning Theory with Implications for Reading

Vygotsky's Model of Learning. Although not a reading model, Vygotsky's (1978) learning theory is influential among literacy educators. Of particular interest is his notion of a **zone of proximal development,** a developmental area where tasks are slightly harder than what students can do by themselves.

Figure 1–3 illustrates this zone of proximal development within a learning continuum. The "easy" end represents what a student can do independently; instructional time spent here is not particularly productive because the student has these understandings under control. The "hard" end of the continuum represents tasks presently far beyond the student's capabilities. Between these is the zone of proximal development, the area where Vygotsky contended that maximum learning occurs—an area where the student is ready to learn, *if given assistance.*

To scaffold instruction, the teacher carefully guides the student through lessons just slightly above what the student could do independently.

Vygotsky believed that a distinct type of assistance is needed, however, a type called **scaffolding.** In the house-building trades, scaffolding temporarily supports a house under construction; in scaffolded instruction, the teacher temporarily supports the learner until independence is achieved in learning a strategy or accomplishing a task (Pressley, 2002). To scaffold learning, the teacher determines a student's present skill level or understanding, then guides the student through lessons at a level just slightly above what he or she can do independently. As the student approaches independence, the teacher increasingly releases more responsibility to the student. Following this

FIGURE 1–3 ***Portrayal of Vygotsky's Zone of Proximal Development***

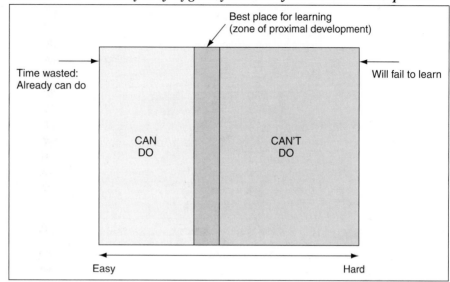

pattern, the student is guided gradually upward to higher and higher levels of achievement.

The form of scaffolding most commonly advocated is what Clark and Graves (2005) call "moment-to-moment verbal scaffolding" in which teacher prompts may spontaneously vary in reaction to student responses during ongoing instruction. Whenever possible, the teacher does not supply solutions to tasks but leads students to discover solutions. The teacher may: (a) model appropriate behaviors, (b) contribute cues about specific elements or strategies, and (c) urge students to think through problem-solving action plans (Beed, Hawkins, & Roller, 1991).

Clark and Graves (2005) suggest another form of scaffolding, which they refer to as use of "instructional frameworks that foster learning." Less frequently discussed, this form is preplanned, taking into account (a) student skill, (b) text characteristics, and (c) lesson goals. Bearing these factors in mind, the teacher structures prereading, during-reading, and after-reading exercises to induce new learning or foster independence, perhaps selecting from activities in Table 1–5.

Another important aspect of Vygotsky's learning theory proposes that developmental levels are not predetermined by student age or intellectual ability. Vygotsky believed that careful student-teacher interactions can advance the levels at which most students operate.

Draw a Schematic.   Research shows the effectiveness of schematic diagrams for enhancing comprehension. Now is an ideal time to try this strategy by drawing a simple diagram to illustrate written text information. Schematics accompany three of the models discussed. Draw your own schematic of the Stanovich model.

TABLE 1–5 *Possible Activities in a Scaffolded Reading Experience*

Prereading	During Reading	Postreading
Relating the reading to students' lives	Silent reading	Questioning
Motivating	Reading to students	Discussion
Activating and building background knowledge	Supported reading	Writing
Providing text-specific knowledge	Oral reading by students	Drama
Preteaching vocabulary	Modifying the text	Artistic and nonverbal activities
Preteaching concepts		Application and outreach activities
Prequestioning, predicting, and direction setting		Building connections
Suggesting strategies		Reteaching

Source: Clark, Kathleen F., & Graves, Michael F. (2005, March). Scaffolding students' comprehension of text. *The Reading Teacher, 58*(6), 570-580. Reprinted with permission of Kathleen F. Clark and the International Reading Association.

Reflections

Reflections   This section, titled Reflections, ends each chapter. It is designed to involve you in decision-making activities related to the chapter content.

Cognitive research indicates that *collaborative learning* is helpful when concepts are novel and complex. This is a technique you can use with students in your own classroom. For now, try this yourself. Divide into teams of two. Each team should discuss a reading model presented in this chapter by doing the following.

1. Examine each step the model suggests a reader goes through to read. Engage in mutual peer tutoring, discussing each step until both partners understand it.
2. Now that you've dealt with details, think about what the main assumptions are that the model maker(s) believes underlie reading processes? Develop a short list with your partner.

2

Causes and Correlates of Individual Differences in Reading Ability

Phonemic awareness is an important prerequisite to reading, spelling, and writing.

A common question asked of reading and learning disability teachers is "What causes a student to have reading problems?" Parents frequently worry that delayed reading development is due to a child's lack of intellectual ability. Others believe a simple intervention such as getting glasses for the child will solve a reading problem. Popular magazines and newspapers frequently feature articles that attribute reading or other learning disabilities to diet, allergies, brain damage, hyperactivity, lack of sensory integration, and many other factors. As Spear-Swerling and Sternberg (1998) say, ". . . when parents are told that a child has a reading disability, they have an understandable desire to seek answers about causation" (p. 230).

What actually causes reading disabilities? How much truth lies in commonly held beliefs about the causes of reading problems?

To answer these questions, first one must understand the differences between *correlation* and *causation.* Although two circumstances may be correlated, one does not necessarily cause the other. For example, suppose a particularly silly researcher decided to undertake a study to determine the relationship between reading achievement and facial hairiness in school-age boys. The researcher probably would find a higher degree of reading achievement in those males with more facial hair because, of course, students who have more facial hair are generally older and normally have had more reading experience. Although a correlation between hairiness and reading achievement could be shown, it certainly would not mean that hairness causes increased reading ability. Nor does it mean that if lack of hairiness could be "corrected" (e.g., giving hormonal treatments to all fourth-grade boys in remedial reading classes), reading achievement would increase. Understanding the concepts of correlation versus causation is important because misunderstanding differences between the two has led to incorrect interpretations of research on causes of reading disabilities and, as a result, to many fruitless teaching procedures.

A related consideration is the teacher's knowledge of research methodology. Teachers working with students who have learning disorders should have coursework that provides information about research procedures and, as well, have opportunities to critique existing research. Some research about causes of reading and other learning disabilities is poorly constructed, and results are simply not credible. Learning to identify faulty research procedures helps teachers avoid accepting fallacious research results.

This chapter presents information about factors that are (and are not) causes or correlates of reading disabilities. Eight general areas are discussed:

1. physiological factors
2. hereditary factors
3. emotional factors
4. sociocultural factors
5. educational factors
6. cognitive factors
7. language factors
8. reading history factors

As you read this chapter, you will find some citations that are older than those elsewhere in this text. Here's why. Over the last century, interest in causes of reading disability/reading delay have moved through cycles and trends (see Table 1–4 in Chapter 1). During a particular time period, high interest in a topic results in much research, and, consequently, often the question being posed becomes a closed issue. As just one example, in the 1930s and particularly the 1940s, many people asked if reading problems were caused by eye defects. But, today, there is little interest in the topic. For instance, it is highly unlikely that research would be undertaken currently on the relationship between nearsightedness and reading difficulties. This is because so much research in the early and mid-20th century indicated there was no connection. Closed issues are a good thing because this allows us to move forward in our quest to solve the puzzling problem of reading delay. However, because much of the public is uninformed about research related to causes of reading problems, reading specialists must be aware of the results and conclusions of both former and present research.

PHYSIOLOGICAL FACTORS

Sensory Impairments

This section on sensory impairments explores visual, hearing, and speech impairments and the effect they have on reading ability.

LEARNING FROM TEXT

> **Make a Prediction.** Before reading the sections on vision and visual perception, make a prediction. Which of the following may be possible causes of an individual's reading disability? Which are not?
>
> - fusion difficulties with the eyes
> - myopia (nearsightedness)
> - faulty eye movements
> - astigmatism
> - eye defects that cause reversals of letters and words
> - limited eye perceptual span
> - visual perception problems

Vision. For certain visual problems, research does show a relationship with reading difficulties, while for others the majority of research shows no connection. Usually when a correlation has been shown, it has been related to **fusion difficulties,** impairments in using two eyes together (Dearborn & Anderson, 1938). One example is aniseikonia, in which the images of an object formed by each eye appear unequal in size and shape. Fusion difficulties occur much more rarely than refractive errors such as nearsightedness, farsightedness, or astigmatism.

Nearsightedness, the most common visual problem, shows no relationship with reading difficulties.

The most prevalent visual problem among school-age individuals, nearsightedness, has no positive relationship to reading difficulties, according to most research (e.g., Taylor, 1937). This is also the case with astigmatism (e.g., Robinson, 1946) and amblyopia (Harris & Sipay, 1980). This means that simply obtaining glasses for a child will not solve reading difficulties. Correcting visual problems may make it possible for students to see printed information more easily, but once the visual difficulty is corrected, instruction is still necessary to help them learn reading strategies.

Another area that has been explored in attempting to explain individual differences in reading ability has involved eye movements. A prevailing hypothesis at one time was that reading difficulties occurred because of inefficient control of eye movements. Actually, it is true that poor readers fixate longer on words and make more eye-movement regressions than do individuals with adequate reading skills. However, much research over several years has laid to rest the assumption that this is a *cause* of reading disabilities; rather, these eye-movement patterns are a *result* of poor word recognition skill (Rayner & Duffy, 1988).

A concern for teachers counseling parents is the effect of visual training exercises on improving reading ability. Ophthalmologists and some optometrists hold opposing views on the value of such training. (**Ophthalmologists** are medical doctors who specialize in diagnosis and treatment of eye diseases and abnormalities, and have passed examinations of the American Board of Ophthalmology; **optometrists** are nonmedical vision specialists trained to diagnose vision defects and prescribe glasses or contact lenses.) Although there are fewer today, some optometrists advocate visual training as a corrective measure in treating reading problems. Most, however, are currently adopting the view of ophthalmologists who believe the training has no value. No research following currently accepted methodological procedures has shown effectiveness of visual training for improvement of reading disability.

Visual Perception. The contribution of visual perception problems to reading difficulties has been much discussed in past years. Allegedly, students with poor visual perception are plagued by confusions and distortions when they look at visual symbols. Some supposed symptoms are listed here.

1. A word appears as a meaningless mixture of letters. The word *music*, for example, might appear as *msuci*.
2. Letters and words are reversed. For example, *b* appears as *d*, or *was* as *saw*.
3. A word may appear as its mirror image.
4. Students may respond to small details of a letter, such as the curve in a lowercase *r*, to the detriment of seeing the letter as a whole.
5. Students may attend to the white spaces between letters in a word instead of the letters themselves.

In looking at the list of symptoms ascribed to students who purportedly have visual perception problems, teachers might ask how one can know a student is responding to the printed page in this manner. What behaviors would students exhibit if they were reading the white spaces between the words? What response would students make if they were reading only the curve in the lowercase *r*? Very little that has been suggested about reading problems resulting from visual perception is observable or measurable. Most is merely conjecture.

Several programs have been proposed for training students with alleged visual perception problems. However, both research and practice have shown that visual perception training does not increase reading ability or remediate other learning disabilities. One well-known program designed to improve students' visual perceptual skills has been the Frostig program, which requires students to match shapes, draw lines within printed lines from one picture to another, and engage in other similar activities. Investigations of the influence of this program on word recognition ability, visual perception skills, and reading readiness of low-achieving students failed to prove its usefulness in any of these areas (e.g., Buckland, 1970).

Note Taking.   Throughout this chapter are indications of procedures to AVOID. These are interspersed within other information, so keep a running list of these to aid recall; also note appropriate teaching procedures.

Another type of training advocated for remediating visual perception difficulties is the use of visual tracking exercises. Such exercises have no value in improving reading skills. For example, Cohen (1972) investigated the use of the Visual Tracking and Word Tracking workbooks of the Michigan Tracking Program with 75 remedial readers and concluded that such exercises did not increase reading achievement.

While it is true that some students with reading delays do reverse letters and words, research also indicates that many average readers make letter and word reversals during preschool and early primary-grade years. Spache (1976) examined 35 studies related to reversals and found that 80% of these showed no difference in the occurrence of reversals in good readers and poor readers. Brown (1982) makes an important point:

> Although the perceptual centers in the brain invert the scene reported to it by the optic nerve . . . they cannot invert some small portion of that scene. If, for example, a person looks out the window onto a beautiful panorama of mountains, trees, and greenery, it is not possible for him to see one tree in an inverted position while all the rest of the landscape is right side up. . . . Although the optic nerve reports everything to the perceptual centers upside down and backward to what is actually there, the entire scene is interpreted right side up and in proper left and right relationship based on the perceptual center's past experience of what is real. The perceptual center cannot interpret all of a page as right side up but leave one small word such as *was* or *saw* upside down and backward. It would be even further beyond belief to imagine that the perceptual center of the brain would interpret sensations received from the optic nerve right side up with the exception of the word *was*, which it would interpret in reversed right-to-left order but not inverted. Such perception would be completely incredible. (pp. 63–64)

When students continue to make reversals beyond the primary years, it is because they fail to use directionality in making discriminations (Moyer & Newcomer, 1977) or fail to read for meaning, not because they have problems with visual perception.

Visual perception is indeed involved in reading, but no specialized kinds of perceptual skills are required. As Smith (1978) states,

> . . . there is, in fact, nothing unique about reading. There is nothing in reading as far as vision is concerned that is not involved in such mundane perceptual activities as distinguishing tables from chairs or dogs from cats. (p. 2)

Based on research evidence, it is logical to conclude that visual perception "difficulties" do not contribute to reading disabilities.

Using Illustrative Aids.   Note that your text suggests that you take time to read over the information in Figure 2–1. Information in figures and tables is placed in informational texts to clarify or to increase understanding. It is a good study strategy to use such illustrative material.

Figure 2–1 provides a summary of points made regarding the impact of vision factors on reading ability. After examining this figure to review the information in the preceding section, reading teachers may want to prepare a handout from the figure to distribute to parents and other teachers.

Hearing.   Students with severe hearing impairment frequently have difficulties learning to read.

The degree of hearing loss that individuals experience varies greatly and can have more or less of an impact on reading ability. Students with a slight hearing loss may only need special attention to vocabulary development and require special seating to hear more easily. Those with a somewhat greater loss may miss much of class discussion, have limited vocabularies, and need special instruction in reading. A marked hearing loss may result in problems with language production and understanding; these students will need special help in reading and all language skills. Students with even more severe losses may be able to

Make a Prediction.   Does hearing impairment cause reading difficulties?

FIGURE 2–1   *The Impact of Vision Factors on Reading Delays/Disabilities*

A Summary of Points for Parents and Educators About Vision and Reading (or Learning) Disabilities

1. Obtaining glasses for a child/student will not solve reading problems.

2. Neither nearsightedness nor astigmatism—common eye defects of school-age individuals—causes reading delays.

3. Poor "control" of eye movements does not cause reading difficulties.

4. There is no evidence, based on studies following accepted research procedure, that visual training exercises improve reading ability.

5. Reading problems are not caused by visual perception abnormalities.

6. Visual tracking exercises do not increase reading achievement.

7. It is common for letter and word reversals to occur with good readers as well as poor readers.

8. Reversals are not caused by vision defects, but by failure to use directionality to make discriminations between letters or between words. Use of directionality can be taught.

9. Reading takes place in the brain, not in the eye.

discriminate vowel sounds but unable to discriminate consonants; since speech does not develop spontaneously for these students, they may need a special program designed for developing language skills. Students suffering the most extreme losses have difficulties with speech and require special training in oral communication, concept development, and all reading and language skills.

Although many individuals with severe hearing impairments reach a high level of educational attainment, some do not, even though they have normal intelligence. In general, students with severe hearing impairments have more difficulty in learning to read and progressing in reading than any other group. Since the reading skills of students with severe hearing impairments are often atypical, special national norms have been developed for interpreting their reading scores on certain tests.

LEARNING FROM TEXT

Make a Prediction.   Do speech disorders cause reading disabilities?

Speech.   The causes of a speech disorder (such as distortions of sounds, stuttering, problems of pitch, and others) include emotional problems, developmental delay, inadequate hearing, imperfectly developed vocal cords, cleft palate, and brain damage.

When a speech problem results from a brain lesion, it is not unusual to find that the affected individual also has a reading delay. Because one of several areas of the brain involved in reading is located near the language center, injury to the language center may also affect the reading area. In these cases, an individual may exhibit both speech and reading difficulties, but the speech disorder does not *cause* the reading problem. Rather, both result from a common cause.

Most speech problems, such as poor articulation (which accounts for about 75% of all speech disorders), stuttering, and lisping, have no direct relationship to reading disabilities. Speech defects are no more prevalent among disabled readers than among average readers.

Neurological Difficulties

Neurology is the study of the nervous system. The human nervous system is comprised of the brain, spinal cord, nerves, ganglia (masses of nerve tissue), and parts of receptor organs. Several types of neurological difficulties have been hypothesized to contribute to reading disabilities—most of them associated with the brain. See Figure 2–2 for a brief description of the workings of the human brain.

LEARNING FROM TEXT

Make a Prediction.   Possible cause of reading difficulties or myth?

- lack of neurological organization
- medically diagnosed brain damage
- food additives
- mixed cerebral dominance
- refined sugar in the diet
- poor motor coordination

FIGURE 2-2 *Information About the Operation of the Brain*

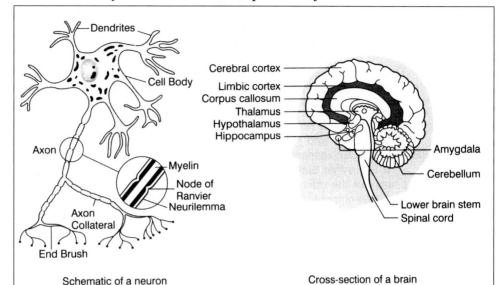

Schematic of a neuron   Cross-section of a brain

Parts of the Brain
1. *Neuron.* A cell consisting of a cell body, dendrites, and an axon.
2. *Dendrites.* Wispy, fingerlike parts surrounding the neuron cell body.
3. *Axon.* A single, taillike portion attached to each neuron cell body.
4. *Neurotransmitter.* A chemical that carries a message from one neuron to another.
5. *Synapse.* A gap between neurons.

Brain Processes
This is a simplified version of what is presently known about how the brain works.
1. Sensory receptors all over the body (e.g., in the eyes and ears) send messages to the brain.
2. When the initial message reaches the brain, neurons further process it in the following way:
   a. Dendrites receive the message and expel an electrical impulse.
   b. This impulse is moved to the axon, which releases a chemical called a *neurotransmitter.*
   c. The neurotransmitter moves across a synapse to the dendrite of the next neuron.
   d. This process is repeated over and over through many of the 5 to 25 billion neurons in the brain, each of which is as complicated as a computer.
The brain comprises many areas, including the cerebral cortex, limbic cortex, corpus callosum, thalamus, hypothalamus, hippocampus, amygdala, and cerebellum, plus the lower brain stem, which is connected to the spinal cord. Specific sections specialize in specific activities, but often more than one brain area is involved in functions and behaviors. Scientists still do not understand the neural codes that translate sensory perceptions into the processing performed in the brain.

Interesting Facts
1. The outer covering of the brain, the cerebral cortex, is only about one tenth of an inch thick, but controls all higher-level mental functions.
2. Memory is stored in cells all over the brain; although in the long run, it may end up in the cortex.
3. More than 50 chemical substances make up the different neurotransmitters that carry messages.
4. An electroencephalogram (EEG) measures the electricity expelled by the brain's neurons.
5. There is white matter as well as gray matter in the brain. Gray matter consists of clusters of neuron cell bodies. White matter consists of bundles of nerve fibers.
6. When a neuron is damaged, a new one does not replace it; it simply ceases to function.

Brain Damage. Brain damage can result from injuries, disease, or toxic substances. Complications during pregnancy can cause some types of neurological damage in the child. Brain damage may also occur during birth. Neurological difficulties related to pregnancy and birth are called **perinatal neurological disorders.** In addition, high and prolonged fevers or poisoning (e.g., lead poisoning) can damage brain tissue. Stroke is the most common cause of brain damage in adults. These various injuries, diseases, or toxins may cause a **lesion**—that is, an abnormal change in the structure of the brain. Lesions may be mild, moderate, or severe and may occur in areas of the brain that do not affect learning to read or in those that do.

A neurological examination by a medical doctor, including an electroencephalogram (EEG) to record electrical activity of the brain, as well as a physician's study of the individual's developmental history, is necessary to determine existence of brain damage. In times past, when a diagnosis of brain damage did not result from a medical examination, sometimes educators insisted that **minimal brain damage (MBD)** was present as evidenced by certain "soft signs" such as inattention, poor motor coordination, and difficulty in left-right discrimination. In addition, poor performance on certain tests administered by psychologists, such as the Bender-Gestalt test, the Draw-A-Person test, and others, often led to a label of MBD. However, there is danger in assuming brain damage without a medical examination, and today it is considered unacceptable to infer brain damage by such means. Inattention, poor motor coordination, and other symptoms may have many other causes than the assumed "medically undetectable" brain damage. The concept of soft signs as an indication of brain damage is not helpful to educators.

The consequences of brain damage that has been medically diagnosed vary. Although some students with diagnosed brain damage may have reading disabilities, most have no difficulty in learning to read. For example, Byers and Lord (1943) reported a study of 13 students with medically determined brain damage caused by lead poisoning; all were making adequate progress in reading. On the other hand, Balow, Rubin, and Rosen (1975–76) found a statistically significant (although low) correlation between perinatal neurological disorders and reading disabilities. In any case, the consensus holds that only in severe cases of reading disability is brain damage a possible factor and, even in these cases, an infrequent one.

> Only in severe cases of reading disability is brain damage a possible factor, and even in these cases an infrequent one.

Even if a neurologist diagnoses brain damage in students with reading disabilities, the diagnosis provides little useful information for teachers. In the past, special instructional techniques, such as training in perceptual-motor coordination, manipulation of visual-spatial configurations, and memory for designs, were used with students who had suffered brain damage. It has since been found that these activities have no positive influence on learning to read for brain-damaged, or any other, students. After reviewing the research on teaching brain-damaged students, Reed, Rabe, and Mankinen (1970) found little evidence to indicate that these students require or benefit from teaching procedures different from those useful for other disabled readers.

Neurological Dysfunctions. Neurological dysfunctions from causes other than brain damage have been studied in relation to reading disabilities. Some of these may result from **atypical maturation of the brain,** in which one area may develop more slowly than others, or from a **congenital brain defect,** in which an individual is born with an underdeveloped area of the brain. Shaywitz et al. (2000) have reported studies in which minor malformations in brain cells of males with severe reading difficulties were found, malformations that they hypothesized to have occurred during fetal development. Individuals with such problems are very rare, however, and these abnormalities may not always cause a reading disability. Ackerly and Benton (1947) reported the case of a man who had very good reading skills despite a serious congenital defect: part of a brain lobe was missing.

Recently there have been a number of explorations of brain structure differences using newly developed technologies such as CT scanning and MRIs. Some of these studies have found differences between reading-delayed subjects and average readers in the size of areas on temporal lobes of the brain located near a site believed to be responsible for some language processing (e.g., Flowers, 1993). In those studies, however, differences have been found only for some reading-delayed individuals, and other studies have not found these differences at all (e.g., Denckla, LeMay, & Chapman, 1985).

One unfortunate notion related to neurological dysfunction is that of "lack of neurological organization." Delacato (1963) and others have proposed a theory based on the premise that development of neurological functions progresses from lower to higher levels. They theorized that the central nervous system may sometimes bypass certain normal developmental stages, resulting in a lack of neurological organization. To remediate irregular neurological organization, the Delacato program proposed a series of motor and other sensory stimulation activities purportedly based on the evolutionary stages of motor development in humans. Clients of this program engage in such activities as cross-pattern creeping and walking (extending the right foot while pointing to it with the left hand and vice versa), one-sided crawling, visual pursuit activities, and sleep patterning. Sleep patterning requires a child to sleep in specific positions; parents check throughout the night and readjust the child's position if necessary.

Delacato contended that these motor activities cause proper neural connections to occur in the central nervous system because of the stimulation to the sensory system. This program supposedly was useful in treating individuals with reading and other learning disabilities, assisting brain-damaged individuals, and increasing IQ. In a number of studies (Foster, 1966; O'Donnell & Eisenson, 1969; Robbins, 1966), the program was not shown to increase reading achievement. Delacato's claims have been censured by major educational, medical, and health organizations, such as the International Reading Association, the National Association of Retarded Children, the American Academies of Neurology, Orthopedics, Pediatrics, Physical Medicine and Rehabilitation, and Cerebral Palsy, all of which have accused Delacato of making undocumented claims of cures. Interest in Delacato's theory has diminished, but recently commercial clinics employing methods similar to Delacato's have opened. These should not be recommended to parents of children with reading disabilities, learning disabilities, or mental retardation.

Mixed Cerebral Dominance. The notion of mixed cerebral dominance is an old idea, once used in an attempt to explain reversals of letters and words. In 1937, Samuel Orton proposed a theory of reading disabilities based on the premise that individuals who have difficulty in learning to read have mixed cerebral dominance. Orton believed that normal readers have an established dominance of one side of the brain, which can be determined by the side of the body the individual prefers for hand, eye, ear, and foot use. That is, if individuals are right-handed and also show clear preferences for use of the right eye and right foot, this is an indication that **lateral dominance** has been established for one side of the body, in this case, the right side.

Orton proposed that students with reading disabilities have not established cerebral dominance. Such lack of dominance is indicated if they are right-handed and left-eyed, or left-handed, right-eyed, and left-footed, and so forth. His premise was that mixed cerebral dominance resulted in a condition he called *strephosymbolia*, which means "twisted symbols." Since supposedly neither side of the brain was dominant, Orton believed that students perceived words or letters appropriately on one side of the brain and at the same time perceived them as their mirror images on the other side. According to this theory, readers with mixed cerebral dominance would sometimes respond to the appropriate image and sometimes to the mirror image. Orton believed that when they responded to the mirror image, they made reversals of letters or words, for example, calling the letter *b* the letter *d* or calling the word *on* the word *no*.

Much research with young beginning readers, adolescents, students with reading and other learning disabilities, and individuals with mental retardation has shown that the lack of established lateral dominance has nothing to do with reading ability (e.g., Belmont & Birch; 1965; Benton & McCann, 1969; Capobianco, 1967).

LEARNING FROM TEXT

Relating Information to Your Own Experiences.   Since ADD is currently a hot topic, at the end of each paragraph in this section, stop and think. Was the information in that paragraph a surprise to you? Was it consistent with what you had previously thought?

Attention Deficit Disorder.   **Attention deficit disorder (ADD)** often is divided into two categories: (a) ADD and (b) ADD with hyperactivity, sometimes called ADHD. The former may be diagnosed when a student exhibits behaviors such as distractibility, impulsiveness, and short attention span. The second may be diagnosed by identifying an unusual degree of motor activity. Some medical professionals contend that neurological difficulties may be the source of ADD; in fact, some question if ADD is a valid diagnosis without evidence of neurological damage (Bohline, 1985).

Determination of the presence of either form of ADD should be made by a medical professional. The use of rating scales by nonmedical personnel to apply this label has been widely criticized, with studies showing that far too many students are misdiagnosed by such a procedure.

Because behaviors associated with ADD also are typical of students who have severe difficulty in learning, the "chicken and egg" question is increasingly being asked: "Does ADD prevent students from learning, or do difficulties in learning simply result in frustration and avoidance tactics such as off-task behaviors and restlessness?" Many educators and medical professionals believe that in the vast majority of instances the latter is the case.

Contrary to certain notions, most students with learning disabilities do not exhibit behaviors that have been associated with ADD. In addition, all students with discipline problems do not have ADD, and neither are all these students in need of drug or other therapy. Many may simply be taking advantage of a teacher who has poor classroom control.

Three types of dietary interventions have been suggested for controlling behaviors associated with ADD: (a) elimination of foods containing certain additives, (b) megavitamin therapy, and (c) elimination of refined sugar. The National

Advisory Committee on Hyperkinesis and Food Additives (1975) and the Committee on Nutrition of the American Academy of Pediatrics (1976) have found that claims for the effectiveness of eliminating additives and of treatments using megavitamins lack objective foundation. They have discounted these therapies for reducing ADD-like behaviors.

No objective evidence supports the theory that eliminating additives or refined sugar from the diet reduces ADD-like behaviors.

The suggestion that refined sugars be eliminated from the diet is based on the assumption that, after eating large amounts of sugar, hyperactive individuals secrete too much insulin, which consequently induces hypoglycemia; the resulting hypoglycemia supposedly interferes with brain functioning. A number of arguments refute this theory. For one, Sieben (1977) points out that no research has shown that abnormal amounts of insulin are secreted in hyperactive or learning disabled students. In addition, Sieben says that "since the body sees to it that the brain has first claim to whatever sugar is available, a truly hypoglycemic person would not be able to sustain the muscular effort required to be hyperactive" (p. 138). In sum, reducing ADD-like behaviors through dietary control has not been effective.

In contrast, drug therapy and behavior modification techniques can be helpful in controlling behaviors associated with ADD. However, because drugs have been overused with some students, there has been a reaction against using them at all. Using certain drugs, such as dilantin and phenobarbital, discriminately is helpful with some students and can effectively eliminate hyperactive behaviors that prevent learning. Behavior modification techniques also provide a promising avenue for working with students who exhibit hyperactive behaviors. For example, such behaviors have been reduced by rewarding students for on-task behavior—and by rewarding classmates for not encouraging off-task behavior. This dual procedure deprives students of reinforcement they receive from peers for inappropriate behaviors and substitutes reinforcement for behaviors conducive to learning. The fact that hyperactivity can be controlled in this fashion indicates that, regardless of its original source, many of its associated behaviors are learned and increased by environmental conditions.

Prenatal Crack/Cocaine Exposure.   For the information in this section, we are indebted to Barone (1999) for her carefully conceived longitudinal study of literacy development in children who were prenatally exposed to crack/cocaine through their pregnant mother's addiction. It is important to communicate this information, if only in summarized form, because the lay public (and sometimes educators) continue to be swayed by myths perpetuated in the media. In addition to her own investigation, Barone provides a comprehensive review of medical and educational studies related to the topic.

Barone's (1999) 4-year study of more than 20 children indicates that prenatal exposure to crack/cocaine is not a cause of reading disability. Of the children studied, five had some difficulty with literacy development, but by the end of investigation only one had not attained age-appropriate reading achievement. The remainder progressed successfully, and four of the children qualified for gifted and talented programs. Barone (1999) attributes the children's triumphs over their unpromising starts in life to two environmental factors—stable foster homes to which they had been removed and early interventions such as Headstart—along with the children's natural resiliency.

Moreover, and relevant for teachers, data show that prenatal crack/cocaine exposure does not lead to hyperactivity, nor is it necessary to teach these students in a low-stimulus environment. The latter is an old idea for working with learning and behaviorally disordered students that seems to have resurfaced in the early confusions about the effects of mothers' drug use on their unborn babies.

Finally, Barone (1999) cites studies in which students who were prenatally exposed to crack/cocaine demonstrated average intelligence on IQ tests (Cohen & Taharally, 1992; Rodning, Beckwith, & Howard, 1989) and average scores on instruments rating cognitive development of babies and toddlers (Griffith, 1992).

Motor Coordination.   Some educators have proposed that poor motor coordination is linked to reading disability. This is not the case, nor does training to improve motor development assist in eliminating reading or other learning disabilities.

Over the years, many programs have been proposed to promote sensory-motor development with the belief that they will increase academic achievement. A widely known example is Kephart's (1960) program of motor activities and body management. Kephart advocated such activities as balance beam walking, performing "angels in the snow" routines on the classroom floor, jumping on trampolines to get a feeling for the body's "position in space," and tracing circles on a board to practice crossing the body's "midline."

Hammill, Goodman, and Wiederholt (1974) reviewed 76 studies relating to the Kephart procedures. They concluded that the effect of this training on achievement in academic skills or on intelligence was not demonstrated. Class time spent on perceptual-motor activities is wasted time that would better be spent on reading practice. After an extensive review of the research, Balow (1971) stated that

> in numerous searches of the literature . . . no experimental study conforming to accepted tenets of research design has been found that demonstrates special effectiveness for any of the physical, motor, or perceptual programs claimed to be useful in the prevention or correction of reading or other learning disabilities. (p. 523)

LEARNING FROM TEXT

Make a Prediction.   Are reading difficulties inherited?

📖 HEREDITARY FACTORS

Some studies have suggested that reading disability is inherited. A number of these have compared the differences in reading ability between identical twins and fraternal twins. Identical twins often share almost indistinguishable personal characteristics; fraternal twins, on the other hand, do not. Several researchers (e.g., Pennington et al., 1991; Plomin, Owen, & McGuffin, 1994) believe their research with reading disabled twins supports the theory of a genetic origin of reading difficulties. These studies show a significantly higher proportion of both twins exhibiting a reading disability when they are identical than when fraternal. However, most educators believe that both biological and environmental influences affect academic learning. Since one fraternal twin may be male and one female, each may be subjected to different environmental influences, which may account for some of the differences found in this research.

Other studies have identified family groups with a high incidence of reading disability (e.g., DeFries, Vogler, & LaBuda, 1985). Some of these studies appear to have procedural problems, but others provide useful information. One group of researchers investigated the reading abilities of the family members of 20 problem readers and found that siblings and parents of these students also had a high percentage of reading problems (Finucci, Gutherie, Childs, Abbey, & Childs, 1976). In Hallgren's study (1950), only 1% of his 122 reading disabled subjects did not come from homes where there was a family history of reading difficulties. Some studies in other countries also have found this relationship. For example, Elbro, Borstrom, and Petersen's (1998) research with Danish families showed that children of parents with severe reading difficulties had an increased risk of having severe reading problems themselves. Results of studies by the Institute of Behavioral Genetics and others seem to support a genetic interpretation of reading problems.

Certain aptitudes do seem to reflect a genetic predisposition. For example, musical ability appears to run in some families, or unusual mathematical facility may be found in a student with a parent having a strong mathematical aptitude. It may be that parents genetically transmit a stronger or weaker aptitude for learning to read, just as they transmit other characteristics to their children. For instance, phonemic awareness, which has a clear link to reading success, may have a genetic as well as an environmental base (Spear-Swerling & Sternberg, 1998). A student with a weak inherited aptitude for a skill may face greater difficulties in acquiring it.

A concept related to genetic transmission of traits (including aptitude for reading) is that of **heritability.** This term refers to the degree to which genes can account for (or be "blamed" for) the trait in question. Studies (see Spear-Swerling & Sternberg, 1998) appear to show that heritability is less likely to come into play in facility with reading comprehension than it is with word recognition skill. And, with respect to word recognition, phonological processing skill seems to be more greatly influenced by heritability than orthographic processing skill. (See Figure 2–3 for a portrayal of these concepts.)

The genetic transmission of an aptitude, or lack of aptitude, may indeed be a tenable explanation for the success or failure of some individuals. However, in some cases, what may appear to be a hereditary cause may be an environmental one. Some of the best predictors of students' success in reading are parents' academic guidance of their children, the intellectual atmosphere in the home, parental aspirations for children, and parental language models, praise, and work habits. This means that parental behavior and the environment parents create may have as significant an impact on their children's reading success as genetic factors.

LEARNING FROM TEXT

Make a Prediction. Does emotional disturbance cause reading disabilities? Possible cause or myth?

FIGURE 2–3 *Relative Degrees of Heritability for (a) Comprehension Versus Word Recognition and (b) Phonological Processing Versus Orthographic Processing*

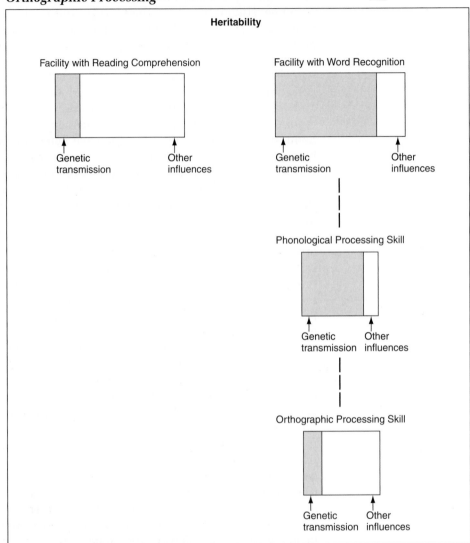

EMOTIONAL FACTORS

The 1940s and 1950s witnessed great interest in the effects of emotional disturbances on reading disability. Despite the cautions of leading educators, emotional maladjustment was considered by many at the time to be the most frequent cause of students' reading problems, and research designed to verify this hypothesis was common. However, results of the research showed that rather than emotional disturbances contributing to reading disabilities, in most cases, the converse was true; that is, reading disabilities contributed to emotional disorders.

Admittedly, a small number of students come to school with emotional problems so severe that their problems have a debilitating effect on their social behaviors and on all aspects of their academic learning. In those rare cases when a student's emotional problems are the initial underlying cause of the reading disability, psychological counseling is called for. However, for most students who are reading disabled and emotionally disturbed, the reading problem is at the root of the emotional disturbance rather than the other way around. These students enter school with emotionally healthy outlooks, but when they have difficulties in learning to read while their peers are progressing normally, they begin to exhibit mild to moderate emotional problems. A circular effect usually occurs; that is, emotional problems stemming from difficulties in learning to read, in turn, contribute to lack of further progress in reading. Problems of motivation become evident. Students may come to believe that they cannot learn to read, that something is wrong with them. The students' motivation to read continues to erode further over time, as does their confidence. This state has been referred to as **learned helplessness** (Johnston & Winograd, 1985). For these students, once the reading problem is remediated, the apparent emotional disturbance disappears. A case that illustrates this phenomenon is Brian's Case Study.

*Brian's
Case Study*

Brian, a fourth-grade boy labeled as having learning disabilities and behavior disorders, could read almost nothing when he was enrolled in a university reading clinic. When Brian's tutors attempted to engage him in any type of reading-related activity, he would spend only a few minutes on task. Then he would engage in a variety of avoidance behaviors, such as putting his head down, saying he was too tired to read, stating that his eyes hurt (although no visual problems of any kind existed), attempting to climb on the desk (even though he was quite large) to peer at students being tutored in other carrels, talking in a loud voice about off-the-subject topics, making abusive comments to his tutor, crawling on the floor, hiding under the desk and grabbing his tutor's legs when she came in, and simply refusing to engage in any planned activity. After 5 months of patient work, during which many instructional techniques were tried and even the smallest bit of progress was praised and visually demonstrated to him, Brian began to read. An almost immediate change in his behavior was seen. He remained on task for the entire 1-hour tutoring session; he asked to engage in specific reading activities; he became eager to demonstrate his reading skill to other clinic personnel; he was quiet, pleasant, and attentive in dealings with his tutor; and before and after tutoring sessions, he wandered about the clinic attempting to read everything in sight. On the day Brian came into the clinic wearing a badge he had received at school that day, a cheer went up in the clinic. The badge said he had been chosen as the good citizen of the month for his entire elementary school. As soon as Brian began to read, his other inappropriate behaviors disappeared. When these behaviors were eliminated, he could focus on tasks necessary in learning to read, and his progress in reading increased rapidly.

📖 SOCIOCULTURAL FACTORS

NCLB

READING
FIRST

Sociological factors are those related to human social behaviors. Cultural factors relate to patterns of behaviors and values characteristic of a population or community. In 1932, Bartlett conducted a classic study that showed how beliefs or values can affect learning. Some sociocultural factors that may affect a student's reading ability are socioeconomic status, ethnic and racial identification, and culturally determined gender roles.

Make a Prediction.   Possible cause or myth?

- failure to adapt instruction to ethnic values of students
- low teacher expectations
- home environment
- mismatch between cultural/linguistic experiences and the stories in standard reading materials
- content of stories in standard reading material reflecting interests of girls, adversely affecting boys' motivation and achievement
- boys' achievement adversely affected when schools have predominantly female staffs

Research has shown that in successful schools in low-income neighborhoods, wide varieties of library books are available to students.

Socioeconomic Status

There *are* differences in reading achievement when comparing students from high, middle, and low socioeconomic status (SES) backgrounds. Studies have shown the incidence of reading disability increases as SES decreases (e.g., Au, 2000; Gutherie & Greaney, 1991).

One home factor correlated with high achievement is high-quality parental verbal interactions with their children.

Many individuals tend to associate low socioeconomic status with race or ethnicity, although in many cases this association does not hold. For this reason, it should be emphasized that low school achievement is linked with low socioeconomic status only, not with racial or ethnic background. Also, traditional ways of viewing SES (education, income, occupation) may be less useful in examining variations in reading achievement than looking at differences in specific practices within homes at any SES level (e.g., Senechal, LeFevre, Thomas, & Daly, 1998). Some home factors correlated with high achievement include:

1. preschool experiences with books
2. parents' interest in reading themselves, thus providing a model for children

3. high-quality parental verbal interactions with the child
4. provision of space and opportunity for the child to read

Some home factors correlated with lower achievement also have been shown:

1. fewer books in the home
2. children less frequently read to by parents
3. unstructured lifestyles regarding home activities such as bedtime, television viewing, and others

For dozens of entertaining preschool literacy activities to share with parents, go to www.ed.gov/parents/academic/help/reader/index.html

Although some of the practices correlated to lower achievement seem to be associated with certain SES levels, that is not necessarily so.

Intellectual deficiencies have been found in African American and Caucasian low-SES children in the United States as early as the preschool years. This is believed to be the result of several aspects of home environment, including lack of intellectual stimulation. In later years, other causes of poor reading achievement may be family environmental patterns that are unresponsive to homework and other school-dictated requirements, as well as social behaviors and values of self-discipline different from those of the mainstream culture. Because of low educational levels of parents, children may not be encouraged to deal with conceptual problems: Children are not asked questions to make them think independently and develop strategies for learning and problem solving. Low-SES preschool children may have less access to opportunities that lead to school success. No one purposely stimulates their interest in reading; therefore, they do not come to school eager to learn to read. Because fewer books are read to them at home, they lack the familiarity with book language and the larger, richer oral language vocabularies of children who have been read to regularly. Senechal et al. (1998) found that young children who frequently heard storybooks read in the home knew the meanings of more words and had better listening comprehension. Heath (1991) also points out the differences in some low-SES homes and those in which mainstream parents engage in game-playing with their preschool children to encourage thinking skills. All of these factors put students from low-SES homes at risk for academic problems. In addition, students from low-SES backgrounds may have poor health care and inadequate diets, leading to health problems and poor school attendance.

Children who have not been read to in preschool years may come to school lacking familiarity with book language and the larger, richer, oral language vocabularies of those who have been read to regularly.

Some school-related factors can also cause poor reading achievement in students from low socioeconomic backgrounds. Lower teacher expectations seem to be a variable leading to failure. Variations in teacher beliefs about whether at-risk students can learn have been shown in some inner-city schools (e.g., Winfield, 1986). Teachers must be trained to assess students' abilities independent of their socioeconomic status. There are successful schools in low-income neighborhoods where reading levels of students are equal to those of students from middle-class backgrounds. Classrooms in these schools are described as quiet and conducive to learning, where there is a high degree of teacher-directed instruction, where teachers have high expectations, and where a wide variety of library books is available to students.

Administrative regulations may be another contributor to lack of reading success for low-SES students. Governmental programs, such as Title 1, which are designed to provide remedial instruction for low-income students, have required that services be provided only to students having the lowest percentiles in reading scores. Students who are eligible one year may not be eligible the next since, because of effective instruction, they are no longer in the lowest percentile of their school population. Although they may not be reading up to their potentials or to the grade norm, and although they both need and have shown they can benefit from special instruction, they are no longer allowed services in the program.

It is important to school achievement that teachers understand language and cultural differences.

Another school-related factor sometimes thought to be a possible contributor to low achievement is the apparent mismatch between cultural experiences of low-SES students and the settings and activities in standard reading materials. Several studies have shown that this mismatch does not affect reading achievement. Ratekin (1978), for example, compared reading abilities of Caucasian, African American, and Hispanic American children instructed in identical reading material (a standard basal reader series). All children in the study were from low socioeconomic backgrounds and were at similar reading levels at the beginning of the study. The cultural experiences conveyed in the stories in the basal readers were for the most part representative of middle-class life and did not reflect the lifestyles of any of the groups. Despite the cultural differences embodied in the reading materials, all groups of children made equal and excellent gains as a result of sound reading instruction. Ratekin believed that an important factor in these gains was that the teachers in the study were prepared to accept and understand cultural differences; that is, they engaged in what Au (2000) and Farr (1991) have called **ethnosensitivity.** In Chapter 14, I discuss ways to accommodate linguistic and cultural differences.

Ethnic and Racial Identification

The culture that a student comes from apparently can have an effect on the ways the student learns best. For example, Au and Mason (1981) reported that verbal interactions in a classroom that were similar to their everyday cultural patterns resulted in Hawaiian children exhibiting more achievement-related behaviors than when interactions were dissimilar. In one classroom, these children were required to wait to be called on by the teacher before speaking in a reading group and were required to speak one at a time—behaviors typical in classrooms of the mainstream culture. In contrast, in another classroom, reading group interactions were allowed to assume the characteristics of a Hawaiian talk story: Students took turns responding to the same question or engaged in joint responses. Children allowed to respond in the second manner had more academically engaged time and made more reading-related responses during group time.

Similar studies have been reported with Native American populations. Children at the Warm Springs Indian Reservation were less willing to participate in school activities if they were directed at individuals and more willing to participate in group activities (Phillips, 1972). Many Native American Indian cultures are family- or group-centered; and students from these cultures are often uncomfortable if required to compete. This culturally determined trait contrasts with the requirements of mainstream-culture classrooms, where individuals are singled out to exhibit their understanding of a topic. Many Native American students respond to singling out by remaining silent rather than by trying to excel over their peers; teachers may incorrectly interpret their silence in response to a question as lack of knowledge.

Heath (1991) described similarities in ways some African American and Hispanic American working-class communities use language in learning.

1. Children learn from daily, real situations rather than from specific information and questions presented by adults.
2. Questions are not asked of children when the answers are already known by adults.
3. Stories are developed by groups, and interruptions are a standard feature of this process.

All of these ways in which learning occurs and is displayed differ from characteristics of mainstream school-based learning.

Bicultural students often appear to lack competence and intelligence in school settings, while they more than adequately demonstrate these traits in their own communities and homes. Good teachers adapt instruction to the ethnic experiences and values of their students and at the same time help them adjust to the mainstream culture. When teachers fail to adapt, their students may not achieve to their potentials.

Culturally Determined Gender Roles

In the United States, overall, girls have superior early reading attainment, although in the general school population the differences tend to disappear by age 10. However, more boys than girls have reading difficulties that necessitate a special program.

Gender differences have been demonstrated in relation to reading achievement. In the United States, girls have superior attainment in early reading progress, although in the general school population these differences tend to disappear by age 10. In addition, more boys than girls have reading difficulties that necessitate a remedial or clinical program. Males enrolled in university-based reading clinics outnumbered females 3 to 1 in one national survey (Bader & Wiesendanger, 1986).

Although biological factors may explain these differences in part, they also may have a sociocultural basis. One premise has been that the content of stories used in reading instruction reflects interests consistent with the culturally determined gender roles of girls rather than boys, and that this in turn affects boys' motivation and achievement. Studies of stories in the most widely used basal reader series have found this assumption to be untrue. Stories do not favor girls' interests over boys', nor do they more frequently describe activities thought of as feminine.

A second premise has been that boys' achievement is adversely affected because schools have predominantly female staffs. Some have suggested that women teachers provide instruction that requires learning styles unnatural for males and that they have lower expectations for boys. A review by Lahaderne (1976) of 22 studies related to this issue laid this myth to rest. What Lahaderne did find was that both men and women teachers seem to operate from the same cultural biases. There were no differences between the perceptions of male and female teachers. Both groups perceived boys as having more problems than girls. There were also no differences in the grades they assigned for academic performance or in their treatment of boys and girls. Boys received more interactions of all types (approval and disapproval) from both groups, and both groups were more directive with boys. Finally, there were no differences in student outcomes between the boys or girls who had male teachers and the boys or girls who had female teachers and no differences in student adjustments.

A third premise is that general cultural expectations related to gender roles reflect larger societal norms. These expectations come from parents, peers, and society as a whole. Specific factors that can affect perceptions of gender roles vary from cultural group to cultural group. In North America, preschool boys and girls view reading as a masculine activity (May & Ollila, 1981), but school-age boys and girls view reading and books as feminine. Culturally determined appropriateness of reading in relation to gender roles may influence the amount of reading done by boys and girls and their motivation to become good readers. Girls seem to have more positive attitudes toward reading than do boys (Greaney & Hegerty, 1987).

EDUCATIONAL FACTORS

NCLB
READING FIRST

Educational factors may contribute to mild or moderate reading difficulties, but are not usually an initial cause of a severe delay. They may, however, lead to a worsening of the condition if appropriate interventions are not undertaken.

Lack of Research Information

We do not yet entirely understand the reading process, and until we do, all the answers teachers need to help students learn best are not available. Instead, teachers must rely on existing research and their own judgments to make instructional decisions. Nonetheless, as we come to understand more about the reading process, procedures commonly used by teachers that once seemed entirely appropriate, as well as procedures suggested by authorities in literacy education, sometimes later have proven to be wrong.

We do have some research evidence about the behaviors and skills of teachers that seem to lead to reading achievement. This body of research has come to be known as **the teacher-effectiveness literature** and deals with such topics as time on task, management skills, grouping, and pacing. Among other findings, these studies show that: (a) direct instruction is important for low-achieving students, (b) effective teachers avoid wasting time, and (c) students learn more when instruction is paced so their success rates are high. Although we do not know all the teacher behaviors necessary to facilitate student achievement, these findings can guide teachers in structuring their attitudes and developing their own skills.

LEARNING FROM TEXT

Make a Prediction.   Can these contribute to reading delays?

- lack of time on task
- use of ineffective teaching methods

Lack of Time on Task

Sometimes administrative policies prevent good teaching. Teachers may be required to carry out so many tasks unrelated to the academic needs of students that they do not have time to treat academic areas comprehensively. Many studies

The amount of time students spend directly engaged in skills they need to learn is significantly related to their achievement.

show that the *amount of time students spend directly engaged in the skills they need to learn is significantly related to their achievement.*

Some nonacademic tasks required of teachers are unnecessary. Administrators should examine what they ask teachers to do and eliminate as far as possible those tasks not directly related to students' learning. Of course, some nonacademic tasks are necessary.

Teachers with good management skills can structure time needed to carry out these tasks so they impinge on students' learning as little as possible. For example, an elementary teacher required to collect students' lunch, milk, and snack money each morning might plan to have students engage in silent reading during the 15 or 20 minutes it takes for this responsibility. While a few students at a time come to the teacher's desk to deposit money, the other students read. By eliminating this educationally dead time, a teacher can add 1 to 1 1/2 hours of learning time during a school week. Perceptive teachers at all levels can turn nonlearning time (such as homeroom in middle schools and high schools) into times of academic engagement.

LEARNING FROM TEXT

Relating Information to Your Own Experiences. For one day, make a list of activities (academic and nonacademic) in your classroom. Beside each, write the amount of time the activity lasted. Also list intrusions from outside and how long they lasted. Are adjustments needed?

Another administrative policy that causes problems of time is the continually increasing number of subjects teachers must cover in a school day. In the 1800s, more than 90% of school time was devoted to reading, writing, and arithmetic. Since then, time allotments for these subjects have decreased markedly. Not only has time devoted to other basic academic areas increased, but also driver's education, sex education, values clarification, productive use of leisure time, and other worthwhile, but time-consuming, topics are subjects included in today's school curriculum. The value of different school programs may vary with the individual. Although the quality of life may be enhanced by learning ways to use leisure time, a nonreader or functionally illiterate individual's quality of life may be more critically affected by increasing his or her reading skills. Teachers must set priorities as to what they teach and how much time they devote to each subject.

Inappropriate Instructional Materials and Techniques

Teachers should question every activity they assign, for example, asking "What does this activity really do to increase students' learning?" or "Is this activity leading to learning of such minor importance that I should substitute one of greater value to this student?"

One educational problem can occur when teachers uncritically follow the dictates of publishing companies. Many reputable companies that publish reading materials use editors who are reading authorities and who screen materials and evaluate the value of suggested activities. Other publishers do not follow this policy and may publish outdated or unsupported suggestions based on a layperson's ideas about what is helpful in reading instruction. When teachers follow such programs uncritically, they waste student learning time. Teachers need to adopt a healthy skepticism. Simply because a suggestion is made in a teacher's manual or an activity is found in a published workbook does not necessarily mean the suggestion or activity is useful.

Direct, teacher-guided instruction often is important with low-achieving students.

Furthermore, teachers should question every procedure they carry out and every activity they assign. They need to ask:

What does this activity really do to help increase this student's learning?

Is this an activity that recent evidence says is not beneficial?

Although this is an activity used for many years, do we now know better ways to accomplish this goal?

Is this an activity leading to learning of such minor importance that I should substitute an activity that will be of greater value to this particular student with a reading delay?

Is this activity designed correctly? Does it really teach or merely test? Is it a time filler or a learning experience?

Engaging students in hours and days of nonproductive activities prevents them from using time constructively. Over weeks and months, this inefficient use of time can contribute to a student's reading problem. The decisions teachers make about instructional planning affect student learning. It is important to become a reflective teacher.

LEARNING FROM TEXT

Relating Information to Your Own Experiences. Consider two teaching activities you have used or seen someone else use—one you believe to be sound and one for which you question its effectiveness. Apply the questions in the preceding list to those activities.

Features of Successful Reading Programs

Reviews of successful reading programs have identified certain characteristics these programs have in common.

Administrative Factors

1. Exemplary programs have administrators who provide time for teachers to plan and carry out instruction.
2. Teachers participate in making decisions.
3. Teachers' instructional behaviors are supervised.
4. Regular inservice sessions are part of the program, and they focus on real problems.
5. Teachers are allowed to observe other successful teachers to use them as role models.

Characteristics of Teachers

1. Teachers devote large amounts of energy and time to carrying out the program.
2. Teachers have had practical training.
3. Teachers employ direct instruction; that is, when the goal is that students learn to read, they give them opportunity to practice reading and reading strategies. They do not have students engage in activities not directly related to the goal.
4. Teachers provide large amounts of instructional time and use time efficiently.
5. The level of complexity of instruction is kept low.
6. Teachers use ongoing evaluation to measure student progress frequently and determine immediate needs.
7. Classes are structured, but teachers maintain a friendly atmosphere.

These characteristics offer clues for establishing educational programs that will not contribute to students' reading failure.

LEARNING FROM TEXT

Relating Information to Your Own Experiences. How do the features of successful reading programs compare with what you see in your own school?

COGNITIVE FACTORS

Cognitive factors for which links to reading disabilities have been suggested include intelligence, preferred learning modality, left and right brain hemispheric functions, and memory. Each is examined in this section.

LEARNING FROM TEXT

Make a Prediction. In regard to reading disabilities, which are possible causes? Which are myths?

- low intelligence
- "right-brained" students receiving instruction that favors "left-brained" learners
- a mismatch between instructional method and a student's preferred learning modality
- poor auditory memory

Intelligence

There is a relationship between intelligence and reading achievement. Generally, an individual whose intelligence quotient, or IQ, is higher needs less practice to learn than an individual whose IQ is lower. In addition, proficient reading requires anticipation of meaning, association of ideas, and perception of relationships—all of which require some degree of abstract thinking, a trait more common in students with higher intelligence. Students with lower mental ages, or MAs, tend to have more specific, or concrete, reactions to words and written text.

The relationship between intelligence and reading ability is variable, however. For instance, the correlations between reading ability and IQ vary at different grade levels. These correlations are relatively low for children in the primary grades but become higher from the intermediate grades upwards due to the increasing complexity of reading tasks at these higher levels. In addition, although higher intelligence is generally associated with higher reading achievement, this is most true when we are considering a fairly wide difference in intellectual functioning levels. For instance, if all other factors are equal, we would expect a student with an IQ of 108 to be a better reader than a student with an IQ of 79. If, however, we are comparing two individuals with IQs of 108 and 99, and all other factors are equal, there should be little significant difference in reading ability.

Does low intelligence *cause* a reading disability? Although a student of low intelligence may be expected to have a lower reading achievement than a student of average intelligence, a lower intellectual functioning level does not necessarily cause a reading disability. Today, expectations of reading achievement are based on an individual's potential, not on grade-level norms. For example, consider Jamie, who has a chronological age (CA) of 13.5, but an MA of only 10.9. Using an appropriate manner for determining potential, we might find that Jamie should be reading at approximately a sixth-grade reading level. Although at age 13.5, Jamie may be in an eighth-grade class, she would not be expected to be reading at eighth-grade level, and she would not be considered a disabled reader if her reading achievement was at or near sixth grade.

Sometimes less intelligent students do become reading disability cases, usually when appropriate adaptations are not made in their instructional programs. Students of less-than-average intelligence need more opportunities to practice and the introduction of new material at a slower pace. If adjustments are not made, these students' reading levels may not reach their individual potentials. In such cases, the contributing cause to the reading disability is educational and not due to intelligence. Almost all students can learn to read, even educable mentally retarded individuals. Today, even persons with intelligence quotients in fairly low ranges of mental retardation are being taught functional reading skills.

The lack of a simple cause-and-effect relationship between intelligence and reading is evident from the number of students of normal intelligence who have difficulty learning to read. In Monroe's (1932) classic work, she found an IQ range from 60 to 150 in reading disability cases she studied. When examining a population of clients enrolled in a reading clinic, one can expect to find that the subjects' IQs conform fairly closely to a standard bell-shaped curve, with the largest number of students having IQs in the average range, a smaller and approximately equal number with IQs slightly above and slightly below average, and a very small and approximately equal number with very high and very low IQs (see Figure 2–4).

Although higher intelligence is generally associated with higher reading achievement, this is most true when considering a fairly wide difference in intellectual functioning.

FIGURE 2–4 *Bell-Shaped Curve Showing IQ Range of Students Typically Enrolled in a Reading Clinic*

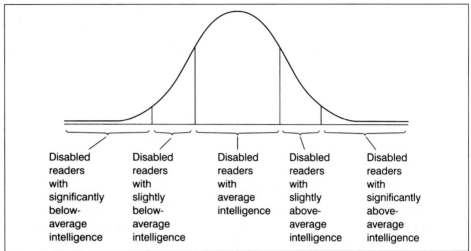

Disabled readers with significantly below-average intelligence

Disabled readers with slightly below-average intelligence

Disabled readers with average intelligence

Disabled readers with slightly above-average intelligence

Disabled readers with significantly above-average intelligence

LEARNING FROM TEXT

Applying What You've Learned. Suppose someone says, "We know the real reason kids are poor readers: They are not as smart as other students." How would you respond based on what you have read here?

Preferred Learning Modality

A **modality** refers to a sensory channel through which information is received. Some educators have hypothesized that individuals have a specific sensory channel through which they learn best; that is, they benefit most from a visual, auditory, kinesthetic (movement related), or tactile presentation of material.

It has been postulated that matching the type of instruction to an individual's preferred modality will enhance learning. This is called **aptitude-treatment interaction.** A well-known study by Ringler and Smith (1973) shows how aptitude-treatment interaction research has been carried out. The New York University Learning Modality Test (Smith, Ringler, & Cullinan, 1968) was administered to 128 first graders. The results indicated that 33 of the children had visual aptitudes, 30 had auditory aptitudes, 28 had kinesthetic aptitudes, and 37 had no preference. Children were assigned to treatment groups to learn word recognition. Students in the visual treatment group matched words to models or to pictures, selected one word from among others, and pointed out salient characteristics of words printed on overhead projector transparencies. Children in the auditory treatment group listened to words in context and isolation as presented orally by the teacher and on audiotape, associated letters with sounds, matched sounds of words, and selected a written word when it was spoken. The children in the kinesthetic treatment group traced words outlined in pipe cleaners or cut from sandpaper, and wrote words on newsprint with crayons. The children in the no-preference group pointed out salient visual characteristics of words, associated pictures with words, compared and contrasted word parts, listened

Studies with many populations show that matching a reading program to students' assessed modality preferences makes no difference to their reading achievement.

to words in context, and traced words. However, results of this study showed that matching the reading treatment to children's assessed modality preferences made no difference in increasing their reading achievement. Other research involving students with learning or reading disabilities has reached the same conclusion. Similar studies also have been conducted with students who have mental retardation and, again, when instruction has been matched to the students' stronger modality, no significant differences have been found in their reading scores.

The folk wisdom that a contributing factor to reading difficulties may be a mismatch between a student's preferred modality and the instruction provided is not supported by research evidence.

LEARNING FROM TEXT

Relating Information to Your Own Experiences.   How many times have you heard it said that we would make progress with reading delayed and learning disabled students if we would match reading instruction to their preferred learning modalities? How often have you seen this done in schools? Should it be?

Left and Right Brain Hemispheric Functioning

In times past, reading specialists were interested in the influence of **lateral dominance,** the preference for use of one side of the body. As discussed earlier research has shown that lateral dominance is not related to reading ability. Not to be confused with this older concept, however, is a newer idea that involves hemispheric dominance and is based on work of neuroscientists exploring functions of the left and right hemispheres of the brain. Their research seems to indicate that each side of the brain has different functions. Reflecting on this work, some educators have hypothesized that certain individuals appear to be more "left-brained" and others more "right-brained" and consequently may have different aptitudes and skills.

Although brain research is far from complete, the functions of the left hemisphere of the brain appear to include: (a) dealing with complex verbal ideas and abstract uses of words; (b) dealing with difficult mathematical calculations; (c) engaging in inductive reasoning—that is, determining whole principles based on observation of parts; (d) dealing with fine motor coordination; (e) segmenting patterns; and (f) carrying out analytical thinking, sequential thinking, and symbolic thinking.

On the other hand, the evidence presently indicates that the right hemisphere's functions may include: (a) dealing with nonverbal ideas; (b) dealing with spatial concepts, including depth perception and sensitivity to geometric forms; (c) dealing with simple uses of words and simple mathematical concepts; (d) visualizing; (e) engaging in deductive reasoning—that is, inferring specific instances based on known general principles; (f) engaging in holistic thinking; (g) dealing with gross motor coordination; (h) making sensory discriminations, such as recognizing environmental sounds and detecting tactile patterns; and (i) performing mechanical types of information processing.

Based on the functions of each hemisphere, some educators have postulated that a "left-brained" person would be more academic and that a "right-brained" individual would be more successful in creative and physical endeavors. These educators are more concerned about "right-brained" students because they believe that typical instruction favors the types of learning in which a "left-brained" individual might be more proficient. They suggest that academic difficulties may be the result of teaching students with a dominant right hemisphere in ways inconsistent with the way they learn best.

Although neuroscientists have made advances in understanding brain functions, complete and definitive evidence does not exist, and many scientists hold contrasting views. Therefore, understanding the implications their findings have for education is little more than speculation. Even though it may eventually be established that certain functions do indeed occur in one hemisphere or the other, the notion that one hemisphere works more efficiently than the other in some individuals is only a guess. Even if future neural research shows that certain individuals have a strong hemispheric dominance, well-controlled educational studies are still needed to determine if specific types of educational experiences enhance learning for those individuals. Some suggestions for teaching "right-brained" students have included:

1. Provide many exposures to the material to be learned.
2. Teach in a one-to-one situation so the student can focus attention on the task at hand.
3. Use dramatization to aid learning.
4. Use audiotapes, films, and pictures.
5. Teach students to finish a task.
6. Allow students to manipulate materials.
7. Provide many opportunities for correct responses; do not let students practice errors.

These suggestions would enhance the learning of any student and simply reflect good teaching practice. Teachers should not regard unresearched suggestions for matching teaching activities to an inferred hemispheric preference as representing a panacea for reading problems. Indeed, many reading educators believe that reading is a "whole brain" activity. Neuroscientists agree that many activities require an integration of both hemispheres' functions.

> Suggested implications of left- and right-brain functioning for educational programs presently are little more than speculation.

LEARNING FROM TEXT

Applying What You've Learned.   If it were suggested that you should teach your "right-brained" students differently from your "left-brained" students, how would you respond?

Memory

Many theorists postulate the existence of three stages in acquiring information. First, information is contained in a perceptual stage, called **sensory store;** after the eye picks it up, information theoretically remains in sensory store for 1 or 2 seconds while the brain makes some decisions about it. Next, information from sensory store is selected and stored in **short-term memory,** which is also called *working memory.* Working memory processes information, holds it until it is stored in **long-term memory,** or sometimes loses information (if it is not important enough to store in long-term memory, or if short-term memory is overloaded). Finally, information is transferred from short-term memory to long-term memory through association with previously stored information. The information in long-term memory is our continuous knowledge of the world.

A number of researchers have investigated whether aberrations in memory processes may be a cause of difficulty in learning to read. Daneman and Carpenter (1980), for example, have suggested that differences in reading comprehension abilities may stem from differences in facility in use of short-term memory. Their research showed that poor readers' short-term memories were less efficient than good readers'; the poor readers processed and stored less information.

Another difference between good and poor readers may be the speed with which they can remember graphic information. In Jackson's (1980) study, for example, better readers had better memory reaction times than poor readers. However, the speed with which readers can retrieve the pronunciation (and meaning) of a word from long-term memory has been correlated with reading fluency, but not with comprehension (Daneman, 1991).

Automatic word recognition is important so that processing efforts are freed for comprehension of text.

Furthermore, some research seems to indicate that poor readers have less available capacity in their working memories than better readers (Daneman & Green, 1986). However, this may simply occur because the poor readers have not developed automatic use of certain reading processes, and, therefore, working memory must divide its actions among several processing functions. For example, reading educators today recognize the importance of automatic word recognition so that processing efforts can be freed for comprehending the messages in a text. Therefore, in associations such as those found in the Daneman and Green study, poor performance on memory tests may be the *result* of reading problems, not their cause.

In fact, an additional word of caution is in order when drawing conclusions about memory processes and reading delays: Many tests purporting to assess memory are only partially related to the memory requirements of reading. Many test batteries available to reading specialists and school psychologists assess only short-term auditory and visual memory. Short-term memory is necessary to reading, but long-term memory is also crucial. Commonly used published tests do not provide any insight into problems of storage and retrieval in a disabled reader's long-term memory.

What is more, results from short-term memory tasks may not provide any useful information to shed light on a reading disability. A case in point would be certain tests of **auditory memory.** The term *auditory memory* has been used to describe the ability to store in the brain what is heard and then later to recall it. In IQ tests and some reading tests, assessment of auditory memory is conducted by asking students to repeat the order of a series of numerals, nonsense syllables, words, or sentences after they have been stated orally to the students. The Detroit Tests of Learning Aptitude include such a subtest. Well-known intelligence tests, such as the Stanford-Binet Intelligence Scale, the Wechsler Intelligence Scale for Children-Revised (WISC-R), and the Wechsler Adult Intelligence Scale, also employ such tasks and refer to them as tests of "digit span" or "auditory memory span." Most research investigating the relationship between these subtests and reading ability has shown the correlations are usually low or nonexistent. For example, certain studies have shown that poor readers have performed better than good readers on the memory subtests of the Stanford-Binet, and disabled readers have scored high on the WISC-R digit span test. In addition, attempts to improve scores on auditory memory tasks have resulted in improved scores on the tests but with no accompanying improvement in reading ability.

Much of the research that discusses the role of memory in reading is based on a **stage model** of cognitive processing, a model in which the brain processes information through several stages from the time of input to the time of output or storage. Analyzing the acquisition of information into sensory store, short-term memory, and long-term memory, as described previously, is an example of a stage model. But psychologists, like reading educators, hold many views, and other models of memory are available. Some of these memory theories may have important applications to reading. Researchers will probably continue to explore these areas.

Other Cognitive Processes

Deficits in some other cognitive processes have been proposed as candidates for causing reading disability: **associative learning,** the ability to associate one thing with another; **pattern analysis,** noting that a pattern remains the same in more than one place; **attention,** the ability to attend to distinguishing features, dependent on acquired knowledge and motivation; and **serial memory,** retaining the order in which things occur. However, because disabled readers do not have difficulties in applying these general processes to types of learning other than reading, the notion of reading disability as caused by difficulties in these areas has been discounted (see Vellutino & Denckla, 1991).

Summarize. What is the main point of the preceding paragraph?

LANGUAGE FACTORS

Make a Prediction. What language factors may be associated with reading delays? Which of these suggested causes are myths?

- lack of phonemic awareness
- lack of skill in using letter-sound relationships
- failure to apply oral language knowledge to reading tasks
- nonstandard oral language dialects

Reading is a language-based activity. The three major aspects of oral language are **phonemes** (sounds), **syntax** (sentence structure), and **semantics** (meaning). In written language, a fourth is added, namely, **graphemes** (letters). Deficits in syntactic and semantic aspects of language processing have at times been associated with reading disability. For example, in some studies poor readers more often than skilled have failed to distinguish between syntactically appropriate and inappropriate sentence structures (Vellutino & Scanlon, 1987), and lack of knowledge of word meanings (semantic knowledge) often has been suggested as causing reading comprehension difficulties (e.g., Vellutino & Denckla, 1991). However, the area most strongly associated with reading problems is related to phoneme use. For one, differences in skill in using letter-sound relationships to identify unknown words has been shown to account for individual differences in reading ability for readers of all ages (Elbro, Borstrom, & Petersen, 1998; Stanovich, 1986), affecting not only word recognition, but often comprehension as well. And, of central concern to discussion of causation is the issue of phonemic awareness.

LEARNING FROM TEXT

Using the ReQuest Procedure.   Phonemic awareness is a critical issue. You should know the information in this section well. Research has shown that good readers make adjustments in their study behaviors based on the importance of the information, whereas poor readers do not vary their study routines. Using the ReQuest Procedure would be helpful in studying this section. You will learn more about this technique in Chapter 11, but for now, here is a brief description and adaptation that might be useful: For every paragraph in this section, stop and see how many questions you can ask (and, of course, answer) about it.

Phonemic Awareness

NCLB
READING FIRST

Our writing system in English is based on the **alphabetic principle:** Written words are made up of letters that have approximate matches with the sounds heard in these words when we speak. One important aspect of learning to read is to understand how written language and oral language correspond in this way.

To understand the alphabetic principle, one must recognize that *spoken words* consist of a sequence of sounds; this understanding is called **phonemic awareness** (Ball & Blachman, 1991). The concept that words are made up of sounds is not necessarily an easy one for young students to grasp because, when we speak, we only rarely pay conscious attention to the sounds we make; rather, we are simply concerned with getting our messages across. Phonemic awareness is not really important to our purposes in spoken language, but it is critical in learning to read.

Authorities are unsure if phonemic awareness or lack of phonemic awareness has an environmental basis or a constitutional basis, but likely the basis lies with both. For instance, studies (e.g., Senechal, LeFevre, Thomas, & Daley, 1998) indicate that one aid to development of adequate phonemic awareness occurs when young children listen to storybooks read aloud by their parents, an advantage enjoyed by some children, but not by all. But other studies suggest that good or poor phonemic awareness may have a genetic origin (e.g., Stanovich, 1986).

There is direct evidence, however, indicating that lack of phonemic awareness is a major cause of word identification difficulties (Ehri et al., 2001; Vellutino & Denckla, 1991). Phonemic awareness permits students to use letter-sound correspondences, employ phonic strategies, and identify unknown words more quickly (Griffith & Olson, 1992). Phonemic awareness also may have a bearing on whole-word learning (Tunmer, Herriman, & Nesdale, 1998). In addition, phonemic awareness is a prerequisite to spelling and writing, which also require hearing and matching sounds. Phonemic awareness is now viewed as a critical variable in emergent literacy (Sulzby & Teale, 1991) and beginning reading acquisition (Juel, 1991). Recognizing that words can be broken into phonemes and syllables, and being able to manipulate these, has a high correlation with reading achievement (Lundberg, Frost, & Petersen, 1988; Perfetti, Beck, Bell, & Hughes, 1987). Research has shown that phonemic awareness is a more powerful determinant than intelligence in predicting whether students will succeed in reading; it is also a stronger predictor than "general" language proficiency (Lomax & McGee, 1987). What is more, the importance of phonemic awareness holds regardless of the type of instructional methodology employed. For example, Klesius, Griffith, and Zielonka (1991) compared a whole-language reading instructional program with a traditional first-grade reading approach and found that neither produced hoped-for results with children who lacked phonemic awareness; likewise, when phonemic awareness was sufficiently developed, students achieved equally well in either program.

Research indicates that a significant discriminator between good and poor readers is poor readers' lack of phonemic awareness.

It is not surprising, then, that a large body of research conducted in the United States and in several other countries indicates that one of the most significant discriminators between good and poor readers is poor readers' lack of phonemic awareness (e.g., Bradley & Bryant, 1985; Cossu, Shankweiler, Liberman, Katz, & Tola, 1988; Ehri et al., 2001; Elbro, Borstrom, & Petersen, 1998; Juel, 1988; Juel, Griffith, & Gough, 1986; Morais, Cluytens, Alegria, & Content, 1984; Pratt & Brady, 1988; Stanovich, Nathan, & Zolman, 1988; Torneus, 1984; Vellutino & Scanlon, 1987; Williams, 1984). Moreover, this holds true regardless of the intelligence level or socioeconomic status of the students.

On the strength of this research, there is little doubt that lack of phonemic awareness is a cause of reading delays in a large portion of students whose difficulties lie with word recognition. Phonemic awareness is a *prerequisite* to adequate word recognition abilities; in addition, more advanced understandings about phonemic awareness develop *as a result* of reading and writing. Because low-achieving students usually read and write less than other readers, the effects are cyclical.

Two levels of phonemic awareness have been identified—simple phonemic awareness and compound phonemic awareness. The knowledge that words can be broken into phonemes and syllables is evident when students can perform these simple phonemic awareness tasks: (a) **isolation of a sound** (e.g., giving the first sound in *camel* after hearing the word pronounced); (b) **blending**—combining, in oral language, separate sounds into a word (e.g., when given the sounds /h//a//m/[1] being able to produce *ham*); and (c) **segmentation**—recognizing the sounds heard in a word (e.g., after hearing the word *bat* pronounced, identifying the three *sounds* heard in this word). Simple phonemic awareness is an important prerequisite to reading and writing.

Compound phonemic awareness involves two operations. One example is **phoneme deletion,** isolating a sound in a word and blending the remaining sounds. For example, the student responds correctly when asked, "What word would be left if the /r/ were taken away from the middle of *brake*?" **Word-to-word matching** entails isolating a sound in a certain position in two words and comparing the sounds. For example, the student responds correctly when asked, "Do *dog* and *dime* begin the same?" Compound phonemic awareness seems to

---

[1] The convention that has been adopted in several fields is to indicate *sounds* by placing the letter between two parallel lines like this.

result from reading experience, but may be important for further advancement in reading and writing.

For disabled readers who are experiencing serious difficulties in developing word recognition and in acquiring word identification strategies, it is important that teachers assess their phonemic awareness. Tests of phonemic awareness are discussed in Chapter 5. Although phonemic awareness is considered a linguistic (i.e., language) skill, it also clearly requires cognitive skill. However, there is evidence that phonemic awareness does not simply occur with maturation or age, but instead results from certain experiences. Furthermore, research indicates that phonemic awareness can be trained. This is good news! Chapter 9 presents suggestions from research for providing instruction that will enhance phonemic awareness.

Oral Language Knowledge

Good readers use knowledge of oral language when they read. They determine whether what they have just read "sounds right." If it does not—that is, if it is not syntactically or semantically correct—the good reader usually rereads and self-corrects. Although all readers can use oral language knowledge when reading, many poor readers do not. When students lack the intuitive use of this strategy or receive no direct instruction to make up for this deficit, they may demonstrate reading difficulties. Grammatical sensitivity, both syntactic and semantic, has been found to be significantly related to reading skill (Willows & Ryan, 1986).

There are more similarities than differences between oral and written language. If this were not so, a reader would not be aided by knowledge of oral language. However, there are differences that have implications for teaching reading. Written language is not simply "talk written down," as some teachers have told their students. Certain types of sentence patterns encountered in written language are seldom, if ever, used during oral language exchanges. Consider these examples of dialogue structures found only in written language.

There are some differences between oral language and written language structures.

- "My kite's flying higher than yours, Dad," laughed Willy.
- "Tomorrow afternoon," Priscilla yelled to her brother, "I'll show you how to really throw a football."

Because patterns like these are not employed in oral language, students are less able to use their oral language knowledge in self-correction. To deal with problems caused by the lack of congruency between oral and written language, students must gain much familiarity with written language patterns. One way this can be accomplished is by reading aloud to children. Young children who have had books read aloud to them frequently and regularly during the preschool years come to school able to respond to written language structures. Students who have not been exposed to the more elaborate formal code of written language lack an important experience.

A study previously cited in this chapter indicated that differences between the oral language dialects of nonstandard English speakers and the written standard English found in texts do not affect reading achievement. Other studies also have shown this to be true. At one time, there was much interest in preparing reading materials in the nonstandard dialects of students who were to use them, and a number of publishers developed materials of this type. In the end, the materials proved not to be useful in increasing the reading achievement of nonstandard dialect speakers.

Many reading materials contain language that is divergent from the oral language of any speaker. For example, no one has ever heard anyone in a real language discussion say:

- See me. See me go. See me go up.
- Dan, the big man, has a fan.

Furthermore, divergences between oral and written language will always exist whether a speaker's dialect is standard or nonstandard, as shown in the earlier examples with Willy and Priscilla.

A student's nonstandard dialect may not contribute to reading difficulties if language differences are handled appropriately. Too often, however, teachers mistake a language difference for a reading error. Teachers' misperceptions of what constitutes reading skill can lead to erroneous evaluations of students' true abilities if teachers do not take into account language differences.

Some researchers have attempted to change the language of students to "correct" the mismatch between oral language and the language of texts. These programs have not brought about an increase in reading achievement. Some commercial language development programs are designed to teach students to speak only in complete sentences. These programs are based on the notion that the failure of students, particularly low-socioeconomic-status (SES) students, to do so makes it difficult for them to contend with the more formal sentence structures they encounter in written material. However, teaching students to use written language structures in their oral language is unnecessary, since, for all speakers, oral language patterns are more informal. Short phrases or even single words appropriately serve as complete communication exchanges in oral language. For example, if a friend asks, "What did you have for lunch today?" you might simply respond, "Chili." It is unnecessary to say, "I had chili for lunch today." Incomplete sentences occur frequently in oral language, even the language of well-educated adults. Oral and written language patterns are well suited to their special purposes, and it is inappropriate to train students to speak in atypical ways. Furthermore, to do so does not expedite their reading progress.

Other myths have developed about the relationship of language problems and their effect on reading ability. One myth is that low-SES students are poor readers because they are less verbal. Sometimes this appears to be so in formal testing situations because students are unfamiliar with the examiner and the testing environment; but when they are tested in more familiar settings, low-SES students are found to be highly verbal. Another myth is that low-SES students have deficient oral vocabularies that interfere with learning to read in the early grades. Although research indicates that low-SES children have more limited vocabularies than middle-class children, these studies may underestimate students' true abilities. Even if these estimates are correct, it has been shown that low-SES students have the oral vocabulary knowledge necessary to deal with the words found in the most widely used beginning books.

A Call for Preventive Measures

A widely discussed report issued by the U.S. Department of Education, *Preventing Reading Difficulties in Young Children* (edited by Snow, Burns, & Griffith, 1998), has accentuated the importance of developing language skills in the critical preschool years, including understanding of the alphabetic principle.

> Misperceptions of what constitutes reading skill can lead to erroneous evaluations of students if language differences are not taken into account.

In regard to kindergarten instruction, the report emphasized the need to provide opportunities for children to engage in oral language interactions, including discussions about books to kindle rich oral vocabularies (which leads to better comprehension later when students read written text), and to begin training in phonemic awareness. This report offers other research-based recommendations for the literacy education of students in preschool through third grade. It is available from the National Academy Press, Washington, DC.

LEARNING FROM TEXT

> **Make a Prediction.** What is "reading history"? Is this a cause of low reading achievement or, in regard to causation, a myth?

READING HISTORY

Research from a multiplicity of areas suggests that a student's reading history is a major source of poor reading ability.

If a young child experiences difficulty in learning the strategies that allow for word identification, this prevents the child from reading ample amounts of connected text, which is important to reading success. Able readers in the middle of first grade may read almost five times as much during a reading instruction session as the poorest readers in the class (Allington, 1984a). This greater volume of reading practice: (a) permits automatic word recognition to develop more readily, (b) improves knowledge of the complex syntactic structures of written language, (c) boosts development of word meanings, and (d) contributes to acquisition of broader background information and improved comprehension. Students who do not learn word identification strategies early do not have these advantages and fall further and further behind their peers. Small differences between individual children progressively develop into larger and larger differences. Educators now use the term **Matthew effects** (e.g., Stanovich, 1986) to describe this occurrence, based on reference to biblical text in the book of Matthew alluding to the "rich getting richer and the poor getting poorer."

The following tracing of events illustrates the series of interrelated, negative cycles in the history of many delayed readers:

- Genetic and/or environmental factors in the preschool years may lead to low phonemic awareness.
- Low phonemic awareness leads to difficulty in establishing word identification strategies.
- Lack of word identification strategies leads to less volume of text reading.
- Less text reading leads to lack of development of automatic word recognition.
- Lack of automatic word recognition leads to slow and laborious reading.
- Slow and laborious reading, again, leads to less text covered when students are required to read in instructional settings and to lack of motivation to engage in independent reading (and therefore, once again, to less text covered).
- Less text covered also means fewer word meanings learned from the context of reading material, less understanding of written syntactic structures, and less background knowledge built from information found in texts.

The greater the volume of reading practice, the better the development of automatic word recognition, knowledge of syntactic structures, development of word meanings, and comprehension.

- Excessive attention to decoding words because of lack of automatic word recognition distracts concentration from comprehending the text. Limited knowledge of word meanings and lack of familiarity with written syntactic structures inhibit comprehension. Lack of a sufficient background knowledge base detracts from comprehension.
- Less text covered leads to slower progress in general reading achievement.

LEARNING FROM TEXT

Verbal Rehearsal. Much discussion recently has focused on students' reading history and Matthew effects. Try to orally repeat the ideas in the previous section. Verbal rehearsal allows readers to monitor their understanding.

Slower progress in reading achievement also appears to lead to more generalized cognitive and linguistic deficits. Many students who enter school with no measured deficiencies in memory, intelligence, or language begin to show evidence of deficits in these areas as the time goes on and they make limited progress in reading. Stanovich (1986) describes these deficiencies as "behavioral/cognitive/motivational spinoffs from failure at reading" (p. 389). The longer the enfeebling reading history continues without successful remediation, the more these other areas are affected. Therefore, a number of authorities today believe that many of the deficient cognitive and language factors shown to be associated with reading disability are actually results of limited reading progress and are not initial causes of this difficulty. This is particularly true of memory factors, verbal intelligence, knowledge of meaning vocabulary, and written syntactic structures, and background information.

Compare. Compare the points in the preceding paragraph with information you read in the sections pertaining to cognitive and linguistic factors. Having read the preceding paragraph, how would you critique the research presented in those sections?

Stanovich (1986) suggests prevention and amelioration of the serious reading-history problem should be undertaken through (a) early identification and remediation of severely underdeveloped phonemic awareness in beginning readers and (b) large amounts and extended practice of connected text reading. The goal of incorporating these two features into reading programs is to counter the cumulative disadvantage that is one of the major causes of reading disability: the debilitating reading histories that progressively weaken an individual's ability to develop.

*R*eflections

Much important information was presented in Chapter 2. To review and reflect on what you have learned, try this exercise.

List these items in the correct column on the following page:

emotional problems;

faulty eye movements;

food additives;

hereditary factors;

home environment;

lack of neurological organization;

lack of phonemic awareness;

low teacher expectations;

Matthew effects;

medically diagnosed brain damage;

mismatch between instructional method and student's preferred learning modality;

mixed cerebral dominance;

nearsightedness;

nonstandard oral language dialect;

poor motor coordination;

poor speech articulation;

prenatal exposure to crack/cocaine;

refined sugar;

severe hearing impairment;

visual perception difficulties.

Possible Causes of Reading Delays	Proposed Causes Rejected by Research
1.	1
2.	2.
3.	3.
4.	4.
5.	5.
6.	6.
7.	7.
8.	8.
	9.
	10.
	11.
	12.

A. For which possible cause are associations with reading delays rare?

_____

_____

B. Which possible cause is more likely to be an effect?_____

_____

ASSESSMENT

3

Assessment for Identification of Reading Problems

Assessment should be carried out over time, in various settings and social contexts, and while students are reading for different purposes.

LEARNING FROM TEXT

Using Textual Features. In informational text, the author often uses certain textual features to highlight information. In this and many texts, words printed in **boldface type** signal that a term is defined right there in the passage for you. Understanding the meanings of technical terms is important when reading informational material. An often-used study strategy is that of underlining significant details; research shows this to be constructive. If you intend to keep this book, underline the boldfaced technical terms and their meanings or, if not, engage in some note taking related to these terms and definitions, paraphrasing the points in your own words.

NCLB **READING FIRST**

A ssessment is the total process of collecting information to make instructional decisions. Testing is one part of assessment.

Formal assessment uses standardized tests. A common type of standardized test is called **norm-referenced.** These are published tests for which norms based on the performances of large numbers of students have been developed. Norms allow comparisons of student performances with those of a sample group.

Informal assessment can employ any number of nonstandardized measures, such as teacher-prepared tests; daily, ongoing observations; published informal inventories; checklists; interest inventories; and interviews; Currently many of these measures are assembled into a student portfolio, allowing assessment of change over time. Unfortunately, there has been less research on these informal measures than on formal assessment procedures, but more studies are being undertaken.

Examples of formal and informal assessment procedures are interspersed throughout all chapters in Part 2. The examples are placed to reflect the pattern and sequence that teachers in real school or clinic settings generally use. The organization in this book, therefore, provides both a scope and a sequence for diagnostic procedures. Part 2 has the following organization:

- This chapter presents information about assessment techniques that are used before students enter a special reading program. These procedures are employed to determine eligibility for placement in a Title I or other remedial reading class, an LD program, or a reading clinic.
- Chapter 4 discusses the first type of assessment usually conducted once students are enrolled in a program—assessment to determine or confirm reading level.
- Chapters 5 and 6 present a variety of tests that are often used next in the assessment process. These are employed to determine specific reading and writing strengths and weaknesses. Chapters 5 and 6 also discuss measures of interest and attitude so teachers can structure environments that facilitate learning.

Informal assessment employs many types of nonstandardized measures, such as teacher-prepared tests and tasks, daily observation, published informal inventories, and others.

SOME GENERAL ISSUES RELATED TO ASSESSMENT

Formal Testing Versus Informal Testing

Periodically there are tensions between educators who advocate formal testing and those who prefer informal measures. Most authorities, however, desire a "reasonable and appropriate balance" between the two, a recognition of the weaknesses—and strengths—inherent in each type, and selection of those tests that are best in their category, whether that category be formal or informal. The most useful assessments of literacy, regardless of category, reflect our present understandings of reading and writing processes, resemble authentic literacy tasks, and reflect the complexity of literacy learning.

In addition, there must be an understanding of the specific purpose for which each category of test is best suited. For example, Figure 3–1 presents Farr's (1992) description of assessment audiences—that is, what different groups or individuals legitimately need to know from tests and what types of tests best fit that aim.

Using Illustrative Aids. What is the main idea of Figure 3–1?

High-Stakes Testing Versus Low-Stakes Testing

While most informed individuals agree that there is a place in the assessment regimen for both formal and informal measures (see Figure 3–1), there is some controversy about high-stakes testing versus low-stakes testing. State-mandated testing has been termed **high stakes** when serious "high-stake" consequences are tied to students' performances (Popham, 1999). These consequences can

FIGURE 3–1   ***Assessment Audiences***

Audiences	The Information Is Needed to	The Information Is Related to	Type of Information	When Information Is Needed
General public (and the press)	Judge if schools are accountable and effective	Groups of students	Related to broad goals; norm- and criterion-referenced	Annually
School administrators/staff	Judge effectiveness of curriculum, materials, teachers	Groups of students and individuals	Related to broad goals; criterion- and norm-referenced	Annually or by term/semester
Parents	Monitor progress of child, effectiveness of school	Individual student	Usually related to broader goals; both criterion- and norm-referenced	Periodically, 5 or 6 times a year
Teachers	Plan instruction, strategies, activities	Individual student; small groups	Related to specific goals; primarily criterion-referenced	Daily, or as often as possible
Students	Identify strengths, areas to emphasize	Individual (self)	Related to specific goals; criterion-referenced	Daily, or as often as possible

Source: From Farr, Roger. (1992, September). Putting It All Together: Solving the Reading Assessment Puzzle. *The Reading Teacher, 46*(1), 26–37. Reprinted with permission of Roger Farr and the International Reading Association.

affect students as well as the educators who work with them and may be positive or negative.

In Texas, school improvement plans are linked to students' reading, writing, and math scores on state-developed tests (Hoffman, Assaf, & Paris, 2001). In some states where legislative ruling ties grade level assignment to test results, test performance can affect students' promotions or retention and even high school graduation. In certain districts, whether their students make a good showing or a poor showing on these tests may influence educators' salaries, or even a school's accreditation. As a result, in some circumstances, teachers and principals say they have felt undue pressures to teach not to children's needs but "to the test."

High-stakes testing emerged in its present form in the 1980s as a result of educational reform movements and has since grown by leaps and bounds (Valencia & Wixson, 2000). Begun with the good intent of improving schooling, policymakers and lawmakers called for standards, and assessments based on these standards, to be developed in order to spur accountability. Today, most U.S. states have responded to that call, some employing commercially produced standardized tests for annual evaluations and others developing their own statewide assessments. (One example of the latter has been the excellent collaborative efforts in Vermont, in which educators at universities, the state department of education, and schools have worked to connect assessment to their state standards.)

Some individuals have been satisfied with the results of high-stakes testing, with the media pointing out the rising test scores in certain states that have strict accountability procedures. In other situations, these results have been contested, with educators contending that improved state test scores do not jibe with test scores of the same students on national standardized measures such as the National Assessment of Educational Progress (NAEP) (Hoffman, Assaf, & Paris, 2001). With the advent of NCLB, high-stakes testing has become one of the dominant issues in education (see the discussion in Chapter 1).

A few states have used low-stakes testing to comply with compulsory state directives for yearly assessments. A hallmark of **low-stakes testing** is that it is *primarily* designed to *plan* for higher-quality instruction and is not used to reward or penalize learning or instruction after the fact. Low-stakes assessment often employs informal, rather than standardized, measures and school districts may select from several informal procedures (e.g., using a published, informal reading inventory [IRI] or having students read from a set of graded books) (Lipson, Biggam, Valencia, Place, & Young, 2000).

Appropriate Interpretation of Test Scores

When using any assessment, teachers must realize that the scores provided are approximations. An important concept when using formal assessment procedures is that of **standard error of measurement.** This term refers to the principle that scores provided by tests are only estimations of an individual's "true" score and that a student's true score lies within a range of scores. Consider this hypothetical case: Jerry's computed score on a standardized reading test is 3.5. However, since the standard error of measurement for this particular test is 7, his "true" score could lie anywhere between 2.8 (seven points below 3.5) and 4.2 (seven points above 3.5). Test manuals report (or should report) the standard error of measurement for their test. Table 3–1 defines other terms commonly used in association with standardized test scores.

TABLE 3–1 *Types of Scores Provided by Common Standardized Tests*

Raw Score The number of questions a pupil has answered correctly on each subtest or on the total test. Raw scores mean little, but provide the basis for determining more helpful scores.	**Grade Equivalent** The score expected of the average student at the grade level designated. For example, a score of 4.2 indicates the student scored at the same level as the average student in the group used for norming who was in the second month of fourth grade.
Percentile Rank The percentage of students in the norming group who had scores lower or higher than this student's score. A percentile rank of 55, for example, means that 55% of the group on which the test was normed scored lower. Percentile rank should not be used to determine growth.	**Stanine** A statistical interpretation of percentile rank useful in examining an individual's score.
Normal Curve Equivalent (NCE) A statistical interpretation of percentile score useful in examining group performance. Unlike percentile scores, these scores have been transformed into equal units of achievement. NCE is often used in Title I programs.	**Extended Scale Score** Scores that can be used to follow a student's achievement over an extended period, even for several years. These scores are not provided by all standardized test manuals.

Remembering that test scores are estimates also is important when using informal measures. Assigning numerical scores to human abilities is not an exact science by any means. A score derived from an assessment instrument represents a good ballpark figure and is helpful because it gives us a place to begin when making instructional or placement decisions. However, such scores should never be interpreted as invariably definitive.

Especially in regard to informal assessment, MacGinitie (1993, pp. 556–558) highlights several common biases that come into play in appraisals of human performance.

1. *Assimilation bias*—tendency to base judgments on early evidence and ignore evidence obtained later.
2. *Category bias*—tendency to assign all attributes ascribed to a category to a person we believe fits that category.
3. *Confirmation bias*—tendency to hold to beliefs, failing to look for other possibilities.
4. *Contrast bias*—exaggeration of differences between earlier and later findings.
5. *Negativity bias*—tendency to allow negative statements or information to take a disproportionate influence over positive.

> Tests scores should be interpreted in light of other available evidence, especially teacher observation.

In addition, sometimes scores obtained from a single test may simply be wrong. Teachers at times are heard to say something like, "Juan's standardized test score indicated he is reading at fourth-grade level, and I don't understand this because he is having no difficulty handling fifth-grade material." They seem reluctant to rely on their own observations if these do not agree with results of formal testing. Test scores should be interpreted in light of other available evidence, especially teacher observation.

Because of limitations of tests and other assessment procedures, teachers need to be tentative in their decisions. Margolis (2001) states this point well when he reminds us that, in particular, "most reading textbooks recommend that group test scores be considered hypotheses to be validated through diagnostic teaching and observation" (p. 377). Decisions should be reappraised periodically, recognizing the biases inherent in both formal and informal evaluations. Furthermore, achievement should not be confused with ability; in remedial students in particular, the two often are not synonymous.

Reading assessment should be conducted in various settings and undertaken while students are reading for various purposes. Interpretations often are more accurate when this is done and frequently are in contrast to interpretations that rely merely on a single measure. It is especially important that students' behaviors be assessed while engaged in real reading in authentic texts and not just when they are taking tests.

📖 ISSUES RELATED TO FORMAL ASSESSMENT

The first assessment task of a reading teacher is to identify those students who warrant remedial services. This is called **assessment for identification.** Since a good deal of assessment for identification involves use of formal measures, teachers should be aware of advantages and limitations of these tests and should be knowledgeble about their proper selection, administration, and interpretation.

When students take either formal or informal tests, teachers should be aware that assigning numerical scores to human abilities is not an exact science by any means.

Judging the Merits of Test Quality

Two categories of standardized tests may be administered to students with reading problems.

1. *Survey tests,* which are designed to determine students' general reading levels.
2. *Diagnostic tests,* which are used to analyze a student's specific strengths and weaknesses in reading strategies, knowledge, and skills.

Issues related to the technical acceptability of tests are of crucial importance.

Teachers need to consider many factors when they choose a standardized survey or diagnostic test. Issues related to the technical acceptability of tests are of crucial importance. The technical acceptability of a test is built on three factors: norms, validity, and reliability.

Norms. **Norms** are scores that represent an average and are used for comparing one student with other students. Test makers develop norms by administering their test to a large sample of individuals. To develop adequate norms, they must use a sample of students who are similar in age, IQ range, and general characteristics to the group with whom the published test is to be used. Most test publishers also try to select their sample from urban, suburban, and rural areas and, if they are attempting to develop **national norms**—that is, norms based on a nationwide sample—they select their sample from many regions of the country. (**Local norms,** based on data from certain schools or certain areas, are occasionally used, but most often school districts use national norms.) Based on performance of students in the sample, **grade norms,** that is, the average score of students from a given grade, are determined.

Test manuals should report the characteristics of the sample on which the test was normed so teachers can determine if the test is appropriate for their students. In addition, norms must be revised at least every 15 years to remain current; check the manual of the test you are considering to see when norms were last revised.

Validity.   The **validity** of a test is the degree to which it measures what it claims to measure. **Content validity** is the extent to which a test assesses all aspects of the subject matter about which conclusions will be made. An example of a test sometimes used in reading assessment that lacks content validity is one consisting simply of a list of isolated words that students read orally. These tests purport to specify a student's instructional level based on this performance and claim to measure general reading ability. However, they obviously do not measure all factors involved in real reading.

Some other types of validity are **construct validity** (the degree to which performance on a test actually measures the extent to which an individual possesses a trait), **concurrent validity** (the degree to which performance on a test predicts performance on a criterion external to that test), and **predictive validity** (the extent to which a test predicts future performance in an area). Test manuals should report evidence of validity.

Reliability.   The **reliability** of a test relates to the degree of consistency of its scores. In other words, if a student took the same test more than once, would he or she make approximately the same score every time? Or, is it likely that a score obtained on this test might just be a chance hit? In the latter case, administering such an unreliable test would be a waste of time because of the good possibility of its providing erroneous information.

Test makers can determine a reliability coefficient for a test by computing a coefficient of correlation between two alternate forms of the test or between scores obtained from repeated administration of the same test. Adequate reliability coefficients for a test used to compare groups should be above 0.60, but should be above 0.90 if used for diagnostic purposes with individual students (Salvia & Ysseldyke, 1982). Reliability coefficients should be reported in test manuals. If they are not, this often means the test developer has not checked the reliability of the instrument. Examine the manual of the test you are considering to see if reliability coefficients are reported—and adequate.

Buros, who edited the *Mental Measurements Yearbook* for 40 years, stated that one of his goals was "to make test users aware of the importance of being suspicious of all tests—even those produced by well-known authors and publishers—which are not accompanied by detailed data on their construction, validation, uses, and limitations" (Mitchell, 1985, p. xiv).

Figure 3–2 provides a checklist for evaluating tests *you* may be considering in order to help you determine if a test(s) is advisable to use.

Advantages of Standardized Tests

Generally, standardized tests save time since they can be administered to many students simultaneously. Group tests may also be used with individual students. In addition, if a standardized test has been properly devised, the test passages and questions have been checked out with numerous students. Some items are discarded in this process, and new items are tested until a final, suitable group of passages and questions is chosen. Most teachers do not have the time to prepare tests with such thoroughness. In addition, many test makers now monitor **passage dependency**—that is, they take care to ensure that a student must actually read a passage to answer the questions, rather than being able to answer based merely on previous knowledge. Finally, standardized tests are usually available in two or more equivalent forms so that students can be retested to measure growth.

FIGURE 3–2 *Checklist for Judging the Technical Acceptability of Tests*

---

* Use the technical manual accompanying a standardized test you are considering to respond to the following items.
* Fill out a sheet like this one for each standardized test you are considering.

NAME OF TEST: _____

	Adequate	Inadequate

✓ Sample on which **norms** are based contains students similar to your students in terms of age, IQ range, and general characteristics.

Comments: _____

_____

_____

✓ Manual discusses **validity,** and statements provide substantiation of validity.

Comments: _____

_____

_____

✓ **Reliability** coefficients are
  • reported.
  • adequate for group comparisons.
  • adequate for diagnostic purposes with individual students.

Comments: _____

_____

_____

While standardized survey tests may provide some measurement of how well a student is performing by specifying an approximate reading level, they do not furnish an analysis of *why* the student is achieving well or doing poorly.

Survey Tests. Group standardized survey tests can be employed to select students who require remedial programs by comparing their performances with the performances of others. In fact, administration of a standardized test is usually required by federal, state, or local mandate for determining eligibility for most LD classes and U.S. Title I remedial reading programs. Figure 3–3 illustrates a typical item found on a group standardized survey test used to determine students' approximate reading levels.

Diagnostic Tests. While *grade scores* on standardized diagnostic tests are not very reliable, if these grade-level scores are ignored and substituted with an analysis of student performance on specific reading tasks, some helpful diagnostic information may be obtained. With careful reflection about each error and its possible causes, a teacher may find these tests to be useful.

Disadvantages of Standardized Tests

There has been an increase in the use of standardized tests every decade since the 1950s. Although standardized tests provide helpful information if they are applied to the appropriate purpose, there also are disadvantages in using them.

FIGURE 3–3   *An Example of the Type of Passage and Accompanying Questions Often Found on Standardized Tests*

Birds are amazing members of the animal kingdom. There is much that is interesting about our feathered friends. For one, they are the only animals that have feathers. This plumage can be dull and used to disguise birds from enemies or bright to attract a mate. Like cows and certain other animals, birds have two stomachs. But they have no teeth. And, of course, we all know of the incredible migrations birds make, sometimes covering thousands of miles. Some, for example, fly back and forth each year from the Arctic to the bottom of South America.

1. **This paragraph tells us that birds are the only animals that**

    Ⓐ migrate.
    Ⓑ have two stomachs.
    Ⓒ have plumage.
    Ⓓ live in the Arctic.

2. **The phrase <u>feathered friends</u> refers to**

    Ⓐ bird lovers.
    Ⓑ the birds themselves.
    Ⓒ those who disguise birds from their enemies.
    Ⓓ birds when they are looking for mates.

3. **This paragraph was probably written by someone**

    Ⓐ who wanted to convince readers that birds are intriguing.
    Ⓑ who was trying to write a fictional story.
    Ⓒ who only knows a little about birds.
    Ⓓ who is not particularly interested in nature.

Survey Tests.   While survey tests do provide some measurement about how well a student is performing in reading by specifying an approximate reading level, they do not furnish an analysis of *why* the student is achieving well or poorly. Usually diagnostic profiles cannot be developed from students' performance on types of items because not enough items of each type are included to make adequate judgments. This is especially problematic for comprehension (e.g., trying to specify that a student has difficulties with a specific comprehension task based on the number of items of that type the student missed). In addition, since test passages become increasingly difficult as the student moves from the beginning to the end of the test, some students may miss items simply because the overall difficulty of later passages is above their reading level, not because they lack the specific skill tested by the items answered incorrectly.

Moreover, most standardized survey tests do not measure all understandings a student needs to perform well on every reading task. For example, the special skills necessary for reading content area texts may not be included in such tests. Furthermore, because passages used are only brief excerpts, the reading task necessary for these tests often does not approximate that of authentic text reading.

Diagnostic Tests.   Grade-level scores obtained on many standardized diagnostic tests commonly used in remedial programs vary from test to test and do not provide an accurate index of reading *level*. One reason for this variance is that criteria for evaluating students' errors differ from test to test.

Improving Test Instruments.   To answer concerns voiced about standardized tests, some groups have directed efforts toward overhauling test instruments in terms of (a) how students demonstrate their knowledge, strategies, and skills, and (b) format and content.

Two examples are those undertaken by educational leaders in Illinois and Michigan (Pearson & Valencia, 1987; Wixson & Peters, 1987). In these cases, university-based reading authorities, members of professional reading associations, and classroom teachers have teamed to develop what may be better assessment instruments for use in their states. In many circumstances, the typical multiple-choice or similar format items have been retained, but students are required to answer in atypical ways, such as marking all plausible answers or ranking answers (e.g., 1, 2, 3) according to plausibility. An emphasis is placed on demonstrating reasoning, and some questions are designed to measure **metacognition**—that is, students' own awareness of the text-processing strategies they are using. There has been mixed success with these atypical instruments. Efforts have been most successful when inservice training has helped teachers understand the rationale and appropriate interpretation of results.

To answer criticisms about lack of task authenticity, some commercial test publishing companies have attempted to address the problem of passage length. Instead of the very short, unrelated passages typically used in standardized tests—which are not representative of much material read in real-world situations—these companies are attempting various approaches to present longer passages. For example, in the fourth edition of the Gates-MacGinitie Reading Tests, at levels 1 and 2, several single stories are divided into a number of paragraphs and comprehension is assessed for each paragraph.[1] New standardized tests also often include informational selections as well as story selections and sometimes listings of teaching suggestions to follow up on test results.

Using Standardized Tests With Students Who Speak Nonstandard Dialects and Those Who Are New English-Language Learners (ELLs)

Another issue about which there has been concern is the degree to which standardized reading tests are suitable for students who speak nonstandard dialects. Some argue that students should not have to take tests in a dialect they do not speak. Educators voicing this view emphasize the differences between sounds (the phonological system) of standard English and those of nonstandard dialects, believing this puts certain students at a disadvantage. For example, some sound-discrimination items found on primary-grade standardized tests are not differentiated in the oral language of a variety of nonstandard dialect speakers. It should be noted, however, that this argument is applicable only to primary-level assessment instruments. Above this level, tests usually do not include items designed to measure how well students can identify letter sounds.

---

[1] Publishers of tests are listed in the test banks found in every chapter of this assessment unit. Addresses of publishers often can be found on the Internet. They also can be found in an appendix of the *Fifteenth Mental Measurements Yearbook* (Plake & Impara, 2003), which is available in any university library.

Instead, they typically contain components that require whole-word recognition and passage comprehension.

Those who favor use of standardized tests with these students assert that students from nonmainstream cultures are really bidialectal; that is, although they speak a nonstandard form of English, they understand standard English when it is spoken to them. These students obviously grasp standard English sentence structures and standard English vocabulary because they can obtain meaning from standard English utterances in everyday situations.

A further point often made in favor of standardized tests is that the material students read in school and later throughout life is written in standard English. Therefore, it seems reasonable to test students in standard English to determine just how well they can handle this task and to plan instruction if tests show they do not handle it well.

> Research has shown that in reading testing, as in reading instruction, nonstandard English dialect differences do not play a major role in affecting performance.

Finally, a substantial amount of research has shown that in reading testing, as in reading instruction, nonstandard English dialect differences do not play a major role in affecting performance. For example, Hochman (1973) compared African American and Caucasian third, fourth, and fifth graders' performances on two forms of the California Reading Test. One form was written in standard English; one was written in a Black vernacular dialect. No differences were found in test scores of African American or Caucasian students on either form. If students did well on one form, they did well on the other; likewise, if they did poorly on one, they did poorly on the alternate form.

While variations seen in standardized test performance may be relatively minor for students who speak a nonstandard form of English—with the one exception being those subtests administered in primary grades that tap into phonological aspects of language—there may be greater difficulties for new English-language learners (ELLs) especially when comprehension is evaluated. Garcia (1991) examined effectiveness of Hispanic fifth and sixth graders of limited English proficiency on a standardized test written in English (the California Tests of Basic Skills). These students performed poorly because they lacked knowledge of vocabulary used in the questions. They also had incomplete background information about a number of topics addressed in the test passages, and this adversely affected their ability to answer inference questions (questions that rely on an individual's prior knowledge as well as on statements provided in the text). In a follow-up interview with the students in which questions were asked orally and in which performances were examined on passages with culturally familiar topics, Garcia found the standardized test seriously underestimated comprehension abilities of limited-English-proficient students. This study provides evidence that teachers should use caution when employing tests for placement, assessment, and AYP decisions with students not yet proficient in English as a second language, and for whom cultural experiences are inconsistent with those targeted by test makers preparing test passages for students in U.S. educational systems.

STEPS IN ASSESSMENT FOR IDENTIFICATION

Chapter 1 noted that the most common method for identifying students who need remedial or clinical reading services, or placement in an LD program, is to assess a student's **potential**—that is, where the student *should* be achieving if the reading problem did not exist—and then to compare this potential reading ability with the student's *present* achievement. Whether the discrepancy between the two is small, moderate, or great is a major deciding factor in place-ment decisions. But, how do you determine an individual's "potential"?

Assessing Potential

To understand the concept of potential, consider a hypothetical case. Teddy is in fourth grade and has average intelligence. There are no indications that he experiences any obvious difficulties that might limit his reading development (e.g., physiological, hereditary, language or possible factors). Thus, there is every reason to expect that Teddy could read at the level of other average fourth graders. Another way to say this is that his *potential*, likely, is fourth-grade level (often expressed as 4.0).

But, what of students who do evidence possibly limiting factors—for example, significantly less-than-average intelligence? It would be atypical for students with substantially lower intelligence quotients (IQs) to be reading at a level similar to students of average intellectual ability who are at the same grade levels. And, con-versely, what of intellectually gifted youngsters? Since their potentials surely are greater than the typical student, they would be expected to be reading above grade level. What would a good estimate of that potential be? Should we expect a sev-enth-grade student with an IQ of 140 to be reading at eighth-grade level? Ninth? Tenth? Or, what would be a useful estimate of potential for the student with an in-telligence quotient 15 or 20 points below the average?

Intelligence seems to come into question often when the problem of deter-mining an individual's potential for achievement is addressed. For this reason, over the years, several mathematical formulas have been developed for esti-mating potential that consider in the equation an individual's IQ score, or a numerical representation of a related concept such as mental age (MA). For example, in the Horn formula (Burns, 1982) MA plus chronological age are the two factors considered to determine **learning expectancy level** or **reading expectancy** (other names for *potential*). In the Bond and Tinker formula (Bond, Tinker, & Wasson, 1979), IQ and number of years in school are used instead.

Several states today employ a different method. Potential is simply equated with intelligence. In these states students' eligibility for special programs is based on a discrepancy of two standard deviations or more between their intel-ligence levels and their present achievement levels. This method is especially used in learning disability programs.

A third way to approach this assessment task has been adopted by other educators who have questioned the wisdom of basing estimates of potential heavily on scores obtained from intelligence tests, a concern voiced both by authorities in the LD field (e.g., Aaron, 1997) and in the literacy profession (Stanovich, 1991a). Arguments against use of IQ scores include (a) lack of con-sensus about appropriate means for measuring intelligence; (b) the fact that being a poor reader seems to cause poor performance on IQ tests (even when no reading is required; and (c) recognition that different types of IQ tests (e.g., verbal vs. non-verbal) tend to identify different students as those with the greatest discrepancy.

Thus, instead, a measure of students' understanding after they have listened to material read to them is the preferred method of some educators for assessing potential (Spring & French, 1990). This measure of **listening comprehension** tells us the level of material students could understand if they were able to read the material themselves. Stanovich (1991a) and others contend that listening tests are sounder reading aptitude measures than IQ or mental age scores.

Assessing listening comprehension is quite simple. Graded passages in an informal reading inventory (IRI) and their scoring criteria often are used for this purpose. (You will learn more about IRIs and how to score them in Chapter 4.) Specific directions for using an IRI to measure listening comprehension are found in the accompanying boxed material titled *STEPS—Administering Assessments in Your Own Classroom: Listening-Level Test.* Or, you may use other measurement instruments that include subtests designed specifically for assessing listening comprehension. Two such instruments are the Diagnostic Achievement Battery and the Stanford Achievement Test.

LEARNING FROM TEXT

Summarize. What is the current view of many literacy educators and special education educators with respect to how potential should be assessed?

STEPS: Administering Assessments in Your Own Classroom

Listening-Level Test (A test of potential)

STEP 1 Obtain an informal reading inventory (IRI). (See Chapter 4 for many sources of these.) IRIs are useful for this purpose because they contain passages written at many grade/reading levels.

STEP 2 Plan to spend some time examining the directions. Although usually easy to follow, directions may vary slightly from IRI to IRI.

STEP 3 Schedule the testing session so students who are targeted for this assessment may be tested individually—and in a setting where others to be tested cannot hear.

STEP 4 Select a passage to begin the assessment, using a passage at the level where you *estimate* the student's potential to be.

STEP 5 Read the passage to the student. Ask the accompanying questions (or follow the IRI's directions for student retelling), asking for oral (not written) responses from the student.

STEP 6 Using criteria established for the IRI you choose, determine if the student's responses indicate—in regard to *listening comprehension*—that the passage was easy, just right, or too difficult for him or her.

STEP 7 If easy, read each successively more difficult passage to the student until the student's listening comprehension responses indicate the passage is just the right level for the student. This is the student's potential.

or

If too difficult, read each successively easier passage to the student until the student's listening comprehension responses indicate the passage is at just the right level for the student. This is the student's potential.

David's
Case Study

An Assessment Case Study

Throughout the four chapters of Part 2, we will follow a student who has been referred to a remedial reading program, calling this hypothetical student David Adams. In this chapter, we will assume that tests must be administered to determine if David does indeed require remedial services. At this stage, the teacher begins an **assessment information form** for him, a form on which diagnostic information is systematically recorded to aid in decision making. Refer to Figure 3–4 to see the beginning notations the teacher has placed on this form. As you will observe, David is in the fourth grade and is 9 years old, information the teacher has placed on the assessment information form. At this time, the teacher has already administered a test of listening comprehension, employing graded IRI passages, and David's potential based on this test appears to be fourth grade. This result may be interpreted to mean that he should be able to read at a level commensurate with his present grade placement. The questions now are, "Does he?" And if not, "How serious is his delay?" Further testing will provide answers to these queries, and we will continue to follow David's test performance to see what the outcomes will be.

Assessing Present Reading Achievement

After assessing a student's listening level, the teacher must determine the student's present reading achievement. Informal procedures are usually unacceptable for designating present achievement level when the purpose is to verify eligibility for programs; administrative regulations frequently require that a standardized test be administered for this purpose.

Research has shown that, for both poor and gifted readers, out-of-level standardized tests provide a more accurate measure of reading achievement.

Entry-Level Assessment. It is good practice to administer **out-of-level** standardized tests to students with reading problems. With out-of-level assessment, the test administered has been designed for students at the grade level that is

FIGURE 3–4 *A Partially Completed Record Form of Assessment Information*

Assessment Information Form

Student's Name: David Adams

Grade Level: 4th

Chronological Age:

   1)   Birth date   February 19, 19—

   2)   Age   9.0

Listening Comprehension Level:

   1)   Method of determination   use of graded IRI passages

   2)   Level   4th grade

equivalent to a student's suspected reading level rather than the student's actual grade level. For example, if we suspect Donna, a fifth grader, is reading at about third-grade level, we would administer the test the publishers have specified for third graders rather than the one prepared for students in fifth grade. Studies have shown that, for both poor readers and for gifted readers, this procedure provides a more accurate measure of reading achievement than using an on-grade-level test.

But, if the purpose of administering a standardized survey test is to determine a student's reading achievement level, how can we decide that level beforehand to administer an appropriate out-of-level test? **Entry-level tests,** quick screening devices that render a rough approximation of a student's reading ability, are used for this purpose. Although entry-level tests should never be used as the definitive specification of a student's reading level, they are useful in suggesting the level of test to be administered for three reasons: They prevent students from possible demoralizing experiences, prevent wasted time, and allow selection of a formal measure that will provide an accurate estimate of reading.

Consider this example: Sixteen-year-old Joseph is enrolled in a reading clinic by his parents. They are quite unsure of his present reading level and only know he is behind the level needed to adequately meet expectations in his 10th-grade class. A call to Joe's school by the clinician, Mr. Ruddell, produces the same information: Joe is apparently behind the other students in reading because he is having difficulty with all assignments involving reading, but neither the counselor nor the classroom teachers have an idea about what his approximate reading level might be. What should the clinician do? Should he choose a test designed for seventh- or eighth-grade students since there is at least agreement that Joe is behind the average readers in his classes? Let's suppose this is the choice. Joe sits down to begin this test only to find he cannot read the first passage. Embarrassed, he tries to hide this deficiency from the clinician and begins putting on a fair imitation of a student reading and answering questions; however, he marks the answers randomly since he cannot read the passages or the question items. As passages become successively more difficult and Joe sees many more words he doesn't know, frustration takes over and he gives up any pretense of reading. He pushes the test a bit to the side, takes the answer sheet in front of him and marks any square on which his pencil happens to fall. As a result, he completes a 27-minute section of the test in 8 minutes.

Mr. Ruddell, who has been observing Joe from the corner of his eye, realizes that any score obtained from this test is obviously of no value in specifying an accurate reading level. He decides that the next day he will give Joe the form of this standardized test designed for fourth- to sixth-graders since he is sure from Joe's behavior that the previous test was too difficult for him.

When Joe sees the test being handed to him the next day, it looks little different than the one with which he had such a disheartening experience the day before. He becomes tense and makes up an excuse for what he expects will be his similarly poor performance: "I've got a terrible headache, Mr. Ruddell." But, because he's a cooperative student, he reluctantly and with feelings of distress tries again. This time he can read the first passage and handles the second passage somewhat, but after that it is all uphill again. Today he makes no pretense of reading. When the third passage turns out to be undecipherable to him, he uses yesterday's strategy. He pushes the test away and marks answers arbitrarily, without having set eyes on passages four through nine. The result is that a 24-minute section of the test is completed in 10 minutes. Having again observed Joe surreptitiously, the clinician, also feeling disconcerted, decides he must administer a primary-level test so Joe can read it and a meaningful measure of his ability can be obtained.

On the third day, Joe is given the second-grade form of the same standardized test. The clinician has to provide many words of comfort and encouragement to get Joe to begin, but when he starts, Joe finds he can read and answer almost all passages and items. He works thoughtfully and when the clinician calls "time" at the end of 20 minutes, he has completed all but the last question. If the clinician had administered an entry-level assessment before choosing the first form of the standardized test, much wasted time and feelings of futility could have been avoided.

Some publishers have established special norms for using out-of-level testing; for example, the Gates-MacGinitie Reading Tests suggest such norms. In addition, the Comprehensive Tests of Basic Skills (CTBS) provide entry-level tests called "locator tests" to facilitate out-of-level testing.

Entry-level tests usually consist of graded word lists. Students read the words orally, and teachers estimate reading levels from their performances. In addition to those supplied with some standardized tests, the published informal inventories described in Chapter 4 furnish good sources for acquiring a graded word list. Because our hypothetical student, David Adams, scored at the second-grade level on his entry-level test, we selected a second-grade form of a standardized test to administer to him.

LEARNING FROM TEXT

Note Taking. What are some things that must be taken into account if you administer a standardized test? Jot down a brief, paraphrased list of these as you read the following section.

Administering a Standardized Test. Standardized tests need to be selected with care. Before tests are purchased, a specimen set should be requested from the publisher. A specimen set usually includes one copy of each level of a test, plus a teacher's manual and technical manual. The technical manual should be examined for information on the norming population, reliability, and validity. Most teachers do not relish the thought of reading a technical manual for a test, but doing so is a critical part of a reading teacher's job.

Furthermore, it is wise to take an additional step before making decisions about which tests will be used in an assessment program: Read published reviews of any tests under consideration. These reviews are written by experts in both assessment procedures and literacy instruction. Reviews of tests can be found in many professional journals, but probably the most valuable resource is the *Mental Measurements Yearbook (MMY)*. This important reference book provides descriptions of reading and other tests currently in print, addresses of the publishers, and critiques of the tests. The critiques are especially helpful because, even though a test has been widely used, that does not necessarily mean it is a good assessment instrument. The adequacy of many tests is discussed throughout Part 2 of this text but because there is an extensive number from which to choose, it is impossible to describe them all. The *MMY*, found in most college and university libraries, offers reports of many tests of potential interest. All school systems should purchase at least one copy of the most recent edition for use by teachers and administrators. The *MMY* is currently in its 15th edition, published in 2003 by the Buros Institute of Mental Measurements and distributed by the University of Nebraska Press. (See Figure 3–5 for an example of a typical entry in the *MMY*.)

LEARNING FROM TEXT

> **Using Illustrative Aids.**   Figure 3–5 covers two and a half pages. Read at least all of the first page to get a feeling for what is covered in the *MMY*.

If the *MMY* is not available to you, test reviews, exactly as they appear in the *MMY*, may be purchased at the Buros Institute website: www.unl.edu/buros/

The Buros Institute of Mental Measurements also publishes a volume called *Tests in Print (TIP)*. Inclusion of a test in the *MMY* is based on whether the test is new or has been revised since the last edition, while *TIP* includes all tests currently available for purchase. *TIP* does not provide critiques of tests, as does the *MMY*, but only a listing and description; therefore, *TIP* cannot be used to determine whether a test is worthwhile but only to establish if it is still published. Another resource produced by the same institute is *Reading Tests and Reviews*, which contains lists, references, and critiques of reading tests that have appeared in all Buros Institute publications since 1938.

When considering test selection to determine a student's eligibility for a special program, a teacher should select a survey test, one that yields information about students' general reading levels, rather than specific information about strengths and weaknesses in strategies and skills. See **Test Bank A** on page 91 for some standardized reading survey tests, along with a brief listing of details for each. The content of survey tests varies, but most include a section on vocabulary and a section on comprehension.

A caution is in order about certain tests that purport to measure general reading achievement level when, in fact, they do not. These tests usually consist exclusively of lists of isolated words that the student reads orally. Two such tests are the Slosson Oral Reading Test–Revised and the Wide Range Achievement Tests–Revised (WRAT-R). These tests cannot be used to determine general reading achievement level, even though they claim to do so, because of the limited type of reading behavior they measure. They include no assessment of a student's understanding of the meanings of the listed words; no measure of general comprehension ability after silent reading, and no appraisal of the ability to read words in context (as found in authentic reading situations). Though often used to specify a reading achievement level, the WRAT-R has been normed by age rather than grade, and the publishers indicate that grade scores given by this test may only be rough clues to instructional level.

The results of many studies to determine the degree of congruency between grade level scores obtained on tests of isolated word recognition and students' actual classroom performance have not been favorable.

Accordingly, a number of studies have been conducted to determine the degree of congruency between grade-level scores obtained on such tests of isolated word recognition and students' reading abilities as seen in actual classroom performance. The results of many of these have not been favorable. While it is true that many standardized tests may overestimate the reading achievement level of certain students, overestimates by the WRAT, for example, have at times been extreme—with reading levels of more than a third of the students overestimated by three or more grade levels (e.g., Bradley, 1976). If these tests measure only a limited type of reading behavior and the scores obtained are often widely divergent from students' actual functioning levels, why are they used? They are used primarily because they are quick and simple to administer.

FIGURE 3–5 *A Sample Review in the Mental Measurements Yearbook*

Burns/Roe Informal Reading Inventory: Preprimer to Twelfth Grade, Fifth Edition.

Purpose: Provides information about the reading skills, abilities, and needs of individual students in order to plan an appropriate program of reading instruction.

Population: Beginning readers—grade 12.

Publication Dates: 1985–1999.

Acronym: IRI.

Scores, 2: Word Recognition, Comprehension.

Administration: Individual.

Levels, 14: Preprimer, Primer, First Reader, Second Grade, Third Grade, Fourth Grade, Fifth Grade, Sixth Grade, Seventh Grade, Eighth Grade, Ninth Grade, Tenth Grade, Eleventh Grade, Twelfth Grade.

Price Data: Available from publisher.

Time: (40–50) minutes.

Authors: Betty D. Roe and Paul C. Burns.

Publisher: Houghton Mifflin.

Cross References: See T5:357 (1 reference) and T4:343; for reviews by Carolyn Colvin Murphy and Roger H. Bruning and by Edward S. Shapiro of an earlier edition, see 10:37.

Review of the Burns/Roe Informal Reading Inventory: Preprimer to Twelfth Grade, Fifth Edition by FELICE J. GREEN, Professor of Education, University of North Alabama, Florence, AL:

The Burns/Roe Informal Reading Inventory: Preprimer to Twelfth Grade, Fifth Edition (IRI) is designed to determine the independent, instructional, frustration, and listening levels of students reading from the Preprimer to the 12th grade level. The listening test can indicate students' reading potential, or capacity to improve reading skills. The rest of the IRI provides information about specific strengths and weaknesses in both reading comprehension and word recognition skills, which enables teachers to plan appropriate reading programs for their students. The inventory is also useful for resource rooms and reading clinics, as well as in the training of preservice teachers in methods courses.

Scores obtained from administering the Burns/Roe Informal Reading Inventory, like other informal reading inventories, are not standardized, or do not yield normed scores. The examinee is evaluated using preestablished standards, and results are reported in grade equivalents.

The passages in this IRI, which include both fiction and nonfiction selections, are well written. Although the passages appear to be on the stated reading levels, passages PP and P are longer than those in many informal reading inventories.

The test writers have included notes to the examiner at the end of passages that include proper nouns—most are people's names—telling the examiner not to count these words as miscue pronunciations. The notes instruct the examiner to pronounce the words for the examinee. This is very good, but there is one thing missing. Many examiners will have trouble pronouncing international names of people CORRECTLY; therefore, phonetic respellings should be provided for all of the names. (One pronunciation is provided in an introductory statement.) One of the positive aspects of the IRI is that it DOES include stories about people from diverse backgrounds.

There are 8 comprehension questions at the end of Passages PP through 2, and there are 10 questions at the end of Levels 3 through 12. There are ample higher order questions at each level, which is not always the case with such tests. Beginning with the PP level, there are inference and cause/effect questions. Other types of questions used to check comprehension at all levels are main idea, detail, sequence, and vocabulary. Teachers can do an analysis of the types of questions missed most frequently to help them decide which comprehension skills need to be taught to individual students.

Directions for administering and scoring the IRI are clearly written and are accompanied by examples. There should be no confusion about administering and scoring the inventory if directions and examples are studied carefully, although some practice for the novice may be necessary.

There are four forms of the IRI, which is good for examiners who wish to measure silent and oral reading at each level. Combining oral and silent reading results yields more diagnostic information than either one alone, if the examiner has the time to administer both, and there are two tests for pretesting and two for posttesting.

FIGURE 3–5 *(continued)*

Another positive aspect of the Burns/Roe Informal Reading Inventory is that it provides several alternative suggestions for using the IRI other than the traditional uses and methods for administering. One such suggestion is that of retelling the reading selections, rather than asking the questions at the end of each passage. A detailed discussion of the use of retelling is included, along with a Free Recall Processing Checklist to use, if this method of checking comprehension is chosen.

An alternate method is also given for asking young readers the Main Idea question when the questions at the end of the selections are used. It is pointed out that young readers may not understand the concept of "main idea"; therefore, they will not be able to answer the question, "What is the main idea of this story?" The novice examiner may not know to reword, or how to reword the question, in order to get the desired response from a young reader.

In addition to testing word recognition and comprehension skills, the IRI can be used to determine the reading rate of a student. Explicit directions are given for obtaining the reading rate.

Excellent forms are provided for tabulating and reporting the results of the IRI. The Worksheet for Qualitative Analysis of Uncorrected Miscues in Context enables the examiner to fill in the three sections of the Summary Form. The three sections of the Summary Form are Miscue Analysis of Phonic and Structural Analysis Skills, the Summary of Strengths and Weaknesses in Word Recognition, and the Summary of Strengths and Weaknesses in Comprehension. These forms facilitate the examiner in analyzing results of the IRI and making the proper educational decisions for their students.

SUMMARY. The Burns/Roe Informal Reading Inventory is an excellent tool for detecting reading strengths and weaknesses of students. It is one of the better IRIs available.

Review of the Burns/Roe Informal Reading Inventory: Preprimer to Twelfth Grade, Fifth Edition by TIMOTHY SHANAHAN, Professor of Urban Education, University of Illinois at Chicago, Chicago, IL:

The idea of the informal reading inventory (IRI) is quite simple. Some texts are harder to read than others, and it is difficult to teach students well from materials that are too hard or too easy. An efficient way of finding out which texts would be best for teaching would be to observe children while they try to read from various books. The IRI is a set of assessment procedures that does just that. For much of the century it was thought that teachers needed to construct their own IRIs on the basis of the materials from which they taught.

Test makers eventually challenged this notion by publishing IRIs that were not linked to particular instructional materials, and studies have shown that reasonable predictions can be made on the basis of commercial IRIs, except at the first grade level. Because of their ease of use, commercial IRIs have grown in popularity over the years. The Burns/Roe Informal Reading Inventory, now in its fifth edition, is among the most popular of these.

The Burns/Roe Informal Reading Inventory (IRI) is an individually administered test that is used to determine a child's frustration, instructional, and independent reading levels, and to identify specific strengths and weaknesses in word recognition, reading rate, oral reading, and reading comprehension. Classroom teachers and reading specialists can use this inventory to discern children's instructional needs, and this IRI is often used in the professional training of teachers. The test can be given in about 40–50 minutes by an experienced administrator. The authors usually provide clear directions for administration and interpretation—including a helpful case study, though the explanatory material could be better organized. The inclusion of previews, a case study, and frequently asked questions lead to repetition and make it difficult to locate specific information.

An IRI is an array of word lists and passages selected to represent varied difficulty levels, and a loose set of qualitative and quantitative observational procedures for interpreting children's performances with these materials. Unlike standardized assessments, the directions are recommendations rather than rules. As these authors point out, informal tests are "not bound by formal directions, defined time limits, or a restricted set of materials or procedures" (manual, p. 1). The purpose is to make good instructional decisions, and users should experiment with the instrument to make the best predictions possible. The authors are usually supportive of such informal use— often, though not always, pointing out alternatives or explaining the reasoning behind their own choices.

The Burns/Roe IRI includes a word recognition test (two forms) and a passage reading test (four forms). The word recognition test includes 14 word lists (Preprimer, Primer, and Grades 1–12). There are 20 words in each list, which should be sufficient to support reliability, though no reliability statistics are provided. These lists are used to determine word recognition skills in isolation from context. The word lists appear to be appropriately difficult for the levels they represent. No data on the equivalence of the two forms are provided. The authors offer no explanation of why they have included word lists through the 12th grade level, a nontraditional approach. It seems doubtful that the higher level lists would reveal much about students' knowledge of sight vocabulary or phonics. It seems that test users could skip these levels of the word test with little loss of information.

(continued)

FIGURE 3–5 *A Sample Review in the Mental Measurements Yearbook* *(continued)*

The passage reading test includes 14 reading passages at the same levels as the word lists. These passages range in length from 53 to 237 words, and each is accompanied by a list of 8–10 comprehension questions. The passages are used to evaluate students' oral and silent reading and listening comprehension. The readability levels of the passages have been tested by formula (Spache or Fry), but there has been no systematic attempt to represent the range of reading demands. For example, some IRIs have narrative and expository test forms, so that both literary and content reading abilities can be examined. This test, however, includes mainly stories or factual narratives, even at the senior high school levels. Only 11 of the 56 passages are expository, no expository tests are used through the first six levels of the test, and there is no systematic representation of content or text type. This is a definite weakness for a test that will often be used with older students.

The oral reading procedures are similar to those of most IRIs, with a couple of notable exceptions. Burns and Roe recommend not counting self-corrections for level setting, but do count repetitions—including those made to self-correct. IRI makers have long disagreed about how to handle repetitions, so I won't quibble with their decision. However, their rationale for doing this is weak—a study by Ekwall (1976) that used contradictory evaluative criteria. Most IRIs use Betts' level-setting criteria. The Burns/Roe IRI, however, uses Powell's criteria at Grades 1 and 2. The difference of accuracy required for instructional level (99% vs. 85%) is considerable, and the Powell criteria have not been widely accepted in the field. Unfortunately, there is no explanation for this choice, and the directions for administering it are unclear. Are these criteria for use with first- and second-grade passages or children? This IRI, in spite of all of its mostly sound advice on the interpretation of oral reading, fails to offer any suggestions for dealing with dialect, an especially important issue for those working with racial and linguistic minorities.

The comprehension questions emphasize recall of main ideas, sequence, details, cause and effect, inferences, and vocabulary. The test encourages analysis of error types, though studies of this topic show no clear differences due to question type. The manual indicates that "teachers should be careful to avoid drawing conclusions from extremely limited samples" (manual, p. 5). They go on to suggest the value of noticing that a student erred 9 of 10 times with a particular question type. The problem with this is that comprehension patterns are rarely this stark, and few students would ever be asked to answer 10 questions of the same type on this test.

SUMMARY. The Burns/Roe Informal Reading Inventory is a practical means for determining reading levels and instructional needs for elementary and secondary students. It provides a useful collection of word lists and carefully graded reading passages for evaluating students' oral and silent reading and comprehension, including some helpful guidance for evaluating students' silent reading speed. The manual is confusing at times, and the authors offer little explanation for several of their recommendations or claims. No evidence is provided concerning any of the psychometric properties of the test such as reliability or concurrent validity, though various design features suggest that these are probably sound. Most of the passages used in this test are stories, so it is questionable how informative this test will be to most secondary school teachers.

REVIEWER'S REFERENCE

Ekwall, E. E. (1976). Should repetitions be counted as errors? *The Reading Teacher, 29,* 365–367.

Source: From Plake, B. S., & Impara, J. C. (Eds.). (2001). *The Fourteenth Mental Measurements Yearbook* (pp. 195–198). Lincoln, NE: The Buros Institute of Mental Measurements, University of Nebraska. Reprinted by permission.

Time is a major problem for teachers, but, since these tests have been inappropriately devised to measure general reading achievement and since the results are often questionable, they should not be used for this purpose.

Administering a standardized survey test correctly is essential. If directions in the administration manual are not followed exactly, the norms will not be applicable. Directions include exact specifications for the length of time a student may work on each test section. At times, teachers feel they should permit a student with learning problems to have more than the specified time, but this is inappropriate. Allowing more or less time, even by a minute or two, invalidates results. Standardized survey tests are designed to be administered to groups of students during the same time period. In a remedial situation, tests can be

A TEACHING RESOURCE

TEST BANK A

Some Norm-Referenced Survey Tests

Name	For Grades	Type of Administration	Time for Administration	Publisher
California Achievement Tests	K–12	Group	Varies by level	CTB/McGraw-Hill
Comprehensive Tests of Basic Skills	K–12	Group	Varies by level	CTB/McGraw-Hill
Educational Development Series	K–12	Group	Varies by level	Scholastic Testing Service
Gates-MacGinitie Reading Tests, 4th edition	prereading-adult	Group	Varies by level	Riverside
Iowa Tests of Basic Skills	K–9	Group	Varies by level	Riverside
Metropolitan Achievement Tests	preprimer–12	Group	Varies by level	Psychological Corporation
Nelson-Denny Reading Test	9–12, college, adults	Group	Varies by level	Riverside
Nelson Reading Skills Test	3–9	Group	35 minutes	Riverside
Stanford Achievement Test	1–13	Group	Varies by level	Harcourt Brace Educational Measurement
Tests of Achievement and Proficiency. This test battery includes subtests on using sources of information, as well as on reading comprehension.	9–12	Group	Varies according to subtests used	Riverside

administered in this way if the same level test is suitable for several students; if not, tests can be administered individually.

Scoring a standardized test is easy since an answer key is supplied. Raw scores for each section, which are simply the number of correct responses, are combined for all sections to obtain a total raw score. The teacher then consults a table in the manual that indicates the grade-level equivalent of the total raw score.

David's Case Study (continued)

For our hypothetical example; after combining the number of correct answers for all sections of a test, the teacher found that David Adams's total raw score was 24 and that the table indicated this is equivalent to 3.0, or beginning third-grade level (see Figure 3–6).

Standardized Test Scores: To Convert or Not to Convert?

Once a teacher has obtained a grade-level score from a standardized test, what should be done with it before comparing it with the student's potential? Since

FIGURE 3–6 *Continuation of a Partially Completed Record Form of Assessment Information for a Hypothetical Student*

Assessment Information Form

Student's Name: David Adams

Grade Level: 4th

Chronological Age:

    1)   Birth date   February 19, 19—

    2)   Age   9.0

Listening Comprehension Level:

    1)   Method of determination   use of graded IRI passages

    2)   Level   4th grade

Entry-Level Assessment Results: 2nd grade

Standardized Survey Test:

    1)   Name of test   Gates-MacGinitie Reading Tests, Level 2, Form S

    2)   Grade score obtained   3.0

Present Reading Instructional Level (based on standardized test results):   approximately 2.0

Discrepancy Between Listening Level and Present Achievement: 2.0

LEARNING FROM TEXT

Self-monitoring.   Compare Figures 3–4 and 3–6. Do you understand what's going on here? If not, reread the text related to each figure.

A score on a standardized survey test helps compare a student's performance with that of others but does not necessarily indicate the level of instructional materials the student can learn from in real classroom situations.

a grade-level score on the standardized survey test is the average score made by all students at that level on whom the test was normed, if a hypothetical student named Robert receives a raw score of 52 and the test manual tells us this is equivalent to 6.0 grade level, this means that the average raw score of all students at the 6.0 grade level who took this test during the norming procedure was 52. This helps us to compare Robert's performance with that of other students. It does not necessarily tell us what level of instructional materials Robert can handle in real classroom situations. Sometimes this standardized test grade-level score is a fair estimation of a student's instructional level, but sometimes it is not. The **instructional level** is the level at which a student can handle material in an instructional situation with normal teacher guidance—that is, with the typical amount of assistance with new vocabulary, help with small comprehension difficulties, and so forth. "Instructional level" is a similar concept to Vygotsky's zone of proximal development (see Chapter 1).

Because teachers have noticed that scores on a standardized test overestimate the instructional level of some students, a number of studies have been undertaken to determine how valid these scores are for specifying the level of functioning of students with actual classroom materials. The data are conflicting. In research with students in grades 4 through 7, several investigators have found that these scores overestimate the actual instructional levels of students by about a year, with the overestimations particularly seen with poor readers (Betts, 1940; Glaser, 1965; Killgallon, 1942; McCracken, 1962). Williams's (1964) study with fourth, fifth, and sixth graders, however, found standardized test scores to be relatively close to students' instructional levels, and Sipay (1964) found that whether these test scores provided a good estimate depended on which standardized test the teacher used and the criteria used to determine actual classroom functioning level.

Teachers who work with poor readers sometimes find that standardized test scores do overestimate instructional levels for many students, although not for all. For this reason, sometimes the score obtained from a standardized test is considered to represent a student's frustration level. **Frustration level** is the level at which the material becomes too difficult for a student. For example, if 4.0 is specified as Elaine's frustration level, material at the fourth-grade level and above should not be selected for her. To determine the student's instructional level based on a standardized test score, sometimes 1 year is subtracted from that score; for instance, if Elaine's standardized test score is 4.0, following this practice, her approximate instructional level would be estimated at 3.0. Further, the student's independent level is estimated by subtracting an additional year. The **independent level** is the level at which a student can effortlessly handle material without teacher guidance; this material is easy enough for the student to read independently. If Elaine's instructional level is 3.0, her approximate independent level is 2.0. (Some standardized tests, for example, the Metropolitan Achievement Tests, provide a table for converting grade-level equivalent scores to instructional levels.)

There is some argument, however, against subtracting a constant of 1.0 (1 year) from the obtained standardized test score to derive an estimate of instructional level. Some have argued that the practice is statistically incorrect. Also, as noted previously, the standardized test score is not an overestimate of actual reading functioning levels for all students. In fact, it may be an underestimate for those students whose reading ability is adequate but whose test-taking skills are poor. Thus, there are two choices when using a standardized test score.

1. *Do not convert the score.* That is, do not subtract a constant of 1 year from the standardized score, but use the score exactly as obtained. Some program regulations require this approach because administrators are unaware that these scores overestimate the actual reading levels of many students, especially poor readers. Or, since the scores are relatively accurate estimates for certain readers, some educators fear that subtracting a year from the score will result in an underestimate of instructional level for certain students.

2. *Convert the scores.* That is, subtract a constant of 1 year from the standardized test score. This practice provides a better estimate for many students with less-than-average reading abilities. Although either choice can result in error, the first choice may result in many students' being denied eligibility for programs they need, while the second choice can result in a few students being placed in special programs when this is unnecessary. The second choice may be the lesser of two evils. If students in a program are found not to require

Because of difficulties interpreting grade-level scores from standardized tests, eligibility for some remedial programs is based instead on percentile rank.

special help, it is easy enough to report this happy finding and dismiss them from the program. On the other hand, if a student is denied placement, it may be a long time before this student is considered for eligibility again—time during which the student may slip even further behind.

Because of this difficulty with grade equivalent scores, some programs require use of a percentile rank instead. If, for example, a student scores at the 63rd percentile, this means the score is better than 63% of the students at that grade level who have taken the test. It is a typical procedure in certain programs to enroll only students who score below a certain percentile rank.

Computing the Discrepancy Between Potential and Achievement

Computing the discrepancy between measured reading potential and measured achievement is easy. The teacher simply compares the student's potential with the present reading instructional level. The result for one student might be

$$
\begin{array}{r}
4.0 \text{ (listening score)} \\
-\underline{2.0} \text{ (present reading instructional level)} \\
2.0 \text{ (discrepancy)}
\end{array}
$$

David's Case Study (continued)

In considering our hypothetical student David Adams, whose partial assessment information form was because in Figure 3–4 and continued in Figure 3–6, we are assuming that David received a grade equivalent score of 3.0 on a standardized test, and we have computed his present reading achievement instructional level to be approximately 2.0. David's discrepancy, therefore, indicates he is approximately 2 years behind the level at which he should be reading according to his estimated potential of fourth grade, and we can see that David warrants special reading services.

Additional information has now been added to David's assessment information form (see Figure 3–6). The teacher has recorded David's entry-level assessment results, which indicated the level of the standardized test to be administered. The name, level, and form of the standardized test that was used is noted for future reference, and his score on this test, the estimate of his approximate instructional reading level, and the discrepancy seen between his estimated potential and approximate reading level are included on the form.

Because David will be placed in a program for special reading services, additional assessment will be undertaken to determine *why* he is not reading up to his potential or, in other words, to discover his present strengths and weaknesses. This further information will help his reading teacher plan an effective program to meet David's needs. We will catch up with David again in the next chapter and learn the results of these additional evaluation procedures.

When determining eligibility for special programs, these other factors should also be considered.

1. What is the best course if the discrepancy indicates that remedial reading or LD services are required, but the student has made little progress in such programs previously? A clinical reading program may be the next step.
2. Is the student's classroom functioning level well above or below test performance level? Remember, even the best test estimates can be in error. All available information should be considered before placement in a special program is accepted or denied.

TABLE 3–2 *A Teacher Checklist for Conducting Assessment for Identification*

	Yes	No
1. Has a listening test been administered and a score obtained?		
2. Has an entry-level assessment been administered?		
3. Has a standardized, group survey test, at the appropriate level, been administered?		
4. Has the constant of 1.0 been subtracted from the grade equivalent score obtained from the standardized test? (optional)		
5. Has discrepancy between potential and present achievement been computed?		
6. Have other factors been considered before a final placement decision is made?		

3. If more students are eligible for a special program than can be accommodated, have you considered all of the students' needs before making the final selection so that first priority may be given to students with the greatest needs?

Table 3–2 suggests some questions a teacher might ask when conducting an assessment for identification.

*R*eflections Discuss these questions:

1. What is the value of assessment?
2. Because appropriate norming procedures and measures of validity and reliability are important if a standardized test is to offer believable information, why do some test producers fail to provide this information?
3. What do *you* see as the major advantage to using standardized tests in reading assessment? The major disadvantage?

4 Assessment for Verifying General Reading Levels

One way to verify general reading levels is to have students read from graded texts.

A *fter completing the assessment procedures described in Chapter 3, teachers will have information available about students' reading ability and will have identified students with reading problems. Refer to Figure 3–6 near the end of the last chapter to review the types of information already recorded for David Adams, our case study student.*

Now teachers must gather further data to design an intervention plan for each student. Two major types of assessment must be undertaken: (a) determining the student's general reading level (or, at this point, verifying the level obtained on the standardized test) and (b) determining the student's strengths and weaknesses in reading strategies, knowledge, and skills. This chapter describes procedures for verifying students' general reading levels.

Literacy educators know that determining a student's reading levels is a critical instructional consideration. If students are to increase their reading achievement, it is essential that they read a great deal of regular, connected material (i.e., reading complete stories, chapters, articles, and books). To assign texts or to help students select materials to read independently, teachers must know students' instructional reading levels and independent reading levels. Texts at a student's approximate instructional level should be used when teachers plan to provide some assistance as the student reads. On the other hand, independent level material is more appropriate if students are to read on their own at home, in study hall, or in any situation without instructional support.

Placing students in texts that are too difficult is a major hindrance to their progress and should be carefully avoided. Reading instruction in which students consistently struggle with texts that are too difficult prevents development of automatic word recognition, depresses comprehension because of necessity to focus on word identification tasks above the student's present ability, and lessens desire to engage in reading experiences (Cunningham & Stanovich, 1998). Thus, determining students' reading functioning levels is a key step in reading assessment.

LEARNING FROM TEXT

Note Taking. Consider this issue: Why is it important to know a student's functioning levels in reading? Make a brief written list of reasons to aid your recall.

As previously noted, research raises some questions about the accuracy of instructional level scores obtained from standardized tests. These furnish a reasonably *good* estimate in many cases, but an overestimate or underestimate in others. In addition, research has shown that using several measures of achievement provides the best approximation of actual reading level. Therefore, a customary diagnostic practice is to use an informal reading inventory, or sometimes a cloze procedure, to verify general reading achievement level. Also, some programs use an informal reading inventory in place of a standardized test rather than in combination with it.

Research has shown that using several measures of achievement (both formal and informal) provides the best estimate of actual reading level.

INFORMAL READING INVENTORIES

An **informal reading inventory (IRI)** is a series of graded passages, each followed by a comprehension check of some type.

Setting a Purpose for Reading. As you read the following section on informal reading inventories, think about the differences between IRIs and standardized tests.

Though once common practice for teachers to prepare their own IRIs, today good-quality, commercially prepared IRIs are available to save teachers preparation time. Most contain graded word lists for determining an entry level—the level at which testing should begin—and also provide some information about students' word recognition. The core of the IRI is a series of graded passages. Many IRIs include two passages at each level, one to be read orally and one to be read silently. These are designed to help teachers further assess a student's word recognition, to examine word identification strategies and comprehension, and to determine the student's independent, instructional, and frustration levels. Passages in many IRIs are relatively short, usually ranging from 100 to 200 words, depending on the level of the passage; however, some recently revised IRIs are featuring longer selections. While readability formulas cannot give an exact level of text, they do offer an approximation, and IRI authors frequently check passage levels using such a formula during test development.

Often the graded passages are followed by questions to assess students' comprehension after oral reading and after silent reading at each level. These incorporate literal questions and various higher-level question types. In other IRIs, comprehension is evaluated by having students simply retell all they can remember about a passage they have read.

A number of IRIs include additional supplementary tests (for example, a phonics test may be packaged at the end of the IRI, or a test of prereading concepts, or others). Today IRIs are available with passages for elementary through college levels. Not all have passages as low as preprimer or primer levels, however; therefore, if these lower levels are needed, you should check before purchasing an inventory to determine if they are available. See Figure 4–1 for important characteristics of several IRIs, including grade levels covered by each; also see **Test Bank B** on page 102 for a brief listing of a number of other available IRIs.

IRIs are available for use with students at all levels, elementary school through college.

Administering an IRI

Some procedures for administering an IRI vary from test to test, but generally the following steps are advised.

1. Steps in preparing for the test
   a. Select a place where no other students can overhear the reading or the responses to questions.
   b. Plan about 30 minutes of testing time for each student.
   c. Set up a tape recorder to record students' responses.
   d. Select the first passage to be used based on the entry-level word lists. Test makers specify the number of words read correctly and incorrectly on a list to indicate the passage on which the student should begin.
2. Before testing
   a. Allow the student to become familiar with the tape recorder for a minute or two by talking into it, listening, turning it off and on, and so on, so he or she feels comfortable with its presence.
   b. Begin with a motivating statement and one that may set a purpose for reading, something like, "Read this passage to find out the funny thing a girl's pet raccoon did." Helping students set a purpose for reading may improve comprehension.
   c. Tell the student ahead of time that you will ask questions after he or she has read the passage.
   d. If the passage is to be read orally, do not allow it to be preread silently.
3. During oral reading
   a. If the student cannot pronounce a word, tell the student to use any strategy he or she knows to figure it out and, if the student still cannot pronounce it, to skip it and continue reading.
   b. Do not mark the student's oral reading errors (often called *miscues*) *while* the student is reading; instead follow along and keep a mental count of these. Tape recording the reading allows you to mark the miscues later when the student is not present.
4. For silent reading
   a. Usually no time limitations are imposed.
   b. It is wise to remain with the student to observe whether all of the passage actually is read and to ensure that the student remains on task.

Name: **Qualitative Reading Inventory, 4**

Reading Levels Covered: *Preprimer through high school*

Features:

- *graded word lists*
- *passages for silent and oral reading, or listening comprehension*
- *narrative and expository passages at every level*
- *at preprimer through second grade, includes selections with and without pictures*
- *comprehension evaluated through retellings, literal and higher-level questions*

- *background knowledge assessed before reading*
- *metacognitive strategy use appraised through text lookbacks and think-alouds*
- *illustrations and maps included with secondary-level passages*
- *validity and reliability data presented in test manual*

Authors: *Lauren Leslie and JoAnne Caldwell*

Publisher: *Addison Wesley Longman; copyright 2006*

Name: **Reading Inventory for the Classroom, 5th edition**

Reading Levels Covered: *Preprimer through 12th grade*

Features:

- *prescreening sentences for passage level selection*
- *same passage for silent then oral reading, levels preprimer through 9; silent reading only recommended for levels 10 through 12*
- *directions provided for administering and scoring passages for listening comprehension*
- *narrative and expository selections for levels preprimer through 9; expository only for levels 10 through 12*

- *comprehension assessed by probed retellings*
- *interest/attitude interviews provided*
- *rubrics included to assess emergent reading behaviors*
- *Spanish version available*

Authors: *E. Sutton Flynt and Robert B. Cooter*

Publisher: *Merrill/Prentice Hall; copyright 2004*

Name: **Basic Reading Inventory, 9th edition**

Reading Levels Covered: *Preprimer through 12th grade*

Features:

- *graded word lists*
- *selections to assess oral reading, silent reading, and listening level*
- *for grades 3 and above, test administrator chooses from short or long passages*
- *questions of topic, fact, inference, evaluation, and vocabulary accompany all passages*
- *procedures and rubrics for eliciting and assessing retellings*

- *special form provides expository selections for grades 3 through 12*
- *early literacy assessments for emergent readers furnished in appendix*
- *formulae provided for determining reading rate for each passage*

Author: *Jerry L. Johns*

Publisher: *Kendall/Hunt; copyright 2005*

FIGURE 4–1 *(continued)*

Name: ***Ekwall/Shanker Reading Inventory, 4th edition***

Reading Levels Covered: *Preprimer through 9th grade (primer level not included)*

Features:
- *San Diego Quick Assessment used for passage level selection*
- *passages for oral and silent reading, or listening comprehension*
- *for preprimer and first-grade levels, 5 to 10 factual comprehension questions accompany selections; for second-grade and above, one vocabulary, one inference, and eight factual questions*
- *supplementary tests in same manual to assess emergent literacy concepts, sight vocabulary in isolation, phonics, structural analysis, and reading interests*

Authors: *James L. Shanker and Eldon E. Ekwall*

Publisher: *Allyn & Bacon; copyright 2000*

Name: ***Analytical Reading Inventory, 8th edition***

Reading Levels Covered: *Primer through 9th grade*

Features:
- *graded word lists*
- *passages (narrative) primarily read orally, but alternate forms allow silent reading and listening level assessment*
- *additional forms feature science and social studies text*
- *comprehension assessed through questions and through retellings*
- *assessment begins with a reading interview to evaluate attitudes and habits (forms provided)*
- *before preparing passages, authors conducted a pilot study to determine topics of interest to students*
- *accompanying CD-ROMs allow for practice in administering before actual use*
- *linked to Standards*

Authors: *Mary Lynn Woods and Alden J. Moe*

Publisher: *Prentice Hall, 2007*

Name: ***Classroom Reading Inventory, 10th edition***

Reading Levels Covered: *Preprimer through 8th grade*

Features:
- *two formats: (1) "subskills" format, with graded word lists, graded paragraphs, and comprehension questions; (2) "reader-response" format, with prediction activities, graded paragraphs, and instructions for student retellings*
- *scoring distinguishes between significant and insignificant errors*
- *many new, longer, contemporary, and multicultural stories in latest editions*
- *separate form for high school and adult education programs available, but not in same booklet*
- *passage difficulty assessed with Harris-Jacobson Wide Range Readability Formula*

Authors: *Nicholas J. Silvaroli and Warren H. Wheelock*

Publisher: *McGraw-Hill; copyright 2004*

5. After student reading
   a. Remove the test before checking comprehension.
   b. Allow the tape recorder to continue running and ask the questions accompanying the passage or ask the student to retell information read.
   c. Note the number of questions the student answered correctly.
   d. Have the student read passages until you identify his or her frustration level. Criteria for making this judgment, based on word recognition and on comprehension, are provided with the IRI directions.

Criteria used with IRIs for making judgments about students' reading ability are based both on word recognition/identification and on comprehension.

Scoring an IRI

To score the test, many publishers supply duplicate copies of the passages that may be photocopied for marking word identification miscues while listening to the tape recording of the student's oral reading. Some commonly used marking procedures appear in Tables 4–1 and 4–2.

To determine percentage of correct word identification, note the difference between the miscue types listed in Table 4–1 and those shown in Table 4–2. Miscues described in Table 4–1 are recorded and scored; that is, the teacher not only marks these on the duplicate copies of the passages while listening to the tape but also considers them when determining percentages of correct word identification. Miscues shown in Table 4–2, on the other hand, often are recorded but not scored; the teacher marks them on the duplicate passages to analyze later to gain as comprehensive a picture as possible of the student's reading strategies, skills, and knowledge, but does not include them when scoring passages to determine percentages of correct word identification. If the student repeatedly makes a miscue on the

---

A TEACHING RESOURCE

TEST BANK B

Some Other Informal Reading Inventories (IRIs)

Name	For Grades	Type of Administration	Time for Administration	Publisher
Burns/Roe Informal Reading Inventory	PP–12	Individual	Varies by student	Houghton Mifflin
Diagnostic Reading Scales	1–12	Individual	Varies by student	CTB/McGraw-Hill
Informal Reading-Thinking Inventory	PP–9	Individual	Varies by student	Wadsworth
McCarthy Individualized Diagnostic Reading Inventory-Revised	K–12	Individual	Varies by student	Psychological Corporation
Secondary and College Reading Inventory	7–college	Individual	Varies by student	Kendall/Hunt
Standardized Reading Inventory	PP–8	Individual	Varies by student	PRO-ED
Stieglitz Informal Reading Inventory	1–9	Individual	Varies by student	Allyn & Bacon

TABLE 4–1 *Marking Procedures Used With IRIs for Miscues That Are Both Recorded and Scored*

Type	Example	Marking Procedure
1. Substitutions	The student says *when* although the text word is *where*.	Write the word the student said above the text word: *when* "I don't know where the cat went."
2. Omissions	The student leaves out a word that is in the text.	Circle the word: "The tall, (old) man was sitting on the bench."
3. Insertions	The student adds a word that is not in the text.	Insert the word with a caret: *big* "That ∧ black dog bit the boy."
4. Use of nonwords	The student substitutes a nonsense word for a real word.	Phonetically write the nonword above the text word for which it was substituted: *pauk* "He sat on the back porch."
5. Word reversals	The student pronounces the word *no* as the word *on*.	Code this as a substitution.

TABLE 4–2 *Marking Procedures Used With IRIs for Miscues That Often Are Recorded But Not Scored*

Type	Example	Marking Procedure
1. Repetitions	The student repeats the same word or phrase one or more times.	Draw a wavy line under the text portion the student repeated: "We saw an elephant at the zoo."
2. Self-corrections	The student makes an error, but then corrects it.	Code the original error in the usual manner, but then place a "C" above it: *c* *sit* "His chemistry set is going to get him in trouble."
3. Hesitations	The student hesitates for a long time before pronouncing a word.	Place a slash in front of the word: "Please hand me my /glasses."
4. Ignoring punctuation	The student appears not to have noticed a period, comma, or other punctuation mark.	Code as an omission (i.e., circle the omitted punctuation mark).

same word, directions for many IRIs recommend that you count it only the first time. Pronunciations that differ from the expected response due only to a student's oral language dialect should not be counted as miscues.

Next, for both oral and silent tests, determine passage comprehension based on responses to questions or responses during retelling. Finally, determine if each passage is at the student's independent, instructional, or frustration level based on percentages of correct word identification and correct comprehension responses. Most published IRIs specify percentages for determining each of these three levels on their test instrument. The percentages vary slightly from IRI to IRI but show strong similarities.

When no specified percentages are furnished by a test maker, based on the best available research evidence and the opinions of authorities, the following criterion levels are suggested:

Level	Word Identification	Comprehension
Independent	100%–96%	100%–90%
Instructional	95%–90%	89%–70%
Frustration	below 90%	below 70%

How Did Our Case Study Student Fare on the IRI?

Setting a Purpose for Reading. Here's David Adams again. Among other information, the discussion of contradictions in test scores is particularly worth noting.

David's Case Study (continued)

Now let's return to David Adams, the hypothetical student for whom we have been gradually completing an assessment information form. On the published IRI chosen by his teacher to verify his general reading levels, we will suppose David's performance indicates his reading levels to be:

Frustration Level	Approximately 2.5 and above
Instructional Level	Approximately 2.0
Independent Level	Approximately 1.0

If we compare David's reading instructional level on the previously administered standardized test with the instructional level obtained from this IRI, we find they are similar indeed (see Figure 4–2). Thus, we can feel relatively confident that placing David in material at approximately the beginning of second-grade level will be appropriate for his initial instruction.

Using Illustrative Aids. What's new in Figure 4–2?

However, such close agreement between two tests is not always found. As an illustration, let's suppose a student's instructional level according to a standardized test is 4.2, but the instructional level based on an IRI corresponds to sixth-grade level. In an instance such as this, you should carefully review any circumstances during administration of the tests that might have resulted in

FIGURE 4-2 ***Continuation of a Partially Completed Record Form of Assessment Information for a Hypothetical Student***

Assessment Information Form

Student's Name: _____David Adams_____

Grade Level: ____4th_____

Chronological Age:

   1) Birth date _____February 19, 19—_____

   2) Age ____9.0_____

Listening Comprehension Level:

   1) Method of determination __Use of graded IRI passages_____

   2) Level ___4th grade_____

Entry-Level Assessment Results: ___2nd grade_____

Standardized Survey Test:

   1) Name of test ____Gates-MacGinitie Reading Tests, Level 2, Form S_____

   2) Grade score obtained ____3.0_____

Present Reading Instructional Level (based on standardized test results): __Approximately 2.0_____

Discrepancy between Listening Level and Present Achievement: ___2.0_____

Verification of General Reading Levels:

   1) Name of test ____Analytical Reading Inventory_____

   2) Grade scores obtained ___Frustration level—approximately 2.5 and above_____

                        Instructional level—approximately 2.0_____

                        Independent level—approximately 1.0_____

---

a score not accurately reflecting the student's reading level. For example, did the student work conscientiously only during the first part of the standardized test, then appear to become bored and rush through questions during the last part? Did you tend to be particularly lenient or stringent in scoring comprehension checks on the IRI when there was doubt about the correctness of a student's response? After answering these types of questions, if incongruities cannot be resolved, you would do best to place the student in materials at a level consistent with the lower of the two scores. Follow this placement with careful daily monitoring; if it appears the lower test score was indeed too low, move the student up through successively more difficult material until you find an appropriate level for instruction. It is better to place the student in material that is too easy at the beginning of a program rather than in text that is too difficult.

Using an IRI to Analyze Specific Strengths and Weaknesses

Although the major purpose of this chapter is to describe procedures for verifying students' general reading levels, some information about specific strengths and weaknesses may also be gained from IRIs, if miscues and behaviors are analyzed as well as counted. Let's assume a teacher is reviewing David Adams's IRI. He or she takes the teacher's copy of each passage on which his miscues were marked, along with a pencil and some blank paper, and begins to appraise David's performance on each passage. The teacher's written comments are found in Figures 4–3 and 4–4.

FIGURE 4–3   *An Analysis of a Hypothetical Student's IRI Performance*

Analysis of David Adams's IRI Performance

Preprimer Level

Oral Reading
Word Identification: One sight word confusion (*there/where*); even though the resulting sentence did not make sense when he made this miscue, David read on with no attempt to self-correct.
Comprehension: All responses were correct.

Silent Reading
Comprehension: All responses were correct.

Primer Level

Oral Reading
Word Identification: 1. One sight word confusion (*get/got*); David did not self-correct although the resulting sentence did not sound like normal language.
2. There was one basic word David could not read at all (*first*). He immediately attempted to "sound it out" when he could not recognize it. However, he was unsuccessful, repeatedly producing the sound of the first letter of the word, but then giving up, omitting the word, and reading on.
Comprehension: All responses were correct.

Silent Reading
Comprehension: All responses were correct.

First-Reader Level

Oral Reading
Word Identification: 1. Four confusions of basic words (*of/off; this/these; black/back; soon/some*). No attempts at self-correction, although in no case did the resulting sentence make sense or sound like normal language.
2. Did not know one basic word (*are*) at all; again attempted to sound it out, saying /ă/ several times and then abandoning attempt and reading on. No attempt to use context, which would have cued the word in this passage.
Comprehension: Missed 1 question out of 10 (a question that required the reader to draw a conclusion).

Silent Reading
Comprehension: All responses were correct.

2₁ Level[1] (First Semester of Second Grade)

Oral Reading
Word Identification: 1. Five confusions of basic words (*everything/everyone; came/come; that/what; eat/ate; because/become*). No attempts to self-correct, although some of the resulting sentences made no sense.

FIGURE 4–3   *(continued)*

2. Two basic words he did not know at all (*were; show*). Attempted to sound them out by using the first one or two letters; did not use context along with these cues. Omitted both words after unsuccessful attempts.

3. After a brief hesitation before the word *doesn't*, omitted it with no obvious attempts to work it out using any word identification strategy.

Comprehension: Missed 2 out of 10 questions (one requiring him to identify the main idea of the passage; the other requiring him to make an inference).

Silent Reading
Comprehension: Missed 1 out of 10 (a question requiring him to draw a conclusion).

2₂ Level (Second Semester of Second Grade)

Oral Reading
Word Identification: 1. Eleven word confusions (*have/had; their/they; stay/start; slid/slide; skin/sky; which/with; something/someone; like/let; soup/soap; when/then; I'll/It's*). No attempts at self-correction.

2. After hesitations before *chipmunk* and *remember*, omitted these with no obvious attempts to use any word identification strategy.

3. On eight other words (*people, smart, stood, birds, waiting, knows, rider, seeds*), he attempted unsuccessfully to sound them out, only producing the sounds of the first one or two letters of the word before abandoning attempt; no attempts to use context clues.

4. Two words were pronounced as nonsense words (*gravel*/"gratel"; *wheels*/ "we-les").

Comprehension: Missed 5 out of 10 questions (two of those missed were literal-level questions; one required him to make an inference; one required him to follow a sequence of events; and one required him to draw a conclusion).

Silent Reading
Comprehension: Missed 4 out of 10 (one literal-level question; one required him to draw a conclusion; one required him to select the main idea of passage; and one required him to make an inference).

---

[1]Numbers with subscripts are used conventionally to denote grade and semester; 2₁, for example, denotes first semester of second grade.

FIGURE 4–4   *A Summary of a Hypothetical Student's IRI Performance*

Summary of David Adams's IRI Performance

Implications for Instruction

David must be taught to use a variety of word identification strategies along with use of the beginning letter(s)/sound(s) of a word (a strategy he already employs). He must be taught to read for meaning and to self-correct when what he reads does not make sense or sound like normal language. Attention should be given to eliminating his many sight word confusions; he substitutes words that look similar (e.g., *of/off; because/become*), even when they make no sense in that passage. He must be taught to use meaning as an aid in word identification.

David appears to need more work in higher-level comprehension tasks rather than in literal-level ones. On this test, he had difficulty with literal-level questions only when he reached his frustration level. He also had slightly more difficulty with comprehension after oral rather than silent reading. Since oral reading requires more attention to word identification than silent reading, increasing his efficiency in word identification strategies also appears to be important so that he can attend more to comprehension of the material.

LEARNING FROM TEXT

Using Illustrative Aids. As you study the next section, consider the facts presented by comparing them to Figure 4–3, and as well, the boxed analysis in Figure 4–4. This is an occasion when the strategy of moving back and forth between the text and illustrative aids will be conducive to clear understanding. An illustrative aid can help you make concrete connections with textual information and thus boost comprehension.

David's Case Study (continued)

From the teacher's analysis as it unfolds in Figure 4–3, we can examine David's performance with material that is easy for him, with material that is at what we now estimate to be his instructional level, and with material at his frustration level, and we can contrast his reading behaviors.

For example, observe from the teacher's analysis that David finds no obstacles with comprehension at the preprimer and primer levels (the easiest levels of first-grade text) and has only minor problems on the first-reader-level passages (a level often used by students near the end of first grade). Although understanding becomes more challenging for him on the beginning second-grade selections, his effectiveness is still within an acceptable range. We also can compare comprehension after oral versus silent reading and note that his confusions at these levels are associated with higher-level comprehension rather than with literal questions. However, a decided difference is detected in his comprehension responses after reading passages designed for second semester of second grade. There is a breakdown in understanding after both oral and silent reading for both literal and higher-level questions.

Some clues to this deterioration in comprehension are found when David's word recognition and word identification abilities are studied from the teacher's written analysis. Looking again at Figure 4–3, we see the same kinds of changes across levels as were seen with comprehension: Word recognition becomes increasingly less satisfactory from the first to the last passages he read. However, we also observe some pervasive difficulties in all levels, even the easiest. In regard to those, it appears that David does not have accurate recognition of basic high-frequency words, those that occur often in all text. He confuses many of these with words that look similar, or is unable to pronounce them at all. Consequently, the meaning of the text is changed.

There is also evidence of deficient word identification strategies. David appears not to know all strategies he might use when encountering an unknown word and is ineffective in using those he does know. All of this has caused him to focus considerable attention on word identification, which can divert concentration from the sense of a selection. What is more, David makes no attempt to self-correct errors, even when these word confusions and omissions result in meaningless sentences. In the easiest test passages, though word recognition miscues do appear, they are relatively infrequent, and therefore, the printed message remains sufficiently intact so that understanding is not interrupted. But as numerous problems with words emerge in more demanding passages, comprehension is adversely affected.

Based on this analysis, the teacher can already reach some conclusions about what is needed in David's instructional program and can make decisions about further testing that should be conducted. The teacher adds a summary statement (see Figure 4–4) to the other written comments and attaches these to the student's assessment information form.

See Figure 4–5 for a sample test passage from an IRI. This sample also shows how a teacher would analyze oral reading errors on this test, and record the student's responses to comprehension questions and during a retelling of the passage.

FIGURE 4–5 Example From a Typical IRI: Student Story as Shown on the Teacher's Promoting and Marking Form

Fluency: Does the Reader . . .

☐ read smoothly, accurately, in meaningful phrases?

☐ read word-by-word, choppy, plodding?

☐ use pitch, stress, and intonation to convey meaning of the text?

☐ repeat words and phrases because s/he is monitoring the meaning (self-correcting)?

☐ repeat words and phrases because s/he is trying to sound out words?

☐ use punctuation to divide the text into units of meaning?

☐ ignore the punctuation?

Rating Scale: Circle One

4 = fluent reading / good pace

3 = fairly fluent / reasonable pace

2 = choppy, plodding reading / slow pace

1 = clearly labored, disfluent reading / very slow pace

Retelling Summary: ☐ many details, logical order ☐ some details, some order ☐ few details, disorder

Retelling

Note: Indicate any probing with a "P"

Story Elements	All	Some	None
Main Character(s)			
Time and Place			
Problem			
Plot Details in Sequence			
Turning Point			
Resolution			

Reader's Thumbnail Summary:

Scoring Guide Summary

WORD RECOGNITION

Independent 0-1
Instructional 3-4
Frustration ..... 8+

COMPREHENSION

Independent 0
Instructional 1-2
Frustration ..... 3+

Emotional Status:

Comprehension Questions and Possible Answers

_____ (RIF) 1. Who are the main characters in this story?   (Sue and Mr. Brown)

_____ (RIF) 2. What are the children planning for their dad?   (a surprise party)

_____ (PIT) 3. Why did the children hurry to hide?   (because Dad was coming home soon, they wanted to surprise him)

_____ (CAR) 4. What do you know about the phrase **all was still?**   (nobody was moving or making a sound)
What does **all was still** have to do with this story? (when Mr. Brown came into the house, nobody was moving or making a sound)

_____ (EAS) 5. What kind of party do you think this was?   (a surprise party for a birthday or a celebration of a special event such as a job promotion or an honor)   You think this because the story says . . . (there were balloons, singing, and the children called, "Surprise!")

_____ (EAS) 6. How do you think Dad felt about the surprise?   (he was happy, pleased)
You think this because the story says . . . (a big smile grew on his face)

Reader Text Relationship (RTR)   From the Text   ☐adequate ☐ not adequate   From Head to Text   ☐adequate ☐ not adequate

Source: WOODS, MARY LYNN; MOE, ALDEN J., ANALYTICAL INVENTORY, 7th Edition, © 2003. Reprinted by permission of Pearson Education, Inc. Upper Saddle River, NJ.

LEARNING FROM TEXT

Self-monitoring. Did you understand the information in the foregoing section by associating statements in the text with those written in the figures (the illustrative aids)? If so, you can answer this question: How did David's word recognition/word identification interact with his comprehension?

ISSUES RELATED TO INFORMAL ASSESSMENT USING IRIs

Advantages of Informal Inventories

IRIs may serve the functions of both a survey test and a diagnostic test since they can be used to determine a student's reading level and also provide evidence of specific strengths and weaknesses in reading strategies, knowledge, and skills. In addition, research shows that grade scores obtained on IRIs are often closer to actual classroom performance of students than scores from standardized survey tests. What is more, since IRIs are individually administered, the teacher can observe students directly while they are responding to reading tasks; direct observation of reading behaviors informs teacher decisions in ways not possible when merely obtaining scores from standardized tests.

Disadvantages of Informal Inventories

Accurate results on an IRI depend on the competence of the teacher administering the test; making judgments based on IRI performance requires more skill than simply scoring standardized instruments. Despite a teacher's efforts to be objective, evaluating student performance on an IRI always involves some subjectivity. For example, when accuracy of a student's response to a comprehension question is in doubt, one teacher may decide the answer is more right than wrong and score it as correct; another might apply more stringent criteria to the same answer and score it as incorrect. Therefore, as research has shown, interpretations of informal measures may not always be consistent from teacher to teacher. Fortunately, however, training for scoring and evaluating student responses on IRIs can increase reliability (Visonhaler, Weinshank, Polin, & Wagner, 1983).

Accuracy of results also depends on careful selection by the author of the passages to be read in the IRI. For example, if the "sixth-grade" passage is actually much easier or more difficult than typical sixth-grade material, the instrument may incorrectly suggest student reading levels. Furthermore, since IRIs must be administered individually, they are more time consuming than group-administered standardized tests. And, like most standardized tests, passages on many IRIs are quite short and therefore may not provide the same task demands as those of authentic reading (Calfee & Hiebert, 1991).

Nonetheless, despite some disadvantages, IRIs are excellent assessment tools if prepared, administered, and interpreted correctly. See Figures 4–6 and 4–7 for a summary of some advantages and disadvantages of standardized survey tests and IRIs.

Like most standardized tests, passages on many IRIs are quite short and therefore may not provide the same task demands as those of authentic reading.

TEST INSTRUMENTS SIMILAR TO IRIs

Currently, with the popularity of informal assessment, a number of instruments are being published that are similar to IRIs. One such assessment package is the Developmental Reading Assessment (DRA) (Celebration Press), which is specifically intended to be carried out individually in one-to-one

FIGURE 4–6 *Some Advantages of Standardized Survey Tests and IRIs*

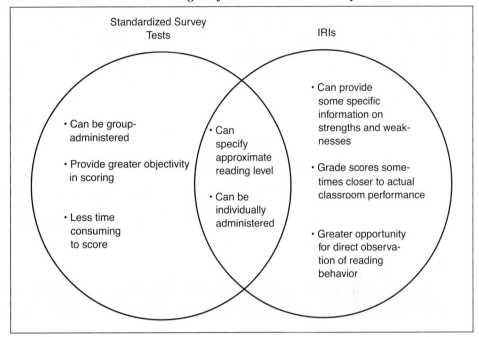

FIGURE 4–7 *Some Disadvantages of Standardized Survey Tests and IRIs*

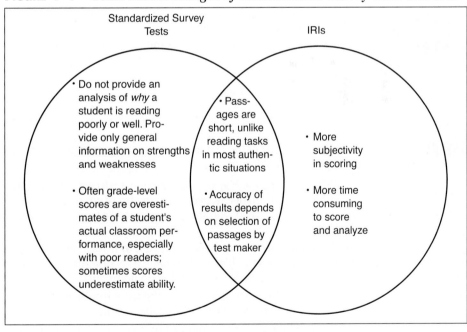

For information on informal assessments of various kinds, visit the changing focus page maintained by the International Reading Association. Go to www.reading.org, then click "Struggling Learners," then click "Assessment."

conferences. Designed by a Reading Recovery teacher, this set of test materials helps teachers pinpoint student abilities and needs at kindergarten through third-grade reading levels. The DRA includes stories for reading, observation guides, pads for recording oral reading behaviors, and other tools to encourage frequent monitoring of reading levels, strengths, and weaknesses for planning instruction.

CLOZE TESTS

In reading programs, the cloze procedure has typically been used for three purposes. One of these is a cloze *test*, sometimes employed to verify reading levels.

The cloze procedure has been used for three purposes: (a) to determine readability levels of texts, (b) to instruct students in use of context clues, and (c) to test students to determine placement. This third use is called a **cloze test,** and such testing is sometimes employed for verifying general reading levels obtained on a group standardized survey test. A cloze test consists of a passage from which words have been systematically deleted. The student is asked to supply the missing words, and an estimate of reading levels is based on accomplishment of this task.

Preparing a Cloze Test

Before administering a cloze test, the teacher must follow some fairly simple directions to prepare the materials needed for this informal assessment measure. These procedures are enumerated in the accompanying box titled *STEPS: Administering Assessments in Your Own Classroom: Preparing for a Cloze Test.* Read these directions now.

STEPS: ADMINISTERING ASSESSMENTS IN YOUR OWN CLASSROOM

Preparing for a Cloze Test

STEP 1 Locate a set of graded materials, such as a basal readers series.

STEP 2 Select two passages of approximately 300 words, which students have not previously read, for each reading level.

STEP 3 Type each passage on a separate sheet of paper, following directions in Steps 4 through 6.

STEP 4 Leave the first sentence of each passage intact (i.e., no words are omitted).

STEP 5 Beginning with any of the first five words in the second sentence, delete every fifth word, following these guidelines:

- DO delete every fifth word, even though a specific deletion may be judged difficult for students. (The guideline to omit every fifth word is not applied when the cloze procedure is used for *instructional* purposes; rather, specific key words are omitted to fit objectives of the lesson.)

- If numerals appear in a passage and are to be deleted, the whole numeral is considered as one word. For example, in the sentence "Native Americans lived in this area 350 years ago," the numeral *350* is treated as a single word.

- Replace omitted words with a line the same length as the deleted word, indicating a blank space the reader is to fill with a suitable word.

- Delete 50 words; fifty words must be deleted to have a reliable measure.

STEP 6 Include one intact sentence after the 50 deletions.

STEP 7 After these materials are prepared, follow the procedures outlined in the accompanying sections presented in this text, titled "Administering a Cloze Test" and "Scoring a Cloze Test."

Administering a Cloze Test

Students can write responses in the blanks or respond orally. See Figure 4–8 for a sample cloze test.

Give the following directions to students:

1. Read over the whole passage, and then go back and fill in words.
2. Try to use the exact word you think the author would have used.
3. Write one word on each line, or tell me one word.
4. If you have trouble guessing a word, skip it, and try again after you have finished the passage.

If desired, a practice passage can be used to ensure that students understand directions and during the test they are given as much time as needed to accomplish the tasks.

Scoring a Cloze Test

On a cloze test, only the *exact* words deleted from the text are scored as correct. Synonyms are not accepted. (This requirement is not used when the cloze procedure is implemented for instructional purposes; instead, any word conveying the same meaning intended by the passages is accepted.) Misspellings of correct words are not considered errors. To determine the percentage of correct words for each passage, the number of correct responses for that passage is divided by 50

FIGURE 4–8 *A Sample Cloze Test*

> Black Barney was the captain of a small, rickety whaling ship. He wore a black _____ over his right eye ____ a pair of old, ____ boots on his feet. _____ at sea, he stomped _____ the deck of his ____ and watched for whales _____ a very long brass _____ .
>
> If many days passed _____ spying a whale, Barney ___ angry and would scream, "___ the best whaling man __ the seven seas. Why _____ I spot a whale __ harpoon and slice and ____ down for its oil?" ____ Barney got mad at ___ whales for not appearing, ___ stomping and shouting made ___ small ship shake like __ was going to break _____ and send the sailors __ the bottom of the ___ . The other sailors became _____ when this happened and ___ day decided they must __ something to help Black _____ find and harpoon a _____ .
>
> Pegleg Sam, so called _____ he had one wooden ___ , was the oldest sailor __ Barney's ship, and he ___ not only the oldest, __ was also the wisest. __ had learned many things ____ his years at sea ___ he thought he had _ good idea for helping _____ find a whale.
>
> He _____ some of the other _____ together and said to _____ , "I have a plan." ___ told them he needed _____ help, but their plan ____ remain a secret. Pegleg ___ reminded them that their _____ , Black Barney, believed he ___ the best whaling man __ the seven seas, and _____ it would make Black _____ very annoyed if he thought he had to take help from the sailors. So, everyone agreed to help, but they also agreed that it was a smart thing to keep their plan a secret from their short-tempered captain.

(the number of deletions). For example, if Dale had 32 correct responses on one passage, his percentage of correct responses is 64% (i.e., 32 divided by 50 = 0.64). The student's percentage of correct responses is averaged across the two passages selected for each reading level. If, for instance, Brian scored 58% correct on one third-grade passage and 50% on the second third-grade passage, his average percentage of correct responses at the third-grade level is 54%. The following criteria are used to determine a student's reading levels (Bormuth, 1968):

Independent level	Over 57%
Instructional level	44% to 56%
Frustration level	43% or less

These criteria are based on the deletion of every fifth word from the text and on accepting as correct only responses identical to the deleted word.

Advantages of Cloze Tests

Use of cloze tests is controversial. Some authorities point to the advantages and others to the disadvantages.

In terms of advantages, cloze tests are easier to prepare, administer, and score than IRIs. Cloze tests also assess a student's ability to use knowledge of language and to comprehend text at the sentence level. In addition, there is some measure of word knowledge inherent in these tests, and they probably furnish a reasonable appraisal of literal understanding. On these bases, studies have shown cloze tests to be valid and reliable measures for determining students' reading levels (e.g., Cziko, 1983). Furthermore, relatively high correlations (between approximately .60 and .80) have been shown when comparing evaluations from cloze tests and scores obtained from standardized tests featuring multiple-choice questions (Shanahan & Kamil, 1984). Considering that reading levels obtained for students are only an approximation on any test, these correlations seem more than sufficient to proponents of cloze tests.

> Use of cloze tests is controversial.

Disadvantages of Cloze Tests

The major criticism of cloze tests is that they do not provide a good evaluation of interpretive (i.e., higher-level) comprehension. This assertion is based on a fairly large number of studies showing that these tests do not measure comprehension that goes *across* sentences—that is, comprehension processes that employ information in one sentence to assist with understanding of another, called **intersentential comprehension** (e.g., Kamil, Smith-Burke, & Rodriguez-Brown, 1986). Using information across sentences makes reading more efficient and aids recall as well as inferential understanding. Because cloze tests do not gauge intersentential comprehension, many authorities do not favor their use on the basis that they are incomplete assessments of comprehension.

A second disadvantage is that cloze tests do not provide a reliable and valid measure for students reading below the third-grade level. A modified cloze procedure that can be used with students reading below this level is called a **maze test.** Suggested as an easier task for younger children and poorer readers, the maze test provides three alternatives for students to choose from for each deleted word. It is recommended that every fifth word be omitted from a passage of about 125 words so that a maze test includes 20 deletions. The first and last sentence remain intact. The three alternatives supplied to students include the correct word, one

> A modified cloze procedure, called a *maze test*, can be used with younger children and poorer readers.

incorrect alternative that has the same grammatical function as the deleted word (e.g., if the deleted word is a verb, this alternative is also a verb), and one incorrect alternative that has a different grammatical function (see Figure 4–9).

Criteria for determining reading levels based on percentage of correct responses on a maze test are:

Independent level	Over 85%
Instructional level	50% to 84%
Frustration level	49% or less

All other procedures for preparing, administering, and scoring maze tests are the same as those for cloze tests.

📖 COMPUTER-ADMINISTERED TESTS

A new type of test is slowly emerging to assess instructional level. This is the *computer-adapted reading assessment.* Though previous attempts had been made at such tests, many came under fire from reading educators for their lack of content and technical adequacy. More recent efforts have attended better to issues of representative norming samples, the need for low standard errors of measurement (i.e., high reliability), and other faults of earlier computerized

FIGURE 4–9   *Example of a Maze Procedure*

The queen told her _____ to go into
                    (servants, friends, sleeping)

the _____ and pick all vegetables
        (woods, dark, fields)

_____ saw lying above the _____ .
  (they, that, he)   (clouds, ground, wet)

Ongoing, daily observation of reading and writing behaviors is an important part of assessment.

renditions. One recent offering is STAR Reading published by Renaissance Learning, Inc., a computer-administered test that features **adaptive branching,** a procedure that evaluates a student's answer for each question and then displays the next question adapted to the correct level of difficulty.

DAILY OBSERVATIONS

One of the most powerful forms of informal assessment is daily observation. This provides teachers with many opportunities to reflect on what students can and cannot do in authentic reading tasks. After a review of assessment research, Johnston, Afflerbach, and Weiss (1993) contend that teachers are the main assessment "instruments" in judging students' needs and growth. However, while research may accept teachers as evaluation "instruments," many teachers feel hesitant to assume that what Goodman, Bird, and Goodman (1991) call "kid watching"—that is, using their own observations and judgments—is a legitimate form of assessment.

Johns (1982) proposed the name *innerocular technique,* or IOT, be used for observations during daily lessons. His tongue-in-cheek suggestion for using this pseudoscientific term is an attempt to legitimize an important diagnostic procedure. Teachers sometimes believe their own judgments lack the value of real tests. This is simply not true. Careful and thoughtful decisions based on students' daily work provide a highly useful form of evaluation that can help teachers verify (or refute) test results, note when growth has occurred, provide clues for changing instructional materials when daily performance does not conform to test performance, and highlight patterns of behavior—all of which have more important implications for instruction than do single or infrequent tests of reading. As such, the IOT can be used to refine decisions about students' reading levels. The additional step of keeping brief anecdotal records, graphs, or charts provides a permanent record of classroom performance that may lend credence to decisions based on this type of informal assessment.

Reflections after observing students during day-to-day instruction should be included in written diagnostic workups, especially if reading behaviors differ from those exhibited on tests.

Occasional reflections after observing students during day-to-day instruction should be included in written diagnostic workups, especially if reading behaviors differ from those exhibited on tests. It should be noted, however, that research suggests that conclusions based on observation are more reliable with experience. Assessment must be informed as well as informal, conducted systematically by a knowledgeable teacher. Preservice teachers need many opportunities to work directly with students to increase their expertise in observational assessment.

Vignette: Real Teachers in Action

The Reading Specialist as Observer

Lyle, a sixth grader, entered Newport School on November 18th and Mrs. Gaspar's special reading class on November 19th. For two reasons, Mrs. Gaspar decided not to administer a standardized test or an IRI to Lyle to determine his instructional reading level: First, the formal and structured assessment period for her class was long over and, second, based on his apparently serious needs, noted by the language arts teacher, Mrs. Gaspar wanted to begin her instruction with him quickly. As an experienced reading specialist, she trusted her own powers of observation.

For a quick screening test to find a place to start her observation/assessment, she pulled from her file drawer copies of the word lists employed with the IRI she routinely used with all students at the beginning and end of the year. While others in her group for that class period were engaged in sustained silent reading, she took Lyle to the library corner where they sat side by side at a small table. Telling Lyle that the rules for this activity require that he start with the first, easiest list and go as far as he could go, she directed Lyle to begin reading the words orally to her.

The first groups of words were indeed a snap for Lyle and he relaxed, seemingly comfortable and confident. By the fourth-grade set, however, he obviously was having an unacceptable amount of difficulty. Mrs. Gaspar's main purpose was to determine Lyle's approximate instructional level to match him with texts as quickly as possible. She could also easily note types of word recognition and word identification problems he was having. As one example, not only did he miss many word in the fourth-grade word set, but it was clear from his responses that words with added prefixes and suffixes were difficult for him.

Because he had missed too many words in the fourth-grade group, Mrs. Gaspar pulled from the nearby library shelves two third-grade books, one at easier level and one at a more advanced level. This was simple to do, because she had coded the books, using colored tape on the spines to indicate an approximate level for each. Beginning with the easy one, she asked Lyle to read a story silently for a few minutes while she helped the other students get started on their oral reading practice for a Readers' Theater activity. As she worked with the others, she cast her eyes on Lyle from time to time to see how he was progressing. She found him quite attentive to the book.

When she returned to Lyle, she found in the short time she was gone he had read a sizable portion of the story. Mrs. Gaspar mentally noted that this was one indication the book was not too difficult for him since it did not appear to have hindered his silent reading fluency. She had him read the small amount remaining aloud to her, during which Lyle accurately and fairly quickly recognized all but one word. As one comprehension check, she simply asked him to retell what he had read. Lyle provided an excellent retelling, complete with fine details. Mrs. Gaspar asked him a couple of higher-level questions and, like his literal understanding as portrayed through his retelling, his interpretive comprehension was of high quality. Mrs. Gaspar's conclusion was that this had been an easy book for Lyle.

She decided to have him read a story from the more advanced third-grade book *with* her, using a guided reading lesson. She briefly chatted with Lyle about his background knowledge in relation to events that would be revealed in the narrative. Then, they did a picture walk through the book, turning the pages, talking about what they saw, and predicting how the actions in the illustrations would play out in the story. Mrs. Gaspar used the picture walk to mention important, and slightly challenging, vocabulary that Lyle would encounter. She wrote these on a yellow legal pad, showing him how to remove prefixes and suffixes to reveal root words he already knew.

Then, Lyle read the story orally to Mrs. Gaspar. Although he read reasonably well, he did not know a number of the words. Mrs. Gaspar promoted various word identification strategies and with this help he was able to read the words and grasp the ideas. In the end she checked his comprehension and found it to be as good as it had been with the easier book, but she doubted that would have been the case if she had not been there to assist with several pivotal words. It was apparent to Mrs. Gaspar that this was a satisfactory book for Lyle— when she was present to help—but important information would have been missed if he had had to go it alone. She concluded that for a start, material at this level would be used for instruction, and materials at the level of the easier book for his independent reading. Thus, she was set to immediately involve him in reading lessons.

This observation/assessment involved only one book at each of the levels and Mrs. Gaspar knew this was not enough. Because assessment should be based on a variety of observations, she would observe Lyle's word recognition, word identification, meaning vocabulary, and comprehension responses closely in additional materials over the next few days, including his reading in a content area book. She would immediately begin a portfolio for Lyle, which, among other items, would include brief comments she would jot down on self-stick notes about his reading responses of various kinds (*"doesn't know -tion"*). She plans to involve Lyle in the Readers' Theater activity the other students are now beginning, giving her more opportunities to monitor his word knowledge and word identification strategies and to see the amount of practice he requires to obtain a fluent reading. So that she can match materials with his interests, she plans to find a little time to talk to him about his likes and dislikes and also take note of the types and topics of books he chooses when allowed to self-select. She also plans to ask Lyle to write something in the next session so she can observe his spelling and writing behaviors.

Mrs. Gaspar knows that it won't take long for her to gain an understanding of Lyle's present level of operation and to get a handle on his needs.

As with her other students, Lyle will participate in more structured informal and formal assessments throughout the year. However, Mrs. Gaspar believes that no test is as powerful an indicator of a student's strengths and weaknesses as an experienced teacher's observations during lessons day after day.

ORAL READING

Since daily observation has frequently meant observing students during oral reading, a few words about oral versus silent reading activities are in order. Today, reading educators recognize the need for both oral and silent reading and avoid using one to the exclusion of the other.

Silent reading practice is important, first, because in most real-life situations, and in school settings as well, students must read material silently. Poor readers need practice in sustaining attention and gaining ideas during silent reading. Second, some students may comprehend better after reading silently because they concentrate on the message rather than on word pronunciation. Finally, students reading silently may move through material at their own pace, perhaps regressing if an idea or word presents difficulty; for this reason, students with reading disabilities sometimes feel less pressure during silent reading.

On the other hand, although some poor readers comprehend more adequately after silent reading, studies have shown that others have greater understanding after reading orally (e.g., Swalm, 1972), perhaps because there is greater likelihood of remaining on task in oral reading (during silent reading readers are on their own to choose whether to attend to the page or not). This may explain why several studies have suggested that time spent in oral reading is more directly tied to increases in reading attainment that are silent reading activities (e.g., National Institute of Child Health and Development, 2000; Reutzel, Hollingsworth, & Eldredge, 1994; Wilkinson, Wardrop, & Anderson, 1988).

> One purpose for having students read orally is to serve as a frequent, ongoing diagnostic tool for the teacher, allowing confirmation of reading development and identification of strategies still needing attention.

Oral reading affords one avenue for the important practice students need in contending with connected text. Another major purpose for oral reading in remedial or clinical programs is to serve as a frequent, informal, and ongoing diagnostic tool. Oral reading reveals clues to a student's changing understandings, thus allowing teachers to identify progress and to discern strategies still needing emphasis and support.

PRE- AND POSTMEASURES

It is routine practice to evaluate the progress students have made after a period of remedial instruction. Comparing performance on pre- and postmeasures is one standard method for judging growth. To make this comparison, the same form, or an alternate form, of the standardized test employed for preassessment is used as a posttest. Or, the student reads a form of an IRI that contains passages not read during the initial appraisal. The student's original test performance is compared with posttest performance to determine gains.

There is some question as to whether using the same form of a test is appropriate for measuring progress. If the identical test is used, some believe "practice effects" will cause students to receive higher scores even if they have not progressed. On the other hand, some have noted that test results can indicate a student has made no progress even when growth is evident; this may occur because students remember answers given on the original test and choose them again with little thought, rather than applying new skills and strategies developed in the remedial program.

Problems also arise from using an alternate form of a standardized test or IRI. Although authors of some tests may claim *statistical* equivalency of their alternate forms, it is doubtful that real equivalency exists between all of the many variables that make up the test. For alternate forms to be exactly equivalent, test makers would have to control factors such as content of test passages, length and complexity of all sentences, word length, vocabulary difficulty, and a large number of other factors. It is impossible to control every component.

Of the two procedures—using the same form versus using an alternate form—it is probably best to use the alternate form, but in doing so, remember that all test scores are approximate. In addition, pre- and postmeasures should be combined with teacher observation when growth is assessed. Finally, to determine if a student has maintained any gains, teachers should conduct posttest measures, not only at the end of a remedial program, but also 3 to 6 months after the student has left the program.

A recently recommended alternate method for appraising growth is the use of portfolios. Portfolio assessment is discussed in Chapter 6.

Reflections

1. Are formal assessment measures better than informal measures? Are informal measures better than formal? After reading the pros and cons of different assessment types in the last two chapters, what do *you* think?
2. There are no perfect assessment procedures. Why is this the case?

5

Assessment for Identifying Specific Strengths and Weaknesses in Reading: Part I

Having students engage in a probed retelling of a story after they have read it is one procedure used for some assessment measures.

A fter verifying students' approximate instructional levels for reading, teachers must next determine their specific strengths and weaknesses. Some indications of strengths and weaknesses are provided when an IRI is administered, as illustrated in the previous chapter.

Compare. Based on the following paragraph, what is the main difference between tests to be discussed in this chapter and those discussed in Chapters 3 and 4?

A student's IRI or standardized test performance also can indicate other tests needed for this purpose because further assessment tools and procedures that are needed vary according to the instructional level of the student. For example, assessing the dictionary skills of a student reading at early first-grade level normally would be a waste of time; a child at such a beginning level of literacy acquisition typically would not be expected to have advanced skills. Likewise, a student reading at sixth-grade level almost certainly would have knowledge of basic high-frequency vocabulary taught in primary grades; otherwise, this student could not be reading at sixth-grade level. Therefore, testing basic sight vocabulary would be unnecessary.

The diagnostic process should include only necessary assessment. Although assessment should be thorough, it should also be completed as quickly as possible so that instruction can begin to alleviate problems. The time needed to conduct a thorough assessment will vary from student to student. In a few uncommon instances, some students may require tests not typically needed for others reading at the same level. Figure 5–1 lists a general outline of basic tests to administer at each reading level; it provides teachers with a starting point, but adjustments should be made for individual students. Both this chapter and Chapter 6 describe tests that help teachers assess a student's specific needs.

Self-monitoring. Of course, you would not be expected to memorize the list in Figure 5–1, but do you grasp the main idea?

Make an Outline. In this chapter you will read about many tests. To lessen confusion, why don't you begin an outline? The effectiveness of outlining is supported by research when the learner includes essential ideas, rather than insignificant ones, in the outline format. Toward that end, use the main headings and subheadings in this chapter as starting points. Later, when you study from the outline, focus first on the major points, and when you understand these, concentrate on the important details.

FIGURE 5–1   *General Outline of Basic Tests to Administer at Each Reading Level*

For students whose scores on a standardized test or IRI indicate that material at the preprimer level is at the student's frustration level:

1. Administer a test of prereading concepts.
2. Administer tests of phonemic awareness.
3. Use the student's own dictated story for assessment.
4. Administer tests of knowledge of basic sight vocabulary.
5. Administer a test of knowledge and use of word identification strategies.
6. Assess writing.
7. Orally administer an interest inventory.
8. Assess background information.

For students whose instructional levels are at the preprimer level:

1. Use an informal test to determine if the student's approximate instructional level is first, second, or third preprimer level.
2. Administer tests of phonemic awareness.
3. Use the student's own dictated story for assessment or use a running record.
4. Administer tests of knowledge of basic sight vocabulary.
5. Administer a test of knowledge and use of word identification strategies.
6. Assess comprehension.
7. Assess writing.
8. Orally administer an interest inventory.
9. Assess background information.

For students whose instructional levels are at the primer level:

1. Administer tests of phonemic awareness.
2. Use the student's own dictated story for assessment or use a running record.
3. Administer tests of knowledge of basic sight vocabulary.
4. Administer a test of knowledge and use of word identification strategies.
5. Assess comprehension.
6. Assess writing.
7. Orally administer a measure of attitudes toward reading.
8. Orally administer an interest inventory.
9. Assess background information.

For students whose instructional levels are at first-, second-, or third-grade levels:

1. Administer tests of phonemic awareness.
2. Administer tests of knowledge of basic sight vocabulary.
3. Administer a test of knowledge and use of word identification strategies.
4. Administer a reading miscue inventory or use a running record.
5. Assess comprehension.
6. Assess writing.
7. Orally administer a measure of attitudes toward reading.
8. Orally administer an interest inventory.
9. Assess background information.

FIGURE 5–1 *(continued)*

For students whose instructional levels are at fourth-, fifth-, or sixth-grade levels:

1. Administer selected portions of a test of knowledge and use of word identification strategies.
2. Administer a reading miscue inventory.
3. Assess knowledge of word meanings.
4. Assess comprehension.
5. Assess writing.
6. Administer an attitude scale.
7. Administer an interest inventory.
8. Assess background information.

For students whose instructional levels are above the sixth-grade level:

1. Administer a reading miscue inventory.
2. Assess knowledge of word meanings.
3. Assess comprehension.
4. Assess reading rate.
5. Assess writing.
6. Administer an attitude scale.
7. Administer an interest inventory.
8. Assess background information.

ASSESSING PREREADING CONCEPTS

An assessment of prereading concepts should be conducted with nonreaders and beginning readers. For students whose standardized test or informal reading inventory (IRI) scores indicate that preprimer material is at their frustration level—that is, they cannot adequately read material even at this easiest level—one of the tests listed in **Test Bank C** may be used. (All Test Banks in this and other assessment chapters include names of publishers and other useful information for choosing and purchasing tests.)

A test that is particularly recommended for nonreaders and beginning readers is Concepts About Print. For this test, a booklet titled *Sand* is read *to* students. During the reading, the teacher asks questions to assess the student's knowledge of several concepts about printed language, such as (a) where the front of a book is found; (b) that the words, not pictures, convey the message; (c) where to begin reading on a page; (d) that it is necessary to move from one line to another; (e) what a "letter" is; (f) what a "word" is; and (g) that the left page should be read before the right. This test also measures knowledge of letter names, which is important prerequisite information, since letter recognition is critical for word recognition and word identification strategies.

Some standardized tests now include a prereading level. For example, the Gates-MacGinitie Reading Tests, 4th edition, provides such a form with four subtests: (a) literary concepts, (b) oral language concepts (phonological awareness), (c) letters and letter-sound correspondences, and (d) listening comprehension. In addition, many new IRIs include an optional subtest for assessing early, related, just-beginning-to-emerge reading knowledge.

📖 ASSESSING PHONEMIC AWARENESS

In Chapter 2, research was cited demonstrating that phonemic awareness is important to reading achievement. Studies show that tests of phonemic awareness are better indicators of students who are at risk for low reading performance than any other commonly assessed factors (e.g., Ehri et al., 2001). This research indicates that a large proportion of poor readers whose difficulties lie with word recognition are particularly lacking in phonemic awareness.

Certain commonly used tests of phonemic awareness may be more useful than others.

Phonemic awareness has been assessed in a number of ways. Yopp (1988) conducted a comprehensive study to determine which methods produce valid and reliable results. Her study investigated both published instruments and common tasks used to test students' sensitivities to phonological aspects of words. Results of this analysis indicate that using the following two tests may be an efficient way for teachers to carry out assessment of phonemic awareness: the Yopp-Singer Phoneme Segmentation Test (Yopp, 1988) and the Bruce Phoneme Deletion Test (Bruce, 1964).

The Yopp-Singer Phoneme Segmentation Test

The Yopp-Singer Phoneme Segmentation Test is administered individually and takes from 5 to 10 minutes. To conduct the test (Yopp, 1988, p. 166), first tell the student: "I will say a word and I want you to break it apart. Tell me each sound in the word, in order. If I say *old*, you would say /o/ /l/ /d/."[1] (In this test, note that students are being asked to give the *sounds* heard in the word, not the letter names.) Give three other examples, using *ride*, *go*, and *man*.

Next, use the word list found in Table 5–1 to administer the test. Keep track of the number of correct answers the student gives. Indicate when the student answers correctly. Consider as correct only those words for which the student gives the expected answer without teacher assistance. When the response is wrong, provide the student with the correct answer before progressing to the next item.

This test assesses **simple phonemic awareness**—that is, phonemic awareness processes that involve a single operation.

TABLE 5–1 *List of Words for the Yopp-Singer Phoneme Segmentation Test*

dog	lay	keep	race
fine	zoo	no	three
she	job	wave	in
grew	ice	that	at
red	top	me	by
sat	do		

Source: From Yopp, Hallie Kay. (1998, Spring) The validity and reliability of phonemic awareness tests *Reading Research Quarterly, 23*(2), 159–177. Reprinted with permission of Hallie Kay Yopp and the International Reading Association.

---

[1] As you probably remember from a previous chapter, when letters are placed between slashes, as is done with /o/ /l/ /d/, this refers to the sound the letter represents, not the letter name.

A TEACHING RESOURCE

TEST BANK C

Some Tests of Prereading Concepts

Name	For Ages	Type of Administration	Time for Administration	Publisher
Brigance K & 1 Screen	5–6	Individual	15–20 minutes	Curriculum Associates
Early School Inventory—Preliteracy	5–7	Individual	Varies with student	Psychological Corporation
Gates-MacGinitie Reading Tests— Levels PR & BR	5–7	Group	Varies according to subtests used	Riverside
Pre-phonics Tests	4–8	Individual	Varies with student	Laguna Beach Educational Books
Sand: Concepts About Print Test	5–7	Individual	5–10 minutes	Heinemann
The Test of Early Reading Ability—2	3–8	Individual	15–30 minutes	Pro-Ed
Test of Kindergarten/First Grade Readiness Skills	3½–7	Individual	20–25 minutes	Psychological and Educational Publications

The Bruce Phoneme Deletion Test

The Bruce Phoneme Deletion Test is individually administered and takes about 10 minutes. Students are asked what word would remain when a specific letter is removed from the word. Yopp (1988, p. 164) suggests using the following practice examples before beginning the test. Ask, "What word would be left if the /c/ in *cat* were taken away?" Follow with these example items: *bright* (remove the /r/); *cried* (remove the /d/). (The teacher should be certain to pronounce the *sound* of the letter to be removed, not the letter name.)

Then use the word list found in Table 5–2 to administer the test. The Bruce Phoneme Deletion Test assesses **compound phonemic awareness**—that is, phonemic awareness processes involving more than one operation.

Teachers also can assess phonemic awareness informally. For example:

1. Can a student respond correctly when asked to identify a word that begins differently when you pronounce a group of three or four words (e.g., "Which word begins differently: *fell, fat, sit, for*?")?
2. Can the learner break a sound from a word and say it in isolation (e.g., "Tell me the first sound you hear when I say *jump*.")?
3. Can the student blend sounds together to form a word when you pronounce the individual sounds (e.g., for the word *got*, you might say "When I say /g/ /o/ /t/, what word is that?")?

Assessing knowledge of prereading concepts is important with some students. These concepts include what a "word" is, what a "letter" is, and that we move from left to right when reading text.

TABLE 5–2 *List of Words for the Bruce Phoneme Deletion Test*

1. *s-t-and* (middle)	16. *c-old* (first)
2. *j-am* (first)	17. *part-y* (last)
3. *fair-y* (last)	18. *we-n-t* (middle)
4. *ha-n-d* (middle)	19. *f-r-og* (middle)
5. *star-t* (last)	20. *n-ear* (first)
6. *ne-s-t* (middle)	21. *thin-k* (last)
7. *f-rock* (first)	22. *p-late* (first)
8. *ten-t* (last)	23. *s-n-ail* (middle)
9. *lo-s-t* (middle)	24. *b-ring* (first)
10. *n-ice* (first)	25. *pin-k* (last)
11. *s-top* (first)	26. *le-f-t* (middle)
12. *far-m* (last)	27. *car-d* (last)
13. *mon-k-ey* (middle)	28. *s-p-oon* (middle)
14. *s-pin* (first)	29. *h-ill* (first)
15. *for-k* (last)	30. *ever-y* (last)

Source: From "An Analysis of Word Sounds by Young Children" by D. Bruce, 1964, *British Journal of Educational Psychology, 34,* p. 170. Copyright 1964 by Scottish Academic Press (Journals) Limited. Reprinted by permission.

4. Can the student tap out the number of sounds heard, indicating the ability to break a word into its single phonemes (e.g., "Listen to this word *mop.* Tap out the number of sounds you hear.")?
5. At a more advanced level, can the learner manipulate phonemes (e.g., ask the student to "Say *has* without the /h/ sound.")?

The teacher is, of course, pronouncing the *sounds* the letters stand for, not the letter names, as indicated by the slash marks on both sides of the letter. Skills demonstrated through these tasks are strong predictors of reading achievement (e.g., Ehri et al., 2001; Liberman, Shankweiler, Liberman, Fowler, & Fischer, 1977; Lundberg, Olofsson, & Wall, 1980; Sweet, 1993; Vellutino & Scanlon, 1987).

USING A STUDENT'S OWN DICTATED STORY FOR ASSESSMENT

Because they can read so little, it is difficult to test, in normal contextual materials, those readers who are in the very beginning stages of learning to read. By using a student's own dictated story for assessment, a teacher can examine reading behaviors and knowledge while the student is reading *connected* text, rather than solely measuring isolated behaviors. Basing assessment processes on student-dictated text has been a successful procedure in many reading clinics and also has been used with illiterate adults (Waugh, 1993). Directions for employing student-dictated stories for this purpose are given in Figure 5–2.

ASSESSING KNOWLEDGE OF BASIC SIGHT VOCABULARY

The term **sight vocabulary,** or sight words, is used in three ways.

1. Frequently the term refers to all words a student recognizes instantly, or "on sight."
2. It also has been used to refer to phonetically irregular words that must be memorized and recognized on sight because the spellings of the words do not conform to typical letter-sound correspondences and, therefore, cannot be identified by "sounding them out." There are many such words in the English language (e.g., *of, night,* and *known*).
3. The term often is employed synonymously with the phrases **high-frequency words, basic vocabulary,** or **core vocabulary words** (i.e., those words that occur frequently in all written material).

LEARNING FROM TEXT

Compare. Understanding the difference in the three preceding definitions can clear up some common confusions.

In the following section, the term *sight vocabulary* refers to that third definition, that is, high-frequency vocabulary. Instant and automatic recognition of these basic words is important to fluent reading because they occur so often in any material an individual reads, from early first-grade through adult materials. A student who requires prolonged deliberation on each individual word to recall it or who has to stop each time to employ a word identification strategy to these frequently occurring words may lose the sense of the material. Immediate recognition of basic words allows students to focus on meaning. Also, because these words appear often, they provide much of the context for other words—context that, at times, may be helpful in identifying less frequently occurring words.

Lists of high-frequency words have been compiled for teacher reference. Some of these include the *Harris-Jacobson Core Lists* (Harris & Jacobson, 1972), *A Basic Vocabulary for Beginners* (Johnson, 1971), the Ekwall list (Ekwall, 1975), *The New Instant Word List* (Fry, 1980), the *Dolch Basic Sight Word List* (Dolch, 1936), and the Durr list of high-frequency words in primary-level library books (Durr, 1973).

The first 200 words (i.e., the 200 most common words) found on all of these lists are about the same—these are basic function words such as *the, and, of,*

FIGURE 5–2 *Using Student-Dictated Stories for Assessment*

1. Materials Needed
   a. Tape recorder with microphone
   b. Blank tape
   c. Object or picture to stimulate discussion
   d. Paper and pencil
   e. Index cards
2. Initiating Procedures
   a. At the beginning of the session, allow the student to talk into the tape recorder, listen to the tape, turn the recorder on and off, and engage in any other activity that will help the student feel at ease with the subsequent taping procedures. Temporarily put the tape recorder aside.
   b. Use an object or picture to stimulate discussion.
   c. Have the student dictate a short "story" based on the previous discussion. For some students, the story may consist of no more than two or three sentences. Other students will dictate a longer narrative. Write down the story for the student exactly as it has been dictated.
3. First Taping Procedure
   a. Turn on the tape recorder.
   b. Have the student read the dictated story.
   c. If the student has difficulty, encourage him or her to
      1. use any procedure known to figure out the unknown word,
      2. guess what word would "sound right there," or
      3. skip the word and go on.

   Student success during the first taping procedure must be assessed subjectively by the teacher. In general, the attempt may be judged successful if the student can read back the sentences within the dictated story in a reasonably meaningful manner. The successful student may not be able to pronounce correctly every word as was originally dictated, but the majority of each sentence will remain intact.

   The behaviors of unsuccessful students may consist of any of the following: the student simply cannot read back any of the dictated story; the student focuses on isolated words in the story, pointing out only those few which are known; or the student may attempt to scan sentences in correct left to right progression, but can only pronounce an occasional word, thus rendering the story meaningless.

   d. Turn off the tape recorder. Write each word from the story on an individual card. Shuffle the cards and present the words to the student in a random order. Record the student's responses by placing a check or an *X* on the back of each word card to indicate a correct or incorrect response. When one word is substituted for another, write the substitution on the back of the card.
4. Second Taping Procedure
   a. If the student had relative success during the first taping procedure, repeat the taping procedure after a short interval (approximately 30–60 minutes) using the *same* story.
   b. If the student has been decidedly unsuccessful during the first taping procedure, do not engage in the second and third taping procedures.

but, for, in, a, that, be, is, to, are, so, it, and *this.* (See how many and how often each of these basic function words occur on the page you are reading right now.)

A test of knowledge of basic sight vocabulary—that is, high-frequency words—should be individually administered with *the student reading to the teacher.* Some published tests of sight word knowledge have been devised so that

FIGURE 5-2   *(continued)*

5. Third Taping Procedure

   a. If the student has had relative success during the second taping procedure, repeat the procedure *the next day* using the *same* story.

   b. If the student has been decidedly unsuccessful during the second taping procedure, do not engage in the third taping procedure.

6. Analysis

   Make one, two, or three copies of the story, depending on the number of taped readings you have obtained. On these copies of the story, write information as you listen to the tapes. As you listen, write down words the student substitutes for other words and note whether the student subsequently corrects the substituted words. Indicate words that are omitted or added.

   Analyze the student's reading behaviors by responding to the following questions and by making other observations and statements that are applicable to a specific student's performance.

   a. How does the student's performance in reading the story compare with his or her performance in reading the isolated words printed on the cards? Are there differences between these two performances during the first, second, and third sessions?

   b. Does the student seem to understand correct directional movements in reading connected printed material (i.e., does he or she attempt to read from left toright across a line of print)?

   c. When the student has substituted words in reading the story, do the words

      1. look similar?

      2. mean about the same thing?

   d. Did the student's behavior in substituting words in the story differ from any substitutions he or she made when reading the isolated words from the cards? What differences were seen?

   e. Each time the student omitted or added words within the story, did the sentence

      1. still make sense?

      2. retain its general meaning?

   f. When the student read aloud a rendition that changed the meaning of the original text, did he or she self-correct? If so, how did the student determine that a correction should be made?

   g. When reading the story, what strategies did the student employ when faced with an unknown word? Did he or she attempt to sound out the word letter by letter? Did he or she use the first one or two letters of the word only, and then pronounce any word that begins with those letters? Did the student pronounce any word that has a general configuration similar to the text word? Guess wildly? Use context to make a choice?

   h. What reading knowledge did the student's performance indicate he or she possessed at the time of the first taping procedure?

   i. What differences were noted in the student's reading behaviors and knowledge when comparing the results of the first, second, and third tapings?

Source: From "Assessment and the Beginning Reader: Using Student-Dictated Stories" by S. McCormick, 1981, *Reading World, 21,* pp. 29–39. Copyright 1981 by the College Reading Association. Reprinted by permission of the author and the College Reading Association.

three or four words are printed by each item number; the teacher pronounces one of these, and the student circles the word. This procedure does not provide an accurate measure because students can often recognize a word when it is pronounced, but are unable to identify it when they must read it for themselves.

There is some controversy over whether words should be read in context or in isolation for these tests. Those who argue for a contextual presentation

For assessing recognition of high-frequency words, there is controversy about whether words should be presented in context or isolation.

correctly point out that, in most reading tasks, words do not occur in isolation and that other words in the sentence or passage provide context clues that aid in word identification. While some words in real life do appear in isolation (such as *Stop* on traffic signs or *Men* and *Women* on restroom doors), the environmental context aids identification in these cases. Certainly, many high-frequency words, such as *of* or *that*, do not occur in isolation in authentic reading tasks. Have you ever found a sign with the single word *of* printed on it, or found the word *that* all by itself on a door, wall, or book page?

On the other hand, those who argue for presenting words in isolation during assessment of sight vocabulary point out, also correctly, that although the context provided by other words can aid word identification, it does not do so in many cases. For example, suppose Don is often confused by the words *was* and *saw*; in the following example, context would not provide any clue to eliminate his confusion.

I _____ a witch on Halloween.

(was, saw)

Although the longer the selection, the more likely context will provide clues, it certainly does not always do so. Since accurate recognition of frequently occurring, basic words is of critical importance, proponents of an isolated presentation of words during assessment contend that we must determine a student's ability to read basic words in any situation, including those where context does not help. Furthermore, one indicator of expert reading performance is the ability to recognize words rapidly; the necessity to identify these words from context may slow down recognition considerably.

A Contextual Test of Sight Vocabulary

One resolution to this problem is to test sight vocabulary both in context and in isolation, if time permits. Poor readers often have particular difficulty with high-frequency words because many are **function words,** such as prepositions and conjunctions. Function words are more abstract than **content words,** such as nouns. Can you define the word *of,* for example? Other than saying it is a preposition, probably not. Function words are more difficult for poor readers to learn initially because they lack the concrete meaning of content words, and they are easier to confuse with similar words for the same reason. Therefore, the teacher may wish to test function words in context initially. Words the student is unable to read, even in context, should have the first priority for instruction. Once a student's basic core vocabulary has been assessed in context, it can be tested in isolation. Words recognized in context but not in isolation can be taught after the first priority words are learned. If time constraints prohibit administration of both a contextual and a context-free test, likely the best course of action is to select the context-free test (described in the next section) since pronunciation of sight vocabulary in isolation provides the most stringent measure of a student's knowledge.

You can use the following procedure to test basic sight vocabulary in context.

1. To *develop* a contextual test of basic sight vocabulary
   a. Use all words from one of the lists of basic high-frequency words. Or select all words from the first preprimer of the material to be used for

instruction to compose section 1 of your test, then do the same for the second preprimer to compose section 2, and so on.

   b. Write sentences that include each word; other words in the sentences should be words the student can identify so that they provide a context for the target word you are testing. In constructing these sentences, you probably will use some of the basic high-frequency sight words several times; that is, they will occur not only as a target word but also in the context of sentences for other target words. In this way, you will have several opportunities to observe the student's response to the same word.

2. To *administer* a contextual test of basic sight vocabulary

   a. Have the student orally read the sentences into a tape recorder.

   b. If a word is not known, tell the student to do anything he or she can to figure it out; if the student still cannot identify the word, tell the student to skip it and continue reading.

   c. If a student begins to exhibit great difficulty as the test progresses, discontinue testing. Plan to provide instruction for those words missed up to the point when you stopped testing. After the student has mastered these words, you can administer the test again to identify additional words to be learned.

3. To *score* a contextual test of basic sight vocabulary

   a. When the student is not present, listen to the tape and mark miscues on a duplicate copy of the test.

   b. Do not mark words only as right or wrong; rather, write down what the student said when a word was mispronounced. For example, if *when* is read as *then*, write *then* above the word *when*.

   c. Circle any word the student is unable to pronounce.

   d. Consider correct only those words for which there was instant recognition. Leslie and Caldwell (2001) specify that for a word to be judged as recognized "at sight" (relatively instantly), it must be pronounced in about one second. If there is a long pause before the student can say a word, or if a word identification strategy must be used, then there is not instant recognition.

   e. Prepare a list of words the student cannot recognize at all and another list of words confused with similar words (such as *on* for *no*, *here* for *there*, etc.). On the second list, note the test word and the similar word.

   f. No grade score is obtained from this type of assessment. Instead, it is used to determine if the student does or does not need instruction on basic sight vocabulary and, if so, how much instruction is required. A contextual test also informs the teacher about the kind of instruction needed: Is initial instruction needed with most words missed because the student cannot identify them at all, or is the principal problem that the student is confusing words with ones that look similar? A contextual test provides lists of specific words for which instruction is needed.

> To score a test of basic sight vocabulary knowledge, it is important to note specific word confusions and not merely produce an enumeration of number right and number wrong.

A Context-Free Test of Sight Vocabulary

If a student has been given a test of basic high-frequency words in context, then that should be followed by one where context provides no clue to aid word recognition; that is, sight words also should be tested in a context-free situation,

FIGURE 5–3   *Example of a Scoring Sheet for a Sight Vocabulary Test*

Student's Name _____ Date _____

1. on _____	1. have _____	1. is _____
2. of _____	2. go _____	2. go _____
3. the _____	3. I _____	3. now _____
4. for _____	4. and _____	4. know _____
5. with _____	5. red _____	5. never _____
6. some _____	6. so _____	6. no _____
7. where _____	7. every _____	7. from _____
8. because _____	8. a _____	8. off _____
9. to _____	9. have _____	9. which _____
10. it _____	10. had _____	10. said _____

or in other words, in isolation. To do so, it is preferable to have each word printed on a separate index card rather than presenting the student with one long list. An extended list of words can overwhelm some poor readers and they may feel defeated before they begin.

1. To *develop* a test of basic sight vocabulary in isolation
   a. Print each word on a card, using correct manuscript writing.
   b. Divide the word cards into sets of 10. In each set, number the cards on the back from 1 to 10.
   c. Make copies of sheets to be used during scoring, with all the words in each set listed on the sheet. One example of such a sheet is shown in Figure 5–3.
2. To *administer* the test of sight vocabulary in isolation
   a. Have the student read from one set of word cards at a time, following the same three procedures used for administering a contextual assessment of sight vocabulary.
   b. Always present the words within a set in the same order (card 1 first, card 2 second, and so on) so they will match the sheets you have prepared for scoring.
3. To *score* the test of sight vocabulary in isolation
   a. Use the scoring sheets.
   b. Follow the same procedures described for scoring the contextual test of sight vocabulary.

ASSESSING KNOWLEDGE OF WORD IDENTIFICATION STRATEGIES

An assessment of word identification strategies should go beyond tests of phonic analysis skill to include measures of structural analysis strategies.

Although we hope students will eventually recognize most words instantly, they will undoubtedly encounter words they do not know during the developmental stages of learning to read. Even skilled adult readers occasionally find unknown words in texts. Therefore, readers must learn strategies to identify words they do not recognize on sight.

Individually administered tests often provide a more accurate assessment than group-administered tests.

FIGURE 5–4 *Methods of Assessing Knowledge of Word Identification Strategies*

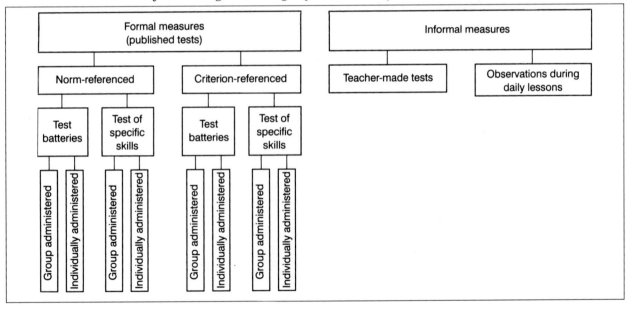

An assessment of students' knowledge of word identification strategies should include tests of phonic analysis and tests of structural analysis. In times past, tests of skill in using context clues also were administered; however, currently, this skill is not deemed as crucial as once believed. (This issue will be discussed in a later chapter.) If a general test of the use of context clues is desired, teachers may use the cloze or maze procedure discussed in Chapter 4.

Analysis of student performance on an IRI provides some incidental information about use of word identification strategies, but there are additional ways to obtain more in-depth information. See Figure 5–4 for a diagram that summarizes several approaches.

Formal Measures

Formal measures (i.e., published tests) for assessing word identification strategies provide *specific diagnostic* information in contrast to the general reading levels that are obtained from the survey tests discussed in Chapter 3. Four types of diagnostic tests are discussed in the following section. Two types are norm-referenced: (a) norm-referenced diagnostic test *batteries* and (b) norm-referenced *tests of specific skills.* The other two types are criterion-referenced: (c) criterion-referenced test *batteries* and (d) criterion-referenced *tests of specific skills.*

Diagnostic tests assess the student's specific strengths and weaknesses in reading. There is no perfectly adequate published diagnostic test, and a variety of problems may occur with those that are available. The tests may not assess all important areas, or they may test areas that research has shown to be unimportant for reading achievement. Some only sample sets of knowledge; for example, they may test only a few consonant sounds instead of all.

Certain tests measure skills and strategies inappropriately. For example, some authorities question the use of nonsense words to test word identification strategies. The argument in favor of use of nonsense words is that students may recognize real words at sight, and thus their performance on the test would not be a true reflection of their knowledge of word identification strategies. Using nonsense words may nonetheless be inappropriate for several reasons. Even though students may be told that the "word" they are to pronounce is a nonsense word, they often attempt to pronounce a real word anyway, rendering the response incorrect. This is, of course, an indication that the student is attempting to use knowledge of the world and language to identify words—strategies we want them to employ. In addition, research has shown that pronouncing a nonsense word may require greater skill than pronouncing a real word (Cunningham, 1977) and is, therefore, an inappropriate test of what a student needs to know in authentic reading situations.

Tests do not always measure what they say they do.

Certain tests do not measure what they say they do. For example, some test the ability to use letter-sound correspondences by presenting a picture instead of a word, and the student is to circle a letter representing the sound heard at the beginning. This is a test of auditory discrimination rather than assessment of ability to produce the sound represented by the letter and use it to identify unknown words.

Today many teachers attempt to resolve some of these problems in assessing letter-sound knowledge by forgoing published tests and, instead, having students write words from the teacher's dictation. When doing so, the teacher is not concerned with misspellings, but only with the use of letters that represent the sounds heard. For example, if the student is asked to write *hammer* and writes *hamer*, the teacher knows this student can correctly match the sounds heard in the word with letters or letter combinations that commonly represent those sounds. When using this procedure, however, teachers must remember that if the student already knows how to spell the word, this method is not a test of ability to match sounds with letters. In addition, it does not test whether the student *uses* this knowledge when reading.

There are no simple solutions to some of these problems. If a formal test is to be used, it is necessary to carefully analyze a number of published tests and select the most adequate for your purposes. In some cases, a teacher may choose to use certain subtests within one test battery and reject others. In other circumstances, it will be necessary for parts of several published tests to be combined and used along with teacher-developed subtests to appropriately assess all word identification strategies. Even then, teachers should verify results of these types of assessments through daily observations.

Summarize.   What are some criticisms of formal (published) tests of word identification strategies?

Some formal diagnostic tests are **norm-referenced** (i.e., standardized with reference to a norm group). However, providing grade scores, as norm-referenced tests do, is not very important information on a diagnostic test since grade levels do not tell us *specifically* what a student needs to learn. In addition, grade scores obtained from various published diagnostic tests often are not comparable; that is, a student can achieve one grade-level score on one published diagnostic test but on another, administered immediately afterward, achieve a different grade-level score. Generally, grade-level scores obtained on norm-referenced diagnostic tests should be ignored. Diagnostic tests should be used only for determining a student's specific strengths and weaknesses in various areas related to reading.

Some norm-referenced formal assessment instruments consist of diagnostic test batteries. (See Figure 5–4.) A **test battery** contains many subtests that assess different skills. Most test batteries provide better tests of word identification strategies than they do of comprehension.

A few norm-referenced test batteries may be group administered. One such battery is the Stanford Diagnostic Reading Test with subtests that include phonic analysis, word reading, listening vocabulary, comprehension, and various measures of word meaning knowledge.

While they do save time, the problem with group-administered diagnostic tests is that they often do not require the same types of performance needed in actual reading tasks. For example, the student's test paper may include a list of numbered items with three or four consonant blends listed beside each; the teacher pronounces a word, and students circle the blend they hear. This task is easier than, and different from, encountering an unknown word in reading and producing a blend sound to aid in identifying the word. In addition, some group-administered tests include multiple-choice items so students may score a correct response by guessing. As a result, group-administered diagnostic tests provide only a ballpark notion of students' needs.

Other norm-referenced test batteries are individually administered. Two are the Diagnostic Reading Scales and the Durrell Analysis of Reading Difficulty. If individually administered diagnostic tests have met other standards for test construction, they provide a more accurate assessment than do group-administered tests because students can be required to perform tasks that are closer to those necessary in authentic acts of reading. For example, students can be asked to read a response to you rather than circle a letter or item in a multiple-choice question. See **Test Bank D** for a listing of some norm-referenced diagnostic test batteries.

Note Taking.   Paraphrase in a note or two (a) the issue related to grade scores on diagnostic tests and (b) the issue regarding group versus individual administration of diagnostic tests.

A TEACHING RESOURCE

TEST BANK D

Some Norm-Referenced Diagnostic Test Batteries

Name	For Grades	Type of Administration	Time for Administration	Publisher
Diagnostic Achievement Battery	Ages 6–14	Individual	60–120 minutes	Pro-ED
Diagnostic Reading Scales	1–7 and disabled readers in grades 8–12	Individual	Varies with student	CTB/McGraw-Hill
Diagnostic Screening Test: Reading. For preliminary screening, not in-depth assessment	1–12	Individual	5–10 minutes	Slosson Educational Publications
Durrell Analysis of Reading Difficulty	1–6	Individual	Varies according to subtests used	Psychological Corporation
Gates-McKillop-Horowitz Reading Diagnostic Test	1–6	Individual	Varies according to subtests used	Teacher College Press
Iowa Tests of Educational Development	9–12	Group	Varies according to subtests used	Riverside
Stanford Diagnostic Reading Test	1–6	Group	Varies by level	Harcourt Brace Educational Measurement
Woodcock-Johnson Diagnostic Reading Battery	Ages 4–95	Individual	20–25 minutes	Riverside

In addition to norm-referenced test batteries, there are also norm-referenced **tests of specific skills.** (See Figure 5–4.) These tests furnish detailed information about one specific area rather than incorporating a number of subtests assessing many diverse areas. For instance, one such test of specific skills may assess only concepts related to word identification with no attention given to sight word reading, listening vocabulary, or other factors, while another may assess only comprehension or only phonemic awareness. Some norm-referenced tests of specific skills may be group administered. An example is Degrees of Reading Power, a test designed to evaluate aspects of comprehension. One norm-referenced test of specific skills that may be group administered or individually administered is the Test of Reading Comprehension (TORC). Intended for grades 2 through 12, this instrument appraises a number of variables, but all are directly related to understanding text (e.g., general and content area-specific knowledge of word meanings, following sequences, understanding syntactic similarities, paragraph reading, reading directions, and a general comprehension measure). See ***Test Bank E*** for some available norm-referenced diagnostic tests of specific skills.

Other published diagnostic tests are **criterion-referenced.** (See Figure 5–4.) Criterion-referenced tests do not compare students' performances with a norm group, but are designed only to provide information about whether students have mastered certain knowledge, strategies, or skills, They often give more

Some criterion-referenced tests assess enormous numbers of skills (and some of these skills have limited usefulness for real reading).

A TEACHING RESOURCE

TEST BANK E

Some Norm-Referenced Diagnostic Tests of Specific Skills

Name	For Grades	Type of Administration	Time for Administration	Publisher
Degrees of Reading Power–Revised. Assesses comprehension; also has criterion-referenced features	1–12+	Group	45–50 minutes	Touchstone Applied Science Associates
The Test of Reading Comprehension (TORC)	Ages 7–17	Group or individual	60 minutes	Pro-Ed

---

specific and comprehensive information about a student's strengths and weaknesses than norm-referenced tests. There are problems with some published criterion-referenced tests, however. For example, enormous numbers of different skills may be tested, with the number of separate objectives sometimes ranging from as many as 300–500. Many skills assessed by such tests are unnecessary. They represent rules and principles of low utility.

On the other hand, some criterion-referenced tests do not include enough items, for example, using only three to five items to measure an important skill. The reliability of tests with so few items per skill is usually low. The Reading Evaluation Adult Diagnosis Test (produced by the Literacy Volunteers of America) has been criticized for this reliability issue, with concerns related to too few items to accurately assess sight word knowledge or word analysis skill (Margolis, 2001; Shanahan, 2001). Moreover, on some criterion-referenced tests, criterion levels set for demonstrating mastery of a skill are subjective and questionable. For important word identification knowledge, 100% mastery may be necessary if the student is to be proficient in using that knowledge when encountering an unknown word. Yet, many criterion-referenced tests specify levels of only 80–90% to indicate mastery. If a student knows only 80% of the consonant sounds, he or she may encounter problems with unknown words that contain the other 20%.

As with all published tests, teachers should carefully analyze criterion-referenced tests to determine which are worth purchasing. In many cases, the teacher may choose to use only certain subtests and may adapt mastery levels set by publishers to more appropriate standards.

Published criterion-referenced tests, like norm-referenced tests, include test batteries. One test of this type, with sections that are group-administered and others that are individually administered, is Bench Mark Measures. This battery has subtests for phonics, spelling, and other areas. One negative feature of this test is that certain portions require producing sounds in nonsense words. An example of a test battery that is individually administered is the Brigance Diagnostic Comprehensive Inventory of Basic Skills–Revised. The Brigance has sections for research and study skills, spelling, and listening in addition to reading. The reading section includes 19 subtests of word identification skills, plus subtests in other reading areas. This test is designed for grades kindergarten through 8. Time needed for testing varies according to the number of subtests administered. Although a popular test, especially in learning disability programs, the Brigance provides no information on the reliability or validity of test scores.

Another individually administered diagnostic test battery is the Diagnostic Assessments of Reading with Trial Teaching Strategies (DARTTS). DARTTS includes subtests for word recognition and word analysis and for oral reading, silent comprehension, spelling, and word meaning. Different levels of this test are suitable for administration in grades 1 through 12. See **Test Bank F** for a listing of some criterion-referenced diagnostic test batteries.

A TEACHING RESOURCE

TEST BANK F

Some Criterion-Referenced Diagnostic Test Batteries

Name	For Grades	Type of Administration	Time for Administration	Publisher
Basic Achievement Skills Individual Screener	1–post-high school	Individual	50–60 minutes	Psychological Corporation
Bench Mark Measures	Ungraded	Some parts group; some parts individual	30–60 minutes	Educators Publishing Service
Botel Reading Inventory	1–12	Group	Varies according to subtests used	Modern Curriculum Press
Brigance Diagnostic Comprehensive Inventory of Basic Skills–Revised. Now also permits norm-referenced interpretations	Ages 5–13	Individual and group	Varies according to subtests used	Curriculum Associates
Brigance Diagnostic Inventory of Essential Skills	6–adult	Individual and group	Varies according to subtests used	Curriculum Associates
Criterion Test of Basic Skills	K–8	Individual	10–15 minutes per subtest	Academic Therapy Publications
Diagnostic Assessments of Reading with Trial Teaching Strategies (DARTTS)	1–12	Individual	20–30 minutes	Riverside
Multilevel Academic Survey Test	K–8	Some parts individual; some parts group	Varies according to subtests used	Psychological Corporation
Reading Skills Diagnostic Test III	2–12	Group	40–60 minutes	Brador Publications
Roswell-Chall Diagnostic Reading Test of Word Analysis Skills. Also includes tests of high-frequency words and spelling	1–4	Individual	10–15 minutes	Educators Publishing Service
Spadafore Diagnostic Reading Test	1–12 and adult	Individual	30–60 minutes	Academic Therapy Publications

A TEACHING RESOURCE

TEST BANK G

Some Criterion-Referenced Diagnostic Tests of Specific Skills

Name	For Grades	Type of Administration	Time for Administration	Publisher
Decoding Skills Test	1–6	Individual	35–40 minutes	York Press
Degree of Word Meaning	3–8	Group	Untimed	Touchstone Applied Science Associates
Phonovisual Diagnostic Tests	3–12	Group	Varies according to subtests used	Phonovisual Product

Certain criterion-referenced tests are tests of specific skills. One example that is group administered is Degrees of Word Meaning, designed to assess knowledge of meaning vocabulary in natural contexts. Another is the Phonovisual Diagnostic Test, which assesses phonics. A criterion-referenced test of specific skills that is individually administered is the Decoding Skills Test. Some criterion-referenced diagnostic tests of specific skills are listed in **Test Bank G.**

In conclusion, published diagnostic tests of word identification strategies present certain problems, but they can be helpful in assessing students' abilities if used judiciously.

> To develop informal assessments of word identification strategies, consider problems of published diagnostic tests and avoid these faults in developing your own instrument.

Informal Measures

Many teachers find developing their own tests of word identification strategies preferable to using published tests. To develop a teacher-made test for this purpose, follow the directions in the accompanying boxed material titled **STEPS— Administering Assessments in Your Own Classroom: Developing Informal Tests of Word Identification Strategies.**

USING THE READING MISCUE INVENTORY

The Reading Miscue Inventory (Goodman, Watson, & Burke, 1987), commonly called the RMI, offers insights about whether students' reading miscues are preventing them from obtaining meaning from text, or if they are relatively inconsequential. While concerns are sometimes raised about the time required for its individual administration (approximately 15 minutes per student) and interpretation (approximately 1 hour per student), many reading specialists use the RMI because it is a productive appraisal of how students are processing print. The RMI assessment procedures are based on the following ideas.

A premise of the Reading Miscue Inventory is that some errors are "better" than others.

1. Some miscues are "better" than others. Compare, for example, these two student responses to the same sentence:

Ralph ran wildly about the room trying to catch his pet mouse before his mother found it was loose.

Ralph ran wildly about the room trying to catch his pet mouse before his mother found it was loose.

The miscue in the second sentence does not change the essential meaning of the sentence as the first one does and therefore is a better miscue.

2. Reading is not an exact process. Even proficient readers change words, omit words, and insert words, with no change in the author's intended meaning.

3. Teachers should not treat all miscues the same way. Miscues should be evaluated according to how much they change meaning; that is, an analysis of a student's reading performance should be qualitative as well as quantitative.

The RMI is different from an IRI in several ways. No reading level is obtained from an RMI, which instead provides information about strengths and weaknesses in the use of specific reading strategies. During administration of an RMI, the student reads a complete selection, that is, a whole story or a complete selection of informational material. In comparison to an IRI, which uses relatively short passages, these longer selections present greater opportunity for the teacher to see how a student interacts with text when more language cues and more meaning clues are available. Also in contrast to an IRI, an RMI bases analysis on oral reading performance only.

Seven items are needed to administer the RMI: (a) a test manual, (b) a passage for students to read, (c) a worksheet copy of the passage for the teacher to mark, (d) a Coding Sheet (provided with the test materials), (e) a Profile Sheet, (f) a tape recorder, and (g) a blank tape.

To administer the RMI, the teacher first selects a passage that is demanding enough so the student will make at least 25 miscues, but not so difficult that it cannot be handled at all. Next, the student reads the selection into the tape recorder, and, while the tape recorder is still running, retells what has been read. The teacher uses an outline in guiding the retelling and then asks specific questions about the story. Later, the teacher listens to the tape and marks the student's miscues on the worksheet copy of the passage and determines the student's retelling score. The teacher codes 25 of the miscues on the Coding Sheet, using these miscues to gain information about how the student is processing print, and transfers a summary to the Profile Sheet. Finally, the teacher plans instruction based on an analysis of the student's performance. Directions for marking and coding miscues, for determining a retelling score, and for other necessary procedures are found in the test manual. (See the sample Coding Sheet in Figure 5–5; also see **Test Bank H.**)

STEPS: ADMINISTERING ASSESSMENTS IN YOUR OWN CLASSROOM

Developing Informal Tests of Word Identification Strategies

STEP 1   List areas you want to assess within the broader areas of phonic analysis and structural analysis. The specific areas listed in Chapter 9 should be helpful to you in doing this.

STEP 2   Examine published tests for appropriate ways of assessing various strategies—ways you can adapt or improve upon in your test. To locate such tests, check with the district office in your school system or a college library with a test collection, or gather samples when you attend teachers' conferences.

STEP 3   Carefully consider the problems of some published diagnostic tests discussed in the previous section in order to avoid those faults in your own instrument.

STEP 4   Develop items for each subarea within your test. (Some teachers start small—developing a test for one or two subareas and trying these out before preparing a more comprehensive instrument.)

STEP 5   Divide the test into logical sections so you have the choice of administering the entire test or only selected sections.

STEP 6   Prepare typed copies of the test for your students. (Sometimes it saves time if you also duplicate student record sheets for indicating their responses.)

STEP 7   Be willing to revise and improve sections if you note inadequacies in the original version as you administer and interpret the test.

A TEACHING RESOURCE

TEST BANK H

A Test of Reading Strategies

Name	For Grades	Type of Administration	Time for Administration	Publisher
Reading Miscue Inventory (RMI)	1–8	Individual	Approximately 15 minutes with pupil; 1 hour for analysis	Richard C. Owen

FIGURE 5–5 *Reading Miscue Inventory Coding Sheet*

MISCUE ANALYSIS PROCEDURE I CODING FORM

READER **Betsy** DATE **Nov. 3**

TEACHER **Mrs. Blum** AGE/GRADE **3** SCHOOL **York Elem.**

SELECTION **The Man Who Kept House**

LINE No./ MISCUE No.	READER	TEXT	1 SYNTACTIC ACCEPTABILITY	2 SEMANTIC ACCEPTABILITY	3 MEANING CHANGE	4 CORRECTION	No Loss	Partial Loss	Loss	Strength	Partial Strength	Overcorrection	Weakness	Graphic H	Graphic S	Graphic N	Sound H	Sound S	Sound N
1	so	some	P	P	1	Y	✓			✓				✓				✓	
2	start	stay	P	P	1	N		✓					✓	✓				✓	
3	house	home	P	P	1	N		✓					✓	✓				✓	
4	keeping	keep	P	P	1	N		✓									✓		
5	we'll	we'll	Y	P	1	N		✓			✓			✓				✓	
6	bread	butter	Y	P	P	N		✓			✓								✓
7		all	Y	Y	P	N	✓			✓		✓							✓
8	well	we'll	Y	Y	N	N	✓			✓				✓			✓		
9	you		Y	Y	N	N	✓			✓				✓			✓		
10	day	morning	Y	N		N		✓				✓				✓			✓
11	job	work	Y	P	1	Y		✓			✓					✓			✓
12	@and	.As	Y	Y	N	N	✓			✓				✓			✓		
13	S churn	churn	Y	Y	P	N			✓		✓			✓			✓		
14	.He	.he	Y	Y	N	N	✓			✓						✓		✓	
15	the	this	Y	Y	1	N	✓			✓					✓			✓	
16	So	Seen	N	N	1	Y	✓			✓									✓
17	.buttermilk	butter	P	P	1	Y	✓			✓					✓			✓	
18	couldn't	could not	P	P	1	Y	✓			✓		✓			✓			✓	
19	There	She	N	N	1	N	✓			✓					✓				✓
20	is	was	Y	P	1	N	✓			✓								✓	
21	into	to	Y	P	1	N	✓			✓						✓			✓
22	forest	far	P	Y	N	N	✓			✓		✓		✓			✓		
23	in	to	Y	Y	N	N	✓			✓								✓	
24	the	his	Y	Y	1	N	✓			✓						✓			✓
25	heard	had	P	P	1	N	✓			✓				✓					✓
			COLUMN TOTAL																
			PATTERN TOTAL																
			PERCENTAGE																

See 1, 2, 4 — GRAMMATICAL RELATIONSHIPS
See 2, 3, 4 — MEANING CONSTRUCTION
5 — GRAPHIC SIMILARITY
6 — SOUND SIMILARITY

a. TOTAL MISCUES ——
b. TOTAL WORDS ——
a ÷ b × 100 = MPHW ——

Source: From *Reading Miscue Inventory* (p. 96) by Y. M. Goodman, D. Watson, and C. L. Burke, 1987, New York: Richard C. Owen. Copyright 1987 by Richard C. Owen Publishers. Reprinted by permission.

RUNNING RECORDS

With the assessment technique called a **running record,** the evaluator uses many strategies similar to those employed with an RMI. A running record is a record the teacher makes as a student reads orally; the record is taken by using check marks to indicate every word read correctly and, for errors, employing a marking system similar to that used for an IRI as described in Tables 4–1 and 4–2 in Chapter 4.

Running record procedures allow teachers to analyze reading performance spontaneously for any story a student is reading.

A running record differs from an RMI or an IRI in a rather notable way: No copy of the story is used for recording the teacher's markings. Rather, the marking is done on a plain piece of paper so the running record can be taken spontaneously with any story, if desired. This means, however, that when an error is made, the teacher must record the text word as well as the student's incorrect response. See Figure 5–6 for a partial sample of a running record.

According to Clay (1985), teachers can learn to take a running record with about 2 hours' practice and can become proficient enough to do so without audiotaping the student's reading. Still, Clay's research also has shown that running records for poor readers characteristically are more complex than those for average readers; therefore, with poor readers, use of a tape recorder may be advisable.

For a preplanned (nonspontaneous) assessment, the teacher often arranges to take a running record with three stories of 100 to 200 words each: one story that will be easy for the student who is to be evaluated, one of average difficulty, and one that will be hard. This allows a range of strengths and weaknesses to be identified. From a calculation of error rate (number of errors divided by all words) and

FIGURE 5–6   *A Sample Running Record From Four Pages of Sample Text*

In this sample the student read most words correctly, as indicated by check marks. At first he miscalls horse as house, but then self-corrects (SC). On the second page, he does not know gone and appeals to the teacher (A); the teacher asks the student to try the word, but he miscalls it as going, whereupon the teacher (T) tells him the word. Complete details on marking procedures for running records, as suggested by Clay, can be found in the 3rd edition of *The Early Detection of Reading Difficulties* (Clay, 1985), which also offers proposed analyses of pupils' reading behaviors based on the errors exhibited during a running record.

an analysis of the errors and other reading behaviors (including nonverbal ones), a teacher may obtain data about whether a particular book is too hard for a student (less than 90% accuracy), the degree of match between a student's oral language skill and the text, reading fluency, the cues and strategies a student uses, and self-correction behavior. Much of this information depends on the teacher examining every error and asking why that error occurred (Clay, 1985, p. 24).

A great many factors in a running record seem analogous to both IRIs and the Reading Miscue Inventory. However, since running records can be undertaken with any story without preparation, a teacher can examine a student's reading behaviors more frequently and thus have a thorough and ongoing set of information to guide instruction.

WRITING ASSESSMENT

"Get Writing with Weekend News," found on the Marco Polo website's compendium of lessons, helps primary grade students develop criteria to self-assess their writing. Go to www.readwritethink.org, then click "Lessons," "Grade Band," and "All Grades." This lesson is alphabetically listed.

Because reading and writing instruction increasingly are being linked in instructional programs, reading teachers may wish to assess students' writing. Large-scale testing of writing (e.g., the National Assessment of Educational Progress) to evaluate school programs does not adequately supply the kinds of information teachers need in order to follow student development. Furthermore, many published writing tests use **indirect measures** that do not assess a student's actual writing but rely on such means as multiple-choice items, which do not reflect students' true writing abilities. While some published tests, such as those specified in *Test Bank I,* do use **direct measurement**—that is, examining actual student writing samples—some ask students to produce these samples under conditions that are atypical from authentic writing situations.

The most widely recommended manner of evaluating writing abilities is to collect examples of student writing when it has been completed in ways advocated by principles of good writing instruction and consistent with procedures

A TEACHING RESOURCE

TEST BANK I

Some Tests of Writing Skill

Name	For Grades	Type of Administration	Time for Administration	Publisher
Integrated Writing Test	2–12	Group	15–20 minutes	Golden Education Center
Stanford Writing Assessment Program	3–12	Group	50 minutes	Harcourt Brace Educational Measurement
Written Language Assessment	Ages 8–18+	Group	15–20 minutes per writing task	Academic Therapy Publications

used by proficient writers: Students should have an opportunity to: (a) choose their own topics, (b) write under untimed conditions, (c) elicit feedback from others, and (d) revise. Teachers should collect chronological samples (dated and over time) to measure ongoing skill but also to involve students in self-evaluation of their writing *processes* as well as their writing *products*.

Using Textual Features. Note that the phrases *indirect measures* and *direct measurement* are printed in the previous section in boldface type. Do you remember that this is a commonly used convention to indicate that a term is defined in text? This also usually signals information that is important to notice and recall. How would you define each of these terms? What is being recommended here?

What is more, to adequately judge patterns of behavior and growth, teachers should collect various types of writing (stories, informational writing, etc.), along with several revisions of single pieces of work. This collection of samples is often brought together into a **portfolio,** a large folder used to collect and organize student products. Portfolios frequently include rough drafts, memos from student-teacher conferences, final drafts, and "published" versions of students' writing—with some of these assigned and others student-selected projects. The length of these may vary from substantial pieces to those that are relatively brief.

Teachers' written observations also should be maintained over time to document students' learning histories, and most important, to guide instruction for individual students. Scala (2001) has provided a rubric that teachers can use for this purpose (see Figure 5–7).

FIGURE 5–7 *Criteria for Rating Student Writing*

	4	3	2	1
Development of Topic	Original, interesting development of topic	Acceptable development of topic	Attempts to develop topic but shows weaknesses	Lacks plan to develop topic
Organization and Use of Support Material	Full development of ideas through excellent use of support material	Adequate use of support material to develop ideas	Little use of support material to develop ideas	Does not use support material to develop ideas
Sentence Variety	Skillful use of sentence variety	Some sentence variety	Little sentence variety	Lack of sentence variety
Language	Uses rich vocabulary and images	Uses general language	Uses incorrect language	Frequently uses incorrect language
Conventions	Few or no errors	Errors do not interfere with meaning	Errors interfere with meaning	Errors seriously interfere with meaning

Source: From Scala, Marilyn C. (2001) Working Together: Reading and Writing in Inclusive Classrooms. *International Reading Association,* Newark, DE. Reprinted with permission of Marlyn C. Scala and the International Reading Associations.

Setting a Purpose for Reading. Knowledge of the spelling stages discussed in the following section has important consequences for interpreting spelling behaviors of reading-delayed students. As you read, think about how awareness of the characteristics of these stages could dispel myths about these students.

SPELLING DEVELOPMENT

Writing also supports opportunities to estimate spelling development. Studies (e.g., Beers & Henderson, 1977; Read, 1975; Zutell, 1998) have shown naturally occurring stages in most children's spelling behaviors, stages that hold true regardless of whether students are average achievers, reading delayed, or learning disabled (e.g., Invernizzi & Worthy, 1989; Zutell, 1998). As investigations of spelling growth have continued from the 1970s to the present, progressively greater understanding has evolved about the earmarks of each stage (e.g., Gentry, 1981; Morris, 1992; Schlagel, 1989; Zutell, 1998). Examination of writing samples over time allows teachers to systematically note these changes in students' spelling growth. Gentry (1981) and Zutell (1998) have described the following spelling stages:

Stage 1. Once termed the *random* stage, now more often called the *preliterate* stage.

Early—"Writing" may consist of scribbling. Shows no knowledge of letter-sound relationships. May not know names of all (or any) letters; selects randomly from those letters that are known—for example, spelling "dinosaur" as "WSA." Diagnostically, some questions the teacher might ask are: Which letters does the student know how to form? Which must still be taught? Does the student discriminate letters from numerals? (At the random stage, some children combine numerals and letters to write "words," e.g., "L6T.") Can the child give names for the letters written? Are the "words" written from left to right?

Later—Begins to show an emerging realization that sounds heard in words are associated with letters, though some sounds heard may not be used, with only a few of the most prominent represented in the student's written form of the word (e.g., spelling "rabbit" as "RBT").

Stage 2. Called the *phonetic* or *letter-name* stage. A much closer association between letters and sounds is seen, with most sounds that are heard being represented in the child's written form of the word (e.g., spelling "ghost" as "gost").

However, some incorrect, but reasoned, letter-sound associations are made. At times, letter names also are substituted for letter sounds. Gentry (1981) gives this example from a sentence actually written by a child at this stage: ADE LAFWTS KRAMD NTU A LAVATR, which should be read as "Eighty elephants crammed into a elevator." Inflectional endings (e.g., -*ed*) are spelled as they are heard (e.g., "jumped" spelled as "jumpt").

Stage 3. Sometimes called the *transitional* stage. Students in this phase are often called *within-word pattern spellers*. The child includes vowels in all syllables, though not always correctly (e.g., "airplane" spelled "arplane"). There is increasing control over short vowel spellings and growing familiarity with common word units (e.g., correct spelling of inflectional endings).

Common letter patterns begin to show up in words (e.g., the final *e* on "arplane"), but not always correctly (e.g., "He *ack*ted bad"). The student at this stage correctly spells a number of consonant blends and consonant digraphs and begins to distinguish spellings of frequently occurring homophones (*to, too, two*).

Stage 4. Called *syllable-juncture* spellers. Zutell (1998) describes students in this stage as exhibiting skillfulness (a) in spelling a large number of single syllable patterns and (b) in spelling multisyllabic words, if syllables contain high-frequency patterns (e.g., *running*). They are, however, lacking skill "with more complex doubling and joining situations (*hindered* but *referred*) and the spelling of unstressed vowels in polysyllabic words (*confide—confidential*)" (p. 221).

Stage 5. Called the *correct* stage, *conventional-spelling* stage, or the *derivational constancy* stage. Students have conquered the confusions of Stage 4. Moreover, they handle spellings of words incorporated into English but derived from other languages, even though the spelling generalizations of English may not apply to these words (e.g., *ballet*).

Most words are spelled correctly. Of course, the student's age and grade must be taken into account, and the likelihood of the amount of exposure to a specific word. Even college students and professors occasionally misspell words when they have had limited exposure to the word in printed form!

Knowing the typical evolution in spelling growth prevents misinterpretation of spelling behaviors.

Understanding this typical evolution in spelling growth prevents misinterpretation of spelling behaviors. For example, at times when students with learning disabilities have exhibited spellings at the preliterate stage, or at other stages consistent with spelling behaviors of younger students, their spelling attempts have been erroneously construed to mean that they have some bizarre neurological anomaly affecting their auditory or visual perception. While it is true that such students must be assisted to move to higher stages of spelling development, quite obviously these are misjudgments about causes of nonstandard spelling. These assumptions are likely made by persons who are unaware that all students follow natural spelling growth patterns. The correct interpretation of such spelling behaviors is simply that these students are moving through the stages more slowly than the norm and not that peculiar mental processes are occurring (Abouzeid, 1992).

Reading and Spelling Connections

A student's stage of spelling development is correlated with reading progress as well. One correlation between the two can be seen in the word features young students use to read (i.e., to *recognize* words), which are the same as those they use to spell (i.e., to *produce* words) (Treiman & Cassar, 1998). Moreover—in the early stages of literacy, at least—children who are good spellers are usually good readers and vice versa (Bear, 1992; Morris & Perney, 1984). This may be somewhat less true at higher grade levels where students must deal with spellings of multisyllabic words that incorporate many ambiguous vowel sounds and must contend with spellings of words less familiar in everyday speaking and reading.

In any case, Zutell (1998) emphasizes the importance of awareness of each student's spelling stage because this, in effect, provides a "window" into the child's thinking about how "words work" (p. 223). For example, an evaluation of spelling development can help teachers answer these questions: Does the student understand that:

letters have names and form words?

letters must be written in left-to-right order to form words in English and recognized and read in the same order?

sounds one hears are represented by letters in words and that there is some consistency to these relationships that helps one write and read words (i.e., the alphabetic principle)?

the *sounds* representing letters are written in words, not the *names* that portray those letters?

common letter patterns often found in words are pronounced in relatively consistent ways?

Even when children use invented spellings, these spellings can provide clues to their cognizance of letter-sound relationships and other crucial word-knowledge principles.

One spelling assessment that provides information on a student's spelling stage is the Qualitative Inventory of Spelling (Schlagel, 1989). See Figure 5–8 for a reproduction of this short assessment instrument. Level I on the inventory indicates Grade 1, Level II indicates Grade 2, and so on. Zutell, who is a spelling researcher as well as a university reading clinic supervisor, says he uses the Qualitative Inventory of Spelling in this way:

> I use Schlagel's Qualitative Inventory as an initial assessment tool for establishing a spelling instructional level and, more importantly, for determining what word features/patterns a student is "using but confusing" in order to guide the selection of word study activities. So, for example, if we were to find that a student was unsure about, or inconsistent in using, long vowel markers, we might develop long vowel versus short vowel word sorting activities to help him/her figure this out. (J. Zutell, personal communication, September 6, 2001)

ASSESSING KNOWLEDGE OF WORD MEANINGS

Formal Measures

Knowledge of word meanings is an important aspect of comprehension. Although most standardized survey tests contain sections on meaning vocabulary, these subtests do not provide a wholly adequate measure of students' word-meaning knowledge. There are several reasons for this. First, because of poor sight vocabulary or underdeveloped word identification strategies, a student may not recognize some test words in their written form—even though the student knows their meanings when these words are used in oral language. Furthermore, most survey tests measure only common word meanings, ignoring

FIGURE 5–8 ***The Qualitative Inventory of Spelling***

Level I	Level II	Level III	Level IV	Level V	Level VI
girl	traded	send	force	lunar	satisfied
want	cool	gift	nature	population	abundance
plane	beaches	rule	slammed	bushel	mental
drop	center	trust	curl	joint	violence
when	short	soap	preparing	compare	impolite
trap	trapped	batter	pebble	explosion	musician
wish	thick	knee	cellar	delivered	hostility
cut	plant	mind	market	normal	illustrate
bike	dress	scream	popped	justice	acknowledge
trip	carry	sight	harvest	dismiss	prosperity
flat	stuff	chain	doctor	decide	accustom
ship	try	count	stocked	suffering	patriotic
drive	crop	knock	gunner	stunned	impossible
fill	year	caught	badge	lately	correspond
sister	chore	noise	cattle	peace	admission
bump	angry	careful	gazed	amusing	wreckage
plate	chase	stepping	cabbage	reduction	commotion
mud	queen	chasing	plastic	preserve	sensible
chop	wise	straw	maple	settlement	dredge
bed	drove	nerve	stared	measure	conceive
	cloud	thirsty	gravel	protective	profitable
	grabbed	baseball	traffic	regular	replying
	train	circus	honey	offered	admitted
	shopping	handle	cable	division	introduction
	float	sudden	scurry	needle	operating
			camel	expression	decision
			silent	complete	combination
			cozy	honorable	declaration
			graceful	baggage	connect
			checked	television	patient

Source: Copyright 1989. From "The Qualitative Inventory of Spelling" by Robert C. Schlagel, *Reading Psychology*, 1989, Vol 10. Reproduced by permission of Taylor & Francis, Inc., www.taylorandfrancis.com

multiple meanings of the same words. Finally, vocabulary items included on such tests represent a very small sample of words.

Nonetheless, a student's general performance on these survey tests can provide clues about whether it is necessary to administer a follow-up diagnostic test of word meanings. If the student has performed poorly on a group, standardized survey test, the teacher is advised to read words from this test to the student and informally check his or her knowledge of their meanings. If, under these conditions, the student performs well, the original poor performance likely has a different basis; that is, the culprit probably is not a deficient meaning vocabulary, but lack of word identification strategies. To further investigate this possibility, a criterion-referenced test battery that may be useful is DARTTS (see ***Test Bank F***), which includes a *listening* subtest of meaning vocabulary.

If, on the other hand, the student performs poorly during the oral follow-up probe with the standardized survey test, more in-depth assessment is advisable. If desired, there are diagnostic tests of specific skills available for this follow-up. One is the Test of Reading Comprehension (TORC). This test assesses vocabulary related to common concepts, as well as words related to several content areas (science, social studies, and math) and vocabulary necessary for reading directions in school work.

Informal Measures

Follow-up assessment of meaning vocabulary also can be undertaken in a number of informal ways. For example, teacher-constructed measures, such as the *knowledge-rating graph* (Blachowicz & Fisher, 2000) seen in Figure 5–9, can be devised to measure general vocabulary or, as in this case, common topics addressed in school. One of the graphs illustrated in Figure 5–9 is designed to

FIGURE 5–9   *Before and After Knowledge Ratings*

Before Reading-Knowledge Rating

Check your knowledge level for each of these terms.

Term	3 Can Define/Use	2 Heard It	1 Don't Know
tipi	✔		
villa		✔	
casa colonica			✔
apartment	✔		
high rise		✔	
dascha		✔	
trullo			✔
dishambe			✔
lean-to		✔	
yurt			✔

After Reading-Knowledge Rating

Term	Rating	Locale	People	Describe	Questions
tipi	3	U.S. Plains	Native American	 ⌂	
villa	3	Mediterranean	Rich Romans, Italian	Large House	
dascha	3	Russia	Peasants-Rich	big house	
trullo	2	Sardinia	?	Not Sure	are they like tipis?
yurt	2	?	Nomads	 ⌂	How can it be felt?

Source: From *Teaching Vocabulary in All Classrooms* (p. 131) by C. Blachowicz and P. Fisher, 1996, Columbus, OH: Merrill. Reprinted by permission of Pearson Education, Inc., Upper Saddle River, NJ.

assess meaning vocabulary before a selection is read and the other afterward to determine how satisfactorily a student develops word meanings from context and concepts of a selection.

In addition, teachers may compile a file of test forms for each grade level. To develop such a file, the first step is deciding on the content for every level. The *general content* should involve these items:

1. knowledge of synonyms
2. use of precision when encountering words with similar meanings (e.g., one person saved money but another hoarded it; what is the difference?)
3. knowledge of multiple meanings of words (Johnson & Pearson, 1984)

Decisions about the *specific content* involve selecting words to be tested. A sample of words may be obtained from one or more of the following sources:

1. *The Living Word Vocabulary* (Dale & O'Rourke, 1976), which provides a listing of approximately 44,000 words with a grade level specified for each that indicates the level at which the meaning of that word is known by most students.

A number of sources for words may be useful in preparing informal measures of meaning-vocabulary knowledge.

2. Word lists from basal readers beginning at grade 4. (Words introduced in basal readers prior to grade 4 are generally selected because they are words that are in the oral language meaning vocabularies of most children; the task in these early years is one of getting students to recognize these known words in printed form. Beginning at grade 4, an additional objective is to introduce words for which meanings must also be learned.)

3. Lists of frequently occurring affixes and roots. One such source is Stauffer's (1969) list of the 15 most frequently occurring prefixes in the English language.

4. Lists of content area words, such as the Carroll, Davies, and Richman list for grades 3 through 9 (Carroll, Davies, & Richman, 1971).

The next step in developing an informal assessment instrument is to choose a method of assessing the words. Kelley and Krey (cited in Farr, 1969, p. 34) suggested one or more of the following methods.

I. Unaided recall
   A. Checking for familiarity
   B. Using words in a sentence
   C. Explaining the meaning
   D. Giving a synonym
   E. Giving an opposite
II. Aided recall
   A. Recall aided by recognition
      1. Matching tests
      2. Classification tests
      3. Multiple-choice tests
         a. Choosing the opposite
         b. Choosing the best synonym
         c. Choosing the best definition
         d. Choosing the best use in sentences
      4. Same-opposite tests
      5. Same-opposite-neither tests
      6. Same-different tests

      B. Recall aided by association
        1. Completion tests
        2. Analogy tests
      C. Recall aided by recognition and association
        1. Multiple-choice completion tests
        2. Multiple-choice substitution tests

Beck and McKeown (1991) have expressed concern about the use of multiple-choice items only to assess meaning vocabulary. While a word may seem to be known on a multiple-choice item, a student may still lack in-depth understanding because such tests provide an easier task than that required in situations where learners must *use* the word. Functional knowledge of a word's meaning is better demonstrated when a student can contrast it with a word having a related meaning, give multiple meanings of the word, and explain what a word means in a specific sentence.

Formal or informal tests should be supplemented with observations during daily work to determine a student's need for remediation in the area of meaning vocabulary.

LEARNING FROM TEXT

Summarize. What are some issues regarding assessment of word meanings?

EVALUATING DIAGNOSTIC TESTS

This chapter has discussed several procedures for determining a student's specific strengths and weaknesses in reading. Some of these use formal, published tests and others informal, teacher-constructed instruments. In either case, assessment procedures should be evaluated with checklists such as found in Figure 5–10 before use. This checklist should also be kept in mind as you read about additional assessment procedures in the next chapter.

FIGURE 5–10 *A Checklist of Adequacy for Diagnostic Tests*

	Yes	No
1. Is the test valid?		
2. Is the test reliable?		
3. Are all important areas covered?		
4. Does the test do more than merely sample a few items within a skill or a knowledge area?		
5. Does the test refrain from assessing areas that research has shown to be unimportant to reading achievement?		
6. Does the test or each subtest within the test assess what it purports to test?		
7. If information is needed to plan programs for moderately or severely delayed readers, is the test individually administered?		
8. As much as is possible, is the performance required on the test like the performance required during the real act of reading?		
9. Does the test provide detailed, comprehensive information about a student's knowledge and skills rather than merely a "ballpark" notion of needs?		

*R*eflections

1. Three hallmarks of exemplary assessment are
   a. use of multiple and diverse procedures to assess knowledge/strategies/skills
   b. thoughtful inspection of reading behaviors
   c. merging of results to obtain as accurate and as complete a picture as possible

   These three could serve as guidelines for your own reading assessment. Based on the tests and procedures described in this chapter, give examples of each of these.

2. What fourth guideline for high-quality assessment might you add?

LEARNING FROM TEXT

Applying What You've Learned. Teachers know that one of the best ways to learn something is to teach it to someone else. Select one of the assessment procedures described in this chapter and assume you are going to teach someone to prepare, administer, and score this assessment. What specific details would you have to convey?

6

Assessment for Identifying Specific Strengths and Weaknesses in Reading: Part II

Talking with students about their interests and attitudes is part of assessment.

*C*ontinuing the topic of Chapter 5, this chapter further describes assessment procedures for determining specific strengths and weaknesses in reading.

Make an Outline. As with the previous chapter, many tests and other assessment procedures are reviewed in Chapter 6. To distinguish them and their different purposes and characteristics, again, a useful study strategy is to start an outline now and complete it as you move through the chapter. Use the headings and subheadings in this chapter as a beginning to frame your outline.

ASSESSING COMPREHENSION

Comprehension assessment can be conducted with conventional tests (both formal and informal) or teacher-constructed instruments and procedures. Each approach has advantages and disadvantages.

Make a Prediction. Poor performance on the comprehension section of a standardized survey test is not always an indication of comprehension difficulties. How can teachers tell whether it is or is not?

Using Conventional Tests

Conventional tests that have some utility for measuring comprehension are survey tests, group-administered or individually administered diagnostic tests, informal reading inventories (IRIs), and the Reading Miscue Inventory (RMI).

Formal Assessments. Formal assessments used to evaluate comprehension consist of (a) standardized group survey tests, (b) group-administered diagnostic tests, and (c) individually administered diagnostic tests. When a student exhibits poor reading performance on the *standardized group survey test* employed during assessment for identification, the comprehension section is often examined to determine if comprehension difficulties exist. This is deemed an appropriate means of appraisal since survey tests measure comprehension after silent reading, which is required in most real-life reading tasks.

However, sometimes the use of group survey tests for measuring comprehension is criticized because these tests are timed. Some researchers question whether they measure speed of comprehension rather than power of comprehension. That is, they are concerned that a student with a slower than average rate of reading (e.g., because of word recognition difficulties or for other reasons) may be penalized, even though the student's comprehension is adequate when the student has all the time needed to complete a reading task. In such cases, these tests would not give a true reflection of the student's comprehension abilities.

Readministering an alternate form of a standardized comprehension test, informally and orally, may allow determination if poor performance has resulted from word recognition difficulties, comprehension problems, or both.

Nevertheless, if other diagnostic tests have indicated that a student has no difficulty with word recognition and word identification strategies, then the time limits of these tests should be sufficient for students to complete them. Therefore, if the student cannot complete the comprehension subtest, that likely indicates comprehension difficulty. If, on the other hand, a student has poor word knowledge skills, an alternate form of the survey test at the same level can be administered for diagnostic purposes after completion of the original form. During this second administration the student is asked to read the test orally and answer the questions. The teacher can then determine whether poor performance results from word recognition and word identification difficulties, from comprehension problems, or from both. Additional insights into the students' thinking processes and background knowledge are obtained if they are asked *how* they arrived at their answers.

Another criticism of group survey tests for assessing comprehension is that they do not measure retention. During these tests, students can refer to the relevant passage to find an answer; because of this, the tests are said to measure only immediate recall. However, retention of comprehended material is often vital, especially in schoolwork. The ideal test probably would include some sections where students can refer to a passage and others where they cannot. Yet some research seems to demonstrate that performance on test passages where students *can* look back to find answers more accurately measures reading achievement.

Other criticisms of group survey tests for determining comprehension ability are:

1. Answers are generally written in a multiple-choice format, allowing for guessing and providing clues that are not available in many authentic situations.
2. While there are exceptions, most measure comprehension of only short excerpts of material (e.g., single paragraphs), which is not representative of most real reading tasks.

In summary, standardized group survey tests are only the beginning point in assessment since the results provide only a general measure of understanding.

Formal, *group-administered diagnostic tests* are also available for assessing comprehension. Most are subtests in larger test batteries. One battery that includes comprehension subtests is the Stanford Diagnostic Reading Test.

Comprehension subtests of test batteries should be examined, however, to determine if they measure what they say they do. For example, the "comprehension" subtest of the Botel Reading Inventory tests only a student's ability to recognize word opposites. An example of a group-administered diagnostic test of specific skills that does assess comprehension is the Test of Reading Comprehension (TORC). In addition to paragraph comprehension, the TORC includes subsections on sequencing sentences and on determining whether sentences have similar meanings although they are syntactically different.

Because standardized, group-administered diagnostic tests are usually timed and read silently, a follow-up in which students orally reread the test or an alternate form, as suggested earlier, yields more specific diagnostic information.

Some *individually administered diagnostic test* batteries that incorporate subtests of comprehension are the Brigance Diagnostic Comprehensive Inventory of Basic Skills, the Diagnostic Reading Scales, the Basic Achievement

Skills Individual Screener, the Durrell Analysis of Reading Difficulty, and the Diagnostic Achievement Battery.

An advantage of individually administered tests is that students can be observed while they are responding. Some of these tests assess comprehension only after silent reading, some after oral reading, and some after both. Most stipulate an oral reply to questions or a retelling of the passage, rather than a written response. This method is advantageous when evaluating students with poor academic skills. Remember, however, that subtests of test batteries do a better job of assessing word identification strategies than of measuring comprehension. In addition, basic information on norming, reliability, and validity should be obtained by checking the technical manual for the test to ensure that the test is suitable for the intended purpose and group. For example, although the test may be suitable for younger children, the validity of the Basic Achievement Skills Individual Screener has been questioned for students beyond eighth grade. The questions suggested for critiquing diagnostic tests, which are listed in Figure 5–8 in the previous chapter, should also be considered before selecting a formal test of reading comprehension.

> An advantage of individually administered tests is that students can be observed while they are responding.

LEARNING FROM TEXT

Setting a Purpose for Reading. Read on to find out how you can use an IRI as a diagnostic measure of comprehension.

Informal Measures. An Informal Reading Inventory (IRI), usually administered to verify students' general reading levels, also supplies some information about a student's comprehension abilities—if the teacher goes beyond merely counting the number of correct and incorrect responses and looks at the types of questions that have been difficult for a specific student. An IRI also enables the teacher to analyze the degree to which comprehension is affected by word recognition and word identification difficulties.

In addition, with many IRIs, the teacher can compare comprehension levels after oral versus silent reading. Differences may indicate several possibilities. Poorer readers sometimes comprehend better after oral reading, perhaps because oral responses keep the student's attention focused on the material. If comprehension is better after silent reading, that may mean the student is focusing on word pronunciation rather than meaning during oral reading. Furthermore, if comprehension after both oral and silent reading is substantially lower than the student's word identification performance on the IRI, instruction in comprehension strategies is almost certainly needed.

Another advantage in using an IRI to assess comprehension is that the test is untimed. The teacher can thus feel confident that power of comprehension is being considered rather than speed of comprehension.

The results of a Reading Miscue Inventory (RMI) also help to estimate comprehension abilities. Because complete selections (whole stories, whole articles) are read, the RMI enables the teacher to measure student comprehension of longer passages than those found in most survey tests, diagnostic tests, or IRIs. In addition, analysis of individual miscues provides data about the degree to which students use sentence structure and background knowledge to gain meaning and the extent to which miscues may affect comprehension. That is, sometimes oral reading mistakes do not affect comprehension at all, and other times they certainly do! The RMI also affords a look at student self-correction. Analysis of self-corrections provides information about the propensity to read for understanding. However, a disadvantage in attempting to capitalize on self-correction data in assessing comprehension strategies, is that some students mentally self-correct a miscue, even though they do not do so orally.

Performance during the retelling of a story selection for the RMI demonstrates the student's proficiency in literal recall of characters and events, understanding of character development, grasp of overall plot, and ability to infer a theme. Effectiveness during retelling of an informational selection assesses memory for specific details, skill in forming generalizations based on stated facts, and ability to extract major concepts from the text.

Developing Teacher-Constructed Instruments and Procedures

Obviously, preparing your own tests and procedures is more time consuming than using published instruments, but doing so has the advantage of allowing teachers to devise assessments that do not contain some of the flaws found in conventional measures. Teachers can improve upon traditional comprehension tests by:

1. determining the types of prompts a student needs to comprehend material
2. designing questions that assess higher-level comprehension of many types
3. using free recall measures followed by probes

It is helpful to know the types of prompts a student needs to correctly answer comprehension questions.

Assessing Types of Prompts Needed. It is helpful for teachers to know the types of prompts a student needs to correctly answer comprehension questions. To investigate this, an assortment of selections is chosen, and questions are written in a multiple-choice format. Students read some passages orally and others silently. After reading, they orally read the alternative answers and attempt to designate the correct one. For those passages when an incorrect answer is chosen, the teacher asks questions and gives prompts as would be done in an instructional situation. The student's responses and the teacher's comments are tape-recorded for later analysis. The appraisal is then used to determine flaws in background knowledge or thinking strategies as well as the types of prompts needed.

Let's look at an example of this technique. See the **Vignette: Real Teachers in Action: Combining Teaching and Testing.**

Vignette: Real Teachers in Action

Combining Teaching and Testing

Mrs. Montgomery asks Bobby to read the following passage and choose the most appropriate response to multiple-choice items. This transcript shows a good example of scaffolding as she combines teaching and testing, assessing the types of prompts Bobby needs to better comprehend material at his instructional level and giving him suggestions for studying and test taking.

In 1849 when gold was discovered in California, many men in other parts of the country left their jobs and families to travel there. The journey to California was often long and hard, but they thought it was worth it. They believed they would strike it rich once they reached California. When these men, called forty-niners, arrived in California, one of the first things they did was to buy supplies

To determine the types of assistance students need to answer comprehension questions correctly, the teacher works with the student during an assessment session, asking questions and giving prompts as would be done in an instructional setting.

needed for mining gold. The most important of these was a mining pan. The miners would take this pan when they went out to try their luck at finding gold in streambeds. They would put water from the stream and sand from the streambed into the mining pan and shake it. Gold can be found in this way because it is heavier than sand and settles to the bottom of the pan while the sand still floats in the water. If the miners did find gold, it was usually in the form of the fine particles called gold dust, but sometimes they found a larger piece that was called a nugget. Many miners stayed in California for years and years before returning to their families. Some of these determined men did find gold, but only a few were found enough to become very rich.

What is the main point of this paragraph?

A. It is written to tell you some things about the forty-niners.
B. It is written to tell you why gold settles to the bottom of a pan.
C. It is written to tell you the year gold was discovered in California.
D. It is written to tell you two forms in which gold can be found.

This dialogue provides an example of assessing the types of prompts students need:

Bobby:	I think the answer's B.
Mrs. M.:	Why do you think so?
Bobby:	It says it in the story.
Mrs. M.:	It does say that, but I want you to read the question to me again.
Bobby:	"What is the main point of this paragraph?"
Mrs. M.:	When you read the question the first time, did you notice the word *main*?
Bobby:	(*Pause*) Not really.
Mrs. M.:	*Main* is a key word in the question. Often when you have to answer questions about what you've read, there's a key word that helps you get the correct answer. Did you know that, Bobby?
Bobby:	(*Laughter*) No.
Mrs. M.:	In this question, *main* is the key word. Do you know what the question is asking you when it asks for the *main* point?
Bobby:	(*Pause*) Important?

Mrs. M.:   Right. *Main* can mean important. So what is the question asking you if it asks you for the main point?

Bobby: The important point?

Mrs. M.:   Right! Or another way to say it is the major point.

Bobby: But it says that right here about the gold settling.

Mrs. M.:   You're right. It does. That *is* one thing that the passage tells you, but there are many other things the author told you, aren't there?

Bobby: Yes.

Mrs. M.:   That's just one small point that was made. When the question asks you for the main point, it wants you to figure out what the whole thing was about. Or, in other words, you could ask yourself, "What was the *main* reason the author wrote this? What was the overall idea he wanted me to learn from this?" What do you think it was?

Bobby: About those men, I guess, about what they did.

Mrs. M.:   Great! Now you've got it. Okay, read the answers to yourself again. Now which one do you think is right?

Bobby: None of them say anything about the men.

Mrs. M.:   Well, let's work on each answer together. Maybe I can help you. Read the first answer out loud to me.

Bobby: "It is written to tell you some things about the forty-niners."

Mrs. M.:   Do you understand that answer, Bobby?

Bobby: I guess so.

Mrs. M.:   Do you remember the paragraph saying anything about the forty-niners?

Bobby: (*Pause*) Yes . . .

Mrs. M.:   Well, let's find the part in the paragraph that mentions the forty-niners, and you read it out loud to me.

Bobby: "When these men, called forty-niners, arrived in California, one of the first things they did was to buy supplies needed for mining gold."

Mrs. M.:   What does the term *forty-niners* mean in that sentence?

Bobby: (*Long pause*) The men!

Mrs. M.:   Right! When you read the sentence the first time, did you realize the sentence was telling you the men were called forty-niners?

Bobby: No.

Mrs. M.:   What did you think it meant when it said, ". . . these men, called forty-niners . . ."?

Bobby: They called it. They said it.

Mrs. M.:   You mean you thought the men called something out? They called out, "Forty-niners"?

Bobby: Yeah.

Mrs. M.:   Okay. I tell you what, let me write a sentence for you that's almost like that, but is about something you're more familiar with. Watch what I write. (*Teacher writes sentence on paper.*) Read that to me.

Bobby: (*Reads sentence teacher just wrote.*) "Our school football team, called the Tigers, is the best team in town."

Mrs. M.:   What does *called* mean in this sentence?

Bobby: (*Rereads sentence silently.*) Named!

Mrs. M.:   Right! Look back at the sentence about forty-niners. Could *called* mean the same thing there?

Bobby: (*Reads sentence silently.*) Yeah. It does.

Mrs. M.:   Okay, let's look at answer A again. What do you think? Is it the right or wrong answer?

Bobby: (*Reads alternative A silently.*) Yeah. It's the right one 'cause the story's about the men.

Mrs. M.:   It seems to me you're right, but let's look at the other answers just to be sure there's not a better one. We've already decided B is not correct. Read C out loud to me.

Bobby: "It is written to tell you the year gold was discovered in California."

Mrs. M.:   What do you think? Right or wrong?

Bobby: Wrong, 'cause . . . (*Long pause*)

Mrs. M.:   Why?

Bobby: Well, it's just a small point.

Mrs. M.:   Super. It *does* tell when gold was discovered, doesn't it? But you're right. It's not the overall or major idea the author wanted you to learn about in this paragraph. What about D? Read that one to me.

Bobby: "It is written to tell you two forms in which gold can be found."

Mrs. M.:   What do you think?

Bobby: It tells you those and I think that's important, but it tells more than that and it's mostly about the men and what they did. (*Rereads alternative D silently.*) So D isn't the right answer.

Mrs. M.:   Excellent. And what happened to them? What did it say happened to the men in the end?

Bobby: Some got rich and some didn't.

Mrs. M.:   Right. Did more of them get rich or more not get rich?

Bobby: (*Has to reread last sentence of passage.*) More didn't.

Mrs. M.:   Super. Now read this next passage silently, and when you get done, I'll ask you to answer a question about it.

LEARNING FROM TEXT

Make a Prediction. When teachers use the procedure illustrated in the Vignette what can they learn?

When a teacher uses questions and prompts in this fashion, it is possible to learn much about students: their approaches to the comprehension task, their test-taking skills, the background knowledge they do or do not possess, the types of prompting necessary to help them understand material, their skills in dealing with written language structures, their abilities to generalize from familiar knowledge to the unfamiliar, and their readiness in picking up on instructional cues provided by the teacher. In short, the teacher can determine rather specifically what is preventing comprehension.

A variation of this process is suggested by Sammons and Davey (1993–94). Some clues about students' comprehension of expository material in content books (such as history, geography, and science) can be gained though an interview procedure they call the Textbook Awareness and Performance Profile (TAPP). In the first portion, students are asked what strategies they use to learn from a book they have been assigned to read in their regular classroom. Next, they are given specific tasks to carry out, such as summarizing, note taking, scanning, underlining, using headings and graphics, using the table of contents and index, and defining vocabulary. TAPP was designed as an assessment measure to be used in clinical and remedial classes so that comprehension instruction in those settings could complement the students' typical daily literacy needs.

Using a Variety of Types of Higher-Level Questions. Many formal tests fail to measure higher-level thinking processes except in a limited manner. One solution is for teachers to develop a series of questions based on the question categories proposed by Sanders (1966) and apply these to graded selections.

Some formal tests fail to measure higher-level thinking processes, except in a limited manner.

Sanders's categories were derived from Bloom's *Taxonomy of Educational Objectives* (1956, p. 3) and are listed here.

1. *Memory.* Recognizing and recalling information directly stated in the passage. Example: The story states that Susie had to wait after school for her mother to pick her up. The teacher asks, "Why did Susie wait after school when the rest of the children went home?"
2. *Translation.* Paraphrasing ideas. Example: The teacher asks the student to put into his or her own words the moral stated at the end of an African folktale.
3. *Interpretation.* Seeing relationships among facts or generalizations. Example: The teacher asks, "Based on what you have read so far, what evidence is there that this is a work of historical fiction?"
4. *Application.* Solving a problem that requires the use of facts or generalizations. Example: The teacher says, "Taking into account the information provided in this science passage, list the steps you would want to carry out for the bean seed you planted to grow."
5. *Analysis.* Recognizing and applying logic to a problem; analyzing an example of reasoning. Example: The teacher asks. "What do you think of Mafatu's solution to his problem of fear of the sea? Why?"
6. *Synthesis.* Using original, creative thinking to solve a problem. Example: The teacher asks, "What are some other ways Mafatu could have overcome his problem?"
7. *Evaluation.* Making judgments. Example: The teacher asks, "Now that you've read several of Chris Van Allsburg's books, which character do you think he has portrayed in the most interesting way? Why?"

Using Sanders's question categories extends the measurement of comprehension beyond responses to literal questions.

Self-Monitoring.   Knowledge of these question types is important for helping teachers raise their questions above the literal level. One of Sanders's questions is literal, however. Which one?

Applying What You've Learned.   Write a question of your own for each of Sanders's question types.

Using Free Recalls, Plus Probes.   Use of **free recalls,** sometimes called **retelling,** is another means for assessing comprehension. To use this fairly simple procedure, the teacher prepares an outline of significant information about the text students will read. The outline is available to the teacher, but not to students. After reading, students are simply asked to retell what they remember. The teacher carefully specifies the task demand; that is, students are directed to tell everything they recall to prevent superficial retellings.

Make a Prediction.   What are the purposes of *probes*?

To further minimize the problem of a cursory retelling, the teacher can follow up by asking about significant understandings the student has omitted from the retelling outline. The follow-up questions are called **probes.** The student's free recall and the answers to probes are tape-recorded. Later, the retelling outline is used in conjunction with the audiotape to analyze the student's performance.

There are several advantages to using free recall measures. They aid you in determining whether students have noted important information, whether they reproduce it in a coherent manner, and whether their background knowledge has an effect on the way they interpret the substance of the text.

These procedures also provide some insights about a student's short-term retention. In addition, if there is a delay between the time when students read some selections and the time when they are asked to retell, a measure of long-term retention can also be obtained. Another advantage is that the teacher's preparation is minimal.

One disadvantage to free recall is that students who do understand the material may nevertheless have difficulty adequately retelling the selection; they may not know where to begin or what sequence to follow in the retelling. This results in a disorganized retelling in which major details are overlooked, conveying the false impression that the student did not comprehend or recall the material. In these cases, the problem is with lack of skill in retelling, not with comprehension. This problem usually can be overcome if students receive some practice and training in retelling. Production problems can also result if students are asked to write their responses during a free recall; although they may understand the material, they may have trouble producing information in written form. When assessing students with poor academic skills, asking for oral responses is usually preferable.

A second disadvantage occurs if relying on free recalls without probes, since this often does not enable assessment of higher-level comprehension. In free recalls, students tend to report only facts and information directly stated in the selection. For example, it would be highly unusual for students during their retellings to say, "Oh, by the way, the theme of this story is _____," or, "Incidentally, an important generalization I drew from the information in this article is that _____." Therefore, using probes to follow up student retellings is important so that higher-level comprehension can be assessed.

Greater demand on memory is required during free recall than with multiple-choice questions. Students should always be told prior to reading a selection that they will be asked to retell it afterward. Four published tests that employ free recalls are the Reading Miscue Inventory (RMI), the Basic Reading Inventory, the Bader Reading and Language Inventory, and the Durrell Analysis of Reading Difficulty.

Teachers can extend free recall procedures beyond the ways in which they are commonly used in published instruments to incorporate these suggestions:

1. Include assessment after silent reading as well as after oral reading.
2. Include methods for measuring long-term retention along with short-term recall.

The best measure of a student's comprehension is gained through a combination of assessments.

A Final Word.   As with other areas, the best measure of a student's comprehension is gained through a combination of assessments. As Johnston (1983) states:

> Given the complexity of the reading task and the number of variables to be assessed and/or taken into account, I believe that a potentially more reasonable approach would be to refine and use the variety of approaches to measurement which we have available already, in the light of our knowledge of the skills and abilities involved in each, though we might want to add some supplementary approaches. By appropriately selecting combinations of these measures, we may gain a clearer picture of what and how a reader comprehends under a given set of circumstances. (p. 54)

ASSESSING METACOGNITION

LEARNING FROM TEXT

Setting a Purpose for Reading.   There is much interest lately in metacognition. Some university students find concepts related to this topic a bit *hard* to understand. One key to understanding is to know the usual definition of the overall concept, but also to realize that metacognition is made up of several factors. Once you can define metacognition *and* those related factors, note an assessment procedure that has been suggested to measure each.

Metacognition is important in all aspects of reading but has been explored most often in relation to comprehension.

Experts have studied comprehension intently to learn what teachers can do to help students better understand what they read. In doing so, they have learned that it is important for readers to engage in metacognitive activity. **Metacognition** can be defined as thinking (consciously) about one's own thinking. Metacognition is important in all aspects of reading, but has been explored most often in relation to comprehension.

Metacognitive activity has three major facets: (a) metacognitive awareness, that is, conscious knowledge about one's own thinking processes, about the specific demands of the task at hand, and about reading strategies; (b) monitoring, or self-appraisal to judge when understanding has broken down; and (c) strategy use, knowing when and why to match specific strategies to specific reading tasks—and doing so (Barr, Blachowicz, & Wogman-Sadow, 1995).

Metacognitive Awareness

Interviews have been suggested for determining students' knowledge about their own thinking (e.g., what is hard for a specific student and what is easy) and knowledge about the nature of reading and writing tasks (e.g., what is important in text and what is not). Garner (1992) proposes the following types of questions for a metacognitive awareness interview. Ask students:

1. Are any sentences in a paragraph more important than others?
2. Is it easier to retell a story if you tell it in your own words, or if you use the author's exact words?

3. Are reading to study and reading for fun the same thing?
4. What things does a person have to do to become a good reader?
5. What makes something difficult to read?
6. How do you answer a question in your textbook if you remember that you read about the topic, but you do not remember the answer?
7. How can you tell what an author thought was important in a passage?
8. How do you write a short summary of a long piece of text?
9. What do you do if you come to an unfamiliar word in something you're reading for homework?
10. How do you put something "in your own words"? (p. 239)

The Metacomprehension Strategy Index (MSI) was developed and validated to measure awareness of reading strategies. This instrument asks students to select statements that indicate important things they should do to aid understanding. The MSI includes 25 items; samples are given below.

1. **Before They Read**

    Example: Before I begin reading, it's a good idea to:
    a. see how many pages are in the story.
    b. look up all the big words in the dictionary.
    c. make some guesses about what I think will happen in the story.
    d. think about what has happened so far in the story. (p. 459)

2. **While They Are Reading**

    Example: While I'm reading, it's a good idea to:
    a. read the story very slowly so that I will not miss any important parts.
    b. read the title to see what the story is about.
    c. check to see if the pictures have anything missing.
    d. check to see if the story is making sense by seeing if I can tell what's happened so far. (p. 460)

3. **After They Have Read**

    Example: After I've read the story, it's a good idea to:
    a. count how many pages I read with no mistakes.
    b. check to see if there were enough pictures to go with the story to make it interesting.
    c. check to see if I met my purpose for reading the story.
    d. underline the causes and effects. (p. 461)

For this complete inventory, see Schmitt (1990).

Monitoring

Comprehension monitoring refers to students' awareness of when their comprehension has broken down.

To ascertain students' abilities to judge when understanding has gone awry, Paris, Wasik, and Turner (1991) and others advocate error detection tasks. Students are given paragraphs containing nonsense statements, sentences that are inconsistent with other information in the paragraph, or statements incompatible with common background knowledge. They are asked to underline anything that does not seem sensible to them. Paragraphs such as these are used.

The cat seemed yellow when you first saw her, although after looking carefully you could see one stripe of orange down her back. She was a good cat and we liked everything about her, except when she began to shed. At those times it was not pleasing to find tufts of black hair on the furniture and on our clothes.

While most people don't like turnips, I love them. Mashed and cooked with butter, I think they make a delicious dish. I always serve chopped turnips with our Thanksgiving turkey and my guests sometimes try to hide their dislike for them as they sip them from their coffee cups.

This comprehension monitoring task can be taken a step further by asking students to edit the paragraphs to make sense.

A self-appraisal of answer correctness also provides an evaluation of ability to monitor comprehension. Manzo and Manzo (1993) advise having students reinspect their answers after completing any test and to display confidence in the appropriateness of their responses by using this marking key:

(+) I'm fairly certain that this is correct.

(0) I'm uncertain of this response.

(−) I'm probably wrong on this item. (p. 120)

Manzo and Manzo call this "the response self-appraisal method."

Strategy Use

Although evaluation of metacognitive awareness may shed light on whether students have knowledge of helpful reading strategies, it is, of course, important to know if they take this knowledge to a higher stage and actually *use* the strategies to foster understanding. The assessment technique most frequently cited for judging strategy use is the **think-aloud.** A think-aloud is a routine in which readers self-report their thinking processes during reading. Sometimes this verbal report is made while they are reading (an *introspective report*); other times immediately after they have read (a *retrospective report*). Wade (1990) has delineated procedures for administering and scoring a comprehension think-aloud; these can be seen in Table 6–1.

Think-alouds have some limitations, as is true with all assessment procedures. These include the difficulties some students may have in expressing the strategies they use; in addition, others may be using strategies about which they are not consciously aware and, therefore, cannot specify them.

ASSESSING READING RATE

An unusually slow rate of reading can hinder comprehension (see the fluency section in Chapter 8). This is also true of an excessively rapid rate. If a teacher suspects that an inappropriate reading rate is compounding a student's reading problems, an assessment of reading rate may be included in the diagnostic procedures.

Formal Measures

When assessing reading rate, it is also important to evaluate comprehension of material at that rate.

Beginning at fourth-grade level, many group survey tests include a test of reading rate along with the usual vocabulary and comprehension subtests. Some IRIs also contain a rate measurement, such as the Basic Reading Inventory. All valid rate tests also require students to answer comprehension questions after

TABLE 6–1 *Procedure for Administering and Scoring a Comprehension Think-Aloud*

I. Preparing the Text

Choose a short passage (expository or narrative) written to meet the following criteria:

1. The text should be from 80 to 200 words in length, depending on the reader's age and reading ability.
2. The text should be new to the reader, but on a topic that is familiar to him or her. (Determine whether the reader has relevant background knowledge by means of an interview or questionnaire administered at a session prior to this assessment.)
3. The text should be at the reader's instructional level, which can be determined by use of an informal reading inventory. Passages at this level are most likely to be somewhat challenging while not overwhelming readers with word identification problems.
4. The topic sentence should appear last, and the passage should be untitled. Altering the text in this way will elicit information about the reader's strategies for making sense of the passage and inferring the topic.
5. The text should be divided into segments of one to four sentences each.

II. Administering the Think-Aloud Procedure

1. Tell the reader that he or she will be reading a story in short segments of one or more sentences.
2. Tell the reader that after reading each section, he or she will be asked to tell what the story is about.
3. Have the student read a segment aloud. After each segment is read, ask the reader to tell what is happening, followed by nondirective probe questions as necessary. The questions should encourage the reader to generate hypotheses (what do you think this is about?) and to describe what he or she based the hypotheses on (what clues in the story helped you?).
4. Continue the procedure until the entire passage is read. Then ask the reader to retell the entire passage in his or her own words. (The reader may reread the story first.)
5. The examiner might also ask the reader to find the most important sentence(s) in the passage.
6. The session should be tape-recorded and transcribed. The examiner should also record observations of the child's behaviors.

III. Analyzing Results

Ask the following questions when analyzing the transcript:

1. Does the reader generate hypotheses?
2. Does he or she support hypotheses with information from the passage?
3. What information from the text does the reader use?
4. Does he or she relate material in the text to background knowledge or previous experience?
5. Does the reader integrate new information with the schema he or she has already activated?
6. What does the reader do if there is information that conflicts with the schema he or she has generated?
7. At what point does the reader recognize what the story is about?
8. How does the reader deal with unfamiliar words?
9. What kinds of integration strategies does the reader use (e.g., visualization)?
10. How confident is the reader of his or her hypotheses?
11. What other observations can be made about the reader's behavior, strategies, and so on?

Source: Wade, Suzanne E. (1990, March). Using think alouds to assess comprehension. *The Reading Teacher, 37(7),* 442–451. Reprinted with permission of Suzanne E. Wade and the International Reading Association.

reading the timed passages since any measure of rate is useless without information on whether students understand what they read at that rate. Rapid word recognition is not helpful if readers do not comprehend the information.

Informal Measures

Informal tests of reading rate also may be used. To do this, the teacher asks the student to silently read a story or informational selection of appropriate

DIBELS is a test of oral reading fluency that measures accuracy, rate, and comprehension in connected text. DIBELS, also available in Spanish, includes additional subtests of phonemic awareness, alphabetic-principle knowledge, and word fluency. For a free download of this test, go to http://dibels.uoregon.edu/

instructional level. At the end of a specified time—for example, 5 minutes—the teacher calls "stop," and the student places a slash mark after the last word read. Rate (words per minute) is determined by dividing the total number of words read by the number of minutes:

$$\frac{\text{Words per minute (WPM)}}{\text{Number of minutes} \;|\; \text{Total number of words read}}$$

Comprehension should also be checked.

Because good reading requires that students vary their rates of reading according to the material and purpose, informal rate assessments should be conducted with different types of material, and readers should be given different purposes for reading. For example, 5-minute rate samples could be taken when the student is reading narrative material, reading selections from content area materials such as history or science texts, skimming an article to determine its overall purpose, or reading to answer several factual questions.

ASSESSING ATTITUDES AND INTERESTS

Conducting an assessment of students' attitudes about reading and their interests in general can help in planning instruction.

Measuring Attitudes Toward Reading

Attitude toward reading has a high relationship with amount of voluntary reading.

An important principle for helping students increase their reading proficiency is to have them engage in a great deal of connected text reading—that is, reading an abundance of whole stories, chapters, articles, and so on. Obviously, teachers must include this critical component daily in their instructional programs, but also, students who do additional reading outside of class usually improve in reading performance more rapidly than those who do not. Attitude toward reading has a high relationship with amount of voluntary reading.

Several reading attitude scales are available. On the popular Estes Attitude Scale (Estes, 1971), which has been validated for students in grades 3 through 12, students rank a list of statements from A to E to indicate attitudes ranging from "strongly agree" to "strongly disagree" (see Figure 6–1). This scale may be readministered after a period of remediation to determine if changes in attitudes have occurred.

For students reading at third-grade level and below, Johns (1982) suggests that statements be read orally to them and that they mark their responses on an answer sheet by circling the appropriate face:

$$(\; \odot \quad \odot \;)$$

Statements he suggests for use with primary students are:

I can read as fast as the good readers.
I like to read.
I like to read long stories.
The books I read in school are too hard.
I need more help in reading.

FIGURE 6–1   ***The Estes Attitude Scale***

| A = Strongly agree | C = Undecided | E = Strongly disagree |
| B = Agree | D = Disagree | |

1. Reading is for learning but not for enjoyment.
2. Money spent on books is well spent.
3. There is nothing to be gained from reading books.
4. Books are a bore.
5. Reading is a good way to spend spare time.
6. Sharing books in class is a waste of time.
7. Reading turns me on.
8. Reading is only for grade grubbers.
9. Books aren't usually good enough to finish.
10. Reading is rewarding to me.
11. Reading becomes boring after about an hour.
12. Most books are too long and dull.
13. Free reading doesn't teach anything.
14. There should be more time for free reading during the school day.
15. There are many books which I hope to read.
16. Books should not be read except for class requirements.
17. Reading is something I can do without.
18. A certain amount of summer vacation should be set aside for reading.
19. Books make good presents.
20. Reading is dull.

| | Response Values | | | | |
Items	A	B	C	D	E
The negative items: Nos. 1, 3, 4, 6, 8, 9, 11, 12, 13, 16, 17, 20	1	2	3	4	5
The positive items: Nos. 2, 5, 7, 10, 14, 15, 18, 19	5	4	3	2	1

Source: From Estes, Thomas H. (1971, November). A scale to measure attitudes toward reading. *Journal of Reading, 15(2),* 135–138. Reprinted with permission of Thomas H. Estes and the International Reading Association.

I worry quite a bit about my reading in school.

I read at home.

I would rather read than watch television.

I am a poor reader.

I like my parents to read to me. (p. 5)

These two procedures measure attitudes by having students rank statements. Attitudes can also be measured through direct observation by the teacher.

Measuring General Interests

Knowing areas of student interest can help teachers select material students will enjoy reading. **Interest inventories** consist of statements to complete or questions to answer so students can express their likes and dislikes. See the accompanying boxed material ***STEPS—Administering Assessments in Your Own Classroom: An Interest Inventory*** for procedures in planning and administering such an inventory.

STEPS: ADMINISTERING ASSESSMENTS IN YOUR OWN CLASSROOM

An Interest Inventory

STEP 1 Plan to use an interest inventory the first time you meet with a student. This is an excellent way to break the ice with shy or reluctant pupils. Many teachers also choose to administer such an inventory at the first meeting because information obtained helps in planning subsequent sessions.

Oral Administration

STEP 2 Sometimes, use oral administration: Plan for questions and answers to be given orally. It is particularly engaging for many students if you use a tape recorder to simulate a radio or TV interview. (Oral administration may be the best course of action if you know nothing about a student's literacy skills, since this lessens the chance of student embarrassment.)

STEP 3 Prepare questions ahead of time (extemporaneous questions logical to include as a result of students' responses also add interest). Use some of these (omitting or adding as seems appropriate for your students):

What do you like to do most after school and on the weekends?

What do you like best in school?

What is your favorite TV program?

What do you like to do with your family?

What is your favorite sport?

Are there any kinds of animals you like?

What is your favorite activity during recess?

What do you and your friends do together?

If someone granted you three wishes, what would you wish?

Has your family ever taken a vacation? Where did you go?

What do you like to read about most?

Written Administration

STEP 4 Sometimes, use written administration: Plan for questions and responses to be written. A written inventory can convey details on interests and attitudes and, as well, yield a brief sample of spelling and writing behaviors early in the assessment process.

STEP 5 A form listing questions like those suggested for oral administration can be used. Or—more appealing to many students—a written inventory similar to that seen in Figure 6–2 can be designed.

📖 OBTAINING BACKGROUND INFORMATION ABOUT STUDENTS

As a part of the assessment process, it is valuable to obtain background information about the student to consider variables outside as well as within the learner that may have a bearing on progress. It is common practice for teachers

FIGURE 6-2 **A Written Interest Inventory**

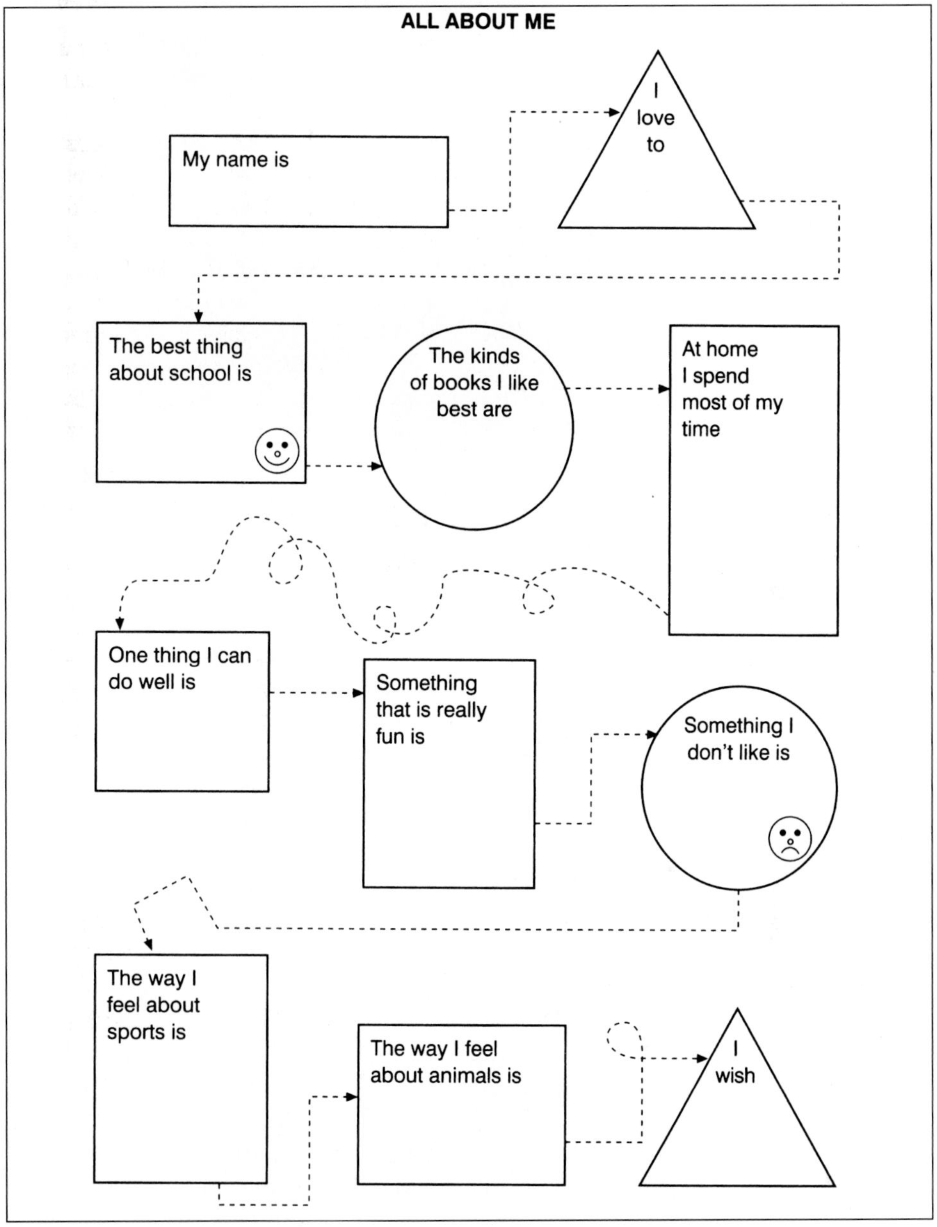

ALL ABOUT ME

My name is

I love to

The best thing about school is

The kinds of books I like best are

At home I spend most of my time

One thing I can do well is

Something that is really fun is

Something I don't like is

The way I feel about sports is

The way I feel about animals is

I wish

working in reading clinics to obtain this information by interviewing parents and by talking with other teachers who work with a student they are assessing and instructing.

Parent interviews can contribute information on a number of relevant factors such as the student's home experiences with literacy events (hearing stories read, activities involving writing, and so on) and the amount of parental support that can be expected in academic pursuits.

Interviews with other teachers may confirm assessment results obtained by the reading teacher and may prompt collaborative effort to alleviate a student's

Reading specialists often begin their first session with a student by conducting an interest inventory; this helps the student to relax, and, also, provides guidance for future lessons.

problems. Conversely, they may show that reading behaviors in a regular class-room setting are different from those seen in a small group or one-to-one situation, and realization of these differences may initiate informative discussion helpful to all teachers involved as to why this is so. Among the information to be shared are types of instruction to which a student has not responded along with topics, activities, and materials that foster the student's motivation. Observation of the student at work within his or her regular classroom also is recommended.

PERFORMANCE ASSESSMENT

One favored type of informal evaluation, called **performance assessment,** seeks to make assessment tasks authentic—that is, to design the content and format of the measures as close as possible to real reading situations. Several of the specific tests and procedures discussed in this chapter and in Chapter 5 may be categorized as types of performance assessment. The following section considers performance assessment generically in terms of general assessment approaches that may be used throughout a program to gain perspective about *all* forms of reading behaviors. Most often, performance assessment involves informal techniques; however, some published measures are available based on this evaluation perspective. One such example is included in *Test Bank J.*

LEARNING FROM TEXT

Using Textual Features. How do you define *performance assessment*? Use the boldface type to help you find and review the definition.

A TEACHING RESOURCE

TEST BANK J

A Published Performance-Based Assessment

Name	For Grades	Type of Administration	Time for Administration	Publisher
Diagnostic Assessments of Reading with Trial Teaching Strategies (DARTTS)	1–2	Individual	50–60 minutes	Riverside

FIGURE 6–3 *Example of a Checklist Used During Observation*

Reading Checklist

Name: _____Jenny_____

Date: _____Dec. 6_____

Situation: _____Oral reading individually to me_____

No   1. Omitted words after *inspecting* them

Yes   2. Omitted words because of *rapid reading*

No   3. Self-corrected when omissions caused a change in meaning

No   4. Appeared to be relaxed during the activity

Classroom Observation

Observations undertaken systematically and carefully analyzed to identify *patterns* of a student's significant reading behaviors serve as a form of performance assessment.

Some tools teachers use during observation are checklists, participation charts, and rating scales. **Checklists** consist of statements used to record specific behaviors; the teacher simply checks off or writes *Yes* or *No* to indicate their presence or absence during a particular observation (see the example in Figure 6–3). A variation of a checklist, called a **participation chart,** can be used when several students are observed (see Figure 6–4). Unlike a simple checklist, **rating scales** (like the one in Figure 6–5) allow the teacher to record quality or frequency of behavior.

The observation form seen in Figure 6–6 has yet another advantage: It allows teachers to record observations across settings. This specific **across-contexts observation form** could be employed with primary-grade students in reading classes or in LD classes.

FIGURE 6–4 *Example of a Participation Chart Used During Observation*

Reading Participation Chart

Situation: _Teacher-directed group of four students; expository passage_

Date: _October 11_

		Karen	Marc	Bob	Al
1.	Participated in prereading discussion	✔	✔		✔
2.	Made attempt to predict story or passage events	✔			✔
3.	Began reading when directed to do so	✔	✔		✔
4.	Read attentively without obvious mind wandering	✔	✔	✔	✔
5.	*Volunteered* information in follow-up discussion	✔	✔		✔
6.	Appeared uncomfortable when *asked* to answer questions			✔	

FIGURE 6–5 *Example of a Rating Scale Used During Observation*

Reading Rating Scale

Name: _Sara_

Date: _May 6_

Situation: _Oral reading of first story in a new book; group situation_

		Yes	Most of the Time	Sometimes	No
1.	Did the student make miscues on words already known to him or her?			✔	
2.	Did the student self-correct?		✔		
3.	Did the student use appropriate word identification strategies when a word was unknown to him or her?			✔	
4.	Did the student appear to be interested in the story/passage?	✔			

LEARNING FROM TEXT

Using Illustrative Aids. As you read the following section, use the strategy of switching back and forth between the figure and the text.

FIGURE 6–6   ***Across-Contexts Observation Form***

Description of child's work and behavior for each context (cite specific indications of skills or knowledge)	
Settings and Activities	*Examples of Child's Activities*
Story Time: Teacher reads to class (responses to story line; child's comments, questions, elaborations)	
Independent Reading: Book Time (nature of books child chooses or brings in; process of selecting; quiet or social reading)	
Writing (journal stories; alphabet; dictation)	
Reading Group/Individual (oral reading strategies; discussion of text; responses to instruction)	
Reading-Related Activities/Tasks (responses to assignments or discussion focusing on word/letter properties, word games/experience charts)	
Informal Settings (use of language in play, jokes, storytelling, conversation)	
Books and Print as Resource (use of books for projects; attention to signs, labels, names; locating information)	
Other	

Source: From Chittenden, Edward, & Courtney, Rosalea. (1989). Assessment of young children's reading: Documentation as an alternative to testing. From *Emerging Literacy: Young Children Learn to Read and Write,* Dorothy S. Strickland and Lesley Mandel Morrow (Eds.), IRA, pp. 107–120. Reprinted with permission of the International Reading Association.

Using the observation form in Figure 6–6, the teacher might make written notation of Shawna's highly motivated responses during story time when the teacher reads to the children, noting her intelligent interpretation of the story line. During independent reading time, he may observe that Shawna chooses books readily, especially fairy tales and folktales, but only looks at the pictures. During writing time, the teacher might note that Shawna willingly participates, but exhibits spelling behaviors at a level more consistent with those typically found in preschool children. In reading group time, the teacher's written observation may reveal that, while Shawna shows extreme reluctance to read orally before the group, she offers astute comments in interpreting meanings underlying the story's message gained from careful listening while other students read. During reading-related activities/tasks, the teacher might note that Shawna's fear of taking risks in oral reading activities subsides a great deal when gamelike activities are used for practicing letter-sound correspondences or for learning new words. In informal settings, the teacher may record that Shawna's oral language skills seem well developed, even advanced, and she is outgoing and confident. In the category of using books and print as resources, the teacher may indicate that he sees little evidence of this in Shawna's case.

Examination of the teacher's comments from this sample observation form begins to build a picture of a bright little girl, interested in books, with excellent oral language skills, who is self-possessed and well adjusted in situations *other than* those in which she is required to read. The teacher's written notations indicate no difficulties with comprehension, but rather that Shawna's problems lie with word recognition and word identification as seen both in reading and writing activities. Clues to interests and motivators also are evident in her choice of books (fairy tales and folktales) and in the lessening of feelings of stress when activities take on a gamelike character.

This structured type of classroom observation focuses on qualitative, not merely quantitative, information.

> Structured classroom observation focuses on qualitative, not merely quantitative, information.

Process Assessment

Process assessment (also called **dynamic assessment**), when viewed in-progress, seems a coalescence of testing and teaching. If a student is unable to respond correctly to a test item, the teacher presents the item differently or gives additional information. If the student remains unsuccessful, a different manner of presentation is tried or even more information added until the correct response is forthcoming. If a student is unable to demonstrate a reading strategy within a given passage, the teacher may even model it with that passage and then ask the student to apply it in a different reading selection. The vignette you read earlier in this chapter provided an example of Mrs. Montgomery employing process assessment when she undertook a comprehension assessment with Bobby.

The purpose of process assessment is not only to determine the student's functioning level in the area being tested, but also to ascertain conditions under which this individual learns best. Popularized by Israeli psychologist Reuven Feuerstein, process assessment has also been explored in Europe, North America, and Australia as an assessment alternative.

Process assessment provides insights into: (a) the amount of guidance needed, (b) the type of guidance needed, and (c) the need for further intervention. It is conducted as a collaborative effort between examiner and student.

One published, individually administered test battery that employs a form of process assessment is the Diagnostic Assessments of Reading with Trial Teaching Strategies (DARTTS). With this test battery, after assessment of six areas of reading and language, the teacher determines, through a set of trial teaching methods and materials, those suitable for students who performed poorly on the subtests.

LEARNING FROM TEXT

Summarize. Condense the information about process assessment by paraphrasing in one sentence an answer to this question: What is meant by the statement that process assessment is a coalescence of testing and teaching?

FIGURE 6–7 *A Literacy Portfolio*

Portfolio Assessment

Using portfolios is another example of performance assessment. As you may remember from an earlier section, a **portfolio** is a large folder containing frequently collected samples of a student's work. A literacy portfolio might contain such items as daily assigned work completed at school or home, tapes of oral reading, or computer disks that provide samples of writing performance (see Figure 6–7).

The notion of collecting samples of student's work is not a new one. William S. Gray, an early and noted authority on reading, suggested in the very first issue of the *Journal of Educational Research* (Gray, 1920) that a monthly sampling of students' oral reading behaviors be accumulated to make possible the identification of (a) patterns of need and (b) patterns of growth. Today the portfolio has become a popular idea for just those reasons—because it allows both *ongoing assessment* and documentation of *progress*—from the beginning to the end of a program, both vital considerations for teachers of delayed readers.

Moreover, portfolios may be the focus of conferences with parents and the student's regular classroom teacher. For example, playing a short tape from the portfolio on which oral reading behaviors have been recorded over the course of time can dramatically demonstrate a student's development.

> One worthwhile procedure of portfolio assessment involves students in self-evaluations of their own products.

One worthwhile procedure of portfolio assessment involves students in self-evaluations of their own products. Teachers schedule brief, but regular, conferences in which "reflective interviews" about the samples of work are undertaken. Paris et al. (1992) suggest these types of general questions in student-teacher conferences:

- Here is a sample of your writing that you did this week. Are you finished with it? What do you like about this piece? What would you change to make it better? Did other students in the class help you to write or revise it?

TABLE 6–2 *Samples of Items That Might Be Found in a Literacy Portfolio*

- Audiotapes of oral reading or of story conferences
- Computer disks containing writing samples
- Comments by student, reflecting self-evaluation
- Different forms of student writing (stories, poems, informational pieces, and so on)
- Several revisions of the same piece of writing, as well as the final product
- Informal reading tests
- Literature logs (lists of books read)
- Charts showing number of pages read
- Journals
- Teacher's notes from reading/writing conferences
- Student's opinions about stories and nonfiction material (written or taped)
- Story discussions that reflect degree of understanding and types of prompts needed (audiotaped)
- Student-dictated stories, written by the teacher

- What book have you read this week? Tell me about it. How did it make you feel? Was there anything surprising in the book?
- Do you think you are a good reader and writer? What makes someone a really good reader? When you think of yourself as a reader, what would you like to do differently or better? (p. 95)

Frequently students, with the teacher, make decisions about which samples of work will be included in the portfolio. This adds the extra advantage of student motivation to do well in areas targeted for inclusion. Sometimes students even voluntarily do extra work at home because they want to add to their portfolios.

In many cases, multiple samples of the same targeted area should be acquired systematically across time, so processes, as well as products, can be evaluated. Materials should be dated to indicate when they were placed in the portfolio. See Table 6–2 for a listing of some of the many items a literacy portfolio might contain.

Based on the portfolio, the teacher can evaluate amount of reading, changes in oral reading strategies, comprehension, growth in word knowledge, students' perceptions of their own growth and needs, skill in various types of writing, types of books enjoyed, and other areas crucial for instructional decisions.

Note Taking. List as many reasons as you can why portfolio assessment might be useful in programs for delayed readers.

Using Illustrative Aids. What's new with David Adams? Read the text, read the figure, read the text, read the figure.

David's Case Study (continued)

At this point, let us assume that initial evaluation procedures with our hypothetical student, David Adams, for whom we have been developing an assessment case study, have been completed. In doing so, the teacher has used several appraisal processes described in Chapters 5 and 6. Examine the additional notations placed on his assessment information form, illustrated in Figure 6–8.

Details in this figure indicate that two tests of high-frequency word knowledge were administered to David, one with the words assessed in context and one with the words in isolation. Both substantiated the brief, preliminary evidence from his earlier IRI, with all three tests pointing to David's need to develop more accurate and automatic recognition of words.

In addition, a word identification strategies inventory was administered. It directed attention to many areas where instruction is needed, also confirming the results of the IRI, but extending those findings in a way useful for planning instruction. David's performance on this latter test allows the teacher to determine areas of phonic analysis and areas of structural analysis where he demonstrates strengths and others where intervention is indicated. Note in the teacher's written comments in Figure 6–8 just what these specific areas are. The RMI results, also recorded there, corroborate other findings: David's miscues disrupted his comprehension of several important elements as he read the story, and he showed a propensity to substitute graphically similar words for the actual text words in many cases, with no self-correction.

As can be seen, the teacher undertook an informal measure of comprehension by having David orally read many of the passages he had previously read silently on the standardized reading test. In doing so, she noted trouble he had in recognizing words in the test selections, in the questions, and in the alternative answers. When assisted with these words, David could answer many questions correctly that he had missed in the original administration of the test. This again leads to the conclusion that the major stumbling block preventing David from reading at grade placement is not with comprehension, but with word recognition and word identification strategies. There were signs, however, that some attention to higher-level comprehension would be useful.

The measures of interests and attitudes reported in Figure 6–8 show that David is aware of his reading difficulties, but that serious problems of motivation have not yet set in. He wants to learn to read better, and this may assist the teacher to move him along more quickly to realizing his potential. In addition, knowing what pastimes and pursuits interest David will guide the teacher in selecting materials in which he will be willing to invest effort.

David's assessment information form concludes with background information the teacher obtained from his parents, from other teachers, and from observations of David while in his regular classroom. One conclusion from this part of the data-gathering process is that David's parents can be a source of assistance. Their sensitivities in exposing David to good books by reading aloud to him and enrolling him in a summer library program may be one reason why David remains interested in reading despite his problems. For example, their help could be enlisted by asking them to provide time for David to read short, easy books to them each day at home.

Reflections by his classroom teacher reveal a concern for David and note that many important adjustments are being made for him. At the same time, this teacher does not have time to furnish adequate individual instruction to meet his requirements, which are untypical of other students in the class. Therefore, the special attention David will receive in the small-group situation of the reading class will be especially critical. By observing David in his regular classroom and by examining notations from previous teachers in his school records, the reading teacher has confirmed her own observations as well as those reported by the present classroom teacher.

David's Case Study (continued)

David has many strengths (e.g., his interest in writing stories and in listening to stories read aloud), and these can be built upon in planning his program. The information provided by other teachers, as well as the on-site observation, gives additional clues to weaknesses that must be alleviated.

FIGURE 6–8   *A Record Form of Assessment Information for a Hypothetical Student*

Assessment Information Form

Student's Name: David Adams

Grade Level: 4th

Chronological Age:

   1)   Birthdate   February 19, 19—

   2)   Age   9.0

Listening Comprehension Level:

   1)   Method of determination   use of graded IRI passages

   2)   Level   4th grade

Entry-Level Assessment Results: 2nd grade

Standardized Survey Test:

   1)   Name of test   Gates-MacGinitie Reading Tests, Level 2, Form S

   2)   Grade score obtained   3.0

Present Reading Instructional Level (based on standardized test results):   Approximately 2.0

Discrepancy Between Listening Level and Present Achievement: 2.0

Verification of General Reading Levels:

   1)   Name of test   Analytical Reading Inventory

   2)   Grade scores obtained   Frustration level—approximately 2.5 and above

                                                    Instructional level—approximately 2.0

                                                    Independent level—approximately 1.0

Specific Strengths and Weaknesses in Reading Knowledge, Strategies, and Skills:

A.   An analysis of strengths and weaknesses determined from David's IRI performance is attached to this Assessment Information Form, along with implications for instruction.

B.   Knowledge of basic sight vocabulary

   1.   On a contextual inventory, David confused 24 words with similar words.

   2.   On a test of words in isolation, David was unable to pronounce 5 words and confused 37 others with similar words.

   3.   Specific words from both tests that David did not know and those he confused with others are listed on a sheet attached to this Assessment Information Form.

FIGURE 6–8 *(continued)*

C. Knowledge and use of word identification strategies
  1. An informal assessment confirmed the finding from the IRI that David does not use context clues to identify unknown words, nor does he seem to have any concept of this strategy.
  2. On a teacher-prepared instrument, strengths in phonic analysis knowledge were seen for
     a. consonant sounds
     b. blends (clusters)
     c. consonant digraphs
     d. naming of vowels
     e. long vowel sounds

  Weaknesses were seen for

     a. short vowel sounds
     b. sounds of r-controlled vowels
     c. combinations with silent letters
     d. use of consonant substitution in combination with phonograms
     e. special vowel combinations
  3. On a teacher-prepared instrument, strengths in structural analysis were seen for
     a. use of inflectional endings
     b. reading contractions and matching these to the words from which they were derived

  Weaknesses were seen for

     a. identifying compound words
     b. identifying words when their spellings were changed before adding an inflectional ending
     c. dividing words into syllables
     d. recognizing prefixes
     e. recognizing suffixes

Specific phonic and structural analysis information David did and did not know is listed on a sheet attached to this Assessment Information Form.

D. Performance on the Reading Miscue Inventory
  1. Most of David's miscues resulted from substituting a graphically similar word for the text word. David self-corrected only 2 of the 25 miscues that were analyzed, even though 15 of these resulted in a loss or partial loss of the intended meaning.
  2. Percentage scores for comprehension were
     a. No loss—40%
        Partial loss—14%
        Loss—46%
  3. Percentage scores for use of grammatical relationships were
        Strength—24%
        Partial strength—30%
        Weaknesses—46%
        Overcorrection—0%
  4. Retelling
     a. Score ___59___
     b. Strengths were seen in recall of characters and remembering events.

(continued)

    c. Weaknesses were seen in stating the overall plot of the story and identifying the theme.

    d. He had some difficulty stating information related to character development because of two miscues he made throughout the story, which caused a misinterpretation of important information.

E. Comprehension assessment

In addition to analysis of comprehension performance on the IRI and RMI, two additional assessments were carried out.

1. David was asked to orally read passages and answer questions from the comprehension subtest of the group standardized survey test that had been used during assessment for identification. This oral assessment showed that the majority of his difficulties on this test had stemmed from word recognition and identification problems. Questions were answered incorrectly because he confused words or could not identify many of them. When the teacher told him the correct word, he was usually able to answer the question. On a few questions, he was unable to respond correctly, even with this assistance. When asked why he responded as he did on these latter questions, he appeared confused by the task of being asked to draw an inference and was attempting to find the answer directly stated in the passage.

2. David was asked to read silently a story selected from a basal reader at his instructional level and then retell it. His retelling was followed by probes. This assessment was used to compare his performance with his retelling after oral reading on the RMI. His performance was somewhat better after silent reading, but only slightly.

F. Measures of attitudes and interests

1. An informal measure of reading attitudes was conducted. David believes he is a poor reader and needs more help in reading, but still says he likes reading and being read to.

2. An interest inventory revealed that

    a. David loves anything having to do with football—playing it, reading about it, watching it on TV. He hopes to be a football player, like his brother, when he gets to middle school.

    b. He likes animals of all kinds. He owns two cats (Scruffy and Stripes) and two ducks (Sally and Ronald). He says he likes to write stories about his animals and likes to look at books that have pictures of animals from Africa.

    c. If he could have three wishes they would be

       1) to get a 10-speed bike

       2) for his sister to leave his stuff alone, and

       3) to have muscles.

3. On Saturday mornings he loves to watch cartoons on TV.

4. In school he likes math, gym, music, and studying about "people of long ago" best.

5. His family takes summer vacations and he loves going to the beach and going fishing.

G. Background information

1. *From David's parents:* David's parents report that there have been no serious illnesses during his preschool and early school years. They have routinely read aloud to David, on most nights providing a bedtime story. In summers since age 4, he has belonged to a library book club where experiences with high-quality children's literature are provided to small groups of children once a week. Mr. and Mrs. Adams try to help David with work sent home from school, but recently he has been reluctant to accept their help, balking and exhibiting avoidance behaviors. The lack of concentration seen during these attempts to assist with most homework is not seen when they read to him or when he is looking at or reading easy books related to topics of great interest to him.

FIGURE 6-8 *(continued)*

2. *From other teachers:* David's classroom teacher says he has had a reputation in the school for having a nice disposition. Though he has a lively nature, he previously has been cooperative. At present, however, she is noticing many off-task behaviors and little effort in many reading-related activities. Her literature-based reading program provides the class much exposure to good books that David enjoys when this involves listening activities, but he is increasingly unable to use many of the books the other students are enjoying in independent activity because of his limitations in word recognition and identification. Because these problems are not characteristic of other pupils in the class, the teacher does not provide time for direct instruction in these areas. She would like to furnish David with individual help, but has difficulty finding time considering the number of students in her class. She gives him some extra attention but worries that it is not enough. The results of her assessments of his reading abilities are similar to ours, and she says when she is occasionally able to find suitable books for their current literature theme which are about two years below the level the other students are reading, David is able to participate more fully. He does engage in writing activities, but she notes that his spelling behaviors are characteristic of those of a younger child.

Observation of David during one morning in his classroom confirmed much of this information. During that time he engaged in no actual reading of text himself, but listened avidly when others were reading favorite parts of the book on which the class was currently focusing. He wandered aimlessly about the room quite a bit, but was diligent in his efforts during a 20-minute math lesson.

Examination of his school records revealed notations by previous teachers indicating slow progress in letter recognition, in gaining control of letter-sound correspondences, and in developing an adequate knowledge of basic words. Although progress was seen in all grades, every teacher had indicated his advancement in these areas was not commensurate with that of other students.

ASSESSMENT PROCEDURES THAT ARE NOT USEFUL

As noted, there are no perfect assessment instruments or procedures for evaluating reading. Even the best techniques available have shortcomings, but when employed judiciously and in combination with other measures, most provide some helpful information.

However, there are some observational tests occasionally suggested for reading programs that simply are not useful. These tests lack value because they are based on faulty ideas or theories about reading and the reading process; their procedures and interpretations are in conflict with research evidence.

In previous sections of this text, some tests that should be avoided have been discussed. Observational procedures to bypass are listed in Table 6–3, along with reasons for their inadequacies.

TABLE 6–3 *Some Observational Tests and Their Inadequacies*

Observational Tests	Test Inadequacies
Tests of visual tracking of a moving object	Ability to visually track a moving object is unrelated to reading ability.
Tests of balance	Balance is unrelated to reading ability.
Tests of eye-hand coordination	Eye-hand coordination is not related to reading ability.
Tests of left-right discrimination	Ability to distinguish between left and right is unrelated to reading ability.
Tests of lateral dominance	Lateral dominance is not related to reading.

The Suitcase Story

It is said that the novice reading teacher or LD teacher arrives at his or her classroom with a suitcase full of reading tests to administer to each student. As time goes by, the teacher begins leaving some of these tests at home. This is possible because more information is obtained during the administration of just a few tests than had been possible early in the teacher's experience: Many incidences of giving tests, over time, heightened the teacher's perceptiveness about numerous reading behaviors that can be observed on any test.

As more time passes, fewer and fewer tests are used as the teacher's skills grow at noting a range of implications from a student's responses, and at thoughtfully asking questions about those responses, going beyond the questions on a specific test being used. Increasing familiarity with student developmental patterns, and with curricular requirements, builds sophistication in analyzing small samples of reading behavior. What, in the beginning of the teacher's test-administration experience, might have seemed only a small kernel of information now furnishes multiple insights.

Astute consideration during assessment—especially when coupled with daily observation in real instructional context—eventually allows the teacher to pare down the number of necessary tests to one or two.

*R*eflections

1. Several criteria suggested for high-quality assessment (e.g., Valencia, McGinley, & Pearson, 1990) are that content and process be: (a) authentic, (b) collaborative, (c) continuous, and (d) multifaceted. What does each of these mean?
2. Compare these criteria to assessment procedures you read about in this and the three preceding chapters. Which tests or procedures would meet one or more of these criteria?

INSTRUCTIONAL INTERVENTIONS

7

Important Principles of Instruction for Delayed Readers

Research on cognition indicates cooperative learning has potential for all learners.

*T*his chapter presents instructional principles that should be considered by reading educators to promote successful reading growth. It also discusses the logistics of organizing and managing remedial and clinical reading programs. It focuses on those teacher tasks, decisions, and behaviors necessary to arrange the learning environment to ensure effective learning. In addition, all principles in this chapter are useful for achieving the goal that no child be left behind.

PRINCIPLES

Principle One: Begin Early

Early intervention is crucial for students who are showing evidence of delays in learning to read. In times past, this was not considered the critical principle that it is today. Previously educators believed that, certain young students simply were not "ready" to learn to read and that, given the curative of time, they would mature into a readiness to do so. However, this conventional wisdom has not been borne out by research (e.g., Juel, 1988). Although it is certainly true that students begin reading acquisition on slightly variable schedules, if delays appear to be outside the normal range, simply waiting for students to catch up is not effective (Clay, 1979; Johnston & Allington, 1991).

Several of the most successful current programs dealing with children who are not progressing adequately in reading share as a central tenet the plan to intervene as soon as a lag is apparent. One such example is the Reading Recovery Program begun in New Zealand (Clay, 1979) and adopted widely with first-grade children throughout the United States (Pinnell, 1989). The Reading Recovery Program initiates instruction with first graders who are below the average of their classes before inappropriate reading behaviors can be firmly entrenched. Reading Recovery, which is undertaken with children who are in the lowest 20% of their classes, is viewed as a preventive tutoring program. The components of this early instruction are described in Figure 7–1, as seen from the point of view of a child. Those components involve connected text reading, development of multiple reading strategies, and writing.

While Reading Recovery implements one-to-one tutoring, Early Intervention in Reading (EIR) is a small-group, early intervention approach that has shown success with struggling first-grade readers (Taylor, Short, Shearer, & Frye, 1995). See Figure 7–2 for components of this program.

See Hiebert and Taylor (2000) for a comprehensive review of a number of other early intervention programs.

LEARNING
FROM TEXT

Verbal Rehearsal. Suppose parents of a child who is not yet reading after a year of reading instruction come to you with a question. These parents are worried, but a neighbor has told them that some children just aren't ready to read at that age, and they should relax and wait until the child matures a bit. They want to know if this is correct. Formulate the response you would give them.

FIGURE 7–1 *Reading Recovery Lesson*

HI! WELCOME TO MY READING RECOVERY LESSON

Fluent Writing Practice

Before my 30-minute lesson begins, I get to write some words on the chalkboard. I'm learning to write little important words as fast as I can so I can write them in my stories. It's fun to write on the chalkboard!

Rereading Familiar Books

In every lesson, every day, I get to read lots of little books. I get to pick some of my favorite stories that I have read before. This is easy for me. I try to read my book like a story and make it sound like people are talking. My teacher says "That's good reading; that's how good readers read."

Taking a Running Record

Now I have to read a book all by myself! My teacher will check on me and won't help me unless I have a hard problem. If I just can't figure out a word or I get all mixed up, my teacher will tell me the word or say, "Try that again." I read this book yesterday. My teacher helped me work hard to figure out the tricky parts. Now I think I can read it pretty good all by myself!

Letter Identification or Word Analysis (optional)

Sometimes I need to do work on learning about letters or important "chunks" of words. My teacher knows all about the things I need to learn. I like to move the magnetic letters around on the chalkboard; they help me understand what I am learning.

FIGURE 7–1 *(continued)*

Writing a Story

Every day I get to think up my own story to write in my writing book. I can write lots of the little words all by myself. My teacher likes my stories and helps me work to figure out how to write some of the words. We use boxes and I say the word I want to write slowly so I can hear the sounds and then I write the letters in the boxes all by myself. I like to read my story when I'm done.

Cut-up Sentence

I read the story and my teacher writes it on a long strip of paper. My teacher cuts up my story so I can put it back together. I have to think real hard to get it all back together, then I have to check myself to see if I got it right. Most of the time I do!

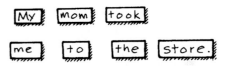

New Book Introduced

I like this part of the lesson the best! My teacher picks out a new story just for me and tells me what the story is all about. We look at the pictures and think about what the people and animals say in this book. My teacher also helps me think about some new, important words in my story. Isn't it fun to hear about the story and look at the beautiful pictures before you read it? I think it helps me read the story too!

New Book Attempted

Now it's my turn to work hard again, but I like this story and I know my lesson is almost over. When I come to a hard part, my teacher will ask me questions to help me think or might show me what I should try to think about or do. My teacher is trying to teach me to do all the things that good readers do. If I have to work real hard on this story, we will probably read it again together so I can just think about the story but I'm not sure there is enough time.

Didn't I do lots of work in my lesson today? I hope you learned something too. Bye!

Source: Mary Fried, Coordinator, Reading Recovery Program, Columbus, Ohio, City Schools.

FIGURE 7–2 *Early Intervention in Reading (EIR)*

Early Intervention in Reading (EIR) was developed to provide special instruction for low-achieving first-grade children (Taylor et al., 1995; Taylor, Strait, & Medo, 1994). The program is conducted by the classroom teacher in the regular classroom setting. Characteristics are as follows.

✔ The teacher is trained to develop the program and works with five to seven low-achieving students in the regular classroom.

✔ Students are assigned to this group on the basis of teacher observation and a phonemic awareness test.

✔ In-class instruction consists of 15–20 minutes of supplemental daily reading instruction. Students also are read to individually by an aide or peer for an additional 5 minutes each day.

✔ Instruction takes place over three-day cycles, using a picture storybook in Big Book format. To begin, readers follow the teacher as she or he reads and tracks (points to the words while reading) the story.

✔ Instructional emphasis is then on choral rereading of the stories, guided writing to develop phonemic awareness and awareness of sound-symbol correspondences, strategic word identification (including sounding and blending), story retelling, and comprehension.

✔ Structured daily observations are used to assess progress and plan instruction.

✔ Transition to independent reading occurs as the teacher works with pairs of students, instead of the group, and as the students read stories that the teacher has not previously read aloud with them.

Source: From *Teaching Children to Read and Write* (4th ed.), by Robert B. Ruddell, 2006, from Chapter 10 by Sandra McCormick. Boston, MA: Allyn & Bacon. Copyright 2006 Allyn and Bacon. Reprinted with permission of Allyn & Bacon.

Principle Two: Consider the Benefits of One-to-One Tutoring

Working with students individually has many advantages because teachers can give undivided attention to the student. The reader's confusions are immediately noted, feedback without delay is possible, and the instructional curriculum can be woven around a specific reader's strengths, weaknesses, and interests. And, after all, responding to individual differences is what remedial programs are all about.

A further value of individual work is the increased opportunities for response. With one-to-one tutoring, the student is doing all of the responding during a lesson rather than sharing the response opportunities with others in a group. Much research has shown that amount of active responding is correlated with achievement (e.g., Greenwood, Delquadri, & Hall, 1984).

Studies conducted to compare the efficacy of one-to-one tutoring with more conventional group instruction have consistently found large differences in learning in favor of the students who are tutored. For example, Burke (1984) found that students in grades 4, 5, and 8 who had one-to-one instruction, on average, scored 98% (or two standard deviations) higher than the group-instructed students. Tutored students also ended the program with more positive attitudes.

Working with students individually has many advantages, for example, ability to immediately respond to confusions, as well as opportunity to design instruction around the reader's specific needs and interests.

The Reading Recovery Program employs only one-to-one instruction. A comparison of Reading Recovery with three other instructional models for educationally at-risk first graders concluded that one of the three variables leading to the success of the Reading Recovery Program was the one-to-one lessons, along with intensive training of teachers and the framework of the lessons themselves (Pinnell, Lyons, DeFord, Bryk, & Seltzer, 1994).

Another successful first-grade intervention program has been designed by Vellutino et al. (1996) to consist of connected text reading, sight vocabulary instruction, and attention to word identification strategies delivered in daily 30-minute, one-to-one sessions. This program has been noted for robust achievement gains that are maintained over time (Hiebert & Taylor, 2000).

LEARNING FROM TEXT

Applying What You've Learned.   Assume that you want to lobby with your school district for more one-to-one instruction for reading delayed students, especially for those in the lowest ranges of achievement. Is there any research information you could use in your advocacy?

Principle Three: Take Into Account the Effects of the Teacher's Instructional Actions During Group Learning

Because one-to-one instruction is not always feasible, many reading teachers work with small groups. Groups are kept small because small class size allows better teaching to occur (Allington, 2001). Individualized instruction can take place in these instructional arrangements since individualized instruction does not necessarily mean working with just one reader at a time. Rather,

individualized instruction is the tailoring of teaching to a student's specific needs. Where more than one student has the same instructional requirements, grouping students is educationally appropriate.

In an examination of several special reading interventions for students in the lowest quartile of achievement, Hiebert and Taylor (2000) concluded that small-group instruction, rather than one-to-one instruction, can be beneficial when carefully planned and carefully focused. In programs they reviewed, although one-to-one instruction produced an 85% success rate for such students, when taught in small groups of three, 75% of low-achieving students were successful (e.g., Hiebert, Colt, Catto, & Gury, 1992), and when in groups of six (e.g., Taylor, Short, Frye, & Shearer, 1992) the success rate for the lowest quartile students—students who usually do not progress adequately with typical classroom instruction—was about 66%.

Grouping for instruction does have some advantages. In addition to efficient use of teacher time, a second benefit is that students often learn from hearing the responses of their peers and by sharing in problem-solving experiences.

Despite some positive features of group instruction, however, the teacher must be certain that readers in the group do not receive unequal treatment. Explanations, prompts, opportunities for response, and support should be directed to all students in a balanced manner to guarantee equitable student participation in learning experiences. Teachers are frequently unaware that they supply more opportunities for active engagement for some students than for others—and studies show that readers who need the most help are the ones who are often ignored.

Principle Four: Provide Opportunities for Collaborative Learning

When group instruction is implemented, positive outcomes can result if readers are allowed at times to engage in collaborative learning. In **collaborative learning,** peers work together in pairs or small groups to write (compose, revise), discuss answers to questions about text, and find solutions to problems. To be effective, teacher guidance should precede—and be available when needed throughout—collaborative learning occasions. Heath (1991) points out that research on cognition indicates cooperative learning has potential for learners of all ages. Presently, collaborative student learning is even suggested in frequently used basal reader series as an activity for accomplishing lesson goals (Barr, 2002).

Cross-age collaborations also have merit. When older and younger students have been paired to work together on reading and writing tasks, gains have been seen, including improvements in cognitive objectives and attitudes toward literacy activities.

Principle Five: Consider the Implications of Independent Work

Research has shown that independent work without teacher supervision is negatively related to academic gains.

Secondary teachers find that students in the age groups they teach sometimes prefer independent practice rather than group activities. Therefore, secondary reading or LD classes at times are managed so that readers carry out assignments independently, with the teacher moving from student to student to provide direct, individual instruction for a part of each period.

It should be noted, however, that research has shown that independent work without teacher supervision is negatively related to academic gains

FIGURE 7–3   *Example of an Individual Assignment Sheet*

<u>**Mike**</u>

  ✔ 1. Reread by yourself the story you read with my help yesterday.

  ✔ 2. Go to the learning center and complete the two activities on recognizing prefixes that have been placed there.

  _____ 3. Write a one-paragraph "story" about your basketball practice last night. I'll be by after you have finished to hear you read this to me and to talk to you about any problems you may have had with sounds of letters. We'll also add words from your story to your word bank. Be thinking of which ones you want to choose.

  _____ 4. There is an activity for sequencing a story in your folder. Do this.

  _____ 5. Choose a new story from the book I have placed on your desk. Begin reading it. I'll come by to work with you on this story at about 10:40.

(e.g., Sindelar & Wilson, 1982). Independent practice can be effective if it follows these principles.

1. It immediately follows teacher-directed instruction.
2. It is at the appropriate instructional level.
3. It is engaged in for short periods of time.
4. It is interspersed with either group or individual teacher-directed instruction.

One way to facilitate good use of time during independent exercise is to prepare personalized assignment sheets for each student (like the one in Figure 7–3) and have students check off tasks as they are completed.

    Although teacher-directed instruction is an important feature of all productive programs, it appears that more teacher-directed time is necessary for delayed readers. For example, Stallings (1980) found that when low-achieving students made high achievement gains, 72% of their instructional time had been spent in teacher-directed experiences, while average readers made high gains when only 49% of their time was spent in teacher-led instruction.

LEARNING FROM TEXT

Summarize.   What are the pros and cons of independent work?

Principle Six: Consider Time on Task

Time on task is a concern closely related to several of the preceding principles. Rosenshine (1980), for example, found rates of academic engagement to be 84% during teacher-led instruction as opposed to only 70% during independent assignments. The amount of time students are actually engaged in academic projects is an important variable in learning.

    When considering the issue of time on task, the differences between *allocated time* and *engaged time* must be taken into account. In discussing the amount of time they have allocated for instruction, teachers may say something like, "In Nicole's daily schedule, I have 20 minutes planned for sustained silent reading." But Nicole is sent to a desk to read on her own while the teacher has responsibilities with other students; Nicole then spends 3 minutes looking through her purse, 5 minutes glancing at pictures elsewhere in her book, 4 minutes daydreaming, and only 8 minutes reading. Allocated time has no impact on learning. Engaged time does.

Another issue related to time on task is the length of group sessions. If students participate in a special reading class for only a limited time each day (e.g., 20 minutes or 30 minutes), substantial increases in learning should not be expected. When group, rather than one-to-one, instruction is necessary, it is more appropriate to plan for 40- to 45-minute periods, every day of the school week.

Principle Seven: Let the Student Read

Teachers who work with poor readers often are so concerned about the skills and strategies the students lack that they allocate the majority of instructional time to specific exercises related to these inadequacies. Yet, while there can be no question that instructional time must be spent on skill and strategy acquisition, it is inappropriate to require students to spend all of their class time on developing specific reading skills while never giving them the opportunity to practice these skills in meaningful material.

One of the most decisive factors for promoting growth in reading competence is the processing of large amounts of regular, connected reading material (Allington, 2001). Harris and Serwer (1966), in their now classic study, found that a critical variable positively correlated with reading success was the amount of time spent "actually reading." In their study, "actually reading" did not mean carrying out supportive activities such as drawing a picture to accompany a language experience story, discussing objects the teachers had brought in to furnish background for a story, or completing other language arts activities. Although the teacher may choose to include these types of experiences in a remedial reading program, time spent on such pursuits should not be counted as part of actual reading time.

In past studies, time spent reading in many regular classrooms has been shockingly small—as little as 7 to 8 minutes a day in elementary classes and 15 minutes a day in middle school programs! (See e.g., Durkin, 1984.) Such limited practice in actual reading is detrimental, especially for students with low aptitudes for literacy learning.

In programs where maximum growth is seen, students spend large portions of time reading regular, connected text.

In those remedial and clinical programs in which maximum reading growth is seen, students spend a large portion of each class period reading regular, connected authentic text. In those programs in which the majority of time is allotted to skills and strategy practice, readers do improve in these specific skills, but the degree to which the skills are generalized to, and applied in, real reading is scant.

Principle Eight: Encourage Outside Reading

Research has frequently reported a significant correlation between the amount of free time reading and reading growth (e.g., Gutherie & Wigfield, 2000). There is no question that poor readers who regularly spend some time outside of class reading books, magazines, newspapers, or anything—even comic book reading (Greaney, 1980)—make more substantial and rapid progress than those who do not. The teacher should have interesting, easy-to-read materials in the classroom and encourage students to check out some of these each time they leave the class. Parents should be asked to have their child read for 15 or 20 minutes daily.

Principle Nine: Incorporate High-Quality Literature Into the Program

Related to the two preceding principles, this axiom is too often neglected with delayed readers despite the fact that high-quality literature can be used in their programs in a number of ways.

Reading Aloud to Students.   Reading to students is beneficial for many reasons. Reviews of research say children who are read to on a regular basis have a larger quantity of vocabulary awareness, a higher quality of vocabulary knowledge, and better comprehension of text. It also motivates their desire to read (Galda, Ash, & Cullinan, 2000) and allows students to enjoy literature they cannot yet read themselves. Here are several instructional suggestions.

> Students who are read to on a regular basis show enhanced vocabulary knowledge and comprehension achievement.

1. *Slip in a little poetry.* Instructional sessions too short? Don't think you have time to read to students? In most sessions you can find time to smuggle in a poem or two. Many reluctant readers tune into the rhythms of poetry. Funny poems like this one may spark a giggle:

CATERPILLAR VIEWINGS

What does a caterpillar see?

When he's curling around a tree?

Maybe it's a butterfly, bird, or bee

But, I really hope it's—me!

2. *Read informational books to students.* Just as reading narratives to students helps them gain a sense of story (which, in turn, aids comprehension), reading informational books to students helps them gain intuitive knowledge of expository text structures, which then assists comprehension of materials that must be read to learn. Try some of these: *My Puppy Is Born* by Cole (primary grades), *If You Sailed on the Mayflower* by McGovern (intermediate grades), *Animal Camouflage* by Nickel (middle school), *Sally Ride, Astronaut: An American First* by Behrens (high school).

3. *Use picture books with older students.* Certain picture books, although usually used with primary-grade students, are suitable for reading aloud to intermediate, middle school, and high school students. These can be completed in a single reading and the illustrations build new concepts. Try these: *Persephone, Bringer of Spring* by Tomainos, *The Firebird* by Bogdanovic, and *The Matchlock Gun* by Edmonds.

Enhancing Motivation, Interests, and Attitudes. Because delayed readers often perceive learning to read as an unpleasant experience, they may have learned to dislike books and to avoid them. At all grade levels, use of charming, funny, fascinating, exciting, compelling literature encourages students to seek out books as friends, rather than regard them as enemies from which to escape. A few of the many ways you can use high-quality literature to motivate students are the following.

1. *Have them read about champions, daredevils, monsters, threats, danger, malevolence, and action.* This sounds like the stuff of which comic books are made, but it's also the stuff of myths. Turn on turned-off intermediate and middle school students by having them read about Greek and Norse gods, goddesses, monsters, and heroes. These are a few examples of books easy enough for many delayed readers to read: *The Hammer of Thunder* by Pyk, *The Gorgon's Head* by Mikolaycak, and *Adventure with the Gods* by Sellew.

2. *Stimulate interest with participation books.* For young students, use books that allow them to make active responses as you read. For instance, use well-known folk songs prepared as picture books (e.g., *Frog Went A-Courtin'* by Langstaff) or books of game chants (e.g., *London Bridge Is Falling* by Spier). Read them, sing them, chant them. For intermediate grade students, try *The Moon on One Hand: Poetry in Song* by Crofut.

Also use "guessing books," in which the reader must participate by making choices. For example, *Two-Minute Mysteries* by Sobel challenges students to arrive at solutions to short mystery selections after they have read them, with the correct explanations given at the back of the book for self-checking.

3. *Use beautifully illustrated books.* Some of your students have excellent artistic skills and are genuinely interested in art. Choosing books with the outstanding illustrations that often accompany fine literature can stimulate interest in books. Before students read the text, teachers can lead discussions of the art forms used in the illustrations (e.g., collage, watercolors, pen and ink drawings). Calling attention to picture content also can add to students' background knowledge and help them develop ways of using illustrative material to comprehend written text. See textbooks on children's literature for descriptions of art forms used in literature for young people and examples of books using each of these types that you can share with your students.

Using Literature to Meet Specific Instructional Objectives. Good literacy skills can be developed with good literature books. For example:

1. *Objective: Improving comprehension.* Use focus units. A **focus unit** is a group of related books organized around a selected topic. Advantages in using

Teacher can stimulate interest with participation books.

FIGURE 7–4   ***Examples of Themes and Books to Be Used in Focus Units***

For Young Students
- Focus Unit: "There's a Mouse in the House"
  - *Walter, the Lazy Mouse* by Flack
  - *Amos and Boris* by Steig
  - *Where Are You Going, Little Mouse?* by Kraus

For Intermediate Grade Students
- Focus Unit: "Super Kids"
  - *Pippi Longstocking* by Lindgren
  - *The Magic Finger* by Dahl
  - *Encyclopedia Brown Takes the Case* by Sobol

For Middle School Students
- Focus Unit: "Characters With Courage"
  - *Sarah Plain and Tall* by Sewall
  - *One-Eyed Cat* by Fox
  - *Roll of Thunder, Hear My Cry* by Taylor

For High School Students
- Focus Unit: "Other Times and Other Places"
  - *The Faraway Lures* by Behn
  - *Adam of the Road* by Gray
  - *Hakon of Rogen's Saga* by Haugaard

sets of conceptually related books are that they encourage students to: (a) compare stories, (b) see relationships, (c) synthesize ideas, and (d) engage in thoughtful reading. Examples of themes and books that might be grouped into focus units are shown in Figure 7–4.

2. *Objective: Increasing knowledge of word meanings.* Authors of good literature employ a variety of ways to help students develop understanding of word meanings. Cohen (1969) identified a number of these techniques, along with books exemplifying their use. Here are a few examples.

• Explanations of word meanings woven directly into the story	*Make Way for Ducklings* by McCloskey; *Middle Matilda* by Bromhall
• Connecting familiar experiences to give meaning to an unfamiliar word	*Millions of Cats* by Gag; *Scaredy Cat* by Krasiloysky
• Giving numerous examples to illustrate meaning	*Crow Boy* by Yashima; *Down, Down the Mountain* by Credle

> Authors of good literature employ a variety of ways to help students develop understanding of word meanings.

3. *Objective: Developing fluency.* Have students engage in Readers' Theater (Keehn, Martinez, & Roser, 2005). After reading a story from a good literature book, students choose parts to play. Independently and with others, they read and reread their parts to practice fluent reading for a final performance. At no time do students memorize their parts; even when the whole group is reassembled for the final

performance they continue to read from the book. This performance can be given for other students or recorded for students to listen to and enjoy their own "play."

   4. *Objective: Learning study skills.* Use high-quality informational books to teach study skills.

   a. Always have students use the table of contents to find chapters rather than simply telling them the page numbers.
   b. Because using an index is confusing for many low-achieving readers, use small steps to teach them to employ this tool. *Secrets*

High-quality children's and adolescent literature has many uses in programs for delayed readers.

Source: From *Snow Bear* by Jean Craighead George. Copyright © 1999 Jean Craighead George. Illustrations Copyright © 1999 Wendell Minor. Reprinted by permission of Hyperion Books for Children.

in Stone by Wyler and Ames is an informational book with a clearly developed index.

   c. Teach students to use subheadings. An informational book for this purpose is *A Natural History of Giraffes* by MacClintock. This book can also be used to teach about glossaries.

Using Literature to Complement Regular Classroom Programs.   The goal of remedial programs is to help students function well in real-life situations. For school-age students, the regular classroom setting encompasses a good deal of their "real life." Furthermore, when two or more teachers, such as the classroom teacher and the reading specialist, work together to accomplish the same goals, strong support for student learning results. Here are several instructional suggestions.

   1. *Use fine-quality informational books related to topics in students' content area classes.* Many content area textbooks are written at reading levels higher than the grade level for which they are intended. This is a particular problem for low-achieving readers. You can help your students learn about topics being addressed in regular classrooms by choosing good informational books about the same topic but written at easier levels. Have students use these books as the reading material for lessons in your reading class. These are examples of potentially suitable books.

> Students can learn about topics addressed in regular classrooms if the reading teacher uses high-quality informational books about the same area, but written at easier levels.

Science:

My Doctor by Rowell (primary)
The Story of Ants by Shuttesworth (intermediate)
The Simple Facts of Simple Machines by James and Barkin (middle school)
The Value in Believing in Yourself: The Louis Pasteur Story by Johnson (high school)

Social Studies:

Abraham Lincoln by Judson (primary)
A Map Is a Picture by Rinkoff (intermediate)
The Hispanic Americans by Meltzer (middle school)
A Weed Is a Flower: The Life of George Washington Carver by Aliki (high school)

   2. *Use fiction related to topics in students' content area classes.* This will broaden, enrich, and help areas come alive for students. For example, when intermediate-grade students are studying pioneers in their history book, reading material for your reading class lessons might include *Carolina's Courage* (Yates). When middle school students are learning about causes of the U.S. Civil War, you might have your students read *Slave Dancer* (Fox) in the reading room.

   3. *Use books as companions to field trips.* Have students read high-quality fiction or informational books in your class before or after taking a field trip with another teacher. It's likely that your students, even if usually reluctant readers, will be interested in this topic. Books also can be sent with students to use *during* a field trip to verify experiences (e.g., to identify rocks, bugs, and plants). This develops the attitude that books are a useful and agreeable part of real-life activities.

> Here is an excellent website to keep you, and your students, abreast of what's new in children's and young adult fiction and nonfiction books: www.ucalgary.ca/~dkbrown/index.html

Principle Ten: Model Effective Reading Behaviors

If students have difficulty accomplishing a task when they are merely told what to do, add another dimension: Demonstrate how to do it. For example, during oral reading, take turns reading with them. It is surprising how quickly a student's oral reading will begin to take on characteristics of the teacher's reading, becoming more fluent, when this is done.

Role-playing in reading situations can also help. For example, the teacher can simulate an encounter with an unknown word and then orally talk through strategies to identify it. For instance, let's suppose the teacher pretends difficulty with the word *bridge:*

> On Sunday our family went for a drive. As we drove along, we came to a bridge we had to cross. It went over a small river.

When the teacher comes to *bridge,* he or she could say, "I'm not sure what that word is, so I'll use some strategies to figure it out." The teacher might continue reading out loud to the end of the sentence and then state, "Well, I know it's something you can cross in a car. It may be a highway or a street or a bridge. I'll look at the beginning letters of the word. They're *br. Bridge* begins with the sounds of those letters, so it's probably *bridge.* I'll read on and see if I can tell if I'm right." After reading the next sentence, the teacher would then say, "Yes, I must be right because it would make sense for a bridge to be over a river." In this kind of role-playing, it is best to choose a word unknown to the student.

Modeling the strategies needed in comprehension is also effective (Ruddell, 2006). If a student has difficulty responding to a question, the teacher may take over the student's role and demonstrate the thinking processes one would use to arrive at the appropriate answer, showing how to select clues, rejecting some answers because of text information, testing possible answers against background knowledge, and so on. Modeling effective reading behavior shows students *how* to learn, not merely what to learn.

Teacher modeling and role-playing can demonstrate to students how to use word identification and comprehension strategies.

LEARNING FROM TEXT

Applying What You've Learned. What reading strategies would be beneficial to model for a student or group you are familiar with? Think of the exact details of the modeling procedures that would be effective for this specific learning goal. That is, what exactly would you do?

Principle Eleven: Stimulate Motivation and Engagement

Motivation is learned. From infancy, children are rewarded for their behaviors. The child learns to crawl, and the ability to move from place to place has all sorts of rewards. Children begin to talk, and their parents reward them with responses and praise. As a result, during the preschool years, natural motivation to achieve and learn new things is established. When some children begin school, however, they fail to develop many of the skills that get rewards in an academic environment. By the time they are identified as needing special instruction, their desire to participate in learning experiences has been stifled (Allington, 2001).

TABLE 7–1 *Attributions for Success or Failure*

	Attributions for Success	Attributions for Failure
Students with high motivation	Ability ("I'm smart." "I'm good at doing this." "I can do things well.")	Lack of effort ("I should have worked harder at this and then I would have done better.")
Students with low motivation	Luck ("I was lucky I got a good grade.")	Lack of ability ("I'm not smart." "I'm not good at this." "I can't do things well.")

Studies have shown two crucial variables affect achievement motivation:

1. whether or not the individual *expects* to be successful in the activity
2. what *value* the individual places on a successful outcome

The amount of persistence a student is willing to deliver for any given pursuit is highly dependent on these factors. These variables are essential for engaged reading, and in turn, reading engagement is highly correlated with reading achievement (Gutherie & Wigfield, 2000).

Another important concept related to achievement motivation is that of **attributions**—that is, to what individuals attribute successes or failures. Table 7–1 shows the attributions often made by persons with high motivation versus those with low motivation.

Plans to stimulate motivation can be classified into two types: (a) those that deal with antecedent conditions and (b) those that deal with consequences.

Antecedents.   **Antecedents,** conditions planned prior to a learning exercise, are important. It is not enough to merely shore up poorly planned or dull programs by rewarding students' performances after a learning endeavor. Students must see value in the outcomes of tasks they are asked to attempt. Here are three examples of approaches to arranging antecedent conditions designed to motivate students to read.

> To help students see the value of tasks they are asked to attempt, assist them in recognizing how reading can help them achieve immediate personal goals.

1. *Instill a need for reading.* Help students recognize how reading can help them achieve personal goals. For example, if Harrison wants to obtain a driver's license, obtain a copy of a driver's manual and work through it section by section. Plan lessons to focus on strategies and skills needed to handle the manual. If, for instance, Harrison needs to enlarge his sight recognition vocabulary, make a cumulative card file, selecting new words for it from each day's lesson; review all words each day. If meaning vocabulary is the need, write definitions of the words on the backs of the cards. Have him discuss how the words relate to questions that might occur on the written driver's test. If word identification strategies are deficient, select words for preteaching before each lesson; in one lesson, have him examine structural elements (prefixes, suffixes, base words); in another, help him to divide multisyllabic words into syllables. Engage him in comprehension tasks after each section.

2. *Understand that a reward can exist within the activity itself.* For example, if the action or plot in a story is intrinsically interesting to a student because of its suspense, excitement, humor, or characters, he or she will be impelled to finish it. **Intrinsic motivation** refers to motivation that comes from within an individual. **Extrinsic motivation** refers to motivation that has been

arranged from an outside source, such as providing a reward for participating in an undertaking. It is very common for individuals to read because of both intrinsic and extrinsic motivation (Gutherie, Wigfield, Metsala, & Cox, 2004). It should be noted, however, that studies have shown when materials are too difficult, interest alone will not provide adequate motivation to sustain the attempt at reading (Anderson, Higgins, & Wurster, 1985); students must expect to succeed.

In nonfiction material, reading for a definite purpose gives students a reason to complete the endeavor. Some examples are reading and following directions to cook, to construct an item, or to play a game.

See Figure 7–5 for books that may have particular appeal for secondary students.

3. *Use student-prepared materials.* Have students dictate books about themselves. Even students who initially pretend to be interested in nothing usually find "self" to be a compelling topic. The book can be used for connected text reading and the focus of strategy lessons. Dictating books may be made more intriguing for some students if you interview them with a microphone and tape recorder to get stories about their lives. Or, have them type chapters for their book on a classroom computer.

Students also enjoy reading stories written by their peers. Establish a classroom mailbox system: A student writes a story and places it in an envelope addressed to a classmate; the student who receives the story reads it, writes a reaction, and mails his or her own story to someone else. Or, simply have

FIGURE 7–5 *Some Recent High-Quality Fiction and Nonfiction Books to Use With Delayed Readers of High School Age*

- *Return to Hawk's Hill* by the adult author, Allan Eckart. Suspenseful. Aimed at average middle school students, this book likely can be read independently by many high school students, even though they are struggling readers. Nineteenth-century drama about a boy swept into Indian territory in his rowboat. This book is a sequel to the Newbery Honor Book, *Incident at Hawk's Hill.*

- *Witness to War: Eight True-Life Stories of Nazi Persecution* compiled by Michael Leapman. Told by adults, these are stories of the authors' lives under Nazi occupation when they were children during World War II. Accompanied by photographs.

- *Dinotopia* by James Gurney. A wild fantasy of another land and another time—a cross between a Jonathan Swift and a Jules Verne story.

- *Ten Queens: Portraits of Women of Power* by Milton Meltzer. Great for a focus unit on "Liberated Women," or to substitute for a more difficult history unit in students' content area classes. Features Catherine the Great, Cleopatra, Elizabeth I, and others. Told with historical accuracy, many parts are quite exciting.

- *Classic Poetry: An Illustrated Collection* selected by Michael Rosen. What makes this anthology more interesting to delayed readers than some is the inclusion of photographs and short biographies of many of the well-known poets that students typically are required to read. Gives students the feeling that poetry is written by real people.

students write letters; these, too, provide text to read. Writing and receiving letters provides high incentives to produce words accurately and to be concerned with communicative content.

> There are many ways to make reading instruction enjoyable and beneficial. Thus, it is unnecessary to select activities that have only an insignificant effect on academic gains.

When planning antecedent conditions to motivate students, teachers should remember that the reason students are in the program is to learn. We want learning to be enjoyable, but the principle of academically engaged time also must be kept in mind. If a potential exercise is heavy on pleasure but very light on learning, that activity should not be selected. There are so many possible ways to make reading enjoyable that it is unnecessary to select practice that has only an insignificant effect on academic gains.

Consequences. **Consequences** are conditions that occur after a learning activity. Consequences can be thought of as rewards. When a behavior, whether personal, academic, or social, is positively rewarded, it will probably occur again.

For some students who have never experienced the joys of reading, extrinsic rewards may serve as temporary incentives into the process. Intrinsic motivation will later supplant extrinsic rewards. Types of rewards, listed from the more intrusive to the less intrusive, are shown in Table 7–2.

TABLE 7–2 *Positive Rewards*

Unconditioned reinforcers are an integral part of life and are effective without any history of specific events; food, water, and sex are examples. Sometimes food (e.g., candy) has been used as a reward in academic programs, but this is inappropriate because of practical problems associated with using edibles. For example, a student may be allergic to a food and have an undesired reaction, or parents may object because it interferes with good nutritional habits.

Conditioned rewards acquire value as a result of experiences.

1. *Tangibles.* The student is given tangible items as a consequence of desired performance. Examples of items that sometimes have been used are inexpensive books or stickers.
2. *Tokens.* The teacher prepares small cards or pieces of construction paper and gives the student one of these tokens for correct responses (e.g., trying a strategy; self-correcting). When a specified number of tokens have been collected, they may be exchanged for a tangible item, activity reward, or natural reward.
3. *Activity Rewards.* As a result of change in academic responses (e.g., a goal is reached in number of minutes during which silent reading is sustained), a favored event is planned. Pupils may have extra minutes of gym time, or view a short cartoon, for example.
4. *Natural Rewards.* A privilege is given in relation to a naturally occurring event, such as (a) choosing the story the teacher will read to the class, (b) sitting at the teacher's desk during sustained silent reading time, or (c) writing a story on the chalkboard instead of paper.
5. *Knowledge of Progress.* Instead of merely telling students they are doing well, a visual display, such as a chart or graph, is used to demonstrate growth. This is often placed in a personal, private folder for the student's daily viewing of his or her progress.
6. *Praise.* The teacher praises effort as well as accomplishment. **Labeled praise** is best. That is, the teacher specifies why the praise is given. Instead of saying, "Good job!" the teacher says "Good job! You tried to use what you know about letter sounds on every hard word today!"

Using Illustrative Aids. The following information will make more sense to you if you read all the way through Table 7–2 before you begin reading the section.

Reading is a hard job for many students in remedial programs and often, in the initial stages, not considered a very pleasant one. Dispensing positive rewards as a result of improved performance or effort can make the task more palatable. In the words of a classic song, "a spoonful of sugar makes the medicine go down in the most delightful way." It is important, however, to use the least intrusive reinforcer that is effective for a specific student. If Brian will expend more effort as a result of keeping a graph of his own progress, it is inappropriate to set up a token system to grant him activity reinforcers (see Table 7–2). If Scott is motivated to learn more basic high-frequency words simply by being told that for each day he shows improved performance, he may sit at the teacher's desk for silent reading, it is inappropriate to give him tangibles as reinforcers. Reinforcers should be gradually faded from the more intrusive to the least as the student moves toward the ultimate goal of intrinsic motivation.

Here are some additional specific suggestions for planning positive consequences.

1. *Give positive recognition.* For example, incorporate a student's name into bulletin boards, stories, and so on, accompanied by praise (see Figure 7–6). What student wouldn't love to walk into a classroom and see that he or she is the focus of the class bulletin board, or that one of the group events that day is reading a short story complimenting him or her?

FIGURE 7–6 *A Colorful Bulletin Board Display to Recognize a Student in a Positive Way*

2. *Visually demonstrate progress.* Use charts, graphs, add-to puzzles, or color-in puzzles. An add-to puzzle is made by cutting a picture into many puzzlelike shapes. For each correct answer, the student selects and lays a piece of the puzzle on the desk, slowly developing the complete picture with each subsequent correct response. A *color-in puzzle* has a shape embedded in the puzzle (see Figure 7–7). The student colors in one section for each appropriate response until he or she has a complete picture.

3. *Help students get through all the tasks of a lesson.* Concentrated effort and on-task behavior can be a problem for unmotivated, unskilled readers. Devise a system in which students can observe their own progress by marking off each responsibility as it is completed. A simple checklist may be sufficient for older students, but an attractive picture to color works well with elementary school children (see the example in Figure 7–8). The student colors in each

FIGURE 7–7 **Example of a Color-in Puzzle**

FIGURE 7–8 **An Imaginative Checklist for Younger Readers**

FIGURE 7–9 *Example of a Contract Between a Student and Teacher*

I, _____Paul_____ , agree to ___study the title and pictures___
          (student's name)   (what)

of stories and make a prediction about each story before I read_____ , to do this for

1 story a day_____ , to do it ___every day for one week___ ,
          (how much)   (when)

and ___not to put my head down and say "I don't want to."_____
                              (under what conditions)

I, _____Mrs. Daly_____ , agree to ___let Paul take home my tape___
          (teacher's name)   (what)

recorder and dictate a story onto tape_____ , to do this for

one night_____ , to do it ___the day after he completes all___
          (how much)   (when)

5 stories as agreed to above_____ ,

and ___to provide the tape, which he may keep._____
                              (under what conditions)

Signed ___Paul Hill___

Signed ___Mrs. Daly___

figure in the picture as each activity ends. They can thus see what has been accomplished and where the lesson is going.

4. *Inform parents about the student's learning.* Some teachers have had success by using daily report cards to motivate students. Each day a report is sent to parents indicating progress their child is making. In addition, on-task behavior may be increased with daily report cards. For instance, a card can be devised on which the teacher places a check mark for each assignment completed during a class period. Parents then may award the student privileges at home based on the number of check marks received.

5. *Use contracts to spell out goals and rewards to the student.* A contract is a written agreement between the teacher and the student designed as a prompt to help the student meet an objective. The contract delineates a task specifically and identifies the reward when the goal is accomplished. An example of a contract is presented in Figure 7–9.

Principle Twelve: Cooperate With the Classroom Teacher

Whether the reading teacher or special education teacher operates within what has been called a "pull-out" program or a "push-in" program, close working

Close working relationships with students' regular classroom teachers support successful learning outcomes.

relationships with the student's regular classroom teacher bode well for successful learning outcomes. Sharing insights, professional knowledge, and plans for intervention is productive.

Principle Thirteen: Enlist Parent Involvement

Often when parents learn their child is having difficulty with reading, they seek a teacher's advice, asking, "What can I do to help with my child's reading problem?" Teachers can offer a variety of practical suggestions. You may wish to make the following recommendations.

1. *Read aloud to your child.* Because reading to their child is such a simple task, parents are often skeptical of its value. For this reason, research specifying positive effects of these interactions can be cited (see Principle Nine).

Scholastic Publishing Company sells "Parent Book Bags" inexpensively; each plastic bag includes a paperback book, a letter to parents, and an activity card for you to send home with their child. These may be a worthwhile investment for a school, or teachers could make a similar kit with plastic food storage bags. You may also suggest that parents read material already in the home, such as comic strips in the newspaper.

2. *Have your child read something orally to someone every day.* Delayed readers also need to process large amounts of print themselves. Oral reading is often the best way to initiate at-home reading because when students are reading aloud, parents can be sure that reading is, in fact, going on.

Permitting students to do their at-home reading in easy material accomplishes many important purposes without the pressure of an instructional-level lesson.

Encourage parents to allow the child to read easy material. Oral reading at home should not be a task that demands substantial effort. Rather, the intent is that readers be exposed to many and varied language structures and gain confidence in their ability to handle print. Permitting students to do their at-home reading in easy material accomplishes these purposes without the pressures of an instructional-level lesson. Moreover, because students are less likely to make errors in easy material, parents are less prone to become impatient and the lesson is less apt to result in tension and frustration on the part of parent and child. Encourage parents to be positive, to use praise, and to remain patient during these short sessions.

Students should also be encouraged to read highly appealing material during these reading sessions. Good children's and adolescent literature is distinguished by its high interest, of course, but if students prefer reading magazines or newspapers or any books on a topic stimulating to them, they should be permitted to do so.

At times, parents' good intentions to supply a helping hand can go awry after initial enthusiasm has diminished. One way to remedy the "parent drop-out" problem is to establish a communication system. Suppose, for example, that Mrs. Adkins has agreed to have her son, Mark, read aloud to her every night for 10 minutes after supper. The teacher can produce a form that Mark delivers back and forth between the school and Mrs. Adkins (like the one in Figure 7–10). Mrs. Adkins writes in the date and the name of the book each evening and Mark returns it to school the next day. The teacher then uses the column at the right to deliver some sort of reward. For example, the teacher may place a sticker there or draw in a happy face. Similar communication systems can be adapted to whatever transactions the parents are conducting.

FIGURE 7–10   *A Sample Form for Reinforcing Parent-Child Activities at Home*

Date	Name of Book Read	
3-15-06	Amigo	
3-16-06	The Murder of Hound Dog Bates	
3-17-06	Emma's Dragon Hunt	
3-18-06	Alistair in Outer Space	

Principle Fourteen: Let Research Guide Your Instruction

Research evidence is not available to answer all questions we have about student's literacy learning, but still there is an enormous database on which we can rely. Topics related to reading instruction have been investigated more than any other area of education! When presented with new ideas for stimulating students' reading development, teachers should ask the question, "Is the advocacy of this method or procedure based on opinion or on research?" Students in remedial programs need the highest quality instruction that is possible to provide. When faced with an educational problem, the teacher should ask, "What does research say about this issue?"

When you seek counsel from a physician about a medical problem, you do not want your doctor to prescribe treatment based on a seat-of-the-pants decision or a personal bias; you want the doctor to make judgments reflecting knowledge of current research. So, too, must teachers who earnestly care about promoting the learning of seriously delayed readers distinguish between opinion, suppositions, speculations, biases, beliefs, feelings, convictions, zealotry, ideas, views, and sentiments versus research. Your watchwords might be: "In God we trust, but all others must present data."

ORGANIZING AND MANAGING REMEDIAL AND CLINICAL READING PROGRAMS

Teachers who employ the 14 principles outlined in this chapter will certainly be well on their way to offering a superior program to those students who are most in need of excellent reading instruction. The following section makes recommendations to assist with day-to-day organizational and management concerns.

Selecting Instructional Materials and Equipment

Materials can influence instruction and, as such, may positively or negatively affect readers' progress.

Materials can influence instruction and, as such, may positively or negatively affect readers' progress. There are hundreds, even thousands, of reading materials from which to choose. Only a few are described in this text. To locate others, teachers can write to publishers or check their websites to ask for free catalogs. Many professional journals also list recommended materials.

Teachers should not assume, however, that commercially published materials always suggest sound teaching procedures. It is a teacher's professional responsibility to carefully evaluate materials before using them. The checklist in Figure 7–11 is helpful in appraising the effectiveness of products designed for reading instruction.

Individual Books. Books are the most important element in any program for remediating reading problems. They should be available for direct instruction, for independent practice, and for students to take home to increase their out-of-class reading. A permanent collection should be kept in the classroom and supplemented by books brought in periodically from the school or public library. The permanent assortment should include picture books, chapter books, and informational books. For beginning readers, **big books,** which are large enough for a group to see, are useful; students can read these with the teacher, chorally in unison. If you integrate writing into your program, wordless picture books are handy for students to write their own original story lines to accompany the pictures.

Knowing students' interests is important to ensure that appropriate books are available. For instance, high-quality children's literature about adventure, animals, fantasy, humor, mystery, games, and sports generally appeal to elementary school children. Some examples are *Martha Speaks* (Houghton Mifflin)[1], a very funny book in which a family's dog begins to speak after eating alphabet soup, and *Snow Bear* (Hyperion Books for Children), a beautifully illustrated fantasy set in the arctic about a young girl and a polar bear (see the illustration on page 198). Intermediate-grade students begin to show

FIGURE 7–11   *Checklist for Evaluating Reading Materials*

Yes	No		
___	___	1.	Does the material provide much opportunity for the student to read in regular, connected text?
___	___	2.	Is it based on current research and not on outdated notions?
___	___	3.	Does it really teach what it says it teaches?
___	___	4.	Does it teach anything important?
___	___	5.	Does it teach anything at all?
___	___	6.	Is the instructional level appropriate?
___	___	7.	Is the interest level suitable for students' maturity levels in terms of topic, pictures, and type size?
___	___	8.	Is it better for initial learning, for practice, or for review?
___	___	9.	Is it attractive and appealing rather than shoddy or dull?
___	___	10.	Are directions easy for students to understand?
___	___	11.	Is it well organized rather than difficult to follow?
___	___	12.	Are lessons of an appropriate length for your students?
___	___	13.	Would something less expensive do the job just as well?

---

[1] Publishers of materials are listed in parentheses. Addresses may be found at your public library through *Books in Print* and often on websites.

an interest in nonfiction. For example, *The Wildlife Detectives: How Forensic Scientists Fight Crimes Against Nature* (Harcourt) is an informational book about how those destroying endangered species are tracked down at Yellowstone National Park, and *Whales* (Scholastic) offers factual information and interesting drawings by Cynthia Rylant.

Children's poetry preferences include poems with humorous themes or those relevant to real-life experiences. Examples are the poetry anthologies by Shel Silverstein such as *A Light in the Attic* (Harper Collins) and by Jack Prelutsky, such as *The New Kid on the Block* (Greenwillow). The **Teachers' Store** feature on this page lists a selection of high-quality children's literature (fiction, poetry, and informational books) that can be used with less-able elementary school readers.

Secondary students often are interested in adventure, humor, and mystery. Girls particularly like romance and historical fiction, and many boys like science fiction and sports. Some examples that may be suitable for older students who are having reading difficulties are *Sarah, Plain and Tall* (Harper Collins), about the life of a mail-order bride at the time of the opening of the American prairie; *Soldier's Heart* (Dell Laurel Leaf), a short novel about the American Civil War written by Newbery Honor winner Gary Paulsen; and *The Maze*

> Secondary students' book interests often include adventure, humor, mystery, romance, historical and science fiction, and sports.

T E A C H E R S' S T O R E

Some High-Quality Literature Suitable for Less-Able Elementary School Readers

Note: Authors' names are given in parentheses.

Where's Spot? (Hill)
Brown Bear, Brown Bear, What Do You See? (Martin)
The Teeny Tiny Woman (Galdone)
The Cat Sat on the Mat (Wildsmith)
A Very Busy Spider (Carle)
Whose Mouse Are You? (Kraus)
Truck (Crews)
The Cat in the Hat (Seuss)
Little Bear (Minarik)
Frog and Toad Are Friends (Lobel)
Mouse Tales (Lobel)
Owl at Home (Lobel)
Uncle Elephant (Lobel)
A Dark, Dark Tale (Brown)
The Chick and the Duckling (Ginsburg)
The Space Ship Under the Apple Tree (Slobodkin)
Danny Dunn and the Anti-Gravity Paint (Williams & Abraskin)
Busybody Nora (Hurwitz)
Superduper Teddy (Hurwitz)
Ramona the Pest (Cleary)

Cornrows (Yarborough)
Amelia Bedelia (Parish)
Tales of a Fourth Grade Nothing (Blume)
How to Eat Fried Worms (Rockwell)
The Secret Three (Myrick)
Something Queer at the Lemonade Stand (Levy)
Encyclopedia Brown Takes a Case (Sobol)
When I Was Young in the Mountains (Rylant)
The Paper Crane (Bang)
Where the Buffaloes Begin (Baker)
Ben's Trumpet (Isadora)
Shadow (Brown)
The Snowy Day (Keats)
My Friend Jacob (Clifton)
A Lion to Guard Us (Bulba)
The First Year (Meadowcroft)
The Courage of Sarah Noble (Dalgliesh)
The One Bad Thing About Father (Monjo)
Benny's Animals and How He Put Them in Order (Selsam)
Wild Mouse (Brady)
I Did It (Rockwell)

Some High-Quality Literature for Less-Able Secondary School Readers

Note: Authors' names are given in parentheses.

Bargain Bride (Sibley)

The Matchlock Gun (Edmonds)

Sounder (Armstrong)

The Philharmonic Gets Dressed (Kuskin)

Journey to Topaz (Uchida)

The Secret Soldier: The Story of Deborah Sampson (McGovern)

Rosa Parks (Greenfield)

Jim Thorpe (Fall)

Cesar Chavez (Franchere)

Sally Ride, Astronaut: An American First (Behrens)

Ol' Paul, the Mighty Logger (Rounds)

The Gorgon's Head (Hodges)

Cupid and Psyche (Barth)

Sir Gawain and the Loathly Lady (Hastings)

Bunnicula (the Howes)

Slaves of Spiegel (Pinkwater)

The Haunted Mountain (Hunter)

Sweet Whispers, Brother Rush (Hamilton)

Playing Beatie Bow (Park)

Cave Beyond Time (Bosse)

The White Mountains (Christopher)

Where the Sidewalk Ends (Silverstein)

Why Am I Grown So Cold? Poems of the Unknowable (Livingston)

Of Quarks, Quasars, and Quirks: Quizzical Poems for the Supersonic Age (the Brewtons)

Sprints and Distances, Sports in Poetry and Poetry in Sports (Morrison)

I Am the Darker Brother: An Anthology of Modern Poems by Black Americans (Adoff)

Songs of the Dream People (Houston)

Call It Courage (Sperry)

Chernowitz! (Arrick)

The Human Body (Miller)

Commodore Perry in the Land of the Shogun (Blumberg)

Castle (Macaulay)

Wolfman: Exploring the World of Wolves (Pringle)

Strange Footprints on the Land (Irwin)

(Avon), which refers both to an area in the desert where a 14-year-old boy meets a bird biologist who is trying to save California condors and the state of Rick's life before his new friend helps him form constructive approaches to coping.

Copious use of authentic texts improves the caliber of remedial instruction. Some high-quality literature that can be used with secondary students who are poor readers is listed in the **Teachers' Store** feature on this page; some quite easy and some slightly more challenging narratives, poetry anthologies, and informational books are included in the list.

High-interest, low-vocabulary books are also worthwhile in remedial programs. These books are easy to read, but have stories and topics that appeal to students with more mature interests. One example is sets of "high-low" books published by Grolier that are geared toward reluctant readers in middle and high school, but with reading levels of 4 through 7. To capture teen interest, themes include celebrity biographies (with titles such as *Leonardo DiCaprio, Brandy,* and *Prince William*), outdoor life (e.g., *Essential Snowmobiling for Teens*), and sports clinics (e.g., *Baseball: Becoming a Great Hitter; Basketball: Outside Shooting;* and *Football: Passing*).

Book Series. Some series of books contain selections to read accompanied by follow-up activities located directly in the student materials. One of these, de-

Some book series contain selections to be read, accompanied by useful follow-up activities located in the student materials.

"It's a book, dear. It's what they use to make movies for TV."
(Reproduced by permission of Mrs. Clem Scalzitti, wife of the artist.)

signed for intermediate grades through high school, is *Reading for Concepts* (McGraw-Hill), in which books ranging from 1.9 through 6.4 reading levels consist of one-page informational articles followed by a page of comprehension questions, with an emphasis on higher-level responses.

Other series of books consist primarily of stories, with the suggestions for practice activities found only in the teacher's manual. *Giant First Start Classroom Library* (Troll) is a series in which each book is written with very few words (e.g., one uses only 34 different words, another 37, and another 47).

Another type of book series—the basal reader series—today includes absorbing, high-quality selections and attractive formats. However, basal readers are used differently in remedial and clinical reading lessons than in classroom developmental programs. In remedial classes, students do not read all stories in a book; instead, certain stories are selected because they complement student interests.

Kits Containing Reading Materials and/or Skills and Strategy Lessons. Many attractive kits for poor readers are on the market. Multimedia kits include audiovisual materials in addition to strategy lessons and reading selections. *Read XL Kit* (Scholastic), for middle school students who are reading below grade level, includes student novels, an audiobook library, a CD-ROM, and assessment materials. Also from Scholastic is *Courtside Reading*, a kit of materials produced in partnership with the National Basketball Association. Student reading materials are comprised of selections on basketball, supplemented with a CD-ROM and basketball trading cards. Reading levels are 3 through 6, but with obvious appeal for older students, as well. The *Reading Advantage* kit offers high-interest theme magazines aimed at middle school students, but written at easier reading levels (Houghton Mifflin).

A different kind of "kit" is *Bella's Mystery Deck* (Mindware), a set of 52 mystery cards with a mini-mystery written on each. The 13-year-old Bella appeals to middle school students, and the fairly easy-to-read stories make this engaging set of materials useful in remedial programs. Students try to unravel the mystery, then hold the solution, printed in reverse type, up to a mirror to check their predicted solutions.

Workbooks and Reproducibles. Educators have been criticized for using workbooks and reproducible worksheets in reading programs. These have received a bad reputation partly because certain teachers have overused them until no time has remained for the most important literacy activity—reading authentic texts. In addition, many of these materials are poorly prepared and dull. Nevertheless, workbooks and reproducibles can be helpful if they are thoughtfully selected and used. Thoughtful use includes employing workbook or worksheet pages only occasionally as part of a much wider variety of materials and selecting only those pages directly related to a strategy or skill in which the student needs specific instruction. Carefully choosing workbooks and reproducible materials with sound and appealing activities is also important. One interesting set of reproducibles is *25 Emergent Reader Plays Around the Year* (Grolier), with each short play reproducible so the multiple copies can be distributed for each group member to read his or her part.

> Workbooks have been criticized when they have been overused to the point where little time is left for reading authentic texts.

Games. Games, carefully selected and appropriately implemented, are good materials for remedial programs. Because most students enjoy games, they attend carefully and often expend more effort to determine correct responses than during more traditional school activities. Games are most advantageous in a *directed lesson*, with the teacher present to prevent students from practicing errors. By playing games with students, teachers can also model correct responses and solution-seeking behaviors.

One caution about games: In most cases they provide few chances to read connected text. Therefore, devoting an entire class period to playing games is never suitable.

Whether bingo games, card games, domino-type games, puzzles, or board games, the majority of games published for school use emphasize practice with words and applications of word identification strategies. For example, Word Scramble (LinguiSystems) provides board game practice with word families and consonant substitution. A few publishers do offer games to accompany comprehension study.

Teacher-Made Materials. Teacher-made materials can include books, strategy lessons, and games.

For example, teachers may write small "books" or short stories stressing specific words certain students need to practice. Other books can be developed from student-dictated stories; some teachers type these directly into a classroom computer as students dictate in order to easily obtain copies for distribution to everyone in the group. When several stories have been produced, they can be bound together and placed in the class library.

Teachers also compose their own strategy lessons. These usually are designed to help students with a single word identification or comprehension strategy. A strategy lesson that has demonstrated success in helping one student can be easily photocopied and placed in a file for future use with students displaying the same need. Teacher booklets containing ideas for strategy lessons are available. For example, *More Ideas for Using Nonfiction Effectively in Your*

Classroom (Grolier) suggests research-based ideas for helping students with expository text comprehension.

In addition, many teachers enjoy constructing learning games and other manipulatives for students. If any of these are to be used independently, they can be designed to be self-correcting so students discover immediately whether they are responding correctly. Teachers' stores, now found in many communities, are sources of materials for teachers who like to make their own games. They sell inexpensive items, such as blank bingo boards, spinners, and game markers, to be used with teacher-prepared projects. Helpful, too, are booklets of word lists, such as *Phonics Patterns: Onset and Rhyme Word Lists* (Laguna Beach Educational Books), which make readily available examples of words following certain patterns (e.g., the teacher wants to develop a lesson activity to emphasize the short /a/ sound in the context of words and refers to a book of such lists to quickly obtain sample words such as *cab, batch, lack, fact, bad,* and *staff*).

Magazines and Newspapers. Some students—especially secondary-level readers—find magazines or newspapers more appealing than books, perhaps because selections are shorter, or because, unlike books, magazines and newspapers may not be associated with failure in the classroom. One newspaper written especially for lower-achieving secondary readers is *Know Your World Extra* (Weekly Reader Secondary Periodicals). With a subscription, multiple copies of this newspaper can be received weekly in the classroom. Scholastic publishes *Action* magazine with articles aimed at students in grades 7 through 12, but with the readability levels of its articles ranging from 3rd- through 5th-grade reading levels. The booklet *Magazines for Kids and Teens–Revised* (International Reading Association) lists many periodicals pertinent for remedial classes.

The community's daily newspaper also can be used as a learning tool. One point of caution, however: Readability levels of newspapers have risen in recent years, although they do vary from newspaper to newspaper and even from section to section. Some research has estimated that front-page stories range from 9th- to 12th-grade levels, and that many help-wanted ads (important to secondary students) are written at about 6th- to 7th-grade levels. Obviously, certain students may have difficulty if asked to read some community newspapers without assistance.

Newspapers may serve many educational goals. Here are just a few examples.

To order a sample copy of the easy-to-read, high-interest magazine, *Action*, go to www.scholastic.com, then click "The Teachers Store," then click "Reading Intervention."

1. For vocabulary study, read a feature story to the students. Then ask them to work collaboratively to change every adjective to a synonym.
2. To address critical reading skills, read an editorial with the students. Ask them to underline facts and circle opinions.
3. Have students cut out bar, circle, line, and pictorial graphs. Ask them to describe how to read each one.
4. White-out the dialogue in a comic strip. Make photocopies to give to each student. Have students write their own dialogues.

Technology and Equipment. Some types of equipment have been used in reading programs for many years. A tape recorder or CD player with sets of headphones is used for students to listen and read along silently or orally with books. A number of publishers offer tapes and CDs of well-known children's and young adult literature with accompanying read-along books for this purpose. One such company is Troll Communications with titles to appeal across age levels,

TABLE 7–3   *Elements That May Serve as a Rationale for Using Technology in Education*

1. Motivation
- Gaining learner attention
- Engaging the learner through production work
- Increasing perceptions of control

2. Unique instructional capabilities
- Linking learners to information sources
- Helping learners visualize problems and solutions
- Tracking learner progress
- Linking learners to learning tools

3. Support for new instructional approaches
- Cooperative learning
- Shared intelligence
- Problem solving and higher-level skills

4. Increased teacher productivity
- Freeing time to work with students by helping with production and record-keeping tasks
- Providing more accurate information more quickly
- Allowing teachers to produce better-looking, more "student-friendly" materials more quickly

Source: From *Integrating Educational Technology into Teaching* (p. 29), by M. D. Roblyer, J. Edwards, and M. A. Havriluk, 1997, Upper Saddle River, NJ: Prentice Hall. Copyright by Prentice-Hall, Inc. Reprinted with permission of Prentice-Hall, Inc.

including *Gift of the Nile: An Ancient Legend; The Gingerbread Boy; Abe Lincoln: The Young Years; Benito Juarez: Hero of Modern Mexico*; and *Can I Have a Stegosaurus, Mom? Can I? Please?* Some of these titles are also available in Spanish. In addition, students can follow prerecorded teacher directions for completing activities, or use recording and playback equipment in many other productive ways.

Since the mid-1980s computers have been used in remedial programs. Computer programs are available to assist with a wide array of classroom instruction, and several publishers also have devised programs for assessment. (See Table 7–3 for several reasons to incorporate computer technology into reading programs.)

Educational software for use with computers is often categorized in the following ways.

1. *Programs for instructional management.* These help teachers track student progress and monitor accomplishments. Programs are also available to estimate readability levels of books. In addition, teachers may use desktop publishing to produce materials for class use, Microsoft® PowerPoint to generate overhead transparencies, and many other programs that support instruction.

2. *Drill and practice programs.* The purpose of this software is to reinforce basic skills and strategies through independent application.

3. *Instructional games.* These are designed to provide drill and practice in a challenging, intriguing manner.

4. *Simulation learning.* These programs simulate real experiences and allow students to role-play hypothetical situations. Exercises encourage problem-solving abilities that may be useful in reading comprehension.

Many types of educational software can accomplish a variety of different purposes.

5. *Tutorial experiences.* Tutorials furnish more instruction than found in drill and practice programs, such as detailed explanations of how to complete an exercise or explanations of why an answer is incorrect. Tutorials often feature *branching,* a technique allowing learners to bypass some instruction or spend additional time when appropriate. Spelling skills, as well as reading skills, are often addressed through drill and practice programs, instructional game programs, and tutorial programs.

6. *Story architecture programs.* Students build their own stories with the computer's assistance.

7. *Telecommunications programs.* The Internet and the World Wide Web allow students to distribute their work through home pages. Teachers are now developing websites for their classrooms for students to do just that and to share ideas with other teachers and classes (Karchmer, Mallette, Kara-Soteriou, & Leu, 2005). Such opportunities encourage students to engage in writing activities more frequently than typically seen with delayed learners as they communicate with others through letters and by sharing stories and original pieces. See "Opportunities for Teenagers to Share Their Writing Online" (Kehus, 2003) for interesting ideas and issues.

Other websites provide information students can use in expository writing, and interactive stories, poetry, and other appealing fiction can be read directly from a number of sites. Websites have other useful potential for special reading classes (see the website margin notes throughout this book as a start). A highly recommended resource is *Teaching with the Internet: Lessons from the Classroom* (Leu & Leu, 2000).

8. *Utility programs.* In these, teachers can select the information to be taught. For example, a teacher might enter a different set of spelling words into the program each week or enter words to make up a crossword puzzle.

9. *Word processing programs and desktop publishing programs.* These help young writers write, edit, read, and print material. The *Kid Works II* (Davidson) word processing software package is suggested for primary grade students, and *Children's Writing and Publishing Center* and *The Writing Center* (both by The Learning Company) are for intermediate grades. Desktop publishing programs extend the appeal of word processing programs with their capability to format text in interesting ways and to include graphics.

There are many new software programs in reading. Although some older software designed for reading instruction (and for related areas such as spelling and writing) was not highly recommended, better quality software is becoming increasingly available. Well-designed programs that provide sound practice for elementary students are the *Playwriter* series (Woodbury Software), *The Vocabulary Game* (J. & J. Software), and *Milliken's Comprehension Power* (Milliken & I/CT). *Reading Around Words* (Instructional/Communications Technology) is a well-constructed program at the secondary level. *Book Brain* is designed to help students find books they would like to read; there are more than 750 tempting book annotations on this database for grades 4 through 6 and 7 through 9. The *Muppet Slate* was designed to encourage writing by first- and second-grade children. Some newer programs, such as *Ghostwriter,* teach outlining before writing as well as revision and editing afterward. *Read 'N Roll* is one of the better drill and practice programs. The *Writing to Read* program (IBM) integrates writing and reading in mutually beneficial ways. Other programs now on the market are for use with adult low-achieving readers, such as *Adult Education Reading* (BLS).

Computer programs can assist the reading teacher with management of classroom instruction and assessment as well as provide students with drill and practice, instructional games, simulation learning, or tutorial experiences.

A number of pros and cons have been voiced about reading programs designed for computers. Some criticisms are that certain software is no more than a set of expensive workbook pages electronically displayed, that drill and practice programs supply little more than an electronic flashcard, and that uninspired program development leads to an inferior educational experience. Some believe there has been failure to harness the potential of computer programs to address problems of the most severe reading disability cases (McCormick, 2002). On the other hand, high-quality software is now valued for supplementary instruction. It provides good practice, allows for instant feedback, serves as an effective tool for review, allows students to control the rate of presentation, and can enable highly individualized teaching. Most reading teachers believe that computers can promote students' thinking skills by engaging them in simulation programs or through use of word processing programs to compose and edit.

Nevertheless, to make the best use of these programs, teachers should not view computers as a panacea. They should preview software before purchasing and integrate computer teaching with teacher-directed instruction.

Many books, magazines, and computer programs are available to provide inservice education to help educators stay abreast of the explosion of new developments in computer uses and technology. And many professional journals now feature columns that give advice for teacher-created lessons, new uses for computers, and lists of recommended software. A book with innovative ideas is *Cartwheels on the Keyboard: Computer-Based Literacy in an Elementary Classroom* (Carroll, 2004).

A good online tutorial to help you learn how to get the most from the Internet for your students is found at www.learnthenet.com/english/

Media. Films, videos, DVDs, and filmstrips add variety to reading lessons. Films can be obtained from commercial educational distributors and for free from public or school libraries. Increasingly videos and DVDs are produced for use in reading classes and are available from a number of companies. Filmstrips are relatively inexpensive; publishers have catalogs of filmstrips suitable for reading instruction.

The brief review in this section is provided to indicate the multiplicity of materials available to enhance reading instruction. Many other excellent choices are available at both higher and lower reading levels.

📖 ORGANIZING THE CLASSROOM OR CLINIC TO TEACH

A well-organized classroom facilitates the use of a variety of materials, permits both individualized and group activities, and encourages on-task behavior of students.

Occasionally a reading teacher is assigned an odd little room in which to conduct classes, perhaps the janitor's former supply room or the abandoned bell tower above the school attic. The reasoning seems to be that since these teachers don't work with a full-sized class, they don't need a regular-sized classroom. Teachers forced to operate in such facilities must take the attitude that good teaching can occur anywhere—which is true—and that students can receive an excellent program even if space is scarce and the room is an architectural mongrel. Nevertheless, the following description assumes the more ideal condition of a normal-sized classroom; teachers with less space can, with ingenuity, make the necessary adaptations to create a well-organized room.

A well-organized classroom facilitates use of materials, permits individual and group activities, and encourages on-task behavior.

Physical Organization

Arrange desks so that some students can work individually while other students are in a group with the teacher. Situate desks for small-group instruction near a chalkboard so it can be used for teaching. If you have a room with no chalkboard, ask for a portable one. Teachers also need a place to display neatly the many books they should have in their room. A revolving metal rack for storing and displaying paperbacks, magazines, and newspapers is an excellent addition to the reading class. If possible, create a comfortable reading area, perhaps equipped with a small rug and a beanbag chair or two near the bookshelves. Use a table or desk for a listening station area; place a tape recorder and earphones on the table and several chairs around it. Find a place to store games neatly so they are convenient for use. Ask that a pull-down screen be installed in the room for showing overhead projector transparencies, or that a portable one be made available. Find a place for neatly placing kits and mechanical devices so that they are accessible. Obtain a file cabinet and file folders for efficiently organizing tests, strategy lessons, information on teaching ideas, forms, and student records.

Devise attractive, organized ways to group supplies. Make supplies accessible to students who are working independently to minimize interruptions when the teacher is working with other readers.

Learning Centers and Writing Centers

Find a place in your classroom for one or more learning centers. A **learning center** is a designated area where students can work independently on activities designed to help them concentrate on a specific knowledge, strategy, or skill area. Here are some points for developing learning centers.

Learning and writing centers should incorporate a multiplicity of response opportunities: reading, manipulating, observing, writing, creating, comparing, and researching.

1. To begin, select a single skill, strategy, or knowledge area (e.g., learning a word identification strategy, reading to predict outcomes, or editing stories). Develop or locate materials and media related to this area. These could include books, pens, pencils, dictionaries, games, teacher-made or commercial audiotapes, a tape recorder and earphones, a filmstrip, a tabletop filmstrip projector,

activity cards, newspapers, a flannel board, and/or a magnet board. (A cookie sheet makes a good, inexpensive magnet board.)

2. To develop a comprehensive learning experience for the topic chosen, include a variety of response opportunities such as reading, observing, writing, creating, comparing, researching, orally answering questions into a tape recorder, or typing into a computer.

3. When possible, devise ways for students to self-correct.

4. Organize materials at a table or desk maintained permanently for student use. Provide space on that table for students to work.

5. Post clear and simple instructions at the learning or writing center so students can complete their activities independently until direct teacher assistance is available.

6. Devise a system for keeping records of what students accomplish. Maintain a scheduling calendar for assigning students to the center.

The design and construction of a learning center requires much thought and effort. Because this process takes time and often requires trial and error solutions to unique problems, it is best to develop a single, successful learning center before attempting to start others.

Bulletin Boards

Devise bulletin boards that teach. There are several functional levels of bulletin boards. The least useful are those that merely provide a colorful visual display in the room, such as one that announces "It's Spring!" accompanied by paper flowers. A second type presents information, such as pictures about the American Southwest with labels beneath them giving facts.

A third, and the most productive, bulletin board is the one around which a learning activity can take place. This third type enables the teacher to teach lessons to small groups of students using the displayed materials. In addition, this bulletin board can serve as a kind of learning center. Students may use it independently to manipulate materials or otherwise engage in activities that have been arranged there. This is a good solution for teachers who would like to have a learning center but cannot because of space limitations. Another excellent way to use a bulletin board is to turn it over to students. They can display work of their own choosing, perhaps the final versions of stories they have composed after they have completed their cycle of editing and rewriting.

A Pleasant Place to Learn

Make the classroom attractive. A bright and pleasant atmosphere seems to students more conducive to learning than a dreary room. When students or visitors come to the classroom, their responses should be, "We can certainly tell that reading is taught here!" and "This would be a nice place in which to learn!"

The basic organizational procedures, equipment, and supplies cited here apply to reading clinics as well as classrooms. Clinics, however, should include more areas reserved for one-to-one instruction, because most teaching in the clinic setting is carried out in this manner. Individual study carrels are often used for this purpose.

PLANNING SCHEDULES FOR INSTRUCTION

Two types of planning of instructional schedules are necessary: (a) devising an overall daily agenda and (b) carefully mapping out what will occur within each class period.

When generating a daily agenda, the teacher should usually group students with similar needs. Because of the seriousness and diversity of poor readers' problems, some individual work is necessary or advisable, but when students have comparable instructional requirements, group instruction also can occur. Working with groups of five to eight students during each class period is common practice, and, in fact, some research has shown that when groups become larger than six, learning diminishes (Payne, Polloway, Smith, & Payne, 1981). Avoid schedules in which reading class conflicts with an activity a student considers highly enjoyable. If the remedial class is arranged as a "pull-out" program, students should be scheduled into the class so that they do not miss relevant reading experiences in their regular classrooms.

Within each class period, reading teachers should follow certain basic guidelines.

1. At least a third of every class period should be devoted to students reading connected text. This means they should read meaningful material with a developed beginning, middle, and end—for example, whole chapters, stories, articles, or short books. It does not mean reading single sentences, isolated words on flashcards, or individual paragraphs in workbooks. Time may be devoted to silent reading and to oral reading. The reading time also may be allotted in variable segments (e.g., 5 minutes at the beginning of the period, 10 minutes during the middle, and 5 minutes more at the end). However it is achieved, the goal is to assure that one-third of the time students spend in reading classes is spent in reading connected text.

2. Allocate time so that all reading is accompanied by comprehension responses. This can be accomplished by asking questions, inviting students to retell the selection, or employing a diversity of ways. (See the comprehension chapters later in this book.)

3. Activities should be based on assessed needs and should be varied throughout the class period. A relatively long time of concentrated effort might be followed by an academically relevant game. In addition, routines and materials should be changed from day to day to prevent boredom.

4. Provide students opportunities to make choices within tasks. For example, *you* may decide that Charles should spend the first 10 minutes of the period reading silently, but *he* may choose from three suitable stories the one he prefers to read. Research has shown that activities are more effective when students are offered some choices within the teacher-selected structure.

5. Spend some time during each class period reading aloud to students or have them listen to taped stories.

6. Daily lesson plans should be modified if students are not demonstrating appropriate progress.

Planning instructional schedules for students enrolled in reading clinics is similar to planning for reading classes. Activities scheduled for clinical reading programs should not be of an unusual or peculiar nature. Clinical reading instruction should exemplify the best of reading instruction, with rich and

Activities scheduled for clinical programs should not be of an unusual or peculiar nature, but should exemplify the best of reading instruction with rich, research-based literacy experiences in abundance.

meaningful experiences in abundance. Clinical programs incorporating current learning theory do not resort to *materials* that are odd or to artificial instructional procedures that too often have only meager relation to authentic reading tasks. In Figures 7–12 and 7–13, two consecutive days' lesson plans are shown for a hypothetical student enrolled in a reading clinic.

FIGURE 7–12 *The First of Two Consecutive Days' Lesson Plans for a Hypothetical Student Enrolled in a Reading Clinic*

Name: Jim Coyne
Age: 10
Approximate instructional level: 2.5
Date: Oct. 31, _____

9:00–9:10 *(CRT = 5 min.)	Jim and I will orally read Chapter 1 of *Max the Monkey* (reading level, approximately 2.5). This book was chosen because of his interest inventory. Jim said he "loves monkeys" and "I wish I could go to the zoo every week to see the monkeys." Since this is his first day with this book, I'll take turns reading with him (I'll read one page, he'll read the next, etc.) to ease him into it. By doing this, he'll hear me pronounce some of the new vocabulary. He'll also begin to get a feeling for the story line so he can make predictions when he reads the book without assistance from me. Also, by hearing him read orally from the first chapter, I'll be able to make some determinations about whether this book is really at the appropriate level for him.
9:10–9:15	Jim will retell the chapter we have just read and at the conclusion I will ask the following inference question: "What are two things that Max's new owner did that tell us he already knew a lot about monkeys?"
9:15–9:25 *(CRT = 10 min.)	Jim will silently read Chapter 2 of *Max the Monkey.* (While he reads, I will silently read a book of my own to model reading behavior.)
9:25–9:30	I will ask him to orally answer four questions I have prepared ahead of time about Chapter 2. One of these is a factual question; one is related to a new vocabulary word whose meaning is implied in the chapter but not directly stated; and two require him to draw conclusions.
9:30–9:40	Jim and I will play a game to review the work we did yesterday on consonant digraphs. He may choose between "Digraph Dominoes" or a digraph bingo game. Then he will read six sentences I have written, each of which contains a word beginning with one of the digraphs in the game.
9:40–9:45 *(CRT = 5 min.)	Jim will orally read a one-page information selection on monkeys from the easy-to-read work text series, *Learn About Your World.* During his reading I will stress the self-correction strategies we have been working on.
9:45–9:50	He will answer the three multiple-choice questions that follow the informational selection on monkeys.
9:50–10:00	I will read aloud to him Chapter 1 of *Follow My Leader,* by Garfield. This is a book of realistic, contemporary fiction of high literary quality and is also very popular with intermediate grade students. The book is written at about 4.0 reading level, which makes it too difficult for Jim to read by himself. He should have no difficulty understanding it, however, based on what I've observed of his listening comprehension. This book was chosen not only because of its interest level, but also because *Follow My Leader* is the story of a boy who is blind; it was chosen from many other good choices because a blind student is to be mainstreamed into Jim's room beginning next week. I'll read a chapter a day to him until the book is completed.

*CRT = Amount of *connected reading time* engaged in by the student.

FIGURE 7–13   *The Second of Two Consecutive Days' Lesson Plans for a Hypothetical Student Enrolled in a Reading Clinic*

Name: Jim Coyne
Age: 10
Approximate instructional level: 2.5
Date: Nov. 1, _____

9:00–9:10	Jim will complete a strategy lesson on predicting and confirming. I have prepared a cloze story, and he will be asked to do the following: 1. Read the whole story silently. 2. Reread it silently and tell me each word that he would supply where words have been omitted; I will write the word in the blank. 3. Orally read the story to me and make changes if any of the original words he supplied do not make sense.
9:10–9:20 *(CRT = 10 min.)	Jim will silently read Chapter 3 of *Max the Monkey.* (I will read my own book as he reads.)
9:20–9:30 *(CRT = 10 min.)	He will orally read Chapter 4 of *Max the Monkey.* I will help him use the word identification strategies we have been working on, but will not take turns reading with him.
9:30–9:40	As a comprehension check over Chapters 3 and 4 of *Max the Monkey,* he will play a game I have devised. I have prepared 10 questions, all of which require him to draw an inference. He will have a game board in front of him that says "Find the Treasure." For each question he answers correctly, he may move one space on the board toward the "treasure." When he reaches it, he can lift a flap where he will find something he can have: a silly looking picture of a monkey I found in *Field and Stream* magazine.
9:40–9:50	I will read aloud to him Chapter 2 of *Follow My Leader.* Afterward, I will ask Jim to orally summarize this chapter.
9:50–9:55	Jim will orally read a one-page story I wrote, which contains 21 words that begin with consonant digraphs.
9:55–10:00	He will dictate a story to me about the Halloween party in his room yesterday. I will write down the story as he dictates and give it to him to take home. His parents have agreed to listen to him read any of his dictated stories that I send home and are filing them in a folder he decorated.

*CRT = Amount of *connected reading time* in which the student engages.

LEARNING FROM TEXT

Using Illustrative Aids.   After reading the two days of lesson plans in Figures 7–12 and 7–13, think about how each time segment relates to the guidelines specified in the preceding section, "Planning Schedules for Instruction."

Reflections   Bloom (1984) and his colleagues, along with other investigators, have conducted studies to ascertain the contributions of various factors to student achievement. The results of this research highlighted the following variables and their relative effects:

- The variable having the greatest effect on student achievement: One-to-one or small-group (two or three students) tutorial instruction

- The variable having the second greatest effect: Provision of reinforcement
- Variables having the third greatest effect:
    a. feedback and correction
    b. cues and explanations
    c. student classroom participation
    d. students' time on task
    e. improved reading and study skills
- Variables having the fourth greatest effect:
    a. cooperative learning
    b. *graded* homework
- Next most important variables:
    a. classroom morale
    b. having initial cognitive prerequisites
- Also important: Home environment interventions (Bloom, 1984, p. 6)

LEARNING FROM TEXT

Compare. Compare the findings in the Reflections section with what you have read in this chapter. Are there any surprises?

Word Recognition

Accurate, automatic, rapid word recognition has positive effects on independent reading and on interest in voluntary reading.

*T*o the layperson, recognition of words seems to be the basis of reading. And it is! Although reading professionals know the purpose of reading is the construction of meaning (i.e., comprehension), word recognition is a necessary, although not sufficient, condition for understanding text.

Word recognition refers to the instant recall of words in which the reader resorts to no obvious mechanisms to recognize the word (although the reader's brain is conducting a number of operations, the reader is not aware of these). When the reader recognizes a word in this way—and can say the word with no hesitation—it is said that he or she has developed **automaticity;** that is, the reader's brain has quickly and automatically processed the word to read it. **Word identification,** on the other hand, refers to those cases in which a reader directly calls into play one or more strategies to help in "figuring out" a word. For proficient readers, the strategies are employed effortlessly and usually go unnoticed by the reader. However, in developing readers, the strategies may be overtly displayed as these readers use phonics, structural analysis, or context clues to figure out a word that is not yet automatically recognized.

As you read this textbook, in the vast majority of cases, you are using *word recognition*. You instantly and accurately recognize almost all of the words. In some cases, however, I have used technical words that may be new to you. In the preceding paragraph, the term *automaticity* was introduced. Unless you have read a great deal on the topics of literacy or psychology, that may have been a novel expression for you. The first time you saw the word, you may have paused and reread for a moment to check the letters—especially, in this instance, at the end of the word—and to think about how the word would be pronounced. If you did that, you were using *word identification* strategies.

Readers must acquire both whole word recognition and word identification strategies. The present chapter addresses word recognition issues and instructional suggestions; Chapter 9 will consider word identification.

> Readers must acquire both whole word recognition and word identification strategies.

📖 THE IMPORTANCE OF RECOGNIZING WORDS AT SIGHT

There are a number of important reasons for recognizing words at sight.

Sight Word Recognition in the Earliest Stages of Reading

Students in the earliest stages of word learning often *must* read words by sight because they do not yet have in place sufficient concepts and skills for reading words through use of word identification strategies (Ehri, 1991). Indeed, not only does recognizing words at sight originate before identifying words through decoding (e.g., using phonic skills), it is a more effortless way for youngsters in the very early period of reading acquisition to read words, even if the readers are in a classroom where instruction in phonics is being presented (Barr, 1974–75; Ehri, 1991).

Sight Word Recognition as a Prerequisite and Aid to Word Identification Strategies

What is more, it appears to be necessary to recognize some words by sight in order to learn word identification strategies. Ehri and Wilce (1985), for instance, found that when students had mastered letter recognition and could read some words in isolation, they then could move to stages of word learning where they were capable of applying letter-sound relationships to read words.

Furthermore, developing readers need to acquire a sight vocabulary because this is necessary in order to employ a word identification strategy beginning readers use until they gain more proficiency. That strategy is use of context clues. As you remember, when implementing this strategy, readers use the other words in a passage to detect what the unknown word should be. Here is an example.

> Elaine and her mother had just moved to the country. Elaine was lonely and missed her old friends. She was sitting in a chair with nothing to do one morning when suddenly someone _____ at the door.

In this example, you can use the surrounding context to guess what the missing word would be, but obviously readers must have accurate recognition of the words surrounding the word they are attempting to identify; otherwise, context provides no help.

Sight Word Recognition Promotes More Word Recognition

Automatic recall of words leads to increased ability to recognize words. This cyclical process is influenced by the fact that, when readers no longer must stop often to puzzle over unknown words, they can read more.

Clay (1967) reported in one study of first graders that good readers read approximately 20,000 words in a year's time, but poor readers read only about 5,000 words. Similarly, Juel (1988) found that over the course of a year, beginning readers who had good word recognition abilities were exposed to twice as many words in the books they read as those who had low word recognition competence. Good readers had more opportunity to practice responding to words and therefore became even better; poor readers had much less practice on the very task for which they needed to gain skill. The amount of contextual reading and the number of opportunities for response are important to word recognition growth.

Sight Word Recognition and "Irregular" Words

While letter-sound correspondences in English are not arbitrary, they are not always consistent with familiar patterns and rules.

Another reason why extensive recognition of words at sight is important is that, while letter-sound correspondences in English are not arbitrary, they are not always consistent with the most familiar patterns or rules.

English words that do not follow common letter-sound correspondences often cannot be "sounded out," such as *of, some, who, learn, they, to, the, other,* and many more. In some cases, context helps the reader identify such words, but often it does not. Words that are not consistent with standard letter-sound generalizations cause exceptional problems for unskilled readers (Vellutino & Denckla, 1991). Sight recognition of these words is needed.

Sight Word Recognition as a Basis of Fluency

Derived from findings of the National Reading Panel (National Institute of Child Health and Human Development [NICHD], 2000), the NCLB legislation requires fluency to be one of the five essential elements included in programs funded by Reading First. Automatic recognition of words is the very basis of fluency (Stahl & Kuhn, 2004). (See the section on fluency later in this chapter.)

Sight Word Recognition and Comprehension

Accurate word recognition is understandably important to comprehension. Beebe (1980) found that the more the subjects in her study substituted text words with other words, the more difficulty they had with understanding the intended meaning. Furthermore, investigations by Biemiller (1970), Blanchard (1980), Calfee and Piontkowsky (1981), Chall (1989), Herman (1985), Juel (1988), Juel, Griffith, and Gough (1986), Lesgold, Resnick, and Hammond (1985), Lomax (1983), Scarborough (1984), Stanovich (1985), and others confirm that automatic word recognition contributes to improved comprehension.

Accurate, automatic word recognition aids comprehension.

Most reading authorities attribute these relationships to the extra concentration readers can give to meaning when they do not have to focus unduly on word identification processes (e.g., Juel, 1991). Attention may instead be given to integration of text information with background knowledge and reflection on the gist of what is read. Comprehension may also be enhanced because fluent word recognition allows one to read much text. On the other hand, if learners must stop often to recall words or to apply word identification strategies, their train of thought may be disrupted and they may disregard the text message as they focus on these lower-level operations—and, furthermore, they will read less.

At times, a strange dichotomy is offered. Arguments arise about the importance of word recognition/identification instruction versus the criticality of comprehension. This dichotomy is false, as demonstrated in all contemporary models of the reading process (e.g., Just & Carpenter, 1980; Rumelhart, 1976; Stanovich, 1980). Word knowledge and meaning interact to produce proficient reading. Stanovich (1991b) points out that "lack of skill at recognizing words is always a reasonable predictor of difficulties in developing reading comprehension ability" (p. 418).

Sight Word Recognition and Independent Reading Ability

Research has shown that a reader needs instant recognition of about 95% of the words in any given text to read the text independently (Adams, 1990a, 1990b). Students must eventually achieve the point where they do not need direct teacher assistance to read. Since there is also research evidence demonstrating that amount of independent or free-time reading is associated with reading growth, this, too, is a vital argument for attention to word recognition in reading instruction.

Sight Word Recognition and Interest in Reading

Finally, reading in which many words are not within a student's automatic recognition vocabulary is simply laborious. In such cases, students may not develop, or may lose, the *desire* to read. Conversely, being capable of reading words easily leads to greater interest in pursuing reading as a pastime and to more extensive reading. A crucial catalyst to easy, fluent reading is the recognition of "whole words, effortlessly, automatically, and visually" (Adams, 1990b, p. 14).

LEARNING FROM TEXT

> **Note Taking.** In the preceding section, several reasons are given to indicate why readers need to recognize words at sight. Would you be able to tell these to someone else? The subheadings for this section provide the reasons; the information within these subsections would give you a sentence or two to explain each reason. Briefly jot down these details and/or perspectives, paraphrasing as you do.

THE BEGINNINGS OF WORD RECOGNITION

Emergent reading and writing behaviors that evolve during preschool years contribute later to literacy acquisition.

Before we examine word recognition development in school, we'll take a step backward for a minute and take a look at prerequisites to word recognition. **Emergent literacy** is a term used to refer to reading and writing behaviors that evolve before formal instruction begins. There is growing awareness that these behaviors contribute later to successful literacy acquisition (Pinnell, Lyons, DeFord, Bryk, & Seltzer, 1994; Sulzby, 1989).

A major literacy activity that should occupy much time in preschool years is listening to books and stories read aloud. During book sharing, those reading aloud should do more than just provide a story. They should highlight linguistic concepts, such as *word* ("Look at what this word says") or *sentence* ("Listen to what the bear says in this sentence"). When reading ABC books to preschool children, adults may focus on letters and the relationship between letters and sounds. Parents should invite their children to inspect print. Asking questions about the meaning of the text also is a particularly helpful interaction, as is relating concepts in books to children's existing background information.

A major literacy activity that ought to occupy much time in preschool years is listening to books and stories read aloud.

Educator M. J. Adams (1990a, 1990b) reports reading aloud to her preschool son 30 to 45 minutes a day. In contrast, Teale (1986) studied families who placed less value on reading to children; on the average, these children were read aloud to only about 20 minutes per *month*. Different backgrounds with reading may account for disparities in knowledge about print that children bring to school.

From listening to repeated readings of favorite books, children frequently move to "pretend" reading where they repeat the words of the story in a "reading-like" manner, often called **emergent storybook readings.** Although such readings may not be conventional (or "accurate") from an adult's point of view, most authorities believe they are important contributors to formal literacy acquisition. During progressive reenactments, children move from attending to pictures to attending to print as they read and show increasingly broader understandings of conventional reading.

Children also exhibit writing behaviors in preschool years. Encouragement of these emergent actions, again, has been linked to success in learning to read. Scribbling, writing strings of letters to represent words, copying, "inventing" spellings based on sounds they hear, and asking adults how to spell words are important precursors to higher levels of conventional writing—and to reading, because the child is playing directly with letters and sounds. Encouraging children to write is important to emerging literacy understandings.

How do emergent literacy activities specifically contribute to word recognition? They do so in several ways. First, students must have a concept of what a "word" is. This understanding may not be as simple as it seems since in speech we run many words together so that "breaks" between them are not obvious to a young child. During adult-guided reading to children, the concept of *word* can be developed by pointing out and discussing words, and this can also transpire by assisting children with writing words. In addition, letter recognition can emerge through these activities. Knowledge of the names of letters is one of the strongest predictors of success in word learning in the beginning stages of reading (Adams, 1990a, 1990b; Biemiller, 1977–78; Blackman, 1984; Chall, 1967; Walsh, Price, & Gillingham, 1988). What is more, this connection has been shown regardless of the method of reading instruction used. (Knowledge of letter names does not merely mean being able to recite the alphabet, but, rather, being capable of telling the name of a letter when it is seen in print.) These early literacy experiences also promote phonemic awareness, which, as you remember from an earlier chapter, is strongly related to word learning. Similar prereading activities are instituted in kindergarten and first grade, especially for students who arrive at school without these experiences.

> Writing strings of letters to represent words, copying, inventing spellings, and asking how to spell words are important precursors to conventional writing.

LEARNING FROM TEXT

Using Textual Features. There are two phrases printed in boldface type in the previous section, an indication in many texts that a definition is provided—right there—for you. Did you note the definitions?

📖 PHASES OF WORD LEARNING

Word learning theory has proposed naturally developing phases as students advance from those prereading experiences to fluent reading.

Phase 1

This is the phase in which word recognition begins. It has been called the **pre-alphabetic phase** (Ehri & McCormick, 2004), the **logographic phase** (Ehri, 1991; Frith, 1985), or the **selective-cue phase** (Juel, 1991). Of these terms, the term *pre-alphabetic* is being increasingly suggested because it, rightly, characterizes these readers as having little knowledge of the alphabetic principle; that is, they do not yet realize that sounds heard in words are usually matched with the letters seen in print. The term *logographic*, previously suggested, is used because students in this phase employ the graphic features of words to read them (from the Greek words *logos* for "word" and *graph* for "writing"). The term *selective-cue* is used because only certain cues are employed at this stage, not all that would be useful. This phase is typified by the following behaviors:

1. The student can read only a few words in a context-free situation (i.e., in isolation).
2. The student uses only minimal, gross clues to a word, such as its length or its shape, to try to recollect it. From word to word, different types of clues may be randomly used to try to remember words.
3. Often *letters* are not used as cues to recognize a word, even though for more advanced readers, these are major clues to reading words.
4. If consideration is given to letters, attention is directed only to certain ones. The student does not use the full sequence of letters in a word to recall it. And letter clues may not be remembered from one encounter with the word to the next.
5. *Sounds* of letters (i.e., letter-sound correspondences) are not used.
6. Words are best learned when only a few are presented at a time; when larger sets are introduced, the student is overwhelmed and fails to learn.
7. Students remember a word only when they have had a good deal of exposure to it. A limited number of exposures produces little maintenance of learning.

In the pre-alphabetic phase of word learning, sounds of letters are not yet used.

Phase 2

The second phase in word learning has been referred to as a **partial-alphabetic** (Ehri & McCormick, 1998), **rudimentary-alphabetic** (Ehri, 1991), or **visual recognition** (Mason, 1980) phase. While the term *alphabetic* refers to the letter-sound associations that learners in this phase use, these relationships begin to be applied only in a partial (or rudimentary) way. At one time, the term *rudimentary-alphabetic* was commonly used to describe this phase; currently *partial-alphabetic* is favored by many researchers involved in investigating and explaining this area of literacy learning. Word recognition behaviors in this phase are characterized by the following:

1. The student recognizes more words in context-free conditions than in the preceding phase.
2. Words are learned and remembered after fewer exposures than are necessary in Phase 1, but still many exposures are needed.
3. There is a breakdown of words into *letters*.
4. There is dependable recall of some letter clues.
5. Beginning and ending sounds are sometimes used as an aid in word recognition.

6. Words are predominately read by sight rather than through application of sounds, but recognition is more accurate than in the previous phase because of improved use of letter cues.

Depending on students' literacy experiences, the word learning traits of Phases 1 and 2 are seen commonly and naturally in preschool or kindergarten children or in students in early first grade. They also may be found in somewhat older students who have reading delays. When such behaviors occur in older students, they should not be interpreted as idiosyncratic or odd. They are merely an indication that the older student is operating in a phase of development natural to all readers, although doing so at a more advanced age than is the norm. A later section of this chapter furnishes instructional recommendations for helping less-able readers to move into and through these first two phases of word recognition.

> In the partial-alphabetic phase, beginning and ending sounds are sometimes used to aid word recognition.

Phase 3

The next phase in reading development is what has been termed the **full-alphabetic** (Ehri & McCormick, 1998), **cipher** (Gough & Hillinger, 1980), or **spelling-sound** (Juel, 1991) phase. In this phase, the following types of performances are noted:

1. Students begin to learn and use more letter-sound relationships (also called *grapheme-phoneme correspondences*).
2. Initially, when students start to use more sound-related cues, they may decode words slowly letter by letter.
3. Eventually, students progress to a phase in which words are decoded more swiftly.
4. Many words are identified through sound-symbol decoding, but words also are learned by sight.
5. There is a significant increase in the number of words a reader can learn in a given amount of time.
6. Word recognition and identification are more consistently correct than in previous phases.
7. When errors do occur, fewer nonsense words are produced; there are more real-word substitutions.

> In the full-alphabetic phase, although students use more letter-sound correspondences, initially they may decode words slowly.

Phase 4

Phase 4 is designated the **consolidated-alphabetic** (Ehri & McCormick, 1998) or **orthographic** (Ehri, 1991) phase. *Orthography* refers to the letters and their *sequences* in words. Students begin to see common sequences or spelling patterns that help them read words. This more advanced step of word learning typically appears in normally achieving readers in about second grade, with more control progressively gained through about fifth grade. The following behaviors occur.

1. Because the student has read many words by this point in time in which the same letter sequences recur, new words can be recognized *by analogy*. For example, after a reader knows *make, bake, take, cake, lake, rake,* and *wake,* he or she may generalize this familiar word unit to *shake, brake,* and *flake* without direct instruction or without resorting to slower letter-by-letter use of the corresponding sounds. You, for instance, can decode these nonsense words in the same way: *clake, prake, splake.*

FIGURE 8–1 *Phases of Word Learning*

1. Pre-alphabetic
2. Partial-alphabetic
3. Full-alphabetic
4. Consolidated-alphabetic
5. Automatic

In the consolidated-alphabetic phase, new words may be recognized by analogy to known words.

2. Through strategies learned in Phases 2 and 3—and through their increasing experiences with print—students accumulate enough exposure to the *spelling patterns* in words that they come to recognize typical units of words. Familiar sequences can be pronounced on sight (such as *-ing, pre-, un-, -tion*). This allows the reader to decode words in bigger units than those used in the letter-by-letter decoding seen in Phase 3. In addition, and partially because of this, more multisyllabic words can be decoded easily and quickly.

Try to read these nonwords for which you know the familiar orthographic units and for which you may apply analogies from common word parts: *undeanful, pregatted, mistavelyment*, or *renickeration*. On this last one, you were able to quickly decode a five-syllable "word" you had never seen before (since I made it up) because you have sufficient knowledge of English spelling patterns.

3. During this phase, more words can be recognized by sight.

4. Reading is more fluent because of skills developed in the previous phases.

Instructional implications for Phases 3 and 4 of word learning are addressed in Chapter 9.

Phase 5

Phase 5 may be thought of as the **automatic** stage (Chall, 1983). Most words are recognized at sight. The reader has stable control over a variety of ways to learn and recognize words—assimilated and practiced in the preceding phases—which can be brought into play in the exceptional cases when a word is unknown. Figure 8–1 reviews the phases of word learning.

WORD RECOGNITION INSTRUCTION FOR DELAYED READERS

NCLB
READING FIRST

Instruction with students who exhibit limited word recognition must take into account students' developmental phases, as described in the preceding section. It is critically important to analyze the means students use to process words at their present stage of development. Such an analysis will suggest instructional procedures to complement the strategies students currently use and will identify those strategies students need in order to move into the next phase. This approach to designing word recognition programs has support in child development theories (e.g., Vygotsky, 1978) and in current theories of word learning (e.g., Ehri, 1991; Ehri & McCormick, 1998; Frith, 1985; Goswami, 1988; Juel, 1991; Stanovich, 1991b; Vellutino & Denckla, 1991). Carefully read the following two case studies to understand how this type of programming can be successfully accomplished and to learn many specific and important instructional procedures that can be used with reading-delayed students.

Bridget's Case Study

> **Setting a Purpose for Reading.** Next you will read a case study of a student in the pre-alphabetic phase of word learning. Be sure to note instructional procedures that are recommended for students in this phase. If you read carefully, you will discover many of these teaching ideas in this case study. Because there are many, and because they are important, it would be wise to keep a running written list of these as you read through the instructional descriptions.

Bridget's Case Study

Bridget was enrolled in a university reading clinic in the middle of first grade by her mother, an elementary school teacher who noticed that her intelligent young daughter was not progressing at a normal rate in reading.

Synopsis of Assessment Information

Preintervention assessments indicated that Bridget was operating at a very early phase of word learning, even though she had received 4 months of first-grade reading instruction. Bridget did understand the concept of *word*. However, on an entry-level test consisting of lists of isolated words, in the set of the 12 easiest, she was able to pronounce only 3, with major hesitations on 2 of these. When Bridget's word recognition was examined in context, only one additional known word was found. Bridget could recite the alphabet, which her mother said she had learned through the "Alphabet Song," but she did not recognize all letters in their printed forms; in print she recognized 18 capitals and 16 lowercase letters. She knew no letter sounds.

Although Bridget did know two to four words, she could not use alphabetic knowledge effectively in word recognition because she could not identify about 35% of the letters of the alphabet, and her overt behaviors also indicated that she was using gross visual clues (the length of the word or its shape) almost exclusively to recognize words.

Instructional Strategies

A program to acquaint Bridget with letter names, to teach her sight recognition of a number of basic words, and to help her focus on letters as cues to words was instituted as the initial phase of her instruction. She participated in 1-hour lessons three times per week. Several steps were taken.

1. Bridget was taught to recognize those letters of the alphabet she did not know. Research demonstrates that awareness of letter names promotes recall of the forms of written words. This occurs because readers are prompted to view words as regular arrangements of letters, rather than trying to remember them by grosser clues, such as word shape or word length (Adams, 1990a, 1990b; Ehri, 1987).

Bridget's Case Study (continued)

Letter recognition was taught explicitly in direct exercises. As one part of these lessons, Bridget practiced printing the letters. Research has shown that writing contributes strong assistance to letter learning (Adams, 1990a, 1990b); also, this helped Bridget develop a skill needed for writing independently. A good deal of attention was given to letters so that Bridget would be confident in her recognition of them; the clinic supervisor and teacher wanted Bridget to have automaticity in letter recognition. These experiences also were expanded by calling her attention to letters in the context of connected text and writing.

Letter recognition also helps students later to learn sound associations of letters more easily, a task made more difficult if they are still trying to remember which letter is which. It also seems to induce interest in playing with writing, with the accompanying curiosity to know letter sounds in order to spell words (Chomsky, 1979).

2. Predictable books were used. Several factors may go into making a book predictable, such as the repetition of subplots in *The Three Bears*. Other books are predictable because words and phrases are repeated on every page. An example of the latter type, the type used with Bridget, is *Brown Bear, Brown Bear, What Do You See?* by Bill Martin (1983). In this predictable book, every left-hand page addresses the featured bear, repeating his name "Brown Bear" twice on each page. Also on all left-hand pages, the bear is asked the phrase "What do you see?" Thus, the student has exposure to the same words repeatedly. On each right-hand page, a different animal in a different color is targeted. From page to page the bear predictably answers in the same phrase "I see a _____," but supplies the name of the animal and its color as depicted in Eric Carle's bright illustrations—for instance, seeing a "blue horse," "red bird," "yellow duck," and others. The repeated word patterns make it easy for a beginning reader to predict what the words will be, with the pictures also making a major contribution to the book's predictability.

Predictable books were a good choice for Bridget for two reasons: (a) words seen recurrently in text are more likely to be later recognized at sight since they have been frequently practiced (Ehri, 1991) and (b) being in the pre-alphabetic phase of word learning, Bridget needed many exposures to words to remember them. Gough, Juel, and Roper-Schneider (1983) found that students at this stage knew best the words they had been exposed to most and remembered least those with which they had the fewest encounters. Remembering words that have been practiced infrequently is hard for pre-alphabetic readers because their strategy of primarily selecting prominent visual hints to a word's identity does not provide efficient clues for recalling it or for distinguishing a word from similar words (for instance, a child may remember the word *look* because it has two "eyes" in the middle, but so do *took*, *book*, and *cook*).

The same predictable book was used repeatedly with Bridget for 3 days, but in a variety of ways, both to prevent boredom and to be commensurate with her growing familiarity with the words in the book over the three sessions. For example, as suggested by Becker (1994):

a. While Bridget followed along, the teacher read the book, pointing to each word. Finger-pointing by the teacher or the child provides an assist during early word learning (Clay, 1985).

b. The teacher read, pausing to let Bridget chime in when she remembered words.

c. Bridget and the teacher read in unison, finger-pointing as they did so.

d. The book was recorded on audiotape, and Bridget read along orally or silently, pointing to each word.

e. The teacher read the left page of the book and Bridget read the right to the end of the story. Then positions were reversed, and Bridget read the left page and the teacher read the right.

f. Bridget read independently, with the teacher chiming in when Bridget was stumped.

g. Pages of the book were printed on chart paper so that Bridget read them without the support of the pictures.

Adams (1990b) indicates that "repeated readings and repetitive texts set the stage for the acquisition of a broad sight vocabulary" (p. 69). At the end of the 3-day cycle, a new predictable book was selected.

3. After Bridget had read several predictable books, each day thereafter she decided on one of her former favorites to read once again. She simply read the book through, with the teacher assisting on words if necessary. This reading was in addition to work with another book that was the instructional focus at the time.

4. To augment practice of words through the context of predictable books, some isolated word exercises also were presented. The words were chosen from the book Bridget was working on during that particular 3-day cycle. This was deemed a better procedure than introducing additional words. Furthermore, there was direct practice on only five words at a time (the first practice set with the *Brown Bear* book contained *see, bear, you, red*, and *a*); until she showed accurate recognition of these, no others were included in the exercises. Both of these procedures were in keeping with Bridget's stage of word learning: Better recall is obtained in the prealphabetic phase through concentration on small sets of words at a given time. Practice of these words outside the book's context was an important addition to the contextual reading because the redundant nature of these texts makes the books easy to memorize by bright children. In such cases, word recognition may appear to be occurring when it is not.

Specific word practice also involved contextual exercises. For instance, sentence building was used; that is, words written individually on cards were placed randomly on the desk and Bridget picked cards and arranged them to form short, but meaningful sentences. These incorporated known words as well as the immediate focus words. For example, since *I* was one of Bridget's previously known words, even with her first practice set, she could create these sentences:

> I see a bear
> you see a bear

The direct practice on words ensured that Bridget would transfer words she was exposed to in the predictable book to other texts.

Some direct word practice exercises also took place *with* the book. In particular, **masking** was used, in which a card with an open rectangle cut into it was placed on a page so only one word could be seen; Bridget attempted to pronounce the word, but if she could not, the card was raised so that she could use the context of the remainder of the sentence to assist in word identification. See the illustration in Figure 8–2.

A different type of "masking" was used in other direct word practice. Words were printed on individual cards, and a blank card was placed on top of one of the words. The blank card was then moved carefully from left to right, exposing one letter of the word at a time. Bridget was to say the word only after all letters were shown.

FIGURE 8–2   *Using a Mask in Word Practice Activities*

The big cat
saw the dog.

saw

←— mask

Bridget's Case Study (continued)

Many word practice activities that were used with Bridget, and that can be used with other students in the pre-alphabetic or the partial-alphabetic word learning phases (i.e., Phases 1 and 2), are outlined in Table 8–1.

LEARNING FROM TEXT

Applying What You've Learned.   Are there any ideas in Table 8–1 that you could use in your own teaching? All of these are better than simply "drilling" students with flashcards.

5. In every session, Bridget's teacher called attention to letters *in words*. The focus was most often on the beginning letter since this is believed to be the most helpful graphic cue in a word, but attention was also systematically directed to the sequence of letters in words. The latter is called *focusing on the internal features of words or focusing on orthographic features*. This was done during word practice activities, but also during connected text reading with predictable books to ensure that Bridget generalized this word learning strategy to real text reading.

    Moreover, when Bridget demonstrated use of nonproductive cues ("I can remember that word is *monkey* because it has a tail."), the teacher switched her attention to more productive cues by saying something like, "Yes, it ends with the letter *y*. What letter does *monkey* begin with? Great! You notice that *monkey* begins with an *m*. Can you spell the letters of *monkey* for me?" Bridget was asked to name and count the letters in words she was working on (as suggested by Ehri & Wilce, 1985) and to engage in other comparable activities. All these procedures were used to shift Bridget's selection of word cues to a higher stage so she would no longer try to exploit visual clues that have limited serviceability—"eyes" (*look*), "tails" (*monkey*), shape, and length—but, rather, would view words as stable arrangements of letters.

6. Bridget dictated a short "story" each day. The teacher attempted to structure the dictation so that some of Bridget's focus words were used. For instance, on the first

TABLE 8–1 *Three Categories of Word Practice Activities*

A Few Examples of Word Practice Activities

1. *Contextual Activities* (Used to promote transfer to connected text.)
   * reading short sentences composed of target words plus known words
   * reading short paragraphs, then short stories (written by teacher) as students progress
   * reading cloze sentences
   * sentence building
   * reading cooperative stories (stories for which the teacher reads most of the text, but that include brief, interspersed sections to be read by the student); see Figure 13–3 in Chapter 13, for an example.
   * guessing words written in "invisible ink" within the context of a sentence, paragraph, or story and coloring in the words to confirm the choice
2. *Focusing on Internal Features of Words* (Used to encourage reflective, rather than impulsive, behavior, and recognition of unique sequences of letters in words. These activities require conscious detection of distinctive and redundant visual and orthographic information.)
   * spelling words with magnetic letters
   * manipulating letter dice to form words
   * linking letters printed on puzzle pieces in arrangements to spell words
   * guessing missing letters in words written with "invisible ink" marking pens, then coloring these in to self-check the choice
   * writing words on a Magic Slate and lifting the paper to rewrite correctly if wrong
   * writing words on small handheld chalkboards
   * filling in missing letters in hangman games
   * tracing words
3. *Games and Manipulatives* (Used to increase attention and to provide a stress-free form of practice. Interest and willingness to take risks positively influence performance.)
   * board games
   * card games
   * bingo games
   * word hunts
   * puzzles
   * concentration games
   * word wheels
   * grab bag activities
   * word checkers
   * games involving play money

Bridget's Case Study (continued)

day of the *Brown Bear* book the teacher said, "We have been reading about a *brown* bear. But let's suppose you saw a *red* bear! Use your imagination. What could you tell me about that *red* bear?" After a little thought, Bridget said, "The red bear ate a man." The teacher then wrote this sentence, with Bridget looking on, and spelled each word aloud as she wrote the letters. She asked Bridget, "What did the red bear say that he saw?" Bridget responded, "He said 'I see a man.'" Thus, four of her focus words appeared in the dictation (*red, bear, a, see*). The teacher wrote, while spelling out loud, the second sentence of Bridget's "story." Bridget then read back her dictation, having little difficulty even though some words were new to her. The teacher helped her finger-point to each word as she read and assisted where necessary.

The next step was to help with more advanced composition skills. The sequence of the two-sentence "story" was discussed, and it was decided that it would make more sense for the bear to see the man first and eat him after that. So, her two sentences were cut apart by the teacher, and they were

Simple composing skills may be taught even to beginning readers.

rearranged by Bridget to show a more logical progression of events. The story now reads:

> He said I see a man.

> The red bear ate a man.

Bridget read the new version of the story. More discussion ensued, with the teacher questioning, "Instead of saying '*He* said I see a man,' could we also say '*The red bear* said I see a man'?" Bridget agreed that this could be said. The teacher then cut each sentence apart into its separate words, and Bridget rearranged them so that the next revision read:

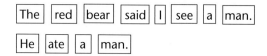

Bridget read the latest "draft" of her story. She thought it did sound good, and the teacher was satisfied that it was acceptable for now (even though in a more mature version, the *a* in the last sentence might have been substituted with the word *the*).

This activity contributed meaningful construction endeavors (by fostering awareness that *the red bear* could be substituted for *he*, for example, and by supplying experiences with logical sequences in composing) and gave Bridget many contextual reading response opportunities with some of her focus words. In addition, because the teacher spelled aloud every letter in each word as Bridget watched her write, this strengthened the concept that words are made of a systematic ordering of letters.

7. The teacher read aloud to Bridget for a few minutes every day from authentic texts. Most often, attractive picture books were used, but poetry and stories from anthologies of famous fairy tales also were read. These included words and sentence constructions slightly above her maturity level, as suggested from research for furthering learning (Chomsky, 1972; Vygotsky, 1978). Occasional word meanings were discussed. Once in a while, the teacher pointed to a word and said to Bridget, "You know this word now! Will you read it to me?" Bridget became attached to many of these books and took them home for her mother to read to her again.

Outcomes of Instruction

After approximately 30 hours of instruction over 9 1/2 weeks, Bridget could name and write all letters of the alphabet in their uppercase and lowercase forms, although she still occasionally confused lowercase *b* and *d*. She had accurate sight recognition of many more words in and out of context. She was learning and remembering words after shorter periods of exposure. She attended to letter cues and had become quite adept at playing the hangman game, which requires attention to orthographic sequences and positions of letters in words.

In short, she was operating rather well in Phase 2 of word learning—the partial-alphabetic phase—with the exception that she was not using letter *sounds* in her word-reading attempts. At that time, objectives for her instruction were changed. She was

*Bridget's
Case Study
(continued)*

engaged in some direct phonemic awareness exercises, and the remainder of the goals for her were similar to those established for Daniel, who is described in the case study that follows. Particular attention was given to help Bridget write her own stories, using invented spellings, with teacher guidance to help her solidify understandings about ways letters and sounds are associated.

Figure 8–3 lists some high-quality books that can be used with students who are in the pre-alphabetic or partial-alphabetic phase.

FIGURE 8–3   *Some High-Quality Literature to Use With Students in Very Early Stages of Literacy Learning*

- There certainly is value in using predictable books to meet certain objectives, books such as:

    Brown Bear, Brown Bear, What Do You See? by Bill Martin

    A Dark, Dark Tale by Ruth Brown

    The Cat Sat on the Mat by Brian Wildsmith

- It also is important for students to begin early to contend with vocabulary without the structured assistance of predictable books. Some recommended literature that beginning readers may be helped to read independently are:

    Little Bear by Else Minarik (and others in the Little Bear series)

    Frog and Toad Are Friends by Arnold Lobel, a Caldecott Honor Book (and others in the Frog and Toad series, such as *Frog and Toad Together, a* Newbery Honor Book)

    Mouse Tales by Arnold Lobel (seven short stories)

    There Was an Old Woman by Stephen Wyllie and Maureen Roffey (lift-up tabs encourage use of context clues and development of word recognition)

Dan's Case Study

LEARNING FROM TEXT

Setting a Purpose for Reading.   You are about to read another case study. This one is about Dan, a student in the partial-alphabetic phase of word learning. This time, note and list not only recommended instructional procedures, but also those that are not recommended. (As you will see, several of those will be mentioned.)

*Dan's
Case Study*

Dan's parents referred him for clinical tutoring in January of first grade, after a conference in which his teacher had broached the subject of retention at the end of that year because of Dan's limited word learning. However, Dan already had attained some reading concepts that Bridget did not have.

Synopsis of Assessment Information

Assessment showed that Dan knew the names of all letters and could print them in both their capital and lowercase forms.

During the assessment period, when asked if he would like to write a story, he eagerly agreed, having had experiences with this in his classroom where the teacher encouraged her first graders to use invented spellings if they did not know conventional forms of words they wished to write. Dan's spellings showed preliminary understandings of letter-sound correspondences, for instance, spelling *monster* as *msr*, but with some letter *names* included in the spellings as well, for example, *seat* spelled *cet*. Most initial sounds in words were represented correctly, but the only words that had conventional spellings in their entirety were *to* and *I*. Dan seemed to like playing with writing and spelling.

On a test of phonemic awareness, Dan had respectable phonemic segmentation skills but could not adequately blend sounds to form words. As seen in his writing, a word identification test confirmed that he knew *some* letter-sound correspondences, but when given simple unknown words to identify, he did not attempt to apply this knowledge in a systematic way by using all sounds he knew to decode the words. What he did do was to use his knowledge of one or two letter sounds and read words that shared these features (for instance, reading *cat* as *car* and *bug* as *big* and *fan* as *farmer*). Most often, consonant sounds were noted at the beginnings of words and were correct, although the rest of the word was not. Occasionally, letter-sound associations in positions other than the beginning of the word also were seen (as in the ending letters of *bug/big*), but use of middle sounds was slight (for instance, he read *pick* for *pink*). When letter sounds were used, they most frequently were at the beginning of a word, and second most frequently the beginning *and* ending letters (called the **boundary letters**) were employed.

During preassessment, Dan could read more words by sight than Bridget, both in context and in isolation. He had solid recognition of about 10. There were several others that he recalled inconsistently, sometimes saying the word correctly, but sometimes confusing it with a similar word.

All these reading behaviors are manifestations of a student in the partial-alphabetic phase of word learning (Phase 2).

Instructional Strategies

Helping partial-alphabetic readers increase their repertoires of sight words allows more comprehensive experiences with reading connected text.

Dan's initial program consisted of helping him increase his repertoire of sight words so he could have more comprehensive experiences in reading connected text. At the same time, instruction was begun that would enable him to make greater use of his rudimentary and emerging sense of letter-sound associations. His lessons included the following.

1. Predictable books were used as one route to word learning with Dan, as they had been with Bridget, but he also read short, appealing, easy-to-read, high-interest books of about first, and later, second, preprimer level. He was shown two or three of these at a time and allowed to choose the book he wished to read on that day. Dan's self-selected book was read at the beginning of each period.

   Before Dan began reading, some attention was directed at pictures that conveyed words found on the accompanying pages. In addition, a few words central to the story were highlighted prior to reading; routinely about two of these were pointed out to Dan, and their forms, sounds, and pronunciations emphasized. For instance, when a story about a lion and a mouse was to be read, both *lion* and *mouse* were presented in this way before he encountered them in the text.

Direct instruction is important, but to be most effective it should teach strategies as well as skills.

At the beginning of Dan's reading instruction, assisted reading was sometimes necessary; the teacher read each page first, with each page consisting of one sentence, finger-pointing as she did. Then Dan repeated the reading, also finger-pointing. During these assisted episodes, the teacher read with expression, and Dan and the teacher stopped to discuss pictures and events to enhance meaning and enjoyment as well as word learning. Because he did know a few words, Dan often jumped in to say a word during the teacher's reading. This fairly intensive assistance was required less as his sight word learning increased.

At times, when Dan missed a word for which he did know most letter sounds, the teacher paused to call attention to the sounds, modeling blending of these to form the word; for example, when *run* was misread as *ride*, she said, "You're correct. This word does begin with the *r* sound (then saying the sound), but you know the sound of *n*, too (pointing to the *n* and saying its sound). This word is *run* (moving her finger under the word as it was said, stressing and blending the sounds)." Direct instruction is important, but to be most effective it should teach strategies as well as skills (Duffy & Roehler, 1987).

Other times when Dan miscalled words that he had correctly recognized on some other occasions, he was encouraged to use context, if the surrounding words or the story line did convey the word. For instance, when *The chick said "There are two of us"* was read as *The chick said "There are two on us,"* he was asked to self-check for meaning by asking if what he had read made sense. Students should be taught to use strategies adaptably, according to the circumstances.

Sometimes the teacher pronounced words that were not yet in Dan's repertoire. This was done when unknown words were not amenable to letter-sound clues he knew, when they were irregular words, or when context did not aid in determining the word's identity. When told a word, Dan was asked to reread the sentence, pronouncing the word himself. Then, he simply got on with his reading.

Dan liked reading whole books—albeit short ones—seeming to feel pleased that he could do so.

2. Next, direct practice on word learning was undertaken. Sets of 10 words were selected from books Dan had read, and these were the focus of practice until he consistently recognized them accurately, with some words moving out of the practice set before others, and with new target words moving in. An ongoing set of 10 was always maintained. Students in the partial-alphabetic phase of word learning can work with slightly larger sets of words than those in the pre-alphabetic phase (Ehri & Wilce, 1987). Words that were dependably recognized were placed in a file box called his "Words I Know!" Word Bank and were periodically taken out, reviewed, and counted to provide feelings of success.

Dan's word practice exercises included contextual activities, activities that focused on internal features of words, and practice with the words in isolation. The practice on words often incorporated games and manipulatives to boost Dan's attention and his willingness to take risks—and because he found these to be fun while learning. Activities also used with Bridget, outlined in Table 8–1, often were employed.

Some care was taken not to include words in a learning set that were very similar, since inclusion of words that look very much alike in the same group to be studied increases the length of time to learn the words (Gough & Hillinger, 1980). For example, when *look* and *like* ended up in the same set, Dan had much confusion in sorting out the two, especially with his propensity to focus on beginning and ending letter-sound associations and to ignore the middles. More than the usual time elapsed before these two words went into his "Words I Know!" Word Bank.

Dan's Case Study (continued)

Many high-frequency words have abstract meanings, making them less easy to learn than words with more concrete meanings.

Also, each set contained words for which it was easy to associate meanings, such as nouns (*elephant, cake*), image-evoking verbs (*jump, play*), and adjectives (*fast, pretty*). The meaningfulness of these types of words makes them comparatively easier to learn and remember than other words. However, many of the most frequently occurring words in written and oral language carry less concrete meanings. These are prepositions, conjunctions, and articles (called **function words**); because of their high frequency, they must be recognized automatically for proficient reading. Therefore, these were included in each set as well. A balance between meaningful words and function words was sought in each set, usually five of each. Because the learning of function words is often difficult, it is useful to know that Ehri and Wilce (1987) discovered that having partial-alphabetic readers *spell* function words helped students to learn them. In addition to this procedure, many of the activities listed in Table 8–1 under the heading "Focusing on Internal Features of Words" had the same effect—and also sped Dan's learning of meaningful words. Dan particularly liked to write his words on a small handheld chalkboard or on a Magic Slate and to form words by manipulating magnetic letters on a cookie sheet used as a magnet board.

Dan could retain words rather well after shorter exposure times than Bridget, probably because using sounds in combination with visual clues, as he was doing, makes it easier to recall words (Ehri, 1991). Still, readers in the partial-alphabetic phase need many practice opportunities for sight word reading to occur (Ehri & Wilce, 1987).

Multiple exposures to words also help students detect differences between similar words. Although, for students in early phases of word learning, learning words initially is swifter when two words that look alike are not practiced at the same time, these words can later be confused if they have not been overlearned to the point of automatic, accurate recognition. Acquiring an adequate sense of letter-sound associations also helps students make distinctions between similar words (Vellutino & Denckla, 1991).

Word exposure is extended through contextual reading (Barr, 1984). However, Juel (1989) cites data demonstrating that achievement of students in early word learning phases depends on how well they read individual words. Only after they have acquired a fair amount of proficiency is word learning affected simply by connected text reading. For that reason, direct practice with words, as well as connected text reading, was included in Dan's program.

3. Following direct word practice, Dan was asked to reread a book he had read on a previous day. Although Dan selected the book for his first contextual reading experience in each session, the teacher chose this book. This was done so a text would be used that either (a) included words he was currently practicing in his word learning set or (b) included ones that had progressed to his known-words word bank. This policy allowed more exposure to the words and prompted transfer to authentic texts. In addition, since function words occur frequently in all written material, any books provided practice with those function words that were a focus of instruction for Dan.

Sometimes a book was picked because Dan now knew all words in the text. It was used to give him the opportunity for an eloquent, highly successful book-reading experience. Other times, a text was selected because it contained several words he was confusing with similar words and therefore required more practice. Since occurrence of words in context can at times help in identifying them, this practice was beneficial, allowing him to make correct responses. But in any case, customarily, Dan found rereading a book easier than reading his new book for the day. His rereadings were rather fluent, and he moved through these books fairly quickly.

*Dan's
Case Study
(continued)*

Writing helps students
achieve reading goals
in a number of ways.

4. Dan wrote something every session. Usually he composed a story of two or three sentences. He was encouraged to use invented spellings because this supported his evolving perspectives about letter-sound associations. These spellings were treated with respect by the teacher, with good associations pointed out. For example, when *job* was spelled *jb*—Dan had written *GD JB!!!* at the top of his own paper—the teacher said, "You're right! *Job* does begin with the *j* sound," and then pronounced that sound for him.

  Some research has shown that on tests of word recognition, students who have had experiences with inventing spellings perform better than those who have not (Baron & Treiman, 1980). In this research, that effect was seen more for *low-readiness* students than for high. It has been hypothesized that when students think about the connections between sounds they hear in words and the letters that could be written for these sounds—and then make active attempts to spell them—their sense of letter-sound associations expands (Adams, 1990a, 1990b). These experiences are good precursors to more formalized instruction with word identification strategies, especially phonic analysis skills. (Many educators today use the term *temporary spellings* to replace the term *invented spellings,* since the former designation elicits a less negative reaction from some who are unaware of the value of students using their own renditions of words as stepping stones to more mature spelling.)

**LEARNING
FROM TEXT**

Verbal Rehearsal.   Formulate a response to someone who questions the use of invented (temporary) spellings by students in early stages of reading and writing acquisition.

  Dan's teacher knew that noting the order of letters in words also bolsters word recognition (Vellutino & Denckla, 1991), so she wanted to use Dan's writing for this objective, too. Therefore, when he wrote a word he had been practicing in his word-learning sets, he was required to spell that word conventionally. To do so, he placed his word card in front of him and copied the sequence of letters in the right order. Cards in his known-words word bank were placed alphabetically behind divider cards with lettered tabs for ease in finding the words. The current practice set was always available on his desk. Examination of the effects of copying words shows that this exercise reinforces students' retention because it requires attention to the complete sequence of letters in these words (Adams, 1990a, 1990b; Whittlesea, 1987). Also, Dan sometimes asked for correct spellings of other words; although this was not required, when he asked, his teacher spelled those words for him.

5. At the end of each day's lessons, Dan and the teacher returned to the book that had been read at the beginning of the session. Dan read it again, with assistance as needed. Because this was the second reading, he commonly showed better word recognition than earlier in the period, often asking for wait time so he could pronounce words without assistance ("Don't tell me. I can get it"). **Wait time** refers to the time a teacher pauses to allow a student to reflect on a problem and to marshal known information and strategies to solve it. Wait time is critical for nourishing students' independence in using strategies for skillful reading.

  Each of Dan's books was read at least three times: (a) an initial reading at the beginning of a session; (b) a rereading at the end of that period, in which growing

adeptness was often seen; and (c) later, when it was chosen by the teacher for the exercise of rereading a book.

If it was time to add words to his learning set, Dan was asked to help select new additions from this book. However, since the goal was to equalize the numbers of meaningful words and function words in those sets, he was allowed to make choices from among those suggested by the teacher. For example, she might say, "Because you knew so many words today, we can add two more to your practice set. From this story shall we include *school* or *boy*?" After his first choice, she might ask, "Should I put in your set *in* or *for*?"

Outcomes of Instruction

After 5 weeks of one-to-one instruction, Dan had consistent, automatic recognition of about 40 words he had not known at the beginning of his tutoring. He sometimes remembered, but did not always recall, other words as well.

Dan was now reading short books with some success. Teacher prompts on words still were needed, but less so than in the initial part of his program. He was using context quite often in word recognition attempts. After successful experiences with books in his tutoring sessions, he liked to take them with him to read to his parents.

During his writing activities, he spelled more words conventionally, especially short words and ones that had been a part of his practice sets.

He was deliberately making more attempts at employing letter-sound associations to come up with accurate pronunciations of words. Although more effective than previously, this was at times still unsuccessful—undoubtedly because, while he seemed to have internalized a few more letter sounds, he still did not know them all.

At this stage, more formal attempts to teach Dan word identification strategies were added to his lessons. These efforts will be described in Chapter 9, where his case study will continue.

📖 MORE ABOUT EXPOSURES TO WORDS

An important question is, how much practice is needed before a word is recognized automatically?

An important question is, how much practice is needed before a word is recognized automatically? First, this question must be considered in light of students' word-learning phases. Basically, the earlier the phase, the more exposures necessary. With each progressive phase, readers learn to use cues and strategies that make recall of words more efficient.

Second, the number of exposures needed for each word varies according to characteristics of the word itself. For example, the level of abstraction influences how easily it is learned; words that carry more highly apparent meanings (nouns such as *horse*, image-evoking verbs such as *run*, adjectives such as *fast*) are generally easier to recall than function words (prepositions such as *of* and conjunctions such as *but*). But, third, the examples provided here for the meaningful words actually are words that students tend to confuse; for instance, these are fairly typical confusions: *horse/house*, *run/ran*, *fast/first*. Those confusions result because the words resemble each other. The degree to which a word resembles a similar word affects the number of exposures needed for accurate, automatic recognition.

In addition, research indicates that a fourth determining factor is a learner's intellectual functioning level. Gates (1931, p. 35), in a now classic study, determined that the following approximate numbers of repetitions were needed, on average, by students in his study, as a function of intelligence levels.

Level of Intelligence	IQ	Required Exposures
Significantly above average	120–129	20
Above average	110–119	30
Average	90–109	35
Slow learner	80–89	40
Upper educable mentally retarded ranges	70–79	45
Middle educable mentally retarded ranges	60–69	55

The general conclusion one should draw is that all students, including those with high intelligence, need many exposures to a word before it becomes part of their sight vocabularies, especially at the automatic recognition level. Three or four opportunities to practice a word are not enough.

Furthermore, these averaged results do not imply that a specific number of exposures is required in isolation, such as 35 opportunities to say a word printed on a flashcard. Rather, it means total exposures of all kinds, including repeated exposures to the same word in a variety of regular, connected reading materials. The goal should be to provide overlearning, not drill. The term **drill** refers to doing the same thing in the same way day after day, as in limiting sight word practice to daily flashcard exercises only. **Overlearning,** on the other hand, refers to practice carried out in a variety of ways and in a variety of materials, including authentic texts. Overlearning facilitates generalization of word knowledge to all reading situations, not just one (e.g., reading flashcards).

Drill suggests that students must do the same thing in the same way day after day. *Overlearning,* on the other hand, implies practice with words in a variety of ways and in a variety of materials.

MORE ABOUT CONTEXTUAL VERSUS ISOLATED PRACTICE

There has been controversy over whether words should be taught in context or in isolation. Some have argued for contextual practice because this method more closely approximates recognition tasks in authentic reading. Others maintain that context-free practice is important, pointing to the need for students to focus specifically on individual words so they may attend carefully to the visual and sound characteristics that distinguish a word from others.

Even research about this issue seems to lead in contradictory directions and fails to provide definite evidence in favor of one side of this argument or the other. For example:

- Kibby (1989) reported research with disabled readers in a reading clinic. On the average, they were 3 years behind their potentials in reading ability. Half the group was randomly assigned to be taught word recognition in context; the other half was taught words in isolation, focusing primarily on the words' distinguishing visual and sound features. There were no significant differences between the groups in age, reading ability, intelligence, or gender. Both groups learned and retained an equal number of words they had not known previously (average number = 64); however, the isolated-word group learned the words at twice the rate.

- On the other hand, Ceprano (1981) found that while introduction of words in context produced slower initial learning, the contextual introduction produced fewer errors later in real text reading.
- Ceprano (1981) also found that if students are to be assessed on words in isolation, practice on words in isolation may produce better results, but if they are to be assessed on words in context, it appears that practicing words in isolation or in context may work equally well.
- An earlier study by Kibby (1977) found that practice in isolation and practice in context were equally effective for transfer of word knowledge to reading in real contextual material.

Some research has shown practice in isolation or in context to be equally effective for transfer of word knowledge to connected text material.

These studies, along with the numerous others reviewed earlier in this chapter, provide many reasons to use *both* contextual and context-free activities in instruction for word learning.

Here are some tentative conclusions about the results of presenting words in isolation.

1. Students focus more attention on letter-sound associations.
2. There is an increased rate of learning.
3. Studying words in isolation may be necessary at some word-learning stages because text coverage alone may not sufficiently develop word recognition.
4. Students can more easily analyze words into their systematic ordering of letters.
5. Students develop phonemic awareness more readily.
6. Students can more readily focus attention on easily confused words.
7. Students can more easily work on blending.
8. Seeing words in isolation helps students with spelling.
9. Students' reading fluency increases.

Both isolated and contextual practice with words is important.

Here are some tentative conclusions about the results of presenting words in context.

1. Students show increased interest.
2. Transfer of learning is promoted.
3. Seeing words in context helps students learn irregular words.
4. Reading words in context provides students assistance with learning function words.
5. Students have opportunities to process many words.
6. Seeing words in context may be suitable for students in some word-learning stages in which words can be internalized from much text coverage.
7. In context, use of multiple cueing systems of language—for example, letters, sounds, and context—is possible.
8. Students can focus on word meaning as well as recognition.
9. Students gain increased fluency.

The obvious conclusion is that both types of word practice are needed. Furthermore, since students need many exposures to words for their recognition to be accurate and automatic, combining the two approaches allows overlearning to occur.

Examples of how contextual practice and context-free word practice can be effectively combined were seen in Bridget's and Dan's programs. Many teachers, as a rule of thumb, follow this routine sequence:

Step 1: *Context.* Each word to be practiced during a session is read in context.

Step 2: *Isolation.* A context-free activity is used to promote careful consideration of the distinguishing features of the words.

Step 3: *Context.* Students read the words in a new context.

This can be called *whole-part-whole* learning.

LEARNING FROM TEXT

Compare. What is the issue concerning teaching words in context versus teaching words in isolation? What is the answer?

MORE ABOUT SPECIFIC TEACHING ACTIVITIES

Using Language Experience Stories

A word recognition program based on student-dictated stories can be instituted, as in the language experience approach. This technique can be used with secondary as well as elementary students; the major difference is simply in the choice of topics for story dictation. With the language experience approach, the student dictates a story, which the teacher writes down as it is dictated. Then the student reads the story.

Lessons are designed to ensure that students develop accurate recognition of words that occur in their dictated stories. The teacher uses a variety of exercises, including in lessons the three word-practice types shown in Table 8–1, each of which serves a different and important need. One effective sequence of activities is shown in Figure 8–4.

Research has shown that a large percentage of words in students' own dictated stories are high-frequency words.

Most high-frequency words will occur in students' dictated stories because they are used so often in oral as well as written language. Henderson, Estes, and Stonecash (1971–72) confirmed this in a study of word acquisition that used a language experience approach. They compared one week's sample of beginning readers' dictated stories with the Lorge-Thorndike Word List and found that 45% of the students' dictated words were in that list's category of highest frequency.

If words a student should learn are failing to occur in the dictated stories, the teacher can structure a situation so that they will be used. For example, suppose the word *green* is one the teacher wants Bradley to know. In one session the

FIGURE 8–4   *Word Practice Based on a Student-Dictated Story*

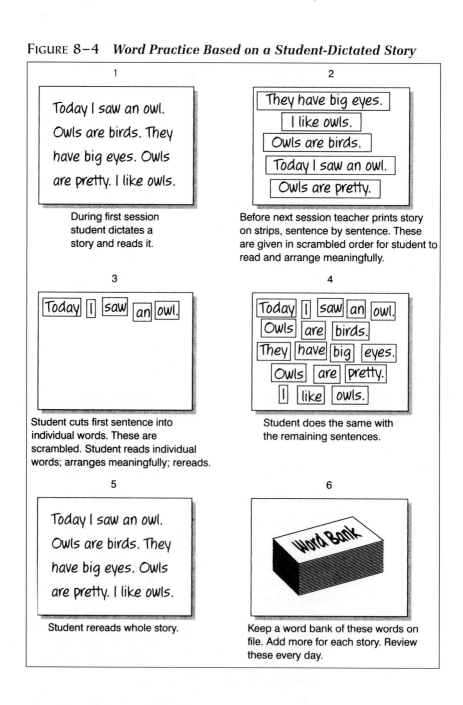

1

Today I saw an owl. Owls are birds. They have big eyes. Owls are pretty. I like owls.

During first session student dictates a story and reads it.

2

They have big eyes.
I like owls.
Owls are birds.
Today I saw an owl.
Owls are pretty.

Before next session teacher prints story on strips, sentence by sentence. These are given in scrambled order for student to read and arrange meaningfully.

3

Today I saw an owl.

Student cuts first sentence into individual words. These are scrambled. Student reads individual words; arranges meaningfully; rereads.

4

Today I saw an owl.
Owls are birds.
They have big eyes.
Owls are pretty.
I like owls.

Student does the same with the remaining sentences.

5

Today I saw an owl. Owls are birds. They have big eyes. Owls are pretty. I like owls.

Student rereads whole story.

6

Word Bank

Keep a word bank of these words on file. Add more for each story. Review these every day.

teacher might bring in several green items (a green leaf, a puppet with a green shirt, a green apple) and say to Bradley (or his group), "Today we are going to write our story about things that are green."

To support word learning activities, students may keep two word banks. A **word bank** is any container (e.g., a metal file box or a manila envelope) in which their personal word cards are placed. One of the word banks can be labeled "Words I'm Working On" and the other "Words I Know."

Words chosen for focus from student stories should, of course, include both high-frequency function words and concrete meaning-carrying words. Word banks help students build a base of words that will enable them to read published books. If other words are learned incidentally (such as from signs, labels, and so on) or in other teaching situations, these can be added to students' word banks.

Throughout the beginning phase, a chart or graph showing the students' progress should be kept so there is a visual record of how many words have been learned. Figure 8–5 shows an example of such a chart. Although it may be

FIGURE 8–5 *Charts Help Students Visualize Progress*

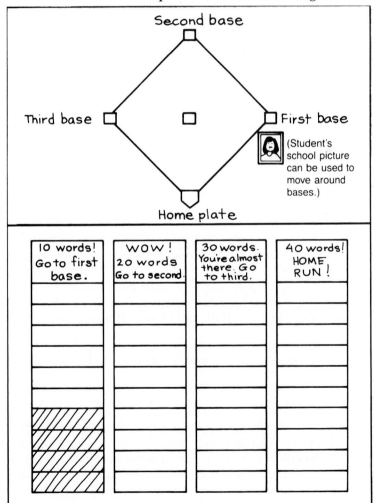

kept in the student's private folder or portfolio, this chart or graph should be available to the teacher and student to use each day. Visually demonstrating progress is highly motivating to most learners.

During the same time that sight vocabulary is being developed, students may benefit from lessons linked directly to their dictated story that help in learning word identification strategies. This knowledge not only is necessary for identifying unknown words not yet in the student's sight recognition but also can actually assist in the initial learning of many sight words.

After the student has learned a number of words, check words in the student's word bank against those in stories found in beginning reading materials. Compare the word bank words to a first preprimer in a basal reader series used in the student's regular classroom or an easy-to-read, high-interest book used in the special program. When the student's story-dictation experiences have helped him or her know most words in the published story, have the student read it. This will provide practice with newly acquired words, an introduction to published material, and a successful experience with a published text because the student learned the words before being asked to read it.

The Four Blocks Program

A systematic program used in many school systems that includes ample amounts of word work is the Four Blocks program (Cunningham, Hall, & DeFee, 1998). Students' literacy instruction is divided into four daily segments, also called *blocks,* consisting of (a) guided reading with whole groups, small groups, and individuals; (b) student self-selected reading; (c) writing; and (d) working with words.

During each of the four time periods, to meet the goals for that block, the teacher furnishes a variety of instructional formats at different levels to meet the needs of delayed readers, average readers, and the most competent readers. Thus, the developers call the program *multi-leveled.*

The "working with words" block addresses both word recognition and word identification. Highly focused daily attention is provided to a certain number of words each week to bring them to the automatic-recognition level. A prominent feature of this work involves a **Word Wall**—classroom space where targeted words are displayed and become the center of intensive and imaginative lessons. In addition, exercises with spelling patterns in words and other activities foster word identification strategies and support word recognition.

A good resource to learn more about the word recognition exercises and other aspects of the program is *The Teacher's Guide to the Four Blocks* by Cunningham, Hall, and Sigmon (Carson-Dellosa Publishing, 1999).

To see how one school system used the Four Blocks program to foster word recognition and other literacy goals, go to www.k111.k12.il.us/lafayette/fourblocks/ Then, click "Working with Words Block."

Other Techniques for Sight Vocabulary Learning

Activities suggested in the following section may be used for introduction and initial learning of words as well as for practice.

Published materials offer a variety of formats for introducing and practicing basic sight vocabulary.

1. Published materials offer the teacher a variety of formats for introducing and reinforcing basic sight vocabulary. For example, the *High Frequency Readers* (Scholastic) are a set of materials featuring lap-sized books, little books, and take-home sheets to read to parents. These all contain several of the same stories to read in different contexts, providing much exposure and review of high-frequency words. These materials are also available in Spanish.

2. The teacher writes cloze sentences, leaving blanks where words on which the student is presently working would fit.

The student places word bank cards on a desk with the single words facing up. Next, the student reads the first cloze sentence and selects a word from the word bank cards that he or she thinks would fit the blank. Finally, the student places that card above the sentence and uses it as a model to write the word in the blank.

| on |
Get <u>on</u> the bus.

3. Make blank bingo boards from oaktag, with squares large enough so that an index card can be placed on each. Students place their individual word bank cards (single word up) on the bingo board in random order (see Figure 8–6).

Before beginning the game, the teacher prints cloze sentences on individual oaktag strips. (For example: This _____ not fun.) These are prepared so there are sentences for all students' word-bank words (the group of words on which each student is presently working). The teacher places one cloze strip on the chalkboard tray. Any student who has a word bank card that makes sense in the sentence raises that card, and reads the sentence pronouncing that word

FIGURE 8–6 **An Example of a Bingo Board With Sight-Word Cards From a Student's Word Bank**

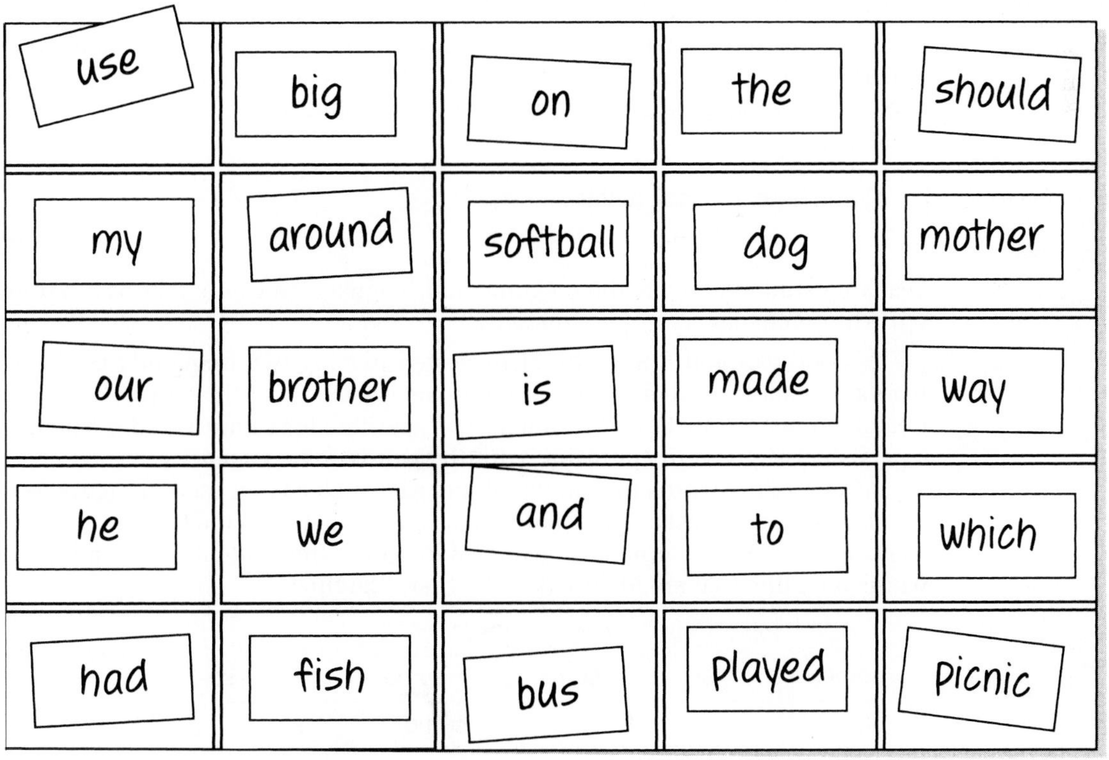

use	big	on	the	should
my	around	softball	dog	mother
our	brother	is	made	way
he	we	and	to	which
had	fish	bus	played	picnic

instead of the blank. If all is correct, the student removes that word card from his or her bingo board. The student who first gets five empty bingo squares in a row or column wins.

4. Mike does not recognize the word *off* when he encounters it twice in the story he is reading orally. At the completion of the story, the teacher asks him to think of some sentences that name things that can be turned off. The teacher asks Mike to begin each sentence with "You can turn off _____." The teacher writes these sentences as Mike completes them, and underlines the word *off* each time.

> You can turn <u>off</u> the stove.
> You can turn <u>off</u> the air conditioner.
> You can turn <u>off</u> the lights.
> You can turn <u>off</u> the TV.

Mike observes as the teacher records the sentences and is then asked to read the sentences orally, finger-pointing to each word as he does. This usually produces successful recognition and response to the problem word every time. To promote generalization of the correct response to other material, the teacher reopens the book Mike had been reading to the places where he had missed the word *off* and asks him to read the word in those sentences.

Elimination of Word Confusions

For many delayed readers the problem with sight vocabulary is not one of needing initial learning experiences with words, but rather one of confusing similar words.

For many delayed readers the problem with sight vocabulary is not one of needing initial learning experiences with words, but rather one of confusing similar words, such as mistaking *of* for *if* or *off*. The following activities may be used to help students eliminate sight word confusions.

1. Encourage students to attend to meaning. In many cases in contextual material, words frequently confused cannot be read for each other and result in a meaningful sentence. An example is this word confusion:

came
Come here and look at this.

Teaching students to use the meaning and language clues the text has to offer will eliminate many word confusions.

2. Goodman and Burke (1972) suggested placing two frequently confused words in a short teacher-written story in such a way that the correct choice is unambiguous. Figure 8–7 offers such a story written for a fourth grader who had a persistent sight word confusion with the words *so* and *some*.

After reading words in contextual material such as that seen in Figure 8–7, the student may be asked to visually discriminate between the two words he or she confuses. An example is an exercise in which the student circles all those words on a line that are identical to the first, like this:

some	so	some	some	so
so	so	so	some	so	some

FIGURE 8–7   ***Example of a Story That Gives Students Many Opportunities to Practice Frequently Confused Words***

> Michael was so glad that it was Friday! He knew that this was the day of the school Christmas party. Some of the other boys were going to stop by his house to walk to school with him today, so he had gotten up early.
>
> The teacher had asked Michael and some of the boys to bring cookies from home, so they were going to go to school early so they could put the cookies on plates and put them out on tables. Some of the girls had been asked to come early so they could make a bowl of punch.
>
> When the other boys got to Michael's house, he went to get his cookies. Much to his surprise some little parts of some of the cookies had been eaten away! He was SO mad!
>
> Crumbs from the cookies were all around the plate. A small line of crumbs led to the edge of the table. Another line of crumbs led from the table to a place under some of the kitchen cabinets.
>
> David and some of the other boys watched as Michael followed this line of crumbs to where they led. Michael got down on his knees. He saw a small hole under one cabinet. "So, that's it," he said. "Some little mouse has already had himself a party." David and some of the other boys laughed. David said, "That's okay. Christmas is for giving, and we just gave part of our party to a mouse."

This lesson may end with another contextual activity to follow the rule of thumb of using context, isolation, and then context again in practice activities. Cloze sentences might be used for the final practice, for example:

  a.   He wanted _____ apples.
                (so, some)
  b.   She had grown _____ big that I did not know who she was.
                (so, some)

3. Use S-S-S: Seeing, Sounding, Sensing. When two words are consistently confused, students may be asked to see how each one *looks* different from the other, to note the differences in the *sounds* of the two words, and to attend to the differences in the *sense* of each.

For example, if a student regularly confuses *on* and *in*, he or she is asked to name the letter at the beginning of each word, to note the difference in the sounds of the two initial letters, and, in order to sense the differences in meaning, to use each word in a sentence, such as "My book is *on* the table" and "I rode *in* a car to come to the clinic." This procedure focuses on graphic and sound clues as well as the important clue of meaning.

4. Use *every-pupil-response cards* along with cloze stories. The purpose of every-pupil-response cards is to increase opportunities for individual responses when groups of children are engaged in the same activity. Each student is given several cards on which possible answers are printed. As the need for a response occurs, instead of one student being called on to give the answer, all students select from their cards the answer they believe to be correct and then hold this card up. Here's an example of how this technique can be used for eliminating sight

Every-pupil-response cards increase opportunities for individual responses when groups of students are engaged in the same activity.

word confusions. Three students are consistently confusing *which* and *with*, so the teacher prepares a cloze story on chart paper such as the one in this example.

> I don't know _____ boys I want to go _____ to the fair. No matter _____ ones I choose, I know I'll have fun. When I go with Al and Bob, though, they never know _____ thing to do first. They can't decide if they want to go see the goats or go get one of those hot dogs _____ onions and peppers on it (_____ make me sick!)

Students print *which* and *with* on separate index cards and place these on their desks. The story is posted for everyone to see and the teacher reads it aloud as the students follow along. The teacher pauses at each blank and the students quickly select and silently hold up the word they believe to be the correct response. The teacher gives corrective feedback when necessary.

LEARNING FROM TEXT

Make a Prediction. What causes word reversals? (The answer is not the mythical visual perception problem.)

5. The first one or two letters of a word often provide the most important graphic clue to that word. Lack of attention to the initial portion of a word can result in word confusions (*would/could, when/then*) and in miscues commonly called **word reversals** (as in *was/saw* and *on/no*). To eliminate habitual confusions of this type, give students activities that require them to attend to the first letters of the confused words.

For example, students could be given words to alphabetize. (Alphabetizing necessitates a focus on the beginning portions of words.)

Another way to deal with these types of word confusions is to use maze exercises in which the possible alternatives differ only in their initial one or two letters so that the student must attend to the beginning of the word to make a choice. For example,

> _____ I get some new jeans _____ I'll throw away these
> (Then, When)   (then, when)
> baggy pants.

Word Recognition and Oral Reading

The importance of guided oral reading is much discussed presently. When the National Reading Panel (U.S. Department of Health and Human Services, 2000) found good results for oral readings' influence on reading achievement, the Panel's report stressed that the positive outcomes were linked to oral reading *undertaken with thoughtful teacher guidance and feedback.*

While guided reading means different things to different educators, in general, most approaches incorporate preparatory work *before* reading (e.g., introduction of a few new words, often within the context of the story; prediction of words and storyline based on the title and pictures; activation of prior knowledge; perhaps, choral or echo reading with the teacher). All guided reading approaches also incorporate careful attention and support to student responses *during* reading (e.g., calling attention to letter sounds in confused words; prompting correction with meaning cues). *After* reading there is direct follow-up to the selection; for example, teachers may explicitly review strategies used during the reading, or students may dramatize or write about the selection.

When teachers' instructional responses to students' word recognition miscues during oral reading have been studied (Spiegel & Rogers, 1980), eight main classifications of teacher prompts have been observed.

1. *Tell.*   The teacher simply tells students the correct words when words are read incorrectly.

2. *Visual.*   The teacher instructs the student to look at the word more carefully.

3. *Visual/context clues.*   The teacher repeats a few words that came before the student's error and says "What?" to indicate that the student is to use context, plus examine the word again. For example:

Text:	Listen to the kitchen clock.
Student:	Listen to the curtain.
Teacher:	Listen to the what?

4. *Sound.*   The teacher prompts students to sound out words they read incorrectly.

5. *Spell.*   The teacher spells the word read incorrectly. For example,

Text:	A bluebird is smaller than a robin.
Student:	A bluebird is smaller then . . .
Teacher:	t-h-a-n

6. *Meaning.*   The teacher asks if what was read makes sense.

7. *Structural analysis.*   The teacher breaks the word into syllables for students or tells them to do this.

8. *Reference to prior use.*   The teacher tells the student that the word was used before, for example, saying something like, "I used that word when I gave you your math assignment after recess."

> Teachers can and do use a number of different prompts when students make miscues.

Prompt 8 seems less than useful since it is little more than an obscure hint that will not lead the student to independence in word learning. A similarly ineffective prod is seen when the teacher points to an item to divulge the word. For instance, Len misses the word *green* and the teacher happens to be wearing a green shirt, so he tugs at his shirt looking at Len meaningfully until he gets the point and says *green*. Because teachers cannot follow students around for the rest of their lives providing little tips to the identities of words, such weak prompts are best avoided.

The other seven types of corrective feedback described can be used legitimately at various times, depending on the skill level of the learner, the word, and the surrounding context. Adams (1990a, 1990b) makes recommendations based on research examining word learning, noting that, contrary to some opinion, the best prompt most often is *not* to direct the student to skip the word. Rather, students should be asked to pause and study, considering letters and sounds to internalize the word pattern for future recognition. If many of these word study pauses are necessary—to the extent that meaning is being seriously disrupted—then undoubtedly the student is reading a selection at his or her frustration level. Use easier material.

While a variety of prompts are needed for students to develop multiple independent strategies, Spiegel and Rogers (1980) found that more than half the time teachers simply told students words when oral reading miscues occurred. Instead, oral reading should be viewed as a chance to help students develop efficient and independent reading strategies—and to practice using these in real texts. Spiegel and Rogers observe that when teachers perceive miscues as spontaneous instructional opportunities, their students show better word recognition and word identification. Although there are certainly some occasions when merely telling the student a word is appropriate, used indiscriminately this teacher response has little long-term value in aiding reading growth.

Another concern is the amount of wait time the teacher allows before providing a prompt. When prompts are given immediately, students employ fewer self-corrections. Positive correlations between reading ability and use of self-corrections have been demonstrated (Clay, 1979; Pflaum & Bryan, 1980). An additional unprofitable practice is seen in group reading instruction when students are allowed to call out a word when one of their peers makes a miscue. This approach has been negatively correlated with progress (Brophy & Evertson, 1981). In both these instances, the very student who requires opportunities for word study is denied them.

MORE ABOUT FLUENCY

NCLB
READING FIRST

Currently, there is much interest in the topic of fluency, partly because of the influence and work of several researchers (e.g., Allington, 1983; Rasinski & Hoffman, 2003; Samuels, 1979; Stahl & Kuhn, 2004), and partly because the National Reading Panel (NICHD, 2000) found evidence that fluent reading is important to overall reading success. Fluency development is considered to be especially important for delayed readers (Hudson, Lane, & Pullen, 2005). A section on fluency is included in this chapter because good word recognition is the major factor underlying fluency.

Different educators approach helping delayed readers (or young readers) to become fluent for different reasons and in various ways. For most, the motive for facilitating fluency is to enhance comprehension; if less attention is given to individual words, the reasoning goes, more attention may be given to text meanings. A second widely accepted purpose for fostering fluency is to allow students to read greater volumes of material; that is, when students are not reading in a slow and plodding manner, they can process more words and cover more text. Research confirms that more reading means more reading growth. For struggling readers, both objectives are important. In addition, some educators are interested in fluent reading to meet another goal—the development of expressive oral reading. This objective is often viewed as one of lesser importance for students who are having serious difficulties with basic skills and strategies for learning to read.

There also are differences in how educators define **fluency.** Some definitions specify the components of fluency as (a) accuracy, (b) automaticity, and (c) prosody (e.g., Kuhn & Stahl, 2004). *Prosody* refers to appropriate phrasing, voice pitch, and stress in oral language and in oral reading. Prosody is important to those whose fluency goals include expressive oral reading and to some who believe that addressing the elements of prosody during fluency training can have a positive impact on comprehension. Other educators argue against including prosody in the definition, saying that use of appropriate phrasing and tones of voice are indications that students *have* comprehended text meanings, and thus, prosody is an effect of comprehension, not a cause.

Certainly most educators agree that word recognition *accuracy* must be considered when defining fluency. It would not be a satisfactory reading if a student read quickly and smoothly, but pronounced many words incorrectly (in all likelihood, disrupting meaning). But, accuracy is not enough. For instance, students' readings would be deemed accurate even if they stopped at numerous words in a selection, decoding each exceedingly slowly—if ultimately the words were decoded correctly. Obviously, this would not be a fluent reading.

Thus, it seems that the crucial key for fluency is *automaticity* (Samuels, 1988). To read fluently, one must recognize the vast majority of words in a text automatically. This allows the reader to move forward at a reasonable rate, attending to overall meanings of the messages with little conscious attention to decoding individual words. Adams (1990a, 1990b) points out that a prominent trait of good readers is that they sweep through material rapidly and easily, appearing to recognize whole words with merely a glimpse. On the other hand, a defining characteristic of many delayed readers is their lack of fluency (Klenk & Kibby, 2000).

> A prominent trait of good readers is that they sweep through material rapidly and easily, appearing to recognize whole words with merely a glimpse.

Word-by-word reading is a normal behavior in beginning reading. Average readers usually progress through four stages.

Stage 1. Initial reading sounds fluent, but students make many errors and are unaware or unconcerned that their reading does not accurately represent the text.

Stage 2. Students become conscious of matching their speech responses to words in the text and, therefore, begin to point to individual words and read in a staccato fashion.

Stage 3. Finger-pointing disappears but word-by-word reading continues as students consciously match their oral responses to each word.

Stage 4. Word-by-word reading disappears as students read in meaningful phrase units (Clay, 1967).

Only when students remain at the second or third stage of this sequence without advancing to the fourth does nonfluent reading become a concern. Because of difficulties some delayed readers have had with initial word learning, they may stay locked in Stages 2 and 3 when no longer necessary. Comparing students' reading rates with broad guidelines for words per minute (wpm) typically read at various grade levels is useful in deciding what and how much instruction might be needed. Some guidelines suggested by Rasinski and Padak (2000, p. 105) are shown in Figure 8–8.

Techniques presented previously throughout this chapter assist readers in developing accurate and, if practiced sufficiently, automatic word recognition. Before reading about additional activities for encouraging fluency, it is important to note a condition that generally should be in place during any fluency-fostering procedure. Unless the teacher, or a competent stand-in for the teacher, can be available to scaffold students through challenging texts during fluency instruction, students should read material at their instructional or independent levels. Students should not read materials that are too difficult for them (O'Connor et al., 2002). If learners encounter an undue number of unknown words in a text, slow and halting reading is to be expected. This is an altogether

FIGURE 8–8   *Estimates of Reading Rates for Six Grade Levels*

By second semester of:	Should approximately be:
Grade 1	80 wpm
Grade 2	90 wpm
Grade 3	110 wpm
Grade 4	140 wpm
Grade 5	160 wpm
Grade 6	180 wpm

Source: From *Effective Reading Strategies: Teaching Children Who Find Reading a Challenge*, 2nd edition, by Rasinski/Padak, 2000. Reprinted by permission of Pearson Education Inc., Upper Saddle River, NJ.

different problem. Word recognition must be accurate before it can become automatic (Rasinski & Hoffman, 2003).

Other fluency-fostering techniques for you to consider follow.

Easy Reading

Many practitioners and researchers obtain particularly good results from having students read daily, not only from instructional-level material, but also for a portion of the reading period, from independent-level text (Allington, 2002b; Clay, 1985). Opportunities to read in "easy" materials remove the task of overt decoding with which many delayed readers struggle. Instead, learners can concentrate on using what they know; they can read all words in a book accurately (or almost all), which allows them to enjoy the ease of reading. This part of the lesson can focus on reading the text relatively quickly, with attention to meaningful portrayal of the content. This simple inclusion in a program leads to greater fluency.

In addition to using independent-level materials, another way to provide an "easy read" is to engage learners in rereading books recently read. Today this is common practice in many programs, such as the Reading Recovery program (Clay, 1979; Pinnell, 1989) and the Book Buddies program (Invernizzi, Juel, & Rosemary, 1996).

Repeated Readings

When suitable texts are used but students' reading is still atypically nonfluent, the method of repeated reading is often suggested. Timed and graphed readings of short selections have enjoyed widespread use since their applications were outlined by Samuels (1979). Rather than reading a new selection at each lesson, Samuels advocated repeated oral readings of the same selection until a criterion had been reached for words read per minute (wpm). With exceptionally nonfluent readers, Samuels advised establishing the criterion at 85 wpm. When that criterion is reached, a new passage is introduced. A half dozen or so repeated readings of a selection are typically needed for students early on, but fewer readings are necessary with more practice. When fluency increases, a higher criterion level is established.

While improved fluency is the primary objective for repeated readings, some positive side effects can occur. Because many exposures to the same words are afforded, word recognition accuracy may improve. Moreover, passage comprehension often improves with each rereading, probably because (a) word recognition becomes automatic and thus attention can be directed to meaning, and (b) rereading the same passage allows opportunity to glean ideas that might be missed in a single reading.

Research on repeated readings has had mixed results, with some students showing good improvement, but others performing no better than with more standard reading lessons. Of interest, these studies generally show that whenever fluency does improve, comprehension improves (Kuhn & Stahl, 2004).

> Research on repeated readings generally indicates that when fluency improves, comprehension improves.

Readers' Theater

Readers' Theater (Keehn, Martinez, & Roser, 2005) is a particularly productive activity for achieving fluency goals. You read about this technique in Chapter 7, on pages 197–198 (take a quick moment to review the procedure briefly described there). There is much to commend Readers' Theater because complete text selections are used (whole stories, short books, sometimes plays) and because there is an authentic purpose for reading and rereading a text many times. Often multiple copies of a children's or young adult literature book are used, but selections from high-quality basal readers also may be employed. Not only do Readers' Theater lessons develop automaticity, teachers find that both younger and older students join in with interest and motivation (Worthy & Broaddus, 2002). Martinez, Roser, and Strecker (1999) conducted a 10-week program to evaluate Readers' Theater with two classrooms of students, finding at the end that these learners substantially outperformed two control groups on measures of fluency.

Modeling

Teacher modeling increases oral reading fluency. In one form that is both successful and easy to implement, the student reads the first page in a story aloud, then the teacher reads the next page orally with the student following along. On page three, it's the student's turn again, as student and teacher continue turn taking. Usually, the student's fluency noticeably improves as the teacher's reading is increasingly imitated page by page over the story.

Several educators have used a group version of teacher modeling, sometimes referred to as an Oral Recitation Lesson (ORL) (e.g., Hoffman, 1987; Stahl & Heubach, 2005). Procedures vary slightly from program to program, but basically, the approach involves the teacher reading a story to students, with students reading parts in an echo fashion. At some point each student is assigned a portion of text to be practiced, independently or in paired reading, until the student can read it fluently to the group. Stahl and Heubach's program, aimed at developing automatic word recognition and fluency, showed particularly good results, especially with delayed readers.

A different type of fluency modeling is called *reading-while-listening*. Students listen repeatedly to recorded tapes of stories or informational material while following along, doing so until they can comfortably read the story to the teacher, on their own and fluently. In Dowhower's (1987) study, students' word recognition accuracy, rate (a measure of automatic word recognition), and comprehension improved with this approach to modeling. When Rasinski (1990) compared the reading-while-listening activity with repeated readings, he found both techniques worked equally well.

Paired Reading

Another procedure conducive to fluency development is paired reading in which learners work together on texts until accurate, fluent readings are produced (Spiegel, 1992; Walley, 1993). In one version, partners with similar reading instructional levels assist each other with word recognition and provide incentive for repeated practice, working as a team. Or, cross-age tutoring is used: Older, better readers read with nonfluent younger readers, in effect, substituting for the teacher as a reading model. An alternate form of cross-age tutoring prepares older poor readers who then read to younger students. For example, in one school system, to lessen feelings of inadequacy in struggling teenage readers who needed to read quite easy books, these books were designated "babysitter books." Teenagers were induced to read the books so they could read to children they were hired to care for. Similar to Readers' Theater tasks, the teenagers practiced reading the books orally until they were prepared to read them fluently to the children.

Choral Reading

Walley (1993) recommends choral reading, with selections practiced in unison as an aid to fluency enhancement. Poetry makes a good choice for choral reading, but teachers have employed many types of relatively short pieces for this activity. Holdaway (1979) used Big Books positioned on an easel and large enough for several students to follow easily. In what he called the "shared-book experience," among other activities, the teacher read to students before the group read the book chorally.

Simultaneous Reading

This technique, originally called the *neurological impress method* (NIM), was developed by Heckelman in 1966. The original name reflects the period in which the procedure was devised, a time when reading difficulties were frequently, and sometimes almost exclusively, attributed to neurological difficulties. Today, although educators are less interested in this causal hypothesis, the fluency technique is still used, but often renamed *simultaneous reading* (e.g., Ruddell, 2006) or *assisted reading* (e.g., Kuhn & Stahl, 2004).

In this technique, the teacher and student simultaneously read aloud from the same material. As they read, the teacher slides a finger under each line to keep both readers at the same place. At first the teacher reads *slightly* faster than the learner, just fast enough to move the student along at a reasonable pace. After the beginning stages, and when the student has demonstrated increased fluency, the student assumes responsibility for sweeping a finger under the words, and the teacher does not read at a faster rate. If the student misses a word, no word identification strategies are used; instead, the teacher who *has* read the word correctly just keeps the student moving along by continuing to read, or the student quickly may be told the word.

The program requires students to have at least a reasonable number of words in their sight vocabularies to read with the teacher in this fashion. Using this technique, students practice making quick responses to words they know and receive immediate feedback on words about which they are unsure from hearing the teacher's reading. Moreover, students process a great deal of regular, connected reading material, more than might be the case if left to their usual inflexibly slow reading pace.

Simultaneous reading is a supplementary technique, usually practiced for 5–15 minutes a session. The method has been used successfully with older as well as younger seriously nonfluent readers (e.g., Mefferd & Pettegrew, 1997; Rasinski & Hoffman, 2003; Topping, 1995).

Silent Reading Fluency

It appears that the development of oral reading fluency also develops fluent silent reading by giving students a feeling for language structure. Additionally, when more words are recognized automatically in oral reading tasks, there is no reason to believe that this automaticity does not generalize to silent reading.

Rasinski (2002) points out that the results of fluent silent reading also are the same as those for oral reading; that is, a fluent silent reading rate allows greater amounts of text to be processed, and comprehension is enhanced. These outcomes likely contribute to results that have been seen with secondary students who are delayed readers: Although oral reading is often associated with instruction for younger students, participation of secondary-level, struggling readers in oral reading activities is correlated with achievement gains (Freeland, Skinner, Jackson, McDaniel, & Smith, 2000; Stallings, 1980).

Fluency Instruction: The Bottom Line

Three factors are key to fluent reading:

1. Unless an activity incorporates a very substantial amount of direct teacher scaffolding, students should read material at their instructional or independent levels.
2. Students need to develop automatic recognition of words.
3. Students need to engage in large amounts of connected text reading.

The second and third factors have a circular relationship: Automatic recognition of large numbers of words are needed to move through large amounts of material, and reading large amounts of material leads to a larger number of words recognized automatically and easily. These three factors should be kept in mind when selecting procedures for fluency instruction.

Reflections   As noted throughout this chapter, interactions occur among word recognition ability, word identification skill, and understanding of text. Accuracy and automaticity with words, at least to a minimum degree, appear necessary for reading to progress into the phases where word identification strategies can develop, which then cultivates additional automatic word learning, which in turn permits students to read more. More reading leads to more word learning, and all of these lead to better comprehension. See the diagram in Figure 8–9.

FIGURE 8–9 *Some Interactions Among Word Recognition, Word Identification, and Comprehension*

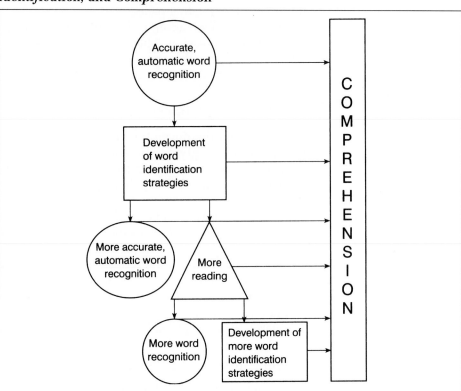

1. Assume you are the literacy coach in your school. How could you use this diagram in a professional development session? What purpose would it serve?
2. For each concept portrayed in the diagram, what practical teaching ideas would you convey to other teachers? When deciding on your answer, among other factors, consider several of the principles of word learning explicitly and implicitly presented in this chapter.

Word Identification

In the alphabetic phase of word learning, students show improved word identification strategies and more conventional spelling as well.

*C*onsider this scene:
Ten-month-old Eddie was extremely excited by the new puppy his father had just placed on the floor in front of him. He waved his chubby arms wildly, stiffened his body, sat up very straight, pointed to the puppy, and said, "Ee-ya-ug!" His 7-year-old sister, Felicia, wanted to help him get the right words, so she looked at him seriously and quietly but firmly said, "Sound it out."

The prod to "sound it out" obviously doesn't provide much help in oral language, and there has been much controversy about whether it is helpful in "getting the right word" in written language. *Does* "sounding it out" help students identify unknown words in written material? Apparently so. After decades of waffling back and forth between approaches that emphasize phonics instruction (or "sounding it out") and instruction that deliberately avoids phonics, it seems that we now have a fairly large body of research that confirms the utility of teaching learners to use letter-sound associations to read words (see Figure 9–1).

This chapter will discuss phonics instruction as well as structural analysis strategies. Research has not identified the best sequence for teaching phonic analysis or structural analysis. As a result, the order in which components of these decoding strategies are taught varies from program to program. However, there are intuitive reasons for selecting which concepts to teach early and which somewhat later. As examples, consonants often provide better clues to words than vowels; therefore, many instructional sequences begin the teaching of phonics with consonants. Short vowel sounds occur more often than long vowel sounds in beginning primary-grade material, so many programs teach short vowels first. The order presented in this chapter is a common one for introducing both phonic analysis and structural analysis concepts (e.g., see Morrow, Holt, & Sass, 2002).

In the previous chapter, **word identification strategies** were defined as those procedures a reader employs when he or she does not recognize a word at sight. For students to gain control of word identification strategies—particularly, learning letter-sound relationships—they must have developed sufficient phonemic awareness (Ehri et al., 2001).

PHONEMIC AWARENESS

NCLB
READING
FIRST

Phonemic awareness is the recognition that *spoken* words can be broken down into their constituent sound units. Understanding how phonemic awareness develops in normally achieving readers furnishes insights for intervention (Ruddell, 2006). It is common for phonemic awareness to mature in many children before they come to school. At home and in preschools, they: (a) hear and memorize nursery rhymes under the auspices of adults who point out the features of rhymes (e.g., "Look! These words sound the same at the end: *jiggle, higgle, piggle!*"); (b) have stories read to them, with adults pointing out words,

FIGURE 9–1 *History of Attitudes Toward Phonics Instruction*

A Minihistory of Attitudes Toward Phonics Instruction

- 1534 = Ickelsamer first suggested use of phonics to assist word identification
- Mid/late 1700s–1840 = ☺
- 1840–1890 = ☹
- 1890–1920 = ☺
- 1920–1930 = ☹
- Late 1930s–early 1940s = ☺
- Mid 1940s–mid 1950s = ☹
- Mid 1950s–1960s = ☺
- 1970–1990 = ☹
- 1990–present = ☺

letters, and sounds; (c) play at writing and ask for spellings of words; (d) manipulate magnetic letters into invented spellings of their own, based on sounds they think they hear; and (e) participate in "lessons" from television programs for young children that include opportunities to play with sounds in language (e.g., *Sesame Street*). These activities also can be incorporated into teaching readers who have not developed ample phonemic awareness.

> To benefit from word identification strategy instruction (particularly, letter-sound relationships), students need an adequate degree of phonemic awareness.

Advice for instruction also is obtained from research programs that have successfully trained children to increase their phonemic awareness. These investigations have been conducted with young children (e.g., Ball & Blachman, 1991), but also with students with reading disabilities (Dewitz & Guinessey, 1990). In many cases, researchers deliberately designed their activities to be gamelike and playful to sustain children's interest (McCormick, 2006). Most emergent literacy programs and beginning reading programs build this instruction from easiest to more complex. For instance, Lundberg et al. (1988) used this sequence: (a) rhyming activities, including those that require learners to produce rhymes themselves; (b) hearing individual *syllables* in words; (c) hearing *initial sounds* of words; and (d) hearing sounds *within* words. In remedial classes, the teacher should begin at the easiest level at which the student is unable to demonstrate phonemic awareness.

The following are a variety of exercises used by researchers.

1. For rhyme production activities, explicitly point out that rhymes sound alike at the ends of words. Griffith and Olson (1992) advocated reading to students daily from rhyming texts, such as *Poem to Mud* (Snyder, 1969): "Poem to mud / Poem to ooze / Patted in pies, or coating your shoes" (p. 317). Students are to use poetry as springboards to orally create their own rhymes.

2. To help students recognize that words may be made up of separate syllables, Lundberg et al. (1988) asked the teacher to pretend to be a troll with an unusual manner of speaking in which words were said syllable by syllable.

The troll had presents to give to the children, but to receive these, the students had to figure out what item was being named—for example, when the troll said "lo-co-mo-tive" or "pen-cil."

For a nice addition, teachers might precede the activity by reading the story *The Three Billy Goats Gruff* to the children to ensure that they understand what a troll is.

3. Ball and Blachman (1991) asked students to match pictures by alliteration (i.e., all those beginning with the same sound) to promote awareness of likenesses and differences of sounds.

4. Yopp (1992) made good use of songs to develop various facets of phonemic awareness. For instance, to increase students' recognition of isolated sounds in words, they sang lyrics, such as these, to the tune of "Old MacDonald Had a Farm":

What's the sound that starts these words:
Turtle, time, and *teeth?*

(Children respond)
/t/ is the sound that starts these words
Turtle, time, and *teeth.*
With a /t/, /t/ here and a /t/, /t/ there,
Here a /t/, there a /t/, everywhere a /t/, /t/.
/t/ is the sound that starts these words:
Turtle, time, and *teeth.* (p. 700)

5. A variation of the troll activity (Lundberg et al., 1988) can be used to develop sensitivity to the principle that words are made up of a sequence of sounds. This modification requires students to mentally blend sounds to produce words. The troll's speaking pattern in this case would consist of pronunciations of the individual phonemes in a word (e.g., /m/ - /o/ - /p/, which the learners must combine to identify the word *mop*).

6. To practice segmenting words into phonemes, students can be given a wooden dowel or a pencil; after hearing a word pronounced, they mentally count and then tap out the number of sounds it contains (Liberman, Shankweiler, Fischer, & Carter, 1974).

7. To refine phonemic segmentation principles, various adaptations of Elkonin boxes (1963) have been used (e.g., Ball & Blachman, 1991; Clay, 1985; Griffith & Olson, 1992). Examples are shown in Figure 9–2.

Prior to this activity, the teacher selects several simple pictures and places them on file cards. Boxes are drawn to represent each sound in a picture. Note in Figure 9–2 that a box is drawn only for the sounds, not for each letter; thus, three boxes are drawn for the second example, *n-ai-l.*

Learners are given counters (e.g., plastic disks, pennies). They move a counter into each box as they hear each sound in a word the teacher slowly pronounces. For instance, as the teacher says *d-o-g,* a counter is moved into the first box as the /d/ sound is heard, into the middle box as the /o/ is heard, and into the last box to represent the /g/ sound.

As students advance in their understanding, they can be instructed to: (a) pronounce the word with the teacher, (b) pronounce it by themselves as they manipulate the counters, and finally (c) write letters in the boxes instead of using counters.

Elkonin boxes are used to help students develop phonemic awareness and spell words needed for writing.

FIGURE 9–2 *Elkonin Boxes That Assist in Phonemic Segmentation Activities*

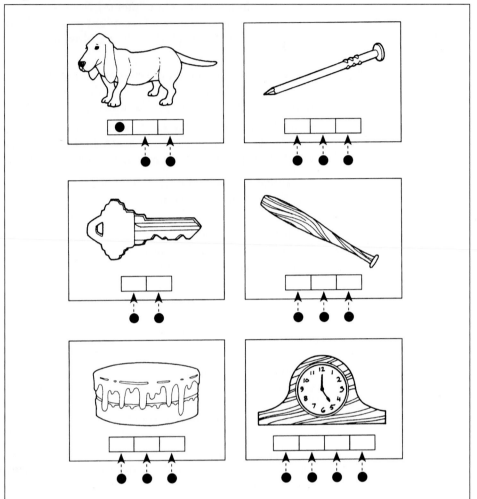

These assignments aid students in hearing individual sounds within words, noting them in correct sequence, and associating them with printed letters. Teachers in some programs, such as Reading Recovery (Clay, 1985), also have learners use Elkonin boxes during writing activities to assist in spelling unknown words.

8. Activities can be used to practice isolating and manipulating sounds through phoneme substitution and deletion tasks.

Yopp (1992, p. 701) had students sing nonsense words, successively substituting beginning sounds:

Fe-fi-fiddly-i-o

Ze-zi-ziddly-i-o

Bre-bri-briddly-i-o

In the same training program, students changed their own names to silly ones by substituting a different initial sound, for example, *Sandy/Tandy, Bobby/Tobby*.

Pictures can be used in phoneme deletion activities. For instance, learners may be directed to "Listen to the word *brake*. Think of the word that would be left if /b/ were taken away. Find the picture of the new word." The student selects from a series of pictures.

9. Other exercises that researchers have used in programs to successfully accelerate students' phonemic awareness include: (a) having students clap out syllables (or sounds) in words; (b) having students march to syllable patterns; (c) using iteration (e.g., if students are to identify the initial sound in *kite*, the teacher says /k/ /k/ /k/ *kite*); (d) using rhymed stories (e.g., certain Dr. Seuss books are useful); (e) having students categorize pictures by rhyme; (f) having students manipulate letter tiles consistent with sounds heard in words; (g) playing board games (such as bingo) focused on sounds; (h) reading books with alliterative patterns to students; (i) using children's literature that playfully deals with sounds in language; and (j) employing riddles and guessing games focusing on sound units in words (Ball & Blachman, 1991; Griffith & Olson, 1992; Juel, 1991; Lundberg et al., 1988; Neuman, 2002; Yopp, 1992).

10. Combining phonemic awareness exercises along with explicit instruction of letter-sound correspondences has been found to be particularly effective (e.g., Bradley & Bryant, 1983). Once students begin noting sounds in words, and when they also recognize written letters, then associating sound cues with visual cues (letters) produces greater growth in phonemic awareness and greater gains in phonics (Fox & Routh, 1984; Hohn & Ehri, 1983).

Using Writing Experiences to Develop Phonemic Awareness

As portrayed with Dan, one of our case study students in Chapter 8, writing experiences using invented spellings help learners "map" written language onto the spoken language they already know. Children develop increasing phonemic awareness as they try to spell words on their own.

Teachers today no longer wait for students to gain some proficiency in reading before beginning writing activities. Instead, they encourage students to use their present level of letter-name and letter-sound knowledge to write words as they think they sound. Not only do students' reading and writing abilities develop together, but playing with writing and spelling assists learning to read in measurable ways.

LEARNING FROM TEXT

Reviewing and Reflecting. Activities suggested in the preceding sections for developing phonemic awareness are research based. What does this mean, and why does it matter? (Consider a principle you read in Chapter 7.)

MOVING INTO PHASE 3 OF WORD LEARNING: THE FULL-ALPHABETIC PHASE

In the preceding chapter, our Phase 2 case study student, Dan, was about to move into Phase 3 when we left him, ready to benefit from more explicit instruction in word identification strategies.

Reviewing and Reflecting. In the previous chapter, characteristics of readers in each of five phases of word learning were enumerated. Flip back to those descriptions and quickly review them now. Doing so will place what follows in perspective and convey its relevance to you. Therefore, you will be more likely to recall the information at a later time. These phases are described on pages 229–232.

The Value of Word Identification Strategies

Skilled readers not only recognize large numbers of words at sight, but they also know what to do when they come to words that are unknown to them. During developmental periods of learning to read, confronting many new words is typical, and doing so is necessary for learning to progress. Knowledge of strategies to employ when new words appear is critical for reading advancement.

When students have attained competency in use of word identification strategies, they can read unfamiliar words independently without the guidance of a teacher. Once students begin using these strategies, considerable strides are made in the number of words they can read (Juel, 1991). Therefore, like word recognition, the development of word identification strategies facilitates comprehension because students can read *more* (Daneman, 1991). On the other hand, when readers have poor word identification abilities, they do not obtain satisfactory practice with higher-level comprehension processes (Daneman, 1991). There is also evidence that when students can associate sounds with the words they read, they can hold the words better in short-term and long-term memory, and thus they have improved recall of what they have read (Mann, Liberman, & Shankweiler, 1980). Systematic instruction on word identification strategies supports comprehension (Ruddell & Unrau, 2004).

Reliable word identification strategies also make recall of words at sight easier. One reason this occurs is because learners have expanded opportunities for exposure to words, and this helps them internalize the forms of more words (Daneman, 1991). With improved word identification strategies, they also make errors less frequently when they read words by sight (Ehri, 1991), and they require fewer exposures to new words to establish their identities; thus, their sight word recognition vocabularies are rapidly extended (Vellutino & Denckla, 1991).

Make a Prediction. How does knowledge of word identification strategies help with irregular words?

Knowledge of word identification strategies even helps somewhat with deciphering irregular words because *portions* of these words *are* regular (Stanovich, 1991b). Vellutino and Denckla (1991) give this example: Based on knowledge of regular spelling patterns, one might expect that *have* would be read so that it rhymes with *gave* and *save*, which is not the case; therefore, in terms of common spelling patterns, the word *have* is an irregular word. But the sounds for *h* and *v* in this word are not irregular; they are the sounds these

Skilled use of word identification strategies assists comprehension.

letters most typically stand for. As a result, the regular segments of the word can help readers get at least within the recognition range of this word if those sounds are known.

Overall, skill in word identification strategies accelerates reading acquisition (Stanovich, 1991b). And, students with dependable word learning strategies also spell with fewer errors (Juel, Griffith, & Gough, 1985).

Word Identification Strategies in the Full-Alphabetic Phase of Word Learning: *Phonic Analysis*

NCLB
READING FIRST

Although various word identification strategies must be assimilated to attain competence in reading, during Phase 3 of word learning, the focus is on **phonological recoding,** also called **decoding.** To "phonologically recode" a word means to look at the letters in the word and turn them into (or *recode* them into) their sounds—that is, the visual code (the letters) is recoded into a phonological code (the sounds). Then these sounds are matched with the pronunciation of a word you already have stored in your memory—stored there because you have heard it in oral language. For example, pretend you do not know the word *swift*, but that you are well established in the alphabetic phase of word learning (Phase 3) and have already learned the sounds of all letters in that word. Therefore, by saying the sounds of the letters ("sounding the letters out") and blending these sounds, you can come up with the correct pronunciation of the word, and because you have heard this word before, it clicks!

You now become aware that the word spelled *s-w-i-f-t* is that word *swift*, which you know because you have heard people say it before or because you heard it when a story was read to you. Maybe you even have used it yourself. This takes care of that word for now, and you can get on with your reading. With enough pairings of *s-w-i-f-t* with the realization "Oh, that's right, this is *swift*," the word will also become established in your memory as a written word you know. This is one reason sight word reading increases rather dramatically when the reader gains control of word identification strategies.

Sight word reading increases rather dramatically when control is gained of word identification strategies.

To make those kinds of associations, though, you must have some important prerequisite information. You must know the sounds of letters, and you must have had practice in blending sounds, both of which are not particularly easy concepts to acquire.

Sequential decoding is learned first, followed by hierarchical decoding (Ehri, 1991). In **sequential decoding,** students learn simple one-to-one correspondences between letters and the sounds the letters typically stand for—for example, they learn that usually the sound associated with *f* is the sound heard at the beginning of *fat*, that usually the sound for *n* is the sound heard at the beginning of *nap*, and so on. Understanding sequential decoding concepts may begin in the partial-alphabetic phase (Phase 2) and expands and solidifies during the alphabetic phase of word learning (Phase 3).

In **hierarchical decoding,** more complicated understandings are developed, such as the concept that sometimes letters give clues to the sounds of other letters, as in certain common spelling patterns. For example, many times when a word—or syllable—ends with an *e*, the vowel preceding it is long, as in "I *made* an attempt to *fade* my jeans in the washing machine, but my mother would always *hide* them because the *price* of those jeans was so high she did not want me to *fake* the *fade*." The words I have italicized in this sentence end with *e* and in all cases the vowel preceding it has the sound that we commonly refer to as "long," or as we sometimes say to students, "it says its own name." (Also notice, though, that the word *machine* in this sentence does not conform to the rule.) Students begin to use hierarchical decoding later in the alphabetic phase.

Instructional Procedures

To gain command of phonological recoding processes, students must have:

1. developed phonemic awareness
2. learned letter-sound relationships
3. had practice with blending

One primary objective when teachers instruct students in phonic analysis strategies is helping them learn letter-sound relationships. There have been vigorous disputes, however, about whether illustrating sounds of letters to students in the context of words or demonstrating the sounds in isolation best facilitates learning. One approach to teaching letter-sound associations is called **implicit phonics instruction,** or **analytic phonics** (Morrow, Holt, & Sass, 2002). When this method is used, letter sounds are never produced separately. Instead, students are given examples of words in which a targeted sound is heard, with the intent that they gain a sense of this sound from hearing many exemplars. The teacher might say, "The sound of *h* is the one we hear at the beginning of *house, horse, had*, and *hi*," often with the targeted sound stressed somewhat when the example words are given. Those who subscribe to this method maintain that letter sounds should be produced only within the context of words because some sounds are difficult to pronounce in isolation (e.g., *b* is always followed by a vowel sound in an isolated pronunciation). There is concern that the distortion in sound will confuse students when they try to apply the sounds to decoding a word.

A different approach is designated as **explicit phonics instruction,** or **synthetic phonics** (Morrow, Holt, & Sass, 2002). In this type of program, letter sounds are taught initially by the teacher articulating them in isolation and with students practicing them both in isolation and in the context of words. For those sounds for which a precise separate pronunciation is difficult, an attempt to minimize the accompanying vowel sound is made by slightly *subvocalizing* (a fancy word for *whispering*) the letter sound and refraining as much as possible from drawing out the vowel that follows. Many consonant sounds can be pronounced in isolation without that accompanying vowel (for example, *f, h, l, m, n, r, s, t, v, x, z*), and all vowel sounds can be enunciated separately. Those who advocate this procedure for teaching letter sounds contend that illustrating sounds only within words does not provide students with information definitive enough for them to distinguish the sounds readily, and then to use them.

Which is best? We can turn to research for the answer. This research shows, with the implicit phonics method, students find it harder to learn the separate sounds and to learn to blend them (Adams, 1990a, 1990b; Anderson, Hiebert, Scott, & Wilkinson, 1984; Johnson & Baumann, 1984; National Institute of Child Health and Human Development [NICHD], 2000). After a review of the research related to the two approaches, Adams (1990a, 1990b) concluded that the advantages to pronouncing and initially practicing letter sounds in isolation outweigh the disadvantages. These research findings substantiating the superiority of explicit phonics instruction—in which students are taught and practice sounds in isolation—may come as a surprise to some, because at certain periods of time in many teacher-training programs, it was recommended that sounds always be taught in context.

Summarize. What are the issues about implicit phonics instruction versus explicit phonics instruction? What does research say?

Some students learn word identification strategies incidentally. Even though strategies have not been specifically taught, after fairly extensive reading experiences, they infer certain word-learning principles themselves, or they may learn these concepts from spelling instruction and writing activities. However, many students require formal instruction to grasp the understandings necessary to apply letter-sound associations (Ruddell, 2006), and this is especially so with poor readers (Barr & Dreeben, 1983; Juel, 1991). For these students, intentional, precise phonics instruction moves students into and through the alphabetic phase of word learning (Ehri, 1991; Gough & Hillinger, 1980).

What, then, can you do to help students learn to decode letters to sounds? A systematic program for learning sounds, combined with explicit instruction in learning to blend sounds, is often necessary (Juel & Minden-Cupp, 2004). Much practice is needed to obtain automaticity with these concepts (Juel, 1991).

Although it may be a good idea to introduce and provide practice with letter sounds in isolation, specific exercises on letter sounds should be viewed as important but not sufficient. Students also must be given opportunities to apply these understandings in the reading of words in real text. As with many cases in high-quality instruction, this is not an either/or matter. Balancing word identification strategy instruction with reading in meaningful text leads to accelerated progress in unskilled readers (Adams, 1990a, 1990b).

Q & A

An Overview of Results from the Meta-analysis of Research on Phonics Instruction Conducted by the NATIONAL READING PANEL

Based on 38 studies including 66 group comparisons, this research provides the following answers:

	Yes	No	Sometimes
Is systematic phonics instruction beneficial for grade K-6 students, generally?	X		
Are kindergarteners too young for phonics instruction?		X	
Is systematic, synthetic phonics instruction more productive for low socioeconomic status students than less-focused approaches?	X		
Does systematic, synthetic phonics result in positive and significant effects for reading delayed and learning disabled students?	X		
Does systematic phonics instruction improve spelling ability for grade K-6 students, generally?	X		
Does systematic phonics instruction improve spelling ability for delayed readers?			X
Does instruction in phonics that is systematic produce more beneficial results than instruction that teaches only a little (or no) phonics?	X		

Providing opportunities for writing in daily lessons also helps cultivate consciousness of letter-sound patterns (Adams, 1990a, 1990b). The reverse is also true: Learning more about reading supports spelling and writing. With practice in reading, students begin to unconsciously note standard spelling conventions—that e comes at the ends of many English words even though it is not heard, for example, and that a u always comes after a q (Nagy, Osborn, Winsor, & O'Flahavan, 1992).

See the accompanying boxed **Q and A** (*Questions and Answers*) material for a brief overview of research findings concerning phonics instruction from the widely discussed meta-analysis conducted by the National Reading Panel (U.S. Department of Health and Human Services, 2000). The report, titled *Teaching Children to Read: An Evidence-Based Assessment of the Scientific Research Literature on Reading and Its Implications for Reading Instruction*, includes other sections addressing research on phonemic awareness instruction, fluency, and comprehension.

Here are some specific suggestions for practice activities sequenced in a common instructional order, beginning with *consonants*. Phonics lessons are more likely to engage students' attention if taught in creative, vibrant, entertaining ways (Ruddell, 2006).

Consonants. Consonant sounds are introduced before vowel sounds in most programs because consonants provide the framework of words. Try to read this sentence.

W_ h__rd h_r wh_n sh_ y_ll_d _t h_r br_th_r.

T E A C H E R S' S T O R E

Materials for Teaching Word Identification Strategies

1. *Consonant Soup Cans* (Gamco)
2. *Group Word Teaching Game* (Garrard)
3. *Corrective Reading* (Science Research Associates)
4. *Rainbow Word Builders* (Kenworthy)
5. *Jumbo Phonics Cassette* Program (EBSCO)
6. *Phonic Rummy Card Games* (Kenworthy)
7. *Building Words* (Lakeshore Curriculum Materials)
8. *Programmed Phonics, Books 1 and 2* (Educators Publishing Service)
9. *Lessons in Vowel and Consonant Sounds* (Curriculum Associates)
10. *Individualized Reading Skills Program* (Science Research Associates)
11. *Sounds, Words, and Meanings* (Steck-Vaughn)
12. *Creature Teachers* (Bowmar/Noble)
13. *Language Lollipop* (Kids & Co.)
14. *Go Fish* (Remedial Education Press)
15. *Sound and Symbol Puzzles* (Developmental Learning Materials)

Although no vowels are given, you were probably able to determine easily that the sentence says "We heard her when she yelled at her brother." Now try this one.

_e_ _ou_ _i_e_ _a_ _e_ _i_e_.

Consonants provide important graphophonic clues to words, whereas vowels and their sounds provide less assistance, as just demonstrated. If you were unable to read the second sentence, try the same one now, when you may use the consonant sounds instead.

H_lp y_r s_st_r w_sh th_ d_sh_s.

Using consonant clues makes it easy to read this sentence: "Help your sister wash the dishes."

Many published materials are available to help students practice consonant sounds. A sampling of these, along with materials suitable for use in developing other phonics understandings, is listed in the ***Teachers' Store*** on this page.

Teachers also like to devise their own activities for teaching phonic analysis skills. Here are some suggestions for practice with consonant sounds.

1. *Composing alliterations.* Alliteration occurs when all words or most words in a phrase or sentence begin with the same consonant (e.g., *Tiny Timmy tied two toads together*). As a first step, read alliterative sentences to students, and ask them to identify the consonant sound heard at the beginning of each word. Next, students compose their own alliterations. Older students of all ages seem to enjoy working with alliterations. This task gives practice with consonant sounds in such a way that it is not viewed as "babyish" by more mature students. If students produce alliterative sentences orally, they should then be written by the student or teacher. To make the best use of any phonic analysis activities, some part of the exercise should always deal with written words or letters (Stahl, 1992).

2. *Self-correcting matching games.* Collect small boxes or other containers. On the outside of each, print a different single consonant sound with a felt-tip pen. On a large index card, paste four small pictures, each beginning with the same sound. (Old workbooks are good sources of small pictures.) Make a card with four pictures for every consonant sound you wish students to practice. Then, turn each index card over and draw a simple picture on the back; the picture should be different on each card and should cover most of the back of the card. Now turn the cards back over and cut the cards into four parts so each small picture is separate (see Figure 9–3).

Mix up all the small pictures from all the cards and have students sort the pictures according to the consonant with which each begins. They should place each small picture in the container labeled with that consonant.

Students check their work by taking the sorted cards from the container, turning them over, and arranging them to form the larger picture drawn by the teacher on the back. Mistakes are immediately apparent because the picture will not make sense if incorrect letters and sounds are mixed together.

3. *Playing Guess and Poke.* Prepare flashcard-sized pieces of oaktag. Each card should have a small picture pasted or drawn at the top. Below the picture, make three holes with a hole punch. Print a consonant letter above each hole. On the back, draw a red star around the hole of the correct answer. (See Figure 9–4 for an example.)

There are a number of ways to devise activities so students can self-check, and self-correct, themselves.

Students are given a pile of cards prepared in this way, plus a knitting needle, pencil, or similar object. They pick up the first card, look at the picture, decide on the consonant with which it begins, and poke the knitting needle through the hole labeled with that consonant. Without removing the knitting needle, they

FIGURE 9–3 *Materials for a Self-Correcting Matching Game*

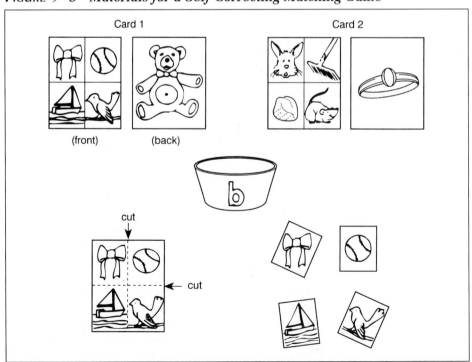

FIGURE 9–4 *An Example of a Card Used in Guess and Poke*

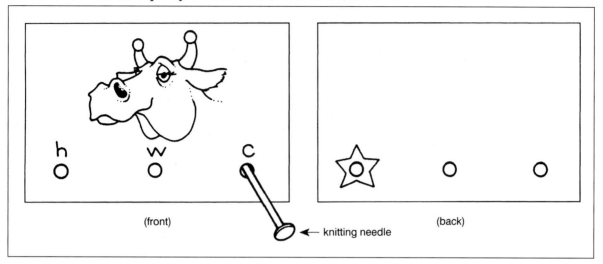

(front)   knitting needle   (back)

turn the card over. If the knitting needle is through the hole with the star, the answer is correct. They continue in this manner with each card in the pack.

Short Vowel Sounds. The "short" vowel sounds are represented in the following words:

ă (at), ĕ (egg), Ĭ (it), ŏ (on), and ŭ (up)

Many programs introduce short vowel sounds before long vowels because the short sounds occur more frequently in words found in beginning reading materials. Knowing short vowel sounds allows students to combine what they have learned about consonants to read many words that appear in simple texts. In fact, since words cannot be read without vowel sounds (all words have at least one), usually a short vowel or two is introduced at the same time consonant sounds are being learned. In any case, most programs teach short vowels early in the instructional sequence (Adams, 1990a, 1990b).

Students often have difficulty learning short vowel sounds, although they may have learned consonant sounds more quickly. Therefore, much and varied practice may be needed to facilitate learning of these sounds.

1. *Practicing vowel sounds in connected text reading.* It is important to choose the right words for practice. In connected text reading, because words with varied patterns are found, students will encounter words containing sounds and patterns they have not yet learned. However, certain books have more words that can be decoded with the sounds a student has already learned. For example, some of the Dr. Seuss books, such as *Hop on Pop*, allow a reader who is practicing consonant and short vowel sounds to apply his or her budding knowledge.

When words in a text are primarily regular ones that follow typical phonetic patterns, this is often referred to as **decodable text.** Many authorities today are calling for more examples of decodable text to use with beginning readers, asking publishers to invest in careful development of such materials so the stories are not only easily "decodable," but also meaningful and interesting.

2. *Direct-practice activities.* In direct-practice activities, in addition to work with letter-sound associations in isolation, the associations also should be

Research shows that working with onsets and rimes provides much important assistance in word identification.

incorporated into words to give practice in applying targeted sounds in ways that will facilitate transfer to real text reading. This, in addition, furnishes opportunities to engage students in that difficult but important skill of blending separate sounds to form words. Teacher modeling of blending is helpful in supporting students with this sometimes confusing task (Juel & Minden-Cupp, 2004).

Onsets and Rimes. An **onset** is the part of a syllable that comes before the vowel (in the one-syllable word *chat*, the *ch* is the onset). The **rime** is the rest of the syllable (in *chat*, the *at* is the rime).

Practice in reading words using onsets and rimes is increasingly viewed as important (Adams, 1990a, 1990b; Fry, 1997; Nagy et al., 1992). When students have some experience with a rime, they can figure out other words that end with the same combination. For example, if they have had sufficient exposures to the words *got, hot, not,* and *pot*—and have been shown the connections among these (the rime *ot*)—they may be able to determine on their own, by analogy, the words *cot, dot, lot,* and *rot* (Morrow, Holt, & Sass, 2002). Having control over a number of rimes helps students quickly expand their repertoires of reading vocabulary. For this reason, onsets and rimes are now typically taught early in the instructional sequence. Like short vowels, when rimes can be added to consonants, this opens up possibilities for identifying many more words.

Rimes are also called **phonograms**[1] and sometimes referred to as *word families*. The word families commonly used in this type of practice are word parts of two or three letters that appear in many different English words (see Figure 9–5). Teachers have students practice adding consonants (and later when these are learned, consonant clusters or consonant digraphs) to the phonograms, calling the process of adding these onsets **consonant substitution**. For example, if students know the words *sat* and *hat* and also know consonant sounds, they can be taken through the following steps:

1. The student reads the known word *sat*.
2. The student is asked to change the *s* to *h* and read the known word *hat*.
3. The teacher points out that words ending with the same group of letters—such as -*at* in these two words—usually rhyme, and this can be a clue to reading unknown words.
4. The student is asked to change *h* in *hat* to *r*, to think of the sound for *r*, and to combine it with the sounds for -*at* heard in the two words already known (*sat* and *hat*) to determine the unknown word *rat*. Teacher modeling of this process is often necessary when the principle is initially being learned.

Phonograms are quite regular from word to word, and large numbers of words can be formed from the same phonogram.

---

[1] The word *phonogram* is pronounced so that the first *o* is long.

5. Several initial consonants are substituted for one another to make various words (*bat, fat, mat, cat, pat,* and so on).

Phonograms are quite regular from word to word and large numbers of words can be formed from the same phonogram; both of these factors make the learning of phonograms a valuable objective (Adams, 1990a, 1990b).

Here are three additional activities for phonogram presentation and practice.

1. *Phonogram tic-tac-toe.* Make many small tic-tac-toe boards from oaktag. Each board should feature a different phonogram. Write that phonogram on every square of the board. Laminate the boards. Give two students who will play each game different-colored washable marking pens: Student A thinks of a word that includes the phonogram and writes in the appropriate consonant to form the word using a green (for instance) marking pen. Student B makes another word by writing in the initial portion of a word with a blue marking pen, and so on. When there are three words in the same color in a row, that student wins.

FIGURE 9-5 *Phonograms That Occur Frequently in Common Words*

-at	hall	-in	test	-ore	bran	drew	top
bat	mall	fin	vest	bore	clan	flew	chop
cat	tall	pin	west	core	plan	grew	crop
fat	wall	sin	zest	more	scan		drop
hat	small	tin	crest	pore	than	-ick	flop
mat	stall	win	chest	sore		kick	shop
pat		grin		tore	-ay	lick	stop
rat	-ing	skin	-ell	wore	bay	pick	
sat	king	spin	bell	chore	day	quick	-oke
vat	ring	chin	cell	score	gay	sick	coke
brat	sing	shin	fell	shore	hay	tick	joke
flat	wing	thin	sell	snore	lay	brick	poke
scat	bring		tell	store	may	chick	woke
slat	cling	-ap	well	swore	pay	click	broke
spat	fling	cap	yell		ray	slick	choke
splat	sling	gap	dwell	-ink	say	stick	smoke
chat	spring	lap	shell	link	way	thick	spoke
that	sting	map	smell	mink	clay	trick	stroke
	string	nap	spell	pink	gray		
-ed	swing	rap	swell	rink	play	-im	-ug
bed	thing	tap		sink	pray	dim	bug
fed		chap	-ear	wink	slay	him	dug
led	-et	clap	dear	blink	spray	rim	hug
red	bet	flap	fear	drink	stay	brim	jug
wed	get	scrap	gear	stink	stray	grim	mug
bled	jet	slap	hear	think	sway	skim	rug
fled	let	snap	near		tray	slim	tug
sled	met	strap	rear	-an		swim	drug
sped	net	trap	year	can	-ew	trim	plug
shed	pet		clear	fan	dew		
	set	-est	smear	man	few	-op	-ip
-all	vet	best	spear	pan	mew	cop	dip
ball	wet	nest		ran	new	hop	hip
call	yet	pest		tan	blew	mop	lip
fall		rest		van	crew	pop	nip

(continued)

FIGURE 9–5 *Phonogram That Occur Frequently in Common Words* *(continued)*

rip	fill	rot	crate	*-ide*	*-ock*	*-old*	*-ave*
sip	hill	plot	plate	hide	dock	bold	cave
tip	kill	shot	skate	ride	hock	cold	gave
zip	mill	slot	slate	side	lock	fold	pave
chip	pill	spot	state	tide	rock	gold	rave
clip	will	trot		wide	sock	hold	save
drip	chill		*-ent*	bride	block	mold	wave
flip	drill	*-ice*	bent	glide	flock	sold	brave
grip	grill	dice	cent	pride	stock	told	grave
ship	skill	lice	dent	slide	shock	scold	shave
skip	spill	mice	lent				slave
slip	still	nice	rent	*-ight*	*-ank*	*-ash*	
strip		rice	sent	fight	bank	cash	*-ab*
whip	*-it*	price	tent	light	rank	dash	cab
	bit	slice	vent	might	sank	hash	dab
-ake	fit	spice	went	night	tank	mash	jab
bake	hit	twice	spent	right	blank	rash	lab
cake	kit			sight	crank	crash	tab
fake	pit	*-ob*	*-ack*	tight	drank	flash	blab
lake	quit	bob	back	bright	prank	slash	crab
make	sit	cob	hack	flight	spank	smash	drab
quake	wit	job	lack	fright	thank	splash	flab
rake	grit	mob	pack			trash	grab
sake	skit	rob	quack	*-eam*	*-ade*		scab
take	slit	sob	rack	beam	fade	*-ace*	slab
wake	spit	blob	sack	seam	jade	face	stab
brake		slob	tack	team	made	lace	
flake	*-ot*	snob	black	cream	wade	pace	
shake	cot		crack	dream	blade	race	
snake	dot	*-ate*	smack	gleam	grade	brace	
stake	got	date	shack	scream	spade	grace	
	hot	gate	snack	steam	trade	place	
-ill	lot	hate	stack	stream	shade	space	
bill	not	late	track			trace	
dill	pot	mate					

(Since the boards have been laminated and washable pens have been used, after the game they are wiped off so that other students may use them.)

2. *Create a crazy story.* Give students a story that has several words containing phonograms. Underline these. Tell students to make a "crazy" story by changing the first part of the underlined words to another letter or letters (see Figure 9–6.) They can illustrate their new and silly version. (Since drawing pictures contributes nothing to learning to read, preparing illustrations to accompany reading activities is best assigned as a "fun" homework activity. Students can return with their pictures the next day and display them on a classroom bulletin board.)

3. *Play with hink pinks.* Cunningham (1991) suggests use of phonograms (rimes) with varied consonants (onsets) to make silly but meaningful descriptions.

FIGURE 9–6   *Imaginative Activity Giving Students Opportunities to Practice Consonant Substitution in an Enjoyable Way*

Make a Crazy Story

Mary went for a walk with her ~~c~~[b]at. They sat in the park for awhile and played with a ~~small~~[t]all dog. Mary decided to go to the hotdog ~~s~~[b]tand and bring back something for her ~~c~~[b]at to eat.

Going for a walk with her bat.

Girl and bat playing with a tall dog.

A hotdog band.

Each combination of two words must end with the same phonogram. Here are some examples to start students on their own hink pinks.

fat cat	quick lick	hot pot	back pack
red bed	nice mice	best nest	tan man
top cop	fake cake	mob job	light fight

Be certain that students write these words or that you write them for the students to see so they attend to the rimes in written form. When they are viewing the words, the teacher should ask students to tell the phonogram they see in both words, underlining it for emphasis.

Cunningham had her students make up riddles about their hink pinks ("What do you get when it rains on your dog?" "A wet pet.") and also illustrate them.

Consonant Clusters and Consonant Digraphs.   A **consonant cluster**, sometimes called a *blend*, is two or more consonant letters that commonly appear together, but even when in this combination, each retains its own sound. Some common clusters are listed in Figure 9–7.

A **consonant digraph** is two consonant letters that commonly appear together, but do not retain their own individual sounds. For example, in the consonant digraph *sh* (as found at the beginning of *ship*), neither the usual sound of *s* nor the usual sound of *h* is heard; rather, the sound that corresponds to these two letters when they appear in combination is an entirely different

FIGURE 9–7 *Some Common Consonant Clusters and Consonant Digraphs*

Consonant Clusters					
bl-	(*blond*)	gr-	(*great*)	sp	(*spit*)
br-	(*brain*)	pl-	(*plate*)	spl-	(*splash*)
cl-	(*clock*)	pr-	(*practice*)	spr-	(*sprain*)
cr-	(*crown*)	sc-	(*scat*)	squ-	(*squirrel*)
dr-	(*drum*)	scr-	(*scram*)	st-	(*step*)
dw-	(*dwarf*)	sk-	(*skate*)	str-	(*straight*)
fl-	(*flower*)	sl-	(*slide*)	sw-	(*swim*)
fr-	(*from*)	sm-	(*small*)	tr-	(*train*)
gl-	(*glad*)	sn-	(*snail*)	tw-	(*twin*)

Consonant Digraphs					
ch-	(*chair*)	gh-	(*rough*)	th-	(unvoiced *path*) (voiced *this*)
sh-	(*shoot*)	ph-	(*phone*)	wh-	(*wheel*)

sound. Some common digraphs are listed in Figure 9–7. Working with these consonant combinations often is seen as a logical next step.

If students can now decode simple words using consonants, short vowel sounds, and phonograms, their prowess will be expanded when they can use consonant clusters and consonant digraph sounds. For example, if they can decode *cat*, this additional knowledge will enable *scat* to be read—and the sentence *Scat, cat!* If they can read *win*, they will now be able to decode *thin*, and so on. If students know the phonogram *-ick* and are familiar with consonant clusters, then they can recognize *brick, click, stick*, and *trick*. When the consonant digraphs are known, then *chick* and *thick* may be determined.

The same teaching activities suggested for working with consonant sounds may also be used by students when they are learning consonant clusters and consonant digraphs. In addition, here are several other ideas.

1. *Word sorts.* Use word sorts (Fresch, 2000) to call attention to blends and digraphs during the introductory phases of learning these letter combinations. Give students a pack of cards in which words beginning with single consonant sounds are intermixed randomly with words beginning with clusters and digraphs. If, for example, the digraphs *ch* and *sh* have been introduced, students may be given the following packs of words to sort.

Pack 1: champ, can, chick, cat, cap, cut, chip, can't, chat
Pack 2: ship, shed, shot, sat, sick, shack, sink, sell

Have students sort cards into piles according to the beginning feature of the words (i.e., according to whether they begin with a single consonant or a cluster or digraph). Next, have students pronounce each word to the teacher and use each one orally in a sentence.

2. *Group-response activity.* The teacher prints consonant clusters or digraphs on flashcards, with a different one on each. A line is drawn after the cluster/digraph to indicate that a word is to be filled in. On the back of each card, the teacher writes several statements, each of which describes a word beginning

with the cluster/digraph on the front. For example, for the *str-* cluster card, some statements on the back might be:

She wore braces; now her teeth are _____.

He is not weak, he is _____.

To conduct the activity, the teacher chooses one cluster/digraph card, holds it up so the front side showing only the targeted letters is seen by the students, reads statements from the back side, and the students call out a word that is a response to each statement and that begins with the appropriate cluster or digraph. After each word is guessed, the teacher quickly writes the word on the board underlining the cluster or the digraph, so students can see the letters representing the sound within a written word.

Long Vowel Sounds.   Long vowel sounds are those represented in the following words:

ā (ate), ē (eat), ī (ice), ō (oat), and ū (use)

Interesting activities for practicing long vowels, complete with animation and sound, can be found at www.bbc.co.uk/education/ wordsandpictures/longvow/ poems/fpoem.shtml/

Because vowels are essential to words and syllables, they must be learned, just as the more easily distinguishable consonants and consonant combinations must be. Fortunately, students seem to find it easier to learn long vowel sounds than to learn the short sounds of vowels, probably because the sound that each long vowel represents is the same as the letter name.

The same suggestions for working with short vowel sounds apply here as well. Introduction and direct practice in isolation are perfectly acceptable, but long vowel sounds should also be practiced in words, with accompanying assists with blending. The Elkonin boxes suggested earlier for phonemic awareness training also can be used for blending practice.

Of course, experiences in applying the new knowledge while reading in real books are vital. By this time, the students should be able to read many words, so the possibilities for appropriate books will have multiplied.

Writing activities can provide opportunities for students to clarify letter-sound associations.

Writing activities can supply opportunities for students to clarify the many letter-sound associations they are now making. Writing should be a part of the learning and reinforcement program for long vowel sounds.

R-Controlled Vowels.   When a vowel is followed by an *r*, often the sound is neither long nor short, but instead results in a special sound called an **r-controlled vowel.** *R*-controlled vowel sounds are those represented in the following words: *ar (star), er (cover), ir (circus), or (for),* and *ur (fur).* Note that the *er, ir,* and *ur* sounds are the same.

One reason vowel-sound concepts are hard to learn is that the same letters have so many variations in sounds. Conversely, the same sounds can be represented by many letters. For example, the *e* in *bead* is long, but the *e* in *bread* is short, although they both are part of the letter pattern *ea.* The short *a* sound is represented by a single *a* in *had,* by *au* in *laugh,* and by *ai* in *plaid.*

R-controlled vowel sounds, on the other hand, are comparatively regular. Clymer (1963) found that for primary material, in 78% of the words that contained a vowel followed by an *r*, the "regular" (i.e., most conventionally taught) *r*-controlled sound was heard. Bailey's (1967) investigation of reading material through sixth grade found 86% of the words with *r*-controlled vowels to be regular, and Emans (1967), in a study of words selected from *The Teacher's Word*

Book of 30,000 Words (Thorndike & Lorge, 1944), found 82% regularity for *r*-controlled vowels in these words. Thus, including *r*-controlled vowels at this point in the instructional sequence is an especially useful practice.

1. *Reading stories incorporating the patterns taught.* After introduction and some practice with *r*-controlled vowel sounds, help students learn to independently use these sounds by preparing stories with many words containing these vowel patterns. Have students circle all words including *r*-controlled vowels and then read the story, using the *r*-controlled vowel sounds to aid in identification of the words. Here is an example. Note how many *r*-controlled vowels are included in this short teacher-prepared passage.

> The worn-out old witch stirred the ugly mess in her old pot. "Heh, heh, heh," she laughed horribly. "I need just one more ingredient, and it must be a living creature!" I shivered as I sat behind a large bush watching her. Then suddenly she pointed her wrinkled finger in my direction. I was stiff with fright. She came closer . . . but she pulled a half-dead bird from off a branch of that bush and dropped it into the boiling pot. I was shocked and wanted to help the poor bird. But just then I was surprised to see the witch's black-furred cat spring up and pull the bird from the pot. I was glad to see that the bird was still alive. The bird flew off through the forest. The cat ran off through the field. And I fell out of bed.

2. *A matching activity.* Another *r*-controlled activity has students complete words with *r*-controlled vowels. The teacher prepares strips with sentences that include a word to be completed with an *r*-controlled vowel. The teacher then punches holes in the strip and attaches them with paper fasteners onto colored posterboard (see Figure 9–8).

FIGURE 9–8 *Example of Teacher-Prepared Materials for an Activity to Help Students Distinguish Among R-Controlled Vowels*

To the left of each strip, punch another hole and put in another paper fastener; attach a length of colored yarn to each of the fasteners at the left. On the right side of the posterboard, list *r*-controlled vowels with a paper fastener in front of each. The student is to read each sentence, then attach the yarn to the paper fastener by the *r*-controlled vowel that would complete the word. Since the sentence strips are attached with paper fasteners, one set may be removed and others placed there after all students have had an opportunity to participate.

Special Vowel Combinations.   In reading programs of the past, students were often required to practice and learn many different diphthongs and vowel digraphs. A **diphthong** is a vowel combination that begins with one sound and moves to another sound in the same syllable, such as *oy* in *toy*.[2] **Vowel digraphs** are formed like consonant digraphs: They are pairs of vowels representing a single sound, such as /ea/ in *heat*.

Using Textual Aids.   What is the correct way to pronounce *diphthong*? Hint: See the footnote on the bottom of this page.

Some vowel diphthongs and digraphs taught in programs of the past are not included in most programs today because research has shown that many of these occur infrequently and/or have many exceptions to the rules about their sounds (e.g., see Clymer, 1963). Today, diphthongs and digraphs usually are not even taught as separate categories. Instead, a small group of these, which occur fairly often and have fewer exceptions, is selected for teaching and given the generic label *special vowel combinations*. Studies by Bailey (1971) and others indicate that the following special vowel combinations are important to teach: *au (caught), aw (raw), oi (boil), oy (toy), oo (cool), oo (foot), ou (out),* and *ow (cow)* or *ow (snow).*

Setting a Purpose for Reading.   The issues about whether and/or how phonics generalizations (i.e., rules) should be taught are somewhat complex. As you read, think about the most effective ways to handle these issues.

Phonic Generalizations.   When students have comprehended a sufficient number of principles of sequential decoding, the more complex generalizations of hierarchical decoding can be presented; that is, helping them recognize special circumstances in which certain letter sounds often occur. Learning generalizations about these circumstances acquaints readers with common spelling patterns found in English, which, in turn, provides important assistance to reading. In addition to calling attention to the generalizations, it is important to

---

[2] Teachers sometimes mispronounce the word *diphthong*. Notice the consonant digraph *ph* in this word. As you know, *ph* represents the /f/ sound, as in *phone*. Therefore, the word is pronounced /dif′thong/.

provide students with opportunities to read many words that conform to the generalizations so that the patterns can be internalized, not merely memorized.

Large numbers of these generalizations involve *vowel rules.* Some commonly taught generalizations are the following:

1. When one vowel is between two consonants, that vowel is short, as in *cat.*
2. When there are two vowels side by side, the long sound is heard for the first and the second is silent, as in *mean.*
3. When a word ends with an *e*, the *e* is silent and the vowel preceding it is long, as in *make.*

Other rules also are sometimes taught, for example:

4. When the letter *g* is followed by *i* or *e*, it sounds like /j/, as in *gin.*
5. When *a* is preceded by *w* it has the schwa sound, as in *was.* (The schwa sound is represented in dictionaries by an upside down *e*, and is pronounced like a short *u* sound regardless of the vowel it depicts.)
6. When *w* is preceded by *e*, the sound is the same as that represented by the special vowel combination *oo* in *shoot*, as in *few.*

Obviously, many of these rules are cumbersome, and, as might be expected, students often have difficulty learning them.

Even when only a few of these generalizations are taught, although students may be able to repeat the rules, they may not actually apply them unless (a) teachers prompt them to do so (e.g., the student has difficulty with the word *held* and the teacher says, "Look, there is one vowel between two consonants, so what sound would the vowel make?") or (b) students are given a specific practice activity that stresses the relevant generalization (e.g., directions on a worksheet say, "When a word ends with an *e*, the vowel in the middle of that word is usually long. Mark all the vowels that are long."). However, when reading independently in regular, connected materials, students may not stop to consciously apply a phonic generalization if they cannot identify a word.

Another obstacle to teaching vowel rules is that many English words are exceptions. For example, note these exceptions to the rules just listed:

Rule 1: told	Rule 4: get
Rule 2: bread	Rule 5: way
Rule 3: gone	Rule 6: sew

Several researchers have investigated the usefulness of the phonic generalizations often taught in primary and intermediate reading programs. They found that many of these rules have so many exceptions that they have low utility. Clymer (1963), for example, found only 45% utility for the generalization that "when two vowels are side by side the first is long and the second is silent." That is, 55% of the words in the four widely used primary reading programs he examined were exceptions to this rule. Another way to say this is that in more than half the attempts by a student to apply this rule to an unknown word, the rule would not work! When Bailey (1967) applied the same vowel rule to words in eight basal reader series through grade 6, only 34% utility was found. In short, some of the rules taught in primary reading programs are even less useful when applied to more difficult words found in higher-level reading selections. The percent of utility found in Bailey's study for the commonly taught rules listed earlier in this discussion were the following: Rule 1, 71%;

Rule 2, 34%; and Rule 3, 57%. Further, of the 45 generalizations taught in major reading programs and examined by Bailey, only 27 were useful at least 75% of the time.

This research indicates that some phonics generalizations may be comparatively useful, but others are not very helpful in identifying unknown words. It is important for students to internalize the spelling patterns of words. Practice with some phonic generalizations may be a useful interim step to assist with this (Stahl, 1992), but many exposures to common word patterns appear also to be productive for this purpose. Students should be given much experience with many words containing those patterns so they can inductively form generalizations about them. Furthermore, practice with onsets and rimes may add much to grasping these concepts and may be easier for students than learning many phonic rules (Adams, 1990a, 1990b). The human brain appears to have greater facility for detecting patterns than for applying rules.

Stahl (1992) suggests these rules of thumb for presenting phonic generalizations.

1. Point out rules to emphasize specific spelling patterns, but do not require students to *memorize* the rules.
2. Be certain that learners understand that these generalizations may help in identifying a word sometimes, but there are exceptions. (This is the reason the qualifier "usually" is employed when reciting these rules: "When a vowel is between two consonants, the vowel is *usually* short.")
3. Highlight only those generalizations that have comparatively high utility.

Dan's Case Study (continued)

A Return to Dan's Case Study

In Chapter 8, we examined a reading program for Dan, who, when he entered the special reading program, appeared to be operating in the partial-alphabetic phase of word learning. After 5 weeks of individualized instruction, he had progressed to the point where it was believed he was entering the full-alphabetic phase.

Instruction was based on the theoretical perspective that matching instruction to a student's learning phase is highly effective (Ehri & McCormick, 2004; Spear-Swerling, 2004). To promote his breakthrough into the critical full-alphabetic phase, explicit teaching of letter sounds that Dan had not learned incidentally through his previous reading and writing activities was now included in his lessons. The sequence for introduction of letter-sound associations discussed earlier was used, along with many of the practice activities that were described. He was taught letter sounds explicitly and given direct practice in blending these into words. A good deal of attention also was given to onsets and rimes, helping him to compare patterns with words he already knew. He was also given some experiences with a few useful phonic generalizations.

In addition to specific phonic analysis practice, writing projects were still used to increase Dan's attention to internal features and order of letters in words. A number of studies have shown that spelling variables are significantly related to students' word reading accuracy and fluency. In Dan's writing, his invented spellings were considered acceptable, but more attention to correct spellings began to be emphasized. The teacher planned to assist with conventional spelling of several words in each of Dan's stories. The words chosen had spellings that were consistent with the letter sounds Dan was focusing on in his direct practice lessons.

After a few days of teacher prompting, Dan began to initiate some of these procedures himself. He would pause and thoughtfully consider the letters to write for

Dan's Case Study (continued)

some of these words. This is not to say that all spellings were correct, but his stories began to exhibit a healthy mix of conventional spelling along with some invented spellings, partly because of teacher reminders of sounds he now knew and partly because of Dan's seeming pleasure in gaining control of these understandings. Furthermore, even words that were spelled incorrectly began to reflect his growing awareness of orthographic conventions as he advanced to higher stages of spelling development. Direct practice in sounding out words, experiences with onsets and rimes, and writing and spelling practice all contribute to awareness of common patterns in words (Stahl, 1992).

An exercise that complemented both his reading and writing activities is one designed by Cunningham and Cunningham (1992). They call this activity "Making Words." After Dan had some experiences with letter-sound relationships, the teacher used the "Making Words" practice with him about once a week. To prepare for the word-making exercise, the teacher decided on a word of several letters (perhaps five or six), and then determined other smaller words that could be formed from the letters of this word.

For example when *plates* was the word for the day, other constituent words were *pets, pat, pest, late, pleat, pale, at, ate,* and *last*. Dan was given magnetic letters in a random order for each of the letters in the long word. He arranged these on a cookie sheet in response to the teacher's directions. For example, the teacher might say "Spell the word *at*." Then, "What letter would you add to that word to make it *ate*? Now, add a letter to make the word *late*. Which of your letters would you use to spell *pets*? How can you rearrange the letters of that word to spell *pest*?" And so on. Generally the progression was to build up words from short ones to the longest one. These steps helped Dan focus very carefully on letter sounds (e.g., think of the careful distinction that must be made to turn *pets* into *pest*). Making words was a popular endeavor with Dan.

As Cunningham and Cunningham note, this activity makes learners quite conscious of the importance of letter sequences in words. It also highlights some phonics generalizations without memorization of the rules (e.g., the silent *e* at the end of *ate* influencing the change in the vowel *a* from short to long). This activity should not be confused with asking students to find small words in big words, which leads to more confusion than enlightenment. For instance, sometimes teachers prod students to look for a small word or words in a longer word they are having trouble identifying. This is less than helpful in many words; for instance, a reader may find that the little words *fat* and *her* or *at* and *he* in *father* do not help with identifying that word at all.

Linking specific exercises on letter-sound relationships to their use in real words and real text is important.

Dan also read authentic, connected texts every day. He read one or two new books or stories in each of these sessions and did a repeated reading of another. During his readings of new books, when words caused him difficulty, the sounds were pointed out to him if they were ones he had worked with in his exercises. He was thus given much opportunity to practice what he was learning in other portions of his lessons and to do so in the context of what the other practice was all about—namely, text reading. Dan showed increasing use of letter-sound associations, though in the beginning he sounded out many words quite slowly, a naturally occurring behavior in the early part of the full-alphabetic phase. As time went by, he decoded words more quickly and began to recognize, at sight, words that previously had required him to apply decoding processes. When he was directed to sound out a word using his developing knowledge, he was also asked to check to see if the word he decided on made sense in the context of the selection he was reading. He did make some word substitutions, but he was not satisfied with nonsense words, and when real words he pronounced did not make sense, he returned to the word to try again. Teacher assistance continued to be necessary, but as Dan practiced more sound-symbol relationships, this support became less frequent. Dan sometimes tried to guess words from context without attempts to decode them, and at times these inferences were correct. When they were not, the teacher asked him to examine the word for letter-sound associations and common-place word patterns.

Dan's repeated-reading experience was given more structure than previously. Following the procedures recommended by Samuels (1988), he read a short story and the teacher graphed the accuracy and fluency of his reading each day until he reached a criterion of 85 words per minute for his reading rate. Reading fluency and accuracy increased each session for every story he read for this repeated-reading activity. When the criterion was reached, usually after about 3 days, a new story was introduced. The intent of this procedure was to continue to increase Dan's automatic recognition of words, which ultimately would allow him to focus on the meaning of text he read. The repeated-reading procedure, along with other exercises in his program, seemed to contribute to his learning more words more quickly than had previously been the case. Increasingly his word recognitions and identifications were correct.

Dan's teacher continued to read aloud to him for 5 or 10 minutes of his 1-hour sessions. Excellent books of narrative and expository selections were used to nurture his motivation to become an independent reader.

Dan worked in the reading program for about a year. At the end of that time, he was skillful at decoding words, was reading at his grade level, and never had any difficulties with comprehension. He had read an enormous amount of connected text by the time he "graduated" from the program. He loved books, with certain favorites for specific periods of time. As he progressed, in addition to the sound-symbol relationships that were a focus of much of his early instruction, structural analysis concepts were introduced. Structural analysis principles, also important to word learning, are considered on pages 290–304 in relation to our discussion about Phase 4 of word learning.

📖 MOVING INTO PHASE 4 OF WORD LEARNING

Typical attributes of readers in Phase 4 of word learning, the consolidated-alphabetic phase, were listed in Chapter 8. You may wish to review those now. Another student, Neal, will serve as an example of a learner moving from the full-alphabetic to the consolidated-alphabetic phase.

Neal's Case Study

LEARNING FROM TEXT

Compare. As you read the following case study, consider how Neal's reading behaviors are different from those of Dan, the student in the preceding case study who had moved to the full-alphabetic phase of word learning.

Neal's Case Study

Neal was a fourth-grade boy of average intelligence who was reading material at approximately a third-grade level with teacher assistance and at about a second-grade level independently. Like a number of the learners seen at the university-based reading clinic he was attending, he demonstrated no problems with comprehension. His knowledge of word meanings in oral language was quite advanced; one basis for his

better-than-average meaning vocabulary was probably his parents' reading aloud to him consistently since he was a toddler.

Neal had a good grounding in letter-sound relationships and was successful in applying these to many words. His decoding of most words was reasonably rapid and he had a sizeable stock of words that he recognized at sight—accurately, automatically, and swiftly.

He also identified common word patterns and was aware of their usefulness in decoding new words. For example, in an early lesson when the word *snug* caused him to pause and puzzle a moment, the teacher supplied this hint: "Look at this word. (The teacher wrote *bug*.) If you removed the *b* and placed the *sn* there, that would be this word." Almost before the explanation had been finished, Neal jumped in, said "snug," and continued reading fluently along. He also appeared to use this strategy without prods, stumbling for a moment over certain words, but then rather quickly blending the beginning sound of the word with the ending part. This behavior was seen for words such as *splat, chore, strip, trot, jade,* and *scrap.* In short, he could read many words by analogy to other words that were known to him. Though it seemed doubtful that Neal could verbalize the principle he was implementing in these cases, he had apparently had enough prior experience with overt and incidental attention to word configurations that he naturally engaged in these word identification behaviors.

Neal's functioning with printed text, as described previously, was typical of students in Phase 4, the full-alphabetic phase of word learning. However, what was not characteristic of this phase were his difficulties with multisyllabic words. He pronounced words of one or two syllables rather fluently, but longer words stumped him. When he encountered words of three syllables or more, he did not use word parts he knew as an aid to decoding. For instance, in one story Neal read during assessment, he was noticeably bothered when he tried to decipher the word *unwilling* and could not do so—though in the same story he read with no complications the words *unlace, unbent, will, paying,* and *hearing,* indicating that he knew all of the individual word parts that made up *unwilling.* He also did not recognize some frequently occurring word patterns, particularly certain prefixes and suffixes. His general fluency in reading was disrupted when he came to multisyllabic words. The serious obstacles he experienced with multisyllabic words were preventing him from moving into fourth-grade selections.

It was thus decided that Neal needed instruction (a) in specific structural analysis concepts and (b) in how to use skills and knowledge he already possessed to decode longer words.

Let's turn now to just what it means to provide instruction in structural analysis as a word identification strategy.

Word Identification Strategies in the Full-Alphabetic Phase of Word Learning: *Structural Analysis*

Structural analysis is a strategy in which attention is given to meaningful word parts so that an unknown word may be identified. Like phonic analysis, the aim is to examine the inner structure of unidentified words. In phonic analysis, the focus is on letter sounds; in structural analysis, the focus is often on larger word parts. Structural analysis helps with word identification, with spelling, and with determining word meanings. It also facilitates speed of recognition; if learners become quite familiar with certain word parts (e.g., *-tion, -less, re-*), words containing these parts can be identified more quickly (Nagy, Anderson, Schommer, Scott, & Stallman, 1989). Instruction in structural analysis deals with: (a) inflectional endings, (b) recognition of words when their spellings have changed because an ending has been added, (c) contractions, (d) compound words, (e) prefixes, (f) suffixes, and, at times, (g) syllabication.

Some work with structural analysis should occur at the same time as with instruction in phonic analysis; other structural analysis concepts may be better understood after the student has obtained expanded understanding of the alphabetic principle. Structural analysis is a major element in skilled reading, allowing learners greater command of the many new words they confront in reading texts. Instruction in use of structural analysis principles should include precise explanations about *how* and *when* to employ them.

Instructional Procedures

Inflectional Endings. **Inflectional endings** are affixes that are added to the ends of words (**affixes** are word parts that are added, or "affixed," to words). Inflectional endings form plurals (*cats, dishes*), third-person singular verb present tense (*runs, washes*), past tense (*jumped*), present participle (*talking*), possessives (*Mary's*), and comparisons in adjectives and adverbs (*smaller, smallest*).

To teach inflectional endings, the teacher simply presents a known root word, and then the same root word in an inflected form.[3] For example, "Here is one duck" and "Here are two ducks." The student is asked to note the word element that changes the word. Practice with many other similar examples, using known words plus inflectional endings, is provided. Most inflectional endings are taught early in a word identification program and generally are easily learned.

One useful manipulative for practicing inflectional endings is the word slide (see Figure 9–9). To make a word slide, cut four slits in a colored 5-inch by 8-inch file card. (You may wish to laminate the card for durability.) Next, make sets of strips containing known root words and inflectional endings. The student inserts the strips into the slits and slides them through attempting to form words. The student reads each pair silently. If the student thinks it forms a word, he or she says so and pronounces the word.

For young students, colorful drawings can be added to the basic file card to make the material appealing (as in Figure 9–9). After the word has been presented using a word slide, each inflected form should be presented in a sentence so the student may read the word in context.

Recognition of Words When Their Spellings Have Changed Because an Ending Has Been Added. Although poor readers may recognize a root word, they may not recognize it as a known word when an inflectional ending (or suffix) is added, particularly if a spelling change occurs in the root word. For example, Iris may know the word *dry* and the ending *-ed*, but because the *y* is changed to an *i* to make *dried*, it may not be apparent to her that this is a known word plus a familiar ending.

---

[3] In structural analysis, the terms *root word* and *base word* are used synonymously.

FIGURE 9–9 *An Example of a Word Slide, With an Alternate Suggestion Suitable for Younger Students*

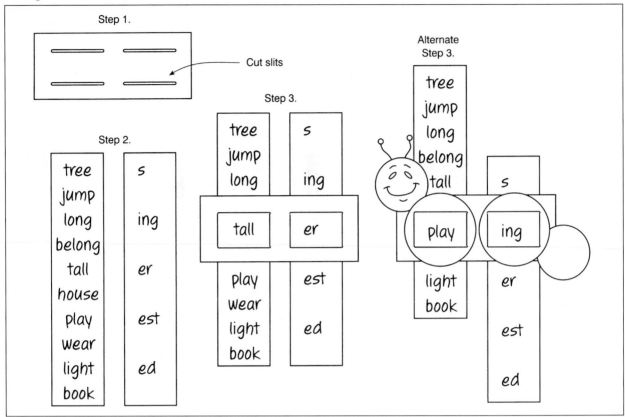

Students often need explicit instruction in the principles of spelling changes when inflected forms are added to their roots—for example, doubling final consonants (*hopping, hitter, wrapped, bigger*), changing *y* to *i* before adding an ending (*married, busily, tried, happily*), dropping the final *e* before adding an ending (*hoping, lived, releasing, freezer*). After initial instruction with these ideas, here are two practice activities you may wish to have students use.

1. *Board game.* To practice recognition of known words when the spellings have been changed before an inflectional ending, have students play board games such as the one in Figure 9–10.

2. *Group ball toss.* Another group game can be played with a plastic ball. On a piece of foam or felt, draw a target and write root words with an indelible marking pen. Obtain a lightweight plastic ball of about golf-ball size. Glue a strip of Velcro around the ball. Mount the target on the chalkboard, using masking tape. Beside the target, write inflectional endings on the chalkboard (see Figure 9–11).

To play the game, students are divided into teams. Students take turns throwing the ball at the target in the same way they would throw a dart; the Velcro causes it to stick to the target. After the student has determined which

FIGURE 9–10 *A Board Game for Practicing a Structural Analysis Word Identification Strategy*

root word the ball has hit, he or she goes to the chalkboard and writes a new word by combining the root with one of the inflectional endings. This is written under the appropriate ending already on the board. To score a point for a team, the student must remember to change *y* to *i*, double the final consonant, and so on, when writing the word.

Contractions. Although contractions occur frequently in oral language, and most contemporary reading programs introduce contractions in early first-grade materials, many students still find them confusing. Perhaps this is because the

FIGURE 9–11 *Game for Practicing Structural Analysis*

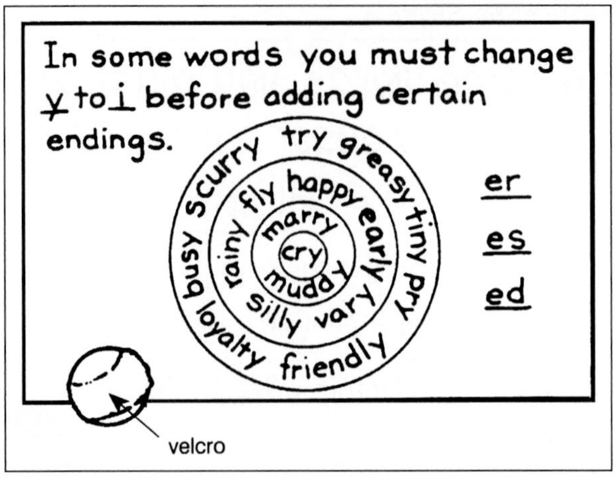

In some words you must change y to i before adding certain endings.

busy scurry try greasy tiny pry
rainy fly happy early tiny
marry cry early
muddy vary
silly vary
loyalty friendly

er
es
ed

velcro

FIGURE 9–12 *Commonly Occurring Contractions*

he's	you've	weren't	you'll
she's	we've	shouldn't	he'll
it's	they've	wouldn't	she'll
I'd	we're	couldn't	it'll
you'd	you're	isn't	we'll
he'd	they're	hasn't	they'll
she'd	let's	haven't	I'm
we'd	don't	hadn't	
they'd	won't	didn't	
I've	that's	I'll	

word form itself is unusual, with its use of an apostrophe. Direct practice in recognizing contractions and their relationships to the words from which they derive often is needed in remedial programs. Some commonly occurring contractions are listed in Figure 9–12.

Compound Words. There are three types of compound words. The type teachers most often describe to students are those formed when two small words are put together to make a longer word (e.g., *butterfly, into*). Hyphenated words are also often compounds (e.g., *self-correction*). The third type are those words not physically connected, but having a special meaning when used jointly, a meaning different from those of the individual words when they are not together. *Ice cream*, for example, means something distinct from just *ice* plus *cream*. In this latter example, although the words are not combined when conveyed by ink marks on paper (i.e., the surface structure of the language unit), they do function as one meaning unit in deep structure and therefore are considered to be a compound word. Here are two exercises for practicing compound words.

1. *Compound Dominoes.* An activity students enjoy when practicing recognition of compound words is Compound Dominoes. The teacher writes compounds on oaktag strips (e.g., *bathhouse, coatroom, fly ball, game bird, lighthouse*). Students try to match compound words so a new compound word

is formed from other compounds. For example, matching *lighthouse* with *fly ball* produces the compound *housefly*, matching *fly ball* with *game bird* produces *ballgame*, and so on. The longest sequence of matches wins.

lighthouse   fly ball   game bird   bathhouse   coatroom

As you can see, this example includes two of the three types of compounds: two words joined (e.g., *lighthouse*) and physically unconnected (e.g., *fly ball*). You may also wish to provide examples containing hyphenated compounds, for instance

lighthouse   fly-fishing   pole bean   bagpipe   dreamland

2. *Twister.* Use masking tape to attach oilcloth or butcher paper to the floor. Draw stepping-stones all over this "playing field" and write parts of compound words in them, with the first part of the compound on one stone and the second on a different one.

A student from Team 1 places one foot on the beginning of a compound and the other foot on the ending. Then the student places one hand on the beginning of another compound and the other hand on its ending. If both words are correct, the student stays in this position, while a student from Team 2 does the same on the same playing field.

Then another Team 1 member joins them, and so on. Soon students have to twist and turn through each other's arms and legs to reach their word parts. Points are lost if a wrong choice is made or students fall down in a happy pile.

Figure 9–13 presents a list of some compound words that teachers can use when preparing exercises for compound words.

FIGURE 9–13   ***Some Compound Words***

afternoon	downhill	mailbox	seaplane
airplane	downstairs	mailman	shoeshine
backbone	downtown	maybe	shoestring
barnyard	driveway	moonlight	snowball
baseball	drugstore	necktie	snowfall
basketball	everyone	neighborhood	snowflake
bathtub	everything	newspaper	sometimes
bedroom	eyebrows	nightgown	sunrise
beehive	firecracker	notebook	sunset
billboard	firefly	outlaw	sunshine
blackout	firehouse	overboard	surfboard
bookcase	fireplace	overcoat	tablecloth
bookmark	flashlight	pancake	toothbrush
bulldog	football	playground	typewriter
chalkboard	fullback	playhouse	underline
checkerboard	goldfish	piecrust	uphill
classroom	hallway	quarterback	waterfall
coffeeshop	headlight	railroad	watermelon
cookbook	highchair	rainbow	whirlpool
cowboy	highway	raincoat	wildlife
cupcake	homesick	rowboat	without
deadline	horseshoe		

Instruction about prefixes should include: (a) recognition of prefixes, (b) identification of words when a prefix is added to a root word, and (c) attention to meaning changes that occur when prefixes are added to words.

Prefixes. A **prefix** is a meaningful word part affixed to the beginning of a word, for example, the *un-* in *unhappy*. Control of larger letter units such as these assists in identifying multisyllabic words (Ruddell, 2006). Work with prefixes should include recognition of prefixes, identification of words when prefixes are added to known root words, and attention to meanings of prefixes and the meaning changes that occur when prefixes are added to words.

Because prefixes are meaning units, for instructional purposes teachers often group those with like meanings. For example, introduction of prefixes might begin with *un-* and *dis-* because both are "negative" prefixes: They mean "not," as in *unsure*, or "the opposite of," as in *untie*.

Stauffer (1942) identified the 15 most commonly occurring prefixes in the English language. These are listed in Figure 9–14. Effective instruction incorporates frequently seen prefixes before those that are used less often. However, some of the prefixes included on Stauffer's list are absorbed prefixes, not active prefixes. An **absorbed prefix** is a syllable that functioned at one time in the English language as a prefix but no longer does so; these

FIGURE 9–14 *The Most Commonly Occurring English Prefixes*

a- or *ab-*	atypical, amoral, abnormal	*in-*	(meaning not) incomplete, inaccurate, invisible, informal, inconvenient, inexcusable, inexpensive, incapable, infrequent, inactive, inadequate, inaccessible, inadvisable, inconsiderate
ad-	adjoining		
be-	beside, befriend, beloved, befitting, bemoan, besiege, becalmed, bedazzled, bedeviled	*pre-*	preschool, prehistoric, precooked, prepaid, prefix, prearrange, pretest, prepackaged, preview, precaution, presuppose, premature, prejudge, prerevolutionary
com-	compatriot, compress, commingle		
de-	dethrone, decontaminate, degenerate, dehumanize, dehumidify, deactivate, decode, decompose, decentralize, decompress, debug, de-escalate	*pro-*	prowar, pronoun, prolong, pro-American, prorevolutionary
		re-	repay, retie, recook, rewrite, reread, reappear, remake, replace, reload, reopen, reentry, review, repopulate, recall, repack, redraw, rearrange, rejoin, reactivate, react
dis-	disobey, disapprove, disagree, disrespectful, dishonest, disconnect, distrust, disarm, disuse, disability, disadvantage, disappear, disbelief, discomfort		
		sub-	submarine, subzero, subtropical, subheading, subsoil, subdivision, substandard, subcommittee, subhuman
en-	encircle, enable, endanger, enforce, entangle, enslave, enclose, entwine, enrobe, enact, enfold, enthrone, encamp, encode	*un-*	unfair, unhappy, uncooked, unlock, untie, uncover, unable, unlucky, untrue, unwrap, uninvited, undress, unfinished, uncertain, unreal, unripe, unwise, unlawful, untruthful, unconscious, unpopulated, undisturbed, unload, unwilling, unsold, unwashed, unspoken
ex-	ex-president, ex-wife, ex-husband, exterminate		
in-	(meaning into) ingrown, inbreed, incoming, inlay, input, inset, intake		

FIGURE 9–15
Worksheet for Students Learning Prefixes

	PREFIX	ROOT
1. disobey	dis	obey
2. enclose		
3. repay		
4. incomplete		
5. prehistoric		

prefixes have been "absorbed" into words; examples are *ad-* in *adjacent* and *com-* in *combine*. An **active prefix,** on the other hand, is one that still functions as a prefix in the manner in which prefixes are generally defined—that is, as word parts that are added to complete root words (such as *re-* in *repay*, or *sub-* in *sub-zero*). When the goal of teaching is to emphasize the identification of words, the majority of instructional time should be devoted to those that are active prefixes. When the objective is to add sophistication to strategies students use to determine word meanings, some attention to absorbed prefixes is appropriate.

Several activities that may be used when working with prefixes follow.

1. *Divide words into parts.* Use worksheets that help students discern word parts. The exercise in Figure 9–15 is an example. Students are to write the prefix and the root in the two separate columns.

2. *Play group games.* On file cards, print prefixes. Pass these out to students. Write root words on oaktag strips. Place one of the root word cards on the chalkboard tray. A student who has a prefix that will fit with the root word comes up and places it in front of the root word card. If it is correct and the student can pronounce the new word, the student may take the root word. The student with the most root word cards at the end of the game is the winner.

3. *Find prefixes in published stories.* Select a story from a sports magazine or any other magazine that might appeal to your students. Have the students circle with a fine-point, red marking pen all prefixes they can find. Give points for each one found. Give additional points for correct pronunciation of each of the words containing a prefix. Then read the article together.

Suffixes.   As you know, a **suffix** is a word part affixed to the end of a root word or base word. Objectives for teaching suffixes are similar to those used for teaching prefixes. Instruction should include recognition of suffixes, identification of words when suffixes are added to known root words, and attention to meanings of suffixes and the meaning changes that occur when suffixes are added to words.

Suffixes, like prefixes, can alter the meanings of words, but they also often change a word's grammatical function. The latter are called *derivational suffixes* (Schumm & Saumell, 1994). For example, the suffix *-ness* changes adjectives to nouns, such as in *dark/darkness* and *happy/happiness*. A listing of some English suffixes is found in Figure 9–16.

Activities used for instruction with prefixes can also be used for work with suffixes. Here are some additional suggestions.

FIGURE 9–16 *Some English Suffixes*

-able	enjoyable, comfortable, enviable	*-ion*	suggestion, graduation, creation, discussion
-age	shortage, leakage, wreckage, breakage	*-ity*	stupidity, humidity, sincerity, productivity
-al	musical, personal, original, removal	*-ive*	productive, expensive, excessive, destructive
-ance	appearance, performance	*-ize*	alphabetize, dramatize, colonize, symbolize
-ant	contestant, attendant, informant		
-ary	imaginary, summary, boundary, missionary	*-less*	spotless, sleeveless, nameless, friendless
-ation	confirmation, information, starvation, relaxation	*-ly*	consciously, quickly, friendly, officially, slowly
-ative	informative, talkative, administrative, imaginative	*-ment*	refreshment, amazement, punishment, enjoyment
-ence	existence, persistence	*-ness*	completeness, wholeness, sickness, darkness
-ent	excellent, insistent, correspondent	*-or*	sailor, actor, inventor, inspector, translator
-er	helper, teacher, player, farmer, miner, follower	*-ous*	joyous, famous, dangerous, nervous, courageous
-ery	bakery, bravery	*-th*	growth, truth, warmth, width, fourth
-ful	delightful, careful, cheerful, truthful, plentiful	*-ty*	loyalty, safety, cruelty
		-ward	homeward, toward, westward, eastward
-fy	classify, beautify, falsify, simplify, purify	*-y*	rainy, windy, noisy, gloomy, curly, snowy

1. *Use flip strips.* On colored strips of construction paper, print root words on the front left-hand side. On the back, print suffixes so the back can be folded over to form a new word with the suffix (see Figure 9–17). When a new suffix is introduced, packs of flip strips can be prepared so that the same suffix is used over and over with different root words, as in example A of Figure 9–17. After readers have become acquainted with several suffixes, flip strips can be prepared with many different suffixes being added to the same root word, as in example B. This demonstrates to students how their repertoires of known words have been substantially extended. Flip strips may also be used for practicing identification of words in which the spelling of the root has changed when an ending has been added, as in example C. After students have read each flip strip from a set, have them read or write each word in a sentence.

2. *Root word tree.* Draw a tree on a large sheet of paper. Attach index cards labeled with root words to the roots (where else!) of the tree by stapling the ends

FIGURE 9–17 *Flip Strips for Practicing Suffixes*

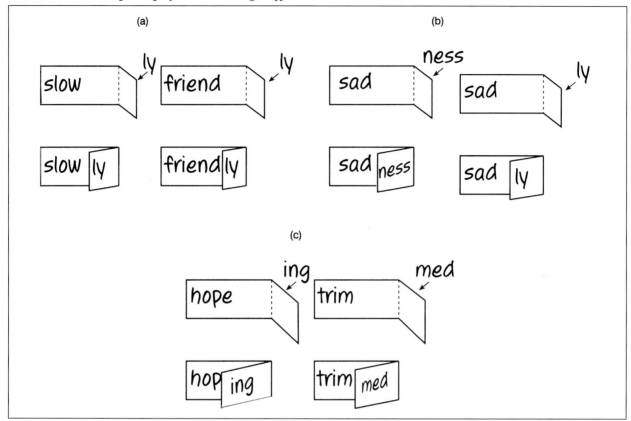

of small strips of oaktag to the tree's roots and simply slipping the index cards behind the strips (see Figure 9–18). Write suffixes on index cards and place these in a pile facedown. Students take a card from this pile and attempt to match it with a root word. If the match is correct, the root word is removed from the roots and attached with the suffix to the leafy part of the tree.

Working With Prefixes and Suffixes. After both suffixes and prefixes have been introduced, give students practice with multisyllabic words that contain both. Not only should delayed readers be taught frequently occurring affixes, they also need teacher-guided practice in using them in words (Ruddell, 2006). Students can be asked to identify and write each part of the word, as in Figure 9–19.

Or, they can be asked to form new words, as in this exercise.

Prefix	+	Root	+	Suffix	=	Word
re	+	fresh	+	ment	=	refreshment
un	+	success	+	ful	=	
re	+	settle	+	ment	=	
un	+	law	+	ful	=	

FIGURE 9–18 *Root Word Tree for Practicing Suffixes*

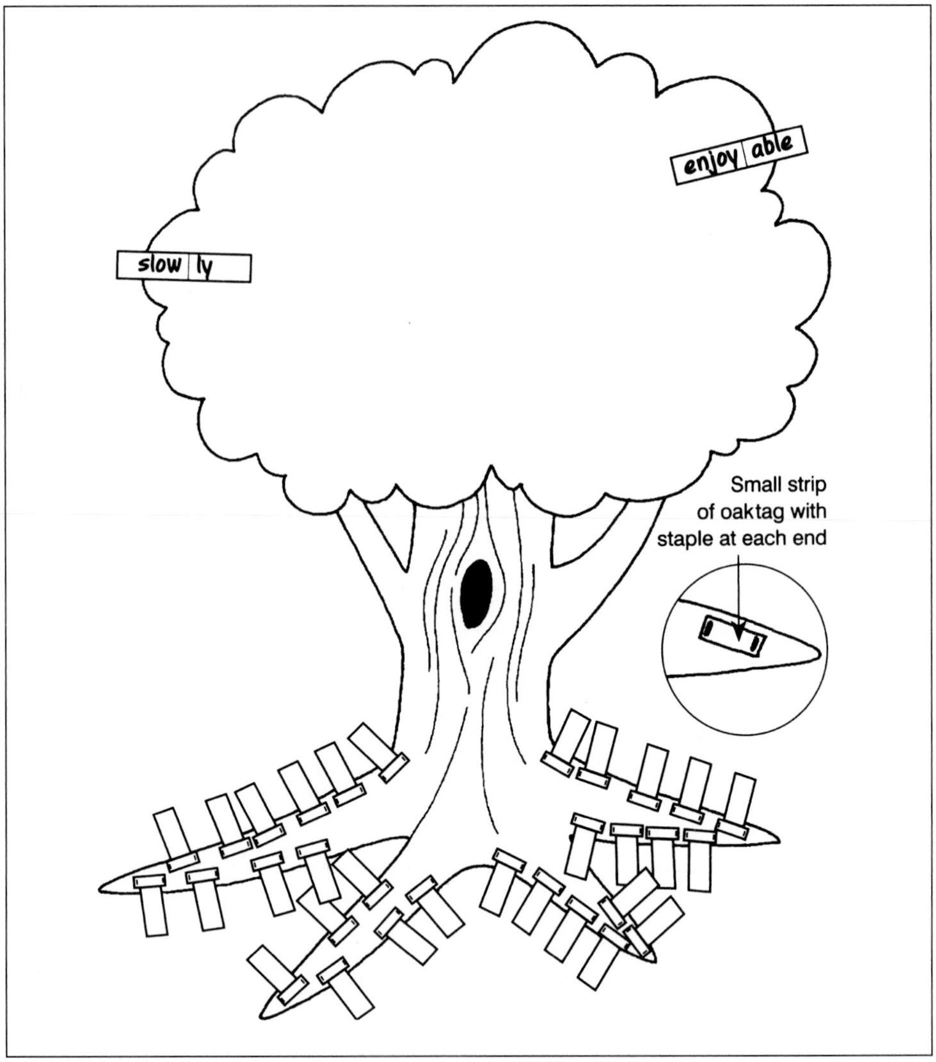

FIGURE 9–19 *Worksheet for Students Working With Prefixes and Suffixes*

	PREFIX	ROOT	SUFFIX
1. unbreakable	un	break	able
2. disgraceful			
3. refillable			
4. previewer			
5. dishonorable			

Students can also be helped to see the relationships of words that are similar to others by building word trees:

joy
enjoyable

joyful

enjoyment

joyous

rejoice

This highlights known word parts for word identification and simultaneously stresses interrelatedness of word meanings.

Syllabication.   **Syllabication,** or dividing words into syllables, is considered a part of phonic analysis instruction in some programs, but a part of structural analysis in others. In the former, the focus is on units of sound, and work with syllabication is believed to be crucial because the ways in which words are divided into syllables are clues to sounds of vowels. In programs that use syllables for phonic analysis, students are taught syllabication rules. Here are some commonly taught rules.

1. When there are two like consonants, divide between them (e.g., *pup/py*). *Exception:* When -ed is added to a word ending in *d* or *t*, it forms a separate syllable (*add/ed*).
2. When there are two unlike consonants, divide between them (e.g., *wal/rus*). *Exception:* Do not divide between consonant clusters or digraphs (e.g., *be/tween*).
3. When a consonant is between two vowels, divide after the first vowel (e.g., *si/lent*). *Exception:* When the consonant between two vowels is *x*, divide after the *x* (e.g., *ex/am*).
4. Prefixes, suffixes, and inflectional endings are separate syllables (e.g., *re/state/ment*). *Exception:* When -*ion* is added to a word that ends in *t*, the *t* joins with the -*ion* to form the final syllable (e.g., *ac/tion*).
5. When a syllable ends in a vowel, the vowel is long.
6. When a syllable ends in a consonant, the vowel in that syllable is short.

By applying a combination of these rules, presumably a reader would be aided in identifying vowel sounds, and, ultimately, unknown words. For example, by applying rule 3 and rule 5, the *i* in *silent* would be pronounced as its long form, which would expedite identification of the word if it was unknown.

However, some students have difficulty learning these rules, and even when they do, they may only use them for specific workbook or teacher-directed exercises. Because they are moderately complex and because of their exceptions, students may not employ the rules in authentic word identification tasks (Cunningham, 1998).

On the other hand, in programs where syllabication is considered a part of the structural analysis component, the purpose of showing students how words can be divided is to demonstrate that a long and possibly intimidating word may be analyzed in terms of its smaller word parts, and thus identified. The focus is on frequent spelling patterns. For example, when a poor reader first encounters in print such words as *enlargement* or *irreplaceable*, the student's first reaction may be, "I don't know that word, and I'll never be able to figure out one that big." On the other hand, the word can seem quite manageable if the student has developed the habit of dividing the word and looking for familiar word parts. For example, the student might go through these steps to identify the word *enlargement*:

"Oh, it begins with *en-*. We worked with a prefix like that. It's /en/."

"The middle of the word is *large*."

"The end is just that suffix, -ment."

"En-large-ment. Enlargement. 'I'll need to make an enlargement of this picture,' the photographer said."

The emphasis in these programs is on looking for known word parts and not on memorizing rules. In such a program, the following activities would occur:

Step 1: Students are told that many long words can be divided into smaller parts to aid identification. This is demonstrated by removing inflectional endings from words (e.g., *entering=enter/ing; darkest=dark/est*). The term and concept of "syllable" is applied to each of these smaller parts.

Step 2: Step 1 is repeated, this time with prefixes (e.g., *disgrace=dis/grace; unselfish=un/selfish*).

Step 3: Step 1 is carried out again, this time with suffixes (e.g., *importantly=important/ly; enrollment=enroll/ment*).

Step 4: Step 1 is carried out with both prefixes and suffixes (e.g., *un/rest/ful, dis/appear/ance*).

Step 5: Students learn about other ways to divide long words and are given brief practice in dividing words based on a few of the most useful rules. The emphasis at this time remains on looking at common word parts. Memorization of the rules is not required. (Knowledge of syllabication rules may actually be more helpful for writing than for reading so that correct conventions of written language may be applied when a word is hyphenated at the end of a line.)

> In many programs today, the emphasis in syllabication is not memorization of rules, but on demonstrating how a long word may be analyzed into smaller parts.

A Return to Neal's Case Study

Neal's Case Study (continued)

Now that we have examined some structural analysis concepts, let's see how these pertain to Neal, our fourth-grade student. With a reading instructional level of approximately third grade, Neal had had more exposures to print than the two other case study students, Bridget and Dan. He also had benefited from direct instruction in phonic analysis and structural analysis strategies in his regular school program. As a result of all these factors, he was familiar with some typical units in words. He recognized, at sight, common inflectional endings, knew all contractions, and had a concept of compound words, easily reading most of those he encountered in the selections that were part of his daily lessons. In addition, spelling changes when affixes were added usually did not confuse him. He recognized certain prefixes and a few suffixes, but there were a number of frequently occurring ones that he did not know. He had not yet grasped how to break a long word into its salient parts, nor was he using what he already did know when he met multisyllabic words.

Many of the strategies for presenting and practicing prefixes and suffixes, discussed in the immediately preceding section, were employed with Neal. The teacher began by focusing on those prefixes and suffixes that are used most often in English words. Neal was given teacher-guided, rather than independent, practice with the use of these affixes. The teacher delivered explicit information about the pronunciations of prefixes and suffixes, and he had many opportunities to add the prefixes and suffixes he was working on to known root words before he was asked to apply them to unknown words.

In addition, Neal received a great deal of assistance with dividing words into syllables or known word parts. Readers' skill at reading multisyllabic words with ease relies on their deftness at separating long words into syllables (Adams, 1990a, 1990b). Again, Neal applied these principles and understandings to words he knew prior to practicing them with new words. For example, the notion that words can be broken into parts was expedited by using the knowledge he already possessed about compound words. The teacher showed him familiar compounds, had him say the separate parts, write the parts separately, and then write the word again in its consolidated form. Neal also worked with word-building notebooks (see Figure 9–20). Next, the same sequence was

FIGURE 9–20 *A Word-Building Notebook for Practicing Compound Words*

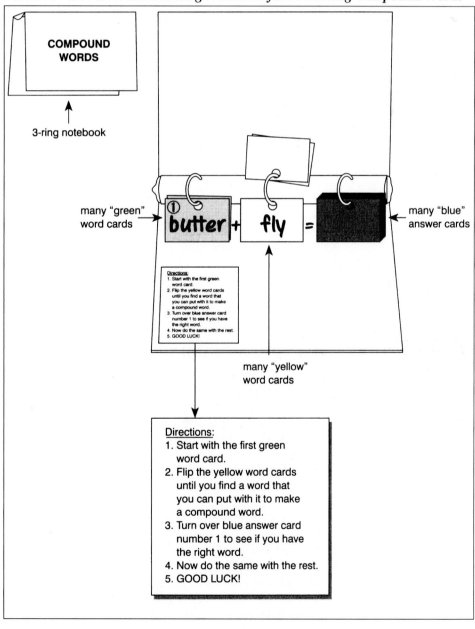

3-ring notebook

many "green"
word cards

butter + fly =

many "blue"
answer cards

many "yellow"
word cards

Directions:
1. Start with the first green
   word card.
2. Flip the yellow word cards
   until you find a word that
   you can put with it to make
   a compound word.
3. Turn over blue answer card
   number 1 to see if you have
   the right word.
4. Now do the same with the rest.
5. GOOD LUCK!

*Neal's
Case Study
(continued)*

followed with two-syllable words that he already recognized. Then longer, unknown words were tackled in exactly the same manner. Word-building notebooks were used in this practice, but in this case with prefixes, roots, suffixes, and parts of multisyllabic words on the cards.

As with all students, Neal's use of new concepts in real text reading was considered critical. He spent one third to one half of his hour-long sessions reading in connected text that included words with prefixes and suffixes and words with three or more syllables. A particular emphasis was placed on teacher modeling to show him how to apply known information to multisyllabic words during his reading of stories and informational selections, as well as during his direct-practice exercises. He was also instructed to use what he already knew about letter-sound relationships when structural analysis strategies were not helpful in specific words. He was taught to use context to self-check the sense of the word his analysis had produced. His good oral language vocabulary aided him in making decisions about whether words he decoded fit into the context.

At the end of one academic term (approximately 9 weeks of instruction), Neal had made considerable progress. Still, he could not readily recall a few prefixes and suffixes. In addition, although he now definitely understood the process of dividing long words into parts to identify them, he was not yet fluently carrying out this skill. He was retained in the clinic for an additional quarter to firm up his understandings and to provide more rehearsals with his newly learned concepts, especially through practice in contextual materials.

By the middle of the next term, he could read fourth-grade materials and became progressively skillful in handling them. At the end of the second 9-week period, special instruction was no longer deemed necessary. His classroom teacher agreed with this assessment, having seen a major change in Neal's word recognition and word identification abilities in his work with her. She agreed to continue instruction in the manner that he had been experiencing. When Neal's progress was checked at the end of his fourth-grade year, he was to be promoted to the next grade level with the confidence that he could read the materials necessary for success in fifth grade.

CONTEXT CLUES AS A WORD IDENTIFICATION STRATEGY

For a number of years, use of context clues was considered the prime strategy for identifying unknown words. Teachers were often advised to direct students' attention to the context surrounding a word *before* prompting other word identification strategies—or sometimes, *in lieu of* any other strategy. Students were routinely asked to skip unknown words, read to the end of the sentence, and then attempt to guess a word that would fit the sentence. For a time, it was assumed that proficient readers did just that, predicting what unknown words would be by using expectancies based on their knowledge of language and the world.

For both skilled and unskilled readers, context clues were presumed to be the most valuable aid to word identification. This theory seemed to hold some logic and was certainly well meaning. However, much to the surprise of many reading authorities, when research investigated widely held assumptions about the value of context clues, this did not prove to be the case (e.g., Adams, 1990a, 1990b; Daneman, 1991; Ehri, 1991; Juel, 1991; Stanovich, 1991b). Proficient readers do not use context as their primary word identification strategy; rather,

Research shows that use of context clues as a word identification strategy is not as helpful as once believed.

identifications are based on visual and phonemic information in the words themselves. And while it is true that context may assist with confirming the meaning of a word that has multiple definitions, this occurs only *after* the word is identified. Context also may help a competent reader use word pattern information more quickly, but it does not replace the need to use letter and sound knowledge.

When research with developing readers investigated the benefits of using context clues, it was found that the strategy is used most by the students who are least skillful (e.g., Allington & Fleming, 1978; Stanovich, 1993–94; Stanovich & West, 1981). Those readers who make the least headway tend to remain in a stage where use of context is the central way to read words (Biemiller, 1970). Biemiller (1970) summarized these findings by saying that "the longer [a student] stays in the early, context-emphasizing phase without showing an increase in the use of graphic information the poorer the reader he is at the end of the year" (p. 95). In fact, use of context clues is now considered to be a compensatory strategy (Stanovich, 1980) since it is used because the reader does not yet have control of more productive methods of word recognition and identification (e.g., Daneman, 1991; Stanovich, 1993–94).

Investigations have also shown that context clues do not provide the support once believed. The easiest words to predict from context are function words (Gough, 1983). These are the words that occur most often in print and, therefore, are the ones that students are most likely to recognize at sight, making the use of context unnecessary. Individual content words occur less frequently, making it more probable that there will be greater challenge in identifying them. However, content words are the words most difficult to determine from context; thus, for those very words where a word identification strategy is most needed, context may not be helpful (Adams, 1990a, 1990b). Quite a number of studies have shown that natural text is not especially predictable (Stanovich, 1991b). The chance that a reader can guess the next word in a passage turns out to be about 20%–35% (e.g., see Gough, 1983; Stanovich, 1991b), and for content words, this percentage may be even less. Gough (1983) found that content words—those that carry the meaning of a passage—could be predicted only about 10% of the time. Juel (1991) notes that no matter how imperfect letter-sound relationships are, they still are more reliable than context in word identification.

One major criticism of encouraging students to use context to the exclusion of other cuing systems is that they will not study a word's letters and sounds and therefore will not have any information to recognize the word the next time they encounter it. This would not be a problem if context habitually conveyed the unknown word, but since it does not, this is a significant issue. Another reason for teachers to refrain from prompting poor readers to use context clues as their chief word identification strategy is that for context to operate productively, the reader must know well the words surrounding the unfamiliar word, and this often is not the situation with unskilled readers (Ehri, 1991).

Use of context does have some value. Until readers are adept at using visual and sound information to determine the identities of many words, there are times when context will provide a clue to an unfamiliar word (though this may be less often than once was believed). Context can also limit the possibilities of what a word might be when a student is trying to identify it; for example, when students are reading independently and their identification strategies lead them to believe a word is one of two similar words but they are not sure which, then context may solve this dilemma. Furthermore, context provides a check on words that have been produced through use of other word identification strategies, and this is indeed a valuable function. Moreover, the use of context to assist comprehension has been upheld by research (e.g., Baker & Brown, 1984). However, context clues are no longer regarded to be as helpful as once was supposed for learning or recognizing words.

*R*eflections

1. Consider this question: Why have many educators been fiercely pro or con in their views about the value of phonics instruction?
2. Based on what you have learned in Chapters 8 and 9, what clues for instruction are obtained by determining a student's phase of word learning? Mention as many specific implications as you can.

10

Knowledge of Word Meanings

Using structured overviews or semantic mapping aids both vocabulary development and comprehension.

R ead Paragraph A.
(A) Apprehension of the semantic fields of morphological units is pivotal for deriving semantic content when reading. This seems to be consummately plausible and most preceptors' ripostes to this attestation would predictably be, "Inexorably so."

You may have had some difficulty getting the gist of that paragraph since it was written with words whose meanings are not commonplace. Paragraph B says the same thing but uses words more frequently found in the meaning vocabularies of the average college student. Now try it again.

(B) Knowledge of word meanings is important for reading comprehension. This seems to be quite logical, and most teachers' responses to this statement would probably be, "Of course."

The contrasting examples in these paragraphs show that ease of comprehension is affected by knowledge of specific word meanings. In Paragraph A the point of the two sentences may have been hidden unless you stopped, reread, and mulled them over somewhat, and even then you may not have understood the full message. On the other hand, Paragraph B was as clear as a bell; with no conscious effort at all, you got the central idea.

Research has confirmed that students' performances on measures of vocabulary knowledge have solid correlations with reading comprehension, and that an individual's understandings of word meanings is a good indication of how well that person will comprehend text (e.g., Anderson & Freebody, 1981; Ruddell, 2006; Sadoski, 2005; U.S. Department of Health and Human Services, 2000).

It would seem to follow, then, that instructional programs specifically designed to teach learners word meanings would make important contributions to the improvement of comprehension. However, somewhat surprisingly, the relationship between vocabulary and comprehension is a bit more complex. When research has tested this idea, initially, results from study to study were conflicting. Sometimes knowledge of new word meanings affected comprehension in positive ways, but sometimes it did not! However, as the number of these studies increased, a pattern began to emerge. This pattern showed that for new word meanings to have any effect on comprehension, students had to know the meanings of the words *well*. Knowing a word well means having breadth and depth of information about the word. This finding has implications for instruction and has helped us understand what is effective instruction and what is not.

An individual's **meaning vocabulary** is defined as the number of words for which that person knows one or more meanings. However, Beck and McKeown (1991) have pointed out that what it means to "know" a word is a complicated concept and that word knowledge can be best expressed on a *continuum*. Figure 10–1 illustrates the continuum they proposed.

Word knowledge develops first in an individual's oral language. Many attempts have been made to estimate the number of word meanings children know when they come to school at age 5 or 6. A number of authorities suggest that the best approximation is between 2,500 and 5,000 (Ruddell, 2006). Recent

FIGURE 10-1 *A Continuum of Word Knowledge*

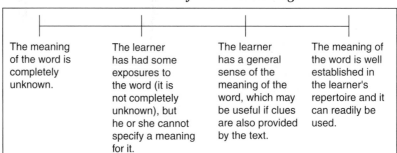

| The meaning of the word is completely unknown. | The learner has had some exposures to the word (it is not completely unknown), but he or she cannot specify a meaning for it. | The learner has a general sense of the meaning of the word, which may be useful if clues are also provided by the text. | The meaning of the word is well established in the learner's repertoire and it can readily be used. |

research seems to show that the average student also adds approximately 1,000 root words during each school year (Biemiller & Slonim, 2000), a more modest figure than previous estimates by educators but still a surprisingly large number of words. In the preschool years, word meanings are obtained from oral language interchanges with parents and peers, from hearing stories read, from television and other media, from illustrations in books and magazines, and even from various print sources. These same sources account for word learning during the school years, along with specific instruction.

Print sources become increasingly important in the school years and beyond. Individuals who read a lot develop more extensive vocabularies than those who do not, and in some cases, word meanings develop in print before they are used in oral language. An example of the latter may be part of *your* experience: If you read a great deal—and what college student can get away with not doing so!— you may read words that you have seen in print many times, words for which you have at some time in the past determined meanings. But because words found in the reading material of a sophisticated reader may not be typically used in oral language, you may have never heard some of these words spoken. The first time you do, you may react, "Oh, so that's how you pronounce that word!" Or, the first time you bravely say one of these words aloud, you may pronounce it incorrectly—even though you know perfectly well what it means. Knowing more words in print than you use in oral language is a characteristic of a competent reader.

Roelke's (1969) research showed that important aspects of vocabulary knowledge affecting comprehension are the following:

1. the sheer number of words for which a student knows meanings
2. knowledge of multiple meanings of words; for example, knowing that *light* can mean "not heavy" as well as a shade of color (as in "*light* pink"), free from worry (as in "*light*hearted"), a source of illumination (as in a "bright *light*"), moderate (as in a "*light* meal"), or a small quantity (as in "*light* rain")
3. ability to select the correct meaning of a word with multiple meanings to fit a specific context

To these, recent researchers have added the insight that understanding of a word's meaning must be adequately *thorough* to affect comprehension. That is, there must be a precise understanding of the concept underlying the word, not a mere parroting of a definition. Partial or hazy conceptions of word meanings are not as useful in producing depth of comprehension.

These findings give clues about instruction necessary to provide effective learning of word meanings. Here are conclusions supported by research.

1.   Instruction should combine several methods for presenting meanings if a complete understanding is to be obtained. For example, simply supplying a definition for a word is not robust enough for students to retain and *use* words. Neither is introducing words in the context of a teacher-prepared sentence, if this is all that is done. Combining these two modes of instruction, however, may help students learn well-developed word meanings, especially if they are accompanied by examples (Stahl & Fairbanks, 1986).

2.   Instruction should include activities that encourage deep processing of targeted words. Students should be actively engaged in relating the words to their prior knowledge (Blachowicz & Fisher, 2000) and in sorting out relationships between the targeted words and other words. They should be involved in seeing connotations (the implied sense of a word) as well as denotations (the literal meaning of a word) and "go beyond the superficial act of memorizing definitions" (Herman & Dole, 1988, p. 42).

3.   Students must have many exposures to words to gain thorough understandings of them (U.S. Department of Health and Human Services, 2000). When studies in which learning new word meanings improves comprehension are compared with those that are less effective, we find that the ineffective programs furnished students with only one or two exposures to a word's meaning, which was not enough to have any lasting consequences. A sole encounter with a word is unlikely to be productive when words are conceptually complex, even if explanations are given of the concepts during this single exposure (Nagy & Scott, 2004). Repetition is important for another reason—so readers can identify a word's meaning speedily and effortlessly when they encounter it in reading.

LEARNING FROM TEXT

Note Taking.   The three points enumerated in the previous section are important. Try to summarize them, paraphrasing as you do, perhaps in writing.

Many studies have established that, in general, unskilled readers have meager meaning vocabularies in comparison with skilled readers. Because an adequate meaning vocabulary is important for reading comprehension, reading teachers must be concerned with this area of instruction.

Three ways students can increase their meaning vocabularies are: (a) through direct instruction, (b) through independent word learning from texts, and (c) through learning words from oral language encounters.

📖 DIRECT INSTRUCTION

NCLB
READING FIRST

Authorities do not agree on all aspects of how word meanings are learned; however, one matter draws strong consensus. Based on their research and their interpretations of the studies of others, most authorities in this area are convinced of the value of direct instruction to facilitate in-depth understanding of word meanings. Beck and McKeown (1991) describe "direct instruction" as including teacher-guided lessons on vocabulary, along with teaching in which students work individually with print materials that are specifically designed to present vocabulary information.

Hittleman (1983) reported that successful programs that incorporate direct instruction of vocabulary development have the following features:

1. A small number of words are taught intensively in a given lesson rather than many words being presented in a more cursory fashion.
2. The instruction is systematic and continuous. Students are exposed to the same word in many different contexts.
3. Gamelike activities are incorporated into the schedule to stimulate students to study vocabulary.
4. Any technique is employed that calls attention to the meanings of word parts.
5. Context, the dictionary, and the derivations of words are studied as means of obtaining word meanings.

Criteria to decide which word meanings merit intensive instruction include (a) the conceptual complexity of the word and (b) the word's present and future utility.

If only a few words are to be taught to allow for intense instruction, how does the teacher decide which words these are to be? Beck and McKeown (1991) suggest that present and future utility be the criteria: (a) Is understanding of the passage dependent on knowing this word's meaning? and (b) Is the word one likely to be useful to know in the future? Since limited time is available in any school day, efficient instruction considers the usefulness of a word as well as its complexity. If the present utility of a word is high, but the future utility is comparatively low, this gives an indication about the amount of attention that should be allotted to instruction of the word. That is, the word cannot be ignored if its presence will hinder comprehension of the immediate reading assignment, but it may not be a candidate for further, more protracted activities.

Direct instruction always includes introductory guidance in which the student is initially acquainted with the word; direct instruction should also involve further rich development of a word's meanings (Ruddell, 2006).

Meaning vocabulary knowledge is enhanced through thought-provoking activities, direct teacher guidance, and instruction that is systematic and continuous.

Introductory Guidance

How should new words be introduced? Some initial presentations result in more lasting acquisitions of words than others.

Use Context—Carefully.   Sometimes students learn words during the natural act of reading without direct instruction. That is, through exposures to a word (usually several of these), the context of the material eventually conveys the meaning. This is normally referred to as **incidental learning** of word meanings. Incidental learning will be discussed in a later part of this chapter, but that is not what we are addressing here.

The present section, instead, considers what is called **pedagogical context,** or **instructional context.** This type of context is used when the teacher introduces the meaning of a new word by placing the word in a sentence or paragraph that is fashioned to communicate the word's definition. The words surrounding the unknown word are expected to assist the student in gaining a sense of the word's definition.

Unless sentences are carefully constructed, however, instructional context may provide only a vague sense of a word's meaning. Sentences must be used that provide enough information so the meaning *can* be derived from surrounding words. Here is an example. To introduce the meaning of the word *matted* the teacher writes this sentence on the board: "The girl's *matted* hair looked dirty and messy," underlines *matted*, and asks the students to guess what *matted* means. *Matted* in this case refers to hairs that are tangled in a dense mass. But even with the use of *messy* in this sentence, that meaning is not really clear. *Matted* in this context could refer to the words *black, blond, red, unwashed, thick, thin, long, short, permed, bleached, frosted,* or, today, even *green.* For the teacher, who already knows the meaning of *matted*, the context may seem sufficient, but for a person unfamiliar with the word, the meaning of the word may not be apparent at all from the context. For this reason, many authorities contend that instructional context as an initial presentation method must be supplemented with other aids, such as definitions or multiple contexts for the same word. In addition, introductory presentations are strengthened if these are followed by having students generate their own example statements.

Sentences offering context clues can take many forms. Dale and O'Rourke (1971) identify the following types of context clues:

1. *Synonyms.* "A martin is a *bird.*"
2. *Antonyms.* "The plastic dish won't *break,* but the glass one probably will *shatter.*"
3. *Apposition* (use of a word or phrase that explains another word and that is set off by commas). "Florida is a peninsula, *a body of land surrounded on three sides by water,* and has many beaches."
4. *Comparison.* "A newsreel is like *a short motion picture* that shows news events."
5. *Contrast.* "A story that *rambles on and on is not concise.*"
6. *Description.* "Flying lizards are *found in Asia and can spread winglike membranes out from the sides of their small bodies so they can sometimes be seen gliding through the air.*"
7. *Example.* "A task force is a temporary grouping of forces, *for example, a military unit that has been called up to achieve a specific objective.*"

8. *Origin.* "*The Italian word* for fresh is *fresco, which gives us the name of a painting done on fresh plaster.*" (Dale & O'Rourke, 1971, p. 34)
9. *Formal definition.* "Lightsome means *buoyant, graceful, light, or nimble.*"

Carnine, Kameenui, and Coyle (1984) found that context clues that are very direct provided the most help for intermediate grade students when compared with types that required learners to make an inference. Determination of meanings also was improved if the clue word or words were placed close to the unlearned word rather than farther away in the text.

Use the Dictionary—Judiciously. Dale (personal communication, November 17, 1974) once conducted a survey asking students which of all activities in school they liked least. The winner of this dubious honor was the exercise of looking up a list of words in a dictionary and writing their meanings.

Should a dictionary even be used as a route to vocabulary learning? Herman and Dole (1988, p. 44) summarize from research answers to that question.

1. If a word represents a complicated or difficult concept about which learners have minimal or no prior knowledge, just looking it up likely will not unravel the mystery.
2. If the students possess a fair amount of understanding of the underlying ideas and know other words that may be used to define it, a dictionary can be useful in pinpointing a word's meaning.
3. If thorough understanding of a word is needed to comprehend a passage, procedures other than obtaining a dictionary definition are preferable.
4. If the word is of only slight importance for understanding the text to be read, then the partial understanding that may be obtained from looking it up in a dictionary can suffice.

Here is an example of ineffective dictionary use. Suppose an article tells about a certain time period in geologic history. As such, it prominently and frequently includes the unfamiliar, potentially difficult word that names it, the *Archeozoic* period. You write the word *Archeozoic* on the board and tell students they should look it up in their desktop dictionaries before they begin to read. The students dutifully begin to thumb through to find the word. As they locate the word, they find that the definition says:

Archeozoic—Of or denoting the earliest of two customary, but arbitrary, partitions of the Precambrian era.

What has this definition told the student who has no prior experience in reading about geologic periods? Almost nothing. Teacher explanations would serve the purpose much better than a trip to the dictionary. Such explanations could involve a brief discussion of the ancient age of the earth and the fact that scientists have divided the time the earth has been in existence into periods in order to study what has gone on at various stages. A geologic map (readily available in most schools) on which time periods have been marked could be briefly shown, pointing out the times during which dinosaurs existed and when humans have lived (since these two points of information are more likely than others to have references in the prior knowledge of learners). The introductory activity might be ended with the statement that the article will show what was happening during one geologic time period, the Archeozoic. With questions peppered throughout this explanation to enhance student involvement and with predictions elicited at the end, this tactic for developing the meaning of a complex, unfamiliar term would be more powerful in building understanding than merely "looking it up."

A second futile dictionary exercise may be one you have experienced yourself. Students go to the dictionary and discover the meaning they are seeking contains a word in the definition they do not know. If they need to understand the term, they look up the other unknown word, only to find that it is defined with yet another term about which they don't have a clue.

For instance, Ronnie's teacher wants him to understand the nuances of difference between the words *pity* and *compassion* because the theme of a story he will be reading hinges on the contrast between the two. Ronnie begins by looking up the word *pity*. He finds the word is defined as "a sympathetic, but sometimes slightly contemptuous sadness for the distress of another." Ronnie doesn't know what *contemptuous* means, so sighing, he wades through the dictionary to find its explanation, which is "a feeling of contempt." "Rats!" Ronnie says. "What is *contempt*?" He looks it up (easy this time since it is on the same page as *contemptuous*) and sees that it means "disdain." "Now, what does *disdain* mean?" mutters Ronnie to himself. "This activity is dumb, or I'm dumb." But, being incredibly motivated, he searches the dictionary for *disdain*, only to see that the word is defined as "a feeling of contempt; scorn." "Oh, no," grieves Ronnie, "that word *contempt* again. And what is *scorn*?" Although this is taking up much of the time allotted for reading, blowing a loud noise through his nose, Ronnie forges on to find *scorn*; the definition states, "vigorous contempt; disdain." "That's it!" he whimpers. "I give up!" And he closes the dictionary with a loud smack.

It is obviously impossible to ferret out meanings that are this circuitous. Plainly, before assigning dictionary work, teachers should look up—in the dictionary students will be using—words they plan to assign. In cases such as this one, a method other than finding dictionary definitions would be more effective.

On the other hand, here is an example where dictionary work could easily help to clarify a distinction. The students are reading *Call It Courage* (Sperry, 1968), the story of a Polynesian boy who fears the sea. A question comes up about the difference between a bay and a lagoon: Are these really just the same thing? The readers already have a concept about different types of bodies of water from their social studies lessons; they know how a lake is different from a river and how both are different from oceans and seas. When they examine the dictionary definition for *bay*, they find it is "a body of water partly enclosed by land but with a wide opening to the sea," whereas the definition for *lagoon* is "a body of water separated from the sea by sandbars or coral reefs." The distinction is forthright and easy to grasp for students who have the underlying concepts.

"Looking it up" also may be an efficient way to handle a quick question about a word of interest that does not particularly merit a well-developed set of lessons to instill its meaning. In a story one class was reading, a young Appalachian girl, Katy O'Toole, was tormented by the teasing of other children in her school when she moved to a big city in Michigan. Among other taunts they called her a katydid ("Katydid! Katydid! You aren't nuthin' but an old katydid," a couple of boys chanted at various times in the book). A visit to the dictionary not only told the students reading this story that a katydid is a green insect related to a grasshopper and a cricket—one that makes a special kind of noise when it rubs its wings together—it also provided a small but nice photograph so they could see what this insect looked like. Satisfied, they were able to understand what the silly taunts had meant, and they moved ahead to concentrate on the important ideas in the narrative.

In short, it is necessary to use dictionary activities judiciously in vocabulary development programs. Certainly, giving long lists of words unrelated to anything and asking students to write out their definitions is not recommended. Furthermore, various other techniques often are more productive than dictionary work (Joshi, 2005). However, under some circumstances, time with the dictionary is well spent.

> Asking students to write out dictionary definitions of long lists of words is an ineffective way to develop knowledge of word meanings.

Use Teacher Explanations. There is no reason at all not to simply tell learners what a word means. Consulting an authority is one way to obtain information. This method is, of course, optimally productive when the explanations of the authority (the teacher) are rich with examples and illustrations. Telling a brief anecdote to elucidate the meaning, showing a visual aid (a picture or map), and pointing out similar words that students already have in their vocabularies are enriching ways to fortify verbal explanations. The example given previously in which the teacher explains the meaning of *Archeozoic* shows the constructiveness of this tactic over some weaker introductory guidance.

Rich Development

Some words simply require a brief mention and a passing exchange with your students to confer enough about their function in a text. Introductory guidance may suffice in these cases, but other words deserve (because of their importance) or need (because of their complexity) deeper development.

General Features of an Intensive Program of Word Development. In-depth development of word meanings involves varied experiences, reflective and dynamic activities, and substantial practice. Such an approach incorporates formal definitions, but also involves students in employing words in a variety of contexts, active use of the words in student-created situations, and seeing relationships with other words (Blachowicz & Fisher, 2000).

A vocabulary program McKeown and Beck (1988) conducted for middle graders exemplifies this type of richness. They describe their approach in the following way (p. 43). Instruction focused on a set of 8 to 10 words each week. Each set contained terms that were related to facilitate useful activities; for instance, one group was based on the theme of "moods" and contained, among others, the words *enthusiastic, indignant,* and *jovial.* Each subsequent part of the weekly activities required successively deeper processing. In one activity, students worked with text that gave examples or actions regularly connected with the words. This is one sample:

> Maria decided that she didn't want to play with Terry anymore. Terry was always being nasty about other people. She'd make a big joke out of the way other people looked or talked. What did Terry do to other people? (McKeown & Beck, 1988, p. 43)

Students were to connect their practice word *ridicule* with this description. The students next generated their own text about focus words based on engaging questions from the teacher. For example, to the challenge "What might a *hermit* have a nightmare about?", first the teacher gave a response to show how logical answers could be derived and then students offered their ideas.

In a later activity, readers were asked questions that combined two of their target words and required that they think about the meanings they had been practicing. Can a *tyrant* be a *miser*? Would you *berate* a person who had *inspired* you? Would you *baffle* someone who tried to *snare* you? (McKeown & Beck, 1988, p. 43). Learners were required to give reasons for their answers.

Such thought-provoking exercises develop sensitivities to a word's connotations and produce a higher level of learning than merely requiring a definition to be stated. Moreover, using words actively facilitates recall of the word's meanings at a later time.

LEARNING FROM TEXT

Verbal Rehearsal. Try to state some general features of an intensive program of word meaning development, a program that promotes rich development.

Some Specific Activities That Require In-Depth Processing. Much interest has emerged recently about the direct instruction of meaning vocabulary. We know that students should build on multiple sources of information to learn words through repeated exposures (Blachowicz & Fisher, 2000). As a result many interesting ideas have been tested and a number have shown good results. Some of those are described here.

1. *Involve students in process-oriented semantic mapping.* Oral or written tasks that help students preview material can aid their vocabulary knowledge. Learning word meanings before reading a selection is helpful (U.S. Department of Health and Human Services, 2000). One way to conduct an oral preview is to use a *semantic map*. There are two broad categories of semantic maps. One type is process oriented and the other is product oriented. Both help students understand terminology and concepts.

In a **process-oriented semantic map,** group discussion precedes reading of a story or informational material. The teacher illustrates the discussion in some graphic manner, often focusing on important concepts related to vocabulary. Process-oriented semantic maps are, in effect, advance organizers (Ausubel, 1960). Here is an example of how this type of semantic map is built.

> *Teacher:* The story you're going to read tells you what happens when a boy uses sarcasm and people think his remarks are serious. What do you think *sarcasm* is?
> *David:* A way of talking that's not serious.
> *Craig:* Smart-alecky talk.
> *Albert:* It seems to me it's being mean.

Teacher writes on board:

```
Sarcasm—Talk that is:
–Not serious
–"Smart alecky"
–Being mean
```

Jana: I had this Girl Scout leader once who would say sarcastic things to us if we didn't do things the way she tried to teach us.

Teacher: How about you, Kimberly? What do you think sarcasm means?

Kimberly: I don't know.

Michael: Sometimes kids say sarcastic things to you on the playground just to act big.

Teacher adds to information on board:

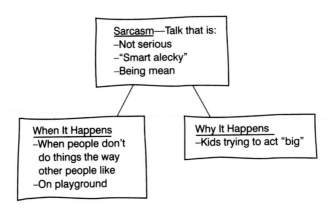

Teacher: Who can think of other times or reasons people have been sarcastic?

David: My dad has been sarcastic to me.

Teacher: When? And why do you think he was?

David: Like, he gets tired of me arguing back when he tells me to do stuff, so he says, "Okay, Mr. Big Shot! No more arguing. Just do it."

Teacher writes more information on board:

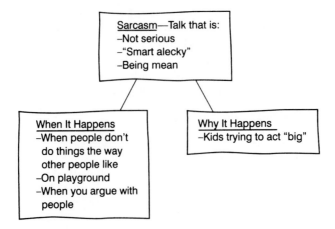

Teacher:	Why do you think David's dad said something sarcastic when David argued with him?
David:	It's his way of getting me to do it in a kind of joking way, but letting me know he means business.
Teacher:	Why do you think Jana's Girl Scout leader sometimes made sarcastic remarks?
Albert:	Maybe she's mean.
Jana:	She wasn't really mean to us, but my mother said she was impatient.

Teacher completes diagram on board:

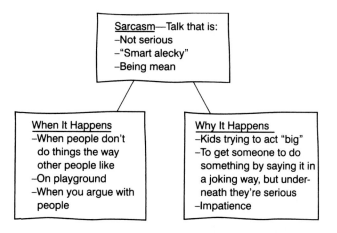

At the conclusion of a dialogue such as this, the teacher points to parts of the diagram the students have developed and directs them to make some forecasts about what they are about to read. For instance, in the example just given, students may be asked to predict whether the boy in the upcoming story will be sarcastic because he is "smart alecky" or because he is mean. The students may also be asked to note whether *when* and *why* the boy was sarcastic are similar to any of the reasons they have suggested. After students read the story, they make these comparisons in a follow-up discussion.

> Both process-oriented and product-oriented semantic maps encourage deep processing of word meanings.

2. *Employ product-oriented semantic maps.* To use a **product-oriented semantic map,** the teacher selects a concept from a selection that will be read. Vocabulary and/or ideas related to the concept are identified and, for student use, the teacher writes each of these on separate cards.

After reading the selection, students develop a product by working in small groups to arrange the cards into a semantic map, which can show relationships among terms and concepts. Figure 10–2 provides an example of a semantic map students used after reading an article on the history of money. Finally, the teacher and students engage in whole-group discussion, examining and critiquing one another's completed semantic maps. Justifications for differences are offered and revisions made when deemed important.

The product developed by students provides reinforcement of vocabulary terms and helps students see the interrelationships among ideas. In this case,

FIGURE 10–2 *A Semantic Map Based on Concepts and Vocabulary From a Reading Selection on the History of Money*

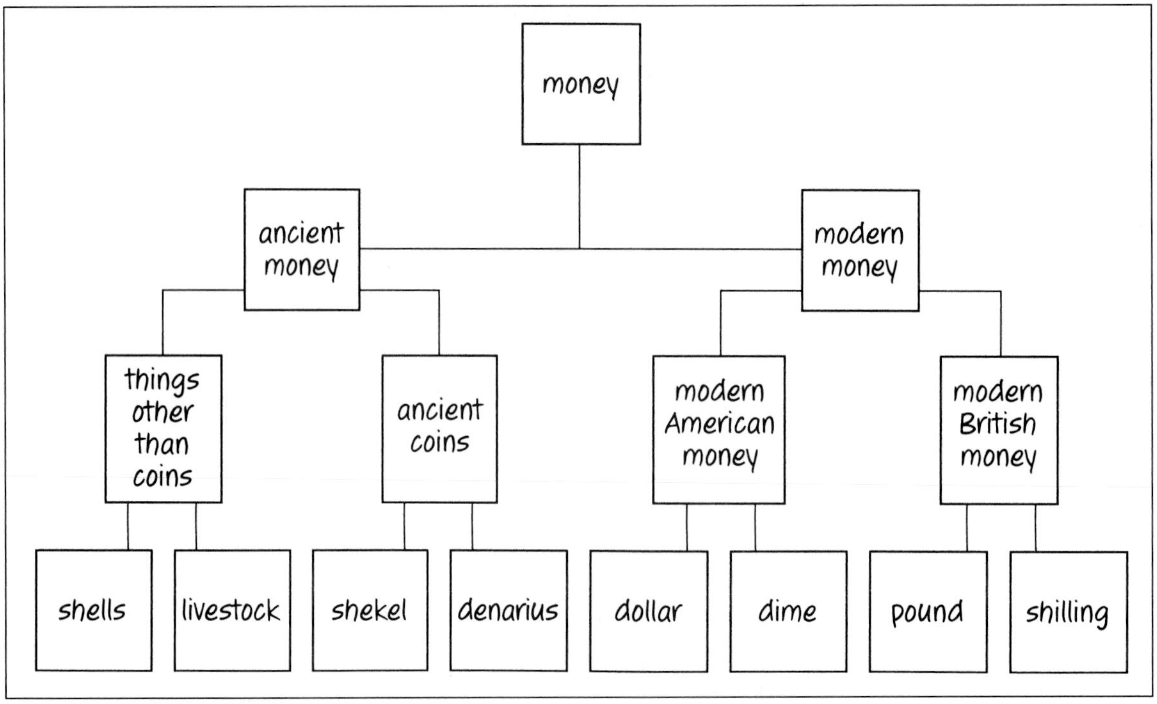

the product itself is referred to as a *semantic map*, whereas in a process-oriented semantic map, the whole procedure is referred to as *semantic mapping*.

Use of either type of semantic map is particularly helpful before or after reading books in which the concept load is heavy, such as science, history, or other textbooks.

3. *Use word maps for different parts of speech.* Duffelmeyer and Banwart (1993) described ways to adapt word maps so they relate purposefully to terms that embody various parts of speech. Figure 10–3 depicts three word maps to exemplify models for words that are nouns, adjectives, and verbs. In each of these maps, the focus word is placed in a center box in the drawing, and terms that suggest attributes and examples of the word are placed in surrounding boxes to fit specific categories. These categories vary according to the part of speech of the focus word.

4. *Engage learners in semantic feature analysis.* Bos and Anders (1990) had middle school readers with learning disabilities compare and contrast groups of semantically related words using semantic feature analysis.

In **semantic feature analysis** (Johnson & Pearson, 1984), readers are helped to see associations and differences between semantically linked words through use of a relationship matrix (see Figure 10–4). A list of semantically similar words is placed along the left side of the matrix. At the top, semantic features are listed. **Semantic features** are properties or meanings that the words listed to the left may share. The task is to determine which are shared and which are not. After discussion, pluses or minuses are placed in columns to indicate group decisions. The value of the activity is, of course, in the discussion. Through these

Semantic feature analysis stimulates students to think, discuss, defend, and learn from one another thorough, rather than vague, definitions of words.

FIGURE 10–3   *Three Word Maps*

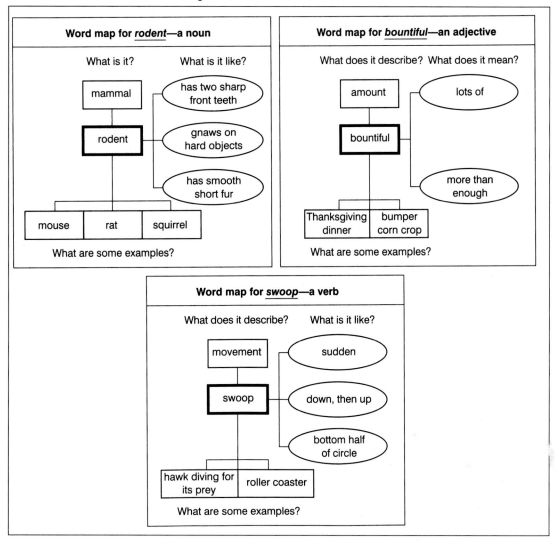

Source: From Duffelmeyer, Frederick A. (1992, December). Word Maps for adjectives and verbs. *The Reading Teacher,* 464, 351–353. Reprinted by permission of the International Reading Association.

FIGURE 10–4   *A Relationship Matrix Used in a Semantic Feature Analysis Activity*

	unknown	unexplained	unfamiliar	unusual	old-fashioned
strange	+	+	+	+	−
peculiar	−	+	−	+	−
quaint	−	−	+	+	+
outlandish	−	−	+	+	?
eccentric	−	+	+	+	?

deliberations, readers must think through their ideas, and argue, and defend, and learn from one another precisions in denotations and nuances of words—a process that leads to complete, rather than vague, definitions. In Bos and Ander's study, use of semantic feature analysis increased students' knowledge of word meanings and reading comprehension on both short-term and long-term measures.

Figure 10–4 shows how one group of learners filled in a relationship matrix for a set of words after much discussion and examples offered by members of the group. The decisions might be slightly different with other students, depending on the illustrations offered by participants and the degree to which particular students have a propensity to split hairs (the latter being a positive behavior and one on which this procedure is designed to capitalize). Most decisions will closely agree with conventional meanings, and, in any case, the discussion is the important part of the learning episode.

5. *Have learners develop Venn diagrams.* Venn diagrams display semantic connections, and also exhibit features that are not shared by two concepts. Figure 10–5 shows a Venn diagram for comparing and contrasting two terms found in geography texts. In the space where the circles of the diagram overlap, shared features of the two words are listed. In the outlying spaces above each term, the features that are different are itemized.

6. *Provide experiences with synonyms and antonyms.* A manipulative activity for practicing synonyms can be made from 8½" by 11" pieces of colored construction paper. Draw two sets of lines across each piece with a marking pen (see Figure 10–6). Write known words on the left-hand lines of each construction paper "board" (e.g., *name, tight, grumpy, winding, sparkle, useless, hothouse*). Cut strips of plain oaktag to a size that will fit on each of the right-hand lines. Write a synonym on each oaktag strip for one of the listed known words (e.g., *sinuous, designation, taut, conservatory,* and so on). Place one set of construction paper "boards" plus the accompanying synonym strips in each of several manila envelopes. Label the envelopes #1, #2, and so forth. Give each student one manila envelope set and a dictionary. Have students use their dictionaries to determine which words are synonyms and then place the oaktag strips next to the matching words on their "board."

Examining and substituting words in written materials can move practice with synonyms beyond the introductory level.

FIGURE 10–5 *An Example of a Venn Diagram Comparing Two Geographical Terms*

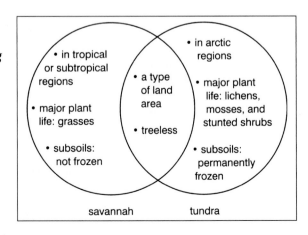

FIGURE 10–6 *A Synonym Board*

name	
tight	
grumpy	
winding	sinuous
sparkle	
useless	
hothouse	

designation

taut

conservatory

This exercise is designed to move word use from a lower to a more sophisticated level. Afterward, ask students why one synonym is better than another.

- Choose the word that would *best* fit the blank.

As the wind _____ through the huge sails, all the sailors shuddered with fear.

  howled   blew   moved

When students are working on synonyms, it is a good time to familiarize them with a thesaurus. Many simplified versions of this functional reference tool are now available for use in elementary classrooms, and abridged paperback editions can be purchased for secondary programs.

Here is one activity for introducing the contents and value of a thesaurus that will get students thinking. Choose a theme, such as *Halloween* or *pioneers* or *basketball*, and ask students to tell you every word they can think of related to that topic. As students contribute words, write them on the chalkboard. When they have exhausted their suggestions and the chalkboard is quite full, tell them they are each to write a short story about this topic, but may not use any of the words listed on the board! The task entails using the thesaurus to locate synonyms for any words on the board they wish to use in their stories. Not only is this fun and challenging, the resulting stories are usually quite interesting.

Writing haiku can also be a stimulus for using a thesaurus and for adding new synonyms to vocabularies. Haiku is a form of Japanese poetry with exactly 17 syllables in three lines. The syllables must follow a prescribed pattern: 5 syllables in the first line, 7 in the second line, and 5 in the third. If students wish to use a word in their poems to express a thought, but it doesn't have the right number of syllables, they use the thesaurus to find a word expressing the same thought but with the right number of syllables.

Being able to specify the opposite of a word is an indication of a good understanding of its meaning.

Many types of practice conducted with synonyms can also be carried out with antonyms. Edgar Dale (personal communication, February 22, 1984) stated that when a person can specify the opposite of a word, he or she truly understands its meaning.

The teacher can prepare antonym cards for students' independent practice. Following are directions for preparing cards for a matching activity that students can correct themselves. On index cards, print single words. Next, write their antonyms on an equivalent set, one antonym to a card. Turn pairs of antonyms over so they are placed next to one another. Paste a paper sticker on the cards so half of the sticker is on one card and half on the other. With scissors, snip the cards apart. Do the same with all pairs. As students practice with the antonym cards they should attempt to line them up by pairs on their desks. At the completion, each pair should be turned over to see if the two half pictures (forming the snipped sticker) on the backs fit together to make a whole; if not, a wrong choice has been made and the student should restudy the cards.

After students have used the cards described in the preceding paragraph, use the same basic set of antonyms, writing them into a short story. The learners are to revise your story by turning each of the focus set of antonyms into a word of an opposite meaning, thus producing a contradictory version. For example, where you may have used the word *bizarre*, they might use *normal*; where you have used *continuous*, they might use *sporadic*.

7. Provide exposures to multiple meanings of words. The difference between the meaning vocabularies of skilled and unskilled readers is often found in the number of meanings the student can provide for a specific word. Poor readers may require direct and imaginative teaching of multimeaning words.

Frequently, a poor reader can give only the most common meaning of a word. Students in remedial programs need work, not only with words they encounter in narrative, story-type material, but also with multiple meanings of words that have specialized meanings in content area fields. A heavy load of unfamiliar vocabulary is characteristic of content area texts (Harmon, Hedrick, & Wood, 2005). For example, although Joe certainly knows the meaning for *mouth* when one is talking about the opening in the head used for eating and talking, he may have no understanding of its meaning when his geography book refers to the *mouth* of a river. Having students draw pictures of right and wrong meanings of such terms helps them remember less familiar definitions of words with multiple meanings.

Discussion of differences in shades of meaning also can help students develop precision in word usage. For example, questions such as the following might be asked:

What is the difference between *soft* fur and *soft* fruit?

What is the difference between *soft* light and *soft* pink?

Games, too, can be used for practice with multiple meanings. One example is the game illustrated in Figure 10–7 called "Multiple Meaning Bingo." This game helps students become familiar with a number of meanings for the same word and gives practice in selecting the correct meaning to fit a specific context. To make this game, the teacher first consults a dictionary to compile a list of different meanings for a single common word. Number and list these meanings as shown in the bottom portion of Figure 10–7. On paper, draw a bingo board as shown in the upper portion of Figure 10–7, and write sentences for each of the listed definitions, writing one sentence in each square. Students are then given a photocopy of the bingo board with a piece of oaktag of the same size. They are to quickly cut apart each square of the photocopy so there are 25 separate squares. These are to be placed on the piece of oaktag in random order, not in the same sequence as on the original paper copy, so that each student has squares in different places on the oaktag, but with five in a row horizontally and five vertically as in typical bingo games. Students are also given 25 numbered markers for covering squares.

To begin the game, the teacher reads definition 1; each student then selects a marker numbered "1" and places it on the sentence whose context is thought

FIGURE 10–7 *A Game for Practicing Multiple Meanings*

(Student's materials)

After praying the man saw the light.	It is ligh[1]	He is one of the brighter lights of American literature.	Evelyn is a light eater.	He gave her a light to start the fire.
His daughter is the light of his life.	The sweater is light blue.	We will get up at first light.	Her eyes lighted up with liveliness.	Her light movements across the ice won her the championship.
He was in the light brigade.	We got a light snow last night.	LIGHT (free space)	The lig[2]	The football missed the goalpost because it was a light kick.
I hate sitting in the dark; I wish it was light.	The Taming of the Shrew is light comedy.	I hope you can shed some light on the subject.	After the good news, Karen felt light at heart.	She felt light-headed.
Her piecrust is always light.	On November 1, 1918 he first saw the light of day.	She now saw things in a different light.	I think that butcher gave me a light pound.	Those women spend their lunch hours engaging in light chatter.

(Teacher's materials)

1. illumination
2. not heavy
3. dawn
4. daylight
5. of less than correct weight
6. means for igniting a fire
7. less than normal force
8. spiritual awareness
9. having less quantity
10. a way of regarding something
11. moderate
12. insignificant
13. adored by another
14. entertainment that is not serious
15. a distinguished person
16. free from worry
17. an expression of the eyes
18. suffering from faintness
19. to be born
20. moving quickly and easily
21. to provide information
22. carrying little military arms or equipment
23. color mixed with white
24. a flaky texture

to indicate a match for the meaning given. When a student has five squares covered in a column or row he or she says "Bingo!" The teacher uses the numbered markers to check the covered sentences against the numbers of the respective definitions on the teacher's master copy, and these must match for the student to win.

LEARNING FROM TEXT

Applying What You've Learned. Do you understand how to use semantic maps, semantic feature analysis, and Venn diagrams? What do you think of the thesaurus activity and the haiku activity? Of those activities suggested so far, which would you like to use in your own classroom?

INDEPENDENT WORD LEARNING FROM TEXT

Incidental Learning

Authorities do not agree about the effectiveness of incidentally learning new word meanings simply from reading text. Some educators point to studies showing that when students read text containing unfamiliar vocabulary, they later can give meanings for only a small percentage of these words, indicating that learners do not easily infer vocabulary meanings from written material. Further, poor readers appear to be less facile at gaining the sense of words from contextual selections than are skilled readers, which is why many authorities believe explicit instruction is especially needed for delayed readers (Biemiller, 2003; Rupley & Nichols, 2005). Finally, some educators argue that natural text that has not been purposely structured to provide a supportive context does not readily convey word meanings.

On the other hand, other authorities counter that some studies of incidental word learning fail to show large gains because readers do not internalize vocabulary understandings from single or brief encounters. Jenkins, Stein, and Wysocki (1984), for example, compared connected text encounters when students were exposed to unknown words either 2 times, 6 times, or 10 times; words were learned incidentally from context only in the cases where there were 6 or 10 confrontations with the words. These educators say learners can derive vocabulary understandings simply from wide reading because of the immense number of words that are processed through natural text reading. In addition, they regard not only reading that occurs in school as a vehicle for development but also reading that takes place in other settings.

Some word meanings can be learned through independent reading.

Currently research does not allow clear answers about the degree to which incidental learning from connected text affects the development of a meaning vocabulary. However, most authorities acknowledge the value of promoting extensive reading (U.S. Department of Health and Human Services, 2000) and a good amount of the disagreement concerns the *degree* to which ample reading affects the learning of new words. In brief, certain educators would claim that not as many words are learned from incidental learning as are often suggested, but that certainly some are. Others would assert that most words are learned from incidental learning, but that certainly many are learned from direct instruction. The bottom line, then, seems to be that most authorities support both direct instruction and incidental learning (e.g., Pressley, 2001) but to different degrees.

Compare. Compare the points in the controversy about learning word meanings incidentally from text. What's the bottom line?

It appears, then, that while knowledge of word meanings can improve reading, interestingly, the converse also is true: Reading can improve knowledge of word meanings. Individuals who read voraciously usually have rich vocabularies that are larger in quantity of known words and broader in quality than the vocabulary of individuals who do not read extensively. This effect is not only seen with common words, but also for words and concepts needed to read content area texts. Wide reading also increases knowledge of multiple meanings of words. It seems, then, that one effective way to help students improve their word meaning knowledge is to stimulate them to read an abundance of books, magazines, articles, newspapers, and any other type of connected text.

Ironically, those poor readers who have deficits in meaning vocabulary are often the very ones who do not like to read. The teacher, then, must find ways to activate interest in reading, prompting this learner to view reading as a worthwhile activity. The following ideas are suggested.

1. *Explore students' interests through interviews and interest inventories.* See examples in Chapter 6 of tools for assessing interests. Start a student's reading program with short, easy books targeted to his or her interests. Use short magazine and newspaper articles along with books.

2. *Provide time for sustained silent reading (SSR).* During SSR, students may read anything they wish, but no other activity except silent reading is allowed. The teacher uses a timer, keeping the interval for reading on the first day quite short, usually about 5 minutes. The timer is placed facing the teacher—so you don't have a room full of clock-watchers—and students read until the timer rings. Every few days the amount of time is increased by a minute or two until students are sustaining their silent reading from about 15 minutes (in elementary level remedial classes) to 30 minutes (in secondary level programs).

The technique works best if the teacher also reads a book of his or her choice to serve as a model for students. Teachers sometimes post a DO NOT DISTURB sign on the door during SSR, and students and teachers often begin to look upon this time period as the best of the day.

If your students are presently turned off by books, let them read stories at the Internet Public Library. For interactive stories, magazines, poetry, short stories, picture books, books in Spanish, and more, go www.ipl.org/ Click "Kidspace" and then "Reading Zone."

In the early phases of an SSR program, reluctant readers may be disinclined to read and instead sit staring at an open page. After a while, this behavior simply becomes too boring, and they begin to look at pictures in the text. If there are captions, they may next be induced to read a few of these. Eventually, previously diffident readers are seduced into the reading material. Thereafter, these students usually participate willingly in SSR. Motivation to read is simplified somewhat because the student is permitted to choose anything at all to read, no matter how easy or short, as long as there is enough text to sustain reading for the duration of the activity.

Although comic books, magazines, and joke books serve legitimate objectives for enticing unwilling readers into SSR, after the incentive to read has been awakened, the teacher may challenge the students to select a book that it will take a week to complete—a book with chapters, for instance.

Arranging some time after SSR for students to share what they have read breeds curiosity about books that peers have enjoyed and may impel students to select longer books or materials of different genres. This can be a rather informal discussion period or may involve more structured projects. For example, several youngsters who have read the same book could make simple stick puppets to dramatize the story to others. Such puppets can be made easily by having students paste tongue depressors on the backs of pictures they have drawn of characters from the book. Preparation of the puppets could occur outside of reading class (a fun homework assignment) so that class reading time is not used.

Another way to augment interest is to have students write brief book reviews. To do this, create a group file box for index cards on which students write the names of books they've read, along with two or three observations about each book. Colored file cards and white file cards should be available. If students really like a book, they "review" it on the colored file cards. If their reaction is that the book was just so-so, the information goes on the white cards. When students want to choose a new book, they can refer to the file box and read the reviews on the colored cards.

3. *Read aloud to students who are at first reluctant to read themselves.* In addition to its other positive effects, reading to students is one of the best ways to get them interested in reading. Have similar books available so that once learners become absorbed with a topic, author, or genre, they can read a comparable text themselves.

Not only does reading to students inspire a desire to read on their own, it is a direct route to vocabulary learning. A good principle to follow when reading aloud to students is to read material slightly above the level they could read for themselves. For example, reading aloud to urban sixth graders from seventh-grade materials resulted in vocabulary gains of approximately 7% in one study (Stahl, Richek, & Vandevier, 1991). Studies also show that reading aloud tends to most affect words that are already slightly familiar.

Some books to read aloud to students who initially do not want to be read to are listed in Table 10–1. These books routinely have been found to engross even the most unenthusiastic students.

Table 10–2 suggests books for reading aloud to middle school students.

4. *Use videos or DVDs of children's and adolescents' books to excite interest in reading the book itself.* Often the original illustrations are depicted as the stories are read in these audiovisuals. Have one or more of these books available

TABLE 10–1 *Some Books to Read Aloud to Reluctant Students*

The Ghost Rock Mystery	Grades 4, 5, 6	Really scary. Leaves you "hanging" at the end of each chapter as something awful is about to happen. A good one to start the year with. Also available in paperback.
The Snake Who Went to School	Grades 3, 4, 5, 6	Funny. A snake gets loose in the school, isn't captured for several days, and is the cause of a number of wild happenings.
Casey, the Utterly Impossible Horse	Grades 3, 4, 5, 6	Ridiculously funny; a horse that talks.
All Pippi Longstocking books: *Pippi Longstocking; Pippi in the South Seas; Pippi Goes on Board*	Grades 3, 4, 5, 6	Even the teacher will laugh while reading these books. Pippi's father is the king of a cannibal island and her mother is dead, so she lives alone in a house in Sweden with her horse, her monkey, and a chest full of gold. And she does *anything* she wants to do.
Julie of the Wolves	Grades 5 and 6	Newbery Award Winner. Exciting, interesting, scary. An Eskimo girl is saved from starvation when a pack of wolves allows her to share their food and shelter. Realistic.
The House of the Sixty Fathers	Grades 5 and 6	Frightening, but realistically told story that takes place during the Japanese occupation of China during World War II when a boy becomes separated from his family and attempts to find them. Runner-up for the Newbery Award.
The Matchlock Gun	Grades 3, 4, 5, 6	A picture book for older children. Very exciting story and dramatic pictures. A settler's cabin is attacked by Indians during the French and Indian Wars. A Newbery Award Winner.

for students to read after they have viewed the video or DVD. On the face of it, it might seem that once students have seen a video/DVD, and know the story, they wouldn't be interested in reading it in a book, but in fact, the opposite effect occurs. A text based on an audiovisual the class has enjoyed frequently becomes the most popular in the room for a time; even learners who generally resist your enticements to read will sign up for their turn with this book.

5. *Use cassette or CD/book combinations to elicit interest in reading.* Cassettes and CDs accompanying books are available commercially. The books are often published in paperback and so are relatively inexpensive. As a result, it is frequently feasible to purchase multiple copies of the books. Students may listen to the tape as a group, and then the book is offered to students who wish to read it.

6. *Use commercial audiotapes and CDs.* Audiotapes have been prepared in which dramas of well-known books are presented, complete with sound effects. One teacher's successful experience with older students in a reading class involved the group listening to a taped drama of the popular H. G. Wells's classic, *The Time Machine*. When easy-to-read versions of this electrifying story were offered to the group afterward, almost all students chose to read the book. Check the school district's central audiovisual library or the public library for similar tapes and CDs.

7. *Have the students join a book club.* Scholastic and other companies sponsor such clubs from which students may order paperbacks monthly at a reasonable price. Engage in SSR on the day the books arrive.

8. *Use books that particularly lend themselves to lessons on word meaning.* The Amelia Bedelia series (Harper & Row), for example, has funny plays on

TABLE 10–2 *Some Books to Read Aloud to Middle School Students*

Some of the books suggested here are most suitable for reading aloud to younger middle school students; some are better for use with older middle school pupils; others are suitable for any student of middle school age. Teachers should skim the first chapter of the book and read the information presented on the dust jacket to determine if a suggested book is suitable for the learners in their classes.

1. *Best Short Shorts,* Eric Berger, Editor (Paperback available from Scholastic. Every story has a surprise ending. Because selections are short, this book would be good to use when there is only a little time for reading aloud to students.)

2. *How to Eat Fried Worms,* Thomas Rockwell

3. *Fifty-Two Miles to Terror,* Ruth and Robert Carlson (Nine tension-packed short stories)

4. *Encyclopedia Brown Takes a Case,* Donald Sobel

5. *Passport to Freedom,* Dorothy Bonnell

6. *Ben and Me,* Robert Lawson

7. *Pegasus, the Flying Horse,* Jane Yolem

8. *Kareem! Basketball Great,* Arnold Hano

9. *The Wonderful Flight to the Mushroom Planet,* Eleanor Cameron

10. *New Sound,* Leslie Waller

11. *Julie of the Wolves,* Jean George

12. *Follow My Leader,* James B. Garfield

13. *Old Yeller,* Fred Gipson

14. *The Lost Ones,* Ian Cameron

15. *Island of the Blue Dolphins,* Scott O'Dell

16. *The Hornet's Nest,* Sally Watson

17. *Earthfasts,* William Mayne

18. *The Last Safe House,* Barbara Greenwood

19. *The House of the Sixty Fathers,* Meindert De Jong

20. *Hunger for Racing,* J. M. Douglas

21. *Incident at Hawk's Hill,* Allan Eckert

22. *Pippi Longstocking,* Astrid Lindgren

23. *Journey Outside,* Mary Q. Steele

24. *Bully of Barkham Street,* Mary Stolz

25. *The Phantom Tollbooth,* Norton Juster

26. *My Name Is Pablo,* Aimee Somerfelt

27. *The Forgotten Door,* Alexander Key

28. *Escape to Witch Mountain,* Alexander Key

29. *A Wrinkle in Time,* Madeline L'Engle

30. *Funny Bananas,* Georgess McHargue

31. *The Witch of Blackbird Pond,* Elizabeth George Speare

32. *The Maze,* Will Hobbs

33. *Eskimo Boy,* Pepaluk Fruchen

34. *The Gift,* Peter Dickinson

35. The Yearling, Marjorie Rawlings

words that students can enjoy and learn from. Amelia is a conscientious, but confused, maid who misinterprets the written directions her employer leaves for her. When told to "dust the furniture," Amelia zips about with a box of powder and a powder puff covering the tables, chairs, and couch with a heavy dose of dusting powder. When told to "dress the chicken," she sews a little dress complete with bows and tucks it around the uncooked roasting hen in the refrigerator. These books may be read just for the fun of it to provoke interest in reading, but follow-up lessons related to the word concepts will be easily tolerated because the books are delightful.

Classroom shelves should be filled with books selected to provide reading levels appropriate for all students in the class.

9. *Fill shelves with books students can check out.* Books should be selected so reading levels appropriate for all students in the class are represented. If students are going to read them on their own, books should be available on their independent reading levels. If there are funds for purchasing books, the Hi-Lo paperbacks (Bantam) are a good choice for adding to a bookshelf collection for very low-achieving high school students. Reading levels in this series range from second through third grade, while the subject matter is of interest to many contemporary teens. Some titles from the series are *Village of Vampires* and *The Bermuda Triangle and Other Mysteries of Nature.*

See Figure 10–8 for research supporting procedures and activities related to use of literature with delayed readers—to improve meaning vocabulary and to facilitate other variables crucial for reading improvement.

Fostering Independent Learning

The topic addressed here is somewhat of a cross between direct instruction and incidental learning. To foster independent learning, teachers provide direct guidance, striving to boost learning when students are on their own. Not only do poor readers need to learn more word meanings, they need to know *how* to learn word meanings (Graves, 2000). As Blachowicz and Fisher (2005) point out, delayed readers often are ineffective at the strategies needed for independent learning of meaning vocabulary, and thus instruction aimed directly at those strategies is important.

Teaching Students About the Uses of Context When Reading Independently. Previously in this chapter, use of context was described as an only moderately useful strategy for introducing words to students in direct instruction activities. Also, it is only moderately useful for deriving word meanings when reading independently—for the same reasons. Sometimes context helps, but sometimes it doesn't. Still, when students are operating independently, it may give an assist on some occasions. Proficient readers use context when it is productive to do so.

Teachers should model how to use context to get word meanings. First, find examples in a book where context does indeed convey an understanding of a somewhat difficult word. Tell students that sometimes the text hints at what a word means. Then, using an example from the selected text, "think aloud" how *you* would use the surrounding words to derive meaning of the one that is unfamiliar. Next, have students take up the modeling role, taking turns to think aloud for their peers how they might do this with other words in the connected text examples you have selected.

Provide other practice activities for gleaning word meanings from context. Here is one. A teacher-made activity can be assembled by cutting manila file folders into four folding strips. A sentence providing context for an underlined target word is written on the outside of each of the strips. The meaning of the target word is written inside each strip. Students are given a pack of these, asked to read the sentence on each, guess the meaning of the underlined word from context, and then open up the file folder piece to find the answer. This activity can be carried out independently and is self-correcting.

For variety, teachers may also prepare games to practice determining words from context before a story is read. For example, develop a card game by printing words, along with context sentences to illustrate the word meanings, on separate index cards (e.g., *hut—He was so poor that he lived in a small, poorly built hut*). Prepare a second pack of cards on which only the word appears. Put both packs together and shuffle them. Deal five cards to each student and leave the remainder on the table as an extra pile. The game is played like rummy; students must obtain pairs of matching cards (one with the word alone and one with the word in a sentence) by drawing and discarding. Before students are allowed to keep a pair to count toward winning the game, they must tell the meaning of the word. To determine the meaning, they use the context of the sentence written on one card of the pair.

FIGURE 10–8 *Selected Research Supporting Procedures and Activities for Using Literature With Delayed Readers*

Reading Aloud to Students

Cohen, D. (1968). Effect of literature on vocabulary and reading. *Elementary English, 45,* 209–213.

A, by now, classic study in which second graders in the experimental group showed significantly improved quality and quantity of vocabulary knowledge, as well as enhanced comprehension, in comparison with control-group subjects when literature was read to them daily for the entire school year. Effects were most pronounced for those in the lowest ranges of reading achievement.

Chomsky, C. (1972). Stages in language development and reading exposure. *Harvard Educational Review, 42,* 1–33.

Also an oft-cited study for children ages 5 to 10, Chomsky's research showed a positive relationship between linguistic stage and exposure to literature.

Morrow, L. M., Sisco, L. J., & Smith, J. K. (1992). The effects of mediated story retelling on listening comprehension, story structure, and oral language development in children with learning disabilities. In C. K. Kinzer & D. J. Leu (Eds.), *Literacy research, theory, and practice: Views from many perspectives* (pp. 435–443). Chicago: National Reading Conference.

Picture books that included well-delineated characters, clear themes, and carefully established plots were read to students with learning disabilities. Students orally retold the stories. Growth in understanding and use of story structure was obtained when retelling was mediated through teacher comments that encouraged attention to sequence, prior knowledge, and elements of story structure.

Byrom, G. (1998). If you can't read it, then audio read it. *Reading, 32,* 3–7.

Published in the journal of the United Kingdom Reading Association, this research explored use of audio-recorded books with 60 failing readers. After reading along with the books for 2 hours per week in a 10-week period, there was marked reduction in errors when students read independently, as well as improvement in fluency and comprehension.

Comprehension Enhancement

Siddall, J. L. (1999). *Fifth graders' story dramatizations during literature study.* (ERIC Document Reproduction Service No. ED 434 373).

Case studies of five students, with data obtained from audiotapes and videotapes, field notes from observations, interviews, student work samples, and detailed transcripts of dramatizations. Data indicated that dramatizations of literature (e.g., *The Slave Dancer* by Fox) led to meaning construction and comprehension.

Wade, S. E., Buxton, W. M., & Kelly, M. (1999). Using think-alouds to examine reader-text interest. *Reading Research Quarterly, 34,* 194–216.

In expository text, information evaluated by subjects as interesting, as well as important, was recalled best.

Spiegel, D. L. (1998). Reader response approaches and the growth of readers. *Language Arts, 76,* 41–48.

Though primarily a discussion article, provides a good review of research and theory related to reader-response approaches to literature and the effects on growth as strategic readers.

Text Coverage/Reading Volume

Wigfield, A., & Gutherie, J. T. (1997). Relations of children's motivation for reading to the amount and breadth of their reading. *Journal of Educational Psychology, 89,* 420–432.

A correlation is shown among the three variables.

Stanovich, K. E. (1986). Matthew effects in reading: Some consequences of individual differences in the acquisition of literacy. *Reading Research Quarterly, 21,* 360–407.

One discriminator between good and poor readers is the number of words read in connected text, with vast differences in reading volume seen for the two groups. More text coverage (i.e., greater number of words processed) is associated with higher reading achievement.

Scott, L. S. (1999). *The Accelerated Reader program, reading achievement, and attitudes of students with learning disabilities* (ERIC Document Reproduction Service No. ED 434 431).

Dissertation research examining use of a computer-based reading management system that includes a database of thousands of books. Students earn points for reading and passing a comprehension assessment of each book. Experimental subjects, who were four classes of middle-school LD students, scored higher on a standardized reading test and on the Estes Attitude Scale than control-group subjects who did not participate in the program.

FIGURE 10–8 *(continued)*

Using Expository Text

Caswell, L. J., & Duke, N. (1998). Non-narrative as a catalyst for literacy development. *Language Arts, 75,* 108–117.

Case studies of delayed readers who increased their willingness to participate in literacy instruction when expository, rather than typical story-type, instructional material was used. Concluded that topics in non-narrative text have greater appeal for some students and that some students saw expository text as being more purposeful (e.g., reading to learn about topics).

Preferences

Daly, P., Salters, J., & Burns, C. (1998). Gender and task interaction: Instant and delayed recall of three story types. *Educational Review, 50,* 269–275.

With 8-year-old and 11-year-old subjects, boys had better immediate and delayed recall of stories of aggressive male protagonists than did girls. Conversely, girls performed better than boys when main characters were female.

Schraw, G., Flowerday, T., & Reisetter, M. F. (1998). The role of choice in reader engagement. *Journal of Educational Psychology, 90,* 705–714.

Reports two studies investigating effects of allowing readers choice in story selection in relation to both cognitive and affective engagement.

Terry, A. (1974). *Children's poetry preferences: A national survey of the upper elementary grades.* Urbana, IL: National Council of Teachers of English.

A well-known and comprehensive study of intermediate grade children's poetry preferences.

Fisher, C. J., & Natarella, M. A. (1982). Young children's preferences in poetry: A national survey of first, second, and third graders. *Research in the Teaching of English, 16,* 339–353.

A partial replication of the Terry study (see previous listing), results for primary-grade children were remarkably the same as for intermediate grade students: Both groups liked limericks, other humorous poetry, poems on topics they were familiar with, poetry featuring animals, and narrative poems.

Both groups disliked poems on esoteric subjects, those using figurative language or requiring thoughtful response to imagery and, in short, any poetry that was hard to understand. Both groups disliked haiku.

Gutherie, J. T., & Greaney, V. (1991). Literacy acts. In R. Barr, M. L. Kamil, P. Mosenthal, & P. D. Pearson (Eds.), *Handbook of reading research* (Vol. II, pp. 68–96). New York: Longman.

Among other topics, includes a thorough review of a body of research on reading preferences (e.g., together this research points to the following literature preferences for elementary age students: Humor, fantasy, animal stories, mystery, adventure, and books about sports and games. Secondary-age students frequently prefer humorous books, mysteries, and adventure, with girls liking historical fiction and romance and boys' preferences running to science fiction and sports.)

Oral Reading Fluency

Millin, S.K., & Rinehart, S.D.(1999).Some of the benefits of Readers' Theater participation for second-grade Title I students. *Reading Research and Instruction, 39,* 71–88.

Research support indicating Readers' Theater experiences using literature books and basal stories resulted in improved oral reading and comprehension. No improvement in reading rate was seen.

Rashotte, C. A., & Torgesen, J. K. (1985). Repeated reading and reading fluency in learning disabled children. *Reading Research Quarterly, 20,* 180–188.

This study showed positive effects when delayed readers engaged in repeated readings of the same texts.

Attention to Illustrations

Day, K. (1996). The challenge of style in reading picture books. *Children's Literature in Education, 27,* 153–165.

With third- and fourth-grade students, illustrations affected students' comprehension of text.

Whether texts help in providing interpretations of vocabulary depends on the complexity of the concept the word is representing. The strength of a particular context is also a factor. Beck, McKeown, and McCaslin (1983) actually found that some contexts were deceptive, leading readers to derive a wrong explanation of a word! Other contexts are neutral, equipping the student with no clues at all. Somewhat serviceable are those that give a general sense of the word; and, of course, the most supportive are contexts that steer the learner to a correct, precise meaning.

Students should be made aware of the limitations of context use and know that, at times, they must use a different strategy.

Increasing Dictionary Skills. When context doesn't help, the dictionary may. While dictionary use alone often is not the best way to initially introduce a word (for several reasons given earlier), certainly no educated person can operate in a literate environment without the skills to use this reference source. We want learners to be able to use the dictionary when it would be profitable and to be willing to do so. One reason students shy away from using a dictionary is that their speed in locating words is slow.

Gamelike activities can provide practice to increase speed in finding words in a dictionary. Try this one. Prepare a list of index cards to be used by the teacher. On each card, write one word for which it is likely that no student in the group will know the meaning and then write a question about the word, along with three possible answers. Here is an example:

If you had a *timbrel*, would you:

1. serve soup in it,
2. plant it in your garden, or
3. play it in a band?

A dictionary should be placed on each student's desk. To begin the game, the teacher selects a card and reads it to the group. The students must vote. For example, the teacher would say, "How many would serve soup in it?" "How many would plant it in their gardens?" and "How many would play it in a band?" The teacher then declares, "All right. Look it up!" Because they've made a commitment to one of the choices, students dive for their dictionaries and try to locate the word rapidly. Giggles begin to be heard from students who chose definition 1 or 2 when they find that a timbrel is a musical instrument like a tambourine. After all have read the meaning, the teacher directs them to close their dictionaries and reads from the next card.

To give practice with the pronunciation key of a dictionary, use jokes or riddles with the answers or punch lines written in dictionary respellings. Here are examples:

A Joke: *Mrs. Hastings:* Robert, I would like to go through one whole day without having to punish you.

   Robert: Yü hav mī pərmishən.

A Riddle: One day two fathers and two sons went fishing and each one caught a fish. Only three fish were caught, however. How could this be?

Answer: Ā boi, hiz fäth̲ər, and grandfäth̲ər wər th̲ə tü fäth̲ərz and tü sənz, sō thaər wər ōnlē thrē fishərmən.

Poindexter (1994) suggests a way to combine use of context and use of the dictionary. With middle school students, she used the following procedures. (a) Difficult words from a text were listed on a chart, students predicted what these words were going to mean in an upcoming story, and their guesses were printed next to the words. (b) The teacher read the story to the class; when each word appeared, students tried to guess from context what each meant, and a column of guesses from context was added to the chart. (c) The dictionary was consulted and definitions were added to the chart for each word. Comparisons were made of the three columns and decisions made about the actual meaning of each word in the text that had been read. Students showed interest in word study during these lessons, likely because of the predictions they had offered (always a good way to engender interest) and because of the active and collaborative nature of the lesson.

LEARNING FROM TEXT

Reviewing and Reflecting. How is Poindexter's procedure an example of providing for deep processing of word meanings?

Working With Important Roots and Other Word Parts. Another beneficial procedure in a word study program is to choose a few roots and word parts to be learned. Knowing these will help students determine meanings of any words in which these word parts appear. Many authorities (e.g., Nagy, Osborn, Winsor, & O'Flahavan, 1992) suggest this as one approach to increasing knowledge of word meanings because of its efficiency. They point out that attempting to learn many unrelated words is a great deal more time consuming than learning several carefully selected roots and word parts that may then be applied to many more words. It also can be of assistance when readers are working independently.

Greek and Latin roots, for example, appear in about a quarter of the words in an English dictionary. One set of word parts often suggested for learning is the set of number prefixes. These are:

mono, uni-	one
bi-, di-	two
tri-	three
quad-	four
quint-, pent-	five
sex, hex-	six
sept-	seven
oct-	eight
novem-	nine
dec-	ten

Students may be asked to write words they already know that begin with each of these prefixes, such as *monorail*, *bicycle*, *bimonthly*, *tricycle*, or *triplets*. Then meanings of the words should be discussed and additional words added to each list. Point out other Latin and Greek roots that appear in many English words. The list in Figure 10–9 is suggested by Voigt (1978, p. 421). See Chapter 9 for additional ideas for working with meanings of other word parts, such as prefixes and suffixes. Although structural analysis is an important strategy for identifying pronunciations of words, it is likewise productive in discovering word meanings (Nagy et al., 1992).

Promoting Out-of-Class Extensions. In several studies, using out-of-class extensions of in-class work has been shown to be a powerful procedure for students to learn vocabulary. McKeown and Beck (1988) describe how this was done in these studies. Rules were established for accomplishing vocabulary tasks outside the classroom for which learners would be rewarded. Specifically, students earned points by being a "word wizard," that is, the student who could either (a) locate and report a word that had been studied in the classroom which he or she had seen or heard outside of school or (b) use the focus words in his or her assigned writings. The benefits from this extra practice were seen when students in a group who had rich instruction plus participation in the word wizard program performed more effectively on tasks involving speed in identifying word meanings than those who had traditional instruction or rich instruction alone.

McKeown and Beck contend that fostering independent word practice in this way may be particularly beneficial for some poor readers who do not have sufficient opportunities for the stimulus of word learning in their homes. They also attested to students' enthusiasm for this activity. This and similar out-of-class extensions are recommended. (See also the suggestion later in this chapter related to oral language development.)

Using Computer Programs. Today, as more and more educational technology finds its way into classrooms, teachers are encouraged to use the computer for enhancing students' word knowledge (U.S. Department of Health and Human Services, 2000). Because students are frequently willing to engage in computer

FIGURE 10–9 ***Common Greek and Latin Roots***

Meaning	Root	Meaning	Root
above	super-	across	trans-
after	post-	again	re-
against	anti-	against	contra-
before	pre-	I believe	credo
between	inter-	book	liber
both	ambi-	capable	-able, -ible
cycle	circle	city	urbs
to carry	port-	disease	-itis
distant	tele-	enough	satis-
for	pro-	foot	ped
I lead, led	duco, ductus	instead	vice-
light	photos	life	bios
not	in-	I make, made	facio, factus
people	demos	out of	ex-, e-
power	kratia	play, I play	ludus, ludo
ripe	maturus	right	dexter
short	brevis	ship	navis
small	micros	single	monos
stone	lithos	star	aster
study, science	logos	suffering	pathos
through	per-	under	sub-
windpipe	bronchos	writing, drawing	graphe
written	scriptum	two	bi-

activities, use of the computer may provide some impetus for independent word learning.

Commercially prepared programs for vocabulary development are available. One such program is *The Game Show* (Computer Advanced Ideas). This program is based on the television program *Password* and is designed for reading levels 2 through 8. The game is used by two students at a time or by two teams and features vocabulary on a variety of topics.

Another software program is *Dictionary* (Microcomputers and Education). Designed for reading levels 2 through 4, this set of activities provides practice in locating words in a dictionary.

Stickybear Opposites (Optimum Resource, Inc.) is a cartoonlike program in which appealing brown bears teach young children such opposite concepts as "happy" and "sad." This software was designed by an author and illustrator of children's books and is accompanied by a hardcover book, a poster, and stickers (see Figure 10–10). Teachers can investigate other computer programs to use in their word study activities.

FIGURE 10–10 *Example of a Computer Software Program Used in a Word Study Program*

Source: From *Stickybear's Early Learning Activities* © 1997 Optimum Resources, Inc., Hilton Head Island, SC 29926. Reproduced by permission.

Promoting awareness of interesting aspects of language may lead the way to a richer vocabulary development.

Instilling an Interest in Words. Helping students learn to love interesting aspects of language can assist them in developing a growing awareness of words that will lead to a richer vocabulary (Blachowicz & Fisher, 2000).

Cleary (1978) had her secondary students engage in Phobia Day to stimulate interest in words. First, students completed a worksheet like the one shown in Figure 10–11. Next they were allowed to invent phobias based on Latin roots (one example: *barbaphobia*, meaning "a fear of whiskers"). Finally, they each chose a phobia and for an entire class period exhibited behavior that would be typical of an individual having that phobia. At the end of the class, of course, students tried to guess which phobias were being dramatized by their classmates.

Many teachers also find that introducing students to information about word origins stimulates interest in vocabulary. A number of books are available that describe the history and origin of words.

Blachowicz and Fisher (2000) suggest several ways of building vocabulary that have good potential for appeal to students, activities like word games, word riddles, puns, and art for word play such as the student drawing in Figure 10–12.

FIGURE 10–11 ***Worksheets to Develop Meaning Vocabulary Can Be Interesting***

PHOBIA: fear, dislike, aversion

The root *phobia* is itself a complete word. Children may have "school phobia" or "ghost phobia" or "lion phobia." Their fear may be real or imagined. Likewise, adults may have a phobia of the dark, a phobia of responsibility, or a phobia of death.

Check the dictionary to determine whether phobias are rational or irrational. (Underline your choice.)

Is a phobia a mild dislike or an extreme fear? (Underline your choice.)

Write a definition for *phobia:* ______________________________

____

Phobia is the root of each of these ten words. Use a dictionary to define them.

acrophobia ______________________________
agoraphobia ______________________________
Anglophobia ______________________________
claustrophobia ______________________________
Germanophobia ______________________________
hydrophobia ______________________________
monophobia ______________________________
phobia ______________________________
photophobia ______________________________
xenophobia ______________________________

Exercise: Complete each of the following sentences.

1. You wouldn't expect a mountain climber to have ______________________________ .
2. As we grow up, we overcome our childhood ______________________________ of the dark.
3. His ______________________________ prevented him from swallowing liquids.

Source: From Cleary, Donna McKee. (1978). *Thinking Thursdays: Language arts in the reading lab.* Newark, DE: International Reading Association. Reprinted with permission of Donna McKee Cleary and the International Reading Association.

FIGURE 10–12 *Interpretation of Possible Multiple Meaning*

Source: From *Teaching Vocabulary in All Classrooms* by Blachowicz & Fisher, © 1996. Reprinted by permission of Pearson Education, Inc., Upper Saddle River, NJ.

LEARNING WORDS FROM ORAL LANGUAGE ENCOUNTERS

NCLB
READING
FIRST

Another potentially effective and lasting way to increase students' meaning vocabularies is through participation in new experiences and engaging in oral language about those experiences (U.S. Department of Health and Human Services, 2000). The "experiences" can be firsthand or indirect. There is a strong association between students' real and vicarious experiences and their meaning vocabulary knowledge (Rupley, 2005).

Real Experiences. When considering new experiences for students, one of the first thoughts to come to mind is probably the field trip. Practical considerations involving time and transportation often make frequent trips of the usual type less than feasible. Teachers should rethink just what a "field trip" is. If any brief excursion away from the confines of the classroom is considered a "trip," then many practical possibilities present themselves.

Using this expanded definition of a field trip, one teacher simply took her students outside to examine the school building in ways they had never done before. One of several things noted was the block above the front door in which a sentence had been carved: New words such as *motto* and *lintel* (the block above the door) emerged. Before each new school year, another teacher makes it a point to drive around the neighborhood of the schools in which she teaches. Her purpose is to locate places of interest within walking distance of the school. This has resulted in walking trips to a doughnut-making shop and an agency that trains guide dogs for the blind, among others. On occasion, she takes a video camera and films a portion of the experience. After the steps in making doughnuts were filmed, lessons on vocabulary and on following a sequence of events were developed based on the film.

A second way to capitalize on real experiences is to use experiences students have had in common outside of school. If many of your secondary students attend hockey or football games, their interests can be the basis of vocabulary development activities. Have them dictate a group story that you write on the board. Challenge the students to revise this first "draft" by thinking of synonyms for common words. (*Jones moved so fast across that ice* can be changed to *Jones moved so swiftly across that ice*). The advantage of a collaborative effort is that students will hear words their peers suggest, each potentially adding some new thoughts about words that previously may have been only in the "partially known" category.

> Advantages of collaborative writing are that students hear words peers suggest, potentially adding new insights about word meanings.

Some real experiences teachers can organize within the classroom include the following:

- food-tasting parties
- bringing in objects (e.g., a weather balloon that fell in your yard; a starfish Ken got on his vacation in Florida)
- science experiments
- displays (e.g., of clothing, artifacts, or art objects from other countries)

Following all such experiences, words describing these experiences must be used in discussion, and oral language activities should be followed by use of the words in written form.

Teachers must also remember the importance of time on task and the specific purpose for providing new experiences, which is to help students expand their meaning vocabularies through development of new concepts and the acquisition of new labels (words) for old concepts. For example, if four reading-class sessions are devoted to an experience with only 20 minutes of follow-up for the development of related vocabulary, this would be an inappropriate division of time. Better planning would call for a briefer experiential activity and more time devoted to work with related words.

Vicarious Experiences. It is not possible for students to experience everything directly. Most people, for example, have not actually seen a volcano erupt firsthand or flown in a helicopter. Nevertheless, they can understand many things about these events and processes, can visualize them, and can use words to discuss them (e.g., lava, altimeter). They know these things because they have had vicarious experiences that help build concepts.

A **vicarious experience** is an indirect experience. For example, although you probably have never directly seen a volcano erupt, you may know quite a lot about eruptions from viewing a film about volcanoes when you were in elementary school, reading about them in a magazine or a high school science book, or seeing TV news clips of erupting volcanoes. All these experiences are vicarious because they are indirect. Nevertheless, they can teach a great deal.

In reading classes, vicarious experiences can be provided in many ways to develop meaning vocabulary. Pictures may be shown to develop concepts before students read a story or article. If, for example, the story to be read includes a horse and mentions its forelock, the teacher may pull from a picture file a photograph of a horse, point to its forelock so that students will see what it looks like, and talk about the meanings of *fore* and *lock* (*fore*, meaning "in front of," combined with *lock*, as in "lock of hair," equals a tuft of hair at the front of the horse's head). Learners should be encouraged to participate in the discussion, suggesting ways the word they see depicted in the picture could be used in oral sentences, offering other words that begin with *fore-* (e.g., *forehead, foreground, forearm, forecast*), and describing the uses of these words. The connection to written language takes place when the learners read the story.

Picture sets designed to help students explore and use new words are on the market. Or, teachers can make their own collections from magazine pictures.

It is critical that students *use* the words they have been exposed to through vicarious experiences. If the words are to become a part of their meaning vocabularies, just hearing them is not sufficient. Students should be induced to employ these new words in their own oral language and ultimately in written activities through reading printed text—either published material or teacher-developed selections.

Reflections

1. Why do *you* read? What incentives make you pick up a book to read it? What implications might this have for your work with reluctant readers?
2. What strategies have helped you to learn word meanings? How can these be used with students you teach?
3. This has been another chapter in which "principles" have been offered, principles for effective instruction of meaning vocabulary. Some of these were enumerated and listed. Others are incorporated within the connected narrative. Could you specify these principles for another teacher?
4. Developing activities that encourage depth of processing and rich understandings of word meanings provides some absorbing challenges for teachers. What suggestions do you have for such activities beyond those given in this chapter?

11

Comprehension of Narrative Text

Comprehension instruction should go beyond only asking questions after material is read; it should also incorporate learning activities that occur before and during reading.

*E*verything we do in reading instruction should be aimed at helping students comprehend written material. It matters not a bit whether students can instantly recognize every word on a page if they cannot understand the message those words are conveying.

Despite a flurry of comprehension research since 1970, findings of this research have not always sifted down to teachers in the schools. As a result, sometimes instructional procedures used by reading specialists have been based only on what has always been done, even though those procedures have not always been effective.

Let's take a look at some of the more recent information on comprehension and how it can help you help your students better understand what they read.

LEARNING FROM TEXT

Using Textual Features. The following section on comprehension processes can seem a bit tricky to some students. One reason is because of the technical vocabulary associated with theoretical descriptions of comprehension processes. Actually the processes themselves are not that odd or hard to understand. They may seem cryptic to some because this technical vocabulary is not in many students' prior knowledge base:

Here's what is suggested: (a) pay particular attention to words in boldface print, (b) read over the information in Table 11–1, and think about whether the "terms more familiar to teachers" clarify the technical term for you.

Also, this is a good time to stop and paraphrase information. For example, after you have read the section on *propositions*, stop and paraphrase what you just read. After you've read the sections on *schemata* and on *mental models*, stop and do that again.

COMPREHENSION PROCESSES

Having some understanding of how we comprehend helps explain the relevance—or irrelevance—of common and/or recommended comprehension instructional strategies. To comprehend, current theory says we employ our knowledge of language and our knowledge of the world (the latter often referred to simply as *background information*). We employ this knowledge to use *propositions*, *schemata*, and *mental models*. We also use inferences to help with these processes, inferences that are based on the text as well as on our *prior knowledge* (prior knowledge is another name for background information) (Anderson, 2004; Kintsch, 1974). (See the definitions of some terminology used in association with comprehension processes and instruction in Table 11–1.)

Propositions are the smallest units of text information that can stand separately and be tested as true or false. They are *ideas*, not the words themselves (McNamara, Miller, & Bransford, 1991).

TABLE 11–1 *Definitions of Comprehension-Related Terms*

Terms Often Used by Researchers About Comprehension	Terms More Familiar to Teachers
Bottom-up processing	Comprehension based on what is in the book—not based on the reader's individual experiences (at least not very much)
Text-driven processing	Same as bottom-up processing
Top-down processing	Comprehension based on what is already in the reader's head (i.e., background information) that helps the reader make intelligent guesses about events, and so on, in written material, and to understand relationships about them
Concept-driven processing	Same as top-down processing
Interactive processing	Comprehension is based on both bottom-up and top-down processing—the reader and the book work together so that student gains meaning
Schema	Background information
Schemata	Background information (plural of *schema*)
Prior knowledge	Background information
Schema availability	The familiarity of the topic to the student
Surface structure	The printed words on the page and how they are arranged within sentences
Deep structure	The meaning conveyed by printed words on a page
Microstructure	1. In regard to surface structure, the words *within* a sentence and how they are arranged 2. In regard to deep structure, the details in a passage
Macrostructure	1. In regard to surface structure, how ideas are arranged *among* sentences to make up the organization of a passage 2. In regard to deep structure, the main idea of a passage
Text structure	How material has been organized by the author into main ideas and supporting details, how these are sequenced, and how they are interrelated
Cohesion, or cohesiveness in text	The way parts of printed text are linked by certain words or statements within and between sentences so the text seems to "hang together" or is seen to be related by the reader
Anaphora	Words that refer to or provide a link to previous words; pronouns, for example, often have anaphoric relationships with nouns, such as in the sentence, "When *Tom* was asked if *he* liked to run, *he* said *he* did" (the noun—*Tom*, in this case—is called a pronoun antecedent)
Proposition	The smallest units of text information that can stand separately and be tested as true or false
Proposition density	The number of propositions (or ideas) in a given piece of written material
Concept load	The same as proposition density
Density	The same as proposition density
Textual features	Things in printed text that relate to reading ease or difficulty, such as vocabulary difficulty, cohesiveness, and density
Textual analysis	Analysis of the things in printed text that relate to reading ease or difficulty (see textual features)
Superordinate units	Sentences
Subordinate units	Words
Lexical item	A word
New information	Ideas with which the reader is unfamiliar

TABLE 11–1 *Definitions of Comprehension-Related Terms* *(continued)*

Terms Often Used by Researchers About Comprehension	Terms More Familiar to Teachers
Old information	Information already in the reader's background knowledge
Reconstructing the author's message	Slightly modifying the author's intended meaning to conform to information already in the reader's background knowledge
Explicit information	Directly stated facts
Implicit information	Information that is not directly stated; it must be inferred since it is only implied
Imagery	Imagining mental pictures of what is read
Mental models	Constructing in our thoughts something similar to what is stated in text
Advance organizers	Material or activities (such as previewing or summarization) presented *before* students read material to help them understand it
Structured overview	A type of advance organizer (see advance organizers) in which vocabulary or ideas are visually related by drawings or diagrams
Hierarchical summarization study strategy	Outlining
Cognition	The process of reasoning
Metacognitive skills	Skills that help students "learn to learn"
Chunk	To organize small pieces of print into larger pieces (e.g., letters into words, or words into phrases)
Prediction strategy	Use of knowledge of language structure and meaning to anticipate words that are upcoming in the text; also, guessing about ideas that will follow, based on prior knowledge about the topic
Retrieval from long-term memory	Remembering
Introspective reporting	Students report the thought processes that occurred when they were reading material

Here is an example.

Ralph went into the autumn woods, which were golden in color.

This sentence has three propositions:

1. Ralph went into the woods.
2. It was autumn.
3. The woods were golden in color.

To comprehend, we consider the propositions in written text. Sometimes this is done rather unconsciously and at other times with more deliberation.

We also employ background information, and yet another name for this is **schemata.** When we know something about a topic, we activate (or mentally "pull up") and think about (usually unconsciously, but sometimes intentionally) our schemata about that topic to understand what we read: Suppose, for instance, that Carolyn is reading a story about basketball. This is a topic she is quite familiar with because she plays on the girls' basketball team at her neighborhood recreation center and also watches games on TV. When she reads that "Judd dribbled the ball but then was called for traveling," she does not think that someone called him on the phone in the middle of the game about his travel plans for vacation. She activates her existing schemata about basketball games and knows just what the author was relating.

Many of the new ideas about comprehension have been based on **schema theory.** (The singular for *schemata* is *schema*.) This theory proposes that what you already know or don't know about a topic can greatly influence your comprehension. This notion was originally advanced by Bartlett (1932) and later developed by Anderson (1977), Rumelhart (1981), and others. It suggests that when readers recognize words on a printed page, they think and react based on their background information (or schemata).

In this view, comprehension is the active construction of meaning. That is, the reader is not an empty vessel into which some words from the page are poured and out comes understanding! Instead, readers actively work to integrate information in a text with what is already stored in their prior knowledge. (Again this may be done unconsciously, or it may be a fairly conscious effort if the text is difficult for a specific reader.) In summary, we must combine old and new information to be good comprehenders. The old information comes from our brains and the "new" information is what we are dealing with from the written text.

Kintsch (1979) has proposed one model (or explanation) of comprehension that is based on schema theory. This model says that the amount of difficulty students have in comprehending a text is related to how much searching of their memories they must undertake to find a schema that closely matches the words the author has presented. If they are quite familiar with the topic, little searching is necessary. If they are not very familiar with it, much searching is required— or they may match the author's information with the wrong schema, or they may not be able to find a match at all. In these circumstances, comprehension is diminished or even absent.

Read the following paragraphs, and try to answer the questions.

> They were obviously Maglemosian, as was evident since the culture was Mesolithic. Given these clues, any budding archaeologist can guess the area of the world in which these shards were found.
>
> 1. To what does the term Maglemosian refer?
> 2. Where were the shards found?
>
> A magnetron tube is of the thermionic type. Its electron beam generates microwaves that are high powered and is influenced by electromagnetic fields.
>
> 1. Write a one paragraph description of a magnetron tube using terminology that can be understood by the general public.
> 2. Given the information about the obvious advantages of thermionic tubes, suggest their possible uses.

If you have some feelings of unease about the correctness of your answers to these questions, this is undoubtedly due to your lack of schema to match the topics. While an electrical engineer may be able to answer questions about the second paragraph, the same engineer might have considerable difficulty answering questions about word identification strategies in reading—a topic for which you should have, at this point, stored information (or schemata).

What practical implications are available from schema theory for reading teachers? First, we can conclude that wide experiences (direct and vicarious) aid comprehension. If experiences with a topic are insufficient, prereading

When students have no schemata stored in their memories about a topic, or only a partial one, they may have difficulty understanding text because the information is "too new" for them.

discussions become very important in supplying information. Second, wide reading on any topic will increase students' comprehension about that topic because over time students will have more and more old information in their schemata to help them understand new information. Wide experience and wide reading relate to what has been called **intertextuality,** a term that refers to use of connections with past written texts to interpret the present text, as well as use of the "texts" of our past experiences. Third, one reason for poor readers' failure to comprehend may be because they fail to *use* the background information they *do* have to comprehend what they read. Teachers should inform students about the need to use prior knowledge and show them how. A number of instructional procedures suggested later in this chapter and the next chapter are based on these premises.

Readers may resort to another process if they find no close match in their schemata for the incoming information from text. To understand unfamiliar topics, it is hypothesized that we can use **mental models.** When we employ this process, we construct something in our thoughts similar to what is presented in the text. Often we, in effect, try (usually unconsciously) to see in our minds what is being described in the selection. Readers can also revise their mental models as they read a story, relying on information found in the selection.

Here is an example of how this might be done. Suppose Sheila reads the statement, "On the first night of the camping trip, Jim sat cross-legged under a huge sycamore tree watching a red squirrel scamper in and out of the hole at the end of the branch." Although Sheila is not familiar with all that she reads here, the author's words may trigger a match with her prior knowledge so that she can fill in her mental model in the following manner.

1. Sheila has not been on a camping trip herself, but from talking with her friend, Theresa, who has, Sheila knows that these trips are often to wooded areas away from a city.
2. She has been to a park with lots of trees and bushes, and she remembers the general impression.
3. She sometimes sits cross-legged herself on her living room floor when she is watching TV and knows the look and feel of the action.
4. She does not know what a sycamore tree is, but there is a huge old oak in her grandmother's backyard and she visualizes it.
5. She has not seen a red squirrel, but there are gray squirrels all around her neighborhood, and she knows what they look like when they scamper on the ground and on the tree trunk.
6. She has not seen a hole in the end of a tree branch, but she has seen a picture in her science book of a hole in a tree trunk with owls peering out.

Sheila has thus developed several schemata that she can match with the words she has just read to get a sense of the meaning of this sentence.

But as can be seen, discrepancies may arise. First, because Sheila's schemata are not parallel to the author's, her mental images may lack precision. For instance, gray squirrels are larger than red squirrels; therefore, the squirrel she visualizes may be larger than what the author intended. Second, readers interpret written words differently according to their varied background experiences. Thus, while Sheila may have visualized an oak tree when she read *sycamore,* if the only large tree Lindsey has seen is an Austrian pine, she might call up that memory from her tree schema; a third reader with greater knowledge about trees, meanwhile, may call upon a schema of exactly what a sycamore tree looks like

A possible cause of poor comprehension is forming inappropriate or meager mental models, which can result in errors in reasoning.

and, therefore, his or her understanding is more likely to agree with what the author meant to convey.

The degree of "closeness" of the schema of the reader to that of the author affects the quality of comprehension as the reader "constructs" meaning. In the squirrel and tree examples given here, this is presumably a "So what?" situation: It probably does not matter how precise a mental model is formed for these minor details. However, if the discrepancy involved a major construct of the story, then comprehension could be hampered. A possible cause of poor comprehension is forming inappropriate or meager mental models, which can therefore result in errors in reasoning.

Actually, another process can occur when readers apply their schemata to words they read: Their schemata can change. Returning to Sheila's schema for squirrels, perhaps squirrels came in only one color (gray) prior to her reading about Jim and the red squirrel. Now she knows that squirrels can also be red; thus, her schema has been altered and expanded. There is an interactive, two-way mechanism: Schemata allow the reader to understand material that is read, and reading new material often changes schemata.

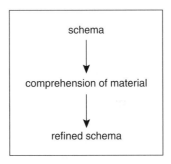

Comprehension, therefore, is an active endeavor that involves "inference making." In this case, inference making is not meant as a specific skill (as in "drawing inferences"), but as a process that permeates all aspects of reading. Inference making is necessary even when attending to single words, such as deciding on the specific meaning of a word like *run*, which has multiple meanings. Using propositions, schemata, and mental models, and employing inferences to hold these processes together, provide the foundation of comprehension.

LEARNING FROM TEXT

Make a Prediction. Why might narratives be easier to comprehend than expository material?

📖 NARRATIVES

This chapter deals with the comprehension of narrative selections and the next chapter with the understanding of expository materials. What is meant by a narrative? **Narratives** are descriptions of events that can be fiction or nonfiction and can be written or oral. Usually we think of stories as narratives (realistic fiction, myths, fairy tales, plays, fables, historical fiction, and legends are examples), but biography, a nonfiction genre, also can be considered a narrative (Gambrel, 2002). Narratives are often written to entertain. Expository material (which you will read about in Chapter 12), on the other hand, is designed specifically to impart new information to readers. The textbook that you are reading at this moment is exposition (or, expository material), but the mystery novel you plan to read during your next vacation is a narrative.

Actually, many instructional procedures that facilitate comprehension of narratives also assist comprehension of expository text, and vice versa. However, there are special features of each text type that merit separate consideration. Several characteristics of narratives make them easier to comprehend than exposition; one of these is that topics they cover may be more familiar than those in, for instance, textbooks. Relatedly, often readers can read narratives more quickly than expository text without comprehension being hindered. The structures of these two types of text differ, and the written language in narrative material is often closer to that of oral language than that found in informational text. Still, a good deal of what you learn about furthering students' comprehension of narratives in this chapter also applies to expository readings, and much that is reported in Chapter 12 is not exclusively recommended for exposition but is helpful for story reading as well.

COMPREHENSION INSTRUCTION: NARRATIVES

NCLB
READING
FIRST

Although more students are enrolled in remedial reading programs because of word recognition and word identification problems than for any other reason, sizeable numbers also are referred because of comprehension difficulties. Students who are identified as having comprehension difficulties often have experienced no undue obstacles with attaining word-learning strategies and often can orally pronounce words in a printed text with facility and fluency. Although not lacking intelligence, these learners exhibit major problems with understanding stories, content area selections, or both.

Frederick's Case Study

Compare. In the case study you are about to read, compare Frederick's reading behaviors with those of the other case study students you've met previously in this text.

*Frederick's
Case Study*

After Frederick's first day in a reading clinic, his tutor came to the clinic supervisor saying she believed he had been "misreferred." During this first session, in addition to activities designed to gain background information about Freddy and to learn something about his interests, the tutor had given Freddy two short tests focusing on word recognition in and out of context. She also had taken to the session a book of high-quality children's literature she planned to read aloud to him. Much to her surprise,

Frederick's Case Study (continued)

Freddy demonstrated a perfect performance on the word recognition tests. And when she began to read to this third grader from the fourth-grade book she had chosen, he wanted to read it to her instead—and did so with no difficulties of any importance!

Having seen such circumstances before, the supervisor asked the tutor if Freddy had been asked to retell the story after reading it, had been asked questions, or had in any other way communicated understanding of what he had read. This had not been done and so the tutor was asked to wait until she had completed more formal and informal appraisals of Freddy's reading abilities.

After the second session, the tutor was still perplexed. Freddy's performance on a test of word identification strategies showed excellent competence in phonic and structural analysis skills. Again he read orally for the tutor from a library book, doing so exceedingly well, and enjoying the activity. On that day, the tutor asked Freddy to summarize what he had read and he gave a brief, literal retelling of events and remembered the main characters. However, no follow-up probes were made to assess higher-level understanding. The tutor agreed with the supervisor that this must be the next avenue of exploration.

Over the next two sessions, Freddy: (a) read silently and completed the comprehension portion of the standardized test; (b) orally read a story for a Reading Miscue Inventory (RMI), which he retold, followed by teacher probes designed to assess higher-order comprehension; (c) read from authentic narrative texts, after which he was questioned about details, but, as well, asked to make inferences and draw conclusions; and (d) read from two well-written expository articles, followed with a variety of question types.

A consistent pattern emerged. Freddy had no apparent difficulties with word recognition, and he could relate some of the literal meanings from all types of materials, although even on these lower-level tasks, information was not complete.

When higher-level reasoning was required, Freddy made almost no adequate responses. When asked questions for which there were no directly stated answers in the text, he appeared confused by the task, saying that he didn't "think that was in there." When asked to use information in his "own good head" to figure out what the answer could be, he drew conclusions that were far too broad for the question being asked or were erroneous. To answer, he seemed to pull out information from the text that was not directly related to the question at hand. When given tasks in which he was expected to explain the general point or significance of the piece, he often focused on ideas of interest to him rather than the main ideas, suggesting that he had concentrated on details of lesser significance. Sometimes his answers to inferential probes merely reflected literal facts, with no reasoning or integration of text details with prior knowledge, thus producing what appeared to be illogical inferences. Often a question would spur Freddy into an anecdotal reply based on something that he had experienced, but that was only tangentially related to the author's intended theme; this resulted in an answer that was clearly unconnected to the question.

Many of Frederick's responses to higher-level comprehension tasks were similar to those found in a study exploring reasons for disabled readers' faulty answers to inference questions (McCormick, 1992). In this investigation, the written answers of 80 fifth-grade students enrolled in a federally funded reading program were analyzed. Students responded to questions for different stories and expository articles they read each week over a period of 20 weeks, answering two inference questions for each. A variety of reasons for unsatisfactory replies were discovered (see Table 11–2). Some

TABLE 11–2 *Sources of Error in Answers to Inference Questions*

A. Reading the Question

A–1: Obviously misread question (omitted word, which made question read differently; substituted one tense for another; didn't read entire question, thereby cuing another question; substituted one word for another)

A–2: Misinterpreted question, thinking that a word referred to a different instance, concept, or object

B. Recalling Text Information

B–1: Apparent that only a part of the text information was recalled

B–2: Did not recall text information that would have cued that the answer was wrong

B–3: Incorrect recall of sequence of information caused incorrect inference

B–4: Answer obviously unrelated to major points in selection

C. Selecting Correct and Sufficient Cues from the Question and the Text

C–1: Selected correct, but incomplete, text information to answer the question

C–2: Misinterpreted question so that answer referred to the overall problem in the selection rather than the specific instance to which the question was referring

C–3: Selected wrong cues from text to answer this specific question

C–4: Did not use written text information; rather, drew inference based on a picture

C–5: Selected wrong cues from the question (focused on less important words in the question)

C–6: Answer suggested recall of information from a different selection

C–7: Responded to only a portion of the question

D. Selecting Relevant, Accurate, and Sufficient Background Knowledge

D–1: Background information selected was inaccurate (an overgeneralization; incorrect concept for a word)

D–2: Information selected was not entirely incorrect, but was too specific and therefore did not reflect the more global or inclusive constructs representing the best answers

D–3: Did not use all available background information in attempt to infer

E. Integrating Text Cues With Background Knowledge

E–1: Too heavy reliance on background knowledge (substantial or complete dismissal of text information in favor of prior knowledge; interpreted text content to conform to prior knowledge; answer given was an opinion rather than an inference)

E–2: Too heavy reliance on text information (substantial or complete dismissal of background information in favor of text information; failure to relate text information to background information that would have cued answer; literal response given with no inference drawn)

F. Writing Responses to Accurately Reflect the Intended Answer

F–1: Words used in written response lacked semantic preciseness, precluding judgment of correctness of answer

F–2: Appeared that student may have inferred correctly but determination could not be made because of lack of specificity in writing response

F–3: Appeared to know answer, but transposed words in written response resulting in incorrect statement

F–4: Answer not fully developed (partially correct, but in writing answer did not provide sufficient information)

G. No Analysis of Response Possible

G–1: Response totally illegible

G–2: No response (answer section left blank; responded "I don't know")

G–3: Merely restated question

G–4: Response incoherent (grammatical order did not approximate English; semantically anomalous)

Source: From "Disabled Readers' Erroneous Responses to Inferential Questions: Description and Analysis," by S. McCormick, 1992, *Reading Research Quarterly, 27*(1), pp. 54–77. Copyright 1992 by the International Reading Association. Reprinted by permission of the International Reading Association.

sources of substandard answers were more prevalent than others. After reading narratives, students made wrong responses most often because they:

1. lacked appropriate strategies for integrating text information with prior knowledge,
2. had difficulty with recall of significant text material,
3. misread the question or misread words in the story,
4. gave answers unrelated to major points in the selection, answers that instead reflected a concentration on more trivial details, and
5. had difficulty in writing out responses that conveyed what they intended to say.

Examine Figure 11–1. Combining those research results with Table 11–2, you can see which error sources most often caused problems for poor readers.

Freddy's score on the standardized test was dismally low in comparison with his oral reading word recognition abilities. On the RMI, his views of the story's plot were simply irrelevant to its significant points, and he was unable to respond to probes designed to determine his understanding of the story's theme. He demonstrated some literal recall of information in the RMI story, but not all important details were given

FIGURE 11–1   *Erroneous Responses for Narrative Selections*

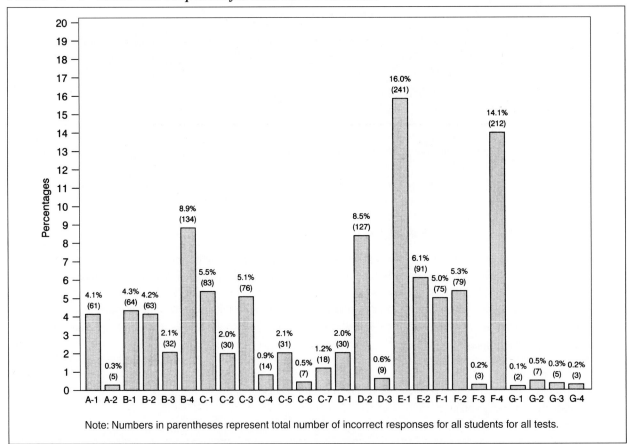

Note: Numbers in parentheses represent total number of incorrect responses for all students for all tests.

Source: From "Disabled Readers' Erroneous Responses to Inferential Questions: Description and Analysis," by S. McCormick, 1992, *Reading Research Quarterly,* 27(1), pp. 54–77. Copyright 1992 by the International Reading Association. Reprinted by permission of the International Reading Association.

or all characters remembered. For the stories read from children's literature books, his performance was similar to that on the RMI. On the expository selections, he could give answers requiring facts and responded to two questions assessing knowledge of word meanings, but he did not draw appropriate conclusions and did not link causes to events.

Frederick had not been misreferred. Although he could give a good imitation of an adept reader, his lack of true proficiency became evident when evaluations went beyond word reading. Freddy's school records indicated a measured intelligence solidly within the average range, yet deriving usable meanings from text was a task baffling for him. He needed a program of special reading assistance. Fortunately, recent research gives many clues about how to help students like Freddy.

Advance organizers consisting of materials or activities, such as previewing, that are presented before students read can aid understanding.

Principles of Good Comprehension Instruction

Pearson and Fielding (1991) offer a bottom-line description of what good comprehension instruction should be: Instruction that is in fact *instructive*. This means that teachers must go beyond asking a few insignificant questions after a student has read. Such procedures may do little more than provide a test; they usually are inconsequential in helping readers learn *how* to comprehend.

Certain principles about the nature of good reading comprehension instruction have evolved from research. Since comprehension is a matter of *constructing meaning*, instruction should emphasize activities that require depth of processing. Furthermore, students should be actively involved in these learning activities before, during, and after reading text (Ruddell, 2006).

A good deal of contemporary research comes out steadfastly in favor of **explicit instruction;** that is, instruction that fully and clearly expresses what must be done (Allington, 2001). While this research shows that extensive reading is important for building background information, lots of reading, alone, does not furnish sufficient practice with strategies necessary for exploring

When students are learning new strategies, precise explanations and guided practice usually are needed before they can practice the strategy independently

deeper meanings, especially for poor readers (The RAND Reading Study Group, 2004). Teachers should offer students guidance on *how* to comprehend, supplying them with specific hints for interpreting texts and doing this in a systematic way. An approach for explicit instruction is emerging in many effective programs and is exemplified by four steps recommended by Pearson and Gallagher (1983).

1. The teacher gives *precise explanations* about a comprehension strategy, frequently modeling or thinking aloud how the strategy is carried out.
2. Readers are given *guided practice* with the strategy.
3. Readers engage in *independent practice* in use of the strategy in specific exercises.
4. The strategy is *applied to regular, connected text.*

This model of explicit instruction is characterized by a gradual release of responsibility. The teacher's role diminishes as time goes on, as students take a more active role in their own learning as their skill develops. It is not that instruction for poor readers should be different; rather, it should be more explicit and guided.

LEARNING FROM TEXT

Self-monitoring. If asked to do so, could you state the four sequential steps recommended for explicit comprehension instruction? (Many of the contemporary comprehension instructional procedures you will read about in this chapter and the next take these principles into account.)

In explicit teaching, students are given something to do that is slightly difficult for them, but as a result of teacher assistance (or, scaffolding), they are pulled up to higher levels of thinking. The teacher engages in **reflective instruction,** that is, noting at any given moment what is puzzling a student or what is contributing complexity to the task for that learner. Students are required to be quite active in the learning events. Teachers solicit much dialogue from the students, but teacher coaching is also evident.

It is not only important to teach students tactics for interpreting text. Students also must be willing to *use* them (which implies motivation), and they must know how to choose the right ones for different situations. To describe this process, to Anderson's (1976) notions of **declarative knowledge** and **procedural knowledge,** Paris, Lipson, and Wixson (1983) added the category of **conditional knowledge.** These ideas were discussed in Chapter 7 in the section on assessment of metacognition, but to review them here: declarative knowledge refers to *what* a strategy is; procedural knowledge relates to *how* a strategy is carried out; and conditional knowledge means knowing *when* and *why* to apply it.

Conditional knowledge allows a learner to be a "strategic" reader. A strategic reader is one who is savvy enough to apply what he or she has been taught when confronting a complicated text (assuming the student had enough practice with the strategy so it is not too laborious to use) and to pick the right one to employ.

Also important to consider is the differentiation between (a) comprehension instruction necessary for understanding the immediate story and (b) comprehension instruction that teaches tactics learners can apply to a wide variety of reading activities, including independent reading. While instruction on how to understand the immediate story is often required, a good comprehension program does not neglect instruction on reading strategies that can be applied with diverse texts.

The National Reading Panel (see introductory discussion of this panel in Chapter 9) evaluated studies of comprehension instruction, careful in their evaluation to include only research that had been conducted according to accepted tenets of research procedure. The accompanying boxed *Q & A* (Questions and Answers) material summarizes some of their findings.

Introductory Guidance

Comprehension instruction should begin before students read a narrative. One goal before reading is to build background information about the story topic, if learners' backgrounds are lacking or scanty. Or, an alternative may be to activate students' prior knowledge—that is, helping them think about background knowledge they do have and helping them associate it with the upcoming selection.

This background building and activating of prior knowledge can consist of any activities that help readers make connections with the narrative, such as discussion, showing pictures, role-playing of ideas, and relating examples to already familiar concepts. Some implications from research for introductory guidance—those activities that can be undertaken before a student reads—are presented here.

LEARNING FROM TEXT

Previewing.   If you have not already examined the illustrative aid labeled Table 11–3 to preview what you will read in the remainder of the chapter, do that now. This table provides a brief framework of the content and organization of the following sections. Previewing can increase comprehension of text.

Assistance With the Immediate Text.   To help students understand a specific text, the teacher can develop a number of procedures to use before students read to promote their comprehension.

1. *Previewing.* Research has shown that written previews can increase comprehension of narratives. One such study was conducted with middle school students who had reading disabilities (Graves, Cooke, & Laberge, 1983). In that

Q & A

Questions Answered by the NATIONAL READING PANEL

Question	Should a particular comprehension strategy be emphasized in reading instruction?
Answer	Instruction that helps pupils develop a variety of strategies is most effective.
Question	Is there any evidence that performance on standardized reading tests is enhanced as a result of comprehension instruction?
Answer	When pupils employ a combination of comprehension strategies, test results can be improved.
Question	Which of the following can be improved as a result of well-developed comprehension strategies: (a) recall of facts, (b) generation of questions, or (c) summarization of main points?
Answer	All of the above.
Question	Since expository text comprehension is sometimes more challenging than comprehension of narratives, could it be effective to teach comprehension lessons within the context of expository material (e.g., using science or history books or selections)?
Answer	Yes.
Question	It has been said that more focus should be placed on comprehension instruction in reading courses offered in teacher education programs. Why?
Answer	Comprehension instruction is complex.

Source: National Institute of Child Health and Human Development (NICHHD), 2000.

program, previews were used before students read short stories. The teaching activity consisted of the following steps:

a. The teacher gave each student a written preview of the story (see Figure 11–2 for a sample preview).
b. The teacher read to the students the statements and questions found at the beginning of the preview. These were designed to arouse interest and link the story to something familiar in the students' backgrounds. The teacher led a brief discussion about these and about the story's topic.
c. The teacher read a summary of the story, which consisted of the middle portion of the written preview, to the students. The summary included the setting, general statements about the characters, and a brief description of the plot up to the ending.
d. Students were asked to look at the chalkboard, where the teacher had previously listed the characters and a short statement about each of them. These were read to the students.

TABLE 11–3 *Examples of Comprehension Instruction for Narratives Before, During, and After Reading Text*

Before

Assistance with the immediate text
- Previewing
- Predicting

Development of strategies that can be used with a wide variety of texts
- Listening activities to practice complex skills
- Guiding selection of main ideas
  - Using heuristics
  - Collaboratively outlining paragraphs
  - Asking key questions and having students combine answers to arrive at implicit main ideas
  - Collaboratively composing paragraph titles

During

Assistance with the immediate text
- Using DRTA
- Accenting content-specific story discussions

Development of strategies that can be used with a wide variety of texts
- Using think-alouds
- Promoting visual imagery
- Engaging students in the ReQuest Procedure
- Using text sets

After

Assistance with the immediate text
- Asking high-quality questions
- Motivating effort for higher-level thinking
- Combining "grand conversations" with teacher questions

Development of strategies that can be used with a wide variety of texts
- Using story maps and story frames
- Using retelling as a route to understanding story structure
- Clarifying question-answer relationships (QARs)
- Focusing questions on complex reading strategies
- Using character maps

e. Student attention was redirected to the written preview. This final portion defined three or four difficult words they would encounter in the story.
f. The previews were put away and students silently read the story on which the preview was based.

As a result of this procedure, students' recall of facts directly stated in the stories increased by 13% and their higher-level comprehension by 38%. In addition,

FIGURE 11–2 *A Written Preview for a Short Story*

Preview for "The Signalman"

It seems sometimes that life is full of dangers! Would you agree? Nearly every day an accident or a disaster of some kind happens somewhere. A plane crashes, an earthquake occurs, or cars pile up on the freeway. Can you think of some accidents or disasters that have happened lately?

Many times before a disaster occurs, a warning is given. For example, lights might blink on the instrument panel of an airplane, or instruments might pick up tremors in the earth that predict an earthquake is about to occur. Can you think of other types of warnings? Were warnings given for the disasters we just talked about?

Some people believe that they are warned of dangers in supernatural ways. They believe in spirits, or voices, or maybe even ghosts guiding them to do—or not do—something. Have you ever heard of someone being warned like this? What did that person say?

Maybe you've been warned about something. For example, have you ever awakened from a dream thinking that what you dreamed would happen? And then—did it? Have you ever had a feeling something bad was about to happen? And then—did it happen? Can you think of any examples?

The story you will read today is about a man who often gets warnings. But, the warnings this man gets don't come from dreams or his mind. The man gets warnings of bad things about to happen from a ghost, or specter. It seems that the ghost always appears before something terrible happens, as if he is trying to warn of danger.

The story takes place in a very lonely and gloomy spot, hidden away in the mountains. The man you will read about lives alone in a hut which is on a railroad line and near a tunnel. The hut has many things the man needs—such as a desk, a record book, an instrument to send telegraphs, and a bell.

The man is a signalman. His job is to signal the trains, watch for danger on the tracks, and warn passing trains of trouble ahead. The signalman works very hard at his job and is quite exact in all his duties. He is nervous, though, because he has seen many people die in train accidents near his post. He wants to be sure that he signals the trains of any danger.

You will learn about what the signalman does and says through the man who tells the story. This man visited the signalman at two different times and learned much about him. The story you will read is the story the visitor tells after meeting the signalman.

The story opens as the visitor calls "Hello! Below there!" to the signalman. He wants to know how to reach the signalman's hut from where he is at the top of a cliff. The signalman hears the man call to him but doesn't answer. He is afraid and looks down the railroad line instead of up to the man.

What does the signalman think he will see? Why is he afraid? Read to find out.

Before you read the story, I want to show you a list of some of the people in it. They don't have names and are described by who they are or what they do. The signalman is the man who lives in a hut near the railroad. The visitor is the man who visits the signalman and who tells the story. Another character is the ghost.

There are also some words I would like to define for you. The signalman is a dark, *sallow* man, with a dark beard and heavy eyebrows. *Sallow* means that he looks sickly and pale.

The signalman's hut is also called a *post* because it is where he is stationed to do his job.

The ghost is also called a *specter*.

Source: Graves, Michael F., Cooke, Cheryl L., & Laberge, Michael J. (1983, Spring). Effects of previewing difficult short stories on low ability junior high school student's comprehension, recall, and attitudes. *Reading Research Quarterly, 18*(3), 262–276. Reprinted with permission of Michael F. Graves and the International Reading Association.

scores on a test of recall of information given after several days had elapsed were significantly higher than when no written previews were used. And, important for poorly motivated readers, an attitude survey showed students liked the technique.

Although the type of previewing just described is conducted in much more depth than the suggestions found in most reading materials, it takes only about 10 minutes to implement. Other studies have shown that written previews are also effective with elementary and senior high school students.

2. *Emphasizing predictions.* Prediction is a strategy that research has shown to foster comprehension (Dole, 2002). For example, in two investigations, one with average readers (Hansen, 1981) and a follow-up study with poor readers (McCormick & Hill, 1984), students' comprehension increased when teachers used a systematic method of focusing on predictions before stories were read.

For the experimental groups, the teacher selected three main ideas from each story students were to read. Two questions were written about each main idea, one requiring students to relate something in the upcoming text to their own background experiences and the second asking students to make a prediction about what might happen in the story. For example, suppose a story concerned two boys who were such good friends they decided to change places for a few days, but the results were not as positive as either boy had anticipated. Based on the theme of the narrative, one of the main ideas the teacher might wish the students to infer could be:

Things aren't always as good for another person as they may seem.

In this case, the *background question* might be this:

Have you ever wished or pretended you were someone else? If so, who and why?

And the *prediction question* that followed might be this:

If two children changed places, what kinds of things, good or bad, do you think might happen?

The three main ideas were never shown or stated directly to the students: They simply served as a way to help the teacher devise important questions. However, the two questions written for each of the main ideas were thoroughly discussed by the group prior to their reading the story. Group discussion was considered critical because: (a) students who at first could think of no responses often could respond after hearing other students' comments; (b) students sometimes modified their original responses after hearing and thinking about other students' answers; and (c) students could use many persons' ideas, not just their own, from which to draw inferences later during reading.

Instead of these systematic prediction exercises before reading, after reading students in other groups discussed answers to one higher-order question and five questions based on details from the text.

Students in the groups emphasizing predictions before reading performed significantly better on weekly tests of higher-level comprehension than those who did not engage in the carefully constructed prediction discussions.

3. *Using story impressions: A writing activity.* McGinley and Denner (1987) developed a combination prediction-writing activity that had favorable results on poor readers' story comprehension. Their research was conducted with children both in primary grades and at the middle school level. This method is called "Using Story Impressions" and is implemented before students read.

To prepare for the lesson, the teacher selects words or phrases that represent important characters, settings, and key elements of the plot for a narrative students will read. The students then use these to compose their own stories, which are to represent a guess or prediction of what the upcoming story will be about. The point of the instruction is not that the learners duplicate the author's story, but rather that they are engaged with the ideas they will encounter in the

> When instruction has emphasized prediction activities, students have significantly improved in higher-level comprehension.

FIGURE 11−3 *Story Impressions (Prereading) Activity Based on Poe's "The Tell-Tale Heart"*

Story Impressions Given to a Class	A Remedial Eighth Grader's Story Guess Written From the Story Impressions
house ↓ old man ↓ young man ↓ hatred ↓ ugly eye ↓ death ↓ tub, blood, knife ↓ buried ↓ floor ↓ police ↓ heartbeat ↓ guilt ↓ crazy ↓ confession	There was a young man and his father, an old man. They lived in a house on a hill out in the bouniey's. The old man hated his son because he had an ugly eye. 　　The young man was asleep in his bedroom when he was awakened by screaming. He went to the bedroom and saw his father laying in the tub. There was blood everywhere and a knife through him. 　　The young man found a tape recording hidden behind the door on the floor. He turned it on there was screaming on the tape. The young man started to call the police, but then he stopped and remembered what his mother had told him. She had told him that he had a split personality. So he called the police and confessed to being crazy and killing his father. His heartbeat was heavy as he called.

Source: McGinley, William, & Denner, Peter R. (1987, December). Story impressions: A prereading/writing activity. *Journal of Reading, 31*(3), 248–253. Reprinted with permission of William McGinley and the International Reading Association.

upcoming reading. This activity is said to activate schema; it is very likely that it also promotes interest, as students read and compare the actual story with their own. Figure 11–3 shows a sample of one student's story "guess," written in response to a set of words the teacher had presented before the middle school students read an adaptation of Edgar Allan Poe's "The Tell-Tale Heart." The clue words are listed in the sequence in which they occur in the published narrative and the arrows between words in the figure are the teacher's indication of the direction in which the action is to flow.

　　Before learners engage in use of story impressions independently, it is recommended that group stories be produced with the teacher's guidance, brainstorming ideas about ways to logically connect the words and phrases.

Development of Strategies That Can Be Used With a Wide Variety of Texts.
Prereading activities may focus on strategies that will be useful in many reading

situations. These prepractice exercises give students opportunities to work with a strategy under teacher guidance before they apply the strategy independently. The objective is to make the text more accessible for students during later real connected reading.

1. *Using listening activities to practice complex skills.* Helping students gain a sense of just what certain strategies entail and doing so within a context that simplifies the task can set students on the road to applying these while reading any text. Two relatively complex strategies that may profit from this type of prereading treatment are drawing conclusions and drawing inferences.

Drawing conclusions involves use of statements expressed in a text. Although the conclusion is not directly stated, all information needed to reach the desired deduction is contained in the material. In contrast, **drawing inferences** is required when part of the knowledge necessary to derive the response is found in the selection, but part of it is not. When making inferences, students must search their schemata to find additional information and combine this with that reported in the story. Generating conclusions and constructing inferences both require interpretive thinking, and the two strategies are closely related. Further, both processes form the basis of, and are interrelated with, other higher-level comprehension skills.

Arriving at conclusions and making inferences may, at times, necessitate fairly intricate thinking. The process may appear particularly enigmatic for some disabled readers, unless they are given explicit instruction. When Hansen and Lovitt (1977) examined performances of students with learning disabilities on literal, sequential, and inferential questions, their scores were lowest when required to draw inferences. Furthermore, Wilson's (1979) study indicated that the differences in effectiveness between average readers and those with reading disabilities were greater on inferential than on literal questions.

Teachers can provide occasions for students to prepractice drawing conclusions and inferences during listening comprehension exercises. As you probably suspect since listening level tests are used to assess students' reading potential, studies have shown that reading comprehension and listening comprehension are related (e.g., Dreyer & Katz, 1992; Hoover & Gough, 1990). In listening exercises, the teacher does the reading while students devote their energies to thinking. Teachers should write or locate short passages, read these to the students, then ask them to draw an inference or conclusion. Here is one example of the kind of paragraph to be used:

> Joe's toothache was making him feel awful. He tried many times to yank the tooth out himself, but he just couldn't do it. He made a big decision. He put on his coat and walked slowly downtown. He came to a building, stopped, sighed, and bravely went up the steps. What was his purpose?

After they have given their response, the teacher should ask students if the correct answer was *stated* in the paragraph, have them name all clues in the text that helped them arrive at the answer, and ask them to tell things from their own experiences (i.e., background information) that helped them determine their reply. This type of practice may be used even with very young students.

Pictures can also be exploited to give students practice with inferring and drawing conclusions (see the example in Figure 11–4). In this example, the student is to draw a picture in the empty box depicting what occurred between pictures 1 and 3.

FIGURE 11−4 *Preliminary Practice in Drawing Inferences or Conclusions Can Employ Pictures: What Happened Between Pictures 1 and 3?*

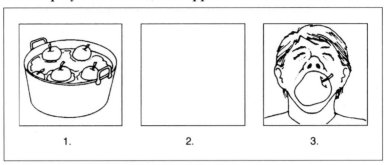

Nontextual practice (listening activities and working with pictures, for instance) should be used only as an introduction to the concept of inferring or drawing conclusions, the goal being simply to give learners a sense of what is called for in these strategies. Nontextual exercises should be followed by students' applying the strategy to written material.

2. *Guiding selection of main ideas.* The **main idea** of a passage is the most important idea the author has given about a topic; it is the idea to which most other information in the passage refers or relates. Determining the main idea of what has been read is also called *getting the gist*; it is the process of deciding on the general significance of the material.

Individual paragraphs in expository (informational) material rather consistently contain a main idea. On the other hand, single paragraphs in narratives may not, because in stories the main ideas sometimes run across several sequential paragraphs.

> Sometimes main ideas are directly stated in text; other times they must be inferred.

At times, main ideas are directly (that is, **explicitly**) stated, as in topic sentences. However, in other cases, the main idea must be inferred from a number of facts that are given; in those circumstances, it is said that the main idea is **implicit.** It's there but not specifically expressed, so the reader must figure it out. In either case, determining the main idea is considered a higher-level comprehension skill because it requires making a generalization. Even when a topic sentence states the main idea, the reader must decide that this statement, and not others, is the central thought.

Learning how to distinguish the main idea of a passage is a valuable strategy because it helps readers identify what is important to know—and to remember. In addition, details are more easily remembered if they are related to a more general point.

Less-skilled readers sometimes have difficulty understanding what is meant by a "main idea." Asked to specify the main point of a passage, they respond with a single, small detail. When the response is deemed inaccurate, they insist, "It does too say that here." They fail to distinguish between factual but less-inclusive supporting information and an idea of significance for the whole selection. The teacher must often illustrate the concepts of "main," "major," and "the most important" in a direct way before learning can progress.

To guide main idea selection, instruction typically begins with single paragraphs. At this stage, teachers should choose paragraphs in which the topic sentence is directly stated. Since authors may place a topic sentence in any of three locations in a paragraph, practice should be given in identifying this main idea statement in each position—at the beginning, at the end, and somewhere in the middle. Teachers should be actively involved to give students immediate feedback about the correctness of responses and to provide direct assistance in deciding why an answer is right or wrong. This method is in contrast to many published activities designed for practicing the skill of determining main ideas. Too often, the latter do little to teach how to ascertain major points, especially if students work the exercises independently. For example, in a typical published lesson, learners read single paragraphs and then answer multiple-choice questions that are later marked right or wrong by the teacher. This is an instance of an activity that is merely a test; it does not enlighten students about the processes necessary for identifying central thoughts (Allington, 2001).

In the second phase, students work with paragraphs in which main ideas are not explicitly presented. Direct teaching, collaborative learning activities, and discussion are important at this stage. All of these can furnish "instruction that is instructive."

Here are some appropriate activities to help students determine main ideas.

   a. *Use heuristic devices.* **Heuristic devices** are tools or mechanisms that help learners discover concepts. At times, these take the form of a visual demonstration. For example, to teach main idea selection, you could demonstrate visually the relationship between the main idea and supporting details by drawing a tree with a trunk and branches on an overhead projector transparency. After students have read a paragraph, they are asked to offer suggestions for the main idea and details. The teacher writes the main idea on the trunk and the details on the branches. (Use a water-based, felt-tip pen for marking on the transparency; when answers are to be changed, dip a tissue in water and erase the previously written answer.)

   b. *Collaboratively outline paragraphs.* Have students work together to outline several single paragraphs to recognize the relationships between main ideas and the details that support them. To introduce the principle, before students read a paragraph, the teacher writes the main idea and each supporting detail on separate oaktag strips. After they read; students arrange the strips in outline fashion to show the main idea and the details.

Abby's measles were making her miserable.

- Abby hated the funny-looking spots on her body.
- Her measles were making her itch.
- The measles made her feel like she had a rash.
- She could not go places she wanted to go because measles are contagious.

Following several such experiences, inaugurate more formal outlining techniques. After learners have read a paragraph, through collaborative discussion, have them decide on the main idea. Next, the teacher writes a Roman numeral I on the board (using typical outlining format), followed by the statement selected as the main idea. The teacher asks for the details that prove or support the main idea. These are listed below the main idea, again in outlining format. This procedure is followed for several paragraphs.

Both categories of outlining practice (informal and formal) reinforce the distinctions between major points and supporting points and demonstrate that all ideas are not of equal significance.

For additional lesson plans to teach a useful comprehension strategy, go to http://reading.indiana.edu/, click "Lesson Plans" and then "Main Ideas and Supporting Details."

c. *Ask key questions and have students combine the answers to arrive at implicit main points.* The *Who? What? When?* and *Why?* questions employed so often in literal comprehension exercises can be used to focus students' attention on main points. They are particularly helpful for paragraphs in which the main idea is not explicitly stated. If a short phrase is written to answer each *W* question, these often can be combined into one statement that reflects the main idea that is not explicitly stated. For example,

Steven was planning to run away from home. He had decided that, if on this birthday, his parents didn't get him the dog he had asked for year after year, that night he would take the Greyhound bus from the station downtown and go off to live on his own.

Who: a boy, Steven
What: planning to run away
When: on his birthday
Why: if his parents didn't get him a dog

Main idea statement: A boy, Steven, was planning to run away on his birthday if his parents didn't get him a dog.

d. *Collaboratively compose paragraph titles.* The teacher can work collaboratively with students to write titles for untitled paragraphs. Revisions can continue until the best title is developed.

Up to this point, the discussion has centered on finding the main idea in single paragraphs. Of course, the next phase in the program should promote transfer of this skill to longer pieces of discourse, material longer than one paragraph. All the activities suggested previously may be used, some with slight adaptations. For example, with *visual heuristics*, the main ideas of individual paragraphs become the supporting details for the main idea of the whole passage. When oaktag strips are used in manipulative outlining activities, the same strips used for main ideas of the individual paragraphs can be physically moved to the slots for supporting details in the passage outline. To ease the way into formal outlining of longer passages, the teacher may wish to print partially completed outlines on the board with the details already given for each paragraph and only the main idea slot for each one left blank. The blank slots are to be filled by the students after group discussion. When asking students to compose titles for passages, teachers can cut headlines off newspaper articles and have them write their own. If students are unable to read the regular community newspaper, any of the easy-to-read newspapers now available may be used.

Baumann (1984) had excellent success in teaching sixth graders to select main ideas of both narrative and expository materials using many of the principles and procedures described here. Working with paragraphs and then short passages, and with explicit main idea statements and then implicit main ideas, students were instructed within a model that embraced the ideas of: (a) clear and complete teacher instructions, (b) guided practice, (c) independent practice, and (d) application to real materials. Students were exposed to heuristics (a table with the main idea written on it and supporting details on the legs that supported the table, a main idea umbrella with details beneath, and so on); they constructed simple, two-level outlines; and they wrote out main ideas rather than merely selecting them. In addition, Baumann directly taught students how to paraphrase. Readers who participated in this program performed significantly better on main idea selection than those who were trained through regular basal reader manual suggestions.

LEARNING FROM TEXT

Review and Reflect. How does Baumann's study show that he used current principles of comprehension instruction?

Schunk and Rice (1992) taught fourth- and fifth-grade students with learning disabilities and with severe reading difficulties a strategy for determining main ideas of passages. They added to the instructional procedures a component that emphasized the benefits of employing the strategy, providing feedback that showed learners how their improved performance was tied to using the strategy they had been taught. These students employed the strategy more and generalized its use to other readings more than students who had not had the value of the strategy demonstrated to them. Including an element stressing the value of the strategy is in line with principles for developing strategic readers who not only know how, but also why, they are to use a learning tactic. Furthermore, in a second experiment, this research team showed another group how to modify the main idea selection strategy for different tasks, and they, too, performed better than a control group who had not received this additional training.

This presentation of recommendations for guiding selection of main ideas is to serve as an example of ways prepractice can be built to prepare youngsters for using complex skills in later connected text reading. Comparable practice activities with other comprehension strategies produce positive outcomes.

Assistance While Reading

What procedures can help a reader interpret text *during* reading? Recommendations from research investigations follow.

Assistance With the Immediate Text. Some techniques are designed to heighten understanding of a specific story students are reading, but in some cases, systematic use of these strategies builds tactics that readers can employ independently with other selections.

1. *Involving students in a DRTA.* The acronym DRTA stands for Directed Reading-Thinking Activity (Stauffer, 1975). DRTA is a carefully organized procedure designed to improve students' comprehension of narrative material and is directed by the teacher. The steps for these lessons are as follows:

   a. Prepare students for what they will be required to do during reading of a text. Have them survey the material by reading the title and looking at pictures. Ask them to predict events in the first portion of the story. To encourage predictions, pose questions such as, "What do you think will happen?" or "After reading the title and looking at these two pictures, what do you think this section is going to be about?" Set a purpose for reading by telling students to check their predictions: "Read to find out if you're right" or "Read to find out who's right."
   b. Have students read a beginning portion of the story silently.
   c. Stop to verify (or reject) through discussion the predictions made before reading. Prediction questions are particularly effective when students compare their guesses with what actually takes place in the text (Fielding, Anderson, & Pearson, 1990).

d. Ask for new predictions before reading the next section. In many cases, these predictions will now be based on what has been previously read in the passage.

e. Continue with a cycle of predicting, reading, and confirming or rejecting through discussion until the material is completed.

DRTA teaches students to consider information, form hypotheses, suspend judgment, find proof, make decisions, and develop critical reading skills. Research has shown that DRTAs help students learn to monitor their own comprehension (Baumann, Seifert-Kessell, & Jones, 1992) and that the quality and quantity of students' answers are better than when using traditional questioning procedures found in basal reader manuals (e.g., see Reutzel & Hollingsworth, 1991). DRTA is useful at any grade level and with any type of text (Dunston & Headley, 2002), and it can be used for listening comprehension lessons as well.

2. *Accentuating content-specific story discussions.* During guided reading of narratives, teachers commonly ask students to pause in their reading at various logical points to discuss events that have transpired so far. Research suggests it is advantageous for these discussions to accentuate *story-specified* content.

An example is seen in a study conducted by Golden (1988). When a teacher and learners engaged in substantial amounts of content-focused dialogue, including discussion of story theme, and when students answered intricate questions based on the story, often with teacher assistance, students remembered considerably more important information than when this was not the case. Readers recalled significantly fewer critical ideas when discussion simply focused on similarities of children's experiences to those of story characters, with students telling personal anecdotes related to experiences described in the text. This is not to say that self-expression is to be denigrated, but this is an example of getting what you teach. If the objective is deep understanding of story information and themes, then emphasizing story information and themes during the reading of narratives is more valuable than less-focused discussion.

Development of Strategies That Can Be Used With a Wide Variety of Texts.   The suggestions here are used during the reading of a specific story, but demonstrate strategies students can "take with them" to subsequent texts they read.

1. *Using think-alouds.* Thinking aloud, or "making thinking public" (Paris, 1986), has been suggested previously in this text, for instance, as a mechanism for assessing students' reading processing. As you remember, a **think-aloud** is a self-report of one's own thinking operations. Think-alouds were also recommended for helping students as they try to employ word identification strategies. Instructional uses of think-alouds vary from the manner in which they are employed in assessment.

In instruction, the teacher is the first person to engage in a think-aloud. The teacher models how to approach a text metacognitively (Brown, Palincsar, & Armbruster, 2004). The teacher states aloud those thinking processes he or she is using. Wade (1990) suggests the following. The teacher: (a) makes predictions before beginning to read, stating these aloud ("From looking at the title and this first picture, I think this story will be about witches"); (b) demonstrates analogy use ("What is being described here makes me think of some things I've been seeing on TV lately about what it's like to live through a hurricane"); (c) admits—or for purposes of instruction, simulates—confusions ("This doesn't quite make

A think-aloud is a self-report of one's own thinking.

sense to me here"); (d) specifies fix-up strategies ("I think I'd better go back to that other part and reread for a moment to see if I can figure out why I don't understand this" or "Maybe if I read ahead this will become more clear"); and (e) describes visual images ("As I read this, I can see in my mind the way that ferocious dog must have looked to Alex, with its teeth bared and its short, wiry hair bristling on its neck as it prepared to attack").

At the onset, focus is on just one strategy at a time. For example, one day the teacher models and asks for analogies ("What does this seem like that you already know about?") with a number of group members offering suggestions about various episodes or descriptions in the story. In another lesson, the teacher solicits visual images that different readers have called up as they read, and so on.

To promote generalization of these strategies to independent and teacher-guided reading of other texts, have readers engage in collaborative learning, using the procedures they have been practicing in daily lessons. Students take turns reading, suggesting their thoughts; others in the group are allowed to add contrasting ideas as they prompt one another through their reading of the text.

Then the teacher puts it all together, asking the learners to follow silently the beginning portion of a story while he or she reads orally, role-playing all five strategies specified here (and perhaps others). After the teacher has illustrated the behaviors of a strategic reader, a student is called on to handle another portion of the narrative in the same manner, and then another student for a next small portion, and so on.

Furthermore, the teacher employs think-alouds as the need arises. When a learner seems confused, the teacher may say, "Well, this is how I would figure that out. I would say to myself, 'Let's see, that idea was talked about in the second part of the story. I'll look back there and see what I may have forgotten'" or "I know they did not give the answer to that question in the book. But I can figure it out if I use what Bobby told Amy about the parrot, and, if I think about what I know parrots can do. Parrots can talk, so . . . Ah ha! The answer must be that it was the parrot who said that crazy thing, and not the man!" This has been called "sharing secrets with students," sharing the ways *you* have learned to figure out text information. Share secrets with learners; don't just test their comprehension. In addition, when students show insightful thinking about a question they have answered well, ask them to tell how they arrived at their answers.

Studies have shown that even elementary school children can learn to think aloud (e.g., Baumann et al.'s [1992] work with fourth graders), and that this helps them detect errors in reasoning. In the Baumann et al. research, readers who had been taught through think-alouds outperformed, in depth and breadth of comprehension monitoring abilities, students who had not received the instruction.

2. *Promoting visual imagery.* Because of the difficulties that some young readers and delayed readers may have with forming visual images, as you may notice during your think-aloud demonstrations, a special word will be said about that strategy. Being able to form visual images seems critical to evoking mental models to comprehend texts.

When most people read a story, they are likely to "see" pictures in their minds of the events they are reading about as they progress through a text. Some poor readers, however, report that they do not see images as they read, perhaps because of exaggerated concern with pronunciation of words or lack of interest in reading. Several studies have shown that when students form mental pictures of the message in a text, both comprehension and recall are aided (e.g., Sadoski, 1983; Williams, Konopak, Wood, & Avett, 1992).

In Sadoski's (1983) study, for example, the role of imagery was shown to be related to higher-level comprehension, which requires deeper levels of the processing of meaning than is required by literal-level comprehension. In this study, fifth graders who reported forming a visual image of a critical part of a story scored better on higher-level comprehension tasks, such as telling the theme of the story, than did students who did not report visual imagery.

Imagery training has helped some poor readers increase their higher-level comprehension achievement. Several suggestions for this training follow.

a. Before students read a story, specifically direct them to try to form pictures in their minds, attempting to "see" the objects and events they are reading about. Tell them why: Because it will help them understand and remember what they read.

b. Read the first paragraph of the story *to* students. Prior to beginning, ask them to close their eyes and attempt to form a mental picture of what they hear as you read. Afterward, discuss these images. (Poetry is also a good choice for this purpose.) Direct students to form pictures in their minds as they read the remainder of the story. At the conclusion, ask for images they "saw."

c. Read the first paragraph to students, again asking them to form a mental image of what they hear. Afterward, request that they quickly draw pictures of what they saw (a very quick sketch, perhaps using stick figures). Briefly compare and discuss the pictures. Lesgold, McCormick, and Golinkoff (1975) reported a study in which third and fourth graders were trained for 4 weeks to draw cartoons about portions of selections they read; after the training period, students recalled more of the stories as a result of this imagery practice.

d. Have students read a paragraph of the story silently themselves. Proceed as in item *b*. And, with another paragraph they—rather than you—have read, proceed as in item *c*. Direct them to attempt to construct the same kinds of images in their minds as they read the rest of the text. Tell them they should try to "see" what the author has described in all stories they read.

e. Have students carry out suggestions *b* through *d*, but with sections of the story longer than a paragraph.

f. Ask students to act out the first portion of a story. Engaging in short dramatizations necessarily induces "seeing" what must be acted out. Henderson and Shanker's (1978) study showed that this activity improved comprehension of students in primary grades more than workbook exercises designed to aid comprehension. Of course, students cannot act out everything they read, but they can "act it out" in their heads. Tell them to try to do this with the rest of the story.

g. Some teachers have assembled stories in this manner—a page of text, followed by a blank sheet of paper; another page of text, followed by another blank page; and so on. The empty sheet is a signal for students to pause and form a mental image of what they have just read on the preceding page.

h. To promote transfer of strategy use, assign a story for students to read independently. Ask that they draw a series of pictures to show the images they formed in their minds as they read. Share and compare these as a group activity.

The ReQuest Procedure helps students monitor their understanding through student and teacher question asking and through teacher modeling.

3. *Engaging students in the ReQuest Procedure.* In this activity, originally developed in a reading clinic by Manzo (Manzo, 1969; Manzo & Manzo, 2002), students are helped to monitor their understanding through asking questions, listening to teacher modeling, and setting purposes for reading.

When a new story is introduced, students and teacher read the title and first sentence and examine illustrations found on the first page! The students are then to ask the teacher as many questions as they can pose about this introductory information. After the teacher answers these, it's the teacher's turn to question. He or she, too, asks questions over the same content, attempting to focus student attention on the major intent of the author and on a purpose for reading.

Next, another small portion of the story is read, followed with the students asking the teacher as many questions as they can about it. Again, when the teacher has answered all of these, he or she directs questions to the students about this section.

The mutual asking and answering continues for approximately a 10-minute period, with the teacher leading the students to frame questions about the purpose and major ideas of the narrative through the types of questions modeled.

Students are then invited to read the remainder of the story silently, and at the conclusion, the teacher inquires, "Did we read for the right purpose?" and asks more questions. In addition to aiding understanding of the current story, the ReQuest Procedure is believed to help students learn to monitor their thinking processes for later independent reading.

4. *Using text sets.* Text sets are groups of books that are conceptually related. For instance, in one study (Short, 1992), students read assortments of books based on shared character types (e.g., specific animals, such as stories about pigs); shared genres (e.g., folktales); shared author (all written by the same individual); shared settings (e.g., stories set in Japan); and shared topic, but different rendition (e.g., various versions of the Cinderella story from around the world).

The advantage in using sets of several related books for a period of time is that story discussions can center on relationships among books, allowing students to draw upon what they have learned from one book to enhance their interpretations of others. This method provides opportunities for analysis and comparison, and the deep processing of text that true understanding requires.

In this procedure, each day during story reading and discussion, the teacher has students focus on connections between the current book and any from the set they have previously read. They should also be guided to look for contrasts as well as likenesses. Correspondences and differences between themes as well as specifics should be included in the discussions. Short believed that collaboratively establishing connections is a positive feature, because readers can springboard from one another's insights to realize more complex links among books and ideas. Teacher guidance can help learners build the connections with some depth.

Understandings should broaden as students read additional books in a set, understandings that can carry over into independent reading of narratives.

Culminating Events

Instructional events *after* students read should be more than the usual "testing" with a few literal questions. Studies of effective comprehension instruction suggest the following approaches.

Assistance With the Immediate Text. Certain culminating experiences strengthen immediate understandings.

1. *Asking questions: general principles and procedures.* For some teachers, a comprehension "program" hinges mainly on asking questions. Morrison (1968), for example, found that teachers ask as many as two questions per minute in a typical reading session. Is all this questioning really useful for improving comprehension? The answer depends (a) on the quality of the teacher's "asking behaviors" and (b) on the types of questions asked.

Asking behavior refers to how teachers foster the environment for question-and-answer sessions. For example, allowing active turn-taking by all members of a group has a beneficial effect on learning (Anderson, Wilkinson, & Mason, 1991). Some good ways and poor ways to set the question-and-answering climate in remedial and clinical reading programs are listed in Table 11–4.

LEARNING FROM TEXT

Verbal Rehearsal. After reading Table 11–4 try to specify, in your own words, some effective question-asking behaviors.

TABLE 11–4 *Asking Questions of Students*

Effective Asking Behaviors	Poor Asking Behaviors
Give students time to think before answering. Also, if they hesitate in mid-answer, be patient.	Demand immediate responses. Call on another student when an immediate response is not forthcoming. Allow other students to sit with hands raised while the first student is trying to think.
When a student gives a correct answer, take it a step further—ask the student to explain how he or she knows it is the correct answer.	When a correct answer is given, always move immediately to the next question.
Ask all students to respond and to respond as often as possible, during any given session.	Only call on students who volunteer.
Require all students to pay attention during answering by another student. When appropriate, involve other students in the answering—for example, by saying something like, "Phillip, do you agree with Judy?" or, "How would you support the correct answer that DeMerrill has already given?"	When one student is answering a question, allow other students to be off-task (looking around the room, talking, working on something else).
If a student doesn't understand the question, rephrase it, break it down into parts, or in some other way assist the student in arriving at the correct response. Researchers (e.g., Guszak, 1967) have found that wrong responses often result because teachers ask questions that are too difficult.	If a student doesn't understand the question, blame the student and call on another person.
When an incorrect answer is given, take time to *teach*: Model how *you* would determine the answer; ask the student to think of a previous answer; explain; give additional information; illustrate. Teach the student *how* to answer questions.	When an incorrect answer is given, immediately call on another student.

The quality of students' comprehension performance is also influenced by the types of questions asked. Obviously, important rather than trivial questions should be the focus. Avoid questions such as "What color was Mary's dress?" Such questions focus on irrelevant details. Emphasize information of significance.

Furthermore, consider the issue of literal questions versus higher-level questions. **Literal-level comprehension** refers to the act or process of understanding information that is directly stated in the material one is reading. For example, if the story states that "Pam was a frog in the class play" and the teacher asks, "What role did Pam have in the play?" the teacher is asking students to respond on a literal level. Sometimes literal-level comprehension is important, and it often provides the basis for higher-level interpretations.

Students are exposed to literal-level questions more than any other type. Guszak (1967) and several other researchers have observed and tabulated teachers' questions. Consistently, researchers have found that about 70% of questions asked by teachers are literal.

Since students have much practice with this question type, one might wonder why a student would have difficulty responding to literal comprehension tasks. If this is the case, first consider if the student has been placed in material that is too difficult, and select alternative reading material. Second, consider whether the student lacks familiarity with the topic, and give special attention to building background if this is so.

Of course, an emphasis should be placed on higher-level questions as well. More students of average ability and below-average achievement encounter greater obstacles with higher-order comprehension questions than with literal ones. Our case study student, Frederick, is a good example. Frederick's attention to literal details was not as well developed as it should have been, but his major impediments arose from his lack of ability to make complex interpretations of the text he read.

Every 4 years when the United States National Assessment of Educational Progress (NAEP) is administered to students in grades 4, 8, and 12, it is found that students show less proficiency with higher-order comprehension skills than with literal interpretations. Therefore, a major concern of teachers of both average readers and students with reading disabilities has come to be higher-level understandings of written text.

Higher-level comprehension involves use of interpretive thinking and, in some cases, evaluative or creative responses. It includes: (a) drawing conclusions and inferences, (b) determining the main ideas of passages, (c) determining cause-and-effect relationships, (d) following a sequence of events, (e) using imagery, and (f) using critical reading skills.

Many different types of questions should be asked about any one story. Higher-level questions ask students to call on their background information, encourage them to seek out the important information conveyed by a story (main ideas), stimulate them to recall directly stated facts, and expand their vocabularies.

Since students must learn how to recall answers (with the book closed) and, as well, to locate answers, practice should be given in answering questions involving both types of tasks.

2. *Motivating effort for higher-level thinking.* On occasion, games may provide an alternative to traditional questioning after stories and may motivate reluctant learners to expend the effort necessary for higher-level thinking. Effective comprehension games involve written text and require concentration on in-depth thinking.

Figure 11–5 shows a board game that focuses on higher-order questions. To play this game, students use a spinner with 1, 2, and 3 on its face. After spinning, the student moves his or her game piece according to the number of spaces indicated by the spinner. The square on which a student lands directs him or her to draw from one of three piles of cards: *Question Cards*, identified on the game board by a question mark, contain questions that require a conclusion or an inference to be drawn; *Creativity Cards* ask for a creative answer; and *Evaluation Cards* request an evaluative response. Sample questions for each set of cards are shown in Figure 11–5. Students attempt to answer the question on each card they draw, and then the next student takes a turn. Some questions, such as those that require students to make judgments about character traits or to give an opinion about the most important event in a story, while termed "evaluative responses," also involve inferring and drawing conclusions. Teachers should require students to defend their answers with reasoning based on text information or their own background knowledge. As can be seen from examining the questions in Figure 11–5, this specific game is generic in nature and could be used after any story.

> When engaged in "grand conversations" about a story, students exchange views about the narrative, with students taking the lead rather than relying on teacher questions.

3. *Combining "grand conversations" with teacher questions.* Studies with average readers show that students can involve themselves in higher-level comprehension tasks without teacher guidance. For example, McGee (1992) had students in regular classrooms engage in "grand conversations" after a story had been read, conversations in which students took the lead without a teacher's questions for the first half of the sessions. The grand conversations consisted of exchanges among the learners about their responses to a narrative. During this part of the lesson, teachers did not launch subjects for discussion; they simply asked, "What do you think?" following the reading of the story and then made encouraging remarks, such as "That's a good idea" or "Interesting comment," as students talked about the book in an open-ended fashion.

The resulting discussions revealed inferences and evaluations that were primarily reader-focused reflections in which students offered personal reactions to the narrative, including beliefs, evaluations, and emotions. Voicing reactions certainly is important, particularly for engendering interest in reading. During the second half of the session, the discussion centered on an interpretative question that the teacher asked to summon higher-order thinking about the meaning of the narrative as a whole. This question was text-focused and attempted to promote inferences, identification of the importance of characters, events, and themes, or, in general, story understanding above the literal level. While student-led discussion did produce interpretations in all conversations, the teacher-posed question drew higher percentages of interpretive responses than open-ended discussions. Supplementing student-initiated responses with teacher-guided thinking appears to have positive effects with students of average ability and would likely prove to be true with students with reading delays.

Development of Strategies That Can Be Used With a Wide Variety of Texts. Certain culminating experiences can strengthen immediate and future comprehension.

1. *Asking questions: general principles and procedures.* Teachers should consider particulars about asking questions that apply to all texts read, not just the text with which students are engaged at the moment. If learners are having little luck with producing suitable responses, there are two questions you might ask.

FIGURE 11–5 *A Board Game That Can Be Used With Any Story to Encourage Higher-Level Comprehension*

Sample Question Cards	Sample Creativity Cards	Sample Evaluation Cards
1. Did anything happen in the story that was unbelievable? Why or why not? If so, what?	1. How would you have solved the problem in the story differently?	1. What character do you like best? Why?
2. Who do you think was the second most important character in the story? Why?	2. What do you think might have happened to the main character after the story was over?	2. What do you think was the one most important thing the main character did. Why do you think so?
3. What kinds of feelings do you think the main character had at different times in the story?	3. How would this story have been different if it had occurred 100 years in the past or 100 years in the future?	3. Choose one character. Tell what kind of person you think this character really is. Why?
4. Choose one of the characters. Tell something this character learned.	4. Make up an ending for the story that is completely different from the one the author wrote.	4. Did you like the story? Why or why not?
5. Was the story fiction or nonfiction? Cite three things from the story to support your answer.	5. Add a character to the story. What would he or she do to change the events in the story?	5. Tell the two events in the story that you think were most interesting. Why?

The first is, "Do the students know they are supposed to be attending to the meaning of the material?" Some students in remedial programs look upon reading as a word-pronunciation task, as in "I said all the words right this time. You mean you wanted me to pay attention to what the words meant, too?" When readers have this attitude, a teacher's effort must be aimed at getting them to understand that the purpose of reading is to gain meaning. For a time, everything these students read should be followed by oral questions posed by the teacher. In addition, specific activities aimed at comprehension of written material—not just word recognition—should be used.

If students have written their answers to questions that have been posed, a second query should be, "Does the problem lie in the form of students' written responses, and not in their actual understanding?" If students' comprehension is evaluated based on written replies (e.g., on workbook pages and to questions found at the ends of chapters), the teacher must take care to separate their skills and their motivation in writing out an answer from their true understanding of the material. When left to their own devices to read and respond independently, some students read the questions before reading the material, search through the material until they find a sentence containing several words also found in the question, and mechanically copy down that sentence for their reply, whether it is a logical answer to the question or not. Suppose, for example, that the question was, "How did the rooster get caught by the fox?" A student may find a sentence in the story that says, "The rooster hoped that he would not get caught by the fox." Note that seven words in this statement are identical to words in the question. Therefore, although this sentence does not respond to the question at all, the student may write it down as his or her reply.

To help students dispense with this unproductive habit, teachers can arrange for group discussions, using questions and statements such as these.

a. What did Mr. Hastings do the next morning?
   1. Mr. Hastings could hardly wait for the next morning.
   2. At dawn Mr. Hastings got out his golf clubs.
b. Describe these two kinds of stores: retail stores and wholesale stores.
   1. Retail stores sell to people like you and me, but wholesale stores sell to people who own retail stores.
   2. There are two kinds of stores: retail stores and wholesale stores.

The teacher reads the questions. Students are instructed to underline those words in each of the possible answers that are identical to words in the question. Count the number of such words for each possible response. Point out the right reply and discuss why the other answer does not resolve the question, despite the number of words the question and the statement have in common. Have the students note that the number of identical words is not necessarily relevant when answering a question.

Another issue regarding evaluation of written responses to comprehension questions is brought out in McCormick's (1992) study of erroneous replies to inference questions. One of the foremost causes for getting answers wrong was that students' written statements did not convey their intended meaning. Because the poor readers in this investigation also had somewhat deficient writing skills—a not untypical circumstance for students with reading difficulties—they left words out of sentences, used words that did not mean what they intended, wrote seriously incomplete statements, and evidenced other similar problems, so that what they started out to write was not stated—even when they appeared to know the correct answers if asked to discuss their meanings orally. This raises questions about the wisdom of evaluating understanding of a text based on written responses for students who lack sufficiently developed writing skills. It also spotlights the need for functional writing competencies to be treated in literacy programs. The NAEP reported that teachers are relying less on multiple-choice questions to judge comprehension (likely a good thing!) and more on having students write paragraphs about what they read. However, it seems that some caution should be exercised with this latter policy of using writing to assess comprehension, particularly with delayed readers. Greater emphases on discussion and reflective observation may be advisable to make accurate evaluations of comprehension.

Teachers can use story maps to devise good questions.

2. *Using story maps.* Beck, Omanson; and McKeown (1982) suggest that teachers use story maps to develop good questions. A **story map** is a sequential listing of the important elements of a narrative and is based on simplified versions of what linguists call **story grammars.** A story grammar is, in effect, a list of "rules" for writing narratives (Fitzgerald, 2002). The "grammar" of narratives consists of the events, ideas, and motivations that direct the movement of stories. Interestingly, the same elements are found to occur in stories across many countries and cultures.

A story usually has the following components:

- characters
- setting
- a problem and a goal to resolve it
- events to solve the problem
- achievement of the goal

Having a sense of this typical story structure is believed to aid understanding and recall. Before writing questions, teachers use this list of story elements as a guide to determine the story map for the specific selection to be read by students. For instance, here is a story map for *The Three Little Pigs.* (There are various versions of this famous narrative. I will use a kinder rendition in which no one gets eaten or boiled.)

- *Characters:* Three pigs and a wolf
- *Settings:* Straw, stick, and brick houses
- *Problem and goal to resolve it:* The wolf keeps bugging these pigs by blowing down their houses, and this has to be stopped!
- *Events to solve the problem:* When the wolf blows down the straw house in which they are living, they build a stronger one of sticks.
- *Achievement of the goal:* When the stick house is also huffed and puffed down, the pigs finally realize they must build a *very* strong house and one of bricks does the trick.

One or more questions is written for each element in a story's map. The questions should be sequenced in the order in which each aspect occurs in the story. This does not mean that only literal questions based on directly stated information are used; higher-level questions should also be written about each element.

In the study conducted by Beck et al. (1982), when questions systematically focused on central story content in this way, students showed better comprehension. In fact, the less-skilled readers who answered questions based on story maps did as well on comprehension performance as skilled readers who answered less-focused questions found in basal reader manuals.

What is more, the best news was that this technique had transfer value. That is, after students had experiences with answering questions based on story maps,

FIGURE 11–6 *Sample Story Frame for Cinderella by Charles Perrault*

The story takes place _in a make-believe kingdom where Cinderella_
lives with her stepmother and sisters in a nice house .
Cinderella, a stepsister, is a character in the story
who _has to do all the chores around the house like a servant_ .
The fairy godmother is another character in the
story who _does magic and helps Cinderella go to the ball_ .
A problem occurs when _Cinderella is hurrying home at midnight and_
drops one of her glass slippers at the ball .
After that, _the handsome prince searches in the kingdom for_
a young lady who can put on the glass slipper and have it fit,
and _the shoe doesn't fit any of the young ladies who try it on_ .
The problem is solved when _Cinderella tries on the glass slipper,_
and it fits perfectly .
The story ends with _the handsome prince and Cinderella getting_
married right away, and they live happily ever after .

Source: Macon, James M., Bewell, Diane, & Vogt, MaryEllen. (1991). *Responses to Literature Grades K-8.,* Newark, DE: International Reading Association. Reprinted with permission of James M. Macon and the International Reading Association.

they showed better comprehension of new stories where the story maps were not used. Thus, although teachers' use of story maps to develop questions has a decided effect on comprehension of the immediate text, this procedure also influences development of mental sets learners may enlist with a variety of narratives.

A different way to structure a story map is by using "story frames." See Figure 11–6 for an example of a story frame.

LEARNING FROM TEXT

Applying What You've Learned. How would you devise questions based on a story map about a narrative students are going to read? You were given an example based on a well-known story, "The Three Little Pigs." Try one yourself: Select another story and think how you would consider that story in regard to the story map components specified.

3. *Retelling as a route to understanding story structure.* Having readers retell a selection after they have read it is usually thought of as an assessment technique; however, some researchers have used this procedure instructionally. Morrow, Sisco, and Smith (1992) taught students with learning disabilities how to retell, and one of the outcomes was increased awareness of story structure.

In this program, learners in an experimental group had training in retelling stories from picture books. For all 12 books used, the teacher provided guidance by helping students tell the narratives in the correct sequence and, in addition, asking specific questions to focus their retellings on elements related to settings, plot episodes, resolution, and theme. During the retelling of the first four stories, students used the book, letting the pictures assist them. For the next four, they used props that represented characters and events as they retold. The last four narratives were retold without the book or props to support them. In contrast, students in a control group drew pictures about each of the 12 books after story reading.

When posttests were administered using another story, learners in the experimental group performed significantly better when asked to retell the story than the control-group students. Students who had experienced mediated story retellings included more information on setting, plot episodes, and resolution and sequenced the story more appropriately as well. There was no difference in the two groups' abilities to give the theme of the story, admittedly a difficult concept. As another part of the posttest, children's listening comprehension was measured; although there was not a difference on general questions, on those related to important story structure components, again the experimental group scored higher.

It appears that use of mediated story retellings has potential. When teachers ask students to retell as a culminating event after narratives are read, the activity can be made instructionally richer by directing their focus to sequence and to significant story elements. That format is preferable to less structured retelling that may be used merely as an assessment of ability to read with comprehension.

4. *Clarifying question-answer relationships (QARs).* Different strategies are needed for answering different kinds of questions. To distinguish task requirements for various question types, Raphael (1986) devised a way to teach students what she called QARs, or question-answer relationships. In this procedure, four subtypes of QARs are described and practiced with students.

    a. *Right There* (or what teachers would call literal questions). Students are told that for these question types the answer is right there in the book, often stated in one sentence. For example:

       Question: "Where did Jimmy find the missing jewel?"

       Answer as stated in the text: "Suddenly, Jimmy saw the missing jewel hanging in the chandelier among the pieces of carved glass."

    b. *Think and Search* (questions that require a conclusion to be drawn). Students are told that the information needed to answer this type of question is found in the story, but statements given in more than one place must be linked; using these accounts, it is possible to conclude an appropriate answer. Teachers often describe this as being a "detective," finding and matching clues to reach a solution.

    c. *The Author and You* (questions for which inferences must be drawn based on text details plus the reader's prior knowledge). For this QAR, learners are told that some of the information is found in the text, but some must come from information they already know; the two must be connected to determine the answer. Such an explanation is an important revelation for many students who have wondered where in the book those other kids were finding the answers they gave because they had looked and looked to no avail.

    d. *On Your Own* (several question types are implied, e.g., evaluative questions, background questions, and creative questions). This category of QARs describes those questions for which most of the response, though associated with the text, is derived from the reader's own experiences or feelings (e.g., *evaluative question:* "Which character did you think was most interesting?"; *background question:* "In a moment we're going to read a story about some animals that showed up in the backyard of a family who lived near a woods. Other than pets, what animals have you seen in your yard?"; *creative question:* "In *Sarah, Plain and Tall,* Sarah's life changes when she moves to a place where she had not lived before and marries a man she had not known previously. How might her life have been different if she had not made those decisions?").

5. *Focusing questions on complex reading strategies.* Hansen (1981) developed a procedure that significantly improved the inferential comprehension of average readers. This procedure was also tested by McCormick and Hill (1984) in 12 classes of students having reading disabilities, with the same positive results. The procedure, called the Question Technique, was based on the hypothesis that students typically do poorly in drawing inferences because they get very little practice with this type of comprehension. (Recall that several researchers have found that about 70% of the questions teachers ask are literal.)

Throughout the several weeks that these research projects were being conducted, students in the experimental group were asked only inference questions after they read stories in their daily lessons. In contrast, students in a control group were asked only one inference question for every five literal questions, a typical practice in many classrooms. In weekly comprehension tests, the students in the experimental group scored significantly higher on inferential comprehension than did the control group.

An implication for reading teachers is that they must provide their students with much more practice in drawing inferences than is usually given. For students who have a weakness in this area, teachers might select only those questions from commercial materials that require students to infer, or they may write their own inference questions to supplement these materials.

One reason students may be exposed infrequently to questions that require them to use inferences or to draw a conclusion is that such questions are often hard to write! It is even more difficult to think of a good inferential question on the spur of the moment to ask orally while working with a group. Therefore, these types of questions should be planned in advance to be ready for use.

> For many students, spending time thoroughly discussing a few higher-level questions may be instructionally more valuable than answering numerous quick and easy questions.

Another reason teachers may ask fewer higher-level questions is that eliciting appropriate answers often takes considerably more time than is demanded for answers to literal questions. When a literal question is asked, students can usually answer quickly. Even when an incorrect answer is given, students may not need much time to locate the correct answer in the text. Questions requiring students to draw conclusions and inferences are not handled so quickly. Students may need to be reminded of, and directed in, an appropriate comprehension strategy. In addition, when a wrong response is given, it is not so easily resolved. Much attention and time may be required to sort out the relevant information in the text, discussions of applicable background experiences may have to ensue, and so on. As a result, a teacher may cover 10 or so literal questions in the same amount of time as only 2 or 3 higher-level questions. Teachers must recognize that the challenges presented by inferential questions are not valid reasons for avoiding them. Spending time in thoughtful, prolonged development of higher-level strategies is one of the most valuable forms of comprehension instruction (Allington, 2001). For many students, time spent in answering 2 or 3 higher-order questions thoughtfully may be more instructionally useful than responding to 10 or more literal questions.

6. *Using character maps.* Character maps are heuristics that provide an additional way to focus students on making inferences. Understanding characters' attitudes and traits opens windows to interpreting actions that occur in stories. Typically authors tell the reader certain snippets of detail about a character, but reveal other attributes in more subtle ways through actions, conversations, and thoughts expressed openly as inner dialogue for the reader to "listen" in on.

Understanding qualities of characters when the information is not directly stated as facts, but instead must be inferred, can be challenging for at-risk readers. Richards and Gipe (1993) had good results using character maps to address this need.

After students read a story, the teacher produced a "map" with four circles on it, each with a different label. The first, marked "Facts About the Character," was used to record statements from the text about one of the main personalities in the narrative. This was a literal-level task.

The teacher modeled ways to determine information to write in the second circle, labeled "What I Know About the Character's Actions." To do so, the teacher helped students point out places in the text where actions were described and showed how these were clues that could help them infer something about the person. For instance, if a narrative describes the character as preferring to spend his Saturdays helping his father who is a carpenter instead of playing games with other boys on his street, the teacher might say, "I suspect from Andy's actions that he likes to build things, because on Saturdays when I have a choice about what I do, I spend my time doing things I like." They would write information based on this inference in the second circle along with inferences offered by the students based on other character actions.

The third circle was tagged "What I Know About the Character's Conversation" and the fourth, "What I Know About the Character's Thoughts." These circles in the map were filled in similarly, using text dialogue and information about thoughts to infer character traits and qualities that the author had not directly discussed.

This exercise teaches readers conventions authors use to reveal characters and provides the necessary practice to draw inferences needed to interpret underlying meanings. After several sessions of collaborative effort, Richards and Gipe found readers were ready to do this on their own. They also recommend extending the project to comparing characters within and between stories and for learners to use in planning the stories they write themselves.

Reflections
Which sections of the present chapter were the hardest for you to understand? Based on what you have learned about comprehension, what do you think were the reasons those segments were more challenging for you than others? Based on what you know about comprehension now, what could you do about it?

LEARNING FROM TEXT

Applying What You've Learned. Consider the questions in the Reflections section.

12

Comprehension of Expository Text

During reciprocal teaching, the teacher first models strategies. Then students in turn assume the role of teacher, instructing their peers as the group works through a section of text.

*I*n the last chapter, the discussion of comprehension centered on one text type—narrative. In this chapter, we will explore instructional approaches for helping students read and learn from expository text, including a bit of attention to studying expository materials. Finally, to tie up the two chapters on comprehension, we will end with additional thoughts about metacognition, since use of metacognitive strategies applies to both the reading of narrative and the reading of exposition.

LEARNING FROM TEXT

Note Taking. The subsequent section expands on information from the last chapter regarding differences between narrative and expository text. Based on the following section, write down several reasons why students often have more difficulty with expository text, noting each succinctly, in a phrase or sentence or even in a single word.

EXPOSITORY TEXT

Expository text—that is, informational text—is written to communicate information. Its main goal is to transmit new facts and ideas.

Textbooks read by elementary, middle school, high school, and college students for content subjects and courses are examples of expository material. In the workplace, adults read training manuals and other kinds of informational text. In everyday life, instances of nonnarrative reading abound, from reading newspapers and business letters to deciphering tax forms.

For several reasons, expository material often is more challenging than narrative, story-type text. One reason relates to **text structure,** which refers to the way concepts are connected in written language to impart meaning. See Figure 12–1 for some text structures found in informational material. Certain text structures occur in both narrative and expository text, but others are unique to expository, including embedded definitions, explanations of technical processes, sequences of logical argument, or procedural descriptions (such as how to conduct a science experiment). Expository structures are commonly more difficult to comprehend than structures used in narrative material.

A second source of difficulty relates to background information (remember schemata?). Expository text is written to convey new information; therefore, it stands to reason that readers may have less prior knowledge to bring to bear on many selections than they do for stories. A third factor is specialized vocabulary found in most textbooks but not in the typical student's oral language. And, fourth, to complicate matters, individuals are not only to comprehend, but often to retain much of the information in expository selections.

Furthermore, these complexities are exacerbated by readability levels of some content area texts written at levels higher than the level for which they are intended. In such cases, the problem is in the material, not the student, when comprehension difficulties arise.

FIGURE 12–1 *Some Types of Expository Text Structures*

> Analysis
> Cause and effect
> Classification
> Comparison and contrast
> Definition
> Description
> Enumeration
> Identification
> Illustration
> Problem and solution
> Sequence

Then there is the problem of **density.** Frequently textbooks present many facts in a small amount of material (a good example is the section you are reading right now), resulting in a heavy concept load and an intensity of reading unnecessary when reading stories. In addition, abstract concepts are discussed; symbols and abbreviations must be read (e.g., in math or science books); and some students lack interest in the material they must read. These problems exist for all learners, but are particularly vexing for poor readers.

Beginning at about fourth grade, students are required to read more expository materials than narratives. Since students we work with find these materials especially demanding, teaching them strategies for reading this text type is an important responsibility. Table 12–1 lists typical characteristics of content area texts.

LEARNING FROM TEXT

Using Illustrative Aids. Read Table 12–1. What is one main idea you could state about all of the information in this table? Based on the table, what could you say about rates of reading in regard to expository text? Are there any teaching ideas in this table you could use with your students?

COMPREHENSION INSTRUCTION: EXPOSITORY TEXT

NCLB
READING FIRST

The key principles of excellent comprehension instruction hold regardless of whether the texts are expository or narrative. For example, explicit teaching, fostering strategic reading, and that bottom-line item—instruction that is instructive (and not merely flimsy question asking)—are imperative. Furthermore, many of the same areas of concern, such as selecting important ideas and drawing conclusions, are similar in reading expository materials and narrative texts, and a number of the instructional methods introduced in Chapter 11 are applicable here. What this chapter will do is report additional teaching suggestions that research has offered when focus has been directed particularly on expository texts. Many of these, of course, can be adapted to narratives. Students should use strategies for constructing meaning *before, during,* and *after* reading (see Table 12–2).

TABLE 12–1 *Content Area Texts: Characteristics and Teaching Implications*

Social Studies

1. Embedded directions

Texts often have directions to follow within a paragraph (e.g., "The Amazon is the longest river in South America. *Turn now to page 67 and trace the Amazon's route through Brazil*").

Teaching implications: Ask delayed readers to follow these directions rather than ignore them. Carrying out tasks specified by the direction will help students visualize, conceptualize, and remember text information. Do this *with* them so they experience the benefits.

2. Pictures, graphs, and maps

Teaching implications: Show students how to use these illustrative materials (Ruddell, 2006). Graphs are relatively easy to read, but many students overlook this source of information. Don't assume that students know how to use map legends or how to learn from maps. Teach them how.

3. Specialized vocabulary

Teaching implications: Encourage classroom teachers to select some words for preteaching before the selection is read. Follow other suggestions given in Chapter 10.

4. Cause-and-effect patterns

Teaching implications: This pattern occurs more frequently in social studies than in other subject areas. Follow suggestions given later in this chapter.

5. Comparative data (e.g., the text asks students to compare the climate, population, and major sources of income in Canada and Mexico)

Teaching implications: To aid recall, show students how to prepare charts on "likenesses and differences." Have them share their charts.

6. Time sequences

Teaching implications: Encourage classroom teachers to have students develop a time line throughout the year in conjunction with their study of topics such as American or world history. Displaying the time line prominently in the classroom will help students gain a perspective about time sequences.

Science

1. Specialized vocabulary

Teaching implications: See the suggestion under "Social Studies." Also, have students in your reading class keep a vocabulary notebook of content-related words, divided by topics such as science or social studies. The reading teacher can obtain textbooks from regular classroom teachers and help students select words for upcoming lessons to discuss, list, define, and illustrate in this notebook.

2. Broad, abstract concepts

Teaching implications: Writers of science texts sometimes incorrectly assume students have more background information than they do. In addition, abstract ideas often are presented without sufficient concrete examples. Alert classroom teachers to these problems and suggest that films and other audiovisuals be used to supplement students' existing background knowledge.

3. Density

Teaching implications: Science material is noted for its density—more facts line for line than in other texts. Since comprehension requires understanding of main ideas as well as each idea that supports this statement, teach poor readers how to prepare simple outlines after reading.

4. Explanations of technical processes (e.g., the workings of an internal combustion engine are explained)

Teaching implications: Students should be told that technical information must be read slowly. (Reading rates used for story-type reading are seldom appropriate.) Since these texts often have diagrams, help students develop the habit of studying these diagrams before, during, and after reading the explanatory passage.

TABLE 12–1 *Content Area Texts: Characteristics and Teaching Implications* *(continued)*

Science (*continued*)

5. Cause-and-effect patterns

Teaching implications: Use suggestions found later in this chapter. Working with students to help them conduct experiments suggested in science books not only concretely illustrates cause-and-effect relationships but also gives practice in following directions, another skill needed for science reading.

6. Classification

Teaching implications: This writing pattern categorizes information, such as dividing animals into mammals, birds, amphibians, and so on. Teach students the concept of categorization, that is, how some ideas or facts can be subgroups of others. Outlining is also helpful.

Mathematics

1. Specialized vocabulary

Teaching implications: Specialized vocabulary is a characteristic of all three types of texts discussed in this table (social studies, science, and mathematics). The most prevalent difficulty for poor readers within all content areas is that of dealing with difficult or unusual vocabulary. In math, the vocabulary is even more specialized. How often, for example, do students use words such as *minuend* and *subtrahend* in their everyday oral language? Context clues don't help much in identifying vocabulary in math texts. All of this implies that direct teaching of mathematics vocabulary is needed, in terms of both word identification and meaning. If the classroom teacher does not do this, the reading teacher can assume this responsibility.

2. Symbols and abbreviations

Teaching implications: Delayed readers must be taught to read symbols and abbreviations embedded in text. For example, "Solve this problem: $3 + 4 = \Delta$" is read, "Solve this problem: Three *plus* four *equals what*" "3% of $39.14 is _____" is read, "Three *percent* of thirty-nine *dollars* and fourteen *cents* is *what*" "$A = \pi r^2$" is read, "*The area equals pi times the radius squared.*" In addition, abbreviations such as *in., ft.,* and *yd.* must be read in problems such as "How many feet of fencing are needed to enclose a garden that is 48 ft. 3 in. long and 28 ft. 7 in. wide?" While these reading tasks may seem quite obvious to most, for students who think reading is what they do in stories, such tasks may be quite difficult.

3. Density

Teaching implications: Math material is characterized by density. Readers cannot skip unknown words and still obtain meaning, as is sometimes possible with narrative writing. In addition, the reading rate must be slow.

4. Unusual writing style

Teaching implications: Vos (cited in Ferguson & Fairburn, 1985) suggested that one language-related factor affecting performance on math story problems is that their writing styles are different from other prose. Practice can be given to familiarize students with this writing style. In Botel and Wirtz's research (cited in Kahn & Wirtz, 1982), students who practiced making up their own story problems did significantly better on these types of math applications than did those who lacked such practice.

Source: Compiled from information in Ferguson & Fairburn, 1985; Kahn & Wirtz, 1982; McCormick, unpublished materials; Piercey, 1976; Ruddell, 2006; Santeusanio, 1983; and N. B. Smith, 1967.

LEARNING FROM TEXT

Previewing. Use Table 12–2 to preview instructional procedures you will read about in the upcoming sections.

TABLE 12–2   *Examples of Comprehension Instruction for Expository Material Before, During, and After Reading Text*

Before

Assistance with the immediate text
- Employing K-W-L
- Using audiovisuals before reading
- Prequestioning

Development of strategies that can be used with a wide variety of texts
- Providing prepractice with cause-and-effect patterns
- Providing prepractice with sequence patterns

During

Assistance with the immediate text
- Using a hierarchical summarization strategy
- Inserting questions in text

Development of strategies that can be used with a wide variety of texts
- Engaging students in reciprocal teaching
- Using schematic diagrams and charts of text structure

After

Assistance with the immediate text
- Instituting learning journals
- Generating questions

Development of strategies that can be used with a wide variety of texts
- Teaching students to summarize
- Helping students compose extended summaries
- Looking back (text reinspection)
- Teaching critical reading concepts

Introductory Guidance

As with comprehension instruction with narrative materials, teacher guidance with expository reading tasks should begin with activities that occur *before* the text is read.

Assistance With the Immediate Text.   It may be even more critical to build new knowledge sets and to evoke students' existing background knowledge for reading expository text than it is for narratives, since there is likely to be more that is new to them (Cote & Goldman, 2004). See the instructional suggestions that follow.

   1. *Employing K-W-L.* The acronym *K-W-L* represents words for steps of an instructional strategy designed to activate prior knowledge and to promote a mental set for expository text so that the reader can interpret and construct meanings (Ogle, 1986, 2004). This teaching model develops active reading by

involving readers in three steps. The first two are undertaken before students read the targeted text. The last occurs after reading:

a. *Assessing What I **Know.*** Students brainstorm what they already know about the subject they will encounter in the selection to be read. Their ideas are classified into categories.
b. *Determining What I Want to **Know.*** With the teacher's assistance, students create questions they want to have answered when they read the text. They also predict what they expect the author to convey.
c. *Checking What I Learned From My **Reading.*** To reinforce information gained, after the material has been read, readers examine what they learned by organizing new knowledge into outlines, semantic maps, and the like.

Activating background knowledge is an important key for effective comprehension of content area text (Ruddell, 2006).

With students who have reading delays, it is effective to have them view audiovisuals *before* they read expository text about the same topic.

2. *Using audiovisuals before reading.* Teachers often use videos and DVDs during study of a topic. However, for students who have comprehension difficulties, it is more effective to allow them to view these audiovisuals *before* they read the written text. The same is often true with computer programs on related subjects.

Because of the complexity of content area materials, reading teachers may provide prereading experiences for assignments their students face in regular classrooms. For instance, when the geography teacher says students will read a chapter about South America soon, in the reading class you may show and discuss a video about this topic, working to build background—and vocabulary— that students lack. Follow up by having students write about word meanings and concepts they have learned.

3. *Prequestioning.* There has been some interest in the use of text questions or teacher's questions *before* students read expository material. A number of educators have seen this as a way to boost comprehension, rather than to merely test it, as is often done with questions used after reading.

Questions asked before students read expository text may boost comprehension rather than merely testing it, as is sometimes the case when questions are only asked afterward.

In prequestioning, teachers have used the questions commonly found at the ends of chapters in content area books, examining these with learners beforehand. Or they have prepared questions of their own about details and impressions they want their students to comprehend and retain. Sometimes teachers transform the questions into a small pretest; after reading, the students address the same questions as a posttest. The belief is that readers' prior awareness of the kinds of information considered to be important will help focus their attention and, thus, support meaning construction. In other words, if you want students to learn something, tell them what it is!

Tierney and Cunningham (1984) reviewed research related to effects of teacher or text prequestions and concluded that prequestions enhance learning in the following circumstances. Prequestions can be beneficial if:

a. the text is difficult to understand;
b. the questions are written about the most significant information in the selection;
c. the concern is that students learn the *specific* information targeted by the prequestions.

In contrast, if the goal is to obtain a more global sense of the information presented, use of prequestions may have a narrowing effect. That is, learners may center on the items in the prequestions to the detriment of gaining overall implications of the text.

Development of Strategies That Can Be Used With a Wide Variety of Texts. Heightening students' awareness of common text structures and patterns is useful with expository text. A number of studies have supported this supposition (e.g., Armbruster, Anderson, & Meyer, 1991; Armbruster, Anderson, & Ostertag, 1989).

Promoting familiarity with text structure includes helping students see how authors organize material into key ideas and supporting statements, how these are sequenced to explain a point, and how they are interrelated (Moss, 2004). Many good readers note and use text structure either intuitively or as the result of reading extensively. Poor readers, on the other hand, do not seem to recognize how the organization of material helps them comprehend, unless they receive direct instruction in the special ways written text is structured to convey ideas.

Because interpretation of expository text relies heavily on recognizing and understanding how to follow certain patterns, some attention to the most prevalent patterns *before* students read provides knowledge that may be used later during reading.

1. *Providing prepractice with the cause-and-effect pattern.* The cause-and-effect pattern is found recurrently in history books, geography books, and science books; it is also found in narratives. This pattern, hence, will be used as our first example of providing prepractice activities directly related to familiarizing students with text structure. Determining causes and effects involves understanding the "why" in relationships and the results of actions and events. In some cases, the significant point to determine is the cause, in others it is the effect, and in still others it is both.

Determining causes and effects can be difficult for students because a number of other higher-level comprehension skills underlie this process. For example, students must be able to draw a conclusion, infer, determine the main idea, predict outcomes, and follow a sequence of events.

To complicate matters, sometimes a passage may relate a single outcome that has more than one cause or a single cause that results in more than one effect. Or, sometimes a chain reaction is described in which a cause produces an effect, but that effect in turn becomes a cause resulting in another effect, and so on.

```
Cause ──────────→ Effect
                    │
                    ↓
              (Cause) ──────────→ Effect
                                    │
                                    ↓
                              (Cause) ──────────→ Effect
```

Furthermore, in longer pieces of material, the cause may be stated in one paragraph and the effect or effects in another.

Authors often use signal words to alert readers to cause-and-effect relationships; words such as *because, if, therefore, so, so that, since, then, as a result of, unless, hence,* and *in order that* can help students see the tie between causes and effects. However, sometimes no signal words are used.

There are additional reasons why this comprehension skill is complex. Sometimes both the cause and the effect are directly stated, but sometimes

In some materials, only the cause *or* effect is directly stated, and the student must infer the other.

although they are both stated, the relationship between the two is not. Therefore, readers must find the relationship themselves. Finally, there are times when only the cause or the effect is stated, but the other is implicit and, therefore, must be inferred by the reader. Students need practice in dealing with passages that exemplify all three cases.

Some specific instructional suggestions for providing prepractice in recognizing the cause-and-effect concept and patterns follow.

a. Begin with causes and effects students already know to promote awareness of the cause-effect concept. Write several "causes" on the chalkboard and have students tell you the effects. List these effects. For example, you may write these sentences:

Water spills in your lap.
A car runs out of gas.

Your students may suggest these effects:

Your clothes get wet.
The car stops.

Then, reverse the process, write a series of familiar effects on the board, and have students suggest causes.

b. Use television programs students watch at home to emphasize the concept of cause-and-effect relationships. Discuss situations in a TV show routinely viewed by your students that indicate these relationships. In addition, bring in examples of statements from commercials that specify cause and effect, such as "strained muscles due to exercise" (cause) and "aching shoulders and neck" (effect). "Taking Whizzy-Fizzy Aspirins (cause) relieves the pain" (effect).

c. Prepare cards, some with causes on them and some with effects. Mix the cards. Have students place the appropriate cards under a label that says *Causes* and then have them match the correct effect card to each, placing these under a label that says *Effects*. For example,

Causes	*Effects*
forest fires	destroy thousands of trees in a short time
meat kept in warm places	often spoils

d. Next, select causes and effects in text. Have students read paragraphs that contain causes and effects. As with the preceding exercises, these should at first be based on experiences familiar to students. Have students locate the statements of cause and underline these in red. Have them do the same with statements of effects, underlining them in blue.

e. Follow the suggestion in item *d*, but this time give paragraphs in which only a cause is explicitly specified. After students have underlined the cause in red, have them write the effect on a line below the paragraph. Next, do this when only an effect is given.

f. Use exercises like the one in Figure 12–2 in which learners must decide if statement 1 (an event) did or did not cause statement 2 (an effect).

g. Interactive stories, as shown in Figure 12–3, can be used to help students perceive cause-and-effect relationships. With these special stories, students choose the path they wish the story to take at certain junctures in the episodes. The path they select causes specific effects

FIGURE 12–2 ***Exercise That Helps Students Distinguish Cause and Effect***

> The library opens at 10:00. When the clock on the wall said ⏱, the doors were opened and the children came in. Brian went to the picture book section, while Kerry looked through magazines. Brian found two books that he took to the table. He looked through these. He liked the second one better than the first, so he put the first book back on the shelf. He took the second one to the librarian and asked to check it out.
>
> A. 1. The library opens at 10:00.
>   2. When the clock says ⏱ the doors are opened and the children come in.
>
>   Yes   No
> Does #1 *cause* #2?   ❑   ❑
>
> B. 1. Brian went to the picture book section.
>   2. He only checked out one of the two books he looked at.
>
>   Yes   No
> Does #1 *cause* #2?   ❑   ❑

to ensue. Rereading and taking different routes reinforces the point even more strongly.

h. By this time, students should have a sense of the cause-effect concept. Now it is time to promote transfer to the real tasks they will confront in reading. Follow the suggestions in the previous items, using topics in which causes or effects are less familiar to students. Through dialogue, help them discover and then relate these causes and effects.

i. Display cause-and-effect relationships by cutting arrows from oaktag strips and affixing these to the chalkboard. After reading a passage with less familiar material, print causes on each arrow and have students write corresponding effects directly on the chalkboard next to the arrow.

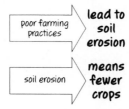

j. Continue to provide students with opportunities to predict outcomes. Predicting outcomes can help students infer indirectly stated causes and effects.

Of course, students need to apply the concepts gained *during actual reading of texts* if the foregoing activities are to have any worth. Teachers should not expect that transfer will occur automatically (Yopp & Yopp, 2000). Direct and guide students, reminding them of the pattern they have been practicing when they encounter it in materials they are reading. Show students how to use their new knowledge to understand principles and facts that appear in their books. Demonstrate how using this new knowledge helps.

FIGURE 12–3 *Interactive Stories Used to Enhance Students' Understanding of Cause and Effect*

giant crickets. Earth crickets were noisy enough, thought Hal. But these giant insects could make sounds that would break his eardrums. Lynn waved her arms at them and mouthed the words. "Stop. Quiet! Please." At once they stopped.

Then, as Hal gazed at the giant crickets, he seemed to hear a voice. But it wasn't really a voice. It was more like someone thinking inside his mind.

Welcome to the Land of the Insects. We are sorry our greeting was too loud for you. Were you sent to help us with our problem?

Hal glanced at Lynn. "Are you getting their message too?"

She nodded, wide-eyed. "Let's beam our thoughts back to them and ask what their problem is.

Our problem is our growth. Each time we double in size, our mass becomes greater but our strength does not increase. So we can hardly carry our weight. You are from a planet where insects live. Can you help us? We can no longer move as fast as we need to.

Hal frowned. "That's quite a problem. We haven't come up against that one on Earth. All our insects are small."

"But maybe we can still help," said Lynn. She aimed her thought question at the nearest cricket. "Do you have termites here?"

Yes.

"And do you have trees?" Lynn went on.

Yes.

Lynn clapped her hands. "Then maybe we can help you invent the wheel." Hal stared at her for a moment, puzzled. Then he broke into a big smile. "Now I get it. Termites can chew through wood. Maybe tree trunks can be chewed into wheels. And insects that are too heavy to carry themselves can ride. It's a long shot, but . . ."

The cricket leader broke in and finished Hal's thought.

It's worth a try. Thank you. You helped us, so you are welcome to come out and explore our land.

Lynn and Hal climbed out of their spaceship as the giant crickets hopped away. Soon they were approached by . . . .

A GREEN MONSTER
*continued
on page 17*

FLYING CIRCLES
*continued
on page 19*

STATUES ON THE MARCH
*continued
on page 21*

TAKE YOUR CHOICE:

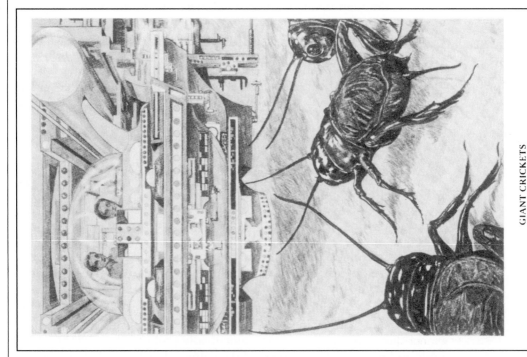

GIANT CRICKETS

Source: From "Star Trip" in *Attention Span Stories*, by L. Mountain. Copyright © 1978 by Jamestown Publishers. Reprinted by permission of Glencoe/McGraw-Hill.

2. *Providing prepractice with the sequence pattern.* As an additional example of prepractice to promote understanding of text structure, we will look at the sequence pattern. Another frequently occurring textual organization, this text structure is seen in social studies books in the form of temporal (time) sequence. In science and mathematics materials, it appears often in explanations of a technical process and in directions for conducting an experiment or computing a problem. Understanding the significance of sequence is important for reading narratives as well, since noting sequence aids interpretation of relationships of events and characters and is also an important aid to recall.

As a preliminary step to heighten awareness of sequences, have students talk through common events and the consequences that would follow incorrect sequencing. Ask them, for example, "What would happen if you put on your shoes and then put on your socks?" or "What would be the problem if you went to the stove to fix your breakfast, broke an egg over the burner, then put on the pan? What could you do to prevent this predicament?" Have students act out several of these garbled sequences so they can see the results.

After establishing this groundwork, you might further instill the relationship between sequence and sense—and move the point to the text realm—by giving to students the sections of a cartoon strip you have cut apart and mixed up (see Figure 12–4). Ask learners to read each section and then sequence the frames correctly.

Before students read a content area selection (e.g., from a history book), list the important events in single sentences on paper, mixing up the correct sequence. Reproduce the list for each student. After students have read the material, they are to cut the list apart and rearrange the sentences to match the order of events in the text. This provides opportunity for the teacher to supply immediate feedback and corrective suggestions as he or she moves about the classroom, noting students needing support and extending assistance while students are working. Comments such as these can promote learning: "Chad, think about it. Does it make sense for this to have happened before that?" or "Holly, I think you need to reread the third paragraph. Then rearrange your sequence and I'll come and check again."

Closely related to following a sequence of events is following written directions, an important academic skill, but also one used in daily life. When

> When instructing students in following written directions, many materials you use should include directions students will actually have to follow in some school activity.

FIGURE 12–4   *Learning to Identify the Proper Sequence of Events Is a Skill Students Need to Understand Causes and Effects and to Follow Explanations and Directions in Informational Material*

instructing students in this area, you are wise to kill two birds with one stone: Many instructional materials you use should include directions students may actually be required to follow in some school activity. Select the directions they will have to read in their spelling book next week, or choose a science experiment they must complete for an upcoming chapter in their regular classroom. What follows is a prototypical activity for practicing following directions.

a. Copy directions for a science experiment onto chart paper. Post these where all students can see them (see Figure 12–5).
b. Read the first sentence aloud to the students and ask, "Does that statement give us a direction to follow?" If they decide that it does, use a colored marking pen to write a large "1" in front of the sentence.
c. Read the next statement, and ask the same question. If it is indeed a direction to follow, number it "2." Continue through the information on the chart; number sentences that give a specific direction, but do not number filler statements often found intermingled with directions. Have students note the many statements interspersed with the instructions they are to follow; this type of writing style, in which authors' comments are mixed among directions (frequently found in textbooks), is difficult for students with poor comprehension. Note in Figure 12–5 the number of statements that are actually directions to follow and the number that are not.
d. Encourage students to find and number (lightly with a pencil so marks can be erased) specific direction statements in their own textbooks when they must follow written directions of any kind.

Practice may also be given in following directions by having students actually construct or assemble something in the classroom. (Figure 12–6 illustrates one activity of this type.) Invest in some inexpensive paperbacks designed to involve students in "making and doing," such as cooking or constructing puppets.

The previous two sections provide examples of prepractice activities to help students gain control of certain widespread text structures. Other expository text organizations also benefit from explicit attention (see Figure 12–1 and the earlier discussion). The examples here are representative of activities and the degree of specificity you should consider when designing instruction with other expository patterns.

FIGURE 12–5 *Give Students Practice Following Written Directions With Exercises Similar to Tasks They Can Expect to Do in Their Regular Classroom*

(1) Take a pan of water. (2) Dip an empty bottle into the pan. You will see bubbles rising from the bottle. These are bubbles of air. Air is all around us and fills any empty space—like an empty bottle. When the water goes into the bottle it pushes the air out. (3) Take the bottle from the water and (4) turn it upside down; (5) let all of the water run out. What is in the bottle now? Right— air. (6) Repeat the experiment by pushing the bottle back into the pan of water.

Assistance While Reading

Probably more than with narratives, poor readers need assistance *during* their reading of expository text.

Assistance With the Immediate Text.   If content area texts used in your students' regular classrooms are not too far removed from their instructional reading levels, it is often productive to use these actual texts in conducting the following approaches in which you support comprehension during students' reading.

Positive research support can be found for almost any type of text structure instruction.

   1. *Using a hierarchical summarization strategy.* After a review of research on strategies designed to assist expository text reading, Pearson and Fielding (1991) concluded that positive support could be found for almost any type of text structure instruction. Taylor and Beach (1984) addressed the problem by helping students attend to text cues such as headings and subheadings. They called their approach a **hierarchical summarization** strategy and found that its use significantly improved understanding and recall of social studies material by middle school students. This strategy was useful when students were reading about

FIGURE 12–6   ***Example of Students Making Something by Following Written Directions***

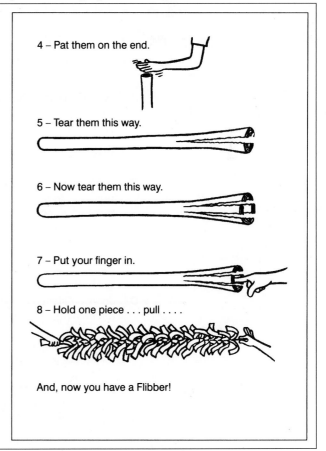

Source: From *The Beginner Book of Things to Make,* by Robert Lopshire, 1964, New York: Random House. Copyright 1964 by Random House. Reprinted by permission.

topics that were quite unfamiliar to them. Hierarchical summarization, an adapted form of outlining, helps students gain sensitivity to text structure, and therefore to the pertinence of specific information. (See Figure 12–7 for a sample of a hierarchical summary.) Hierarchical summarization is accomplished in the following way:

a. An outline is begun by drawing a line at the top of the chalkboard. (The line is not filled in at this time; a heading representing the key idea of the entire passage is written there later.)

b. A letter is written for each subheading found in the selection.

c. Students begin by reading the first section (as designated by the first subheading) and then decide on a main idea for that section. The teacher writes the main idea in the outline next to the letter for that section.

d. Two or three important details about the main idea are listed under the main idea.

e. This is done as learners read all sections of the assigned lesson.

f. Then topic headings are selected and these are written in the left margin, along with lines connecting main ideas related to the same topic. (See Figure 12–7 to see how this is done.)

g. The key idea for the entire selection is chosen and written on the blank line at the top of the chalkboard.

FIGURE 12–7 *Example of a Hierarchical Summary for a Three-Page Social Studies Text Segment With One Heading and Six Subheadings*

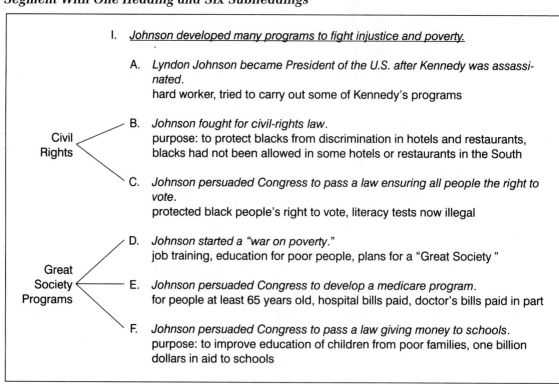

Source: From Taylor, Barbara M., & Beach, Richard. (1984 Winter). The effects of text structure instruction on middle-grade students' comprehension and production of expository text. *Reading Research Quarterly, 19*(2), 134–146. Reprinted with permission of Barbara M. Taylor and the International Reading Association.

After a few sessions, students work independently, completing a hierarchical summary on their own. When individual summaries have been completed, collaborative discussion, in which the summaries are critiqued, should follow. Additionally, paired learning can be employed: Students work as partners, each telling the other as much as they can about their summaries and other information they remember from the selection.

Using this strategy for one hour per week, students in Taylor and Beach's study improved their comprehension of unfamiliar topics more than a control group not having the instruction. However, if the assigned topic was familiar, this fairly complex strategy was no more productive than the more traditional procedure of simply having students write answers to questions about main ideas and details after reading the selection.

2. *Inserting questions in text.* In the chapter on narrative comprehension, we discussed the use of a teacher's oral questions interspersed during students' readings of stories. Some suggestions were made for the structure of those questions.

Teachers may also want to try the technique of inserting written questions within informational material. This is done by providing students with typed copies of text passages with questions written in at logical junctures. These questions are highlighted by setting them off from the remainder of the prose, for example:

Access the **R**ead**W**rite**T**hink site through www.reading.org for innovative lessons for teaching comprehension of informational material. Click "web resources," then "lesson plans," then "**R**ead**W**rite**T**hink," then "lessons." (New lessons appear each month.)

> When the settlers arrived in the Northwest Territory, many Native Americans were resentful of their presence. The French had come first for furs, believing that it gave them some claim to the land because they were the first Europeans to arrive there. Then the English came to live permanently. Since they were developing permanent settlements, they thought this gave them a right to the area. The Native Americans felt they had to protect their homes, hunting grounds, and their way of life.

> • **When more than one group of people believe they have claim to the same land, what can happen?**

> Certain Native American tribes tried to make a stand for their lands. Attacks by these tribes against the settlers made life difficult in some parts of the Northwest Territory. In addition, the French and English had been fighting in Europe and they now carried that fight to the New World.

> • **What would have been the reason for the French and English to declare war against one another in the Northwest Territory?**

> Newcomers who had come to the Ohio Country and other Northwest Territory regions may have at times wished that they had never left the East as they fought the Native Americans and the French, who both wanted the land. The Native Americans had lived in the area for many, many years and it was, in truth, their homeland. Whether the French had a greater right to any part of that land than the English or vice versa seemed an unimportant issue to the Native Americans.

The inserted questions can prompt a prediction of upcoming text information (as in the first question) or promote a reflection on details previously given (as in the second question), helping students to synthesize ideas.

Research supports use of inserted questions. Tierney and Cunningham's (1984) review of several such studies concluded that literal questions inserted in text help students respond better to those questions after reading. Positive benefits were also seen when higher-level questions were interspersed.

Compare. Is the technique of inserting questions similar or different from these pedagogical aids called "Learning From Text" which I have inserted in the text that *you* are presently reading? How?

Development of Strategies That Can Be Used With a Variety of Texts. Although used during the reading of a specific text, the ideas in this section also have the purpose of helping learners obtain strategies they can apply to texts they will read in the future. Indeed, research has shown that they do so.

1. *Engaging students in reciprocal teaching.* This instructional approach involves teacher modeling and has most often been applied to expository text. In this as-they-read technique, first the teacher and then the students are responsible for leading the lesson, which is composed of definite sequences of learning events. Palincsar and Brown (1984) successfully used these steps with poor readers whose decoding skills were adequate, but whose comprehension levels were 2 to 3 years below their grade levels.

After students have read silently the beginning section from a longer informational piece, the teacher:

    a. explains parts of the beginning section that are difficult to understand
    b. demonstrates how to summarize the information in the section
    c. shows how to develop important questions about that material
    d. makes a prediction about what will be found in the section that follows

Reciprocal means shared. Next, students share the instructional responsibility. For subsequent sections, students are assigned a portion of the text (usually a paragraph) and, in turn, each assumes the teacher's full role and applies these same four steps to the part they are accountable for, teaching others in the group about their assigned piece by (a) explaining difficult ideas, (b) summarizing the section, (c) asking important questions about their portion, and (d) making a prediction about the upcoming part. Then the student turns the teacher's role over to a peer for the next segment of the text. And so on until the targeted lesson is complete.

If adequate summarization of a section does not occur, then fix-up strategies are used, such as rereading or clarifying. Teachers *and* students give feedback to each other. In the original research with this technique, students self-graphed their successes. Graphing is a powerful motivator because it provides students a visual demonstration of the benefits of the strategies. All practice takes place in the context of actual text reading. Students are consistently reminded to practice these activities while reading independently.

In the Palincsar and Brown study, dramatic increases were seen in students' selection of important ideas for their oral summaries and in the quality of their questions, significant increases occurred on standardized reading comprehension test scores, and the improved results were maintained over time. Excellent success has been obtained by many other researchers and by many teachers using reciprocal teaching with readers at many grade levels and with students having reading difficulties.

2. *Designing and using schematic diagrams and charts of text structure.* A number of educators have used various types of schematic and pictorial diagrams and charts to help students gain control of expository structures and to

LEARNING FROM TEXT

Setting a Purpose for Reading. In the next section, you will read about schematic diagrams. Because students like working with these, greater cognitive effort is expended, attention improves, and greater depth of processing occurs. As you read, consider whether you could use these ideas with your own students.

conceptualize ideas presented in expository materials (e.g., Armbruster et al., 1991; Naughton, 1993–94).

One example is use of *semantic mapping* (Ruddell, 2006). In Chapter 10, semantic mapping was discussed as a previewing process for understanding word meanings. You may want to review the semantic map in Figure 10–2. To facilitate comprehension of whole texts, semantic mapping focuses on broader constructs so that students have deeper understandings of the topic. It also has proven a viable method for visualizing important points and subordinate ideas. Mapping has been one of the most widely researched content area text reading strategies.

Schematics and charts are often designed to accent specific text patterns. Teaching students to organize information from comparison and contrast structures onto comparison-contrast charts is relatively simple (see Figure 12–8).

FIGURE 12–8   *Comparison-Contrast Chart*

	CANADA	MEXICO	Similar or different?
Population			
Climate			
Products			
Size of country			

1. The main ways the countries are similar are _____

_____

because _____

_____.

2. The main ways they are different are _____

_____

_____

because _____

_____.

Venn diagrams, also introduced in Chapter 10, are particularly useful to compare and contrast likenesses and differences (see Figure 10–5 to review the structure and use of a Venn diagram).

Classification boxes are similar to comparison-contrast charts (see Figure 12–9) and concretely depict the relationship of ideas in text.

A heuristic for a sequence pattern might be stair steps (depicting the steps in the sequence), as in Figure 12–10. As students come upon statements relating the sequence of occurrences, they write these on the *sequence stair steps,* one statement on each step. For instance, in the sample in Figure 12–10, after reading the first bit of information about the formation of glaciers, students would write on the bottom step, "Winters turned particularly cold," or a similar idea conveying the essence of the details given. As they read farther and find the next occurrence, they pause and write that on the next step. The statements

FIGURE 12–9 *Classification Boxes*

	REPTILES	MAMMALS
Characteristics	• cold blooded • young born live or from eggs • •	• warm blooded • young born live • •
Examples	• snakes • alligators • • •	• humans • cats • • •

FIGURE 12–10 *Sequence Stair Steps*

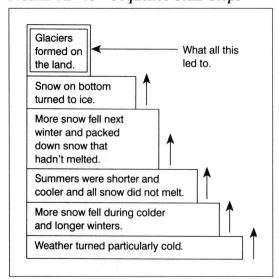

on the steps ultimately lead to the outcome, written at the top. The outcome can be placed at the top of the steps before the sequences leading to it are determined or placed there at the end when the conclusion is drawn that it is the consequence of this set of sequences. Engaging in sequence stair steps as a group activity before assigning it as independent practice is recommended.

As may be apparent, a diagram of a sequence structure fits nicely with examination of cause-and-effect patterns. In the example in the figure, students could be directed to write in the terms *cause* and *effect* at appropriate places on the stair steps after they have organized the sequence (i.e., the bottom step might have *cause* written above the statement, with an arrow pointing upward to the next step; the second step might have *effect* written below the statement, with an arrow pointing to the statement and *cause* written above the same statement with an arrow pointing upward toward the third step; and so on).

Figure 12–11 shows a problem-solution web used to represent this common expository structure. When the problem is discovered in the text, it is written in the center circle. As solutions are proposed in the reading material, they are written in the ancillary circles. In some texts, all solutions are intermeshed to solve the problem; in others, one of the possible solutions is selected. When the solution becomes clear in the passage, students write the final outcome on the bottom line. Creating a diagram illustrating key concepts and connections facilitates understanding and retention.

Armbruster, Anderson, and Ostertag (1987) used another type of instructional graphic to convey the problem-solution pattern as applied specifically to social studies material. Three items are commonly reported in this pattern: (a) problem of a person or group, (b) the attempt to solve the problem, and (c) the results. Since some social studies material can resemble stories (i.e., in

Having students develop schematics of sequence structures fits nicely with examination of cause-and-effect patterns.

Creating diagrams illustrating key concepts and connections facilitates understanding and retention.

FIGURE 12–11   ***Problem-Solution Web***

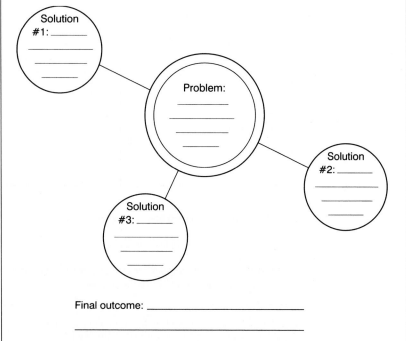

history books), it is not surprising that this structure resembles the elements in a story map. Armbruster et al. used the frame in Figure 12–12 to advance students' understanding of this particular problem-solution pattern. The frame visually portrays the form of the significant information in this text structure.

Fifth graders were taught to follow three steps with each lesson.

a. While reading silently, they were to search for information that should be included in the problem-solution frames they had been given.
b. They wrote this information in the appropriate boxes in the frame diagram.
c. They wrote a paragraph based on the information they had recorded in the frame.

Students were taught to do this during daily lessons over a 2-week period in which principles of explicit instruction were followed (teacher modeling, guided practice, teacher monitoring and feedback, and independent practice). Then students were evaluated on the ability to comprehend new social studies materials that employed a problem-solution pattern. Trained students scored

FIGURE 12–12 *Problem-Solution Frame*

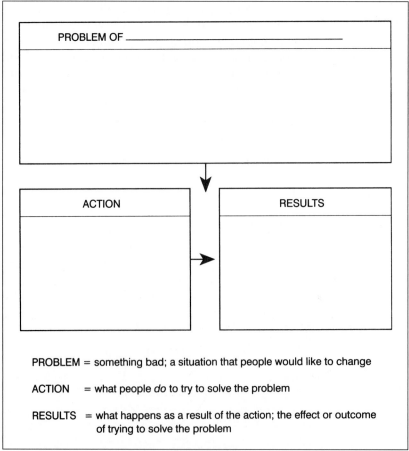

PROBLEM OF _____

ACTION

RESULTS

PROBLEM = something bad; a situation that people would like to change

ACTION = what people *do* to try to solve the problem

RESULTS = what happens as a result of the action; the effect or outcome of trying to solve the problem

Source: From Armbruster, Bonnie B., Anderson, Thomas H., & Ostertag, Joyce. (1987, Summer). Does text structure/summarization instruction facilitate learning from expository text? *Reading Research Quarterly, 22*(3), 331–346. Reprinted with permission of Bonnie B. Armbruster and the International Reading Association.

significantly higher on comprehension of passages they had not previously read than learners who had been exposed to traditional postquestions instead. The differences were seen in the skills for grasping main ideas in the selections and in writing paragraphs that included more ideas of importance about the text. No differences were seen between the two groups in recalling literal details. Armbruster et al. (1991) extended this study to include other types of frames, such as sequence flow charts and comparison boxes, which also were successful with intermediate grade students.

Many other schematic diagrams have been used. You can design additional ones to logically fit the structure and aim of a lesson, making certain that they focus on the central ideas of the reading selection. Sometimes student work with schematics serves as the culminating event after reading. However, often the best use is in assistance as you work with the learners during reading or for their independent use while reading silently. Collaborative group activity or partnerships (working in pairs) fits quite naturally with the task of completing instructional graphics. Berkowitz (1986) found that an excellent learning experience is for students themselves to design a diagram that will fit the pattern and the notions in a written text.

Diagrammatic representations of information aid comprehension of the immediate text, but the major purpose of comprehension instruction is to provide strategies that can be used in the future to conquer other difficult material. Diagramming and charting pivotal elements in text seems to be such a strategy. By producing diagrams and charts, readers are given the opportunity to internalize processes for recognizing text structures and organization (and, thus, important ideas) and have tools to use when they encounter new text.

Culminating Events

As with the foregoing activities, the culminating events recommended in this section have a research base supporting their value in assisting comprehension.

Assistance With the Immediate Text. The first suggestion provided here is based on a relatively recent practice—journal writing. The second has been recommended by comprehension studies for some time.

1. *Instituting learning journals.* Jennings (1991) formulated a procedure to be carried out after students read expository text—having students write in learning journals. This was described as a way for students to "think on paper." In Jennings's program, students reacted to social studies text by writing journal entries. They were asked to think about what they had gained from the material just read and to engage in writing a personalized response to it. This was seen as a way of bonding new schema with old information already known by the reader. In their learning journals, students simulated roles, made conjectures concerning incidents they had read, and wrote about other reflections on their learning episode. Learners shared their journal entries with peers, and the teacher wrote individual replies to the entries.

Jennings provided research evidence for the constructiveness of this type of reflective writing. Students participating in the learning journals activity scored higher than students receiving a more traditional method of instruction when assessed on immediate comprehension of the text, based on end-of-chapter tests. Journal writers also showed superior recall of knowledge after time had passed on a test over all chapters in the social studies unit.

Positive results of writing in learning journals was believed to result from interest bred from personal writing (in contrast to writing responses to teacher-produced tasks) and to speculations about events students engaged in and personal viewpoints they brought to occurrences, the latter thought to help tie old and new information. Content area journal writing has become an accepted practice across the grades (Duke & Bennett-Armistead, 2003).

2. *Generating questions.* This means *students* generating questions, not teachers. Asking students to generate questions after they have read text has become quite a popular idea and is believed to enhance recall because students focus on ideas that they think teachers will judge to be important. Generating questions has been suggested as a way to facilitate comprehension of informational material and as a study skill.

Choosing ideas about which to write questions prompts student attention to the principal information in a text. Having to select important facts and concepts increases students' cognitive effort and thoughtfulness about the text. Several of the instructional methods recommended thus far in this chapter have included procedures for student-generated oral questions before reading (e.g., as with K-W-L) and during reading (e.g., in reciprocal teaching).

> There are positive advantages of student-generated questions after reading—if students are taught how to write questions of appropriate significance.

However, there is one caveat: Students must be taught *how* to generate questions. Some investigations have shown positive advantages of student-generated questions after reading and some have not—the difference often being whether this training was provided. To explore that issue, Andre and Anderson (1978–79) had one group of secondary school students write their own questions after being taught how to generate questions that were appropriately significant, another group created questions but with no training, and a third did not write questions. Both groups who wrote questions did better than those who did not, but readers with low- and middle-level skills did not experience the benefit unless they had been taught how to write questions that focused on important ideas. See Figure 12–13 for some types of questions McLaughlin and Allen (2002) suggest that students be taught to generate before, during, or after reading in both narrative and expository text.

Development of Strategies That Can Be Used With a Wide Variety of Texts.
Independent reading is a fact of life, in school and through adulthood. Students are asked to read silently in their classrooms and are later called upon to answer oral questions about what they read. Students are sent to study hall to read a chapter from a geography book and to write answers to the questions found at the end of the chapter. In homework assignments, when textbooks must be read and questions must be answered, students are usually on their own, receiving little help from their parents or peers.

When reading income tax forms, reports, or other material, adults usually do not have the luxury of another person to guide and prompt them through what may at first seem incomprehensible. The majority of comprehension strategies taught to students should be aimed, therefore, at enabling them to internalize those strategies to be used when reading on their own.

1. *Teaching students to summarize.* Summarizing, a traditional task that has been assigned to myriad students over years past, also interests reading authorities because, under certain conditions, this has proved to be a powerful way to help students improve comprehension of expository texts (Ruddell, 2006).

FIGURE 12–13 *Generating Questions: A Skill That Supports Comprehension Strategies*

Comprehension Strategy	Narrative Text *(The True Story of the Three Little Pigs)*	Expository Text (Chapter: "The American Revolution")
Previewing	What is this story about? What might happen in this story?	What do I already know about the Revolutionary War?
Self-Questioning	Why is the wolf telling this story?	Why did this war occur?
Making Connections	How does this little-pigs story compare or contrast to the original?	How does the text description of Washington crossing the Delaware compare or contrast to the film we saw? To the article we read?
Visualizing	Is my mental picture of the wolf still good? Why should I change it?	What did an American soldier look like? A British soldier?
Knowing How Words Work	Does the word make sense in the sentence?	What clues in the text can I use to figure out the word *representation*?
Monitoring	Does what I'm reading make sense? If not, what can I do to clarify?	Does what I'm reading make sense? Did French soldiers fight in this war? How can I find out?
Summarizing	What has happened so far?	What is the most important information in the chapter?
Evaluating	Do I believe the wolf's story? Why? How does this story rank with other little-pigs stories I've read?	How would my life be different if we had not won this war?

Source: From McLaughlin, Maureen, & Allen, Mary Beth. (2002). *Guided Comprehension: A Teaching Model for Grades 3–8*, Newark, DE: International Reading Association. Reprinted with permission of Maureen McLaughlin and the International Reading Association.

One condition that influences positive outcomes is training learners *how to* summarize. Brown and Day (1983) developed plans for teaching summarization that have been tested with readers of many age levels and with a variety of content area texts. To teach your students the rules Brown and Day devised about summarization, do the following:

a. Show learners how to omit *insignificant* information from material they are summarizing.
b. Demonstrate how to omit *redundant* details.
c. Help them develop an *overarching, general label* for specifics (e.g., "deciduous trees" used in place of "oaks, maples, sycamores, hickories, beeches, ashes, and buckeyes").
d. Help them determine main ideas the author has stated and use these in the summary.
e. Teach them how to express the main ideas when the author has not stated these explicitly.

Good results have been found following Brown and Day's plan for enhancing comprehension of the immediate material, and positive effects have also carried over to comprehension of other selections. When readers have been asked to summarize after reading but have not been explicitly taught how to do so, these favorable findings have not followed. Another condition on which success depends relates to the type of comprehension to be emphasized. Training and practice in summarizing enhance understanding of main ideas or the general significance of a passage rather than recall of minor facts.

2. *Helping readers compose extended summaries.* After learners have conquered the basics of summarizing and can do so with a single portion of text (e.g., a short chapter), practice with extended summaries can help students determine interrelationships among several associated subjects (e.g., several chapters). For example, content area texts often structure chapters into units of similar topics. Pulling together overlying meanings can broaden understanding.

An extended summary can be composed by summarizing the component parts of targeted text and then, in effect, summarizing the summaries. Using a super summary form organizes the process (see Figure 12–14).

3. *Looking back.* Strategies that may seem obvious to good readers and that they derive intuitively may not be so apparent to less-skilled readers. A case in point involves what have been called "text lookbacks" (Garner, Wagoner, & Smith, 1983), or more formally "text reinspection." A **text lookback** simply means looking back in the material when a question cannot be answered.

When you need to respond to a question whose answer is given in a selection you've read, but you don't recall the particulars necessary for your reply,

> Strategies that may seem obvious to good readers—strategies they may have developed intuitively—may not be so apparent to less-skilled readers.

FIGURE 12–14 *A Super Summary Form*

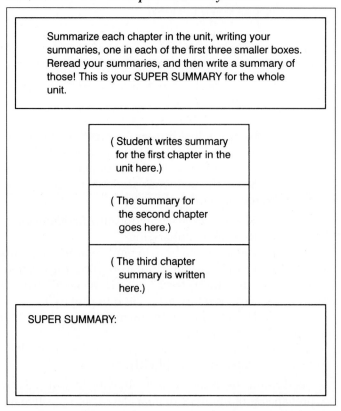

what do *you* do? You *look back* and see what it said there, of course! Some unskilled readers do not use this fairly simple solution. In some cases, they may believe checking back into the text is a "forbidden" resolution to their problem; they think they are required to remember the details that they have read. Or they may have experienced previous trial-and-error attempts to reinspect text for answers, only to find that the random search method they have employed is unproductive. Or they may have previously used an inefficient approach in which they simply began at the beginning, reading *everything* all over again until they found the answer—and this seems too great an effort to expend. As with many other comprehension strategies, it may be necessary to directly teach those with reading disabilities to look back systematically.

Table 12–3 shows results from a lookback study with fourth and sixth graders by Garner et al. (1983). The results of this study have implications for the instruction of students with poor comprehension strategies. A three-phase approach to such instruction follows.

a. Select a short, expository selection. Have students read it. Next, ask five literal questions. They should be of sufficient difficulty to require students to look back at the text for at least some questions. When a student is "stumped," ask what should be done to get the answer. Encourage the response, "Look back at the page where the answer is found." Have students do this. After several sessions in which lookbacks are practiced, move to the second phase.

b. In the second phase, students must learn to distinguish between questions for which a text lookback will do the trick (e.g., literal-level questions) and those for which only their own background information can be used. Again present short passages followed by five questions, some literal and some that require the student's prior knowledge to obtain a correct response. Through discussion, aid students in deciding which is which. Confirm their decisions by looking back in the text and underlining the answers to literal questions, while noting when there is no answer to underline for the background-dependent questions. Have students answer the questions. Practice these activities for several sessions before moving to the third phase. (Recall the exercises with QARs described in Chapter 11; those may also be in order here

TABLE 12–3 *Lookback Study With Fourth and Sixth Graders*

	Good Comprehenders	Poor Comprehenders
Looked back in text for unknown answers	Often	Seldom
Looked back at the right time: a. did look back when answer was in text b. did not look back if answer had to be determined from student's own background information	Good differentiation was made	Poor differentiation was made
Knew how to sample text when they looked back (i.e., they looked back to the specific area where answer could be found and did not just reread whole passage until answer appeared)	Yes	No

Source: Adapted from information in "Externalizing Question-Answering Strategies of Good and Poor Comprehenders" by R. Garner, S. Wagoner, and T. Smith, 1983, *Reading Research Quarterly, 18*, pp. 439–447.

since some questions require text information and background knowledge to be combined.)

c. Follow the next sets of materials by asking only literal-level questions. Tell students all these questions can be answered by looking at the passages. The questions should again be written at a difficulty level requiring students to engage in at least some text lookbacks. In this phase, however, before each lookback, tell students that looking through the whole passage takes too much time. They should be asked to try to remember where the answer occurred and be required to guess where they will find it (e.g., near the beginning, middle, or end; right after the part about . . .). Category selection also is important here ("Since the article is divided into sections on religion of the Aztecs and social life of the Aztecs, and the question asks about Aztec gods, in which section should we look?"). Dreher (1992) reports that many students have difficulties with category selection during a text search. Points can be awarded for a correct guess about where to locate the specific information needed to answer a question. Practice this strategy for several sessions.

Until the strategies are firmly internalized and to ensure generalization across other materials, prompt students to use them whenever appropriate and remind students about the strategies before they read independently. When students have missed or forgotten details, text lookbacks do a remarkably good job of repairing the problem. Reviewing a number of studies, Garner (1987) found the lookback strategy to have a beneficial effect on reading comprehension.

4. *Teaching critical reading concepts.* **Critical reading** is defined as "the process or result of making judgments in reading" or "reading in which a questioning attitude, logical analysis, and inference are used to judge the worth of text according to an established standard" (Harris & Hodges, 1995, p. 49).

To teach critical reading skills, have students read several newspaper accounts of the same incident and contrast the details reported.

Critical reading of expository material means judging the believability of what has been read. Poor readers often believe that anything presented in print is true. As adults, they may be bilked by vague, misleading language found in advertising and news articles. They may be influenced adversely because they do not trust their own judgments if they find opposing ideas in print. Good comprehension involves realization that text is written with different goals in mind and that authors may use propaganda techniques to persuade readers to a certain view.

Critical reading concepts are no more difficult to grasp than other higher-level comprehension understandings. An added benefit is that the reasoning and thinking exercises employed to teach critical reading may positively affect other types of comprehension tasks. It has also been suggested that instruction in critical reading concepts, because of the emphasis on evaluation skills, may facilitate the important metacognitive strategy of monitoring reading.

Many teachers begin a program of teaching critical reading concepts by providing practice in recognizing the seven propaganda techniques identified by the Institute of Propaganda Analysis (Robinson, 1967).

a. *Bad names.* Name calling designed to cause dislike: "Americans are capitalist imperialists."

b. *Glad names.* Using "names" or descriptions of people to generate positive feelings: "The candidate can be trusted. He was a Boy Scout in his youth."

c. *Transfer.* Suggesting approval because other people purportedly approve: "Use Acid-O Aspirin. Nine out of ten doctors do."

d. *Testimonial.* Using public figures to endorse ideas or products: "Melvin Mish, pole vaulting champion in the Olympics, drives the new Ford Taurus."

e. *Plainfolks.* Suggesting that an important person is just like the average person, and, therefore, can be trusted, or indicating that average folks (just like you) prefer a certain product or idea: "Senator Kitten's campaign manager says he spent Sunday at the family farm where he ate a fried chicken dinner and played with the dog."

f. *Stacking the cards.* Not giving the full truth by omitting details or focusing attention on one detail: "The Chinese press reports the American economic system is on the verge of collapse because unemployment is high."

g. *The bandwagon.* Suggesting that since "everybody" is doing something you should, too: "Over 1 million people have bought the Higglely Pigglely screwdriver."

To acquaint students with propaganda devices, teachers use newspapers, magazine articles, and ads. After students read these, they attempt to identify statements representing the various devices. Students are guided to make inferences about the believability of the statements, their purposes, and their relevance to the point being made.

Work with critical reading concepts should not be limited to practice in recognizing propaganda techniques, however. Other important abilities and skills include:

• understanding that because something is found in print does not necessarily mean it's true (Practice in recognizing propaganda devices is a beginning, but developing this understanding should be carried further. For example, ask students to examine several newspaper accounts of the same incident, some of which may report contradictory information, or review several different reports of an event in history, such as might be found in an encyclopedia or textbook in contrast to a work of historical fiction.)

- identifying fact versus opinion
- detecting faulty generalizations
- detecting overgeneralizations
- identifying the effects of quoting out of context
- detecting false causality
- discerning writers' purposes and biases (Do they want to inform—or influence?)
- asking questions about the writer's qualifications (Does the author of an article about learning disabilities in a women's magazine have the background and expertise for his or her statements to be believable?)
- learning to ask these questions: Where's the proof? What facts support this? What data back this up?

Poor readers have significantly improved their critical reading skills when teachers have worked directly with them, using principles of active teaching, providing feedback and guidance.

Seeking to settle debate about whether critical thinking can be taught or is a result of natural reasoning powers, one group of researchers set out to determine if critical reading could be improved through explicit instruction (Patching, Kameenui, Carnine, Gersten, & Colvin, 1983). They compared two instructional approaches. Fifth graders in one group received workbooks containing lessons for learning three critical reading concepts. After students completed exercises, the teacher marked right and wrong answers and gave them back to the students. This method did not prove to be very effective.

A second approach—a systematic instruction method—did prove valuable, however. Teachers worked directly with the students during each lesson, employing principles of active teaching, providing feedback about responses, and guiding readers to deduce logical responses. At the end of the program, students who engaged in the systematic instruction method scored significantly higher on a critical reading test than did the group using the workbook method. Furthermore, the systematic instruction method was most effective with the poorer readers in the group.

The important implication of this study for the remedial teacher is that students (including poor readers) can develop critical reading concepts, but the specific method chosen may well determine success or failure. Students who frequently participate in discussions about what they are reading are more likely to become critical readers than those who do not.

📖 STUDYING

Studying is certainly related to comprehension. It involves the interpretation and construction of meaning based on what the author has told the reader and what knowledge the reader can bring to the text. Unlike typical reasons for reading narratives, the focus of studying is on recall for some purpose—to take a test, write a paper, carry out an experiment correctly, give an oral presentation, or use the information in one's job or other real-life situation. Often studying is done with expository materials.

Throughout these last two chapters on comprehension, you have read suggestions for helping learners develop comprehension strategies that can be used with a wide variety of reading materials. Many of these suggestions can be useful approaches in interpreting and recalling information (e.g., summarizing, employing text lookbacks, diagramming, and charting). This section extends these discussions to common study techniques. Study skill instruction is best accomplished in real texts for real needs (Bean, 2000).

Research on the most common study routines has produced many conflicting results, and the conclusion to be drawn from research findings is that there is simply no one system that is better than another. Some investigations show, for instance, that a technique works well and other studies show that the same study method is no better than several others the student could use. The difference in whether a study behavior is successful depends in part on the recall response the student must later produce. For instance, certain circumstances necessitate understanding and retention of specific data, as in some science learning or in introductory information in texts and courses in many subject areas. Other situations require retention of the main ideas only, and in others, both the main ideas and the details share importance.

Another factor on which success of the study system hinges is the depth of processing. As with learning word meanings and with approaches that truly influence comprehension, deep processing is key. Some study techniques induce the learner to concentrate and expend more cognitive effort, both of which are associated with greater recall of information than, for example, a single reading of material.

Here are some examples:

Paraphrasing and reorganizing written text requires deeper levels of processing than merely copying an author's words verbatim.

1. *Note taking.* In some investigations, note taking has been no more productive than other study procedures. However, when students paraphrase the author's words or reorganize the author's text, rather than recording words verbatim, the process is effective (Bretzing & Kulhavy, 1979). Paraphrasing and reorganizing require deeper levels of processing.

2. *Outlining.* Outlining requires reorganization of the author's presentation and, as such, has been one of the more constructive study techniques according to several, but not all, studies. One difference here seems to hinge on whether readers have been trained to outline. Once again we see comparable results with other comprehension research: To be effective, many of the most functional strategies must be taught directly—and fully—for worthwhile consequences to occur. When there is no training in selecting ideas of importance, although students may employ outlining formats, they may process information only superficially and therefore not recall significant information (Anderson & Armbruster, 1984).

3. *Underlining.* Underlining is carried out simply by the student marking lines in a book (or highlighting with transparent pens). Why would this study routine help? Perhaps it is because critical details are signaled. With this hypothesis in mind, investigators have tried underlining portions of passages before giving them to students to emphasize essential facts or concepts. But this has not proved to be helpful. Thus, it has been concluded that when students do their own underlining (and must necessarily make choices about the importance of text statements to underline), deep processing is encouraged (Anderson & Armbruster, 1984).

4. *Using study guides.* Good results have been seen when study guides are used. You might confer with classroom teachers about the value of these aids and encourage their use, especially for the poor readers with whom you work. Herber (1992) suggests that study guides are most effective when they serve both content

learning and strategy learning, that is, when they help students understand the subject addressed at the time and, as well, teach general ways for ferreting meanings out of text that can be used in the future. When this is the case, they also are suitable for reading teachers to implement in strategy lessons for reading expository text. An example of such a study guide is shown in Figure 12–15.

Many new types of study guides are currently being developed, with some of these based on the effectiveness that has been found for using schematic diagrams to enhance comprehension. See Figure 12–16 and Table 12–4.

Research shows that study guides are excellent resources, but not a cure-all for problems with learning from text. Study guides should be used during reading, not afterward; and though more often applied in independent study, they are particularly well suited for collaborative learning activities.

📖 METACOGNITION

Metacognition has been discussed earlier in this book, particularly in relation to assessment, but the topic will be revisited and expanded here. As you recall, **metacognition** refers to two things: (a) knowledge individuals have about their own thinking and (b) control individuals have over their own thinking (Baker & Brown, 1984).

Knowledge implies that you are aware of basic characteristics of your thinking and of literacy processes ("When I read a physics text, I usually have to read more slowly and carefully than when I read a history text."). It also refers to being aware of what you are thinking and mentally doing at any given time—that is, that you monitor your reading. *Awareness* may not always occur at a conscious level—if you are "getting it," you just move on through the reading. For the good reader, awareness may migrate to the conscious level only when understanding breaks down—you may say "Huh! What was that? Let's read that again!"

Control means doing something about those thinking processes, if a need for change arises. And you must have strategies to do that something.

Some metacognitive strategies involve *planning*.

1. Thinking about the purpose: "The reason I'm reading this is to determine if dinosaurs existed in what is now the United States" or "When I'm reading this, I can't just understand it. I also have to remember it for that quiz."
2. Determining and focusing on what is important and not trivial: "This is important information for figuring out what I need to know so I'd better attend to this part carefully."

Some metacognitive strategies involve *monitoring* (Ruddell, 2006).

1. Being alert to when understanding occurs but also to problems: "I get it, so I can read on" or "That doesn't make sense to me!"
2. Taking corrective action: "That doesn't make sense to me, so I'd better reread this."

Metacognition requires complex processes. Research, not surprisingly, has shown that poor readers are inferior to good readers in metacognitive activity

FIGURE 12–15 *Sample of a Study Guide*

Fossils

Names _____   Date(s)_____

_____

Strategy Codes:

RR — Read and retell in your own words
DP — Read and discuss with partner
PP — Predict with partner
WR — Write a response on your own
Skim — Read quickly for purpose stated and discuss with partner
MOC — Organize information with a map, chart, or outline

Self-Monitoring Codes:

__✔__ I understand this information.

__?__ I'm not sure if I understand.

__X__ I do not understand and I need to restudy.

1. ____ PP   pp. 385–92. Survey the title, picture, charts, and headings. What do you expect to learn about this section?

2. ____ WR   As you are reading, jot down three or more new words and definitions for your vocabulary collection.

3. ____ RR   pp. 385–86, first three paragraphs.

4. ____ DP   pp. 386–87, next three paragraphs.
   a. Describe several reasons why index or guide fossils are important.
   b. How can finding the right type of fossil help you to identify it?

5. ____ MOC   Map pp. 387–89. Make an outline of the information.

1._____   2. _____   3. _____
   a. _____   a._____   a._____
   b. _____   b._____   b._____
   c. _____   c._____   c._____

6. ____ Skim   p. 390, first three paragraphs
   Purpose: To understand the role of the following in the formation of fossils
   _____ a. natural casts
   _____ b. trails and burrows
   _____ c. gastroliths

7. ____ DP   pp. 390–91
   As an amateur fossil collector, describe:
   a. where to find fossils
   b. what to use to find them
   c. how to prepare them for display

8. ____ WR   p. 392, next to last paragraph
   Define *pseudofossil*. Jot down three other words that contain the prefix "pseudo."
   Use the dictionary if necessary.

9. ____ DP   Examine the fossil collection being passed around and list eight things you have learned by analyzing it.

Source: Used with permission from National Middle School Association. From "Helping Students Comprehend Their Textbooks" by K. D. Wood, 1987, *Middle School Journal, 18*(2), pp. 20–21. Copyright 1987 by National Middle School Association.

FIGURE 12–16 *A Sample Schematic Diagram Study Guide*

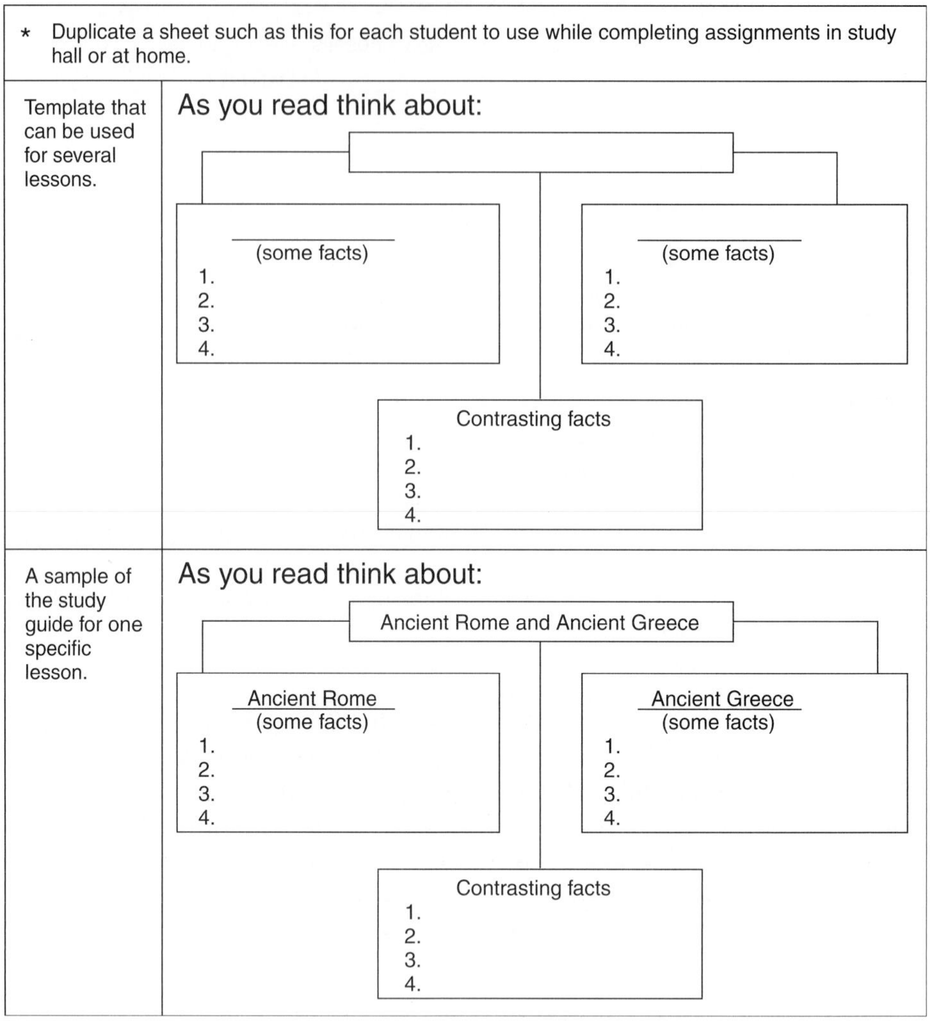

✳ Duplicate a sheet such as this for each student to use while completing assignments in study hall or at home.	
Template that can be used for several lessons.	**As you read think about:** _____ (some facts) 1. 2. 3. 4. (some facts) 1. 2. 3. 4. Contrasting facts 1. 2. 3. 4.
A sample of the study guide for one specific lesson.	**As you read think about:** Ancient Rome and Ancient Greece Ancient Rome (some facts) 1. 2. 3. 4. Ancient Greece (some facts) 1. 2. 3. 4. Contrasting facts 1. 2. 3. 4.

TABLE 12–4 *Other Schematic Diagrams for Independent Study Found in This Text (Chapters 10, 11, and 12)*

Objective	Use
• You want students to focus on details.	Figure 12–9; Figure 12–15
• You want students to focus on main ideas.	Figure 12–13
• You want students to focus on both details and main ideas.	Figure 12–8
• You want students to make comparisons.	Figure 10–2; Figure 10–5; Figure 12–8; Figure 12–9; Figure 12–16
• You want students to note causes and/or effects.	Figure 12–10
• You want students to consider problems and solutions.	Figure 11–6; Figure 12–11; Figure 12–12
• You want students to note sequences.	Figure 12–10

(e.g., Brown, Armbruster, & Baker, 1986). And, younger readers are less skilled than older.

Early research cast some doubt about whether metacognition could be trained. These studies seemed to show that students could be taught to apply metacognition to specific tasks but did not continue to do so once they were no longer prompted through the training program to exercise the skill. Nor did they generalize what they had learned to new types of texts. Later research has identified the problem: The complexity and effort required for metacognitive skills to be internalized requires a lengthy training program. When researchers and teachers work with students over an extended period, provide much opportunity for practice, and furnish explanation of the value of the activity, metacognitive strategies have been learned, maintained, and employed in new situations (Derry & Murphy, 1986; Miller, 1987; Palincsar & Brown, 1984; Schunk & Rice, 1987).

LEARNING FROM TEXT

Self-Monitoring. Early research with metacognitive strategy instruction did not always produce good results, while later studies have shown much success. What has been the difference?

Metacognitive Strategies

A variety of suggestions for increasing students' metacognition can be found in the professional literature. You will see some familiar entries in this discussion because some of these recommendations are incorporated in many of the successful comprehension strategies you have learned in this chapter and the previous one; others are of a broader nature and relate to any type of intentional learning. These strategies should be applied in both narrative and expository text reading. All, also, could be useful to college students when studying assigned texts.

Before Reading

1. Survey the materials before you read by looking at the title, pictures, and headings.
2. Think about your purpose; allot time for reading based on this purpose (Ruddell, 2006).
3. Think about the topic; allot time and select strategies to be used based on your familiarity with the topic.
4. Be aware of your strengths and weaknesses; if you are not interested in the topic, plan strategies to keep yourself on task.
5. Predict what you think the text will tell you.
6. Think of some questions you'd like answered by the selection.

During Reading

1. Use visual imagery; try to picture in your mind what the text is describing.
2. Use visual aids supplied in the text (don't just skip over them); relate these to the written information.
3. Think about the text cues. How can these help you understand? Are main points numbered? Are there words and ideas printed in bold and italics?

4. Think about text structure. Is it important to remember the sequence? Are things compared to one another to help you understand?
5. Keep making predictions; ask yourself if your guesses so far are right or wrong.
6. Pause to think about important points; part way through, stop and try to retell main points made so far.
7. When encountering something you don't understand, select a strategy to resolve this difficulty. For example:
   a. Slow down; reread the difficult part.
   b. Look back in the text and reread (text reinspection).
   c. Temporarily read ahead to see if difficult concepts are clarified.
   d. Work with a partner; talk through your understandings and confusions.
   e. Underline the parts you don't understand; consult an external source (e.g., the teacher).

After Reading

1. Think about your predictions. Which were correct?
2. Summarize the selection to aid in noting important information and in recalling it.
3. Try to think of questions that could be asked about the selection; focus questions on important rather than trivial information. Try to answer the questions to evaluate your understanding and to aid later recall. Try to think how you would "prove" to someone that your answers are correct.

All of these strategies would, of course, be overwhelming if you tried to teach them in their entirety to poor readers at one time. Instead, you should select one or two that seem to be of particular relevance for a student or group.

To practice use of metacognitive strategies, students may work as partners.

Make these strategies the focal point of lessons until students are comfortably operating with them. Then introduce another one or two. The optimistic news is that delayed readers *have* been taught to approach text metacognitively and, with skillful teaching, can achieve proficiency.

Reviewing and Reflecting.   Throughout this chapter there have been recommendations for good questioning procedures. Do you remember other ideas from other sections of this text? What could you add from Chapter 12?

Applying What You've Learned.   Read the entire Reflections section that follows, thinking over your answers to the questions you find there.

Reflections

Reflections   Much of the information in the two preceding chapters should be helpful to college students studying and learning from text. Which of these strategies do you intuitively use or have you learned to employ? Which might you want to try in the future?

	Already Use	A Strategy to Try
1. Previewing a chapter before reading.	_____	_____
2. Establishing a purpose before beginning to read (e.g., for the present chapter, one purpose should be to learn instructional procedures you can use in your own teaching to help poor readers who have difficulties with comprehension. However, another immediate, practical purpose might be to remember information well enough to discuss it on a test or in a paper your instructor asks you to prepare).	_____	_____
3. Meshing your own background information with text information (e.g., What do you already know about the material given in the text? How does the text information apply to actual situations you know of with children or adolescents?).	_____	_____
4. Stopping at the ends of major sections to put the information in your own words.	_____	_____

	Already Use	A Strategy to Try
5. Summarizing the entire chapter by thinking of the major points that were conveyed.	_____	_____
6. Reinspecting the text for important details omitted in your summarization attempt.	_____	_____

READING INSTRUCTION FOR SPECIAL POPULATIONS

13

The Severely Delayed Reader and the Nonreader

Greater explicitness may be necessary when instructing severely delayed readers.

LEARNING FROM TEXT

Setting a Purpose for Reading. As you read this chapter, think about all the ways mentioned in which there is diversity in learning needs among students enrolled in remedial programs.

*D*isabled readers are not all cut from the same cloth. There is great diversity in the characteristics and needs of students enrolled in remedial reading and learning disability programs. One way they vary is according to the severity of their difficulties with literacy attainment.

The majority of students with reading problems face challenges that are fairly *mild* (see Figure 13–1). In fact, they may not be in a remedial program; instead, when the classroom teacher supplies perceptive, individualized attention, these students progress. The second largest group are those whose difficulties may be described as *moderate*. They make up a fairly substantial portion of the learners who are considered to be poor readers. Most students receiving special instructional services in remedial reading classes, in learning disability programs, and in reading clinics are those experiencing moderately serious obstacles in learning to read.

A third group is much smaller in number, perhaps only 3% to 5% of the reading disabled population; these are individuals whose lack of reading achievement constitutes a decidedly severe delay in learning (Torgesen, Wagner, & Rashotte, 1997). How a severe disability is defined differs among authorities and agencies providing services. When this specification is *discrepancy based* (based on differences between actual level of reading and expected level), some have suggested a lag in reading level that is 3 years or more below the individual's potential constitutes a severe delay; others specify two standard deviations below the norm on standardized measurement instruments. Originally, learning disability programs were established to serve this bottom 3% to 5% of students, but in common practice today, many students enrolled in LD classes fall within the moderate range of needs. Some research attention has been given to the instructional predicaments of severely delayed readers, but not nearly so much as given to those with moderate difficulties.

The smallest group—those with the gravest problems—are *nonreaders* who make up perhaps 1% or less of the reading disability group. Obviously, they too are severely delayed, but these learners are a special segment of those with severe problems because they can read almost nothing at all. Although few in number, they represent the most needy students we serve and without special care are quite likely to grow up to join the ranks of the "unexplained" adult illiterate. Research on instruction for nonreaders has been exceedingly scant.

Assessing students' needs by examining the severity of the problem may be a constructive way to gain insights for program planning because it does seem that severely delayed readers, and particularly nonreaders, need somewhat

FIGURE 13–1
Proportions of
Students With
Literacy Problems

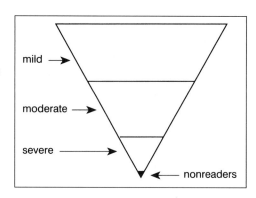

modified routes to learning (Stahl, 2002). This is not to say that outlandish instruction is called for (like walking balance beams, tossing bean bags, or other such approaches suggested in times past). However, instruction for severely delayed learners may need to (a) focus on prerequisites over which moderately disabled readers may have gained control (e.g., letter recognition, phonemic awareness), (b) provide more than the usual number of opportunities for practice, and (c) provide more than the typical amount of direct guidance, since in the earliest stages these students seem to engage in little self-generative learning. Furthermore, since the problems of severely delayed readers customarily lie with word recognition and word identification, it is particularly crucial to consider their stages of word learning (Spear-Swerling, 2004). Finally, lack of motivation, bred from persistent failure, can cripple instructional efforts if motivational variables are not given attention along with cognitive concerns.

GENERAL CHARACTERISTICS OF SEVERELY DELAYED READERS AND NONREADERS

Typical general characteristics of both severely delayed readers and nonreaders are the following:

1. Their problems may result from multiple and differing causes.
2. They are found in all IQ ranges, but most have average intelligence.
3. Some are unusually reticent about making attempts at reading, likely due to feelings of insufficiency and embarrassment. They *do* have a desire to learn to read, although their overt behaviors often belie that conclusion. Initially, they may avoid reading, exhibit off-task behaviors, and sometimes be uncooperative with attempts to instruct them.
4. Habitually they are demoralized, believing they cannot learn to read. Many have acquired this belief as the result of statements and actions of well-meaning but misinformed individuals and because of past experiences. For example, Eric, a university football player referred to a college of education reading clinic, said to the staff at the first meeting, "I can't learn to read. They told me at the medical facility I have dyslexia." Eric was nevertheless asked to try to read a short selection, which he could do, although with some difficulty. After reading he was told, "You can learn to read. You just don't recognize some long words. We'll teach you how to figure those out." Later

assessment determined that Eric was reading at about fifth-grade level. This is certainly an indication of a severe delay for a college student, but it also indicates that he did not have some malady that made it impossible to learn to read. Further evaluation demonstrated he had little difficulty with word meanings or comprehension. Eric, a mature young man with average intelligence who wanted to read better, was delighted to find he wasn't "dyslexic" and cooperatively engaged in activities suggested for remediation.

5. Severely delayed readers and nonreaders usually require one-to-one instruction (Brown, Morris, & Fields, 2005). Frequent instructional sessions are needed (Allington, 2002b), and the typical severe reading disability case must be enrolled in a program for an extended period of time (Olson, Wise, Ring, & Johnson, 1997).

6. They can learn to read. It is not unusual for these students to make consistent, but relatively slow, progress during early remedial instruction; then a breakthrough occurs, and growth is rapid. Some reach "plateaus" periodically, during which progress continues but slows considerably. These plateaus are followed by periods of return to rapid learning. Recognition of this cycle in learning rate is important to ensure continued motivation to persevere.

Vellutino et al. (1996) presented research evidence confirming that severely delayed readers who are viewed as difficult to remediate can reach their reading potentials if instruction is intensive, and preferably begins early.

LEARNING FROM TEXT

Note Taking. While this chapter will make recommendations for teaching severely delayed readers and nonreaders, it will also tell you some "instructional" procedures to avoid. Jot down activities to avoid as you encounter this information in your reading of the chapter.

A GENERAL PRINCIPLE: INSTRUCTION SHOULD APPROXIMATE THE REAL ACT OF READING

The principle that reading instruction should approximate authentic reading certainly holds true for all students, but deviation from it has most often occurred with nonreaders and severely disabled readers. When students face uncommonly serious barriers to learning, some programs have advocated activities far removed from the act of reading. These approaches have employed body management and perceptual training, including activities such as visual tracking practice, walking balance beams, lateral dominance exercises, discriminating the left sides of their bodies from their right, visual-motor integration drills, crawling, jumping, climbing, hopping, and eye-hand coordination workouts (e.g., throwing bean bags or drawing lines). The stated purpose of this training is to provide a prereading perceptual-motor foundation that ultimately will foster reading. Yet, whatever the intended goal may be, research has shown these procedures provide no assistance to academic learning of any kind for those with reading disabilities and learning disabilities or with developmentally disabled students. The Council for Learning Disabilities has adopted a position statement opposing training of perceptual and perceptual-motor functions as part of remedial programs ("Measurement and Training," 1986).

FIGURE 13–2 *Visual Discrimination Exercises*

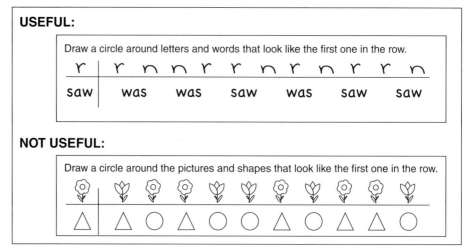

In addition, certain kinds of visual discrimination activities that have been used in prereading programs are not prerequisites for reading. One such activity requires students to visually discriminate between shapes and pictures. A typical exercise of this type asks students to look at the first shape or picture and find all others in a line that look the same or to find all the shapes or objects of one type in a picture. Numerous studies have shown that matching shapes and pictures as preliminary instruction for letter and word discrimination is useless (e.g., Barrett, 1965; Gates, 1926). If we want students to visually identify the distinguishing features of letters and words, the exercises should include letters and words and not nonword forms (see Figure 13–2).

Similar findings have resulted from research on certain types of auditory discrimination training. These studies have shown that instruction with nonverbal sounds does not transfer to the phonemic skills needed for reading. Training with nonverbal sounds may consist of exercises in which students are asked to distinguish between environmental noises, for example, by asking them to close their eyes while the teacher taps on several objects (such as a desk, the chalkboard, and a window) and then to guess the object being tapped. Another exercise is having them listen to tape recordings of sounds such as the typical sound of an alarm clock, lawn mower, or bird call and guess each sound. Such exercises simply do not have any relation to reading. These activities should be distinguished from helpful phonemic awareness training that involves discrimination of phonemic elements of letters and words. Appropriate instructional decisions prevent waste of learning time.

SEVERELY DELAYED READERS

Predicting the precise needs of severely delayed readers is not possible without knowing the learner. The term *severely delayed* is a rather general designation that can describe a wide range of differences (McCormick, 1999). Just as examples, a severely delayed high school student with an instructional level of, let's say, approximately third grade may have advanced through the alphabetic stage of word learning, but is not yet reading words orthographically. On the other hand, a severely delayed sixth-grade student reading at beginning second-grade level may just be making his or her way through the alphabetic stage (or neither of these statements may describe these specific students' reading behaviors).

When word recognition and word identification are sources of the problem, as is most commonly the case (Torgesen, Wagner, & Rashotte, 1997), considering word learning stage yields clues for teaching. These stages suggest the reader's current strengths (how he or she can best learn words at this point in time) and needs (what he or she needs to learn to proceed to the next stage). The description of typical reading behaviors associated with each stage, provided in Chapter 8, can serve as a checklist for estimating word-learning level. (Time for you to do a text lookback!)

Important to note, too, is that students need work with both word recognition and word identification. Some research investigating instruction for severely delayed readers has devoted the majority of instructional time to learning phonic analysis skills. Results have shown that while students in these studies have increased their decoding skill, the transfer to reading of whole words with automatic recognition has not occurred (e.g., Lovett et al., 1994; Torgesen et al., 1997; Wise & Olson, 1995). On the other hand, when severely delayed readers have engaged in abundant connected text reading in independent and instructional level materials, with assistance on specific difficult words, automatic word recognition has improved (Wise & Olson, 1995). The point is that you get what you teach and students need to be taught both.

Although less frequent with severely delayed readers, it is possible that some students with extreme reading discrepancies may have grade-appropriate word knowledge but show acute deficiencies in comprehension. There may also be differences in how you work with a student whose reading attainment is 3 years below his or her expected achievement versus one who is 5 years, or 6 years, or 8 years delayed, for instance—instructional differences related to issues of motivation. In any case, individual evaluation is requisite for determining needs of severely delayed readers and for structuring beneficial programs.

LEARNING FROM TEXT

Drawing a Schematic. The next several pages will provide suggestions for addressing the problem that "severely delayed readers' difficulties lie mainly with word recognition/identification." Generate your own diagram, using a problem-solution schematic, as illustrated in Chapter 12. This diagram should include the problem stated here and some brief statements of solutions that you derive from the information in these pages.

Instructional Suggestions for Word Learning

A far too insufficient body of research is available to inform our instruction of severely delayed readers. Some of the instructional studies that do exist are reviewed here.

Word Self-Selection. A motivational element was a factor in one word-learning program with severely reading delayed students in a laboratory clinic (Noble, 1981). Intermediate grade students with good oral language skills but seriously limited reading vocabularies participated in a plan based on a well-known word self-selection concept used earlier by Sylvia Ashton-Warner (1964) with Maori children in New Zealand. Students, described as being discouraged from being "left out and left behind," selected some of the words they wanted to learn, a procedure that was intended to be beneficial because of the learners' interest in those words.

The instructional approach was as follows. The young students orally read short passages at their instructional levels and the teacher recorded unknown words. Each student selected a few of the unknown words he or she wanted to learn, and the teacher chose an equal number of these to be studied. Word study took up 10 to 20 minutes in each session. Each word was written in isolation on one side of an index card and in context (using the sentence from the reading material) on the reverse side. After initial instruction using what the researcher described as "appropriate techniques for teaching sight vocabulary" (p. 387), words were reviewed through games and flashcard activities.

The majority of students learned more of the words they had chosen than those selected by the teacher, although with a few students no difference was seen. For students who are reluctant to try after repeated failure, the researcher suggested word self-selection as a motivating procedure.

No information was given on the specific words chosen by the students versus those selected by the teacher, although a partial list of one student's combined group of words was provided as an example: *then, while, came, exhibit, forced out, complete* (p. 386). Knowing whether the student's choices had more easily distinguished characteristics than those picked by the teacher would make it easier to evaluate the power of this approach. The word *then*, for instance, might be harder to discriminate (because of similar words such as *than, them,* and *when*) than the phrase *forced out* or a word with distinctive letters and more concrete meaning, like *exhibit*. Still, with excessively reluctant learners who have endured many failures, the approach of self-selection might prove to have some usefulness.

The PASP Program. A Phonological Awareness Plus Synthetic Phonics (PASP) program was undertaken by Torgesen, Wagner, and Rashotte (1997) with young children for $2\frac{1}{2}$ years, focusing primarily on the Auditory Discrimination in Depth method devised by Lindamood and Lindamood (1984). Following this approach, children were intensively taught sounds of phonemes, including how to place their mouths in the correct positions to pronounce them, to consciously hear the sounds in words, and to associate the sounds with particular letters.

Also included in PASP was instruction in decoding words while reading books written with words that were phonologically regular, as well as spelling instruction with "regular" words—that is, those that did not contain irregular spelling patterns.

In general, this program significantly improved phonics skills of the subjects but did not improve whole-word reading. These researchers concluded that training in phonetic reading skills is a necessary but not sufficient condition for improvement of overall reading abilities of severely delayed readers. They suggested that students also need word-learning instruction centered on units larger than single phonemes.

Analogy Use. Wolff, Desberg, and Marsh (1985) obtained positive results by teaching analogy strategies to fifth-grade learning disabled students who were reading three grades below their actual grade placements (i.e., at about second-grade reading level). Learners were taught to compare unknown words with words already known and make comparisons about letter combinations (e.g., the unknown word *fight* might be recognized by comparing it with the known word *light*). The learning disabled students in the study gave many indications of being in the rudimentary-alphabetic stage of word learning (they guessed at words using letter name cues and partial sound cues, using only a first letter or two; they seldom employed more complete, sequential decoding or use of sound-symbol generalizations). As you noted in your review of the word learning stages in Chapter 8, analogy use often begins at about second-grade level, but usually not by those who haven't yet reached the orthographic stage. These researchers saw their instruction as a way of "speeding up" reading development. They believed that while competent readers may develop analogy use intuitively, severely delayed readers must be systematically taught the strategy.

One of their two procedures was effective. The following steps helped students learn analogy use and generalize the strategy to new words.

1. Students were shown an unknown word and directed to think of a word that would look like it, if the first letter were changed: If they could not recall such a word, they were given three examples and then asked to think of a word of their own.
2. They were directed to pronounce the unknown word like the known word they had given, changing only the sound of the first letter.

Here is the procedure that did *not* work.

1. A known word that had been written in red by the teacher was pronounced by the student.
2. An unknown word with a similar letter pattern with the exception of the first letter, written in blue, was then to be pronounced by the student.

When teaching analogy use, greater gains have been seen when students generate their own examples rather than merely reading words supplied by the teacher.

Can you already guess what made the difference in the two procedures? It's that same old theme—the importance of depth of processing. The researchers credited the superior effectiveness of the first set of procedures to students' generating their own words in contrast to merely reading words that had been supplied by the teacher. They believed this helped the learners form better mental sets for generalizing the strategy to new situations.

It should be noted, however, that severely delayed readers would be able to use this strategy only with letter-sound associations they knew. This is because the technique described earlier called *consonant substitution* must be employed (e.g., substituting the /f/ sound for the /l/ sound when *light* is changed to *fight*). All common consonant letter-sound associations would have to be known for the strategy to be most effective.

Some aspects of this program seem reminiscent of the Glass Analysis approach (Glass & Glass, 1978). The Glass Analysis method has at times been recommended for use with severely delayed readers because of its focus on frequently occurring word parts larger than single letters. It is believed to be a simpler avenue to decoding than some other conventional systems that involve smaller phonic elements and somewhat cumbersome phonics rules. The Glass Analysis program is based on letter clusters that are for the most part phonograms (see Chapter 9 for a list of phonograms), although a few clusters represent other types of letter combinations.

Instruction begins with one cluster. A number of words containing the cluster are analyzed, centering first on letters that stand for certain sounds and then on sounds heard for certain letters (e.g., for the cluster *ing*, the following might occur: "Here is the word *rings*. What letters make the /ing/ sound? What letter makes the /r/ sound? What letter makes the /s/ sound?" and conversely, "What sound does *ing* make? What sound does *r* make? What sound does *s* make?" Then other words containing the *ing* phonogram are analyzed in this same way). Although suggested by a number of authorities, currently there is no research available to confirm the actual effectiveness of the Glass Analysis method. Rather, Glass based the approach on his observations of children and believed it to be valuable when used with students who had chronic reading problems.

Self-Correction of Errors Based on Meaning.   Pflaum and Pascarella's (1980) work involved students with learning disabilities in the primary and intermediate grades as well as some of middle school age. These were students who were reading 3 years below their actual grade levels despite normal intelligence. Learners were taught procedures aimed at inducing self-correction of oral reading errors based on meaning of passages read. In 24 lessons, students did the following:

1. They listened to tape recordings of another reader and underlined oral reading errors, first in lists of sentences, then in paragraphs, and then in stories.
2. They listened to their own taped readings and did the same.
3. They underlined errors made by another recorded reader, underlining twice when the errors changed the intended meaning, underlining once when they did not.
4. They did the same with their own taped readings.
5. Next, the focus moved from simply noting errors to self-correction. To introduce this, students marked with a small *c* those errors that were corrected by a recorded reader.
6. Some attention was given to using letter cues plus context to correct errors.
7. Learners corrected the errors made by a recorded reader, using the sense of the passage.
8. In paired learning situations, students worked together to correct errors on a worksheet prepared by the teacher.
9. Students recorded and analyzed their own reading. When they heard a miscue, they stopped the tapes and corrected it.

For ideas on prompting severely delayed readers during reading when they are having difficulty identifying words, go to www.bankstreet.edu/ literacyguide/early.html. Click "Reading Strategies," then click "During Reading Strategies."

Students receiving this instruction were contrasted with another group who were given phonics instruction in which they were taught individual sounds of letters and how to blend these sounds together to decode words.

The self-correction instructional procedures used with the first group represent a good example of systematic, carefully sequenced, intensive instruction. And they worked—for students whose reading levels were second grade and above. For that group of students, posttest scores on word recognition and comprehension were significantly higher for students taught to self-correct than for students receiving phonics instruction. However, for the students reading below second-grade level, the phonics group scored higher. This points again to the fact that the reader's level of word learning must be taken into account. What is most constructive instruction for students who are in the earliest stages may not be for those in later stages, and vice versa. This is true although all the students may be deemed as severely reading disabled, each having a significant delay between his or her own expected achievement and actual attainment. One can assume that there may be differences in what is appropriate as instructional techniques for a seventh grader reading at fourth-grade level and what is appropriate for a fourth grader reading at first-grade level, although both have a 3-year lag in learning.

Computer–Assisted Instruction. Wise and Olson (1995) conducted a computer-assisted instructional study with students in grades 3 through 6 who had scored below the 10th percentile in word recognition. Students read stories on a computer, with a third of the time spent reading aloud to the teacher and two thirds reading silently. When difficult words were encountered, students could click on a word and use color coding provided by a program titled a Reading with Orthographic and Speech Segmentation (ROSS) to help in sounding out the word. If still unsuccessful, another click caused a speech feedback feature to pronounce the word for the student. These students thus engaged in accurate, supported reading experiences. Although their problems emanated from word-learning difficulties, high-quality comprehension activities accompanied the stories. The students spent most of their off-computer time reading books.

At the end of the study, when results were contrasted with those from a group whose program centered heavily on explicit phonics training, the computer-assisted story reading group scored less well on decoding skills, but better on automatic whole-word recognition. Once again, students learned what they were taught—and they need to learn both (McCormick, 2006).

Programming Based on Psycholinguistic Principles. Eldridge (1985) focused on one middle school student, providing an in-depth case study of instruction and learning of a severely delayed reader in seventh grade. The student was of average intelligence but with a seriously restricted word recognition vocabulary; he was reading at about first-reader level, able to use materials customarily read by children near the end of first grade. This student had received instruction in learning disability classes since first grade with obviously limited success, and the school had concluded that he was "unable" to learn.

Eldridge's plan was to modify instruction the boy had previously received by basing lessons on psycholinguistic theories of reading. **Psycholinguistic processes** are those that combine thinking processes with language knowledge (Smith, 2002). In the reading field, approaches based on psycholinguistic research emphasize meaning as a means and an end to reading and generally advocate instruction based on a whole-language orientation (Goodman, 2002). (Note that the term *psycholinguistic* is used differently by educators in special education, where it once referred to training involving body management and perceptual activities, radically different instruction from that used by Eldridge.)

Eldridge's program consisted of (a) emphasizing the axiom that reading should make sense (and stressing the correction of errors based on meaning); (b) demonstrating to the reader that he could combine several sources of information to read—visual and orthographic cues (including the spelling of the word), semantic clues (meaning), and syntactic cues (sentence structure); and (c) ensuring that the boy read copious amounts of connected text material at his instructional level, carried out orally in the early stages. Eldridge also provided one-to-one instruction for 2 hours per day.

Eldridge's program in the early stages of the lessons used a language experience approach, having the student dictate and read his own stories, and while reading, finger-point to individual words. The teacher read sentences when difficulties arose, followed by the student reading (sometimes called **echo reading**). Other specifics included (a) words targeted for learning based on those in the student's stories; (b) words practiced in the context of stories or sentences, never in isolation; (c) the student writing out copies of his dictated sentences; and (d) many rereadings of the same story, with the student prompted to use various strategies with unknown words or sometimes simply told the word.

All these tactics together gave the student many exposures to the same sets of words. Stanovich (1986) and others have provided evidence that frequent exposures positively affect word recognition accuracy and latency. A **latent period** in psychological research refers to the interval between a stimulus and a response; in plain language, *latency* simply means how quickly the reader recognizes a word after it is seen. If a student must pause and study before recalling a word, the period of latency is likely longer than desired. A shorter period is the goal; the ultimate objective is automatic word recognition.

Later, Eldridge used "integrated" stories. Words from the student's dictations were written into new stories by the teacher and read by the boy. Eldridge's goal in doing this was to give the student repeated encounters with the words in a variety of contexts; this also precluded the student's simply memorizing his own dictated stories (and thus making it appear that he had attained word recognition when he had not). Writing was emphasized throughout the program, permitting the student to focus on distinctive features of words.

Fluency was promoted through rereading of the same stories and with timed 1-minute readings of short passages, where the aim was rapid recognition of words. Eldridge noted that automatic recognition of words was fostered in these ways.

At the next stage, the student read commercially published stories, which were introduced when he had gained enough sight vocabulary from working with his own stories. Over the 3-year period during which Eldridge worked with him, the student eventually progressed to reading short novels at his increasingly higher instructional levels. When these "chapter books" were first introduced, shared reading was employed: The student read some and the teacher read some, each taking turns throughout the lesson. Eldridge also had a rule of thumb called the "50-page limit": The student had to stick with the novel for 50 pages; then, if he did not like it, a new novel was selected. Gradually expanded amounts of silent reading were included in the sessions.

At the end of the 3-year program, this severely delayed reader attained scores on an informal reading inventory indicating a word recognition level of 6.5; scores on a standardized test were equivalent to a fifth-grade level.

This was an excellent success story for a reader who previously had profound difficulties. No doubt, the amount of instruction available to him—2 hours per day of one-to-one instruction—was an influential factor. However, quality of instruction is also a crucial ingredient in learning. The procedures employed by Eldridge were sound and would be recommended by most contemporary reading educators. This instruction indisputably affected this student's life in positive ways. The school had believed this boy was destined to be an adult "functional nonreader." After this instructional experience, that no longer would be the case. He had shown clear evidence that he was "able" to learn.

Still, after 3 years of instruction, this student would have been a tenth grader and therefore a reading level of fifth or sixth grade continued to represent a severe lag between potential and achievement. Had he persevered with the program beyond the 3-year period, that may have resolved the difference. However, one also wonders if explicit instruction with sound-symbol correspondences would have hastened his learning. Given new information on the criticality of

Writing helps students focus on distinctive features of words.

phonemic associations for adequate reading, it seems reasonable that such phonics instruction would have been a fruitful addition to the tutoring.

Instruction With Adult Severely Delayed Readers.   Bruner (1983), Watson (1982), and Meyer (1982) all targeted adult severely disabled readers in their research. Bruner reported step-by-step procedures of a technique that aided word identification for a 43-year-old man who had a critical sound-symbol decoding deficit; explicit instruction of letter-sound correspondences and their uses in word identification, as described in Chapter 9, were employed.

A 21-year-old intelligent college student with a severe reading handicap was the subject of Watson's work. Learning events and tenets of instruction were similar to those described in Eldridge's program, with Watson designating this as instruction based on whole-language principles. After 10 months of one-on-one instruction with reading and writing activities, the student showed improvement.

Adults reading at an elementary-school level were aided in Meyer's study by a technique she called Prime-O-Tec, an adaptation of the simultaneous reading technique (see Chapter 8). Prime-O-Tec produced significant gains in vocabulary recognition and in comprehension over gains made by a control group of adults not receiving this instruction.

Even with adults, stages of learning must be considered. Types of miscues made by severely delayed adult learners have been shown to vary with their degree of reading development, with major differences seen in error types between those adults who read at or above third- to fourth-grade levels and those who read below these levels (Norman & Malicky, 1987).

NONREADERS

Nonreaders are unable to read any connected text. Despite normal intelligence, lack of sensory deficits, absence of obvious neurological defects—and much reading instruction—they have not learned to read.

"Nonreaders" may recognize a very few words, but recall of even these few may be sporadic.

Taken literally, the description *nonreader* suggests that the individual can recognize no words. In some cases, however, by the time the student has been referred to a remedial program he or she has learned a word or two or even a few, but not many. Students with extreme delays may recognize their own names or a word or so they have picked up because of its frequent occurrence in their environment, such as *Boys* or *Girls* on restroom doors. As a result of instruction, some nonreaders may have spotty knowledge of several words typically taught in beginning reading programs, such as color words, a few function words from a high-frequency word list, or a couple of words learned from a preprimer. However, recognition is occasional and recall is sporadic.

Experience has shown that the number of words known by a nonreader may range from about 2 to 50; however, because nonreaders know so few words and because of the nature of the words they do know, the words cannot be combined into any kind of meaningful reading. Take the case of Peter, an 8-year-old boy with a measured intelligence of 116 and a superior oral language vocabulary. Peter could distinguish four written words when he was enrolled in a university reading clinic during the summer after his second-grade year. In spite of 2 years of schooling and above-average intelligence, the only words he knew were *I, a, and,* and *but.* Thomas, an 8-year-old third grader with a high average IQ of 107, recognized more words, 21, but most were function words such as *at, the, no, has, to, a, it, is, as,* and *in.* He had managed to learn these 21 words with great effort over $2\frac{1}{2}$ years, perhaps because of their frequent appearance in early reading lessons. In neither student's case, however, could the known words result in the reading of any kind of meaningful text, even simple sentences.

The term *nonreader* should be distinguished from the term *prereader.* The reason **prereaders** cannot read is simply because they have not yet been exposed to reading instruction; for example, many 5-year-olds are prereaders. A nonreader, on the other hand, has had reasonably extensive instruction and still is unable to read in any meaningful sense. Older individuals who are often labeled as illiterates are sometimes nonreaders, but in other cases are really prereaders, that is, they do not read because they have not had the opportunity to learn. (The term *preliterate* is sometimes used synonymously with the designation *prereader,* especially if referring to an adult.)

Nonreaders also should be differentiated from students like Bridget and Dan, our case study students in earlier chapters. Bridget and Dan each had gotten off to a slow start in first grade, and early intervention was instituted to prevent successively larger gaps in their reading growth. Nonreaders have had a good deal more instruction than those case study students. The description *nonreader* is not applied unless a student has had a minimum of 1 full year of instruction with virtually no reading development.

A typical route for nonreaders is a move to a remedial reading program after no increases in learning occur despite substantial assistance in their regular classroom work. When other students in the remedial reading class progress and the nonreader does not, he or she may be tested to assess eligibility for a learning disabilities program. With the continued lack of advancement after a year or so in an LD class, if a reading clinic is available, the student may be referred there. After having had much attention by a number of educators, the student still arrives at this clinic unable to read at all. Conversations with previous teachers who have worked with a nonreader generally uncover a variety of futile programming attempts to resolve the student's problems. The nonreader's difficulties seem highly resistant to instruction.

Can these students be helped? We are slowly learning more about how to set the learning environment for nonreaders in such a manner that they can learn to read. Special care must be taken to provide word study in ways that are appropriate to the student's stage of development (McCormick, 2006). In addition, it must take into account the resistant behavior the student may exhibit toward typical instruction; that is, motivational factors must be considered (Spear-Swerling, 2004). Because of recurring failures, many nonreaders cease to try. Not only may there be lack of task persistence (Friedman & Medway, 1987), but these students may simply refuse to engage in reading-related activities at all. All these factors should be considered in the design of early phases of programs for nonreaders to ensure positive outcomes.

It is unfortunate that the majority of research concerned with nonreaders has been directed to issues of causation (e.g., attempts to determine if visual perception aberrations are impeding their word learning or if brain malformations are the source of their problems—the latter usually assessed during autopsies, and therefore, a little late to do anything about it!). Another research approach has been to describe nonreaders' learning characteristics, such as assessing their speed in naming letters or ability to read non-words in comparison with the aptitudes of more competent readers. This is *not* to say that exploring causes for the nonreading enigma or the response behaviors of these individuals is without worth. At some time, these studies taken together may provide clues that will allow preventive efforts or suggest ways in which instruction should be structured. In the meantime, however, teachers need information on how to teach those who seem "unteachable." Sadly, *instructional* studies to examine what does and does not facilitate learning for nonreaders are exceedingly scarce.

LEARNING FROM TEXT

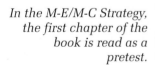

Verbal Rehearsal.   What would you say if asked to define the term *nonreader*?

The Multiple-Exposure/Multiple-Context Strategy

Among the small amount of instructional research available on nonreaders are two studies investigating the Multiple-Exposure/Multiple-Context (M-E/M-C) Strategy (McCormick, 1991, 1994). In both, use of this program had positive results with nonreaders. The M-E/M-C Strategy consists of the following interventions.

1. A high-interest, easy-to-read book *series* is used for instruction, a series in which the easiest book is written at a simple preprimer level. Typically these books consist of a single short story divided into five or six small chapters. The same major characters often appear throughout the series, having different adventures in each succeeding book. Such series are intended for remedial work; although written at easy levels with new words introduced at a moderate pace, they focus on topics designed to appeal to somewhat older learners. A series of this type is used because stories intentionally repeat words from earlier books. Thus, when a student has completed one small book, he or she may move to the next and there find familiar words learned in previous stories in the series.

In the M-E/M-C Strategy, the first chapter of the book is read as a pretest.

This is preferable to using a number of different unrelated books in early stages of instruction with nonreaders. A very moderate rate of word introduction and many opportunities to review the same words is necessary for initial instruction to take hold.

2. The first chapter in the easiest book is used for a pretest. The student reads the chapter as best he or she can and the teacher records words that are unknown. To allay student anxiety, the teacher simply says, "Don't worry about words you miss. I'll teach those to you later."

Even a nonreader may know a few of the words (perhaps *I, a,* and one or two more). Each chapter at the easiest level in this type of series is notably short, with approximately five pages per chapter and one or two brief sentences per page. Chapters also are written so that only 10 or so different words are used. Therefore, even if the student does not know most of these, the number of unknown words that the student needs to learn is in an acceptable range.

3. The teacher's task for the next several sessions is to teach the unknown words from the first chapter. Because the targeted words are tied directly to the book, once the student learns these words, he or she can successfully read a selection of connected text—a first-time occurrence in the life of a nonreader.

Word recognition is accomplished through providing students with multiple exposures to the words, but using techniques other than drill. Rather, the words are presented in multiple contexts. Although nonreaders require many occasions for practice, flashing word cards at them 40 or 50 times is not the path to learning.

Three major categories of practice are used to study words.

    a. *Contextual activities.* Practice of words in context is undertaken to boost generalization from recognition of individual words to recognition of these in connected text. Practicing words in context is difficult in the earliest stages because students know so few words, but simple sentences usually can be written by combining unknown words from the chapter and the few words the learner already knows, including, perhaps, his or her own name. **Cooperative stories,** as seen in Figure 13–3, are also useful; to use cooperative stories, the teacher reads most of the text and the student reads only the boxed material, which includes his or her practice words and known words. As more words are learned over time, contextual practice involves increasingly larger pieces of text, moving to paragraphs and short stories written by the teacher.

    b. *Practice that focuses on the internal features of words.* This consists of writing, spelling, manipulating letters to form words, tracing words, and other activities that encourage attention to the orthographic elements of words.

    c. *Use of games and manipulatives.* These are used to provide a stress-free form of practice and to motivate discouraged learners to expend maximum effort. Some of these activities offer contextual practice, but more afford exposures to words in context-free situations (i.e., in isolation).

Table 8–1, found in Chapter 8 of this text, lists word practice activities similar to those used in the M-E/M-C Strategy. These suggested activities are found on page 237.

FIGURE 13-3   ***Sample of a Cooperative Story***

Larry was running to Dan's house. Dan lived in a neighborhood where all the houses looked the same. Larry was in a hurry and wasn't thinking very carefully. As he scooted up to the gate in front of one house, he paused for a moment and said to himself:

- This is Dan's house.

Larry rushed through the gate, up onto the porch, and pushed the doorbell. When a woman appeared he did not recognize her, but thought maybe she was Dan's aunt. Larry wasn't sure, though, so he said:

- Is this Dan's house?

The unfamiliar woman said, "No. Dan lives next door." Down the steps and out the gate Larry ran, then into the next yard and up onto that porch. Another unfamiliar woman was sitting right on this porch, in the porch swing. Larry asked again:

- Is this Dan's house?

"Right!" said the woman. "Do you want me to call him?" "Yes," replied Larry.
    "Dan!" the woman called. And in a moment or two a tall, baldheaded man with large muscles and a beard appeared. "Who are you?" asked Larry politely. "I was looking for Dan." The woman responded by saying:

- This is Dan.

Flustered, Larry sputtered, "Dan is a guy who plays softball with me." The bald-headed man laughed. He said:

- I work.

He went on to say, "I think you have the wrong house and the wrong Dan." But the woman quickly added with a smile and a twinkle in her eyes:

- This Dan plays, too.

She asked Larry, "Would you like to take him to your softball game instead of your friend?" Larry looked at the tall man with his large muscles and thought how neat it would be to have *him* on their team. They'd probably win every game. "Wish I could," said Larry, also with a twinkle in *his* eyes, "but the other team would never allow it. Guess I'd better find the right house and the right

- Dan.

During the several days when unknown words from the first chapter are practiced, the lessons focus only on that small set of words (never more than 10). An attempt is made to include all three practice types at least once in each session (contextual practice, attention to the internal features of the words, and use of games and manipulatives). Thus, the student has repeated practice with the words but in a variety of ways, each of which is designed to satisfy specific goals.

Changing activities frequently throughout the lesson also maintains attention. Because of nonreaders' all too frequent reluctance to participate in any reading activities, capturing interest is important in the early lessons. This reluctance, born of previous failure, lessens when successes begin to occur. Moreover, identification of distinctive features of words under a variety of stimulus conditions has another advantage: Transfer of learning is strengthened. It is more likely that a learner will recognize the word in another context than if all learning had been limited to one form of exposure, such as seeing the word many times on a flashcard.

A vital feature related to word study is visual demonstration of progress. Throughout sessions, the student is helped to realize that gains in learning are occurring. Simply telling a nonreader, "You are doing well," is not a potent indicator to these students who never before have "done well." Being intelligent individuals, they are aware of their deficiencies when they compare themselves with peers. A verbal pat on the back in the form of statements such as "You are doing a good job" simply may not be believed. Therefore, progress charts and graphs, the counting of newly learned words, and the like, are used abundantly. By self-charting the number of words known from one day to the next, a student can see that headway is being made. If the known words in a word bank are counted every day, the increase in number is plainly discernible to the student. Motivational incentives are considered critical in the M-E/M-C Strategy and should not be overlooked.

In addition to word practice, one other element is included each day. The teacher reads aloud to the nonreader to provide exposure to real narratives or expository selections at a time when these students cannot yet access connected text themselves. A standard one-hour lesson may include 10 minutes of the teacher's reading aloud from a well-known book of children's or adolescent literature and 50 minutes of varied word practice. Figure 13–4 depicts three successive days of lessons with one nonreader when the M-E/M-C Strategy was inaugurated with her.

Following the plan outlined previously, on the average, a nonreader learns the small set of words from the first chapter of a book in about 3 to 5 hour-long sessions. When words are known, the student returns to the chapter, reading it again, this time successfully! Early on, emphasis is placed on learning the words well before returning to the book to reread in order to demonstrate to the student that he or she can indeed learn to read. Effective chapter reading does just that. Although strong emphasis on word study is necessary to launch the reading effort, this method also allows a relatively quick return to connected text reading in comparison with some alternate approaches to teaching nonreaders.

Along with an emphasis on word study, the M-E/M-C Strategy allows a quick entrée into connected text reading.

4. The second chapter of the book is approached in the same way: Pretesting the words by a contextual reading of them, practicing the words repeatedly but in a variety of ways (some of which are highly appealing to disinclined readers), and rereading the chapter triumphantly when words are known. Each chapter of the first book is completed in this way.

5. When all chapters in the book have been undertaken in this manner, the student rereads the entire book in one sitting. Because this is the first time a nonreader has conquered an entire book, it is a red-letter day!

6. At this point, the student is ready to move to the next book in the series. By this time, the student knows a reasonable corpus of words, which is composed

FIGURE 13-4   *Three M-E/M-C Sessions*

<u>Session 1 for Kerry</u>

<u>9:00-9:05</u> – Talk with Kerry about the events of her weekend.

<u>9:05-9:15</u> – Work on Kerry's 7 targeted words: (<u>house, this, Dan, work,</u>
<u>too, plays, is</u>). I have made flashcards with these words. For the 4
words that can be illustrated, I drew a picture for the word on one
side and put the word only on the other side:

The other 3 words will have no picture. To give successful experiences I
included in the flashcard pack the 3 words Kerry already knows (<u>a,</u>
<u>and, I</u>). To provide a strong support system to introduce these words
we'll do the following:

   <u>First</u> – She'll read the word (using the picture if one accompanies
      it). I'll pronounce those without pictures and use each one
      in a sentence before <u>she</u> reads it.
      – She'll trace the word.
      – She'll read the word again.
      – She'll use each one in an oral sentence.
  <u>Second</u> – I'll scramble the word cards.
      – She'll read them all again.
      – When she cannot, I'll pronounce those words and have her
      trace again. I'll point out important features of the word
      and have her say it once more.
   <u>Third</u> – We'll go through the second step again; this time <u>one</u> of the
      pictures will be turned over so she must read the word
      without help from the picture.
 <u>Fourth, Fifth, Sixth</u> – Same as step 2, but each time we'll turn over
      one more of the picture words.

<u>9:15-9:25</u> – Continue practice on her targeted words: I have made a game
    board with a track. The words are written on file cards. Correct
    responses will allow Kerry to move along squares to the final goal.

<u>9:25-9:35</u> – I will read <u>to</u> Kerry: <u>Amigo</u> by Byrd Baylor (rdg. level = approx. 3.5).

<u>9:35-9:40</u> – I have written short sentences with Kerry's words. Examples:
                 Dan plays.
             Dan and I work, too.
    She will read these to me orally.

<u>9:40-9:50</u> – Kerry will play Word Bingo using her words and a blank bingo
    board I have made. I will lay file cards with the words on the blanks.
    Since she doesn't have enough words to cover all squares, some words
    will appear more than once. I will call the words and she will cover them
    with pennies.

<u>9:50-10:00</u> – End-of-session check:
      1) Using words written on index cards, I will check Kerry's recognition
    of the words at the end of this session.
      2) Words she knows instantly will be placed on a word bank ring.
    She will help me do this. We will count the number she has on the ring
    today and talk briefly about trying to add more the next day.

(continued)

FIGURE 13–4 *Three M-E/M-C Sessions* *(continued)*

Session 2 for Kerry

9:00-9:05 – We will talk about Kerry's success in the last session in getting some words on her word bank ring. For a beginning-of-the-session review I will have Kerry read the words already on the ring. I will show her two games I have made for word practice today and ask her to choose which game we play first. Game #1 = "Grand Slam"; Game #2 = "Rotten Apple."

9:05-9:15 – We will play the game Kerry chooses to use first.

9:15-9:20 – I have written a "cooperative" story which both Kerry and I will read. I will read most of it, but I have interspersed her words in brief sentences throughout. She will read these.

9:20-9:30 – We will play the other game specified above.

9:30-9:40 – I will read to Kerry Once A Mouse by Marcia Brown (rdg. level = approx. 3.0).

9:40-9:50 – Play Word Hunt. I will write her words on red construction paper rectangles the size of a small file card. Before class I will hide these around the clinic materials room. Kerry will look around the room and find her word slips (I used red so finding them would be easy). As she finds each one she will bring it to me and READ it.

9:50-10:00 – End-of-session check:
1) Using flashcards I will check her recognition of the words.
2) She will assist in adding those she recognized instantly to her word bank ring.
3) We will count these and make goals to add more tomorrow.

---

of a variety of types (e.g., nouns, verbs, and function words). Contextual practice activities have expanded and have begun to look very much like natural text. Rate of word learning accelerates as students proceed through the chapters of the books, and fewer practice sessions are needed before returning to read the chapter. Furthermore, the student typically shows a will to try and exhibits less avoidance behavior.

7. As the learner moves through the series, there comes a time when it is apparent that the strong support system of the M-E/M-C Strategy is no longer needed. The student is then moved into a more typical reading program with attention to sound-symbol correspondences, ample amounts of connected text reading every day, and instruction to meet other assessed needs.

One study conducted with the M-E/M-C Strategy (McCormick, 1994) examined the learning of Peter, introduced on p. 429 who could read only four words

LEARNING FROM TEXT

Self-Monitoring. Having read the steps for the M-E/M-C Strategy, can you say *why* each element is included? If you cannot, it's time to do a "text lookback."

FIGURE 13-4 *(continued)*

<u>Session 3 for Kerry</u>

<u>9:00-9:10</u> – I will read aloud to her <u>Frederick</u> by Leo Lionni (rdg.
level = approx. 3.0-3.5). Afterward I'll have Kerry compare
Frederick, the mouse, and the mouse in Marcia Brown's story I
read to her yesterday. How were they alike? How were they different?

<u>9:10-9:15</u> – For a beginning-of-the-session review Kerry will read the
words on her word bank ring to me. Yesterday all of her remaining
words were added except <u>this.</u> I think that after today's session of
word practice she will be ready to reread the first chapter of the
book tomorrow. Yesterday she even knew the word <u>this</u> after some
hesitation and a self-correction. Although she did <u>correctly</u> read all
of the other words when I checked her at the end of the period, there
was also a hesitation on a couple of these. I thought one more day of
practice on all of them was wise to be sure she really knows them so
she'll have a success experience with the book tomorrow.

<u>9:15-9:25</u> – Special work on the word <u>this:</u>
   1) I will show the word on a flashcard and say it.
   2) She will read it, trace it, and say it again.
   3) We will compare <u>this</u> and <u>is</u> on 2 flashcards since she has often
      confused <u>this</u> with <u>is</u>. We will talk about differences in how the
      words look and she will use each one in an oral sentence.
   4) I will give her sentences to read in which both <u>this</u> and <u>is</u> appear.
      The sentences will use her targeted words and sometimes
      pictures. Examples:

                Is this Dan?

                This is a house.

                Is this a 🐱 ?

<u>9:25-9:35</u> – Practice with <u>all</u> words in her set: Since we have read about
mice for the last 2 days we will have a "mouse" game. In this game,
cloze sentence strips will be used. Kerry must say the correct word
that will fit into the context of the sentence, then match this word
with the correct one written on a construction paper mouse. Correct
responses allow these mice to move across a game board to a large
piece of cheese.

<u>9:35-9:45</u> – Special practice with the word <u>this</u>: Manipulate letters on
a magnet board. The purpose of this activity is to highlight the features
that distinguish <u>this</u> and <u>is</u>. After deciding which of these fits into
each of several cloze sentences I show her, she will spell it on the
magnet board.

<u>9:45-9:55</u> – Work with <u>all</u> of her words: Puzzle Activity. I have written
the words on puzzle pieces I made. She will read each word; when it
is read correctly she will fit it together with other pieces to form an
animal (a camel). After she identifies the animal, I will tell her that
tomorrow I'm going to read her a book called <u>The Camel Who Took A
Walk</u>.

<u>9:55-10:00</u> – End-of-session-check: Hopefully the word <u>this</u> can be added
to her word bank ring. To check for this I will lay out cards on the desk
with all her words on them. The word <u>this</u> will be placed somewhere
in the middle. I'll ask her to quickly read over them all.

after completing second grade. Peter's mother understood the importance of emergent literacy activities in the years before he came to school; as a result, experiences with hearing stories, trips to the library, and the like had been an important part of his formative years. The usual good effects of these activities were not realized with Peter if measured in terms of his reading attainment: In his first 2 years of school, he attained no reading competence at all. After experiences with a basal reading program, a language experience approach, an intensive phonics procedure, and the Fernald Method (described later in this chapter) were carried out by a classroom teacher, an LD tutor, and two reading clinicians—all to no avail—the M-E/M-C Strategy was tried as the frame for his instruction. Learning commenced quickly, and by the end of 16 weeks (56 hours) of one-to-one instruction, he had learned 170 words and was reading material at a second-grade level.

At that point, Peter's program was modified to one that is more standard in remedial instruction, and a follow-up study was undertaken to monitor his progress. The heavy emphasis on word recognition early on did not have adverse effects, but rather allowed him to learn. Peter had excellent comprehension throughout his participation in the clinic, learned decoding strategies, and eventually read with fluency. He read a large variety of narrative and expository materials, developing interest in different genres and topics as time went by. Peter participated in the clinic program for $3\frac{1}{2}$ years in all, including the early period during which instruction was not effective, the time of the M-E/M-C Strategy application, and the follow-up period. He was "graduated" from the program at age 12, reading at seventh-grade level.

Another research investigation with the M-E/M-C Strategy (McCormick, 1991) was undertaken with Thomas (p. 429) who, before beginning the program, recognized 21 function words (plus his first name, but not his last). Thomas, like Peter, came from a home where he enjoyed preschool years rich with books. He showed clear abilities in mathematics computation and logic, and although his speech development had been delayed, after its onset he had acquired a broad expressive vocabulary. Thomas also had several experiences with different methods of reading instruction, each instituted when he had not responded favorably to a previous one. In an early one, Thomas had opportunities for writing experiences, but he was not yet able to recognize or write most letters and was unable to profit from these opportunities to any productive degree. By the time he enrolled in a reading clinic, he had control over letter recognition, but he scored below first preprimer level on an informal reading inventory (IRI) and was unable to read the easiest first-grade material, although he was in the middle of third grade.

While being instructed with the M-E/M-C Strategy, Thomas completed a preprimer and primer-level book and learned automatic recognition of 90 words over a period of 11 weeks. Tests of word recognition in isolation and in context administered 1 month after the intervention had been terminated showed he had maintained knowledge of words he had learned. After approximately 10 additional months of clinical work, he progressed to third-grade reading before his mother removed him from the program. Five months later his parent reported that he had continued to progress.

The Fernald Approach

Probably the best-known clinical procedure for nonreaders is an approach developed in 1921 by Grace Fernald and Helen B. Keller, known as the Fernald Method. This is also sometimes known as the VAKT, approach because it is carried out in four stages that employ the v̲isual, a̲uditory, k̲inesthetic, and t̲actile senses (from which come the acronym VAKT). Since a number of senses are involved, it is often referred to as a multisensory approach. The Fernald Method uses the following four stages:

A positive feature of the Fernald approach is that, from the beginning, students focus on both orthographic (visual) and phonological (auditory) aspects of words.

Stage 1: *Tracing.* The program is begun with whole words, not letters. Students choose a word to learn. This can be a short word, long word, easy word, or hard word. The teacher prints the word on a card and the students trace it. As they trace, they say the *sounds* of the word parts (this does not mean spelling the word letter by letter). The process is repeated until the students can write the word without looking at it. If they cannot do this, they are given the card again and must repeat the original process. When they can write the word from memory, it is typed and they read it in typed form. Finally, the word on the card is filed alphabetically in a box for later review. After a number of words have been accumulated, the student uses these to write a story. The story is immediately typed to be read. Instruction in Stage 1 may occur for a few days or several weeks before it appears that the student can learn without tracing and can be moved to Stage 2.

Stage 2: *Writing.* The teacher prints the word on a card, saying the parts as this is done. Students observe the process. The students are given the card, study the word, try to visualize it with their eyes closed, and silently "say" it to themselves. Next they write the word without looking at the card, saying the word parts as they do. If an error is made, they are given the card again to compare the error with the correct form. They continue to study, visualize, and say the word until they can write a story using this word and those previously learned. The story is typed, and the students immediately read it silently and then orally.

Stage 3: *Recognition from print.* The teacher no longer writes the word on a card. Instead, the students choose a word from a book, are told its pronunciation, study it, visualize it, "pronounce" it silently to themselves, and then write it from memory. If they cannot do this, they study and pronounce the word until they can. Reading in first preprimers begins during Stage 3.

Stage 4: *Recognition without writing.* In this stage, each new word is not written. Instead the students are taught to study new words and note their similarities to familiar words. Silent reading precedes oral reading. During oral reading, if students do not know a word, it is pronounced for them. After the reading, only these "problem" words are pronounced and written by the student.

Research on the Fernald Method has produced contradictory findings, with some studies not indicating favorable results. In other studies, conversely, this approach has helped nonreaders when a variety of other procedures had proved unsuccessful (Bryant, 1979; Hulme, 1981). However, it is a method in which progress sometimes seems to be rather slow. For this reason, other instructional plans might be tried before the Fernald Method is implemented.

One factor that may contribute to the Fernald Method's lack of success with some nonreaders is the limited interest they have in the learning activities. Some aspects do not capture the attention of students who have developed antagonistic attitudes toward reading. They become quickly bored with the repeated tracing, sounding, visualizing, and copying from and have some difficulty seeing the point of these procedures. Although you may know that doing this can lead to word learning, they are skeptical and do not think this is going to help them read books. After a session or two, students may exhibit avoidance behaviors, seem reluctant to engage in the activities, and make only half-hearted attempts, limiting the amount of practice they obtain and the serious attention they give to the words. No participation, no learning.

Remember who you are working with here. These are students who have met roadblocks in their every attempt at reading. Day after day, week after week, month after month, maybe year after year, they have been frustrated in their efforts to do what others around them can do. While they may believe that nothing is going to make the difference, give a game to the same students who are bored with less involving activities and they will participate for the fun of it whether they think it will help their reading or not. In the meantime, a little learning sneaks in. Give the same students a manipulative (arranging magnetic letters on a magnet board, for example), and they will concentrate because they are actively engaged with a concrete operation. Creative teachers probably can modify the procedures in the Fernald Method to figure motivation into the learning equation for nonreaders.

LEARNING FROM TEXT

Reviewing and Reflecting.   Do you agree with what has been said in the last two paragraphs about the Fernald approach?

Reading Mastery: DISTAR Reading

The Reading Mastery: DISTAR Reading program employs a grapheme-phoneme method based on a synthetic phonics approach. It has often been used in classes for students with learning disabilities. In general, its use had been bypassed by reading teachers because the procedures are viewed by some to be undesirably mechanistic. Still, research with DISTAR has routinely produced favorable results (e.g., Meyer, 1984). It is unclear whether students in some of the research investigations of this program consisted of severely disabled readers in the more general sense with serious delays of varying degrees or consisted of nonreaders, but it appears likely both categories have been included in the groups studied. The first stage of the program assumes the student is not reading.

In initial stages, students learn the sounds of 40 symbols. These include the lowercase letters, certain letter symbols designed by joining letters that are sounded together, such as *ng*, and long vowel sounds with their diacritical marks. Silent letters appear in small type. (Later in the program a transition is made to more conventional forms of print.) After learning the sounds of these symbols, students sequence and blend them to form words. Still later, two- and three-word sentences are read. One of the first of these is

hē rēads.

Eventually the students progress to reading stories.

One advantage of the DISTAR program is that an ample amount of instructional time is provided: (a) daily lessons are considered a basic requirement (if students miss a day, they must have two lessons the next); (b) lessons last for 40 minutes—twice the length of sessions in many beginning programs; and (c) procedures are conducted to ensure that every student responds during every lesson. Another advantage is immediate feedback to each student response.

The disadvantage of the DISTAR program is that instruction begins with the abstract task of learning the sounds that letters stand for, and students do not read words until they have mastered the sounds. For some students, this means that it is a long time before they are in contact with meaningful material.

The Orton-Gillingham Approach

In 1966, Gillingham and Stillman developed a program for working with seriously delayed readers based on theories about causes of reading disability advanced in the late 1920s by Samuel Orton. This is generally known as the Orton-Gillingham Approach. In 1976, Slingerland proposed certain adaptations to the program. The adapted program is referred to as the Gillingham-Slingerland Approach or the Orton-Slingerland Approach. If the programs are followed as outlined, students receive instruction 5 days a week for a 2-year period. Sessions last 1 hour and the activities are changed at least every 10 minutes. This latter is a plus with off-task students, keeping them involved and the lesson moving. A grapheme-phoneme orientation is employed and includes four basic steps:

1. Students trace single letters and then learn the sounds they commonly stand for. An extended period of time is spent on working with letters and letter-sound associations.
2. Students are taught to blend consonants and short vowels into words that have a consonant-vowel-consonant pattern. They blend the first two letters and then add the last: /ma/+/t/. Finally, they spell the word.
3. Sentences composed of the resulting words are read.
4. Phonetically irregular words are learned through tracing.

Though Orton's theories are no longer considered tenable, some aspects of this program are consistent with more recent research indicating the need for development of phonics understandings. The advantage of the Orton approaches is that students obtain explicit instruction with sound-symbol associations and help with blending these to read words. A principal disadvantage is the lack of opportunity for students to read meaningful, connected text until after they have mastered a large number of skills. On occasion, the basic forms of the programs have been modified by various educators to incorporate additional principles and procedures that vary, or add to, the fundamental models.

As with DISTAR, the precise characteristics of the populations in research studies on these approaches are somewhat vague, but the programs in the studies direct their instruction in the beginning to students who, though they have had instruction, are not reading. Although these programs have been successful with some students, Ruppert's (1976) research showed that the Orton-Slingerland Approach had produced no better reading achievement in that study than a more flexible, eclectic method when used with students who had been classified as learning disabled.

Using Predictable Books

Predictable books have become a common vehicle for instruction with beginning readers (Bridge, 2002). Research has shown favorable results in sight vocabulary learning when they have been used with poor readers having moderate delays in learning (Bridge, Winograd, & Haley, 1983). Their use has been recommended with nonreaders.

A number of elements can make a book "predictable," and a variety of types have come under this rubric. When language patterns in books are very repetitive, when there are cumulative structures (that employ, for example, adding new lines to old in a systematic way, as in *The House That Jack Built*), if there are sequential episodes, or if there is rhythmic and rhyming language, the books all may be designated as predictable. When a book, like the classic *Three Billy Goats Gruff*, for instance, has sequential episodes in a plot in which events repeat themselves with only a little variation, this helps students to predict story lines, which often aids comprehension. However, this does not assist nonreaders with their basic problem—severe difficulties with word recognition. Thus, when predictable books are recommended for use with seriously delayed readers, the type of predictable book is an important consideration.

Predictable books that may provide assistance with word learning are those with very repetitive language. An example is *Brown Bear, Brown Bear, What Do You See?* (Martin, 1983). In such books there is a high degree to which the same words are consistently repeated. Routinely, after initial use of a predictable book with emerging readers, the book is read over again several times in a variety of ways. The frequent repetition of words in the text and the rereadings of the book may foster word learning because of recurrent exposures students have to a limited number of words.

The positive effects of highly repetitive predictable books have been seen with students whose word-learning difficulties are less extreme. Nonreaders, however, have not always experienced good results. Perhaps this is because, despite serious reading delays, nonreaders are usually very bright individuals who have learned alternative strategies to survive in academic and real-world environments. They have mastered a good deal of information through listening. When the teacher reads a predictable book to a nonreader, with its easy-to-discover pattern of words, and the learner then "reads" it in unison with the teacher, and he or she then "reads" it with teacher assistance, and so on, soon, as a result of all these readings, the student can give an excellent rendition of the book. It appears that the student is indeed reading the text because he or she says all the words correctly. The performance is even fluent. Unfortunately, when the student later confronts the same words in another text, the words are not recognized at all. Clues to what has occurred can be seen in the cases in which nonreaders have had "read and reread" experiences with a predictable book and then recite the book word for word with perfect accuracy—while the book is closed, or even when it is in another room! They have learned the exceptionally uniform book pattern through listening, not through attending to the written words.

Remember, nonreaders usually are in the pre-alphabetic phase of word learning (see Chapter 8, p. 230 for a review of characteristics of that phase): They have not found productive ways of attending to word clues. Something more than rereading of easily memorized books is needed to establish word knowledge that is functional—word knowledge that can be used in real reading of other books.

A number of elements can make a book "predictable," and a variety of types of books have come under this rubric.

Becker (1994) has developed a plan for working with nonreaders using predictable books. The multiple rereading of stories is maintained to provide many contextual exposures to words—as well as experiences with connected text in the early phases of their learning. But between each reading, direct attention is given to recognition of specific words found in the book, both through isolated and in-context practice exercises. In addition, explicit focus on word clues is promoted (i.e., centering on clues within words, such as letter sequences). During introductory reading of a text, the nonreader is directed to the illustrations, but, in addition to six repeated oral readings of the book in a variety of ways over a 3-day period, chart-story versions of the book are used. To do so, the teacher reproduces the exact story on chart paper for the student to read without the aid of illustrations; this procedure is used after the learner has had several contextual and noncontexual exposures to the words.

Many activities are employed with the predictable book in Becker's plan: Briefly discussing the author, illustrator, and title; making predictions before reading based on illustrations, the teacher reading the text while the student follows along; finger-pointing; checking predictions and asking questions; word games; shared reading; visual cloze activities; assisted reading; matching word cards to text; looking for repeated words in the text; using masks or frames to focus on orthographic sequences or on specific words or phrases; matching sentence strips to the text; silently reading along while listening to the story on tape; independent oral reading of the book; and innovating on the text by adding, deleting, or substituting words and phrases to produce new sentences on the chart story. Given the inordinate difficulties of nonreaders, this plan has greater promise for developing generalizable word knowledge than plans in which learning is expected to occur incidentally from numerous rereadings alone.

LEARNING FROM TEXT

Summarize.   What is the reason why use of predictable books has sometimes been ineffective with nonreaders? What is the remedy?

One carefully conducted, in-depth case study has been undertaken using these procedures with a nonreader (Becker, 1994). The participant was a second grader who, at the beginning of the program, recognized only 15 words, most of which were function words (e.g., prepositions and conjunctions). After instruction with 10 predictable books following this plan, at the end of 10 weeks, the student had automatic recognition of 75 words. The researcher reassessed the student's knowledge of these words after a lapse of 1 month during which no intervention occurred, finding that the student had maintained recognition of 71 words.

A myriad of predictable books are now published commercially and are widely available. Even among books for which "predictability" is grounded in very repetitive language structures, there still are differences in difficulty. Becker (1994) has made a careful analysis of recommended predictable texts and proposes a sequence to inaugurate a program with nonreaders. The sequence begins with books that have the fewest number of different words and progresses to those that have slightly more. (A book, for example, might have 90 total words, but only 9 that are different from one another.) The 10 predictable books to establish reading behaviors with nonreaders suggested by Becker are the following, in this order (numerals in brackets behind the publisher's name indicate the number of different words in the book):

1. *Have You Seen My Duckling?* (Greenwillow) [8]
2. *Have You Seen My Cat?* (Picture Book Studio) [9]
3. *I Went Walking* (Harcourt Brace Jovanovich) [28]
4. *The Cake That Mack Ate* (Joy Street Books) [30]
5. *Brown Bear, Brown Bear, What Do You See?* (Holt) [32]
6. *The Chick and the Duckling* (Macmillan) [32]
7. *Where's Spot?* (G. P. Putnam Sons) [33]
8. *10 Bears in My Bed* (Random House) [34]
9. *Polar Bear, Polar Bear, What Do You Hear?* (Holt) [36]
10. *Dear Zoo* (Four Winds Press) [42]

Other Instructional Possibilities

In addition to research, the professional literature also includes suggestions from educators for instructing nonreaders. Although no supporting research is offered to confirm the effectiveness of the approaches, they are usually based on direct experiences in working with nonreaders and are, for the most part, in conformance with current educational thinking.

Cunningham's Method.   Cunningham (1988) suggests combining language immersion, explicit and targeted sight vocabulary teaching, and phonemic awareness training in a program for nonreaders.

Following Chomsky's (1976) suggestion, Cunningham recommends that a nonreader listen to a book the teacher has taped until he or she has learned it well. Repeated listening/reading procedures are often referred to as **language immersion programs;** that is, the student is immersed in large amounts of oral and written language (Ruddell, 2006). Chomsky worked with very poor readers who had beginning reading skills, but who had failed to progress beyond the introductory level. She had students follow along in books while they listened repeatedly to taped stories. The students engaged in multiple listenings of the same narrative until they became familiar enough with the words to read the story orally with ease. Most students required about 20 listenings before they could fluently read their first narrative; but, thereafter, they could read each successive book with facility after fewer and fewer listening sessions. Not only did fluency increase, but students participating in this program acquired confidence and increased interest in reading. Chomsky reported that one parent said her daughter, who had previously avoided reading, had begun to read with great frequency at home and that "she even reads to the dog and cat" (p. 291).

Cunningham (1988) recommends language immersion with nonreaders and further proposes extending this experience by giving the learners a blank tape on which they record any small portion they can read themselves as they progress from learning by listening to the teacher's version.

In addition, specific words are selected for instruction. These are taught to mastery, using a variety of techniques, so they can be identified independent of the book. Furthermore, when the number of words learned reaches 25, these are used as a basis for phonemic awareness exercises and later phonic analysis training. The phonics instruction begins with the teacher selecting two of the learned sight vocabulary to serve as key words to letter sounds, slowly adding more as student understanding of decoding principles grows. Phonograms and consonant substitution also are introduced and are based on words from the fund of known sight words.

After earliest stages of the program, some silent reading is encouraged with short selections of text, allowing the student to engage in "mumble reading." **Mumble reading** consists of saying the words quietly; this serves as an intermediate phase between oral reading and true silent reading.

Cunningham's method is founded on the premises that one learns to read by opportunities to engage in reading of real texts and that word recognition and letter-sound associations are best taught by linking them with something that is already known.

An Adapted Language Experience Approach.   One standard reading method, the language experience approach (LEA), has been useful with some severely delayed readers (Eldridge, 1985 [see research account presented earlier in this chapter]; Stauffer, 1970). Stauffer (1970) reported that certain students enrolled in the university reading clinic with which he was associated made progress with LEA. However, this often has not been the case with nonreaders.

LEA, based on student-dictated stories, does not seem to provide the support needed by many of the most delayed learners. Nonreaders typically have well-developed oral language skills. Thus, the stories they dictate tend to be lengthy, interesting, and difficult to read. There are too many words. Even if the teacher structures a situation so the story is maintained to a shorter composition, there are not enough repetitions of individual words for the nonreader to learn, remember, and retain them. Rereadings of the stories produce easy memorization, but not true word learning in which the knowledge of words transfers to any other situations.

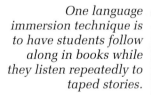

One language immersion technique is to have students follow along in books while they listen repeatedly to taped stories.

However, adaptations of the typical LEA program may be useful for non-readers. To develop a functional program, short selections must be used; students must continue to work with the same story until words are known, in contrast to frequent dictation of new stories. Furthermore, direct practice with individual words from the stories is necessary. Providing a strong reinforcement program to motivate the students through the difficult early phases of the process also is recommended. Reinforcement can come about from visual demonstrations of progress and small appropriate awards when short-term goals are met (see Figure 13–5).

LEARNING FROM TEXT

Summarize. What are reasons that use of the language experience approach has sometimes been ineffective with nonreaders? What is the remedy?

FIGURE 13–5 *A Bar Graph Charting the Number of Words Known by a Student*

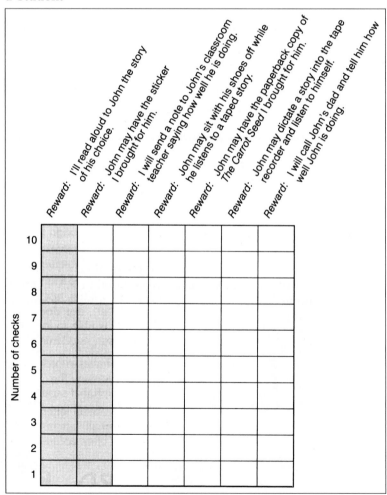

Other Concerns

There are certain specific teaching and learning problems that often occur with readers who are severely delayed in their progress, regardless of the general approach used. Suggestions for remediating these follow.

Letter Recognition. While not often a problem with older nonreaders, if students enter a program immediately after a year of first grade or even after a slightly more extended period of schooling, they may not yet have obtained accurate, not to say, automatic, recognition of all letters of the alphabet. The importance of this knowledge has been previously discussed. In summary, recent research indicates that "reading depends first and foremost on visual letter recognition" (Adams, 1990b, p. 21). For some time, large numbers of studies have shown that knowledge of letter names is the single best predictor of success in first-grade reading (see Adams, 1990a, 1990b; Johnson, 1969; Venezky, 1975; Walsh, Price, & Gillingham, 1988). This is not to say that other factors are unimportant in the complex act of reading, of course; however, it is difficult for nonreaders to gain control of these other factors without letter recognition. It would certainly be cumbersome to go through a student's instructional program referring to letters in ways other than by their names (e.g., for the letter *f* asking something like "What sound does that upside-down candy cane with a line across it make?" or, for the letter *g*, saying something like "Notice that this word begins with a ball with a tail." and so forth).

The term **letter recognition** does not mean learning the correct alphabetical sequence (as in saying the alphabet), nor does it mean the sounds of the letters are known. It simply means a student can look at a letter, recognize it, and name it. Here are some suggestions for assisting students with letter recognition.

1. The ability to say the alphabet in order is helpful because written symbols can be tied to the names already known. The "Alphabet Song" is an easy way for young students to learn the alphabet sequence.

Letter recognition is not easy; the task of letter recognition causes learners to grapple with a great many abstractions.

2. Many of the uppercase (capital) letters are easier to distinguish than the lowercase (small) letters. Note the differences between the capital and lowercase forms of these often confused letters:

BD   bd

For this reason, capital letters often are taught first to preschool children. However, once students are enrolled in school and face the task of reading, the preferred choice is usually to begin with lowercase letters because lowercase letters are encountered more frequently in printed text.

3. One of the best ways to help students learn names of letters is through writing. They learn to form each one and associate it with the name from the "Alphabet Song." Writing the letter calls the student's attention to its distinguishing features and fosters recall.

4. Another technique that will help students note the distinctive forms of individual letters is tracing while saying the name. Several variations of letter tracing that may be employed are tracing letters written on paper, tracing cardboard cutouts of letters (these may be purchased through a teachers' supply catalog), and placing a light layer of sand in a cafeteria tray and having students trace letters in the sand. Using several methods provides variety in lessons. It should also be noted that there has been some misunderstanding about the

purpose of tracing activities. Tracing is not used because certain students learn in an odd and unusual manner; that is, it is not because they learn with their fingertips instead of their brains. Tracing is used simply because it aids students who might not attend *carefully* to specific details if asked merely to look at letters as they are learning them.

5. Relate lessons on letter recognition to other materials that are meaningful to students. For example, write Susan's name and call attention to the letter it begins with. Then have her find all the words in the day's lesson that begin with that letter.

6. Work with only a few letters at a time—perhaps two or three—and introduce new letters only after these are learned.

7. Help students eliminate letter confusions. When students confuse similar letters, this is often the result of a reversal of the left and right directions of letters (e.g., confusing lowercase *b* and lowercase *d*). At other times, the confusion is an inversion; that is, the tops and bottoms of letters are inverted (e.g., in confusing *b* and *p*).

In the past, when students mistook *b/d, n/u, d/p, M/W,* and so on, this was often attributed to a visual perception problem, mixed lateral dominance, or a neurological processing difficulty, and it was an easy way to get a student labeled as "dyslexic." Research in the fields of education, neurology, and psychology has shown these views to be incorrect. In the first place, reversals and other letter confusions are found in only about 10% of reading disability cases (Harris, 1970). In any case, letter confusions are as common with young average readers as with poor readers. Most educators today believe that these confusions simply result from inexperience with directionality as a way of making discriminations (Moyer & Newcomer, 1977). For identification of concrete objects like chairs, birds, or cars, the direction of the object does not affect its name. A chair facing right, a chair facing left, or a chair placed upside down is still a chair. To discriminate among many similar letters, however, direction is important. A line with a circle on its right side is a *b,* but a line with a circle on its left side is a *d,* while an "upside-down" line with a circle on its right side is a *p.* With training in the importance of directionality, even preschool children can be taught to distinguish reversible and invertible letters.

Confusion of letters is a fairly typical behavior pattern during the early stages of learning to read. It should not be presumed to be a danger signal indicating a major or unusual problem. However, such confusions should not be ignored; instructional procedures can be implemented to ensure that they do not persist. Some suggestions for helping students eliminate letter confusions follow.

   a. If students confuse *b* and *d* (probably the most common reversal), prepare a capital *B* and a lowercase *b,* each cut from oaktag. Show students how the small *b* could fit on top of a capital *B.*

Tell them that if the letter they are looking at does not fit on top of the capital *B* correctly, it is not a *b.*

b. Use file cards. Print *b*s on some cards and *d*s on the others, or do this with whatever letters are confused. Mix up the cards. Have the students sort all the *b*s into one pile and all the *d*s into the other. When they can do this accurately, then time them to see how quickly they can make the discriminations in order to build speed of recognition.

c. Make up worksheets containing rows of letters. Have the students circle all the *b*s, or *m*s, or whatever letter they are confusing. When they can do this accurately, time them to see how quickly they can do this correctly. For example:

w   o   h   w   ⓝ   s   o   ⓝ   u   p   l   o   ⓝ   g   i   u   l   ⓝ   u

p   r   u   t   u   o   v   ⓝ   k   a   b   t   z   ⓝ   h   u   j

The worksheet should contain both letters the students are confusing, for example *n* and *u,* but the students should be asked to circle only one of the two.

d. Have the students go over a page from a magazine and circle with a marking pen every occurrence of one of the letters in the pair they are confusing.

e. Don't forget the helpfulness of context once the student begins to read a bit. Suppose a student frequently confuses *b* and *d*. If the student is reading for meaning, context frequently will not allow these confusions. For example, reading *big* as *dig* would not make sense in this sentence:

That big dog ran away.

When context provides a clue to letter identification, encourage learners by asking, "Did that make sense?" Then, follow the lesson with specific attention to the two confused letters.

LEARNING FROM TEXT

Applying What You've Learned.   Suppose you were asked to talk to other teachers about the problem of reversals. What would you say? Frame a comprehensive answer.

Phonemic Awareness and Orthographic Processing.   The critical role of phonemic awareness has been stressed at several places in this text. In alphabetic languages, there is strong and convincing evidence that a root of the problem for many poor readers—even those with more moderate disabilities—is lack of phonemic understandings (Spear-Swerling, 2004). Unquestionably, assessment of phonemic awareness should be undertaken with nonreaders and with other individuals with severe learning delays. Practice activities proposed earlier for developing phonemic awareness very likely should be a part of the interventions for a large number of delayed learners.

However, there also is evidence that deficiencies in **orthographic processing** may be the locus of the problem for certain individuals (Solman & May, 1990; Stanovich, 1991b). For these learners, deficits may lie heavily in the visual domain, not the phonological—although this group of learners may be much smaller in number. These learners have difficulties in recognizing words using visual and orthographic cues—that is, recognizing and remembering letters, noting and recalling sequences of letters in words, and using other productive cues that help them visually distinguish word patterns (Stanovich & West, 1989).

It is hypothesized that this subgroup of students may have complications in storing patterns of words in memory. Or, on the other hand, they may have failed to learn prerequisite information that allows visual cues to be employed. For instance, it is difficult to remember the sequences of letters in a word if you don't know the letter names. Let's suppose you are trying to do this with the word *word,* not knowing letter names. You say to yourself, "This begins with that squiggly mark that has lines pointing downward, then there is a circle, then there is a squiggly mark that is a straight line with a little piece of curve at the top, then there is a circle with a long line stuck on the back of it." And if you had to do that with very many words—whew! You might give up trying to read right then. Another hypothesis is that, although words might be stored in memory, there may be unique difficulties in retrieving the patterns that have been stored. It is interesting to note that in non-alphabetic languages, such as Chinese, a defining characteristic of poor readers seems to be an orthographic deficit (Ho, Chan, Leung, Lee, & Tsang, 2005).

Stanovich (1991a) cautions that these obstacles should not be confused with the "visual perception enigmas" that were once proposed as a cause of reading problems but that have since been refuted. It is not suggested that students perceive print in any eccentric manner, but, rather, that learning the visual abstractions of writing and recalling word patterns is uncommonly troublesome for them.

In summary, while it seems that a prevalent problem among many disabled readers is lack of phonological awareness, some readers may have orthographic processing problems instead. It is interesting to speculate about nonreaders. Perhaps the reason their reading delays are so abnormally pronounced is that they have both phonological and visual processing impediments.

Independent Activities for Nonreaders.   There are two reasons why nonreaders may be asked to work on activities independently. First of all, although instruction is best carried out individually with these students, a clinical reading program may not be available in the area where the student lives. Therefore, enrollment in a remedial program in which most instruction is conducted in a group setting may be the only recourse. Some instruction for the students may be undertaken individually, but there will be times when each student must work alone so the teacher can provide instruction to others. Second, nonreaders spend only part of the school day in the reading teacher's class; during the remainder of the day, they are in regular classrooms with many other students. Obviously, the regular classroom teacher cannot spend all of the day working on a one-to-one basis with any one student.

Appropriate independent activities are difficult to devise for nonreaders because they can read so little. Unfortunately, this results too often in students receiving independent work that provides no assistance to academic learning (such as coloring pictures unrelated to any reading skill or activity).

The instructionally relevant activities that follow are especially useful to reading specialists in their reading programs, but also prove successful in the regular classroom. Most teachers are perplexed about how to handle students who read very little (if at all) and welcome good ideas for independent student activities. Reading teachers can make copies of these suggestions and give them to classroom teachers who have students in the earliest stages of reading acquisition. Used in the regular classroom, these activities provide the nonreader with reading-related experiences to supplement those provided in the special clinical or remedial program.

1. Ask a skilled reader to record a story onto an audiotape. Have the non-reader listen to the story, using earphones. After the story is completed, the non-reader is to fold a piece of paper into four sections, then draw pictures about the story in four parts that follow the sequence of main occurrences. This provides opportunity for seriously delayed readers and nonreaders to hear connected text and to focus on comprehension of what was heard.

2. Place labels on objects around the room, for example, *clock, chalkboard, door, chair, desk.* Give the student index cards with the same words written on them, and ask him or her to match the word cards with the labels around the room. Next, the student scrambles the cards and attempts to read each one without looking at the labels. After silently reading each word, the student checks it against the labels in the room. The student places the cards back in the pack and continues to practice until he or she feels confident of correctly reading all cards without looking at the labeled objects. A peer tutor can listen to the words read and place those recognized correctly into a file box of known words. The other words are retained for more practice.

3. After hearing the teacher read a story to the whole group, the nonreader can use the tape recorder at the room's listening center and record retellings of the story. The student may be given different instructions at different times such as, "Be sure to tell something about all of the important characters," "Tell the story exactly in the order things happened," or, "At the beginning, tell the main idea of the story, then give as many details as you can." At a later time the teacher listens to the taped retellings and provides feedback during the next individual session with the student.

4. Write words on one-half of the front side of an index card. Place an illustration of the word on the other half of the card's front side. Make a cut between the word and its illustration, jigsaw-puzzle fashion. The cut should be slightly different for each card. Students are to try to read the words, but when they cannot, they match the illustration to the word by finding the jigsaw cut that fits. Students continue reading and matching until they can say each word without using the illustration. Here are two examples of such word-picture cards.

A number of creative approaches can make independent work academically useful for nonreaders.

5. Have the student use a wordless picture book. A **wordless picture book** illustrates a story from beginning to end but contains no words. Many of these are available. A particularly delightful one is *The Chicken's Child* (Scholastic) in which a hen mistakenly hatches an alligator egg and the pictures convey the unusual problems she faces as her new child grows—and grows. The learner should be asked to study the pictures of a wordless picture book from beginning to end and silently develop his or her own stories. In the next individual session with the teacher, with the book used as an aid, the student dictates a story for the teacher to write. This story is used as the focus of a language experience lesson for one or several days.

6. Ask the student to listen to a tape recording of an informational selection the teacher or an aide has previously taped. Include questions on the tape about the selection and ask the student to draw answers. Example: "According to what you have just heard, which of these is a reptile: A bird, a dog, or a snake? Turn off the tape recorder now and draw a picture of the right answer. When you have finished, turn on the tape recorder again to hear the next question."

7. Give the student a magazine along with an envelope labeled with a letter, such as *f*. Have the student cut out all the pictures in the magazine he or she can find that begin with the sound of that letter and place them in an envelope to take home for parents to check. The teacher can talk with the parents or enclose a note so they understand the task. Also, it is important to set up a system, such as requiring a parent's signature on the envelope, for determining whether the check was made.

8. Collect old reading books that can be cut apart. In one session, have a peer tutor read a story to the student from one of the books. Before the next session, cut out the pictures from the story. In the second session, during which the student works independently, give him or her the pictures in a scrambled order. Ask the student to sequence them correctly and paste them on hole-punched notebook paper, one picture to a page. By tying yarn through the holes in the paper, the student can assemble his or her own wordless picture book. In a third independent session, the student can use this "book" to dictate the story into a tape recorder to be checked later by the teacher for accuracy in remembering details.

9. Cut pictures from old reading books or magazines so that pairs of pictures represent words that rhyme. Paste the pictures on colorful construction paper squares and give them to the student in random order; have the student match those that rhyme.

10. Tape-record a series of word pairs, some of which begin with the same sound and some which do not. Prepare a worksheet like this:

As students listen to the tape, they circle the happy face if the paired words begin with the same sound or the unhappy face if they do not.

11. Paste two pictures on a card side by side and draw frames around each, cartoon style. The pictures should be related to one another and placed to show a logical progression of events or action. (Old reading books are a good source for these.) Draw one more frame, following the other two, but leave this third frame blank. To aid in story prediction, ask the student to draw a picture in this frame depicting what might logically occur next.

The suggestions here are only a sampling of ideas for providing reading-related independent work for nonreaders. These ideas were selected to demonstrate a variety of alternatives to direct teacher intervention (by use of peer tutors, taped material, self-correcting materials, and so on) and to list ways in which non-readers *can* respond (by drawing, circling happy faces, coloring, and so on). These suggestions were chosen to illustrate several different skill, strategy, and knowledge areas—following a sequence of events, developing a sense of story, recognizing words, relating reading activities to the real world, noting details and main ideas, relating words to concrete objects, using picture clues, recognizing the messages conveyed by books, making letter-sound correspondences, dictating stories, and gaining familiarity with the book language of narrative and expository material. Teachers can add to these suggestions and maintain a file of ideas for academically relevant, independent activities that can be used with nonreaders.

📖 A FINAL WORD AND VITAL POINTS TO REMEMBER

With the right combination of features, instructional programs can be structured so that severely delayed readers and nonreaders *can* learn to read.

NCLB
READING FIRST

Working with severely delayed readers and nonreaders of any age can be one of the most rewarding of all tasks for the reading specialist. With the right combination of features, instructional programs can be structured so that these students *can* learn. And remember, the goal of NCLB is that *no* child be left behind. See Figure 13–6 for a summary of vital points to remember when working with severely delayed readers and nonreaders.

FIGURE 13–6 *Reminders for Working With Severely Delayed Readers and Nonreaders*

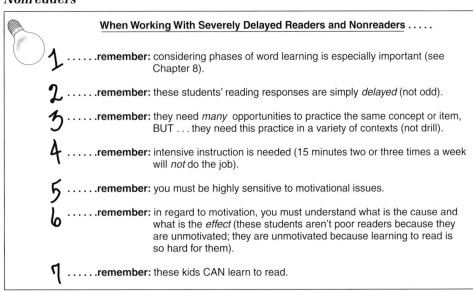

When Working With Severely Delayed Readers and Nonreaders . . . . .

1 . . . . . .**remember:** considering phases of word learning is especially important (see Chapter 8).

2 . . . . . .**remember:** these students' reading responses are simply *delayed* (not odd).

3 . . . . . .**remember:** they need *many* opportunities to practice the same concept or item, BUT . . . they need this practice in a variety of contexts (not drill).

4 . . . . . .**remember:** intensive instruction is needed (15 minutes two or three times a week will *not* do the job).

5 . . . . . .**remember:** you must be highly sensitive to motivational issues.

6 . . . . . .**remember:** in regard to motivation, you must understand what is the cause and what is the *effect* (these students aren't poor readers because they are unmotivated; they are unmotivated because learning to read is so hard for them).

7 . . . . . .**remember:** these kids CAN learn to read.

Reflections

1. Why do you think there have been so few instructional research studies focusing on severely delayed readers and nonreaders?
2. If you could design an *instructional* study with severely delayed readers or nonreaders, what would the study investigate?

14 Other Learners With Special Needs

Across the country, reading teachers today are providing instruction to students, preschool through adults, who are from cultural and linguistic backgrounds differing from the mainstream culture.

*T*oday's teachers often provide reading instruction to students whose linguistic and cultural backgrounds differ from the mainstream population. Some are immigrants or children of recent immigrants, and some are native-born Americans—but many in either group are at risk for educational failure. While most are children and older youth, some adults with similar personal histories have compelling literacy needs as well.

STUDENTS WITH LINGUISTIC AND CULTURAL DIFFERENCES

NCLB
READING
FIRST

Students with culturally diverse backgrounds include (a) those who speak Standard English, (b) those who speak nonstandard English, (c) those who are bilingual, and (d) those who do not speak English at all. While the families of some language-minority students are well educated and financially secure, many such students are from low-social status, low-income homes.

Newcomers currently prevalent in North American schools include Asians, Latinos, Pacific Islanders, Middle Easterners, Africans, East Indians, and Europeans. Once, most immigrants to the United States established themselves near their points of entry (California, New York, Florida, and Texas, as prominent examples), but recently, various groups—some living at the poverty level and some not—have settled in most states in both rural and urban areas.

There also are American-born students who are better served when there is sensitivity to the linguistic and cultural variations they bring to school, for example, some whose heritages are Appalachian or African American and those of native American peoples (Indian, Eskimo, and native Hawaiian). This is particularly true if poverty or other factors have prevented their families from moving into mainstream society.

LINGUISTIC DIFFERENCES

This section addresses oral language and literacy concerns for new English-language learners (ELLs), followed by a discussion of issues related to nonstandard dialects among American-born students.

English Language Learners

In the mid-1980s approximately 1.5 million students in the United States were new ELLs (IRA, 2001). This figure began increasing dramatically in the 1990s when the number of individuals immigrating to the United States was the largest of any decade on record (Gray & Fleischman, 2005). By 2003, Garcia and Beltrán reported that 42% of U.S. classrooms were serving one or more ELLs. And the numbers keep growing—in 2005 this population had risen to about 5 million (Goldenberg, 2005).

In many districts, students with several different first languages are found in the same classroom, along with native English speakers. As just one of numerous examples throughout the country, Devonshire Elementary School in Columbus, Ohio, a large Midwestern city in the U.S. heartland, serves students from Mexico,

Czechoslovakia, Egypt, and several sub-Saharan African nations (L. J. Weaver, personal communication, June 8, 2005). While approximately 70% of school-age English learners are Latino, the Latinos residing in North America are themselves diverse in regard to place of origin (e.g., Mexico, Central America, Cuba, Puerto Rico, and South America) and in terms of Spanish language use, culture, and economic status (Goldenberg, 2005).

There is much interest in improving educational levels of these students. In fact, this group is one of those heavily targeted by the NCLB legislation. The growth in language-minority populations presents interesting challenges for reading specialists and other teachers. Table 14–1 summarizes selected research relevant to oral language and literacy instruction of new English learners.

Oral Language Instruction.   Although opinions differ about some aspects of ELL instruction, almost everyone agrees about one thing—the importance of oral language development. Obviously needed for communication, a solid oral language foundation also is a major building block for literacy (see the oral language citations in the Research Box, Table 14–1).

Thus, there has been concern among educators that programs for ELLs too often provide insufficient time devoted exclusively to expanding knowledge of English vocabulary and structure. In many cases, language learning occurs only as a spin-off of other content area instruction. To satisfactorily address this fundamental area, Garcia and Beltrán (2003) make a strong case for reserving time each day dedicated solely to learning oral English. Referring to the successful Four Blocks reading program used in many regular classrooms (Cunningham, Hall, & Defee, 1998) they suggest that to those four blocks (guided reading, independent reading, word work, and writing), a fifth block be added for language-minority students—namely, English language development.

> It is important to remember that, while new to English, ELLs are fully competent in their own language.

In working toward oral language goals, educators should remember that, while new to English, these students bring with them rich knowledge of their first language. Jiménez (2004) describes the type of instruction to which teachers should aspire. After looking at studies of how teachers worked with Spanish-speaking ELLs, he stated:

> Teachers who were successful with their students recognized them as fully competent speakers of a particular variety of Spanish. Such recognition helped avoid many of the difficulties associated with a deficit perspective. In other words, they did not treat their students as linguistic incompetents—or solely as non-English speakers—but rather as individuals involved in the very natural process of second-language development. (p. 216)

It is also important to understand that when students acquire English, this does not mean they must lose their first language. Many students and their parents prefer bilingualism, and there are numerous reasons why this is advantageous. Furthermore, for very young ELLs, many successful programs in the United States, Canada, and other countries begin by strengthening development of the students' first language before moving into English learning.

New English learners operate at various English language proficiency levels. Gunderson (1991) suggests these descriptions. Some have *no or negligible English knowledge*, and are unable to respond to questions or name objects. Others exhibit *very limited English knowledge* but can produce two- to three-word phrases. Some who are more advanced, while still considered to have *limited English knowledge*, can speak a fair amount of English but often use ungrammatical structures.

Research Box

Reading

- Some data show that it is more effective for ELLs' first reading instruction to occur in their native language (Willig, 1985); other data indicate English-only immersion programs (Rossell & Baker, 1996) or structured immersion programs (Gersten, 1985) promote better reading progress. In Slavin and Cheung's (2005) review of several studies, most favored bilingual programs, but some found no difference between these and English-only programs; these authors called for additional studies carefully conducted over longer periods to better resolve the question.
- Reading skills learned for one language can transfer to reading in another language (Moll & Diaz, 1987), but students should be *taught* to transfer these skills (Goldenberg, 2005).
- Overall, skills and strategies needed to learn to read in one's native language or in a second language are about the same (Fitzgerald, 1995).
- When entering early grades, ELLs from low-income families often understand fewer traditional preliteracy skills (e.g., knowledge of alphabet letters) than mainstream students (Goldenberg & Gallimore, 1995). However, upon their children's school entrance, low-income parents increase, or begin to implement, a number of literacy activities with their children (Baker, Serpell, & Sonnenschein, 1995).
- Several studies with minority parents show their willingness to help their children in academic areas (Chavkin, 1989; Goldenberg, 2004) and their capabilities to do so (Guerra, 1998).
- In middle grades, successful reading achievement in English appears to be strongly associated with degree of proficiency in spoken English (Weber, 1991).
- Middle school bilingual students who are high achieving make connections between their two languages, for example, using the cognate vocabulary connections between English and Spanish (Jiménez, 2004).

Oral Language

- Children learning English for the first time in preschool at ages 3 through 5 go through the following stages: (a) continuing to use native language; (b) when they determine they are not being understood, becoming nonverbal and communicating through pointing and mime while simultaneously listening and developing *understanding* of the new language; (c) *speaking* single English words and phrases; and (d) using English to speak in sentences, although these may contain grammatical errors (Tabors & Snow, 2004).
- Young students who stop participating in oral language development activities before they have adequate control of English begin to do poorly in school in about fourth grade when language demands become greater (McCardle, 2005).
- Oral English learned outside of school may not entirely suffice because English used in classrooms differs in a number of ways from speech used in everyday settings (Piper, 1993).
- The time needed to develop fluent English varies with individuals. Some studies have shown that this can take from 2 to 6 years on the average (Wong-Fillmore & Valadez, 1986). Others have broken this accomplishment down and found it took about 3 to 5 years for general oral language development, but 4 to 7 years for academic English (Hakuta, Butler, & Witt, 2000).
- Teachers tend to spend too little time enhancing oral language proficiency when language development is undertaken only as a by-product of content instruction (Gersten & Baker, 2000).

Other Instructional Strategies and Stances Supported by Research

- Excellent teachers of ELLs (a) have high expectations for students, (b) are knowledgeable about reading instruction, (c) make use of cooperative learning, (d) include reading and writing in content area studies, and (e) are willing to participate in innovative/experimental instructional practices (Carter & Chatfield, 1986; Gersten & Jiménez, 1994; Goldenberg, 1996; Lucas, Henze, & Donato, 1990).
- Associations have been shown between a teacher's respect for students' native language and their achievement (Lucas, Henze, & Donato, 1990).
- There are no effects for achievement from simply matching students and teachers from the same ethnic or racial background (Vierra, 1984, cited in Goldenberg, 2004).
- There are cognitive benefits of bilingualism (Rossell & Baker, 1996).

Still others may be described as having *limited fluency*; although not at the level of native speakers, they use complex sentences that, for the most part, are consistent with English grammar.

Many practical ideas for oral language development, useful for native English speakers or ELLs, are described in the final section of Chapter 10. Teachers also find the following strategies helpful:

- At earliest stages of English learning—for students who possess no or negligible knowledge of English—use objects and pictures to teach nouns; develop an item collection and a picture file for these lessons. Engage in pantomime and role-playing to teach action words. Include puppets in lessons for young ELLs who are shy about practicing their new language. Use videos such as the Baby Einstein series designed to enhance language development for very young native English speakers. Employ computer software intended to teach simple vocabulary (see the illustration in Chapter 10, p. 337). Teach survival vocabulary (e.g., language to request bathroom visits and to satisfy other basic needs). Arrange for many, varied repetitions of targeted vocabulary and targeted language structures. Make directions clear and short.
- Plan for daily discussions. Here's why. Students will reach a point where they *understand* a moderate amount of English even though they are not *speaking* it. The key to advancement at this stage is *production* of language. As examples, have students engage in cooperative learning, explain directions to a buddy, or employ wordless picture books to structure conversations.
- Employ good books as springboards to oral language. Read simple, high-quality books to students who are in early stages of English development (e.g., the *Little Bear* series by Minarik). Reading whole stories to students exposes them to English syntax as well as vocabulary. Have students dramatize stories after they are read, encouraging use of vocabulary they heard in the story. Draw upon simply illustrated concept books designed for young children and linguistically predictable books like *Brown Bear, Brown Bear, What Do You See?* (Martin, 1983). Make pictures visible as you read by using Big Book versions or holding books so all can see; point to salient items and actions mentioned in the text. Gradually choose more sophisticated picture books as students' English expands. Take a "picture walk" before reading any book: page by page have students make statements or say words for what they observe (Garcia & Beltrán, 2003). To read about a highly effective oral language lesson using a Big Book, see the accompanying *Vignette: Real Teachers in Action*—"*A Sheltered English Lesson*" (p. 461).
- Attend to special language concerns. Explain English idioms. Confusions result from literal interpretations of phrases like *she came out smelling like a rose* or *he bit her head off*. Homonyms also cause problems (*two/too; hole/whole*). Explain the differences. After common meanings of words are well learned, introduce alternate meanings ("There are leaves under the trees"; "She put leaves in the table").
- Be aware of the demands of academic language. Explicitly teach word and phrase meanings ("*top* of the page"; "See the map *legend*"; "*Illustrate* your answer with an *example*"). Invite students to work together, problem solving through academic assignments. Many ELLs do not feel comfortable asking

Vignette: Real Teachers in Action

A Sheltered English Lesson

Programs that adapt instruction to foster learning for those who have control over some English but are not yet fluent are called *sheltered English programs.*

Gersten and Jiménez (1994) describe an effective sheltered English lesson using Big Books, which sit on an easel and are large enough for a group to see the pictures and print. The teacher they describe read to the students using a slightly slower than normal pace, stopping every two or three pages to determine students' understanding of word meanings and ideas. Meanings of key words were demonstrated (e.g., for the word *pierce*, the teacher pierced a hole in paper with scissors) and related to known concepts (the teacher pointed out the pierced ears of girls in the class). Only words particularly significant for understanding the story were highlighted rather than overwhelming students with many words. Questions were interspersed throughout the story, at the literal and inferential levels. After reading, the highlighted vocabulary was written on the board and students used the words in context. Finally, each drew a picture based on the story and described it to the group, an activity to promote extended English use.

teachers for help, or they may indicate they do understand when they do not. Working with a friend may ameliorate difficulties.

- Have students create and produce. Ask them to make scrapbooks by cutting pictures from magazines representing words they can say in English; weekly, team classmates to share their growing scrapbooks and pronounce the words. If students have writing skills, they can construct illustrated dictionaries.
- Once students are reading and writing in English, sentence scrambling (rearranging mixed-up word cards to make a sentence) and cloze or maze activities are helpful for gaining control of English syntax. An important follow-up is *oral* use of the same sentence structures.
- Finally, pay attention to correct usage. Students may be disadvantaged academically and in the workforce when they are hampered by what some consider to be "broken English" (Wong-Fillmore & Snow, 2000).

Reading Instruction.   Literacy instruction for ELLs requires (a) decisions about the general approach to adopt and (b) knowledge of instructional strategies to enhance learning within the general approach chosen.

There are three widely used general approaches for teaching reading to ELLs in U.S. and Canadian schools. These approaches offer contrasting viewpoints about how much a student's native language should be involved in reading instruction. In **transitional bilingual programs,** reading instruction begins in the students' native language, while at the same time they are helped to develop oral English. Later, students are guided through a transition into English literacy. As seen in Table 14–1, research supports the premise that reading skills learned in one language can transfer to another language although students often must be explicitly taught to make that transfer. Educators who advocate this approach believe it is unreasonably challenging to learn to read English when students have minimum understanding of its oral vocabulary and structure.

A second approach, **immersion programs,** introduces reading instruction in English immediately and concurrently with oral English instruction. No literacy instruction takes place in the students' first language. In **structured immersion programs,** the third general approach, there is immediate English literacy

Reading skills learned in one language can transfer to another language, although students often must be taught to make that transfer.

instruction, but, when deemed necessary, the first language is employed in reading as well as in oral interchanges. English predominates, however, because educators who subscribe to this approach believe that students become English speakers and readers more quickly if they are immersed in the language—the view also held by proponents of immersion programs.

A fourth general approach, less frequently used but found in some school districts, is the **two-way bilingual program** in which native English speakers and students with a different first language are in the same class. Instruction is conducted in English during half of the class time and in the other language for the remainder of the day, resulting in both groups becoming bilingual and biliterate.

Which general approach should one select? Obvious factors to consider are (a) effectiveness and (b) feasibility. In regard to effectiveness, research shows that the first three, widely used, general approaches discussed in the preceding paragraphs all have been successful with ELLs (see the Research Box, Table 14–1). As for the fourth, less-used general approach, Slavin and Cheung's (2005) synthesis of research on reading instruction for ELLs found positive results for these programs.

In regard to feasibility, this factor is most often judged by the number of first languages other than English to be accommodated. For example, a bilingual transition program works well if, for instance, all students speak Spanish but is likely to be unworkable if students use many different native languages. Whether there are bilingual teachers and materials in the needed language(s) also are feasibility factors that must be accounted for when choosing a general approach to ELL literacy instruction.

Equally important in planning reading programs for ELLs is knowledge of *specific instructional strategies* to enhance learning within the general approach that has been selected. As a starting point, it is important to understand that all you have learned in this book is applicable to ELLs. Basically, reading instruction in a student's second language is the same as reading instruction in a first language.

However, in addition to the processes and strategies you read about in this text, there are certain special considerations for literacy lessons of new English learners. Note, first, Table 14–2 to see variables that are the same for reading instruction in all alphabetic languages (and primarily the same in non-alphabetic ones), but also note unique challenges ELLs meet in second-language reading.

One minor difference is sound-symbol dissimilarity between English and many other languages. This may cause ELLs to *pronounce* certain printed words differently than an English speaker, even though they do correctly recognize the words. For example, a speaker of certain Chinese dialects may pronounce English long /$\bar{a}$/ sounds as short /$\breve{a}$/, /$\breve{e}$/, or /$\breve{u}$/; or a Spanish-language speaker may pronounce the English /j/ as /ch/, and other variations (Ruddell, 2006). These differences are regarded by some individuals as examples of one language "interfering" with another. However, in terms of reading instruction, at least, and at the phonological (i.e., sound) level, dissimilarities are inconsequential if handled appropriately by the teacher. Although it is useful during oral language instruction to teach sound variations between the student's first language and English, such pronunciation differences have little importance to understanding what is read. During reading, if a student obviously knows a word and a "mispronunciation" is merely a sound-level variation, the teacher should ignore it.

TABLE 14–2 *Similarities and Differences in First- and Second-Language Reading*

Requirements of first- and second-language readers:
- alphabetic understanding
- decoding skills
- automaticity of sight vocabulary
- overall fluency
- development of metacognitive strategies that foster fluency and comprehension
- text matched to reading level and interests
- engagement in extensive reading

Unique challenges second-language readers face:
- sounds/symbol dissimilarity or interference
- oral vocabulary constraints
- limitations due to background knowledge
- difficulties with text structure

(Bamford & Day, 1998; Carrell & Grabe, 2002; Eskey, 2002; Grabe, 2002; Hudson, 1998; Wallace, 2001).

Source: From Lenters, Kimberly. (2004, December). No half measures: Reading instruction for young second-language learners. *The Reading Teacher, 58*(4), 328–336. Reprinted with permission of Kimberly Lenters and the International Reading Association.

A second special consideration is the student's adeptness with oral English vocabulary. Remembering Gunderson's (1991) English-knowledge levels specified in a previous section, it is easy to understand that reading materials and methods must necessarily differ for ELLs with no English (or negligible amounts) versus those who have advanced to limited fluency. Lenters (2005) cites information indicating that an ELL must have oral knowledge of 95% of the English vocabulary words in a text to read with understanding.

A related issue is unfamiliarity with English text structures. As students learn English, there are levels of growth in the English syntax (i.e., sentence structures) they understand and use, in the same way there are levels of vocabulary growth. Furthermore, written sentence structures can vary from oral. Combinations of written structures forming typical English text may be novel to students at certain levels of English development. In these cases, teacher guidance in teasing out text meanings may be necessary to ensure comprehension (remember scaffolding!).

The language experience approach (LEA) is a popular method for accommodating the oral English vocabulary and syntactic levels of beginning ELLs who also are beginning readers. In the LEA, after the teacher uses discussion to stimulate dictation, students dictate stories or informational pieces as the teacher records them on a chart or chalkboard for all to see. The dictated material becomes the text for subsequent reading lessons. Thus, the students' own words and the English sentence structures they presently control are used for instruction. When students make sufficient progress in reading English, lessons are refocused to incorporate more typical text materials.

After ELLs advance beyond earliest reading levels, a highly recommended technique to accelerate acquisition of both oral vocabulary and reading vocabulary is cognate matching (e.g., Jiménez, 2004). **Cognates** are words in two languages that are spelled similarly, sound similar, and mean the same, such as *alphabet* (English) / *alfabeto* (Spanish) and *tobacco* (English) / *tabac* (French). Various languages have cognates with English, but there is an especially large number with Spanish. It has been estimated that of the 10,000 most frequently used words in English, 3,000 are cognates with Spanish words. (See the website

For a list of Spanish-English cognates, use your search engine (e.g., Netscape or Google) and enter "*Cognates-Spanish and English*," then click "Espangles."

margin note for a source of Spanish-English cognates.) Whatever the targeted language, one school system advises their teachers to capitalize on these connections by progressively generating a *cognate word wall*, putting up linked pairs of words as students are introduced to cognates over the school year (Monongalia County, WV Board of Education, 2005). This makes for easy reference when students are reading (or speaking) and is a source for teacher prompting and review.

A third special situation is the background knowledge ELLs bring to the classroom, some of which is dissimilar from what is typically expected of North American students. Since prior knowledge is an important ingredient for text comprehension, teachers should use a two-pronged approach to address these variations. For one, take advantage of the rich experiences students bring from their home countries. For example, teachers might include culturally relevant themes in LEA stories and use multicultural literature as reading texts. Some books reflecting students' backgrounds and cultural knowledge also incorporate their first language, making particularly good choices for students who are still in transition to English reading and speaking. An example is *I Love Saturdays y domingos* (Ada, 2002), which features a young girl who spends Saturdays with her English-speaking grandparents and Sundays (domingos) with her other set of grandparents, who speak Spanish. English words and phrases are seen on each left-hand page as she relates her Saturday events and are repeated in Spanish on the right-hand page as she describes her Sunday adventures, which, though similar, reflect a slightly different cultural bent (see a two-page illustration in Figure 14–1 on pages 466 and 467).

Using Multiple Information Sources. In what ways could parents of ELLs also be resources for cultural knowledge and language?

For the other part of your two-pronged approach, consciously build new background for each English reading experience. Examine materials beforehand and provide discussions, demonstrations, media, modeling, and the like to fill in missing links.

To these three special considerations, this principle is added: Have high but reasonable expectations for ELLs as they learn to read English. Assign tasks at which—with teacher help—they *can* be successful, and openly celebrate their growing progress.

Assessment. Reading assessment for ELLs employs much the same types of procedures and tools as for native English speakers. However, there are certain factors to bear in mind.

For purposes of judging whether adequate yearly progress (AYP) has been made, the No Child Left Behind law requires reading tests to be administered in English to ELLs, if students have been in the United States for 3 consecutive years. In such situations, when interpreting results for new English learners, one should be aware of data indicating that ELLs are more often negatively affected on standardized test passages by topics that are outside their prior knowledge base than are native English speakers. In addition, they have more confusion concerning certain text structures, such as information paraphrased from passages to questions (García, 1991). Outcomes from these tests, therefore, may provide only minimum guidance to teachers for understanding students' true levels of literacy accomplishment and, thus, for discerning their present needs.

For program planning, teachers should employ informal procedures since these commonly provide a truer picture of day-to-day functioning than do formal tests. In particular, *process assessment* can be a particularly revealing informal diagnostic practice with ELLs (see Chapter 6, p. 176).

Nonstandard Dialects

In our discussion of students with linguistic backgrounds that differ from the mainstream population, next we turn to those who speak nonstandard dialects. Questions sometimes arise about the communicative impact of these dialects and about their relationship to reading achievement.

There are a number of English-language dialects spoken in the United States and Canada. The most dominant one is referred to as "Standard English," but there are others as well.

Phonological variations of English are heard throughout the United States (e.g., differences in vowel pronunciations in the Southeast, Northeast, or Midwest may be referred to as a Southern "accent," New England "accent," or Midwestern "accent"). *Semantic variations*, that is, variations in vocabulary, also are prevalent, for example, speakers from different parts of the country may refer to the same beverage as "pop," "soda," or "a soft drink." None of these are considered nonstandard English forms but, rather, regional dialect variations.

Although there are some semantic and sound considerations, a nonstandard English dialect is most often perceived in terms of *grammatical variation*. For instance, when a student drops or adds morphological units (e.g., "He land on his feets" versus "He landed on his feet"), uses archaic language forms (e.g., the Elizabethan English *ain't* versus the modern English *isn't*), or does not use standard subject-verb agreement (e.g., "Charles like it" versus "Charles likes it"), the student usually is tagged a nonstandard dialect speaker.

Most people have a positive attitude toward regional dialects, viewing them as interesting products of our diverse heritage ("You say to-mā-to, I say to-mah-to" or "What a charming Southern accent she has"). But many Standard English speakers have decidedly negative feelings about the grammatical (and sometimes semantic and sound) variations of nonstandard American dialects, probably because these often are associated with low socioeconomic levels. The attitude is that nonstandard dialects should be changed (although this is considered unnecessary for regional dialect variations).

Linguistically sound arguments could be made against such change. Research shows that nonstandard dialects are viable language forms in their own right with their own rules and complexities. They communicate as well as the dialect known as Standard English. Language studies clearly show that these dialects are in no way linguistically deficient or a substandard language form; they are only *different* from majority speech.

However, pressure to adopt the standard dialect comes not only from Standard English speakers, but also from many nonstandard dialect speakers themselves. Parents in homes where a nonstandard dialect is spoken often believe the school's role is to teach children the "standard" manner of speaking as a prerequisite to upward social mobility.

All of this suggests that reading teachers adopt dual goals. One goal relates to oral language—helping students add a second dialect (Standard English) for

A number of English-language dialects are spoken in the United States and Canada. The most dominant dialect is referred to as *Standard English*.

FIGURE 14–1 *First of Two pages from a Book Featuring Both English and Another Language in Comparable Text*

On Saturdays, Grandma serves me breakfast:

milk, scrambled eggs, and pancakes.

The pancakes are spongy. I like to put a lot

of honey on my pancakes.

Grandma asks me, "Do you like them

sweetheart?"

And I answer, "Oh, yes, Grandma, I love

them!"

(continued)

Source: I love Saturdays y domingos, by Alma Flor Ada; illustrated by Elivia Savadier. New York: Atheneum Books for Young Readers, © 2002.

social and, probably, economic reasons. A second goal is to understand how nonstandard dialects should be handled in regard to reading instruction.

There is no exact match between any oral dialect, including Standard English, and written language. Therefore, it is not surprising that research shows that lack of an exact match between nonstandard English and the language of instructional materials does not affect reading achievement. Attempts to change written materials to match students' dialects also have made no difference. For example, writing instructional materials in African-American dialects has failed to change the reading ability of African-American dialect speakers, and rewriting standardized tests in various dialects has made no difference in reading scores. Furthermore, attempts to change the oral language of students

Research shows that lack of an exact match between nonstandard English and the language of instructional materials does not affect reading achievement.

FIGURE **14–1** *(continued)*

Los domingos, Abuelita serves me a large glass of papaya juice and a plate of eggs called *huevos rancheros*. The *huevos rancheros* are wonderful. No one makes them better than *Abuelita*.

Abuelita asks me if I like them: —¿*Te gustan, hijita?*

First I need to swallow, and then I answer: — *Sí, Abuelita, ¡me encantan!*

Source: I love Saturdays y domingos, by Alma Flor Ada; illustrated by Elivia Savadier. New York: Atheneum Books for Young Readers, © 2002.

who are nonstandard dialect speakers to Standard English also have failed to promote reading growth.

Students who speak nonstandard dialects understand Standard English even if they do not produce it. They understand television. They understand their teachers and others who speak Standard English. They also understand printed English. When students read a statement so that it conforms to their oral speech, this is an indication that they understand the author's message. If the text reads, "She isn't at home," and a rural Appalachian student reads, "She ain't home," the student had to understand the printed sentence to translate its meaning to the spoken form of his or her own oral language.

Teachers should distinguish between language differences and reading errors. In language arts lessons it is certainly appropriate to discuss alternative ways to express meaning (e.g., pointing out that another way to make the statement "She ain't home" is "She isn't home"). But, in the case of reading, the nonstandard English performance does not affect its ultimate purpose—getting meaning. When oral reading is evaluated, dialect renditions should be assessed for what they are—variations of the most common dialect, not reading errors.

In sum, research does not show that use of a nonstandard dialect is a cause of reading difficulties.

CULTURAL DIFFERENCES

Addressing teachers, Alvermann and Phelps (1998) observe that

> . . . without knowledge of the different norms, values, myths, traditions, and symbols that have meaning for different cultural groups, you will find it difficult to access or build on your students' rich and diverse backgrounds when introducing new concepts and strategies for learning from texts. (p. 44)

Two aspects of cultural diversity relevant to teachers and education are (a) differences in concept development and (b) differences in value systems.

The development of concepts and the vocabulary attached to those concepts vary with background experiences. The two-pronged approach previously suggested for addressing prior knowledge disparities during reading instruction with ELLs can be adopted across subject matters and across culturally diverse groups who come from within or out of the country. That is, be alert to ways in which to incorporate students' experiences into learning activities, and concomitantly, be alert to possible misunderstanding due to lack of prior concept development.

Value systems can affect how individuals learn and perform in relation to school expectations.

A second hallmark of cultural diversity—that is, variations in value systems—can affect how individuals learn and perform in relation to school expectations. Most schools promote views consistent with middle-class American principles of hard work, delayed gratification, achievement orientation, and meeting one's responsibilities on time. These contrast with the ideals of a number of other cultures whose children are educated in American schools. The culturally instilled beliefs of some nonmainstream groups lead them to value anonymity rather than recognition; to try to experience the joys of life each day rather than work to experience them at some future time; to act for the good of the group rather than strive for individual attainment; and to adopt an unhurried approach to meeting commitments.

Upon consideration, some of these beliefs might cause harried, stress-ridden, middle-class Americans to see the good sense of alternative points of view. However, these values are different from those of most professionals in American educational systems, and problems arise if teachers are insensitive to the traditions of students they teach. Ogbu (1992) contended that groups whose cultural references differ from the cultural frameworks of mainstream society face genuine obstacles in spanning cultural lines at school to learn.

To promote learning, teachers should respect differences in value systems and help students acculturate to mainstream values if, in some situations, their own values are deterring learning. When possible, they may adapt teaching to students' value systems, if this facilitates the educational experience. Teachers should also remember that there are different cultural traditions and standards among members of the same ethnic group, such as between urban and rural low socioeconomic status (SES) African Americans, among different Native American peoples, or among various Asian or Hispanic groups.

Add books to your classroom library that reflect the traditions, values, and prior experiences of ELLs and native-born North American students from diverse backgrounds. Use these books with students from different cultures and also with mainstream students to introduce them to their classmates' cultures. Books help students avoid misleading overgeneralizations and distorted views if they realistically reflect a group's way of life and avoid stereotypes. Table 14–3 lists excellent children's and adolescent literature representing diverse cultural groups.

SPECIAL CONSIDERATIONS FOR AT-RISK STUDENTS

NCLB
READING
FIRST

Students may be academically at risk for reasons unrelated to linguistic and cultural differences, such as physical impairments, emotional disturbance, or drug abuse. However, many at-risk students are from nonmainstream groups with specific ethnic, racial, and linguistic identities and often represent the urban or rural poor.

TABLE 14–3 *Some Excellent Children's and Adolescent Literature Representing Diverse Cultural Groups*

And Now Miguel by Krumgold (Hispanic American)
Blue Willow by Gates (migrant families)
Hannah Elizabeth by Rich (Amish)
The Cornrows by Yarborough (African American)
Child of the Owl by Yep (Asian American)
When Thunders Spoke by Sneve (Native American)
First Snow by Coutant and Vo-Dinh (Asian American)
When I Was Young in the Mountains by Rylant (Appalachian)
To Stand Against the Wind by Clark (Vietnamese refugee families)
Sing Down the Moon by O'Dell (Native American)
Plain Girl by Sorenson (Amish)
Where the Lillies Bloom by the Cleavers (Appalachian)
Tough Tiffany by Hurmence (African American)
Judy's Journey by Lenski (migrant families)

Differences That May Originate From the Home Environment

Special considerations are needed when providing reading instruction for students from low socioeconomic status (SES) backgrounds if they lack the breadth of experiences with books and other building blocks of literacy normally expected in schools. One way to support at-risk pupils is through parent involvement and parent education. McConnell's (1989) work with Northern Cheyenne and Latino children concluded that parental involvement can have a pivotal influence on literacy accomplishments for minority students.

Parental involvement can have a pivotal influence on literacy accomplishments for minority students.

Provide parents with information about home behaviors that have helped other at-risk students. Parents need to know that successful students:

- are read aloud to by older brothers and sisters
- come from homes where discipline is evident, but fair
- come from homes rich in books
- come from organized homes
- have parents who are aware of local, national, and world events (and presumably model an interest in these events with their children)
- have parents who themselves read
- have parents who understand the value of education to their own lives and the lives of their children
- have parents who show an interest in each of their children's needs and interests

A second way to support at-risk pupils is through adaptations at school. Not only does the school lack control over certain home conditions, but data indicate that teachers' attempts to compensate for home-originated limitations should concentrate directly on educationally related variables. Some suggestions for adaptations within the school setting follow.

For at-risk students, it is important to encourage heavy involvement in authentic reading tasks, as opposed to an emphasis on workbook activities.

1. In your classroom make available many books of high appeal and in wide variety. Include fiction and nonfiction books that are easy, short, funny, colorful, scary, and engaging in other ways. Research has shown that at-risk students who are second-language learners have significantly improved comprehension when books are of interest to them (Elley & Mangubhai, 1983).
2. Structure your program so that independent activity time and free time are spent in reading (or even just looking at) books.
3. Set up learning centers with listening stations so students can hear taped books read to them as they follow the words and/or pictures.
4. Take students to the school library regularly to check out books (even if the books are sometimes lost). Library use significantly increases the number of books read by at-risk students who don't have books bought for them in the home (Rodriguez-Trujillo, 1986). Also, make a field trip to acquaint students (and parents) with the free services of the public library.
5. Help students acquire and own books. Use school or PTA/PTO funds to purchase inexpensive books and give them to students.
6. Have magazines in your room intended for both young people and adults. Bring in your own magazines rather than discard them and give them to students to take home.
7. During sustained silent reading (SSR), students will see you reading. Before or after an SSR session, take the opportunity to talk to students about books you loved as a child, and have them available for your students to read. Tell them about books you are reading and enjoying now.
8. Read aloud to students every day. Choose high-quality children's or adolescent literature. Scaffold information by comparing ideas from several books and linking text to background experiences. Use story-comparison charts as seen in Figure 14–2; have students write in comparisons of books they have shared as a group.
9. Allow students to engage in paired learning. Process writing furnishes a good occasion for this if you encourage peer conferences for planning, revising, and editing written work.
10. Decrease the assignment of worksheets and workbooks; increase the amount of direct teacher instruction in authentic reading tasks.
11. Establish an organized classroom. Establish set procedures and plan the day so there is no wasted time. Let every minute of the school day include interesting, intellectual stimulation.
12. Help students learn self-discipline and learn to organize their own tasks and time.
13. Try to understand students' problems, but remember that the kindest thing you can do for at-risk students is to help them obtain a first-rate education. You have control over what happens in your classroom, and education is the business of schools.
14. If disruptive behavior occurs, be firm, consistent, and fair about refusing to accept those behaviors in an educational setting.
15. Expand students' interests. Try to intrigue them with experiences beyond their own homes or neighborhoods.

Problems That May Originate at School

Problems in low SES students' learning also may be caused by attitudes of educational personnel. Unfortunately, some teachers and administrators hold

FIGURE 14–2 *Story Comparison Charts*

Books We Have Read About Mice			
Title	Once A Mouse by Brown	Frederick by Lionni	Mouse Tales by Lobel
Main characters	A mouse, a man	Frederick, the mouse	
Other characters	A bird		
Problem			
How the story ends			

Our Favorite Folk Tales			
Name	Country of origin	Human or animal characters?	Moral or lesson

lower expectations for these students than for their counterparts from higher socioeconomic households. Low expectations lead to low achievement. Studies of poor minority children who become successful readers show that students from low-income homes are most likely to read at or above grade level when schools give special attention to reading—and when they maintain high expectations for students. Although teachers may find it necessary to provide compensatory activities for low SES students, their ultimate expectations for these students should equal those for others. A watered-down program or a willingness to adapt to a lower set of standards does an injustice to at-risk students.

In schools where large numbers of pupils come from populations that historically have not fared well in the educational system, reading teachers can take a leadership role in assessing the school reading program. Schoolwide

> Students from low-income homes are more likely to be successful readers if schools (a) emphasize reading and (b) maintain high expectations for these students.

LEARNING FROM TEXT

Setting a Purpose for Reading. In the following section, read to find answers to these questions about the program described: (a) How much reading instruction do students receive each day? (b) Is connected text reading a part of the program? (c) Is oral reading used? (d) What is the purpose of specially written stories? (e) Who participates in the tutoring portion of the program, and how is it carried out?

efforts to adopt a goal of high achievement for all and to provide a careful, systematic, and rich reading program in every classroom have had an appreciable impact in low-income areas.

The Success for All Program

The Success for All program (Slavin, Madden, Karweit, Dolan, & Wasik, 1992) is an intervention used in inner-city schools with high-risk students. The Success for All plan encompasses two components: (a) regular classroom reading instruction and (b) tutoring.

Regular classroom reading instruction is organized so that teaching occurs in groups of about 15 children in grades 1 through 3. Though grouped heterogeneously during the rest of the day, the children move to their special reading class—grouped so that students of only one reading level are in the room—where they receive instruction for 90 minutes, 5 days a week. Direct teacher guidance is employed throughout the period, and no independent seatwork is used. Classroom teachers, Title I reading teachers, special education teachers, and tutors who are certified teachers all share responsibility for teaching the reading sections; thus, class size is kept to a reasonable number.

Instruction consists of: (a) reading to students; (b) discussions of story structure; (c) oral language development; (d) connected text reading, with an emphasis on oral reading in early stages; (e) systematic instruction with phonics, including work on phonemic awareness and on letter sounds and blending; (f) teaching error-correction strategies; (g) development of an instantly recognized sight vocabulary; (h) repeated reading of texts to promote fluency; (i) writing to facilitate word recognition and identification, and process writing; (j) attention to comprehension and to metacognitive strategy use; and (k) partner reading and paired-practice activities (Wasik & Slavin, 1993).

Basal reading materials are used along with specially written stories that emphasize the phonic understandings being taught in class. For some time, reading researchers have called for texts in which there is a relation between decoding lessons and what students must read. This recommendation is based on studies showing the helpfulness of this practice (e.g., see Adams, 1990a, 1990b; Anderson, Hiebert, Scott, & Wilkinson, 1984). The trick is to write engaging stories that have natural language structures, while at the same time including words that incorporate sounds and phonic generalizations learners have been practicing. This is what the Success for All program has tried to do.

Student progress is evaluated every 8 weeks. Parental involvement is a part of the program, including use of parent support teams. Parents see that students meet requirements, such as the assignment to read a library book at home each night for 20 minutes. There also is a part-day preschool and a full-day kindergarten as a part of Success for All.

Teachers are trained for the program for 2 days before school begins and receive an additional 4 days of training later in the year.

The goal of Success for All is that all students learn to read "the first time they are taught" and that they do not require remedial services at a later time. To assist with this objective, the second major component is a one-to-one tutoring program for students who are in the lowest 25% of their classes.

FIGURE 14–3   *Success for All: Framework for a Tutoring Session*

- The session begins with the student reading orally from a familiar story previously read in the regular reading class.
- This is followed by a 1-minute drill on letter sounds that are being practiced in the regular class.
- Most of the session is spent on the oral reading of specially designed "shared stories" that are written to be predictable and interesting. The stories contain phonemically controlled vocabulary written in large type and other words written in small type. The student reads the large-type words; the teacher reads the small. The teacher provides assistance with sounding out words when needed. The stories correspond to work in the regular class.
- Comprehension questions are asked and answered.
- Passages from the story are reread to promote fluency.
- The student engages in writing activities.

Source: Summarized from "Preventing Early Reading Failure with One-to-One Tutoring: A Review of Five Programs," by B. A. Wasik and R. E. Slavin, 1993, *Reading Research Quarterly, 28*, pp. 179–200.

Tutoring begins in first grade and, if needed, continues into second and third grades. Tutoring supplements the reading instruction children receive in the regular classroom program and is closely integrated with it. Teachers in the classroom program use a communication system to let tutors know what tutored children have been working on in the regular reading class. Tutors all are certified teachers who receive the same Success for All training as the other school personnel. Tutoring activities are based on the belief that one learns to read by reading, but specific attention also is given to skills and strategy work. Tutoring occurs for 20 minutes, 5 days a week. Figure 14–3 describes the framework of each tutoring session.

Excellent results have been attained with the Success for All program (Slavin, 2002). Participating students have scored significantly higher on end-of-year reading measures than previously had been the case. What is more, a growing difference is apparent after each year the children are in the program. This effectiveness has been seen for all learners, even those in the bottom one-fourth of the class (Wasik & Slavin, 1993).

A Spanish-language version of Success for All is designed for use with new ELLs.

The America Reads Program

America Reads (Smith, Levin, & Cianci, 1997) is another tutoring program implemented to support literacy for at-risk students. See the Vignette: Real Teachers in Action in the accompanying boxed material titled "America Reads . . . Everyone Benefits" for an overview of a model America Reads program. Research has indicated that low-achieving children do benefit from this program—if they take full opportunity to participate in it consistently (Fitzgerald, 2001).

Vignette: Real Teachers in Action

America Reads . . . Everyone Benefits

One enters a large, bright classroom at Norfolk State University and finds 12 undergraduates receiving instruction on how to teach reading. The instructor is Dr. Carmelita Williams, former president of the International Reading Association and full professor at Norfolk State. The students are atypical. Only three are education majors, with the rest enrolled in programs ranging from biology to home economics to marketing. However, these four men and eight women have two things in common. First, they all are work/study students. Second, as students who need financial assistance to attend college, they all have chosen to earn their monthly government stipend by tutoring youngsters who have literacy problems as part of the America Reads Challenge initiated in 1996. This program, a collaboration between U.S. universities and the U.S. Department of Education, has developed numerous sites where universities train, college students who need financial aid tutor, and children with literacy problems learn.

The program at Norfolk State has a three-pronged approach, addressing: (a) training for tutors, (b) instruction with children in grades K–6, and (c) community service activities related to literacy. Dr. Williams has organized her reading class so tutors in the Norfolk State America Reads program are trained with the latest, soundest, most effective instructional methods. A textbook typically assigned in graduate classes is read and discussed. Other assignments and activities include: engaging in simulations of various teaching strategies, such as DRTA and use of QARs; peer practice in administering IRIs; development of materials they can use in their tutoring; and developing a portfolio of resources for tutoring. During the 2 days the author of this text visited the program, a portion of one morning was spent on developing a short, costumed dramatization of a well-known book of high-quality children's literature. Because it was near the end of the summer session, this drama would be acted by tutors as well as children who were their tutees in a brief program for parents.

It is summer, and so the Norfolk State Reading Clinic is in progress. After a full morning of their reading instruction class, the tutors move down the hall to the clinic where they each meet the elementary school student with whom they have been working. The children receive literacy instruction from these America Reads tutors for one hour a day on a one-to-one basis, 5 days per week. Tutoring is individualized to the needs of each tutee, based on instruction and activities undertaken in Dr. Williams's class and supervised by Dr. Williams. Examples seen on the days this author visited were varied. One child read a myth and used vocabulary from the story to study multisyllabic words. Another child played a phonics game and then read a tutor-prepared story containing the elements practiced in the game. A third used K-W-L with a social studies text. Other teaching activities included reading poems, writing a language experience story and selecting five words from it for spelling study, writing a story extension, and listening to a story read aloud by the tutor and then reading a story on a similar theme at an easier level.

In addition to guidance from Dr. Williams, graduate students at Norfolk State, who also tutor at this clinic, serve as mentors to the America Reads undergraduate tutors as part of their course requirement—a component referred to as TTT, or Teachers Training Tutors. The graduate students and America Reads tutors also work together to plan three workshops for parents of clinic children.

The assistance of the America Reads tutors does not stop with this clinical instruction. During the school year, the tutoring occurs in local elementary schools the children attend. This community-based portion of the effort may also include working as aides to teachers in literacy activities, providing guidance for parents, and participating in distribution of books for the Reading Is Fundamental (RIF) program. These college students, once they have progressed into their training, have even taught high school students to tutor other children in an Americorp Project in their hometown.

One unexpected outcome of America Reads programs all across the country also has been seen with the Norfolk State tutors: Several of the undergraduates have decided to switch majors and make education their career.

One leaves with the impression that this is a program from which everyone benefits.

ILLITERACY AND FUNCTIONAL ILLITERACY IN OLDER YOUTHS AND ADULTS

Because of geographic isolation, unusual economic factors, immigration from an underdeveloped nation, or other reasons, illiterate or functionally illiterate individuals often have been denied the intensive schooling enjoyed today by most people in our society. There are other adults who did participate in school experiences but did not benefit from those during their normal school years. In either case, reading instruction at the acquisition level or very early stages is needed.

An **illiterate** individual lacks ability to read and write. This term usually refers to older individuals rather than school-age students. **Functional illiterates,** on the other hand, are older youths and adults who read, but to such a limited extent that they cannot understand basic written information needed to function in adult daily life. They may be able to read easy primary-level stories, but are unable to cope with writing found on packages, medicine bottle labels, bank statements, advertisements, bills, maps, telephone books, or recipes.

To be lacking in literacy is difficult in this society. In addition to satisfaction of basic needs, literacy is needed to increase occupational knowledge, attend to one's health needs, use community resources, and understand government and law. A strong correlation exists between adults reading at the lowest levels and poverty-level incomes (Elish-Piper, 2002). In addition, many fewer illiterate and functionally illiterate individuals vote than those at middle and higher literacy levels. See the Vignette: Real Teachers in Action, titled "An Adult Literacy Tutor and Her Pupil" for a real-life story that furnishes a poignant example of illiteracy and the effect it had on one life.

Illiteracy Rates in the United States

The United Nations has estimated that the illiteracy rate in the United States is approximately 4%, comparable to that of other industrialized countries. Although much lower than in developing nations, this statistic does not include people who are functionally illiterate. An often-cited guess at the incidence of

For adults, literacy—both reading and writing—is needed to increase occupational opportunities, attend to one's health, use community resources, and understand government and law.

Vignette: Real Teachers in Action

An Adult Literacy Tutor and Her Pupil

Catherine Gillie of Columbus, Ohio—wife of a judge, mother of four, and part-time nurse—heard a radio commercial. "It said 77,000 persons in central Ohio did not know how to read. I didn't believe there was anyone like that."

She and the judge took the four Saturday morning training sessions offered by the Columbus Literacy Council.

Gillie: "Then I was assigned a student, and I called her. Her voice was so soft I could hardly hear her. It was obvious that I had awakened her, but when I said, 'I've been assigned to be your tutor,' a shriek of joy came over that telephone.

"She was so delighted. Several times before, she had tried to get help. Once she even telephoned the Columbus Board of Education to say she couldn't read, and the secretary there wouldn't believe her. Because of her use of language and the way she presented her ideas so well, the secretary was sure she was a college graduate playing a prank."

The student was Betty Elliott, something over 30 years old (she isn't sure because there are no records), who was orphaned at 3 weeks and taken to New York City by a woman who wanted her to help around the house. She remembers having to stand on a chair to wash dishes and diapers. Whenever the truant officer came around, the woman would say, "Don't bother with her; she's not right, you know."

Never a day in school and not able to read a word, Elliott recalls: "I get surprised when I think back to when I had to memorize things and wasn't able to put them down on paper."

What she did was fake it a lot. She "wrote" her name, but actually she drew the letters. She made reports at the end of her night shift as a cottage mother at Franklin Village, a children's home, by calling a friend and telling her what she wanted to say. Slowly the friend would spell out the letters, and laboriously Betty would print them in capitals.

"I had no idea you could picture letters because I didn't know what reading and writing were all about. Now I can close my eyes and see that *a* and *b* and you know, that's marvelous."

Gillie would go to the Elliott home for lessons: "We both cried a great deal at the beginning. We spent many sessions with not too much time reading but with her telling about her life. Never before, she said, had any individual been personally interested in her. Many friends, because she's a very friendly person, but never anyone that interested."

Elliott: "People think if you can't read or write, you're stupid."

To cover up, she learned numbers. She counted on her fingers and found how to make change. She couldn't read labels at the grocery, but she knew how to shake the cans. If the contents rattled, they were peas. If the can was heavy, it was fruit. She even could tell pears from peaches without pictures.

Gillie: "It's fascinating, the extent to which people learn to cope and work around the printed word. It takes immeasurable use of energy and brainpower and time and money, but to a small extent, it can be done.

"After 2 months, I asked her whether she was able to see any difference at work or anywhere else because she could begin to read. Betty answered: 'I notice now that when I look in the mirror, I'm smiling.'"

Over about 3 years, there were some 80 tutoring sessions, 90 or so minutes each, sometimes twice a week, sometimes only once a month when both were very busy.

Elliott: "Another surprise, when you see on paper the word that you have been holding up here in your mind and rattling it around, then you see it there and begin to make some sense out of it. It's surprise; it's happiness.

"The first day I was able to do one word, one word as I have in my book, to know that I could spell it out; it stood out so much for me, just to know I could spell it and hear it. That was so neat, the way the sounds came together. I can see it; I can hear the letters."

(The word was s-p-y.)

Gillie: "She's such an intelligent person, with such compassion, such wisdom. She could write a psychology book about working with children. And she accomplished all this with no models. A very wise, very smart person."

Elliott: "If I could just tell it all, if people only knew exactly how I felt then and also bring it up to now, it would be some story. It would be like—like it's not the truth. I have all intentions some day to write that for others to know."

Gillie: "I've been involved in all the things you do as your children are growing up, and I've thought they were good causes, and you put your shoulder to the wheel, and that's fine.

"But this is different, seeing a whole world open up to one person who had been seeing the world through a long tube without much light at the end. That's the most exciting thing that can happen."

Betty Elliott's book, the one from which she read her very first word, is *The New Streamlined English Series: In the Valley.*

Happy ending: Elliott won a prize for reading the most books of any student in the literacy program in her first year. (Sabine & Sabine, 1983, pp. 49–51)

Source: From *Books That Made the Difference* (pp. 49–51) by G. Sabine and P. Sabine, 1983, Hamden, CT: Library Professional Publications. Copyright 1983 by Library Professional Publications. Reprinted by permission of G. Sabine and P. Sabine.

functional illiterates in the United States is about 5% of the population. The exact number of illiterates or functional illiterates is difficult to ascertain because criteria used to determine illiteracy are different for various organizations and authorities.

Reading Level. Some definitions assume a reading level one must attain to read everyday printed matter successfully, but opinions vary about just what this level is, ranging from fourth grade to eighth grade. Obviously, the level chosen changes the number of illiterates or functional illiterates estimated.

Grade Completed. A more questionable criterion for defining literacy is the number of school years completed. For example, in Canada, literacy has been assumed if a person has completed eighth grade and the United Nations has cited 4 years of schooling as the necessary requisite. However, as any reading teacher knows, the fact that students have completed a particular grade is not necessarily an indicator that they are reading at that grade level.

Skills Mastered. Others define literacy in terms of ability to perform reading tasks associated with real-world experiences. Suggested basic tasks have included ability to read: (a) forms; (b) letters, memos, and notes; (c) newspapers; (d) manuals and instructions at work; (e) information while shopping; and (f) signs when traveling.

School-Based and Nonschool-Based Programs

School-based programs designed to fight illiteracy and functional illiteracy often are Adult Basic Education (ABE) or English as a Second Language (ESL) classes administered by local school systems (Smith, 2002). Classes are taught by certified teachers and usually are held in public school buildings. In or near major metropolitan areas, entire schools may be devoted to this purpose. One example is the ESOL Transitional High School in Fairfax County, Virginia, which serves adult ELLs. Many adults enrolled in this program were not literate in their own countries, and they, and many others in the school, are instructed in reading at the earliest levels (K. C. Adkins-Hastings, personal communication, July 11, 2005). Typically more than 4 million adults enroll in school-based programs annually; however, about half drop out before completing 30 hours of instruction (Comings, 2002). Furthermore, every year more than 2 million individuals are added to the number of adult illiterates and functional illiterates in the United States as the result of immigration and through school dropouts. Considering these figures, the number of participants in school-based adult literacy classes is strikingly few.

There also are nonschool-based literacy programs which rely heavily on volunteers. Two of the largest and most well-known volunteer programs, Literacy Volunteers of America and Laubach Literacy International, merged in 2002 to become ProLiteracy Worldwide. See the margin note for their website.

Whether the program is school based or nonschool based, it is important to realize that successful programs are not short term. At times, promises of unrealistically rapid acquisition of literacy are fostered by uninformed literacy program workers, materials developers, and the media. Those who promise quick fixes may raise false hopes, which rapidly develop into frustrations and program dropout. The most successful programs are gradual and long term.

> **Summarize.**   What does the text say about short-term adult literacy programs? Why?

Instructing Illiterate Older Youths and Adults

Organic primers, used both in the United States and in many developing countries, are one avenue for providing early level reading instruction in a nonpatronizing manner to illiterate adults. **Organic primers** are stories, written by the teacher, to reflect experiences and concerns of students in the literacy class. To prepare organic primers, teachers write short, simple stories about themes of adult interest, such as marriage or job-related concerns. To use the primers, the following steps are taken:

1. The story content is discussed prior to reading.
2. The teacher reads the story aloud to the students.
3. With teacher assistance, the teacher and students read and reread the story in unison until the learners can read it alone.
4. Students read the story individually.
5. Activities are employed (a) to ensure that word recognition will generalize to other reading materials, (b) to emphasize meaning, and (c) to practice word identification strategies related to the story words.

This technique has some similarities to language immersion techniques used with seriously delayed readers (see Chapter 13).

The language experience approach (LEA) also has shown utility with adult illiterates. A variation of LEA was used in the Adult Literacy Project at

While sizable numbers of individuals are enrolling in adult literacy programs, considering the numbers of new immigrants and school dropouts, many more could benefit from these programs.

To learn more about ProLiteracy Worldwide and ways you can help, go to www.proliteracy.org.

LEARNING FROM TEXT

the University of New Orleans (Wangberg, Thompson, & Levitov, 1984). Following introduction to reading through the LEA, adults wrote stories on computers, assisted by software with prompts programmed into it. After the computer lesson, each adult student took the story to a teacher station for reading and help in editing. The edited story was entered into the computer and a printout displayed the story, a list of words used by the student, and a set of follow-up activities. A composite list of words used most frequently when writing language experience stories was developed as a spelling reference.

Some instructors have used song lyrics in adult reading programs, and poetry has also proved to be particularly motivating to adult clients. Such language forms often have less negative associations than typical school reading materials.

Reading *strategies* advocated throughout this book are appropriate for adult clients. While suitable *materials* may be different in format (e.g., no childlike pictures) and content (e.g., passages at higher maturity levels), adults must still learn to identify unknown words and comprehend the message. Many published instructional materials are currently available to use in literacy programs for older individuals. Steck-Vaughn Publishing Company is one good source.

Instructing Functionally Illiterate Older Youths and Adults

Functional literacy programs are undertaken with older individuals who have mastered the rudiments of beginning reading strategies but who need assistance with literacy tasks encountered in everyday environments. These tasks demand decidedly more reading skill than functionally illiterate older teens and adults have attained. Instead of a general, basic program focusing on word recognition, strategy use, and universal comprehension abilities, functional literacy emphasizes direct teaching of reading tasks dictated by specific needs.

An example of functional literacy instruction aimed at a specific reading/writing task is seen in a program developed to teach students of high school age with severe reading disabilities or mild retardation to read and complete job applications (Joynes, McCormick, & Heward, 1980). Both populations were residing in a residential facility for male delinquent youth. As a preliminary step, a Master Employment Application was developed to introduce items occurring with highest frequency on real applications. The Master Employment Application is shown in Figure 14–4.

This job application was divided into four sections to teach students to read a few items at a time and to teach them to correctly fill in the requested information. The program required 11 class periods of 40 minutes each and entailed several steps employing explicit instruction, modeling, and gradual release of responsibility to the students. Before the program, students were able to read and complete an average of 13 of the 35 items on the application. Afterward, correct reading and completion ranged from 29 to 35 items.

Abbass (1977) analyzed 50 common forms and found that many words on them are not on word lists used in basic reading programs and, further, that the forms' readability levels ranged from 8.0 to above college level. When the NAEP Assessment of Functional Literacy examined the performances of 17-year-olds,

FIGURE 14–4 *Master Employment Application Using Terms That Often Appear on Actual Application Forms*

MASTER EMPLOYMENT APPLICATION

Please print

PERSONAL

Name: Last / First / Middle / Date

Date of Birth / Age / Social Security Number / Sex ☐ M ☐ F

Married ☐ Yes ☐ No / No. of Dependents ___ / Weight / Height

Are you a citizen of the U.S.? / Phone No.

Present Address: No. / Street / City / State / Zip Code

Previous Address: No. / Street / City / State / Zip Code

PHYSICAL

Do you have any physical disabilities? _____ If yes, describe.

Have you had any major illness in the past 5 years? _____ If yes, describe.

In case of an emergency, notify, Name _____

Address / Phone No.

EDUCATION

	Name of School	Attended From - To	Did you graduate?
Elementary			
High School			
College or University			
Other			
Other			

Do you plan to continue your education?

Last grade completed _____ Grade point average _____

Extracurricular activities _____

List any special office skills that you have. _____

EMPLOYMENT HISTORY

List below your last three employers:

Name and Address / Salary / Position / Date From - To

1. _____
2. _____
3. _____

MILITARY

Have you ever served in the U.S. armed forces? ☐ Yes ☐ No

If yes, what branch? _____

Dates of Duty: From _____ To _____

Rank at Discharge _____

REFERENCES

List below three names of people not related to you, whom you have known at least one year.

Name	Address	Phone No.	Years Acquainted
1.			
2.			
3.			

Do you have any relatives in this company? _____

JOB PREFERENCE

Type of work desired _____

Date available _____ Hours available _____

Starting expected salary _____

Why do you want this job? _____

GENERAL INFORMATION

Have you committed any felonies or violations? _____

If yes, explain. _____

Are you a licensed driver? ☐ Yes ☐ No

List here any additional comments that you think are important to us in considering you for employment: _____

SIGNATURE

To the best of my knowledge the above statements are complete and are true. False statements may be cause for dismissal.

Date _____ Signature _____

these students scored more poorly on the reading of forms than on any other area except reading reference material. Functionally illiterate individuals should be taught to complete other types of forms requiring biographical information (e.g., health insurance applications or credit card applications). A temporary survival strategy used with very low-literacy individuals is to write basic information on the front and back sides of a small index card, such as his or her Social Security number and the correct spelling of the individual's street address. The card is laminated and carried in a billfold to provide individuals with an aid in filling out forms.

Other examples of functional literacy instruction include teaching students to read road signs; driver's license manuals (many states have a simplified version that makes excellent instructional material); help-wanted ads; bus schedules; recipes; and other practical reading tasks. Mini-steps and moderately slow progression are important factors when teaching minimally literate individuals.

One issue in the adult education field is a debate about whether the "functional literacy" approach is too narrow, since literacy has a much broader scope than does reading for specific tasks. The U.S. Armed Forces, in fact, have attempted two approaches with low-literacy enlistees—one that deals with general literacy and the other with on-the-job literacy. In the general literacy program, students retain about 40% of the material taught, but those in the job-related reading courses retain about 80% (Sticht, 1981).

While functional literacy goals are designed to deal with immediate tasks, once these goals are realized, students can work to improve their abilities with all dimensions of reading.

Intergenerational Literacy

Recently there has been much interest in combating low reading skills in families with recurring illiteracy cycles—parents (and probably grandparents) who have limited literacy levels and their children also potentially growing to adulthood in the same debilitating situation (IRA, 1992). Efforts called **intergenerational literacy programs** have been instituted to attack the reading problems of the older and younger generations together.

Intergenerational literacy initiatives are conducted in several ways. For example, children and parents may attend a center in the evenings and on weekends where they receive reading instruction by different teachers and in different rooms, but with the whole family attending at the same time.

Another version teaches low-literacy adults several basic reading skills, then coaches them in how to tutor their young children in these areas. Thus, the children learn and the parents' learning is reinforced.

In yet another variation, parents are taught how to promote emergent literacy. They are apprised of activities that foster reading success; shown how to read aloud to their preschool children in ways that promote understanding, language development, and concepts about print; and given tools and instructions for promoting writing activities.

A related area is *family literacy*, which deals more broadly with literacy events in any family, whether reading problems are evident or not. Sometimes the terms *intergenerational literacy* and *family literacy* are used interchangeably.

There is currently much optimism about the potential of intergenerational programs for adults and for children, and these programs are spreading.

Reflections Linguistic and cultural diversity has always been a hallmark of the United States. At the time the United States gained its independence, many languages were spoken. Weber (1991) reminds us that not only were there speakers of English, but people speaking languages of the many countries from which the new United States was receiving immigrants, as well as, persons from the nearby New World colonies of Spain and France and

Native American speakers. Throughout the years, individuals, languages, and cultural practices have arrived from all over the world. Canada has a similar richly diverse cultural and linguistic history.

Consider the following:

1. Why is it difficult for people to accept differences? What are the responsibilities of educators in this regard?
2. What specifically can you do as a teacher with respect to the linguistic and cultural differences experienced in classrooms?

Outline for Preparing Case Reports

This appendix presents an outline for preparing case reports based on remedial assessment and instruction.

CASE REPORT OUTLINE

This outline has been used at The Ohio State Psychoeducational Clinic, Ohio State University, Columbus, Ohio.

The Case Study

A case study is a comprehensive report that integrates a student's case history and the results of previous studies. It also includes inferences about behavior observed during teaching and intensive analysis of patterns of behavior as revealed through achievement tests and observation. This type of report ordinarily relates the subject's behavior to a specific educational problem. A case study must point toward recommendations—that is, toward what can be done to help the student.

The Outline

IDENTIFYING DATA

Name of Student: Quarter and Year:

Age: Grade: Tutor:

I. HISTORY

    A. Developmental

        1. Prenatal and postnatal health and medical history

        2. Speech and language development

        3. Other pertinent data obtained from parents

The Case Study (Cont.)

B. Educational
1. Age of school entrance, summary of progress in school, including retentions and areas of difficulty
2. Summary of teacher's or principal's remarks concerning student's behavior and adjustment in school

II. RESULTS OF PREVIOUS TESTS OR DIAGNOSTIC EXAMINATIONS

If your student has previously attended this clinic, for the last quarter (semester) of attendance, list tests administered and summarize results.

If your student has attended the clinic for more than one quarter, make the following statement: "(Dave) also attended the clinic during (Winter) and (Spring) Quarters of 20_____. Case studies for those quarters are on file at the clinic."

If your student has not previously attended this clinic, simply say so.

III. GENERAL OBSERVATIONS

Summarize observations of the student in the following areas:
A. Interpersonal response to the tutor
B. Perceptiveness
C. Attention and concentration

IV. TESTS ADMINISTERED DURING THE QUARTER

List the tests administered and, for each, state the scores and other descriptive classifications. If test results are questionable, give evidence and show reasoning. Analyze test items and patterns for best and poorest abilities, significant variability, and so forth.

V. INSTRUCTION DURING THE QUARTER

Include the following:
A. Objectives of instruction
B. Methods used (This section is the most important section of the case study and should be comprehensive. Give specific information on all instructional activities.)
C. Materials covered (with reading levels of materials)
D. Evidence of gain

VI. RECOMMENDATIONS

Make specific recommendations to help others understand and work with the problem (e.g., the classroom teacher or future tutors).

(Name) _____
                        Tutor

Approved by _____

Date _____

References

Aaron, P. G. (1997). The impending demise of the discrepancy formula. *Review of Educational Research, 67,* 461–502.

Abbass, M. (1977). The language of fifty commonly used forms. *Dissertation Abstracts International, 37,* 5655A. (University Microfilms No. 77–6197, 520).

Abouzeid, M. (1992). Stages of word knowledge in reading disabled children. In S. Templeton & D. Bear (Eds.), *Development of orthographic knowledge and the foundations of literacy* (pp. 279–306). Hillsdale, NJ: Erlbaum.

Ackerly, S. S., & Benton, A. L. (1947). Report of a case of bilateral frontal lobe defect. *Proceedings of the Association for Research on Nervous and Mental Disease, 27,* 479–504.

Adams, M. J. (1990a). *Beginning to read: Thinking and learning about print.* Cambridge, MA: MIT Press.

Adams, M. J. (1990b). *Beginning to read: Thinking and learning about print: A summary.* Urbana-Champaign, IL: Center for the Study of Reading, University of Illinois.

Allington, R. L. (1983). Fluency: The neglected reading goal. *The Reading Teacher, 37,* 556–561.

Allington, R. L. (1984a). Content coverage and contextual reading in reading groups. *Journal of Reading Behavior, 16,* 85–96.

Allington, R. L. (1984b). Oral reading. In P. D. Pearson (Ed.), *Handbook of reading research* (pp. 829–864). New York: Longman.

Allington, R. L. (1993). Michael doesn't go down the hall anymore. *The Reading Teacher, 46,* 602–604.

Allington, R. L. (2001). *What really matters for struggling readers.* New York: Longman.

Allington, R. L. (2002a). Remediation. In B. J. Guzzetti (Ed.), *Literacy in America* (pp. 545–547). Santa Barbara, CA: ABC-CLIO.

Allington, R. L. (2002b). What I've learned about effective reading instruction. *Phi Delta Kappan, 83,* 740–747.

Allington, R. L., & Fleming, J. T. (1978). The misreading of high frequency words. *Journal of Special Education, 12,* 417–421.

Alvermann, D. E., & Phelps, S. F. (1998). *Content reading and literacy.* Boston: Allyn & Bacon.

Anderson, G., Higgins, D., & Wurster, S. (1985). Differences in the free reading books selected by high, average, and low achievers. *The Reading Teacher, 39,* 326–330.

Anderson, R. C. (2004). Role of the reader's schema in comprehension, learning, and memory. In R. B. Ruddell & N. J. Unrau (Eds.), *Theoretical models and processes of reading* (5th ed., pp. 594–606). Newark, DE: International Reading Association.

Anderson, R. C., & Freebody, P. (1981). Vocabulary knowledge. In J. Gutherie (Ed.), *Comprehension and teaching: Research reviews* (pp. 77–117). Newark, DE: International Reading Association.

Anderson, R. C., Hiebert, E. H., Scott, J. A., & Wilkinson, I. A. G. (1984). *Becoming a nation of readers.* Washington, DC: National Institute of Education.

Anderson, R. C., Wilkinson, I. A. G., & Mason, J. M. (1991). A micro-analysis of the small-group guided lesson: Effects of an emphasis on global story meaning. *Reading Research Quarterly, 26,* 417–441.

Anderson, T. H., & Armbruster, B. B. (1984). Studying. In P. A. Pearson (Ed.), *Handbook of reading research* (pp. 657–679). New York: Longman.

Andre, M. E. D. A., & Anderson, T. H. (1978–79). The development and evaluation of a self-questioning study technique. *Reading Research Quarterly, 14,* 605–623.

Armbruster, B. B., Anderson, T. H., & Meyer, J. L. (1991). Improving content-area reading using instructional graphics. *Reading Research Quarterly, 26,* 393–416.

Armbruster, B. B., Anderson, T. H., & Ostertag, J. (1987). Does text structure/summarization instruction facilitate learning from expository text? *Reading Research Quarterly, 22,* 331–346.

Armbruster, B. B., Anderson, T. H., & Ostertag, J. (1989). Teaching text structure to improve reading and writing. *The Reading Teacher, 43,* 130–137.

Ashton-Warner, S. (1964). *Teacher.* New York: Bantam.

Au, K. H. (2000). A multicultural perspective on policies for improving literacy achievement: Equity and excellence. In M. L. Kamil, P. B. Mosenthal, P. D. Pearson, &

R. Barr (Eds.), *Handbook of reading research* (Vol. III, pp. 835–851). Mahwah, NJ: Erlbaum.

Au, K. H., & Mason, J. M. (1981). Social organizational factors in learning to read: The balance of rights hypothesis. *Reading Research Quarterly, 17,* 115–152.

Ausubel, D. P. (1960). The use of advance organizers in learning and retention of meaningful material. *Journal of Educational Psychology, 51,* 267–272.

Bader, L. A., & Wiesendanger, K. D. (1986). University-based reading clinics: Practices and procedures. *The Reading Teacher, 39,* 698–702.

Bailey, M. H. (1967). The utility of phonics generalizations in grades one through six. *The Reading Teacher, 20,* 413–418.

Bailey, M. H. (1971). Utility of vowel digraph generalizations in grades one through six. In M. A. Dawson (Ed.), *Teaching word recognition skills.* Newark, DE: International Reading Association.

Baker, L., & Brown, A. L. (1984). Metacognitive skills in reading. In P. D. Pearson (Ed.), *Handbook of reading research* (pp. 353–394). New York: Longman.

Baker, L., Serpell, R., & Sonnenschein, S. (1995). Opportunities for literacy learning in the homes of urban preschoolers. In L. M. Morrow (Ed.), *Family literacy connections in schools and communities* (pp. 236–252). Newark, DE: International Reading Association.

Ball, E. W., & Blachman, B. A. (1991). Does phoneme awareness training in kindergarten make a difference in early word recognition and developmental spelling? *Reading Research Quarterly, 26,* 49–66.

Balow, B. (1971). Perceptual-motor activities in the treatment of severe reading disability. *The Reading Teacher, 24,* 513–525, 542.

Balow, B., Rubin, R., & Rosen, M. J. (1975–76). Perinatal events as precursors of reading disability. *Reading Research Quarterly, 11,* 36–71.

Bamford, J., & Day, R. R. (1998). Teaching reading. In W. Grabe (Ed.), *Annual review of applied linguistics: Volume 18.* Foundations of second-language teaching (pp. 124–141). New York: Cambridge University Press.

Barganz, J. C., & Dulin, K. L. (1970). Readability levels of selected mass magazines from 1925 to 1965. In G. B. Schick & M. M. May (Eds.), *Reading process and pedagogy. Nineteenth Yearbook of the National Reading Conference* (pp. 26–30). Washington, DC: National Reading Conference.

Baron, J., & Treiman, R. (1980). Use of orthography in reading and learning to read. In J. Kavanaugh & R. Venezky (Eds.), *Orthography, reading, and dyslexia.* Baltimore: University Park Press.

Barone, D. (1999). *Resilient children: Stories of poverty, drug exposure, literacy development.* Newark, DE: International Reading Association.

Barr, R., Blachowicz, C. L. Z., & Wogman-Sadow, M. (1995). *Reading diagnosis for teachers: An instructional approach* (3rd ed.). New York: Longman.

Barr, R. C. (1974–75). The effect of instruction on pupil reading strategies. *Reading Research Quarterly, 10,* 555–582.

Barr, R. C. (1984). Beginning reading instruction: From debate to reformation. In P. D. Pearson (Ed.), *Handbook of reading research* (pp. 545–581). New York: Longman.

Barr, R. C. (2002). Ability grouping. In B. J. Guzzetti (Ed.), *Literacy in America* (pp. 1–5). Santa Barbara, CA: ABC-CLIO.

Barr, R. C., & Dreeben, R. (1983). *How schools work.* Chicago: University of Chicago Press.

Barrett, T. C. (1965). The relationship between measures of prereading visual discrimination and first grade reading achievement: A review of the literature. *Reading Research Quarterly, 1,* 51–76.

Bartlett, F. C. (1932). *Remembering.* Cambridge, MA: Harvard University Press.

Baumann, J. F. (1984). The effectiveness of a direct instruction paradigm for teaching main idea comprehension. *Reading Research Quarterly, 20,* 93–115.

Baumann, J. F., Seifert-Kessell, N., & Jones, L. A. (1992). Effect of think-aloud instruction on elementary students' comprehension monitoring abilities. *Journal of Reading Behavior, 24,* 143–172.

Bean, T. W. (2000). Reading in the content areas: Social constructivist dimensions. In M. L. Kamil, P. B. Mosenthal, P. D. Pearson, & R. Barr (Eds.), *Handbook of reading research* (Vol. III, pp. 629–644). Mahwah, NJ: Erlbaum.

Bear, D. (1992). The prosody of oral reading and the stages of word knowledge. In S. Templeton & D. Bear (Eds.), *Development of orthographic knowledge and the foundations of literacy* (pp. 137–190). Hillsdale, NJ: Erlbaum.

Beck, I. L., & McKeown, M. (1991). Conditions of vocabulary acquisition. In R. Barr, M. L. Kamil, P. Mosenthal, & P. D. Pearson (Eds.), *Handbook of reading research* (Vol. II, pp. 789–814). New York: Longman.

Beck, I. L., McKeown, M. G., & McCaslin, E. S. (1983). Vocabulary development: All contexts are not created equal. *Elementary School Journal, 83,* 177–181.

Beck, I. L., Omanson, R. C., & McKeown, M. G. (1982). An instructional redesign of reading lessons: Effects on comprehension. *Reading Research Quarterly, 17,* 462–481.

Becker, E. (1994). *Using predictable books with a non-reader: Cognitive and affective effects.* Unpublished doctoral dissertation, Ohio State University, Columbus, OH.

Beebe, M. J. (1980). The effect of different types of substitution miscues on reading. *Reading Research Quarterly, 15,* 324–336.

Beed, P. L., Hawkins, E. M., & Roller, C. M. (1991). Moving learners toward independence: The power of scaffolded instruction. *The Reading Teacher, 44,* 648–655.

Beers, J., & Henderson, E. (1977). A study of developing orthographic concepts among first graders. *Research in the Teaching of English, 11,* 133–148.

Belmont, L., & Birch, H. G. (1965). Lateral dominance, lateral awareness, and reading disability. *Child Development, 36,* 57–71.

Benton, C. D., & McCann, J. W. (1969). Dyslexia and dominance: Some second thoughts. *Journal of Pediatric Ophthalmology, 6,* 220–222.

Berkowitz, S. J. (1986). Effects of instruction in text organization on sixth-grade students' memory for expository reading. *Reading Research Quarterly, 21,* 161–178.

Betts, E. A. (1940). Reading problems at the intermediate grade level. *Elementary School Journal, 15,* 737–746.

Biemiller, A. (1970). The development of the use of graphic and contextual information as children learn to read. *Reading Research Quarterly, 6,* 75–96.

Biemiller, A. (1977–78). Relation between oral reading rates for letters, words, and simple text in the development of reading achievement. *Reading Research Quarterly, 13,* 223–253.

Biemiller, A. (2003). Vocabulary: Needed if more children are to read well. *Reading Psychology, 24,* 323–336.

Biemiller, A., & Slonin, N. (2000, July). Estimating root word vocabulary growth in normative and advantaged populations: Evidence for a common sequence of vocabulary acquisition. Paper presented at the meeting of the Society for the Scientific Study of Reading, Stockholm, Sweden.

Bittner, J. R., & Shamo, G. W. (1976). Readability of the 'Mini Page.' *Journalism Quarterly, 53,* 740–743.

Blachowicz, C. L. Z., & Fisher, P. (2000). Vocabulary instruction. In M. L. Kamil, P. B. Mosenthal, P. D. Pearson, & R. Barr (Eds.), *Handbook of reading research* (Vol. III, pp. 503–524). Mahwah, NJ: Erlbaum.

Blachowicz, C. L. Z., & Fisher, P. J. (2005). Vocabulary instruction in a remedial setting. *Reading and Writing Quarterly, 21,* 281–300.

Black, W. F. (1974). Achievement test performance of high and low perceiving learning disabled children. *Journal of Learning Disabilities, 7,* 178–182.

Blackman, B. A. (1984). Relationship of rapid naming ability and language analysis skills to kindergarten and first-grade reading achievement. *Journal of Educational Psychology, 77,* 610–622.

Blanchard, J. S. (1980). Preliminary investigation of transfer between single-word decoding ability and contextual reading comprehension of poor readers in grade six. *Perceptual and Motor Skills, 51,* 1271–1281.

Bloom, B. S. (Ed.). (1956). *Taxonomy of educational objectives.* New York: Longman.

Bloom, B. S. (1984). The 2 sigma problem: The search for methods of group instruction as effective as one-to-one tutoring. *Educational Researcher, 13*(6), 4–17.

Bohline, D. S. (1985). Intellectual and affective characteristics of attention deficit disordered children. *Journal of Learning Disabilities, 18,* 604–608.

Bond, G. L., Tinker, M. A., & Wasson, B. B. (1979). *Reading difficulties: Their diagnosis and correction* (4th ed.). Englewood Cliffs, NJ: Prentice Hall.

Bormuth, J. R. (1968). The cloze readability procedure. In J. R. Bormuth (Ed.), *Readability in 1968.* Champaign, IL: National Council of Teachers of English.

Bormuth, J. R. (1973–74). Reading literacy: Its definition and assessment. *Reading Research Quarterly, 9,* 7–66.

Bos, C. S., & Anders, P. L. (1990). Effects of interactive vocabulary instruction on the vocabulary learning and reading comprehension of junior-high learning disabled students. *Learning Disability Quarterly, 13,* 31–42.

Bradley, J. M. (1976). Evaluating reading achievement for placement in special education. *Journal of Special Education, 10,* 239–245.

Bradley, L., & Bryant, P. E. (1983). Categorizing sounds and learning to read—a causal connection. *Nature, 301,* 419–421.

Bradley, L., & Bryant, P. E. (1985). *Rhyme and reason in reading and spelling.* Ann Arbor: University of Michigan Press.

Bretzing, B. B., & Kulhavy, R. W. (1979). Note taking and depth of processing. *Contemporary Educational Psychology, 4,* 145–153.

Bridge, C. A. (2002). Predictable books. In B. J. Guzzetti (Ed.), *Literacy in America* (pp. 450–452). Santa Barbara, CA: ABC-CLIO.

Bridge, C. A., Winograd, P. N., & Haley, D. (1983). Using predictable materials vs. preprimers to teach beginning sight words. *The Reading Teacher, 36,* 884–891.

Brophy, J. E., & Evertson, C. M. (1981). *Student characteristics and teaching.* New York: Longman.

Brown, A. L., Armbruster, B. B., & Baker, L. (1986). The role of meta-cognition in reading and studying. In J. Orasanu (Ed.), *Reading comprehension: From research to practice* (pp. 49–75). Hillsdale, NJ: Erlbaum.

Brown, A. L., & Day, J. D. (1983). The development of plans for summarizing texts. *Child Development, 54,* 968–979.

Brown, A. L., Palincsar, A., & Armbruster, B. B. (2004). Instructing comprehsion-fostering activities in interactive learning situations. In R. B. Ruddell & N. J. Unrau (Eds.), *Theoretical models and processes of reading* (5th ed. pp. 780–809). Newark, DE: International Reading Association.

Brown, D. A. (1982). *Reading diagnosis and remediation.* Englewood Cliffs, NJ: Prentice Hall.

Brown, K. J., Morris, D., & Fields, M. (2005). Intervention after grade 1: Serving increased numbers of struggling readers effectively. *Journal of Literacy Research, 37,* 61–94.

Bruce, D. (1964). An analysis of word sounds by young children. *British Journal of Educational Psychology, 34,* 158–170.

Bruner, L. G. (1983). The remediation of a graphophonic decoding deficit in an adult. *Journal of Reading, 27,* 145–151.

Bryan, T. H. (1974). Learning disabilities: A new stereotype. *Journal of Learning Disabilities, 7,* 304–309.

Bryant, S. (1979). *Relative effectiveness of visual-auditory versus auditory-kinesthetic-tactile procedures for teaching sight words and letter sounds to young disabled readers.* Unpublished doctoral dissertation, Teachers College, New York.

Buckland, P. (1970). The effect of visual perception training on reading achievement of low readiness first grade pupils. *Dissertation Abstracts International, 31,* 1613A (University Microfilms No. 70–15, 707).

Burke, A. J. (1984). Students' potential for learning contrasted under tutorial and group approaches to instruction (Doctoral dissertation, University of Chicago, 1983). *Dissertation Abstracts International, 44,* 2025A.

Burns, E. (1982). Linear regression and simplified reading expectancy formulas. *Reading Research Quarterly, 17,* 446–453.

Byers, R. K., & Lord, E. E. (1943). Late effects of lead poisoning on mental development. *American Journal of Diseases of Children, 66,* 471–493.

Calfee, R. C., & Hiebert, E. (1991). Classroom assessment of reading. In R. Barr, M. L. Kamil, P. Mosenthal, & P. D. Pearson (Eds.), *Handbook of reading research* (Vol. II, pp. 281–309). New York: Longman.

Calfee, R. C., & Piontkowski, D. C. (1981). The reading diary: Acquisition of decoding. *Reading Research Quarterly, 16,* 346–373.

Capobianco, R. J. (1967). Ocular-manual laterality and reading achievement in children with special learning disabilities. *American Educational Research Journal, 2,* 133–137.

Carnine, D., Kameenui, E. J., & Coyle, G. (1984). Utilization of contextual information in determining the meaning of unfamiliar words in context. *Reading Research Quarterly, 19,* 188–202.

Carrell, P. L., & Grabe, W. (2002). Reading. In N. Schmitt (Ed.), *An introduction to applied linguistics* (pp. 233–250). London: Edward Arnold.

Carroll, M. (2004). *Cartwheels on the keyboard: Computer-based literacy instruction in an elementary classroom.* Newark, DE: International Reading Association.

Carroll, J. B., Davies, P., & Richman, B. (1971). *American Heritage word frequency book.* Boston: Houghton Mifflin.

Carter, T. P., & Chatfield, M. L. (1986). Effective bilingual schools: Implications for policy and practice. *American Journal of Education, 95,* 200–232.

Ceprano, M. A. (1981). A review of selected research on methods of teaching sight words. *The Reading Teacher, 35,* 314–322.

Chall, J. S. (1967). *Learning to read: The great debate.* New York: McGraw-Hill.

Chall, J. S. (1983). *Stages of reading development.* New York: McGraw-Hill.

Chall, J. S. (1989). Learning to read: The great debate 20 years later. *Phi Delta Kappan, 70,* 521–538.

Chang, T., & Chang, V. (1967). Relation of visual-motor skills and reading achievement in primary grade pupils of superior ability. *Perceptual and Motor Skills, 24,* 51–53.

Chavkin, N. F. (1989). Debunking the myth about minority parents. *Educational Horizons, 67,* 119–123.

Chomsky, C. (1972). Stages in language development and reading exposure. *Harvard Educational Review, 42,* 1–33.

Chomsky, C. (1976). After decoding: What? *Language Arts, 53,* 288–296, 314.

Chomsky, C. (1979). Approaching reading through invented spelling. In L. B. Resnick & P. A. Weaver (Eds.), *Theory and practice of early reading* (Vol. 2, pp. 43–65). Hillsdale, NJ: Erlbaum.

Clark, K. F., & Graves, M. F. (2005). Scaffolding students' comprehension of text. *The Reading Teacher, 58,* 570–580.

Clay, M. M. (1967). The reading behavior of five-year-old children: A research report. *New Zealand Journal of Educational Studies, 2,* 11–31.

Clay, M. M. (1979). *Reading: The patterning of complex behavior* (2nd ed.). Auckland, New Zealand: Heinemann.

Clay, M. M. (1985). *The early detection of reading difficulties* (3rd ed.). Portsmouth, NH: Heinemann.

Cleary, D. M. (1978). *Thinking Thursdays: Language arts in the reading lab.* Newark, DE: International Reading Association.

Clymer, T. (1963). The utility of phonics generalizations in the primary grades. *The Reading Teacher, 16,* 252–258.

Coaches, controversy, consensus. (2004, April/May). *Reading Today,* pp. 1, 18.

Cohen, D. (1968). Effect of literature on vocabulary and reading. *Elementary English, 45,* 209–213.

Cohen, D. H. (1969). Word meaning and literary experience in early childhood. *Elementary English, 46,* 914–925.

Cohen, D. K. (1972). *The effects of the Michigan Tracking Program on gains in reading.* New Brunswick, NJ: Rutgers University. (ERIC Document Reproduction Service No. ED 064 700)

Cohen, S., & Taharally, C. (1992). Getting ready for young children with prenatal drug exposure. *Childhood Education, 69*(1), 5–9.

Comings, J. P. (2002). Adult literacy programs. In B. J. Guzzetti (Ed.), *Literacy in America (Vol. 1,* pp. 22–25). Santa Barbara, CA: ABC-CLIO.

Commission on Emotional and Learning Disorders in Children. (1970). *One million children: A national study of Canadian children with emotional and learning disorders.* Toronto: Leonard Crainford.

Committee on Nutrition of the American Academy of Pediatrics. (1976). Mega-vitamin therapy for childhood psychoses and learning disabilities. *Pediatrics, 58,* 910–912.

Cook, W. D. (1977). *Adult literacy education in the United States.* Newark, DE: International Reading Association.

Cote, N., & Goldman, S. R. (2004). Building representations of informational texts: Evidence from children's think-aloud protocols. In R. B. Ruddell & N. J. Unrau (Eds.), *Theoretical models and processes of reading* (5th ed., pp. 660–683). Newark, DE: International Reading Association.

Cunningham, A. E., & Stanovich, K. E. (1998, Spring/Summer). What reading does for the mind. *American Educator,* pp. 8–15.

Cunningham, P. M. (1977). Investigating the role of meaning in mediated word identification. In P. D. Pearson & J. Hansen (Eds.), *Reading: Theory, research, and practice.* Clemson, SC: National Reading Conference.

Cunningham, P. M. (1988). When all else fails . . . . *The Reading Teacher, 41,* 800–805.

Cunningham, P. M. (1991). *Phonics they use: Words for reading and writing.* New York: HarperCollins.

Cunningham, P. M. (1998). The multisyllabic word dilemma: Helping students build meaning, spell, and read "big" words. *Reading and Writing Quarterly, 14,* 189–218.

Cunningham, P. M., & Cunningham, J. W. (1992). Making words: Enhancing the invented spelling-decoding connection. *The Reading Teacher, 46,* 106–115.

Cunningham, P. M., Hall, D. P., & Defee, M. (1998). Non-ability grouped, multilevel instruction: Eight years later. *The Reading Teacher, 51,* 652–664.

Cunningham, P. A., Hall, D. P., & Sigmon, C. M. (1999). *The teacher's guide to the Four Blocks.* Lindon, UT: Carson-Dellosa Publishing.

Cziko, G. A. (1983). Another response to Shanahan, Kamil, and Tobin: Further reasons to keep the cloze case open. *Reading Research Quarterly, 18,* 361–365.

Dale, E., & O'Rourke, J. (1971). *Techniques of teaching vocabulary.* Palo Alto, CA: Field Educational Publications.

Dale, E., & O'Rourke, J. (1976). *The living word vocabulary.* Elgin, IL: Dome.

Daneman, M. (1991). Individual differences in reading skills. In R. Barr, M. L. Kamil, P. Mosenthal, & P. D. Pearson (Eds.), *Handbook of reading research* (Vol. II, pp. 512–538). New York: Longman.

Daneman, M., & Carpenter, P. A. (1980). Individual differences in working memory and reading. *Journal of Verbal Learning and Verbal Behavior, 19,* 450–466.

Daneman, M., & Green, I. (1986). Individual differences in comprehending and producing words in context. *Journal of Memory and Language, 25,* 1–18.

Daniels, P. S., & Hyslop, S. G. (Eds.). (2003). *Almanac of world history.* Washington, DC: National Geographic Society.

Dearborn, W. F., & Anderson, I. H. (1938). Aniseikonia as related to disability in reading. *Journal of Experimental Psychology, 23,* 559–577.

DeFries, J. C., Vogler, G. P., & LaBuda, M. C. (1985). Colorado Family Reading Study: An overview. In J. L. Fuller & E. C. Simmel (Eds.), *Behavior genetics: Principles and applications II* (pp. 357–368). Hillsdale, NJ: Erlbaum.

Delacato, C. H. (1963). *The diagnosis and treatment of speech and reading problems.* Springfield, IL: Charles C. Thomas.

Derry, S. J., & Murphy, D. A. (1986). Designing systems that train learning ability: From theory to practice. *Review of Educational Research, 56,* 1–39.

Dewitz, P., & Guinessey, B. (1990, December). *The effects of phoneme awareness training and repeated readings on the oral reading of disabled readers.* Paper presented at the meeting of the National Reading Conference, Miami, FL.

Dolch, E. W. (1936). A basic sight vocabulary. *The Elementary School Journal, 36,* 456–460.

Dole, J. A. (2002). Comprehension strategies. In B. J. Guzzetti (Ed.), *Literacy in America* (pp. 85–88). Santa Barbara, CA: ABC-CLIO.

Dole, J. A. (2004). The changing role of the reading specialist in school reform. *The Reading Teacher, 57,* 462–470.

Dowhower, S. L. (1987). Effects of repeated reading on second-grade transitional readers' fluency and comprehension. *Reading Research Quarterly, 22,* 389–406.

Drame, E. R. (2002). Sociocultural context effects on teachers' readiness to refer for learning disabilities. *Exceptional Children, 69*(1), 41–53.

Dreher, M. J. (1992). Predicting the location of answers to textbook search tasks. In C. K. Kinzer & J. D. Leu (Eds.), *Literacy research, theory, and practice: Views from many perspectives* (pp. 269–274). Chicago: National Reading Conference.

Dreyer, L. G., & Katz, L. (1992). An examination of "the simple view of reading." In C. K. Kinzer & D. J. Leu (Eds.), *Literacy research, theory, and practice: Views from many perspectives* (pp. 169–175). Chicago: National Reading Conference.

Dufflemeyer, F. A., & Banwart, B. H. (1993). Word maps for adjectives and verbs. *The Reading Teacher, 46,* 351–353.

Duffy, G. G., & Roehler, L. R. (1987). *Improving classroom reading instruction: A decision-making approach.* New York: Random House.

Duke, N. K., & Bennett-Armistead, V. S. (2003). *Reading and writing informational text in the primary grades: Research-based practices.* New York: Scholastic Teaching Resources.

Dunn, L. M. (1973). Children with mild general learning disabilities. In L. M. Dunn (Ed.), *Exceptional children in the schools: Special education in transition.* New York: Holt, Rinehart, & Winston.

Dunston, P. J., & Headley, K. N. (2002). Directed reading activity and directed reading-thinking activity. In B. J. Guzzetti (Ed.), *Literacy in America* (pp. 133–135). Santa Barbara, CA: ABC-CLIO.

Durkin, D. (1984). Is there a match between what elementary teachers do and what basal reader manuals recommend? *The Reading Teacher, 37,* 734–744.

Durr, W. K. (1973). Computer study of high frequency words in popular trade journals. *The Reading Teacher, 27,* 37–42.

Ehri, L. C. (1987). Learning to read and spell words. *Journal of Reading Behavior, 19,* 5–31.

Ehri, L. C. (1991). Development of the ability to read words. In R. Barr, M. L. Kamil, P. Mosenthal, & P. D. Pearson (Eds.), *Handbook of reading research* (Vol. II, pp. 383–417). New York: Longman.

Ehri, L. C., & McCormick, S. (2004). Phases of word learning: Implications for instruction with delayed and disabled readers. In R. B. Ruddell & N. J. Unrau (Eds.), *Theoretical models and processes of reading* (5th ed., pp. 365–389). Newark, DE: International Reading Association.

Ehri, L. C., Nunes, S. R., Willows, D. M., Shuster, B. V., Yaghoub-Zadeh, Z., & Shanahan, T. (2001). Phonemic awareness instruction helps children learn to read: Evidence from the National Panel's meta-analysis. *Reading Research Quarterly, 36,* 250–287.

Ehri, L. C., & Wilce, L. S. (1985). Movement into reading: Is the first stage of printed word learning visual or phonetic? *Reading Research Quarterly, 20,* 163–179.

Ehri, L. C., & Wilce, L. S. (1987). Does learning to spell help beginners learn to read words? *Reading Research Quarterly, 22,* 47–65.

Ekwall, E. E. (1975). *Corrective reading system.* Glenview, IL: Psychotechnics.

Elbro, C., Borstrom, I., & Petersen, D. K. (1998). Predicting dyslexia from kindergarten: The importance of distinctness of phonological representations of lexical items. *Reading Research Quarterly, 33,* 36–60.

Eldridge, B. H. (1985). Reading in context: An alternative approach for the adolescent disabled reader. *Journal of Reading, 29,* 9–17.

Elish-Piper, L. (2002). Adult literacy. In B. J. Guzzetti (Ed.), *Literacy in America* (*Vol. 1,* pp. 19–22). Santa Barbara, CA: ABC-CLIO.

Elkonin, D. B. (1963). The psychology of mastering elements of reading. In B. Simon & J. Simon (Eds.), *Educational psychology in the U.S.S.R.* (pp. 165–179). London: Routledge & Kegan Paul.

Elley, W. B., & Mangubhai, F. (1983). The impact of reading in second language learning. *Reading Research Quarterly, 19,* 53–67.

Emans, R. (1967). The usefulness of phonic generalizations above the primary grades. *The Reading Teacher, 20,* 419–425.

Eskey, D. (2002). Reading and teaching of second-language reading. *TESOL Journal, 11,* 5–9.

Estes, T. H. (1971). A scale to measure attitudes toward reading. *Journal of Reading, 15,* 135–138.

Evans, M. M. (1982). *Dyslexia: An annotated bibliography.* Westport, CT: Greenwood Press.

Evensen, D. H., & Mosenthal, P. B. (1999). *Reconsidering the role of the reading clinic in a new age of literacy.* In P. B. Mosenthal (Ed.), *Advances in reading/language research* (Vol. 6). Stamford, CT: JAI Press.

Farr, R. (1969). *Reading: What can be measured?* Newark, DE: International Reading Association.

Farr, R. (1991). Dialects, culture, and teaching the English language arts. In J. Flood, J. M. Jensen, D. Lapp, & J. R. Squire (Eds.), *Handbook of research on teaching the English language arts* (pp. 365–371). New York: Macmillan.

Farr, R. (1992). Putting it all together: Solving the reading assessment puzzle. *The Reading Teacher, 46,* 26–37.

Felton, G. S., & Felton, L. S. (1973). From ivory tower to the people: Shifts in readability estimates of American presidential inaugural addresses. *Reading Improvement, 10,* 40–44.

Ferguson, A. M., & Fairburn, J. (1985). Language experience for problem solving in mathematics. *The Reading Teacher, 38,* 504–507.

Feuerstein, R. (1979). *The dynamic assessment of retarded performers: The learning potential assessment device, theory, instrument, and techniques.* Baltimore: University Park Press.

Fielding, L. G., Anderson, R. C., & Pearson, P. D. (1990). *How discussion questions influence children's story understanding* (Tech. Rep. No. 490). Urbana-Champaign: University of Illinois, Center for the Study of Reading.

Finucci, J. M., Gutherie, J. T., Childs, A. L., Abbey, H., & Childs, B. (1976). The genetics of specific reading disability. *Annals of Human Genetics, 40,* 1–23.

Fitzgerald, J. (1995). English-as-a-second-language learners' cognitive processes: A review of research in the United States. *Review of Educational Research, 65,* 145–190.

Fitzgerald, J. (2001). Can minimally trained college student volunteers help young at-risk children to read better? *Reading Research Quarterly, 36,* 28–46.

Fitzgerald, J. (2002). Narrative text. In B. J. Guzzetti (Ed.), *Literacy in America* (pp. 388–392). Santa Barbara, CA: ABC-CLIO.

Flowers, D. L. (1993). Brain basis for dyslexia: A summary of work in progress. *Journal of Learning Disabilities, 26,* 575–582.

Foster, J. M. (1966). Effects of mobility training upon reading achievement and intelligence. *Dissertation Abstracts International, 26,* 3779A (University Microfilms No. 66–00, 336).

Fox, B., & Routh, K. D. (1984). Phonemic analysis and synthesis as word-attack skills: Revisited. *Journal of Educational Psychology, 76,* 1059–1064.

Freeland, J. T., Skinner, C. H., Jackson, B., McDaniel, C. E., & Smith, S. (2000). Measuring and increasing silent reading comprehension rates: Empirically validating a repeated readings intervention. *Psychology in the Schools, 37,* 415–429.

Fresch, M. J. (2000). What we learned from Josh: Sorting out word sorting. *Language Arts, 77,* 232–240.

Friedman, D., & Medway, F. (1987). Effects of varying performance sets and outcomes on the expectations, attributions, and persistence of boys with learning disabilities. *Journal of Learning Disabilities, 20,* 312–316.

Frith, V. (1985). Beneath the surface of developmental dyslexia. In K. E. Patterson, J. C. Marshall, & M. Coltheart (Eds.), *Surface dyslexia* (pp. 301–330). London: Erlbaum.

Fry, E. B. (1980). The new instant word list. *The Reading Teacher, 34,* 287–289.

Fry, E. (1997). *Phonics patterns.* Laguna Beach, CA: Laguna Beach Educational Books.

Galda, L., Ash, G. E., & Cullinan, B. E. (2000). Children's literature. In M. L. Kamil, P. B. Mosenthal, P. D. Pearson, & R. Barr (Eds.), *Handbook of reading research* (Vol. III, pp. 361–379). Mahwah, NJ: Erlbaum.

Gambrel, L. B. (2002). Narrative and expository text. In B. J. Guzzetti (Ed.), *Literacy in America* (pp. 385–388). Santa Barbara, CA: ABC-CLIO.

Garcìa, G. E. (1991). Factors influencing the English reading test performance of Spanish-speaking Hispanic children. *Reading Research Quarterly, 26,* 371–392.

Garcia, G. G., & Beltrán, D. (2003). Revisioning the blueprint: Building for the academic success of English learners. In G. G. Garcia (Ed.), *English learners: Reaching the highest level of English literacy* (pp. 197–226). Newark, DE: International Reading Association.

Garner, R. (1987). *Metacognition and reading comprehension.* Norwood, NJ: Ablex.

Garner, R. (1992). Metacognition and self-monitoring strategies. In S. J. Samuels & A. E. Farstrup (Eds.), *What research has to say about reading instruction* (2nd ed., pp. 236–252). Newark, DE: International Reading Association.

Garner, R., Wagoner, S., & Smith, T. (1983). Externalizing question-answering strategies of good and poor comprehenders. *Reading Research Quarterly, 18,* 439–447.

Gaskins, I. W. (1998). There's more to teaching at-risk and delayed readers than good reading instruction. *The Reading Teacher, 51,* 534–547.

Gates, A. I. (1926). A study of the role of visual perception, intelligence, and certain associative processes in reading and spelling. *Journal of Educational Psychology, 17,* 433–445.

Gates, A. I. (1931). *Interest and ability in reading.* New York: Macmillan.

Gentry, J. R. (1981). Learning to spell developmentally. *The Reading Teacher, 34,* 468–474.

Gersten, R. (1985). Structured immersion for language minority students: Results of a longitudinal evaluation. *Educational Evaluation and Policy Analysis, 7,* 187–196.

Gersten, R., & Baker, S. (2000). What we know about effective instructional practices for English language learners. *Exceptional Children, 66,* 454–470.

Gersten, R., & Jimènez, R. T. (1994). A delicate balance: Enhancing literature instruction for students of English as a second language. *The Reading Teacher, 47,* 438–447.

Gillet, J. W., Temple, C., & Crawford, A. N. (2004). *Understanding reading problems* (6th ed.). Boston: Allyn & Bacon.

Gillingham, A., & Stillman, B. W. (1966). *Remedial training for children with specific difficulty in reading, spelling, and penmanship* (7th ed.). Cambridge, MA: Educators Publishing Service.

Glaser, N. A. (1965). A comparison of specific reading skills of advanced and retarded readers of fifth grade reading achievement. *Dissertation Abstracts International, 25,* 5785A-5786A (University Microfilms No. 65–2467).

Glass, G. G., & Glass, E. W. (1978). *Glass Analysis for decoding only: Easy starts kits.* Garden City, NY: Easier to Learn.

Golden, J. M. (1988). The construction of a literacy text in a story-reading lesson. In J. Green & J. Harker (Eds.), *Multiple perspective analyses of classroom discourse* (pp. 71–106). Norwood, NJ: Ablex.

Goldenberg, C. (1996). Latin American immigration and U.S. schools. *Social Policy Report of the Society for Research in Child Development, 10,* 1–29.

Goldenberg, C. (2004). Literacy for all children in the increasingly diverse schools of the United States. In

R. B. Ruddell & N. J. Unrau (Eds.), *Theoretical models and processes of reading* (5th ed., pp. 1636–1666). Newark, DE: International Reading Association.

Goldenberg, C. (2005, April). *Improving literacy outcomes for Latino students: Idealogy, research, and practice.* Paper presented at the meeting of the Reading Research Conference of the International Reading Association, San Antonio, TX.

Goldenberg, C., & Gallimore, R. (1995). Immigrant Latino parents' values and beliefs about their children's education: Continuities and discontinuities across cultures and generations. In P. R. Pintrich & M. Maehr (Eds.), *Advances in motivation and achievement: Culture, ethnicity, and motivation* (*Vol. 9*, pp. 183–228). Greenwich, CT: JAI Press.

Goodman, K. S. (2002). Whole language and whole-language assessment. In B. J. Guzzetti (Ed.), *Literacy in America* (pp. 673–677). Santa Barbara, CA: ABC-CLIO.

Goodman, K. S., Bird, L., & Goodman, Y. M. (1991). *The whole language catalog.* Santa Rosa, CA: American School Publishers.

Goodman, Y. M., & Burke, C. L. (1972). *Reading miscue inventory manual.* New York: Macmillan.

Goodman, Y. M., Watson, D., & Burke, C. L. (1987). *Reading miscue analysis.* New York: R. C. Owen.

Goswami, U. (1988). Orthographic analogies and reading development. *Quarterly Journal of Experimental Psychology, 40,* 239–268.

Goswami, U. (2000). Phonological and lexical processes. In M. L. Kamil, P. B. Mosenthal, P. D. Pearson, & R. Barr (Eds.), *Handbook of reading research* (Vol. III, pp. 251–268). Mahwah, NJ: Erlbaum.

Gottlieb, J. (1974). Attitudes toward retarded children: Effects of labeling and academic performance. *American Journal of Mental Deficiency, 79,* 268–273.

Gough, P. B. (1983). Context, form, and interaction. In K. Rayner (Ed.), *Eye movements in reading* (pp. 203–211). New York: Academic Press.

Gough, P. B., & Hillinger, M. L. (1980). Learning to read: An unnatural act. *Bulletin of the Orton Society, 30,* 179–196.

Gough, P. B., Juel, C., & Roper-Schneider, D. (1983). A two-stage model of initial reading acquisition. In J. A. Niles & L. A. Harris (Eds.), *Searches for meaning in reading/language processing and instruction* (pp. 207–211). Rochester, NY: National Reading Conference.

Grabe, W. (2002). Reading in a second language. In R. Kaplan (Ed.), *The Oxford handbook of applied linguistics* (pp. 49–59). New York: Oxford University Press.

Graves, M. F. (2000). A vocabulary program to complement and bolster a middle-grade comprehension program. In B. M. Taylor, M. F. Graves, & P. van den Broek

(Eds.), *Reading for meaning: Fostering comprehension in the middle grades* (pp. 116–135). Newark, DE: International Reading Association.

Graves, M. F., Cooke, C. L., & Laberge, M. J. (1983). Effects of previewing difficult short stories on low ability junior high school students' comprehension, recall, and attitudes. *Reading Research Quarterly, 18,* 262–276.

Gray, T., & Fleischman, S. (2005). Research matters/Successful strategies for English language learners. ASCD. Retrieved January 7, 2005, from www.ascd.org

Gray, W. S. (1920). The value of informal tests of reading achievement. *Journal of Educational Research, 1,* 103–111.

Greaney, V. (1980). Factors related to amount and type of leisure-time reading. *Reading Research Quarterly, 15,* 337–357.

Greaney, V., & Hegerty, M. (1987). Correlates in leisure-time reading. *Journal of Research in Reading, 16,* 3–20.

Greenwood, C. R., Delquadri, J. C., & Hall, R. V. (1984). Opportunity to respond and student academic performance. In W. L. Heward, T. E. Heron, D. Hill, & J. Trap-Porter (Eds.), *Focus on behavior.* Columbus, OH: Merrill.

Gresham, F. M., & MacMillan, D. L. (1997). Social competence and affective characteristics of students with mild disabilities. *Review of Educational Research, 67,* 377–415.

Griffith, D. (1992). Prenatal exposure to cocaine and other drugs: Developmental and educational prognoses. *Phi Delta Kappan, 74,* 30–34.

Griffith, P. L., & Olson, M. W. (1992). Phonemic awareness helps beginning readers break the code. *The Reading Teacher, 45,* 516–523.

Guerra, J. C. (1998). *Close to home: Oral and literate practices in a transnational Mexicano community.* New York: Teachers College Press.

Gunderson, L. (1991). *ESL literacy instruction: A guidebook to theory and practice.* Englewood Cliffs, NJ: Prentice Hall.

Guszak, F. J. (1967). Teacher questioning and reading. *The Reading Teacher, 21,* 227–234.

Gutherie, J. T., & Greaney, V. (1991). Literacy acts. In R. Barr, M. L. Kamil, P. Mosenthal, & P. D. Pearson (Eds.), *Handbook of reading research* (Vol. II, pp. 68–96). New York: Longman.

Gutherie, J. T., Wigfield, A., Metsala, J. L., & Cox, K. E. (2004). Motivation and cognitive predictors of text comprehension and reading amount. In R. B. Ruddell & N. J. Unrau (Eds.), *Theoretical models and processes of reading* (5th ed., pp. 929–952). Newark, DE: International Reading Association.

Gutherie, J. T., & Wigfield, A. (2000). Engagement and motivation in reading. In M. L. Kamil, P. B. Mosenthal, P. D. Pearson, & R. Barr, (Eds.), *Handbook of reading research* (Vol. III, pp. 403–424). Mahwah, NJ: Erlbaum.

Hakuta, K., Butler, G. Y., & Witt, D. (2000). *How long does it take English learners to attain proficiency?* University of California, Linguistic Minority Research Institute, Policy Report 2000–1.

Hall, M. (1970). *Teaching reading as a language experience.* Columbus, OH: Merrill.

Hallgren, B. (1950). Specific dyslexia: A clinical and genetic study. *Acta Psychiatrica et Neurologica* (Supplement No. 65). Copenhagen, Denmark.

Hammill, D. D., Goodman, L., & Wiederholt, J. L. (1974). Visual-motor processes: Can we train them? *The Reading Teacher, 27,* 469–478.

Hammill, D. D., & Larsen, S. C. (1974). The effectiveness of psycho-linguistic training. *Exceptional Children, 41,* 5–15.

Hansen, C., & Lovitt, T. (1977). An applied behavior analysis approach to reading comprehension. In J. T. Gutherie (Ed.), *Cognition, curriculum, and comprehension.* Newark, DE: International Reading Association.

Hansen, J. (1981). The effects of inference training and practice on young children's reading comprehension. *Reading Research Quarterly, 16,* 391–417.

Harmon, J. M., Hedrick, W. B., & Wood, K. D. (2005). Research on vocabulary instruction in the content areas: Implications for struggling readers. *Reading and Writing Quarterly, 21,* 261–280.

Harris, A. J. (1968). Five decades of remedial reading. In J. A. Figurel (Ed.), *Forging ahead in reading* (pp. 25–34). Newark, DE: International Reading Association.

Harris, A. J. (1970). *How to increase reading ability* (5th ed.). New York: David McKay.

Harris, A. J. (1976, May). *Ten years of progress in remedial reading.* Paper presented at the meeting of the International Reading Association, Anaheim, CA. (ERIC Document Reproduction Service No. ED 182 465)

Harris, A. J. (1981). What is new in remedial reading. *The Reading Teacher, 34,* 405–410.

Harris, A. J., & Jacobson, M. D. (1972). *Basic elementary reading vocabularies.* New York: Macmillan.

Harris, A. J., & Serwer, B. L. (1966). The CRAFT Project: Instructional time in reading research. *Reading Research Quarterly, 2,* 27–56.

Harris, A. J., & Sipay, E. (1980). *How to increase reading ability.* New York: Longman.

Harris, T. L., & Hodges, R. E. (Eds.). (1995). *The literacy dictionary.* Newark, DE: International Reading Association.

Heath, S. B. (1991). The sense of being literate: Historical and cross-cultural features. In R. Barr, M. L. Kamil, P. Mosenthal, & P. D. Pearson (Eds.), *Handbook of reading research* (Vol. II, pp. 3–25). New York: Longman.

Heckelman, R. G. (1966). Using the neurological impress method of remedial reading instruction. *Academic Therapy Quarterly, 1,* 235–239.

Henderson, E. H., Estes, T. H., & Stonecash, S. (1971–72). An exploratory study of word acquisition among first-graders at midyear in a language-experience approach. *Journal of Reading Behavior, 4,* 21–31.

Henderson, L. C., & Shanker, J. L. (1978). The use of interpretive dramatics versus basal reader workbooks for developing comprehension skills. *Reading World, 17,* 239–243.

Herber, H. L. (1992). Foreword. In K. Wood, D. Lapp, & J. Flood, *Guiding readers through text: A review of study guides* (p. v). Newark, DE: International Reading Association.

Herman, P. A. (1985). The effect of repeated readings on reading rate, speech pauses, and word recognition accuracy. *Reading Research Quarterly, 20,* 553–565.

Herman, P. A., & Dole, J. (1988). Theory and practice in vocabulary learning and instruction. *The Elementary School Journal, 89,* 41–52.

Hiebert, E. H., Colt, J. M., Catto, S. L., & Gury, E. C. (1992). Reading and writing of first-grade students in a restructured Chapter I program. *American Educational Research Journal, 29,* 545–572.

Hiebert, E. H., & Taylor, B. M. (2000). Beginning reading instruction: Research on early interventions. In M. L. Kamil, P. B. Mosenthal, P. D. Pearson, & R. Barr (Eds.), *Handbook of reading research* (Vol. III, pp. 455–482). Mahwah, NJ: Erlbaum.

Hildreth, G. (1965). Experience related reading for school beginners. *Elementary English, 42,* 280–297.

Hinshelwood, J. (1896). A case of dyslexia: A peculiar form of word-blindness. *Lancet, 2,* 1451–1454.

Hirshoren, A., Hunt, J. T., & Davis, C. (1974). Classified ads as reading materials for the educable retarded. *Exceptional Children, 41,* 45–47.

Hittleman, D. R. (1983). *Developmental reading, K–8: Teaching from a psycholinguistic perspective* (2nd ed.). Boston: Houghton Mifflin.

Ho, C. S., Chan, D. W., Leung, P. W. L., Lee, S., & Tsang, S. (2005). Reading-related cognitive deficits in developmental dyslexia, attention-deficit/hyperactivity disorder, and developmental coordination disorder among Chinese children. *Reading Research Quarterly, 40,* 318–337.

Hochman, C. H. (1973). Black dialect reading tests in the urban elementary school. *The Reading Teacher, 26,* 581–583.

Hoffman, J. V. (1987). Rethinking the role of oral reading. *The Elementary School Journal, 87,* 367–373.

Hoffman, J. V., Assaf, L. C., & Paris, S. G. (2001). High stakes testing in reading: Today in Texas, tomorrow? *The Reading Teacher, 54,* 482–492.

Hohn, W., & Ehri, L. (1983). Do alphabet letters help prereaders acquire phonemic segmentation skill? *Journal of Educational Psychology, 75,* 752–762.

Holdaway, D. (1979). *The foundations of literacy.* Sydney, Australia: Ashton-Scholastic.

Hoover, W. A., & Gough, P. B. (1990). The simple view of reading. *Reading and Writing: An Interdisciplinary Journal, 2,* 127–160.

Hoskins, R. L. (1973). A readability study of AP and UPI wire copy. *Journalism Quarterly, 50,* 360–363.

Hudson, R. F., Lane, H. B., & Pullen, P. C. (2005). Reading fluency assessment and instruction: What, why, and how? *The Reading Teacher, 58,* 702–714.

Hudson, T. (1998). Theoretical perspectives on reading. In W. Grabe (Ed.), *Annual review of applied linguistics: Volume 18. Foundations of second-language teaching* (pp. 43–60). New York: Cambridge University Press.

Hulme, C. (1981). The effects of manual tracing on memory in normal and retarded readers: Some implications for multi-sensory teaching. *Psychological Research, 43,* 179–191.

Institute for Education Sciences. (2001). National Center for Education Statistics (NCES) Home Page. U.S. Department of Education. Retrieved May 28, 2005, from http://nces.ed.gov/

International Reading Association [IRA]. (1992). *Adult literacy volunteer tutors* [Position statement]. Newark, DE: Author.

International Reading Association [IRA]. (2001). *Second-language literacy instruction* [Position statement]. Newark, DE: Author.

International Reading Association [IRA]. (2004a). *The roles and qualifcations of the reading coach in the United States* [Brochure]. Newark, DE: Author.

International Reading Association [IRA]. (2004b). *Standards for reading professionals–Revised.* Newark, DE: Author.

Invernizzi, M., Juel, C., & Rosemary, C. (1996). A community volunteer tutorial that works. *The Reading Teacher, 50,* 304–311.

Invernizzi, M. A., & Worthy, M. J. (1989). An orthographic-specific comparison of spelling errors of learning disabled and normal children across four grade levels of spelling achievement. *Reading Psychology, 10,* 173–188.

Jenkins, J. R., Stein, M., & Wysocki, K. (1984). Learning vocabulary through reading. *American Educational Research Journal, 21,* 767–787.

Jennings, J. H. (1991). A comparison of summary and journal writing as components of an interactive comprehension model. In J. Zutell & S. McCormick (Eds.), *Learner factors/teacher factors: Issues in literacy research and instruction* (pp. 67–82). Chicago: National Reading Conference.

Jimènez, R. T. (2004). Literacy and the identity development of Latina/o students. In R. B. Ruddell & N. J. Unrau (Eds.), *Theoretical models and processes of reading* (5th ed., pp. 210–239). Newark, DE: International Reading Association.

Johns, J. L. (1982). The dimensions and uses of informal reading assessment. In J. L. Pikulski & T. Shanahan (Eds.), *Approaches to the informal evaluation of reading.* Newark, DE: International Reading Association.

Johnson, D. (1995). Dyslexia. In T. L. Harris & R. E. Hodges (Eds.), *The literacy dictionary* (pp. 64–65). Newark, DE: International Reading Association.

Johnson, D. D. (1971). A basic vocabulary for beginning readers. *Elementary School Journal, 72,* 31–33.

Johnson, D. D., & Baumann, J. F. (1984). Word identification. In P. D. Pearson (Ed.), *Handbook of reading research* (pp. 583–608). New York: Longman.

Johnson, D. D., & Pearson, P. D. (1978). *Teaching reading vocabulary.* New York: Holt, Rinehart, & Winston.

Johnson, D. D., & Pearson, P. D. (1984). *Teaching reading vocabulary* (2nd ed.). New York: Holt, Rinehart, & Winston.

Johnson, R. (1969). The validity of the Clymer-Barrett Prereading Battery. *The Reading Teacher, 22,* 609–614.

Johnston, P. H. (1983). *Reading comprehension assessment: A cognitive basis.* Newark, DE: International Reading Association.

Johnston, P. H., & Allington, R. (1991). Remediation. In R. Barr, M. L. Kamil, P. Mosenthal, & P. D. Pearson (Eds.), *Handbook of reading research* (Vol. II, pp. 984–1012). New York: Longman.

Johnston, P. H., Afflerbach, P., & Weiss, P. (1993). Teachers' assessment of the teaching and learning of literacy. *Educational Assessment, 1,* 91–117.

Johnston, P. H., & Winograd, P. N. (1985). Passive failure in reading. *Journal of Reading Behavior, 17,* 279–301.

Joshi, R. M. (2005). Vocabulary: A critical component of comprehension. *Reading and Writing Quarterly, 21,* 209–220.

Joynes, Y. D., McCormick, S., & Heward, W. L. (1980). Teaching reading disabled students to read and complete employment applications. *Journal of Reading, 23,* 709–714.

Juel, C. (1988). Learning to read and write: A longitudinal study of 54 children from first through fourth grades. *Journal of Educational Psychology, 80,* 437–447.

Juel, C. (1989, December). *The longitudinal study of reading acquisition: Grades 1–4.* Paper presented at the meeting of the National Reading Conference, Austin, TX.

Juel, C. (1991). Beginning reading. In R. Barr, M. L. Kamil, P. Mosenthal, & P. D. Pearson (Eds.), *Handbook of reading research* (Vol. II, pp. 759–788). New York: Longman.

Juel, C., Griffith, P. L., & Gough, P. B. (1985). Reading and spelling strategies of first-grade children. In J. A. Niles & R. Lalik (Eds.), *Issues in literacy: A research perspective* (pp. 306–309). Rochester, NY: National Reading Conference.

Juel, C., Griffith, P. L., & Gough, P. B. (1986). Acquisition of literacy: A longitudinal study of children in first and second grade. *Journal of Educational Psychology, 78,* 243–255.

Juel, C., & Minden-Cupp, C. (2004). Learning to read words: Linguistic units and instructional strategies. In R. B. Ruddell & N. J. Unrau (Eds.), *Theoretical models and processes of reading* (5th ed., pp. 313–364). Newark, DE: International Reading Association.

Just, M. A., & Carpenter, P. A. (1980). A theory of reading: From eye fixations to comprehension. *Psychological Review, 87,* 329–354.

Kahn, E., & Wirtz, R. W. (1982). Another look at applications in elementary school mathematics. *Arithmetic Teacher, 30,* 21–25.

Kamil, M. L., Smith-Burke, M., & Rodriguez-Brown, F. (1986). The sensitivity of cloze to intersentential integration of information in Spanish bilingual populations. In J. A. Niles & R. V. Lalik (Eds.), *Solving problems in literacy: Learners, teachers, and researchers* (pp. 334–338). Rochester, NY: National Reading Conference.

Karchmer, R. A., Mallette, M. H., Kara-Soteriou, J., & Leu, D. J. (2005). *Innovative approaches to literacy education: Using the Internet to support new literacies.* Newark, DE: International Reading Association.

Keehn, S., Martinez, M. G., & Roser, N. L. (2005). Exploring character through Readers Theatre. In N. L. Roser & M. G. Martinez (Eds.), *What a character!* (pp. 96–110). Newark, DE: International Reading Association.

Kehus, M. J. (2003). Opportunities for teenagers to share their writing online. In B. C. Bruce (Ed.), *Literacy in the information age* (pp. 148–158). Newark, DE: International Reading Association.

Kephart, N. C. (1960). *The slow learner in the classroom.* Columbus, OH: Merrill.

Kibby, M. W. (1977). *The effects of context emphasis on teaching sight vocabulary.* Unpublished manuscript, State University of New York at Buffalo, Buffalo, NY.

Kibby, M. W. (1989). Teaching sight vocabulary with and without context before silent reading: A field test of the "Focus of Attention" hypothesis. *Journal of Reading Behavior, 21,* 261–279.

Killgallon, P. A. (1942). *A study of relationships among certain pupil adjustments in language situations.* Unpublished doctoral dissertation, Pennsylvania State University, University Park.

Kilty, T. K. (1976, March 17). Many are found unable to comprehend instructions on grocery store package. *The New York Times,* p. 49.

King, C., & Quigley, S. (1985). *Reading and deafness.* San Diego, CA: College-Hill.

Kintsch, W. (1974). *The mental representation of meaning.* Hillsdale, NJ: Erlbaum.

Kintsch, W. (1979). On modeling comprehension. *Educational Psychologist, 14,* 3–14.

Klenk, L., & Kibby, M. W. (2000). Re-mediating reading difficulties: Appraising the past, reconciling the present, constructing the future. In M. L. Kamil, P. B. Mosenthal, P. D. Pearson, & R. Barr (Eds.), *Handbook of reading research* (Vol. III, pp. 667–690). Mahwah, NJ: Erlbaum.

Klesius, J. P., Griffith, P. L., & Zielonka, P. (1991). A whole language and traditional instruction comparison: Overall effectiveness and development of the alphabetic principle. *Reading Research and Instruction, 30*(2), 47–61.

Klingner, J. K., Vaughn, S., Schumm, J. S., Hughes, M., & Elbaum, B. (1997). Outcomes for students with and without learning disabilities in inclusive classrooms. *Learning Disabilities Research and Practice, 13,* 153–161.

Kuhn, M. R., & Stahl, S. A. (2004). Fluency: A review of developmental and remedial practices. In R. B. Ruddell & N. J. Unrau (Eds.), *Theoretical models and processes of reading* (5th ed., pp. 412–453). Newark, DE: International Reading Association.

Kwolek, W. F. (1973). A readability survey of technical and popular literature. *Journalism Quarterly, 50,* 255–264.

Lahaderne, H. M. (1976). Feminized schools—Unpromising myth to explain boys' reading problems. *The Reading Teacher, 29,* 776–786.

Lenters, K. (2005). No half measures: Reading instruction for young second-language learners. *The Reading Teacher, 58,* 328–336.

Lesgold, A. M., McCormick, C., & Golinkoff, R. M. (1975). Imagery training and children's prose learning. *Journal of Educational Psychology, 67,* 663–667.

Lesgold, A. M., Resnick, L. B., & Hammond, K. (1985). Learning to read: A longitudinal study of word skill development in two curricula. In G. E. Mackinnon & T. G. Waller (Eds.), *Reading research: Advances in theory and practice* (Vol. 4, pp. 107–138). New York: Academic Press.

Leslie, L., & Caldwell, J. (2001). *Qualitative reading inventory–3.* New York: Longman.

Leu, D. J., & Leu, D. D. (2000). *Teaching with the Internet: Lessons from the classroom.* Norwood, MA: Christopher-Gorden.

Liberman, I. Y., Shankweiler, D., Liberman, A. M., Fowler, C., & Fischer, F. W. (1977). Phonetic segmentation and recoding in the beginning reader. In A. S. Reber & D. L. Scarborough (Eds.), *Toward a psychology of reading* (pp. 207–225). Hillsdale, NJ: Erlbaum.

Lindamood, C. H., & Lindamood, P. C. (1984). *Auditory discrimination in depth.* Austin, TX: PRO-ED.

Lipson, M. Y., Biggam, S. C., Valencia, S. W., Place, N. & Young, K. (2000, May). *Early reading assessment: Three states' efforts to implement second-grade reading evaluations.* Papers presented at the meeting of the International Reading Association, Indianapolis, IN.

Literacy Volunteers of America. (2001, July). Retrieved from http:/www.literacyvolunteers.org

Lomax, R. G. (1983). Applying structural modeling to some component processes of reading comprehension development. *Journal of Experimental Education, 52,* 33–40.

Lomax, R. G., & McGee, L. M. (1987). Young children's concepts about print and meaning: Toward a model of word reading acquisition. *Reading Research Quarterly, 22,* 237–256.

Lovett, M. W., Borden, S. L., Deluca, T., Lacerenza, L., Benson, N. J., & Brackstone, D. (1994). Treating the core deficits of developmental dyslexia: Evidence of transfer of learning after phonologically and strategy-based reading training programs. *Developmental Psychology, 30,* 805–822.

Lucas, T., Henze, R., & Donato, R. (1990). Promoting the success of Latino language minority students: An exploratory study of six high schools. *Harvard Educational Review, 60,* 315–340.

Lundberg, I., Frost, J., & Petersen, O. P. (1988). Effects of an extensive program for stimulating phonological awareness in preschool children. *Reading Research Quarterly, 23,* 264–284.

Lundberg, I., Olofsson, A., & Wall, S. (1980). Reading and spelling skills in the first school years predicted from phonemic awareness skills in kindergarten. *Scandinavian Journal of Psychology, 21,* 159–173.

MacGinitie, W. H. (1993). Some limits of assessments. *The Reading Teacher, 36,* 556–560.

Madden, N. A., Slavin, R. E., Karweit, N. L., Dolan, L. J., & Wasik, B. A. (1991). Success for All: Ending reading failure from the beginning. *Language Arts, 68,* 47–52.

Mann, V. A., Liberman, I. Y., & Shankweiler, D. (1980). Children's memory for sentences and word strings in relation to reading ability. *Memory and Cognition, 8,* 329–335.

Manzo, A. V. (1969). The ReQuest procedure. *Journal of Reading, 13,* 123–126.

Manzo, A. V., & Manzo, U. C. (1993). *Literacy disorders: Holistic diagnosis and remediation.* Fort Worth, TX: Harcourt Brace Jovanovich.

Manzo, A. V., & Manzo, U. (2002). Mental modeling. In B. J. Guzzetti (Ed.), *Literacy in America* (pp. 344–345). Santa Barbara, CA: ABC-CLIO.

Margolis, H. (2001). [Review of the test Reading Evaluation Adult Diagnosis]. In B. S. Plake & J. C. Impara (Eds.), *The fourteenth mental measurements yearbook* (pp. 987–989). Lincoln, NE: University of Nebraska Press.

Martin, B. (1983). *Brown bear, brown bear, what do you see?* New York: Holt, Rinehart, & Winston.

Martinez, M., Roser, N., & Strecker, S. (1999). "I never thought I could be a star": A Readers Theatre ticket to reading fluency. *The Reading Teacher, 52,* 326–334.

Mason, J. (1980). When *do* children learn to read: An exploration of four-year-old children's letter and word reading competencies. *Reading Research Quarterly, 15,* 203–227.

Matthews, M. M. (1966). *Teaching to read: Historically considered.* Chicago: University of Chicago Press.

May, R. B., & Ollila, L. O. (1981). Reading sex-role attitudes in preschoolers. *Reading Research Quarterly, 16,* 583–595.

McCardle, P. D. (2005, May). *Research findings on teaching reading to English language learners: Preschool interventions.* Paper presented at the meeting of the International Reading Association, San Antonio, TX.

McConnell, B. (1989). Education as a cultural process: The interaction between community and classroom in fostering learning. In J. B. Allen & J. Mason (Eds.), *Risk makers, risk takers, risk breakers: Reducing the risks for young children* (pp. 47–56). Portsmouth, NH: Heinemann.

McCormick, S. (1981). Assessment and the beginning reader: Using student dictated stories. *Reading World, 21,* 29–39.

McCormick, S. (1991). *Working with our most severe reading disability cases: A strategy for teaching nonreaders.* Paper presented at the meeting of the National Reading Conference, Palm Springs, CA.

McCormick, S. (1992). Disabled readers' erroneous responses to inferential comprehension questions: Description and analysis. *Reading Research Quarterly, 27,* 54–77.

McCormick, S. (1994). A nonreader becomes a reader: A case study of literacy acquisition by a severely disabled reader. *Reading Research Quarterly, 29,* 156–177.

McCormick, S. (1999). Severely delayed readers in clinical programs. In P. B. Mosenthal (Ed.), *Advances in reading/language research (Vol. 6,* pp. 273–289). Stamford, CT: JAI Press.

McCormick, S. (2002). Delayed readers. In B. J. Guzzetti (Ed.), *Literacy in America: An encyclopedia* (pp. 123–127). Santa Barbara, CA: ABC-CLIO.

McCormick, S. (2006). Instructing delayed readers in a regular classroom setting. In R. B. Ruddell (Ed.), *Teaching children to read and write: Becoming an effective literacy teacher* (4th ed., pp. 363–394). Boston: Allyn & Bacon.

McCormick, S., & Hill, D. S. (1984). An analysis of the effects of two procedures for increasing disabled readers' inferencing skills. *Journal of Educational Research, 77,* 219–226.

McCormick, S., & Cooper, J. O. (1991). Can SQ3R facilitate secondary learning disabled students' literal comprehension of expository text: Three experiments. *Reading Psychology, 12,* 239–271.

McCracken, R. A. (1962). Standardized reading tests and informal reading inventories. *Education, 82,* 366–369.

McGee, L. M. (1992). An exploration of meaning construction in first graders' grand conversations. In C. K. Kinzer & D. J. Leu (Eds.), *Literacy research, theory, and practice: Views from many perspectives* (pp. 177–186). Chicago: National Reading Conference.

McGinley, W. J., & Denner, P. R. (1987). Story impressions: A prereading/writing activity. *Journal of Reading, 31,* 248–253.

McKeown, M. G., & Beck, I. L. (1988). Learning vocabulary: Different ways for different goals. *Remedial and Special Education, 9,* 42–52.

McLaughlin, M., & Allen, M. B. (2002). *Guided comprehension: A teaching model for grades 3–8.* Newark, DE: International Reading Association.

McNamara, T. P., Miller, D. L., & Bransford, J. D. (1991). Mental models and reading comprehension. In R. Barr, M. L. Kamil, P. Mosenthal, & P. D. Pearson (Eds.), *Handbook of reading research* (Vol. II, pp. 490–511). New York: Longman.

Measurement and training of perceptual-motor functions. (1986). *Learning Disabilities Quarterly, 9,* 247.

Meyer, C. (1982). Prime-O-Tec: A successful strategy for adult disabled readers. *Journal of Reading, 25,* 512–515.

Meyer, L. A. (1984). Long-term academic effects of the direct instruction project Follow-Through. *Elementary School Journal, 84,* 380–394.

Miller, G. E. (1987). The influence of self-instruction on the comprehension monitoring performance of average and above-average readers. *Journal of Reading Behavior, 19,* 303–316.

Mitchell, J. V., Jr. (Ed.). (1985). *The ninth mental measurements yearbook.* Lincoln, NE: The Buros Institute of Mental Measurements.

Moats, L. C., & Lyon, G. R. (1993). Learning disabilities in the United States: Advocacy, science, and the future of the field. *Journal of Learning Disabilities, 26,* 282–294.

Moll, L. C., & Diaz, S. (1987). Change as the goal of educational research. *Anthropology and Education Quarterly, 18,* 300–311.

Monongalia County, WV Board of Education. (2005). Tips for teaching second-langauge learners in the classroom. *Classroom Strategies.* Retreived June 16, 2005, from http://boe.mono.k12.wv.us

Monroe, M. (1932). *Children who cannot read.* Chicago: University of Chicago Press.

Morais, J., Cluytens, M., Alegria, J., & Content, A. (1984). Segmentation abilities of dyslexics and normal readers. *Perceptual and Motor Skills, 58,* 221–222.

Morris, D. (1992). Concept of word: A pivotal understanding in the learning to read process. In S. Templeton & D. Bear (Eds.), *Development of orthographic knowledge and the foundations of literacy* (pp. 53–78). Hillsdale, NJ: Erlbaum.

Morris, D., & Perney, J. (1984). Developmental spelling as a predictor of first grade reading achievement. *Elementary School Journal, 84,* 441–457.

Morrow, L. M., Holt, T., & Sass, A. C. (2002). Phonics instruction. In B. J. Guzzetti (Ed.), *Literacy in America* (Vol. 2, pp. 428–431). Santa Barbara, CA: ABC-CLIO.

Morrow, L. M., Sisco, L. J., & Smith, J. K. (1992). The effect of mediated story retelling on listening comprehension, story structure, and oral language development in children with learning disabilities. In C. K. Kinzer & D. J. Leu (Eds.), *Literacy research, theory, and practice: Views from many perspectives* (pp. 435–443). Chicago: National Reading Conference.

Moss, B. (2004). Teaching expository text structures through information trade book retellings. *The Reading Teacher, 57,* 710–718.

Moyer, S., & Newcomer, P. (1977). Reversals in reading: Diagnosis and remediation. *Exceptional Children, 43,* 424–429.

Nagy, W. E., Anderson, R. C., Schommer, M., Scott, J., & Stallman, A. (1989). Morphological families in the internal lexicon. *Reading Research Quarterly, 24,* 262–282.

Nagy, W. E., Osborn, J., Winsor, P., & O'Flahavan, J. (1992). *Guidelines for instruction in structural analysis* (Tech. Rep. No. 554). Urbana-Champaign, IL: University of Illinois, Center for the Study of Reading.

Nagy, W. E., & Scott, J. A. (2004). Vocabulary processes. In R. B. Ruddell & N. J. Unrau (Eds.), *Theoretical models and processes of reading* (5th ed., pp. 574–593). Newark, DE: International Reading Association.

National Advisory Committee on Hyperkinesis and Food Additives. (1975). *Report to the Nutrition Foundation.* New York: The Nutrition Foundation.

National Institute of Child Health and Development. (2000). *Report of the National Reading Panel: Teaching Children to Read* (NIH Publication No. 00-4769). Washington, DC: U.S. Government Printing Office.

Naughton, V. M. (1993–94). Creative mapping for content reading. *Journal of Reading, 37,* 324–326.

Neuman, S. (2002). Early literacy. In B. J. Guzzetti (Ed.), *Literacy in America* (Vol. 1, pp. 157–160). Santa Barbara, CA: ABC-CLIO.

Noble, E. F. (1981). Self-selection: A remedial strategy for readers with a limited reading vocabulary. *The Reading Teacher, 34,* 386–388.

Norman, C. A., & Malicky, G. (1987). Stages in the reading development of adults. *Journal of Reading, 30,* 302–307.

O'Connor, R. E., Bell, K. M., Harty, K. R., Larkin, L. K., Sackor, S. M., & Zigmond, N. (2002). Teaching reading to poor readers in the intermediate grades: A comparison of text difficulty. *Journal of Educational Psychology, 94,* 474–485.

O'Donnell, P. A., & Eisenson, J. (1969). Delacato training for reading achievement and visual-motor integration. *Journal of Learning Disabilities, 2,* 441–447.

Ogbu, J. V. (1992). Understanding cultural diversity and learning. *Educational Researcher, 21,* 5–14, 24.

Ogle, D. M. (1986). K-W-L: A teaching model that develops active reading of expository text. *The Reading Teacher, 39,* 564–570.

Ogle, D. (2004, May). *Essentials for effective content area reading.* Paper presented at the meeting of the International Reading Association, Reno, NV.

Olson, R. K., & Gayan, J. (2002). Brains, genes, and environment in reading development. In S. B. Neuman & D. K. Dickinson (Eds.), *Handbook of early literacy research* (pp. 81–94). New York: Guilford.

Olson, R. K., Wise, B., Ring, J., & Johnson, M. (1997). Computer-based remedial training in phoneme awareness and phonological decoding: Effects on the posttraining development of word recognition. *Scientific Studies of Reading, 1,* 235–253.

Orton, S. T. (1937). *Reading, writing, and speech problems in children.* New York: Norton.

O'Sullivan, P. J., Ysseldyke, J. E., Christenson, S. L., & Thurlow, M. L. (1990). Mildly handicapped elementary students' opportunity to learn during reading instruction in mainstream and special education settings. *Reading Research Quarterly, 25,* 131–146.

Palincsar, A. S., & Brown, A. L. (1984). Reciprocal teaching of comprehension-fostering and comprehension-monitoring activities. *Cognition and Instruction, 1,* 117–175.

Paris, S. G. (1986). Teaching children to guide their reading and learning. In T. E. Raphael (Ed.), *The contexts of school-based literacy* (pp. 115–130). New York: Random House.

Paris, S. G., Calfee, R. C., Filby, N., Hiebert, E. H., Pearson, P. D., Valencia, S. W., & Wolf, K. P. (1992). A framework for authentic literacy assessment. *The Reading Teacher, 46,* 88–99.

Paris, S. G., Lipson, M., & Wixson, K. (1983). Becoming a strategic reader. *Contemporary Educational Psychology, 8,* 293–316.

Paris, S. G., Wasik, B. A., & Turner, J. C. (1991). The development of strategic readers. In R. Barr, M. L. Kamil, P. Mosenthal, & P. D. Pearson (Eds.), *Handbook of reading research* (Vol. II, pp. 609–640). New York: Longman.

Patching, W., Kameenui, E., Carnine, D., Gersten, R., & Colvin, G. (1983). Direct instruction in critical reading skills. *Reading Research Quarterly, 18,* 406–418.

Payne, J. S., Polloway, E. A., Smith, J. E., & Payne, R. A. (1981). *Strategies for teaching the mentally retarded* (2nd ed.). Columbus, OH: Merrill.

Pearson, P. D., & Fielding, L. (1991). Comprehension instruction. In R. Barr, M. L. Kamil, P. Mosenthal, & P. D. Pearson (Eds.), *Handbook of reading research* (Vol. II, pp. 815–860). New York: Longman.

Pearson, P. D., & Gallagher, M. C. (1983). The instruction of reading comprehension. *Contemporary Educational Psychology, 8,* 317–344.

Pearson, P. D., & Valencia, S. (1987). Assessment, accountability, and professional prerogative. In J. E. Readence & R. S. Baldwin (Eds.), *Research in literacy: Merging perspectives* (pp. 3–16). Rochester, NY: National Reading Conference.

Pennington, B. F., Gilger, J. W., Pauls, D., Smith, S. A., Smith, S. D., & DeFries, J. C. (1991). Evidence for major gene transmission of developmental dyslexia. *Journal of the American Medical Association, 266,* 1527–1534.

Perfetti, C. A., Beck, I., Bell, L., & Hughes, C. (1987). Children's reading and the development of phonological awareness. *Merrill Palmer Quarterly, 33,* 39–75.

Pflaum, S. W., & Bryan, T. H. (1980). Oral reading behaviors in the learning disabled. *Journal of Educational Research, 73,* 252–257.

Pflaum, S. W., & Pascarella, E. T. (1980). Interactive effects of prior reading achievement and training in context on the reading of learning disabled children. *Reading Research Quarterly, 16,* 138–158.

Phillips, S. U. (1972). Participant structures and communicative competence: Warm Springs children in community and classroom. In C. Cazden, V. John, & D. Hymes (Eds.), *Functions of language in the classroom.* New York: Teachers College Press.

Piercey, D. (1976). *Reading activities in content areas.* Boston: Allyn & Bacon.

Pinnell, G. S. (1989). Success of at-risk children in a program that combines reading and writing. In J. M. Mason (Ed.), *Reading and writing connections.* Boston: Allyn & Bacon.

Pinnell, G. S., Lyons, C. A., DeFord, D. E., Bryk, A. S., & Seltzer, M. (1994). Comparing instructional models for the literacy education of high-risk first graders. *Reading Research Quarterly, 29,* 9–39.

Piper, T. (1993). *Language for all children.* New York: Macmillan.

Plake, B. S., & Impara, J. C. (Eds.). (2001). *The fourteenth mental measurements yearbook.* Lincoln, NE: The Buros Institute of Mental Measurements, University of Nebraska.

Plomin, R., Owen, M. J., & McGuffin, P. (1994). The genetic basis of complex human behaviors. *Science, 264,* 1733–1739.

Poindexter, C. (1994). Guessed meanings. *Journal of Reading, 37,* 420–422.

Popham, W. J. (1999). *Classroom assessment: What teachers need to know* (2nd ed.). Boston: Allyn & Bacon.

Pratt, A. C., & Brady, S. (1988). Relation of phonological awareness to reading disability in children and adults. *Journal of Educational Psychology, 80,* 319–323.

Pressley, M. (2001). *Effective beginning reading instruction.* Executive summary and paper commissioned by the National Reading Conference. Chicago: National Reading Conference.

Pressley, M. (2002). *Reading instruction that works: The case for balanced teaching* (2nd ed.). New York: Guilford.

Professional Standards and Ethics Committee. (2004). *Standards for reading professionals.* Newark, DE: International Reading Association.

RAND Study Group. (2004). A research agenda for improving reading comprehension. In R. B. Ruddell & N. J. Unrau (Eds.), *Theoretical models and processes of reading* (5th ed., pp. 720–754). Newark, DE: International Reading Association.

Raphael, T. E. (1986). Teaching question-answers relationships, revisited. *The Reading Teacher, 39,* 516–522.

Rasinski, T. V. (1990). Effects of repeated reading and reading-while-listening on reading fluency. *Journal of Educational Research, 83,* 147–150.

Rasinski, T. (2002). Fluency. In B. J. Guzzetti (Ed.), *Literacy in America* (pp. 191–193). Santa Barbara, CA: ABC-CLIO.

Rasinski, T. V., & Hoffman, J. V. (2003). Oral reading in the school literacy curriculum. *Reading Research Quarterly, 38,* 510–522.

Rasinski, T., & Padak, N. (2000). *Effective reading strategies: Teaching children who find reading difficult.* Columbus, OH: Merrill.

Ratekin, N. (1978). A comparison of reading achievement among three racial groups using standard reading materials. In D. Feitelson (Ed.), *Cross-cultural perspectives on reading and reading research.* Newark, DE: International Reading Association.

Rayner, K., & Duffy, S. A. (1988). On-line comprehension processes and eye movements during reading. In M. Daneman, G. E. Mackinnon, & T. G. Waller (Eds.), *Reading research: Advances in theory and practice* (Vol. 6, pp. 13–56). New York: Academic Press.

Razik, T. A. (1969). A study of American newspaper readability. *The Journal of Communication, 19,* 317–324.

Read, C. (1975). *Children's categorization of speech sounds in English.* Champaign, IL: National Council of Teachers of English.

Reed, J. C., Rabe, E. F., & Mankinen, M. (1970). Teaching reading to brain-damaged children. A review. *Reading Research Quarterly, 6,* 379–401.

Reutzel, D. R., & Hollingsworth, P. M. (1991). Using literature webbing for books with predictable narrative: Improving young readers' prediction, comprehension, and story structure knowledge. *Reading Psychology, 12,* 319–333.

Ribovich, J. K. (1978). Teaching reading fifty years ago. *The Reading Teacher, 31,* 371–375.

Richards, J. C., & Gipe, J. P. (1993). Getting to know story characters: A strategy for young and at-risk readers. *The Reading Teacher, 47,* 78–79.

Ringler, L. H., & Smith, I. L. (1973). Learning modality and word recognition of first grade children. *Journal of Learning Disabilities, 6,* 307–312.

Robbins, M. P. (1966). A study of the validity of Delacato's theory of neurological organization and reading. *Exceptional Children, 32,* 517–523.

Robinson, H. A. (1966). Reading: Seventy-five years of progress. *Proceedings of the 29th Annual Conference in Reading, Vol. 38* (Supplementary Educational Monographs No. 96). Chicago: University of Chicago.

Robinson, H. M. (1946). *Why pupils fail in reading.* Chicago: University of Chicago Press.

Robinson, H. M. (1967). Developing critical readers. In M. L. King, B. D. Ellinger, & W. Wolf (Eds.), *Critical reading.* Philadelphia: Lippincott.

Rodning, C., Beckwith, L., & Howard, J. (1989). Characteristics of attachment organization and play organization in prenatally drug-exposed toddlers. *Development and Psychopathology, 1,* 277–289.

Rodriguez-Trujillo, N. (1986, May). *Effect of availability of reading materials on reading behavior of primary school students.* Paper presented at the meeting of the International Reading Association, Philadelphia.

Roelke, P. L. (1969). Reading comprehension as a function of three dimensions of word meaning. *Dissertation Abstracts International, 30,* 5300A–5301A (University Microfilms No. 70–10, 275).

Roller, C. M. (1996). *Variability not disability.* Newark, DE: International Reading Association.

Rosenshine, B. V. (1980). How time is spent in elementary classrooms. In C. Dunham & A. Lieberman (Eds.), *Time to learn* (Publication No. 695–717). Washington, DC: U.S. Government Printing Office.

Rossell, C. H., & Baker, K. (1996). The educational effectiveness of bilingual education. *Research in the Teaching of English, 30,* 7–74.

Ruddell, R. B. (2006). *Teaching children to read and write: Becoming an effective literacy teacher* (4th ed.). Boston: Allyn & Bacon.

Ruddell, R. B., & Unrau, N. J. (2004). Reading as a meaning-construction process: The reader, the text, and the teacher. In R. B. Ruddell & N. J. Unraw (Eds.), *Theoretical models and processes of reading* (5th ed., pp. 1462–1521). Newark, DE: International Reading Association.

Rumelhart, D. E. (1976). Toward an interactive model of reading. In S. Dornic (Ed.), *Attention and performance* (Vol. VI, pp. 573–603). Hillsdale, NJ: Erlbaum.

Rumelhart, D. E. (1981). Schemata: The building blocks of cognition. In J. T. Gutherie (Ed.), *Comprehension and reading*. Newark, DE: International Reading Association.

Rumsey, J. M., Nace, K., Donohue, B., Wise, D., Maisog, J. M., & Andreason, P. (1997). A position emission tomographic study of impaired word recognition and phonological processing in dyslexic men. *Archives of Neurology, 54,* 27–38.

Rupley, W. H. (2005). Vocabulary knowledge: Its contribution to reading growth and development. *Reading and Writing Quarterly, 21,* 203–207.

Rupley, W. H., & Nichols, W. D. (2005). Vocabulary instruction for the struggling reader. *Reading and Writing Quarterly, 21,* 239–260.

Ruppert, E. T. (1976). The effect of the synthetic-multisensory method of language instruction upon psycholinguistic abilities and reading achievement. *Dissertation Abstracts International, 37,* 920A–921A. (University Microfilms No. 76–18, 223)

Sabine, G., & Sabine, P. (1983). *Books that made the difference: What people told us.* Hamden, CT: Library Professional Publications.

Sadoski, M. (1983). An exploratory study of the relationships between reported imagery and the comprehension and recall of a story. *Reading Research Quarterly, 19,* 110–123.

Sadoski, M. (2005). A dual coding view of vocabulary learning. *Reading and Writing Quarterly, 21,* 221–238.

Salvia, J., & Ysseldyke, J. E. (1982). *Assessment in special and remedial education* (2nd ed.). Boston: Houghton Mifflin.

Sammons, R. B., & Davey, B. (1993–94). Assessing students' skill in using textbooks: The Textbook Awareness and Performance Profile (TAPP). *Journal of Reading, 37,* 280–286.

Samuels, S. J. (1979). The method of repeated readings. *The Reading Teacher, 32,* 403–408.

Samuels, S. J. (1988). Decoding and automaticity: Helping poor readers become automatic at word recognition. *The Reading Teacher, 41,* 756–760.

Sanders, N. M. (1966). *Classroom questions: What kinds?* New York: Harper & Row.

Santeusanio, R. P. (1983). *A practical approach to content area reading.* Reading, MA: Addison-Wesley.

Saphier, J. D. (1973). The relation of perceptual-motor skills to learning and school success. *Journal of Learning Disabilities, 6,* 583–591.

SAT, ACT scores steady. (2004, October/November). *Reading Today, 22*(2), 17.

Scala, M. (2001). *Working together: Reading and writing in inclusive classrooms.* Newark, DE: International Reading Association.

Scarborough, H. S. (1984). Continuity between childhood dyslexia and adult reading. *British Journal of Psychology, 75,* 329–340.

Schlagel, R. (1989). Constancy and change in spelling development. *Reading Psychology, 10,* 207–229.

Schmitt, M. C. (1990). A questionnaire to measure children's awareness of strategic reading processes. *The Reading Teacher, 43,* 454–461.

Schreiner, R., & Tanner, L. R. (1976). What history says about reading. *The Reading Teacher, 29,* 513–520.

Schumm, J. S., & Saumell, L. (1994). Learning the meaning of common English suffixes. *Journal of Reading, 37,* 390.

Schunk, D. H., & Rice, J. H. (1987). Enhancing comprehension skill and self-efficacy with strategy value information. *Journal of Reading Behavior, 19,* 285–302.

Schunk, D. H., & Rice, M. J. (1992). Influence of reading-comprehension strategy information on children's achievement outcomes. *Learning Disability Quarterly, 26,* 417–441.

Senechal, M., LeFevre, J., Thomas, E. M., & Daley, K. E. (1998). Differential effects of home literacy experiences on the development of oral and written language. *Reading Research Quarterly, 33,* 96–116.

Shanahan, T. (2001). [Review of the test Reading Evaluation Adult Diagnosis]. In B. S. Plake & J. C. Impara (Eds.), *The fourteenth mental measurements yearbook* (pp. 989–991). Lincoln, NE: University of Nebraska Press.

Shanahan, T., & Kamil, M. L. (1984). The relationship of three concurrent and construct validities of cloze. In J. A. Niles & L. A. Harris (Eds.), *Changing perspectives on research in reading/language processing and instruction* (pp. 334–338). Rochester, NY: National Reading Conference.

Shaywitz, B. A., Pugh, K. R., Jenner, A. R., Fulbright, R. K., Fletcher, J. M., Gore, J. C., & Shaywitz, S. (2000). The neurobiology of reading and reading disability. In M. L. Kamil, P. B. Mosenthal, P. D. Pearson, & R. Barr (Eds.), *Handbook of reading research* (Vol. III, pp. 229–250). Mahwah, NJ: Erlbaum.

Shaywitz, S. E., & Shaywitz, B. A. (1996). Unlocking learning disabilities: The neurological basis. In S. C. Cramer & W. Ellis (Eds.), *Learning disabilities, lifelong issues* (pp. 255–260). Baltimore MD: Paul H. Brookes.

Short, K. G. (1992). Intertextuality: Searching for patterns that connect. In C. K. Kinzer & D. J. Leu (Eds.), *Literacy research, theory, and practice: Views from many perspectives* (pp. 187–197). Chicago: National Reading Conference.

Sieben, R. L. (1977). Controversial medical treatments of learning disabilities. *Academic Therapy, 13,* 133–147.

Sindelar, P. T., & Wilson, R. J. (1982, October). *Application of academic skills as a function of teacher-directed instruction and seatwork.* Paper presented at the meeting of the Applied Behavior Analysis in Education Conference, Columbus, OH.

Sipay, E. R. (1964). A comparison of standardized reading scores and functional reading levels. *The Reading Teacher, 17,* 265–268.

Slavin, R. E. (2002). Mounting evidence supports the achievement effects of Success for All. *Phi Delta Kappan, 83,* 469–471, 480.

Slavin, R. E., & Cheung, A. (2005). A synthesis of research on language of reading instruction for English-language learners. *Review of Educational Research, 75,* 247–284.

Slavin, R. E., Madden, N. A., Karweit, N. L., Dolan, L., & Wasik, B. A. (1992). *Success for All: A relentless approach to prevention and early intervention in elementary schools.* Arlington, VA: Educational Research Service.

Smith, F. (1978). *Understanding reading* (2nd ed.). New York: Holt, Rinehart, & Winston.

Smith, I. L., Ringler, L. H., & Cullinan, B. L. (1968). *New York University Learning Modality Test.* New York: New York University.

Smith, M. C. (2002). Adult literacy testing. In B. J. Guzzetti (Ed.), *Literacy in America* (*Vol. 1,* pp. 25–28). Santa Barbara, CA: ABC-CLIO.

Smith, M. S., Levin, J., & Cianci, J. E. (1997). Beyond a legislative agenda: Education policy approaches of the Clinton administration. *Educational Policy, 11,* 209–226.

Smith, N. B. (1965). *American reading instruction.* Newark, DE: International Reading Association.

Smith, N. B. (1967). Patterns of writing in different subject areas. In M. L. King, B. D. Ellinger, & W. Wolf (Eds.), *Critical reading.* Philadelphia: Lippincott.

Smith, W. E. (2002). Psycholinguistics. In B. J. Guzzetti (Ed.), *Literacy in America* (pp. 462–464). Santa Barbara, CA: ABC-CLIO.

Snow, C. E., Burns, M. S., & Griffith, P. (Eds.). (1998). *Preventing reading difficulties in young children.* Washington, DC: National Academy Press.

Snyder, Z. (1969). *Today is Saturday.* New York: Atheneum.

Solman, R. T., & May, J. G. (1990). Spatial localization discrepancies: A visual deficiency in poor readers. *American Journal of Psychology, 103,* 243–263.

Spache, G. D. (1976). *Investigating the issues of reading disability.* Boston: Allyn & Bacon.

Spear-Swerling, L. (2004). A road map for understanding reading disability and other reading problems: Origins, prevention, and intervention. In R. B. Ruddell & N. J. Unrau (Eds.), *Theoretical models and processes of reading* (5th ed.). Newark, DE: International Reading Association.

Spear-Swerling, L., & Sternberg, R. J. (1998). *Off-track: When poor readers become "learning disabled."* Boulder, CO: Westview Press.

Speece, D. L., & Shekitka, L. (2002). How should reading disabilities be operationalized? A survey of experts. *Learning Disabilities Research & Practice, 17,* 118–123.

Sperry, A. (1968). *Call it courage.* New York: Macmillan.

Spiegel, D. L. (1992). Blending whole language and systematic direct instruction. *The Reading Teacher, 46,* 38–48.

Spiegel, D. L., & Rogers, C. (1980). Teacher responses to miscues during oral reading by second-grade students. *Journal of Educational Research, 74,* 8–12.

Spring, C., & French, L. (1990). Identifying children with specific reading disabilities from listening and reading discrepancy scores. *Journal of Learning Disabilities, 23,* 53–58.

Stahl, S. A. (1992). Saying the "p" word: Nine guidelines for exemplary phonics instruction. *The Reading Teacher, 45,* 618–625.

Stahl, S. A. (2002). Reading clinics. In B. J. Guzzetti (Ed.), *Literacy in America* (pp. 502–506). Santa Barbara, CA: ABC-CLIO.

Stahl, S. A., & Fairbanks, M. (1986). The effects of vocabulary instruction: A model-based meta-analysis. *Review of Educational Research, 56,* 72–110.

Stahl, S. A., & Heubach, K. M. (2005). Fluency-oriented reading instruction. *Journal of Literacy Research, 37,* 25–60.

Stahl, S. A., & Kuhn, M. R. (2004). Fluency: A review of developmental and remedial practices. In R. B. Ruddell & N. J. Unrau (Eds.), *Theoretical models and processes of reading* (5th ed., pp. 412–453). Newark, DE: International Reading Association.

Stahl, S. A., Richek, M. A., & Vandevier, R. J. (1991). Learning meaning through listening: A sixth-grade replication. In J. Zutell & S. McCormick (Eds.), *Learner factors/teacher factors: Issues in literacy research and instruction* (pp. 185–192). Chicago: National Reading Conference.

Stallings, J. A. (1980). Allocated academic learning time revisited, or beyond time on task. *Educational Researcher, 9*(11), 11–16.

Stanovich, K. E. (1980). Toward an interactive-compensatory model of individual differences in the development of reading fluency. *Reading Research Quarterly, 16,* 32–71.

Stanovich, K. E. (1985). Explaining the variance in reading ability in terms of psychological processes: What have we learned? *Annals of Dyslexia, 35,* 67–96.

Stanovich, K. E. (1986). Matthew effects on reading: Some consequences of individual differences in the acquisition of literacy. *Reading Research Quarterly, 21,* 360–407.

Stanovich, K. E. (1991a). Discrepancy definitions of reading disability: Has intelligence led us astray? *Reading Research Quarterly, 26,* 7–29.

Stanovich, K. E. (1991b). Word recognition: Changing perspectives. In R. Barr, M. L. Kamil, P. Mosenthal, & P. D. Pearson (Eds.), *Handbook of reading research* (Vol. II, pp. 418–452). New York: Longman.

Stanovich, K. E., Nathan, R. G., & Zolman, J. E. (1988). The developmental lag hypothesis in reading: Longitudinal and matched reading-level comparisons. *Child Development, 59,* 71–86.

Stanovich, K. E., & West, R. F. (1989). Exposure to print and orthographic processing. *Reading Research Quarterly, 24,* 402–433.

Stauffer, R. G. (1942). A study of prefixes in the Thorndike list to establish a list of prefixes that should be taught in the elementary school. *Journal of Educational Research, 35,* 453–458.

Stauffer, R. G. (1969). *Teaching reading as a thinking process.* New York: Harper & Row.

Stauffer, R. G. (1970). *The language experience approach to the teaching of reading.* New York: Harper & Row.

Stauffer, R. G. (1975). *Directing the reading-thinking process.* New York: Harper & Row.

Sticht, T. G. (Ed.). (1975). *Reading for working: A functional literacy anthology.* Alexandria, VA: Human Resources Research Organization.

Sticht, T. G. (1981). *Basic skills in defense.* Alexandria, VA: Human Resources Research Organization.

Sulzby, E. (1989). Assessment of writing and children's language while writing. In L. Morrow & J. Smith (Eds.), *The role of assessment and measurement in early literacy instruction* (pp. 83–109). Englewood Cliffs, NJ: Prentice Hall.

Sulzby, E., & Teale, W. (1991). Emergent literacy. In R. Barr, M. L. Kamil, P. Mosenthal, & P. D. Pearson (Eds.), *Handbook of reading research* (Vol. II, pp. 727–758). New York: Longman.

Swalm, J. E. (1972). A comparison of oral reading, silent reading, and listening. *Education, 92,* 111–115.

Sweet, A. P. (1993). *State of the art: Transforming ideas for teaching and learning to read* (GPO Document No. 065-000-00620-1). Washington, DC: U.S. Department of Education, Office of Educational Research and Improvement.

Tabors, P. O., & Snow, C. E. (2004). Young bilingual children and early literacy development. In R. B. Ruddell & N. J. Unrau (Eds.), *Theoretical models and proceses of reading* (5th ed., pp. 240–267). Newark, DE: International Reading Association.

Taylor, B. M., & Beach, R. W. (1984). The effects of text structure instruction on middle-grade students' comprehension and production of expository text. *Reading Research Quarterly, 19,* 134–146.

Taylor, B. M., Short, R. A., Frye, B. J., & Shearer, B. A. (1992). Classroom teachers prevent reading failure among low achieving first-grade students. *The Reading Teacher, 45,* 592–597.

Taylor, B. M., Short, R. S., Shearer, B., & Frye, B. (1995). First grade teachers provide early reading intervention in the classroom. In R. L. Allington & S. A. Walmsley (Eds.), *No quick fix: Rethinking literacy programs in America's elementary schools* (pp. 159–176). New York: Teachers College Press.

Taylor, E. A. (1937). *Controlled reading.* Chicago: University of Chicago Press.

Teale, W. H. (1986). Home background and young children's literacy development. In W. H. Teale & E. Sulzby (Eds.), *Emergent literacy: Writing and reading* (pp. 173–206). Norwood, NJ: Ablex.

Thompson, L. J. (1966). *Reading disability: Developmental dyslexia.* Springfield, IL: Charles C. Thomas.

Thorndike, E. L., & Lorge, I. (1944). *The teacher's word book of 30,000 words.* New York: Columbia University Teacher's College.

Tierney, R. J., & Cunningham, J. W. (1984). Research on teaching reading comprehension. In P. D. Pearson (Ed.), *Handbook of reading research* (pp. 609–655). New York: Longman.

Topping, K. (1995). *Paired reading, spelling, and writing.* New York: Cassell.

Torgesen, J. K., Wagner, R. K., & Rashotte, C. A. (1997). Prevention and remediation of severe reading disabilities: Keeping the end in mind. *Scientific Studies of Reading, 1,* 217–234.

Torneus, M. (1984). Phonological awareness and reading: A chicken and egg problem? *Journal of Educational Psychology, 76,* 1346–1358.

Treiman, R., & Cassar, M. (1998). Spelling acquisition in English. In C. Perfetti, L. Rieban, & M. Fayol (Eds.), *Learning to spell: Research, theory, and practice across languages* (pp. 61–80). Mahwah, NJ: Erlbaum.

Tunmer, W. E., Herriman, M. L., & Nesdale, A. R. (1988). Metalinguistic abilities and beginning reading. *Reading Research Quarterly, 23,* 134–158.

U.S. Public Law 107–110. (2002). 107TH Congress, 1st session, 8 January 2002. No Child Left Behind Act of 2001.

Valencia, S. W., McGinley, W., & Pearson, P. D. (1990). Assessing reading and writing. In G. G. Duffy (Ed.), *Reading in the middle school* (2nd ed.). Newark, DE: International Reading Association.

Valencia, S. W., & Wixson, K. K. (2000). Policy-oriented research on literacy standards and assessment. In M. L. Kamil, P. B. Mosenthal, P. D. Pearson, & R. Barr (Eds.), *Handbook of reading research* (Vol. III, pp. 909–936). Mahwah, NJ: Erlbaum.

Vaughn, S., Bos, C. S., & Schumm, J. S. (1997). *Teaching mainstreamed, diverse, and at-risk students in the general education classroom.* Boston: Allyn & Bacon.

Vellutino, F. R., & Denckla, M. B. (1991). Cognitive and neuropsychological foundations of word identification in poor and normally developing readers. In R. Barr, M. L. Kamil, P. Mosenthal, & P. D. Pearson (Eds.), *Handbook of reading research* (Vol. II, pp. 571–608). New York: Longman.

Vellutino, F. R., & Scanlon, D. B. (1987). Phonological coding, phonological awareness, and reading ability: Evidence from longitudinal and experimental study. *Merrill Palmer Quarterly, 33,* 321–363.

Vellutino, F. R., Scanlon, D. M., Sipay, E. R., Small, S. G., Pratt, A., Chen, R. S., & Denckla, M. B. (1996). Cognitive profiles of difficult-to-remediate and readily remediated poor readers: Early intervention as a vehicle for distinguishing between cognitive and experiential deficits as basic causes of specific reading disability. *Journal of Educational Psychology, 88,* 601–638.

Venezky, R. L. (1975). The curious role of letter names in reading instruction. *Visible Language, 9,* 7–23.

Venezky, R. L. (1991). The development of literacy in the industrialized nations of the West. In R. Barr, M. L. Kamil, P. Mosenthal, & P. D. Pearson (Eds.), *Handbook of reading research* (Vol. II, pp. 46–67). New York: Longman.

Verrengia, J. B. (2004, September 3). Study of dyslexia in China challenges biological cause theory. *San Francisco Chronicle,* p. A7.

Vierra, A. (1984). The relationship between Chicano children's achievement and their teacher's ethnicity. *Hispanic Journal of Biological Sciences, 6,* 285–290.

Visonhaler, J. F., Weinshank, A. B., Polin, R. M., & Wagner, C. C. (1983). *Improving diagnostic reliability in reading through training* (Research Series 176). East Lansing: Michigan State University, Institute for Research on Teaching. (ERIC Document Reproduction Service No. ED 237 934)

Voigt, S. (1978). It's all Greek to me. *The Reading Teacher, 31,* 420–422.

Vygotsky, L. S. (1978). *Mind in society: The development of higher psychological processes.* Cambridge, MA: Harvard University Press.

Wade, S. E. (1990). Using think-alouds to assess comprehension. *The Reading Teacher, 43,* 442–451.

Wallace, C. (2001). Reading. In R. Carter & D. Nunan (Eds.), *The Cambridge guide to teaching English to speakers of other languages* (pp. 143–160). Cambridge, UK: Cambridge University Press.

Walley, C. (1993). An invitation to reading fluency. *The Reading Teacher, 46,* 526–527.

Walsh, D. J., Price, G. G., & Gillingham, M. G. (1988). The critical but transitory importance of letter naming. *Reading Research Quarterly, 23,* 108–122.

Wangberg, E. G., Thompson, B., & Levitov, J. E. (1984). First steps toward an adult basic word list. *Journal of Reading, 28,* 244–247.

Wasik, B. A., & Slavin, R. E. (1993). Preventing early reading failure with one-to-one tutoring: A review of five programs. *Reading Research Quarterly, 28,* 179–200.

Watson, D. J. (1982). In college and in trouble—with reading. *Journal of Reading, 25,* 640–645.

Waugh, J. C. (1993). Using LEA in diagnosis. *Journal of Reading, 37,* 56–57.

Weber, R. (1991). Linguistic diversity and reading in American society. In R. Barr, M. L. Kamil, P. Mosenthal, & P. D. Pearson (Eds.), *Handbook of reading research* (Vol. II, pp. 97–119). New York: Longman.

Whittlesea, B. W. A. (1987). Preservation of specific experiences in the representation of general knowledge. *Journal of Experimental Psychology: Learning, Memory, and Cognition, 13,* 3–17.

Wiener, R., & Hall, D. (2004). Adequate yearly progress: Is it working? *Principal, 83*(5), 12–15.

Wilkinson, I., Wardrop, J. L., & Anderson, R. C. (1988). Silent reading reconsidered: Reinterpreting reading instruction and its effects. *American Educational Research Journal, 25,* 127–144.

Williams, J. (1984). Phonemic analysis and how it relates to reading. *Journal of Learning Disabilities, 17,* 240–245.

Williams, J. L. (1964). A comparison of standardized reading test scores and informal reading inventory scores. *Dissertation Abstracts International, 24,* 5262A. (University Microfilms No. 64–4485)

Williams, N. L., Konopak, B. C., Wood, K. D., & Avett, S. (1992). Middle school students' use of imagery in developing meaning in expository text. In C. K. Kinzer & D. J. Leu (Eds.), *Literacy research, theory, and practice: Views from many perspectives* (pp. 261–268). Chicago: National Reading Conference.

Willig, A. C. (1985). A meta-analysis of selected studies on the effectiveness of bilingual education. *Review of Educational Research, 55,* 269–317.

Willows, D. M., & Ryan, E. B. (1986). The development of grammatical sensitivity and its relationship to early reading achievement. *Reading Research Quarterly, 21,* 253–266.

Wilson, M. M. (1979). The processing strategies of average and below average readers answering factual and inferential questions on three equivalent passages. *Journal of Reading Behavior, 11,* 235–245.

Winfield, L. (1986). Teacher beliefs toward academically at-risk students in inner-city schools. *Urban Review, 18,* 254–268.

Wise, B. W., & Olson, R. K. (1995). Computer-based phonological awareness and reading instruction. *Annals of Dyslexia, 45,* 99–122.

Wixson, K. K., & Peters, C. W. (1987). Comprehension assessment: Implementing an interactive view of reading. *Educational Psychologist, 22,* 333–356.

Wolff, D. E., Desberg, P., & Marsh, G. (1985). Analogy strategies for improving word recognition in competent and learning disabled readers. *The Reading Teacher, 38,* 412–416.

Wong-Fillmore, L., & Snow, C. E. (2000). What teachers need to know about language. Special report from ERIC Clearinghouse on Languages and Linguistics [Online]. Available: www.cal.org/ericcll/teachers/teachers.pdf

Wong-Fillmore, L. W., & Valadez, C. (1986). Teaching bilingual learners. In M. C. Wittrock (Ed.), *Handbook of research on teaching* (pp. 648–685). New York: Macmillan.

Worthington, J. S. (1977). The readability of footnotes to financial statements and how to improve them. *Journal of Reading, 20,* 469–478.

Worthy, J., & Broaddus, K. (2002). Fluency beyond the primary grades: From group performance to silent, independent reading. *The Reading Teacher, 55,* 334–343.

Yopp, H. K. (1988). The validity and reliability of phonemic awareness tests. *Reading Research Quarterly, 23,* 159–177.

Yopp, H. K. (1992). Developing phonemic awareness in young children. *The Reading Teacher, 45,* 696–703.

Yule, W., Rutter, M., Berger, M., & Thompson, J. (1974). Over- and under-achievement in reading: Distribution in the general population. *British Journal of Educational Psychology, 44,* 1–12.

Zigamond, N., Jenkins, J., Fuchs, L. S., Deno, S., Fuchs, D., Baker, J. N., Jenkins, L., & Couthino, M. (1995). Special education in restructured schools: Findings from three multiyear studies. *Phi Delta Kappan, 76,* 531–540.

Zutell, J. (1998). Word sorting: A developmental spelling approach to word study for delayed readers. *Reading and Writing Quarterly, 14,* 219–238.

Index